ESSAYS

CRITICAL AND HISTORICAL

ESSAYS

CRITICAL AND HISTORICAL

BY

JOHN HENRY CARDINAL NEWMAN

VOLUME I

with an Introduction, Notes and Textual Appendix
by

ANDREW NASH

GRACEWING

Individual essays first published 1829-1841
Collected in two volumes:
First edition 1871
Revised editions 1881, 1885

Published in the Birmingham Oratory Millennium Edition
in 2019
by
Gracewing
2 Southern Avenue
Leominster
Herefordshire HR6 0QF

www.gracewing.co.uk

ISBN   978 0 85244 457 3

CONTENTS

ACKNOWLEDGEMENTS

I am grateful to Rev. James Tolhurst, D.D., the General Editor of the Millennium Edition of Newman's works, for having commissioned me to edit this volume and also for his generosity in allowing me to incorporate the notes to his edition of Tract 73 in *Newman's Tracts for the Times* (Gracewing, 2013) into my notes for Essay II here. My thanks too to Mrs. Camilla Macnab and Rev. Guy Nicholls for translations of Latin and Greek quotations in the text, and to the latter also for information about Newman and music; and to my wife Dora, not only for explicating some complex 18th century genealogy for Essay IX but most of all for her constant interest, wise advice and unfailing support.

A.J.N.

EDITOR'S INTRODUCTION

This book is the first of two volumes of some of Newman's occasional writings from 1829 to 1841, brought together by him as *Essays Critical and Historical* in 1871. They thus all date from the Anglican period of his life (Volume II contains just one published after his conversion), and Newman explains in his Advertisement that he was republishing them now so that he could 'reduce what is uncatholic in them'[1] by adding his own Notes to answer his earlier self. He was worried that without the theological content of the Essays being 'satisfactorily answered' in this way, there was the danger that after his death the original versions of them might be quoted in support of the Anglican position which he now no longer held.[2] Pusey had already done this in his *Eirenicon* in 1866.

Actually, Newman's deeper motive for republishing these Anglican writings was far from defensive, as we shall see. And in fact, there was not that much that needed to be corrected in the theological content of these Essays in Volume I (though there was more in Volume II). What is of more significance is just how consonant much of what he was writing was with his later Catholic faith. In particular, his critique of trends within Protestant Christianity from a Catholic, even if not yet Roman, standpoint now looks strikingly perceptive, even prophetic. Both the consistency of Newman's principles and the trajectory of their development are therefore evidenced here.

Volume I shows us some of the theological topics which engaged Newman as the Oxford Movement developed (including Essay I on Poetry, even though it was written before the public start of the Movement and at first sight appears purely literary). These writings are more combative than his title 'Critical and

---

[1] p.[viii]
[2] Cf. p.[vii]

Historical' essays might suggest. They are not academic studies. Some of them could almost be termed journalism, albeit of a much more substantial nature than can be found in today's journals. Apart from Essay I which was written for another journal and Essay II which was one of his *Tracts for the Times*, they were originally articles in the *British Critic* magazine, of which Newman himself became the Editor in 1838.

When the Oxford Movement began, Newman was writing with the 'supreme confidence' that he describes in the *Apologia* in the 'momentous and inspiring cause' of 'upholding that primitive Christianity which was delivered for all time by the early teachers of the Church, and which was registered and attested in the Anglican formularies and by the Anglican divines.'[3] Certainly, in these essays he engages with his subjects with vigour, forensic skill and wit—sometimes even with satire. However, as the essays are in chronological order we can also detect the approaching crisis of Newman's Anglican belief. Particularly in Essays VII and VIII, his tone towards the Church of England becomes markedly more critical.

It is also interesting to see how much Newman revised the essays for his 1871 collected edition. Hitherto, when critics have quoted from these writings in the standard edition, they may have been unaware that they were not always looking at the words of Newman's original 1830s and 1840s texts. In some cases his revisions only make minor differences to his expression, but in others the differences are significant, as the Textual Appendix to this edition demonstrates, with whole passages omitted, added or re-written. In the case of Essay III he completely rewrote substantial amounts of his original article, as I discuss below, but still dated the essay 'July, 1836' which may catch out the reader who is unaware of the full extent of the changes. In other essays Newman carried out judicious shortening for which the reader who consults the original version in the Textual Appendix may often be grateful.

But it is not only for such textual matters that these essays deserve a full critical edition now. They are also worth reading for their own sake. First, Newman knew that he now had many

---

[3] *Apologia Pro Vita Sua*, p.43.

Anglican readers; the wide popularity of the *Apologia* on its publication in 1864 had caused a new sympathetic interest in him. So his strategy behind the republication in 1871 of his Anglican essays was to influence this Anglican audience—to show them, as the *Apologia* had argued throughout, that his Tractarian principles had led him to Rome and therefore should lead other Anglo-Catholics to Rome too. This is evident from his letter to Sir William Cope about the addition of Essay III 'Apostolical Principles' to the fifth edition of the *Essays* in 1881 (see below p.xxi). These Essays were therefore now intended by Newman as further witnesses to the development and direction of his thought during the years of the Oxford Movement. They could perhaps be seen as a series of appendices to the *Apologia*, giving the evidence of where his Anglican thought was going over the years he wrote them. He was hoping that his readers would follow him.

For readers today, whether Anglican, Catholic or other, Newman's analyses of trends in the Christianity of his day have continuing resonance. Indeed, one could call some of his writing here prophetic, such as Essay II 'On the Introduction of Rationalistic Principles into Revealed Religion'. Far from being of historical interest only, they are evidence of why Newman is a guide of such great stature amidst the religious issues of our own times too.

I. Poetry, with Reference to Aristotle's Poetics

The opening essay in this volume was originally an article published in 1829 in the first issue of the short-lived journal The London Review edited by Joseph Blanco White who was a Fellow of Oriel.[4] Newman wrote the article in the early autumn of 1828,[5] though Robert A. Colby has pointed out that Newman's earlier private annotations of Thomas Tyrwhitt's 1817

---

[4] Joseph Blanco White (1775-1841), born in Spain, had been a Catholic priest but had gradually lost his faith. He came to England and became a Church of England clergyman. He and Newman got to know each other well as Fellows of Oriel. Newman gives an account of White in his *Lectures on the Present Position of Catholics in England* (Gracewing/Notre Dame, 2000, ed. Andrew Nash), pp.142-160. Newman and White were moving in opposite religious directions: White later became a Unitarian minister and ultimately had no religious belief at all.
[5] Cf. *Letters and Diaries*, Vol.II, p.101: 'finished article for B.White'.

edition of Aristotle's works 'taken together amount to a first draft of his famous essay'.[6] This perhaps accounts for the less mature style of some of this article, reflecting especially his undergraduate enthusiasm for Greek tragedy. Later he refreshed his knowledge of the Greek drama in a formidable reading list he set himself for the Long Vacation of 1827 in preparation for becoming Examining Master for the B.A. degree.[7] Newman was now commissioned by White to review *The Theatre of the Greeks* by Philip Buckham,[8] but, as was usual in book reviews of that period, he used this only as the starting point for giving his own views. In his 1871 revision, he omitted the first two paragraphs of his original article which had dealt with Buckham's book (see the Textual Appendix).

He begins by criticising Aristotle's rules for Tragedy from what we can immediately identify as a Romantic standpoint: they 'tend to withdraw the mind of the poet from the spontaneous exhibition of pathos or imagination'[9]; and Aristotle 'treats dramatic composition more as an exhibition of ingenious workmanship, than as a free and unfettered effusion of genius'.[10] He compares and contrasts a number of the tragedies of Aeschylus, Sophocles and Euripides and judges the varying effectiveness of their structures and language. Nevertheless, he goes on to praise Aristotle's 'general doctrine' that 'poetry ... is a representation of the ideal'.[11] It has been pointed out that this is a Platonized version of Aristotle's definition (as Blanco White himself told Newman[12]). Indeed, Alba Warren concludes that 'Newman's theory of poetry is Platonic and romantic, and is fundamentally opposed to the theory of the *Poetics*.'[13]

---

[6] 'Newman on Aristotle's *Poetics*', *Modern Language Notes*, Vol. 71, No.1 (Jan. 1956), p.23.

[7] Cf. *Letters and Diaries*, Vol.II, p.21. The list of twenty-seven titles includes, Aeschylus, Euripides and 'Greek Theatre' presumably (the book White asked him to review), as well as Keble's *The Christian Year*.

[8] *Theatre of the Greeks; or the History, Literature, and Criticism of the Grecian Drama. With an Original Treatise on the Principal Tragic and Comic Metres*, Philip Wentworth Buckham (d.1829), Cambridge, 1827.

[9] pp.[4]-[5]

[10] p.[7]

[11] p.[9]

[12] Cf. p.[29]

[13] *English Poetic Theory, 1825-1865* (Princeton, New Jersey; Princeton University Press, 1950); quoted in W. David Shaw, 'The Optical Metaphor: Victorian Poetics and

Newman applies his definition in a way that shows him to have imbibed thoroughly the critical doctrines of Romanticism. T. R. Wright[14] finds echoes of Coleridge as well as Plato in Newman's discussion of how poetry 'recreates the imagination by the superhuman loveliness of its views'.[15] Throughout, Newman uses the word 'poetical' to express a quality which some poetry has while other poetry does not. The poetical mind 'is one full of the eternal forms of beauty and perfection'; it 'feels a natural sympathy with everything great and splendid in the physical and moral world' and so it 'speaks the language of dignity, emotion and refinement'.[16] On this criterion of judgment, 'a poem may be but partially poetical; in some passages more so than in others; and sometimes not poetical at all'.[17]

Newman proceeds to use this doctrine to judge a variety of writers, of prose as well as poetry, under the headings of descriptive poetry; narrative; character; opinion, feelings, manners and customs; and philosophy of mind. The essay shows the breadth of his reading: not only does he have a close knowledge of ancient Greek tragedy, but he has read widely in the English literature of his own day, as well as of earlier centuries as far back as Spenser. Not all his critical judgments have stood the test of time. He ranks Keble equally with Milton as showing 'the charm of the descriptive poetry of a religious mind.'[18] He judges that Pope was 'not ... a poet.'[19] And his personal favourites, the novels of Walter Scott and the poetry of Southey, are both out of critical favour today and rarely read. Nevertheless, we see Newman enthusiastically engaged with a range of literature and making interesting comparisons and contrasts.

However, he also had wider purposes in mind for this essay. There is a moral element to Newman's criticism. He states that 'A right moral state of heart is the formal and scientific

the Theory of Knowledge', *Victorian Studies*, Vol. 23, No. 3 (Spring, 1980), p.297.
[14] 'Newman on Literature: Thinking out into Language', *Journal of Literature & Theology*, Vol j, No 2, June 1991, pp.184-5.
[15] p.[10]
[16] Ibid.
[17] p.[11]
[18] p.[12]
[19] p. [25]

condition of a poetical mind'.[20] This does not mean, he adds, that a depraved man may not write a poem; but he affirms that 'frames of mind short of virtuous will produce a partial and limited poetry'.[21] This comes out especially in his ambivalence towards Byron. He praises the 'unweariness and equable fullness of accomplished eloquence'[22] in *Childe Harold*; but when it comes to *Manfred*, 'the delicate mind shrinks from the spirit which here and there reveals itself, and the basis on which the drama is built'. Newman argues that this is because we can infer that 'there was right and fine feeling in the poet's mind, but that the central and consistent character was wanting'. And he adds, 'From the history of his life we know this to be the fact'.[23]

This moral basis of the truly 'poetical' leads him to a further important conclusion: that Revealed Religion is 'especially poetical'. This is because it 'presents us with those ideal forms of excellence in which a poetical mind delights'. Here we have moved beyond a strictly literary critical assessment. Newman tells his readers that 'With Christians, a poetical view of things is a duty,—we are bid to colour all things with hues of faith, to see a Divine meaning in every event, and a superhuman tendency.' He goes on to identify the Christian virtues such as meekness and gentleness as 'poetical', whereas the 'ruder' feelings such as anger, martial spirit and love of independence are 'the instruments of rhetoric more justly than of poetry'.[24] For Newman, the 'poetical' and the spiritual are ultimately the same thing.

This is the key to why in 1871 Newman included this apparently non-religious piece of writing among the other Essays in this volume which are all theological in subject matter. Newman was to see poetry as playing an important part in the Oxford Movement's influence, and indeed some poetry, that of Southey and Wordsworth, as having been one of the causes of its rise.[25] He himself wrote, and more importantly published, his

---

[20] p.[21]
[21] pp.[21]-[22]
[22] p.[18]
[23] p.[22]
[24] p.[23]
[25] Cf. Essay VII, p.[268]ff.

own poems in *Lyra Apostolica*, many of which were composed during his trip to Italy in 1833 during which he was thinking about the religious situation back in England and the need for action. This volume of poetry was intended to help create a more Catholic-minded ethos within the Church of England and also included poems by John Bowden, Richard Froude, John Keble, Robert Wilberforce and Isaac Williams, all of whom were to play some part in the Oxford Movement. Keble's *The Christian Year*, published the year before this Essay, had quickly become popular and was to prove very influential in creating a Tractarian spirituality; it is part of this wider strategy that Newman promotes Keble as a 'gifted poet' here.[26] In Essay VII in this volume he commented that 'poetry of a religious kind has in modern times in a certain sense taken the place of the deep contemplative spirit of the early Church.'[27] So this Essay is by no means as different in intention from the rest of the pieces in this volume as might first appear.

His final section on the actual composition of poetry contains the startling statement that 'the art of composition is merely accessory to the poetical talent.'[28] A 'poetical mind', he claims, is sometimes 'overpowered by a rush of emotions' but too indolent to describe them. He perhaps moves to surer ground when he describes the poet as 'a compositor; words are his types; he must have them within his reach, and in unlimited abundance'. He goes on, 'Hence the need of careful labour to the accomplished poet ... that the language may be subjected to him'.[29] This is a tentative step towards his later, more mature, thought on this subject in *The Idea of a University*, where he says that 'Thought and speech are inseparable from each other. Matter and expression are parts of one: style is a thinking out into language'.[30]

When Newman came to republish the text in 1871, he made a number of changes, but few of them were major. As he explains in his Note on the Essay, he restored several sentences

---

[26] Cf. p.[12]
[27] p.[290]
[28] p.[24]
[29] p.[25]
[30] *The Idea of a University*, Longmans, 1905 edn., p.276.

which Blanco White had altered, including one instance where, as Stephen Parrish argues,[31] White must have altered Newman's text about Rousseau to make him say the opposite of what he had originally written.[32] However, it is interesting that Newman chose to republish this early essay in literary criticism without substantial revision. He did not repudiate or 'answer' the ideas in it, though he says in his appended Note that it 'omits one of the essential conditions of the idea of Poetry, its relations to the affections'; and he then gives a new definition of poetry: it 'may be considered to be the gift of moving the affections through the imagination, and its object to be the beautiful'.[33]

One critic, Joshua Hochschild, even sees in this essay a seed of Newman's last work, the *Grammar of Assent*: Newman notes, he says, that Aristotle

> understood that "a word has power to convey a world of information to the imagination, and to act as a spell upon the feelings". Newman not only appreciated this point, he made it a central feature of his *Grammar of Assent*: mere ideas tend to be "abstract" and "notional," but vivid thought, and effective communication, makes use of images, concrete and "real."[34]

This essay's presence, therefore, among the other weighty theological pieces, does more than illustrate Newman's abiding interest in and love of literature and the spiritual function it can have. It also contains some germs of his later fully developed epistemology.

II. The Introduction of Rationalistic Principles into Revealed Religion

This Essay was originally Tract 73 of the *Tracts for the Times*, published in 1836. It expresses one of the central concerns of the Oxford Movement—the spread of liberal or rationalistic theological opinions. Newman was not, of course, opposed to

---

[31] cf. '*Newman* on Rousseau: Revisions in the Essay on *Poetry*', Notes and Queries 199, no. 5 (May 1954): 217–18.

[32] See the Textual Appendix for page [23].

[33] p.[29]

[34] 'The Re-Imagined Aristotelianism of John Henry Newman', *Modern Age*, Fall 2003, p.341.

using one's reason in matters of religion, but he defines rationalism as 'a certain abuse of Reason ... To rationalize in matters of Revelation is to make our reason the standard and measure of the doctrines revealed.'[35] In the passage where Newman argues what is the legitimate use of reason and what is not, Ian Ker notes his 'sharply antithetical rhetoric' as 'an early example of the kind of tension that is so marked a characteristic of Newman's developed style and thought.'[36]

Newman is concerned about the habit of mind whereby 'the Rationalist makes himself his own centre, not his Maker'[37] and he illustrates this in an extract from a populariser of science who rhapsodises over astronomical knowledge while implicitly disparaging knowledge given by Revelation. Newman then moves to the first of his targets in this essay, the Scottish Episcopalian theologian Thomas Erskine, whose *Remarks on the Internal Evidence for the Truth of Revealed Religion* had made a considerable impact on its publication in 1820. Erskine's starting principle was: 'I cannot believe anything which I do not understand.'[38] Everything in the Gospel should therefore be susceptible of clear and systematic understanding. He decides at the outset that 'The object of Christianity is to bring the character of man into harmony with that of God';[39] and also that this ethical message appeals to humanity's innate sense of what is good and reasonable. In this view Christ's life is a 'manifestation', a sort of sketched or acted out picture, which makes God's ethical character intelligible and which each reader then responds to subjectively.

So in this view, Newman summarises, 'Revelation, as a Manifestation, is a doctrine variously received by various minds, but nothing more to each than that which each mind comprehends it to be.'[40] He is pointing out that Erskine's approach subjects the content and indeed truth of the Gospel to a human standard of judgment. To use a modern term, it is reductive. Newman contrasts this 'manifestation' theology with

---

[35] p.[31]
[36] *John Henry Newman* (Oxford, 1990), p.121.
[37] p.[33]
[38] p.[40]
[39] p.[50]
[40] Ibid.

the concept of 'mystery' which is 'a doctrine *lying hid* in language ... entered into more or less by this or that mind, as it may be [but] ... one and the same, independent and real, of depth unfathomable, and illimitable in its extent.'[41] The Gospel, he says, is not reducible to one simple ethical message but reveals many doctrines, and therefore we should 'avoid all rash theorizing and systematizing'.[42] He quotes from the great Anglican theologian Joseph Butler to make this critique of Erskine; and this is an important part of his strategy as he wishes to demonstrate that traditional, mainstream Anglican teaching does not support Erskine's theology.

Newman argues that Erskine's 'manifestation' Christology in fact amounts implicitly to Sabellianism, the 3rd century heresy in which Jesus is seen just as a mode of God's revealing himself, almost a mask, rather than as actually God made man.[43] Newman's accusation of this is carefully argued, bringing out the implications of Erskine's assumption that all revelation is solely for the purpose of revealing God's *moral* nature and therefore man's *moral* improvement. Does the doctrine of the Holy Trinity do this, Newman asks? Ultimately, yes, but that is not its *sole* purpose. It is not just a 'manifestation' to help us behave better. The Incarnation is central to the Christian faith, to our salvation and redemption. But so far from recognising the centrality of professing this faith, Erskine regards all 'creeds and Church articles' as originating from 'the introduction of doctrinal errors and metaphysical speculations into religion.'[44] Newman goes on to trace out how Erskine's reductive and anti-credal Christology leads him to an equally reductive understanding of the Atonement.[45]

In this analysis, Newman sees the Rationalism of his own day as a re-playing of controversies of the early centuries of Christianity. In his *Arians of the Fourth Century*, published only three years earlier, he had shown how an over-rationalising theology had led to Arius's denial of the divinity of the Son.

---

[41] p.[41]
[42] p.[47]
[43] Cf. pp.[55]ff.
[44] p.[58]
[45] pp.[65]ff.

Newman's patristic study had thus given him the prism through which to view the effects of an over-rationalising approach to Revelation in contemporary protestant writers.

Throughout his analysis of Erskine's theology, Newman never accuses him of intentional heresy. Rather, he shows the assumptions underlying Erskine's approach and suggests the tendencies towards which it leads. Stephen Thomas argues that this was a deliberate rhetorical strategy by Newman:

> This impressionism and diffidence of tone in the handling of Erskine shows Newman modifying polemic into a critique which sounds not unfriendly, and avoiding the implication of Tractarian bigotry which some of his less unequivocal contributions to contemporary debate had provoked'.[46]

In his controversy with the liberal Renn Dickson Hampden,[47] Newman had been accused of such bigotry – though it has to be said that Hampden was quick to take personally what was a theological dispute. Nevertheless, however gently Newman put it, he saw Erskine's theology as in fact dangerous to the very heart of Christianity. It was, he said, a 'narrow-minded, jejune, officious, and presumptuous human system' which in its attack on 'metaphysical' doctrine 'dishonours our holy faith.'[48]

He found this even more to be the case in the second writer he next moved to critique. Jacob Abbott (1803-79) was an American Congregationalist minister whose writings were popular rather than scholarly. He was widely read in England, the *English Churchman* newspaper describing him as well-known. He was a highly prolific author, going on to write a large number of books for children. For Newman, he represents the popular devotional Protestantism of the day.

---

[46] Thomas, S., *Newman and Heresy: The Anglican Years* (Cambridge, 2003), p.122.
[47] Cf. Newman, J.H., *Elucidations of Dr Hampden's Theological Statement* (Oxford, 1836). Hampden (1793–1868) was an Anglican divine whose unorthodox views on the Trinity were expressed in his Bampton Lectures of 1832. His theological principles in *Observations on Religious Dissent* (1834) were described by Newman, in a courteous letter to him, as 'tending ... in my opinion altogether to make shipwreck of the Christian faith' (*Letters and Diaries*, Vol. IV, p.371).
[48] p.[70].

From Newman's quotations from Abbott's *The Corner-Stone, A Familiar Illustration of the Principles of Christian Truth*, which had been published in 1835, it is immediately apparent that he follows the same 'manifestation' theology as Erskine. He considers Jesus' 'exalted nature as the great moral Manifestation of the Divinity to us'.[49] But is this the same as saying that he is God made man? Newman sums up the key doctrinal issue: 'If we wish to express the sacred mystery of the Incarnation accurately, we should rather say that God is man, than that man is God'.[50] And he quotes an extract by a Unitarian who had previously been a believer in the Trinity, Joseph Blanco White, in illustration of the difference in these two ways of speaking. What is particularly striking about the extract from White is his admission that he had tried to pray to God in a Sabellian way but now realised that 'Sabellianism is only Unitarianism disguised in words.'[51] White's movement away from orthodox Christianity (via Unitarianism ultimately to unbelief) greatly distressed Newman who knew him well at Oriel, as did the similar doctrinal movement of Newman's own brother Frank. Behind Newman's theological controversy there thus lay his personal experience of the way theological rationalism led to loss of orthodox Christian belief.

In the case of Jacob Abbott, Newman's Note added in 1871 records the evidently considerable impact of Tract 73's critique of Abbott's writing on the author, who later came to visit Newman at Littlemore in 1843. Abbott expressed

> his deep and sincere obligations to Mr.Newman for the severe strictures which had been made upon his work some time since in the 'Tracts for the Times'. He confessed that they had the greatest effect upon his mind, and that he should write very differently now.[52]

It is notable that Abbott's many subsequent writings mostly kept to secular topics—perhaps Newman's criticisms made him

---

[49] p.[73]; the italics are Newman's.
[50] p.[74]
[51] p.[79]
[52] p.[100]

feel that he had got his theological fingers burnt. For his part, Newman slightly softened his language towards Abott when he revised the Tract for republication in *Essays Critical and Historical*, as the Textual Appendix to this edition indicates.

Nevertheless, Abbott's implicit Christology is found severely lacking by Newman; it is 'something very like Socinianism'[53]—the heresy which denied the Divinity of Christ. Indeed, even more fundamentally, Abbott's description of how God acts in nature, of which Newman quotes a lengthy extract, 'savours unpleasantly of pantheism' since it 'treats the Almighty, not as the great God, but as some vast physical and psychological phenomenon'.[54] He also quotes from Joseph Blanco White again to demonstrate that Abbott's 'is a philosophy under which Socinianism may *lie hid* even from a man's own consciousness'.[55] One can see Newman's point. Abbott describes Christ as 'this personification of [God's] moral attributes' and 'the personification of the divinity for us'[56]—phrases which fall well short of the historic orthodox doctrine of the Incarnation.

Newman also analyses Abbott's account of the Atonement. In this, Christ's death is not seen as an expiation for sin but as a kind of moral example for his followers. But perhaps the most striking parts of this critique are when Newman quotes Abbott's descriptions of Jesus which reduce him to human categories. Jesus 'had a taste for beauty, both of nature and art'; he admired the Temple's architecture and he dressed rather well;[57] he enjoyed a 'lonely ramble at midnight'.[58] All this makes Jesus sound like a cultured middle-class Victorian gentleman. And Abbott goes so far as to praise Jesus' 'peculiarly new and original style of public speaking'[59] and even compares him to Napoleon. Newman concludes, 'Surely such passages as these are simply inconsistent with faith in the Son of God'.[60] This is

---

[53] p.[75]
[54] p.[78]
[55] p.[79]
[56] p.[82]
[57] p.[86]
[58] p.[88]
[59] p.[89]
[60] p.[90]

the key issue: if we take seriously the concept that Jesus is God himself come amongst us as man, we cannot write about him as if he were just a rather superior sort of human being.

Newman's purpose is not to single out Abbott personally for attack. He concludes with a lengthy extract from a leading Congregationalist theologian endorsing Abbott, thus demonstrating that:

> There is a widely, though irregularly spread School of doctrine among us … based upon error, that it is really a specious form of trusting man rather than God, that it is in its nature Rationalistic, and that it tends to Socinianism.[61]

Through Abbott and Erskine, Newman is in fact fighting a theological battle with opponents nearer home such as Hampden and others of the Liberal school of theology within the Church of England and other non-Catholics. Newman has shown the implications of a religion which is aiming solely to have a moral effect, rather than a doctrinal one, and especially one which is impatient with the creeds and ritual which have historically protected the traditional teaching about the Incarnation.

Tract 73 is thus important among Newman's writings, and one can see why he thought it worth republishing in 1871. Indeed, the continuing movement of thought within Protestant Christianity during the decades after he wrote it makes it seem not only perceptive but also prophetic. Abbott's popularising depiction of a rather less than divine Christ would become the 'quest for the historical Jesus'. As Colin Gunton puts it, 'It must be acknowledged that Newman's fundamental rejection of the shape the modernist quest took has been amply justified by history'.[62]

III. Apostolical Tradition.

'If in Newman's view rationalism is the chief enemy of religious truth in his day,' writes Victor Lams, 'its antidote is the constant voice of the Church over the centuries, a voice which he defends

---

[61] p.[95]
[62] Gunton, C., *Theology Through the Theologians: Selected Essays, 1072-1995* (T. & T. Clark, 1996), p.30.

in "Apostolical Tradition"'.[63] Originally an article, 'The Brothers' Controversy', in *The British Critic* of July 1836, this essay was added by Newman to the fifth edition of *Essays Critical and Historical* in 1881. Newman had listed this article among others for possible inclusion in the *Essays* early during his correspondence with the publisher Basil Pickering about the volumes.[64] However, it was not included in the first edition in 1871, presumably for lack of space. When Newman revised the volumes for the 1881 Fifth edition, he decided to remove the lengthy Note to 'The Theology of St. Ignatius' on the genuineness of Ignatius's epistles because he had now transferred it to his *Tracts Theological and Ecclesiastical*, as he explains on p.[262]. This left a thirty page gap in Volume I which he now filled with 'Apostolical Tradition'.

In a letter of 17th September 1880 to Sir William Henry Cope, a Tractarian who had not followed Newman into the Catholic Church but remained sympathetic to him, Newman wrote:

> I am publishing in my first volume of Essays an additional article, which I propose to send you when it is ready. It is nothing very good but you are so kind in wishing to have what I have written, that I should be sorry not to send it you.[65]

He evidently hoped that the article would help to bring such sympathetic Anglicans into the Catholic Church, since he added:

> You must excuse me on the ground of my being a Cardinal, and of my feeling it my duty to be bolder and more urgent with you than when I was a simple priest. And I am older than you, and have less time left me testify my deep conviction that there is but one Church and that is the one called by the whole world Catholic.

The article reviews an exchange of letters between a Unitarian minister and an Anglican clergyman on the divinity of Christ.

---

[63] Lams, Victor J., *Newman's Visionary Georgic* (Peter Lang, 2006), p.xix.
[64] Cf. *Letters and Diaries*, Vol. XXIX, p.237
[65] *Letters and Diaries*, Vol.XXIX, pp.300-1.

What concerns Newman is that both of them base their arguments on the common assumption that

> if we would ascertain the truths which Revelation has brought to us, we have nothing else to do but to consult Scripture on the point, with the aid of our own private judgment, and that no doctrine is of importance which the Christian cannot find for himself in large letters there.[66]

The Anglican clergyman, arguing on this Bible-only approach, is thus very much handicapped—he has not availed himself of the Anglican belief in Tradition, handed down directly from the apostles, as also being a source of doctrine. Newman's frustration at this is palpable, such as when the Anglican disputant at one point actually refers to 'that which they [early Christians] received from the mouths of the apostles' but fails to realise that this is Apostolic Tradition. Newman exclaims:

> The writer not only *burns*, he has the truth in his hands; yet, as his whole argument shows undeniably, he scarcely has caught hold of it but he lets it go again. It is a game of Blind-man's Bluff. The notion of an Apostolical creed authoritatively interpreting scripture is, after all, quite beyond him.[67]

Newman's main objective in this article, therefore, is not to engage with the Unitarian disputant, but to demonstrate the real doctrine of Tradition which the Anglican disputant should have made use of. Without it, the Anglican disputant 'is obliged to look about for philosophical evidence, and fortifies his scheme of doctrine by the shallow and dangerous arguments of Mr. Erskine'.[68] Of course, Newman was well aware that most Anglicans of his day would also have adopted this Bible-only approach, and he is trying to make them aware of how weak it is and how open to the opposing arguments of Unitarians and others it leaves them. He shows the intellectual roots of this

---

[66] p.[103]
[67] p.[108]
[68] p.[110]

approach in Chillingworth and Locke and its radical modern version in Hampden.

Newman shows how Tradition is not, as Hampden had argued, just an accumulation of the Church's comments and reasonings on Scripture. Rather, 'Had scripture never been written, Tradition would have existed still; it has an intrinsic, substantive authority, and a use collateral to Scripture'.[69] Although he quotes Cardinal Bellarmine on the true Catholic view of Tradition, he also quotes an Anglican bishop of the time, John Kaye, in support of this view and sums up: 'This is the doctrine of genuine Anglicanism'.[70] The whole thrust of this article, therefore, is aimed at persuading Anglicans of the necessity of their grasping the importance of Apostolical Tradition in order to defend orthodox Christian doctrine.

To demonstrate that the idea of a tradition, to be handed on faithfully, existed in New Testament times, he quotes St. Paul urging Timothy to 'Keep the deposit.'[71] The usual translation of this and similar verses is 'Keep that which is committed to thy trust', but Newman is correct in his translation, which is also that used by St.Vincent of Lérins whom he also quotes. The Greek word used here is $\pi\alpha\rho\alpha\theta\dot{\eta}\kappa\eta\nu$, meaning something which has been deposited, for example a sum of money. In a parallel text this noun has an adjective added to it, $\kappa\alpha\lambda\dot{\eta}\nu$,[72] meaning noble or beautiful; so it is clear that this deposit is a *thing*, not just a personal action of entrusting by Paul to Timothy. Newman is showing that the concept of the 'deposit of faith', familiar in Patristic writings and in contemporary Catholic theology, was to be found this early in Christianity and was not a late innovation. Although Newman was not a Scripture scholar in our modern sense, this shows his perceptive understanding of how the meaning of specialised terms in Scripture can be inferred from the use of the same term later. He argues similarly about St. Ignatius of Antioch's use of theological terms in Essay VI. Newman's insight here is that the meaning of key terms in Scripture and the Fathers can be

---

[69] p.[118]
[70] p.[120]
[71] I Tim 6:20.
[72] II Tim 1:14.

missed by those who read them out of context, and with Protestant preconceptions, rather than understanding them in the historic continuum of Christian thought.

He goes on to demonstrate the significance of Tradition in the early centuries of the Church, particularly when the Church had to deal with the Arian crisis. He points out that:

> the great Council of Nicæa was summoned, not to decide for the first time what was to be held concerning our Lord's nature, but, as far as enquiry came into its work, to determine the fact whether Arius did or did not contradict the Church's teaching.[73]

And he points out how bishops from different parts of the Church, even those who disagreed with each other on other matters, witnessed to the same doctrine in their tradition:

> The unanimity at Nicæa, then, was not a mutual sacrifice of views between separate churches for the sake of peace; not merely the decision of a majority; but simply and plainly the joint testimony of many local bodies, as independent witnesses to the separate existence in each of them, from time immemorial, of that great dogma in which they found each other to agree.[74]

This is the principle expressed in the dictum of Vincent of Lérins: true doctrine is 'quod ubique, quod semper, quod ab omnibus creditum est'—that which has been believed everywhere, always and by all—a principle which was to play a key role in propelling Newman towards the Catholic Church.

In his Note appended in 1871 Newman says:

> The doctrine of the foregoing Essay is, on the whole, so consonant with what I should write upon the subject now, that the reasons which are given above in the Advertisement, for preserving the original text in these volumes generally, do not apply here. Accordingly I have availed myself of the liberty thus allowed me to make large alterations in it of a literary kind.[75]

---

[73] p.[125]
[74] p.[128]

This is in fact one of the most interesting aspects of this Essay. For some sections of it, Newman did a complete re-write: the Textual Appendix shows that for much of the 1871 version of this 1836 article we are really reading a new text. It is extraordinary that the Catholic Newman could so completely throw himself into his former position, even writing 'as Anglicans, we maintain … '.[76] This is a very bold act of imaginative recreation. It does result in a sharper presentation of his argument, but why does he do it? Why was he so keen not only to fight again, in this republished essay, the theological battles of the 1830s, especially the controversy with the liberal Hampden, but even to sharpen up the weapons with which he had fought them?

The reason was that he could see that subsequent events had vindicated his fears of the time. By the 1870s, liberal theology was widely and increasingly influential in the Church of England, especially following the publication in 1860 of the controversial (and best-selling) *Essays and Reviews*, and the subsequent acquittal of its Anglican authors on a charge of heresy. These essays had questioned the reliability of Scripture and denied the reality of miracles. Newman 'deplore[d] it extremely'[77], because of its effect on the bible-based religion of most English people, so that 'to strike a blow at its [Scripture's] inspiration, veracity or canonicity, is directly to aim at whatever there is of Christianity in the country.'[78] And this was why Newman 'could never hope to defend Christianity on the Anglican basis.'[79] By contrast, Catholics had greater freedom on matters of Scriptural interpretation (for instance about the early chapters of the Book of Genesis) because they had the tradition and authority of the Church to guarantee the truths of Christianity. But basing their faith on the Bible alone made Protestants very vulnerable to liberal re-interpretations of Scripture.

---

[75] p.[137]
[76] p.[103]
[77] *Letters and Diaries*, Vol. XIX, p.482.
[78] Ibid.
[79] Ibid.

So in 1871 Newman was very conscious of his continuing Anglican readership, especially among the heirs of the Oxford Movement. In this revised Essay he was showing that the principles on which he had defended Apostolic Tradition in the 1830s were ones that he could do full justice to now as a Catholic. It is the same as he did in the *Apologia*: not only showing his personal continuity of principles, but also demonstrating that it is only on these principles that Catholic-thinking Anglicans can defend the Christian faith; and implicitly, therefore, that these principles will lead them where they had ultimately led him—to the Catholic Church.

IV. The Fall of La Mennais

It is easy to see why Newman found the French priest Félicité de Lammenais (1782-1854) such an interesting figure. This gifted priest had been the brightest star of the French church in the first two decades of the nineteenth century. His *Essai sur l'indifférence en matière de religion* (four volumes, 1817-24) was a brilliant work of apologetics which attracted wide attention, the first volume selling 40,000 copies within the first few weeks of its publication and influencing a number of conversions to Catholicism. Visiting Rome, he was warmly commended by Pope Leo XII who even offered to make him a Cardinal, though de Lamennais declined the offer. Other works followed, and he was now one of the best known priests in France. Yet his career ended in catastrophic failure; he left the Church and died unreconciled.

De Lamennais deeply lamented the subservience of the Church in France to the State. The 'Gallican' tradition, which dated back to at least the seventeenth century, saw the State having extensive powers over the Church, including the appointments of bishops, the selection of the clergy, and even the promulgation of Papal decrees. What had been barely tolerable under the 'most Christian' Bourbon monarchy was now intolerable under a state whose ministers were sometimes outright enemies of Catholicism. There was an obvious parallel with the establishment of the Church of England under the crown as Supreme Governor, which in reality meant the majority party in Parliament. One of the key concerns of the Oxford Movement was precisely the encroachment by the Whig government over the rights of the Church of England. Keble had famously denounced such moves as 'National Apostasy' in his Assize Sermon which had effectively launched the Movement in 1833. Lamennais' account of how he had tried—and failed—to bring about a new approach by the Catholic Church clearly struck Newman as having lessons for the Church of England. It is, he wrote, 'curious and instructive, as setting before us the actual state of the Roman Communion, both ecclesiastically and morally; and in consequence, as holding out to us some warning of what may come on ourselves.'[80]

Lamennais' proposed solution was that the Catholic Church should break her reliance on the State, and the Pope should put himself at the head of the democratic and revolutionary forces which were at work in European society. The corollary of this was that the Papacy should also renounce its temporal power—the Papal States which Popes had ruled for many centuries and which had been restored by the Congress of Vienna after the depredations of the Napoleonic years. This radical approach—a sort of Liberation Theology—had found an echo in the early days of the Oxford Movement. Hurrell Froude (whose early death was to rob the Movement of one of its most radical thinkers and Newman of a close friend) had come across Lamennais' ideas in France and wrote enthusiastically about them to Newman, adding 'Don't be surprised if one of these days ... [we turn] Radicals on similar grounds.'[81] In a subsequent article in the *British Magazine* in 1833 he drew a parallel between the situation of the Church in France and in England and urged that the English bishops should break their financial reliance on the state.[82] Newman was attracted to these ideas, writing to a friend that if the Church's traditional supporters, the monarchy and the aristocracy, were abandoning

[80] p.[139]
[81] R.H. Froude, *Remains of the Reverend Richard Hurrell Froude, M.A., Fellow of Oriel College, Oxford*, ed. J.H.Newman and John Keble, 2 vols. (London, 1838), i. 311-12.
[82] Cf. O'Connell, Marvin R., 'Newman and Lamennais', in *Newman after a Hundred Years*, ed. Ker, I. and Hill, A.G. (Oxord, 1990), p.184.

it, then "'lo! we turn to the people.'" — perhaps even to become 'long-headed, unfeeling, unflinching radicals.'[83] He later moved away from this brief espousal of radicalism, but he continued to see the Church of England as weakened by her subservience to the State.

Lamennais' views, propounded in his newspaper *L'Avenir*, had caused controversy among French Catholics, and he decided to go to Rome to present his case personally to the Pope for judgment. Newman is scathing about Pope Gregory XVI's political manoeuvres to hold on to the Papal States, even negotiating with the Russian Czar for his support in return for a papal condemnation of the Poles who, as fervent Catholics as much as nationalists, were struggling to free themselves from Russian rule. There was no interest in Rome at all in Lammenais' vision of the papacy as the champion of liberty. The outcome was the condemnation of his teachings in the encyclical *Miravi Vos*. While his followers accepted this, Lamennais himself in bitter disappointment withdrew from the exercise of his priesthood, recording the whole business in his book *Affaires de Rome* which Newman was reviewing in this 1837 article in the *British Critic*.

For all his sympathy with Lamennais' analysis of the French Church's situation, Newman's own political outlook was fundamentally conservative, and he strongly disagreed with Lamennais' endorsement of revolution:

the elementary error of M. de la Mennais ... [is that] he does not seem to recognise, nay to contemplate the idea, that rebellion is a sin. ... Accordingly what we, in our English theology, should call the lawless and proud lusts of corrupt nature, he almost sanctifies as the instinctive aspirations of the heart after its own unknown good.

Newman compares this rebellion to 'the cravings of Eve after the forbidden fruit' and sees Lamennais as 'Hence ... able to draw close to the democratical party of the day, in that very

---

[83] *Letters and Diaries*, vol. iv, p.44, quoted in O'Connell, p.184-5.

point in which they most resemble antichrist.'[84] His final verdict on Lammenais is that he was a 'heresiarch'.[85]

Nevertheless he agrees with Lammenais' identification of the pope's temporal power as the reason why the papacy had, in his view, lost its spiritual power:

> whatever be thought of the duty of the Pope under his circumstances ... no one can doubt that his temporal power is in fact the immediate cause of his pusillanimous conduct ... the Papal monarchy proper so depends upon the renunciation of mere temporal dominion, that while the Pope has the latter, he cannot aspire to the former.[86]

It is interesting that Newman republished these sentiments without any comment now that he was a Catholic. And it is even more striking that he should do so in 1871, shortly after the First Vatican Council which had been interrupted by the withdrawal of French troops from Rome (to fight in the Franco-Prussian war) and the consequent loss of the Papal States to the forces of King Victor Emmanuel, thus completing the unification of Italy. As a Catholic, Newman had never been a supporter of the pope's temporal power. Its maintenance by means of 'foreign bayonets' was 'a great scandal.'[87] It was a repression, which forced unbelief underground, leaving Rome in such a state as 'to honeycomb the population of Italy with unbelief, under the outward profession of Christianity.'[88] When the Vatican Council passed the definition of papal infallibility, Newman felt that 'the definition of July involved the dethronement of September.'[89] Presumably his republication of the essay on Lamennais was a way of indicating that he had not changed his mind on the temporal power since his Anglican days.

In fact this essay leaves open even more interesting questions about the extent of the Pope's authority. When Pope Gregory

---

[84] pp.[157-8]
[85] p.[178]
[86] pp.[155-6]
[87] *Letters & Diaries*, vol. xxv, p.217; quoted in Ker, op. cit., p.658.
[88] Ibid., p.239.
[89] Ibid, p.245.

XVI gave his judgment against Lamennais' ideas, Lamennais had been left in a quandary:

> A Roman Catholic is bound to believe the Pope's decision as true in matters of doctrine, and to submit to it as imperative in matters of discipline; but the critical question is, what are matters of doctrine? ... what are the limits of the revelation, and of [the Church's] message? Are the questions of civil liberty, the liberty of the press, and the like, included in it? Can they in consequence be turned into points of faith?[90]

Lamennais eventually gave up the priesthood and left the Church (just as Newman feared in 1837 would be the final outcome), but initially he had tried to avoid the dilemma by '*interpreting* the Pope's words in *accordance* with *his own* interpretations of the Church'. The Anglican Newman then adds, 'This is worthy of attention, because it shows that objections brought by Protestants in controversy against the Roman theory of infallibility, are not so unreal and subtle as Romanists would represent them.'[91] And almost Newman's final words in this article are that Lammenais had demonstrated that 'Rome has taken up a position which goes far towards involving a *reduction ad absurdum* of her claim to infallibility', and Newman adds 'We agree with him.'[92]

This should not make us think that Newman did not believe in Papal Infallibility. His realisation of the role of the Papacy in the early history of the Church had been crucial in his conversion to Catholicism. His explanation of the historical development of the authority of the popes is one of the most striking elements in his *Essay on the Development of Christian Doctrine* of 1845; and in his *Apologia Pro Vita Sua* in 1864 he had made an eloquent avowal of his belief in the Church's infallibility. So why did he not now in 1871 add any gloss to this Anglican comment of 1837 on infallibility, when the issue had now been put into even more acute form by the Vatican Council's definition? The Ultramontanists who had pushed for

---

[90] p.[169]
[91] p.[170]
[92] p.[172]

the definition were now interpreting it very broadly to cover all the Pope's utterances on any subject whatever, not just on matters of doctrine: W.G.Ward had famously said that he wanted an infallible statement from the Pope with his *Times* at breakfast every morning. Many Catholics now assumed that this was indeed the scope of the 1870 definition and were accordingly very disturbed and looked to Newman to give his view. However, he was not yet ready to do so in public. From his knowledge of history, he knew that the extreme Ultramontanist interpretation of papal infallibility was untenable. But he presumably thought that a note or comment added to this republished Anglican essay was not the place to discuss the controversial question of how papal decisions are to be interpreted. Or rather, perhaps one could see the republication of the essay at this time as itself an indirect way of indicating his approach to this delicate issue. The only addition that he made to the article was his Note which shows how none of Lammenais' followers left the Church. This is perhaps an implicit reassurance to his Catholic readers. It was not to be until 1874 that he published his *Letter to the Duke of Norfolk*[93] which deals with which papal decisions are covered by infallibility and which are not. His detailed and nuanced analysis of the issue there effectively answers the questions raised at the end of his Lammenais article.

The case of Lammenais had other implications. It threw into sharp relief questions about the Church's attitude to social issues which were not to be addressed until Leo XIII initiated the modern tradition of Catholic social teaching with his encyclical *Rerum Novarum* published the year after Newman's death. The Church's teaching on questions of social justice since then has developed rapidly, and Vatican II's Declaration on Religious Liberty, *Dignitatis humanae*, would have delighted Lammenais. Interestingly, shortly after the republication of this Essay, Newman commented in a letter to Matthew Arnold, 'perhaps la Mennais will be a true prophet after all.'[94]

---

[93] Later republished in *Certain Difficulties Felt by Anglicans in Catholic Teaching*, Vol.II.

[94] *Letters and Diaries*, Vol.XXV, p.442.

V. Palmer on Faith snd Unity

William Palmer (1803–1885) was an Anglican divine and theologian of the High Church party, known for his work on early liturgy and admired for his great learning. He initially supported the Oxford Movement, contributing 'On the Apostolic Succession in the English Church' (which Newman revised and completed) as Tract 15 of the *Tracts for the Times* in 1833. In the *Apologia* Newman was later to write:

> Mr. Palmer had many conditions of authority and influence. He was the only really learned man among us. He understood theology as a science; he was practised in the scholastic mode of controversial writing; and, I believe, was as well acquainted, as he was dissatisfied, with the Catholic schools. He was as decided in his religious views, as he was cautious and even subtle in their expression, and gentle in their enforcement.[95]

But Palmer wanted the nascent Movement to be organised under a committee and for the Tracts to be approved by them, a procedure which Newman strongly opposed. Although he had contributed to them, Palmer became increasingly worried by the Tracts and eventually tried to stop their publication (though later when Tract 90 came out to a storm of protest, he wrote Newman a warmly supportive letter about it). He was essentially a man of the establishment. He became very critical of the younger Tractarians such as W.G.Ward, accusing them—rightly, as it turned out—of heading towards Roman Catholicism in their theology.

On the publication in 1838 of Palmer's *Treatise on the Church of Christ designed chiefly for the use of students of theology*, the subject of this review, Newman wrote to John Bowden: 'Have you seen Palmer's book? It is quite overcoming—his reading—and makes one feel quite ashamed. It will do a great deal of good, for just at this moment we need ballast.'[96] And to Samuel Wood he called it 'a tremendous

---

[95] *Apologia Pro Vita Sua*, p.40.
[96] *Letters and Diaries*, Vol VI, p.215.

magazine of learning'.[97] In the *Apologia* he was later to describe it as:

> a most learned, most careful composition; and in its form, I should say, polemical.... it was one which no Anglican could write but himself,—in no sense, if I recollect aright, a tentative work. The ground of controversy was cut into squares, and then every objection had its answer. This is the proper method to adopt in teaching authoritatively young men; and the work in fact was intended for students in theology.[98]

So in reviewing the *Treatise* in this article for *The British Critic*, Newman adopts a respectful tone: 'No one indeed is a good critic about the ability of a writer to whom he has to come as to a teacher; this is our position towards Mr. Palmer, and this is our disadvantage.'[99] He admits that the work may initially appear 'a useful book of reference for facts and nothing more,' but those who persevere with closer study will find it to be

> an attempt, well weighed and wrought out with great patience and caution, to form ... a theory of the Church, which shall be at once conformable to ancient doctrine on the subject, and to the necessities of the modern English communion.[100]

What Newman likes about Palmer's approach is that it does not take the typically Protestant view about the Bible being the sole guide for Christians but rather that the Church is 'our great divinely-appointed guide into saving truth.'[101] But then, of course, comes the question of where the Church is to be found. Palmer says that it is to be recognised by its Notes of being One, Holy, Catholic and Apostolic, in whatever country it is to be found. This leads him to a 'branch' theory of the Church, with the Church of England being one branch, along with the Roman and Greek branches. This was Newman's own view, and he comments that the Anglican Church's true nature had survived

---

[97] Ibid, p.217.
[98] Ibid., p.65.
[99] p.[188]
[100] p.[189]
[101] p.[190]

despite the actions of the State to enforce its established status and Protestant spirit. But he then discusses the objections which can be made to the theory that the Church exists all over the world despite differences between its branches. The question is:

> whether local bodies which have separated from each other can possibly be part of one and the same body; for if they cannot, we shall be driven perforce either to deny that there is a Catholic Church, or else to deny either the Roman Communion or our own to be part of it.[102]

Here we see Newman struggling with what was to become the central issue of his ultimate conversion to Catholicism. Palmer argued that 'misunderstandings and quarrels' between the different branches of the Church were bound to occur but since 'there is no centre of unity, that therefore such estrangements cannot be schisms.'[103] He also argued from divisions in the Church of the patristic age that such had always been the case. All this buttressed Newman's current position as an Anglican.

Newman was evidently much taken with Palmer's view that the '*formal* doctrine [as opposed to 'superstitious practices'] of the Roman Church' was not 'of so erroneous a nature as it is often considered.'[104] Newman grants both that 'those [Catholic] additions are great and serious; and, on the other hand, we may grant without embarrassment the existence of defects in our own system.'[105] He adds in his 1871 revision of the text, 'This is the doctrine of the *Via Media*', while noting that Palmer does not hold it. This addition shows Newman realising that in reviewing Palmer's work on the church in 1838 he was really expressing his own ecclesiology. Indeed, Newman's interpretation of Palmer was over-confident. After this review was published, Palmer wrote to the *British Critic* to disavow two things which Newman had claimed he said,[106] both of which made Palmer out to be more favourable to current Catholic

---

[102] p.[197]
[103] p.[199]
[104] p.[203]
[105] p.[204]
[106] Cf. pp.[169] and [176]

teaching than he really was. Newman added in his 1871 Postscript to Volume II of the *Essays*, 'Neither at the time did they lead me, nor do they lead me now, to change the judgment which I formed of the direct drift of his teaching.'[107] Nevertheless, it seems evident that Palmer's reputation and mainstream respectability were being used by Newman to support the Oxford Movement's catholicising theology.

Newman goes on to contrast Palmer's view with the more widely held view of 'Fundamentals'. These were held to be doctrines which constitute the essentials of the Christian faith, existing separately from the Church, and 'the property of each individual'. The difficulty with this theory was in agreeing just what such fundamental teachings actually are. Newman uses Palmer to criticise the theory, which appealed to more Protestant-minded Anglicans. He opposes to it 'the theory that the Church is absolutely our informant in divine truth' as being 'most simple and unembarrassed certainly.' But he notes that it puts Anglicans at a disadvantage in controversy with Catholics because 'unless we appeal to the past, how can we condemn the present [i.e. Roman 'corruptions']? And how can we detect additions unless we know what it is which is added to?'[108] Here we see the crucial issue which Newman was only finally to address in his *Essay on the Development of Christian Doctrine* in 1845 which took him into the Catholic Church. For the moment, he refers to Palmer's view that the Church can have 'additions' in doctrine but only those which have the consent of the whole church, East as well as West. And Palmer argued that General Councils such as Lyons and Florence, which had approved such 'additions', only really had Western approval, and that since the Eastern (Greek) Church was in fact just as numerous, if not more so, than the West, universal approval had in fact been lacking. Palmer went on to find Catholic writers who did not endorse Catholic teaching on transubstantiation—all of which was grist to Newman's mill as an Anglican. It is significant that this is part of the review that

---

[107] Vol. II, p.[454].
[108] p.[212]

the Catholic Newman replies to in the Note which he added in 1871.

In Newman's Anglican days he had found Palmer to represent some of the best and most authoritative theology that the Church of England could produce. His 1838 review reveals his enthusiasm for Palmer's theology, and yet in retrospect such theology in fact expressed what he was later in his 1871 Note to call 'the Anglican paradox'. This was the position of those in the Church of England who 'Though they think it a duty to hold off from us ... cannot be easy at their own separation from the *orbis terrarum* and from the Apostolic See, which is the consequence of it.'[109] So his final words in this Note are aimed squarely at such Anglicans, the High Church heirs of Palmer. Newman has:

> a serious apprehension that there are those among them who make that paradox the excuse for stifling that enquiry which conscience tells them they ought to pursue, and turning away from the light which otherwise would lead them to the Church.[110]

This sums up Newman's strategy (albeit unstated) behind his republishing of this article, as with so much of his republished work: to show Anglican readers where the principles of the Oxford Movement and the High Church Party really led—to the Catholic Church.

VI. The Theology of St. Ignatius

This Essay was originally a review in the *British Critic*, January 1839, of an edition of the Apostolic Fathers, Saint Clement, Saint Ignatius and Saint Polycarp, edited by Rev. William Jacobson, an Anglican divine who was to become Regius Professor of Divinity at Oxford and later the Bishop of Chester. However, the article in fact incorporated a lot of material from two papers which Newman had read to the Theological Society in Oxford, the first on 11th November 1836 entitled 'Ignatius, a witness for Catholic doctrine', and the second on 10th February 1837 just entitled 'Ignatius'.[111] Newman was interested in the

[109] pp.[210-20]
[110] p.[220]

Epistles of St. Ignatius of Antioch (c.50-98/117) because of the theology of the Church, the episcopate and indeed the sacraments, which they contain and thus the doctrine of first generation of Christians after the apostles. Paul Misner remarks that these Epistles 'had an influence on Newman's interpretation of the church's life from the beginning which can hardly be exaggerated.'[112]

Indeed, the whole article has a more personal background for Newman than might be imagined on first reading. In it Newman describes how people can misunderstand the early Fathers of the Church by reading them through the prism of Protestant doctrines:

Their [Protestants'] notion of the matter of divinity is so different from what prevailed in primitive times, that the surface of their minds does not come into contact with what they read; the points on which they themselves would insist slip on one side, or pass between those of the Fathers; their own divisions of the subject are cross-divisions, or in some way or other inconsistent with theirs. Thus they are ever at cross-purposes with the author they are studying; they do not discern his drift; and then, according as their minds are more or less of a reverent character, they despise or excuse him. ... we know a person who, when he entered on them, read and analyzed Ignatius, Barnabas, Clement, Polycarp, and Justin, with exceeding care, but who now considers his labour to have been all thrown away, from the strange modern divisions under which he threw the matter he found in them.[113]

This 'person' was in fact Newman himself. Later, as a Catholic, he described his experience:

When ... I first began to read their [the Fathers'] works with attention and on system, I busied myself much in analysing them, and in cataloguing their doctrines and principles; but, when I had thus proceeded very carefully and minutely for some space of time, I found, on looking back on what I had

---

[111] Cf. *Letters and Diaries*, Vol.VI, p.25.
[112] Misner, P., *Papacy and Development, Newman and the Primacy of the Pope* (Leiden, 1976), p.31.
[113] p.[227]

done, that I had scarcely done anything at all; I found that I
had gained very little from them, and I came to the conclusion
that the Fathers I had been reading, which were exclusively
those of the ante-Nicene period, had very little in them. At the
time I did not discover the reason of this result, though, on the
retrospect, it was plain enough: I had read them simply on
Protestant ideas, analysed and catalogued them on Protestant
principles of division, and hunted for Protestant doctrines and
usages in them. My headings ran, "Justification by faith only,"
"Sanctification," and the like. I knew not what to look for in
them; I sought what was not there, I missed what was there; I
laboured through the night and caught nothing.[114]

Newman goes on to paint a picture of an imaginary Protestant
writer who decides to produce a book on the Fathers. He reckons
he knows in advance what he wants to say, reads up some of
the standard Protestant authors on the subject, finds he is
running out of time to read the actual Fathers themselves and
gets his book into print. His Protestant readers find their various
prejudices confirmed by it, and so the result is that his book is
'a specimen how the age of railroads should behave towards
the age of martyrs.'[115] The whole passage shows Newman's
satire at its most effective.

In this article Newman is revisiting the letters of St. Ignatius,
now that he has learnt to read them in a more objective—and
indeed more scholarly—way. He focuses on Ignatius' use of key
theological words and phrases and demonstrates how they are
not mere rhetoric but dogmatic terms with specific meanings.
These expressions bore witness to the earliest tradition of the
Catholic faith and also went on to become standard in the
Church's theological vocabulary. Those who are ignorant of this
theology thus miss the significance of what Ignatius was saying.
Newman's detailed discussion of the Greek text shows what an
acute scholar he was, making use of the tools of textual
interpretation which were (and are) used in dealing with all
ancient texts. He comments, 'when an author is hard to be
understood, it is fair to adduce other authors to illustrate his

---

[114] *Certain Difficulties Felt by Anglicans in Catholic Teaching*, Vol, I, pp.370-1.
[115] p.[232]

meaning: is not this what we always do in critical or antiquarian researches?'[116] Protestant commentators had not done this with Ignatius.

Newman brings out such real significance most strikingly in the passage where Ignatius is writing about the Eucharist.[117] Vincent Blehl makes an interesting point about Newman's method of argument here:

> It should ... be noted that in dealing with these various 'dogmatic expressions', Newman uses the argument from converging probabilities, a theory he would later develop in the *Grammar of Assent*. Passing from the form of St. Ignatius' teaching on justification is the Catholic, not the Protestant, teaching that salvation is communicated to man, not merely by the atonement of Christ, but by the risen Christ, present to man in the sacraments.[118]

Ignatius' closeness to the apostolic age makes him a fundamental witness of the early development of the Catholic faith. Newman sums it up: 'St. Ignatius' view of the Gospel truth was very much the same as that taken in "the Catholic religion," and not that of ultra-Protestantism'.[119] Indeed, he comes to the very striking conclusion: 'It is hardly too much to say that almost the whole system of Catholic doctrine may be discovered, at least in outline, not to say in parts filled up, in the course of [St. Ignatius' epistles]'.[120] He references the doctrines that Ignatius teaches in them which everyone would now recognise as distinctively Catholic:

> the principle of dogmatic faith, the doctrine of the Incarnation ... the dissemination of a new and divine nature in the fallen stock of Adam, and that by means of the Eucharist ... the divine authority of the bishop ... the doctrine of the three orders [bishop, presbyter and deacon] ... the doctrine of unity ... the doctrine of the Church's Catholicity ... the diocesan system

---

[116] p..[250]
[117] cf. pp.244-254
[118] Blehl, Vincent Ferrer, *Pilgrim Journey – John Henry Newman 1801-1845*, (London, 2001), p.241.
[119] p.[235]
[120] p.[255]

... the sin of going by individual judgment in matters of faith ... the sacramental character of unity ... the consecrating power and authority of bishops over all Church appointments ... the importance of united prayer ... his implied praise of virginity, and his implied countenance of formal resolves for that purpose ... the *disciplina arcani* ... the *Limbus Patrum* ... the Lord's Day ... the acceptableness of good works ... grace as inherent, not merely external ... ecclesiastical councils ... departed saints remembering or at least benefitting us ... communion with them in life and death'. [121]

Unfortunately one has to add that the list concludes with 'and not least important as throwing a light on all that has been said by the contrast, his hatred and condemnation of Judaism.' It is shocking to read this apparent anti-semitism in Newman, but we must not rush to an anachronistic judgment. Historians explain the early Church's polemical need to distinguish itself from Judaism, and Newman is reflecting this. However, after centuries of bad treatment of Jews by Christians in many places, one might have hoped that the humane Newman would have written more sensitively; but he is thinking of the 1st and 2nd centuries when Christianity and Judaism were rival faiths in the pagan world, and it should be emphasised that he is not recommending hatred towards Jews in his own time.[122] The charge of anti-semitism in Newman's Anglican writing is discussed by Steven Aguzzi who summarises: 'Though Newman's language betrays the prejudices of his day ... scholarship pegging Newman as anti-semitic tends to be anachronistic and one-sided, and considers only a narrow and limited amount of his writing.' Newman also 'stressed the positive characteristics of Judaism, illustrated the continuity between Judaism and Christianity, and pointed out that the religious system of Judaism was divinely inspired and contained worthy examples for Christian living.'[123] Nevertheless, Newman's comment is an aspect of his writing which we today need to critique in the light

---

[121] pp.[255]-[257]
[122] See, for instance, his appreciation of the sympathetic presentation of the exiled Jew in Byron's 'Hebrew Melody' in Essay I, p.[16].
[123] 'John Henry Newman's Anglican Views on Judaism', *Newman Studies Journal*, Volume 7, Issue 1, Spring 2010, pp.56-72.

of the Second Vatican Council's Declaration *Nostra Aetate* which states: 'the Church, mindful of the patrimony she shares with the Jews … decries hatred, persecutions, displays of anti-Semitism, directed against Jews at any time and by anyone.'[124]

Overall, St. Ignatius's letters contains so much Catholic doctrine that Newman asks rhetorically:

> is any further witness wanting to prove that the Catholic system, not in an inchoate state, not in doubtful dawnings, not in mere tendencies, or in implicit teaching, or in temper, or in surmises, but in a definite, complete, and dogmatic form, was the religion of St. Ignatius; and if so, where in the world did he come by it? How came he to lose, to blot out from his mind, the true Gospel, if this was not it? How came he to possess this, except it be apostolic?[125]

And he concludes: 'Give us, then, but St. Ignatius, and we want nothing more to prove the substantial truth of the Catholic system.'[126]

The whole article shows that at this stage Newman was already thinking in the way that was to culminate in the *Essay on the Development of Christian Doctrine* six years later. It is significant that he quoted a lengthy extract from this article in the first edition of the *Essay* (he removed it from his revised 1878 edition, perhaps because he had so recently republished this article in *Essays Critical and Historical*). All that is missing from his 1839 analysis of St. Ignatius is a discussion of the saint's reference to the church of Rome as the one which 'presides in the place of the region of the Romans, worthy of God, worthy of honour, worthy of the highest happiness, worthy of praise, worthy of obtaining her every desire, worthy of being deemed holy, and which presides in love.'[127] The Anglican Newman was not yet ready to apply the same principles to this

---

[124] Op. cit., 4.
[125] p.[258]
[126] p.[261]
[127] *Letter to the Romans*, Introduction.

text evidencing the primacy of the Roman church as to the other Catholic doctrines found in Ignatius's epistles.

VII. Prospects of the Anglican Church

In the *Apologia* Newman makes significant use of this Essay, quoting from it extensively. He says:

> What will best describe my state of mind at the early part of 1839, is an Article in the British Critic for that April. I have looked over it now, for the first time since it was published; and have been struck by it for this reason: — it contains the last words which I ever spoke as an Anglican to Anglicans. It may now be read as my parting address and valediction, made to my friends. I little knew it at the time. It reviews the actual state of things, and it ends by looking towards the future.[128]

The article originated as a response to various critics and defenders (mostly the former) of Tractarianism — a number of such works are listed at the head of the original 1839 *British Critic* article (see the Textual Appendix for p.[263]). Newman sees the chorus of hostile criticism as itself tribute to the extent of the Movement's influence: one alarmed bishop had declared that 'there are few towns of note, to which they [Tractarian doctrines] have not extended.'[129]

Newman proceeds to explain this success. He sees it partly as a reaction to the theology of the previous century, but he also identifies other reasons: first, on the one hand, the growing hostility by the government of the day towards the privileges of the Church of England; but also, on the other, a wider phenomenon, 'a growing tendency towards the character of mind and feeling of which Catholic doctrines are the just expression.'[130] What he means is the cultural shift which we today term the Romantic movement. He cites Walter Scott, Coleridge, Southey and Wordsworth as writers who have contributed to this new sensibility. He also quotes the Church of Ireland lay theologian Alexander Knox as having foreseen a

---

[128] *Apologia pro Vita Sua*, p.94.
[129] p.[265]
[130] p.[268]

restoration of 'primitive truth' — the doctrines of the early Church — in the Church of England. These deeper trends in society and in the church mean, Newman argues, that it is 'plainly idle' to blame the rise of Tractarianism on 'the acts of two or three individuals'[131] as its critics did. He shows the different backgrounds of the Oxford Movement's leading exponents (including himself), stressing their 'independence and individuality'[132] and arguing that 'They are one and all in their degree the organs of One Sentiment, which has risen up spontaneous in many places very mysteriously.'[133] Newman is thus creating the Oxford Movement's own historical narrative, the implication being that it is a providential development.

However, beneath the apparently confident tone of this article are tensions which become apparent during it. Newman becomes more defensive in tone as he deals with the accusations that the Oxford Movement was producing adherents who were 'enthusiastic, extravagant or excessive'. The young, in particular, he admits, 'will be very apt to attach themselves to particular persons, to use particular names ... to act in a party-spirited way.'[134] He was evidently aware of and embarrassed by his own, unwanted, status as a leader in Oxford. He probably knew that his undergraduate followers declared 'Credo in Newmanum.'[135] However, he defends 'the preachers of neglected truth' (i.e. the leading Tractarians such as himself), saying that 'They are not answerable for the dust and din which attends every great moral movement.' He adds, 'The truer doctrines are, the more liable they are to be perverted,'[136] a characteristic Newmanian thought. He also argues that the doctrines of the Movement actually discourage irresponsible individualism because they 'elevate the Church, but they sink the individual.'[137] Nevertheless, in these sections of the article, one somewhat has the impression that Newman knows that the Oxford Movement has started something of which he cannot see the outcome. He is aware of

---

[131] p.[272]
[132] p.[273]
[133] p.[274]
[134] p.[277]
[135] Cf. J.A.Froude, *Letters on the Oxford Counter-Reformation*, p.274.
[136] p.[281]
[137] p.[282]

the emotional appeal of the Catholic doctrines being preached, of 'mere sentiment, romance and the perception of the beautiful, acting powerfully upon ... persons, and being the cause of the present revolution in religious opinions'; but

> if this quality in Catholicism ... does carry men away, we see no harm in persons obeying the higher perceptions and impulses of their minds for the time being ... provided always that they are ready to go on with what they have begun; to acquiesce in consequences when they come upon them; to take up with a course as a whole. [138]

He also defends the Movement against the accusation that, because it found its doctrines in the early Fathers, it wanted to force the Church into an impossible return to Antiquity. This leads him into an early attempt to work out the relation between primitive doctrine and its later fuller expression. It is an awkwardly expressed argument, using less than convincing analogies from mathematics and the law; and in his 1871 Note following the article Newman says that these sections contained the material which he had 'borrowed from the papers of my friend'[139] — almost certainly Henry Wilberforce (see page [308]n) — and in an added 1871 footnote to the main text he says that 'what is said above goes ... further than I habitually went myself as an Anglican.'[140] He emphasises that the theory he uses here 'of a certain *metamorphosis* and recasting of doctrines into new shapes' was 'not mine.' It is interesting to see the Anglican Newman grappling with this topic of the relation between primitive doctrine and that of the Church today which was only to resolve itself in his *Essay on the Development of Christian Doctrine*.

The article picks up pace and fluency again as he turns to the future, surveying the Church of England's different parties: the liberals, the Evangelicals and the Tractarians. About Liberalism he is confident that 'the formularies of the Church will ever ... keep it from making any serious inroads' but adds in a

---

[138] p.[283]
[139] p.[308]
[140] p.[288]

somewhat rueful 1871 footnote that 'It must be confessed that these formularies have not excluded it from the Anglican Church.'[141] He gives most attention to the Evangelicals (though he is reluctant to use that title), whom he sees as the most powerful party. He judges their theology to be inconsistent, occupying 'the space between the contending powers, Catholic truth and Rationalism'[142] and thinks that it will not last. But he turns his most withering satire on the attitude of mind within the Church of England that avoids all definiteness of doctrine:

> In the present day mistiness is the mother of wisdom. A man who can set down half a dozen general propositions, which escape from destroying one another only by being diluted into truisms ... who never enunciates a truth without guarding himself against being supposed to exclude the contradictory ... this is your safe man and the hope of the Church; this is what the Church is said to want, not party men, but sensible temperate, sober, well-judging persons, to guide it through the channel of no-meaning, between the Scylla and Charybdis of Aye and No.[143]

He goes on to use what Ian Ker has called 'grotesque physical imagery, not unreminiscent of Dickens'[144] as he describes the position of such a people: 'they cannot go on for ever, standing on one leg, or sitting without a chair, or walking with their legs tied.' This part of the article, which has been much praised by critics,[145] reminds us that Newman was a highly effective satirist.

But there is also some wishful thinking by Newman in this part of the Essay. He wants to paint a picture of Catholic principles everywhere gaining influence and invites his reader to look at the nation's universities. At Cambridge, he claims that views are shifting, 'edging forward and forward ... to a more Catholic theology'[146]. But a private letter of his at the time expresses scepticism about this, as I have indicated in a footnote. Similarly, he claims that at Dublin (Trinity College), there are

---

[141] p.[294]
[142] p.[297]
[143] p.[302]
[144] Ker, I.T., op.cit., p.175.
[145] For example, Augustine Birrell, 'Cardinal Newman', *Res Judicatæ* (1892), p.160.
[146] p.[304]

'no uncertain tokens of a great and happy change' among 'able and serious men of various characters of mind'[147], but in reality the number of such men was limited. He quotes an opponent's alarm as evidence of the growth of Tractarian ideas,[148] and concludes that this all 'exemplifies the march of the whole of educated Europe.'[149]

This surely overstates the case, but it is more than a rhetorical flourish. It marks a sudden change of direction in the article. Newman says that there is a Europe-wide current of opinion which points not towards Protestantism but everywhere to 'Dogmatism, to Mysticism, or to Asceticism'[150], i.e. to Catholicism, and that the only alternatives to this are 'democracy' (French secular republicanism) or 'pantheism' (German non-Christian philosophy). This change of focus to the European context brings Newman to switch from a tone of inevitable triumph among Anglicanism at home to one of warning about the revival of the Roman Catholic Church in other parts of Europe: 'The spirit of Luther is dead; but Hildebrand and Loyola are still alive.'[151] And so he ends the article with a warning question to his Anglican readers about what will happen if the principles of the Oxford Movement are not allowed to flourish in the Church of England: 'Would you rather have your sons and daughters members of the Church of England, or of the Church of Rome? This is the real alternative.'[152] But whom was he really warning — his readers, or himself? It was in reality himself, though he did not realise this as he wrote. As he later reflected in the *Apologia*:

> while I was thus speaking of the future of the Movement, I was in truth winding up my accounts with it, little dreaming that it was so to be; — while I was still, in some way or other, feeling about for an available *Via Media*, I was soon to receive a shock which was to cast out of my imagination all middle courses and compromises for ever.[153]

---

[147] p. [304].
[148] Cf. pp.[304-5]
[149] p.[305]
[150] Ibid.
[151] p.[306]
[152] p.[307]
[153] *Apologia*, p.100.

This shock was his reading of an article by Nicholas Wiseman in September of 1839 on the Monophysite controversy which quoted the saying of St. Augustine 'securus judicat orbis terrarum' - 'the whole world [i.e. the universal Church] judges justly' - by which, says Newman, 'the theory of the Via Media was absolutely pulverised'[154]; and he began to wonder whether '"The Church of Rome will be found right after all."' [155]

VIII. The Anglo-American Church

Newman had long been interested in the Anglican Church in America - the Protestant Episcopal Church, as it was called, though Newman disliked this title. As early as 1824 he had dined in Oriel with Bishop Hobart of New York who had given him 'a good deal of information' about the church there.[156] Indeed, Raymond Albright thinks that Hobart 'may have influenced this young potential leader [Newman] far more than has hitherto been admitted.'[157] Later, meeting an American Episcopalian during his trip to Italy in 1833, Newman pondered the purpose of the American Church in the Divine scheme.[158] The Oxford Movement men were keen to spread their ideas in America. Supporting the initiative of Walter Hook, the Tractarian Vicar of Holy Trinity, Coventry, to send a complete set of the Fathers to the Episcopal College of New York in 1835, Newman wrote to Hook: 'They [the American church] have a great gift and do not know how to use it'; and he suggested that 'two or three men who agree with us ... go over to New York and make it their head quarters for several years'[159], though nothing came of this idea. According to George Demille, the *Tracts for the Times* were far more favourably received in America than in England,[160] though Larry Crockett has argued that 'the *Tracts* were less influential than has usually been

---

[154] Ibid., p.111.
[155] Ibid., p.118.
[156] *Letters and Diaries*, Vol. I, p. 173
[157] Albright, Raymond, *A History of the Protestant Episcopal Church* (New York, 1964), p. 230.
[158] Cf. *Letters and Diaries*, Vol. III, p. 225.
[159] *Letters and Diaries*, Vol. V, p. 180.
[160] Cf. Demille, George E., *The Catholic Movement in the American Episcopal Church* (Philadelphia, 1941), p.41.

supposed because a fair number in the American church had already reached, in part or in full, many of the ecclesiological views advocated in the *Tracts for the Times*.'[161] Whichever way round it was, it is interesting that Bishop Doane of New Jersey was to defend Tract 90 when he visited England in 1841.

But Newman was also made aware that the American church could not always be relied on. In April 1839 he was visited by the Bishop of Vermont, John Henry Hopkins, and they evidently got on well together. However, Newman was soon much disturbed by reports of how the bishop had subsequently presided at meetings of Evangelical clergy in Dublin which were promoting a society to send preachers round the country in defiance of the bishops. Newman wrote Hopkins letters of pained remonstrance,[162] though he later sent him a friendly farewell, together with some books, when the bishop returned to America.

Newman's article in the *British Critic* of October 1839, reviewing a number of publications about the American church (see the Textual Appendix for p.[309]), thus reflected an ongoing interest that may surprise readers who think of him in a solely English context. That summer the North American church had been much on his mind. In August he wrote to Bishop Hicks of Nova Scotia[163] and Bishop Strachan recently appointed to Toronto[164] who were in England for consecration by the Archbishop of Canterbury, though he never met them. On 30th August, writing to Tom Mozley about the *British Critic*, Newman says 'I think I shall keep American publications, when any come',[165] and by 8th September he writes to his sister Jemima, Tom's wife, that he has written an article on the American church,[166] so presumably the article was written in the first week of that month.

---

[161] Crockett, L., 'The Oxford Movement and the 19th-Century Episcopal Church: Anglo-Catholic Ecclesiology and the American Experience', *Quodlibet Journal*, Volume 1 Number 5, August 1999.
[162] Cf. *Letters and Diaries*, Vol. VII, pp.67, 71, 74.
[163] Ibid., p. 121.
[164] Ibid, p. 122. This bishop had assured Newman of his 'adhesion to the Tracts almost in toto' (ibid., p.123).
[165] Ibid, p. 128.
[166] Cf. Ibid., p. 138.

The timing of the article is significant. Alone in Oriel during the Long Vacation, he had been reading the history of the Monophysite crisis in the fifth century. As he read, 'for the first time a doubt came upon me of the tenableness of Anglicanism'.[167] Comparing the various theological parties of the fifth century with those of the sixteenth and nineteenth, he suddenly saw the parallels: 'I saw my face in that mirror, and I was a Monophysite.'[168] He did not tell his friends of his doubts, though on 1st September he did admit his anxiety about the Church of England to Manning, writing about a female friend of Manning's who was on the brink of becoming a Catholic: she had doubts about the Church of England's catholicity, and Newman wrote somewhat desperately, 'can she deny that the hand of God is with our Church, even granting *for argument's sake* Rome has some things which we have not. Is it dead? has it the signs of death?'[169] One can see why it was just at this time that he wished to write about the American church: there, in the New World, there seemed to be evidence that Anglicanism was alive. Looking 'across the western wave' and seeing the American off-shoot of the Church of England now flourishing 'gives us some taste of Catholic feelings, and some enjoyment of Christian sympathy'.[170] One can feel here Newman's theological isolation and need for reassurance. More importantly for Newman, concerned at the Church of England's status, 'We have the proof that the Church, of which we are, is not the mere creation of the State, but has an independent life'.[171]

Of course, this fact of vitality and of geographical extension was actually a rather weak argument for the Anglican Church, as the Catholic Newman was so easily able to point out in his 1871 Note on this essay:

> as to success in various countries, which, when attaching to an idea or undertaking, is under conditions a genuine evidence of truth, it must be recollected that, if Anglicanism has spread among its kindred population in the United States, there have

---

[167] *Apologia*, p.114.
[168] Ibid.
[169] *Letters and Diaries*, Vol.VII , p.134.
[170] p.[312]
[171] p.[313]

been, I think, Wesleyans in Sweden, and Friends in the Low Countries, places strange to England in climate, language, and mental habits. Nestorianism, a Greek heresy, lasted for many centuries, and extended from China to Jerusalem. It had twenty-five archbishops, and its numbers, with the Monophysites, surpassed those of the Greeks and Latins together.[172]

In the *Essay on the Development of Christian Doctrine* he had gone even further in describing how in various times and places the Catholic Church has been much outnumbered by heretical or schismatic communions, and he actually used this as an argument for the continuity of identity of the present day Catholic Church, very much a minority in Protestant countries like England, with the church of the early centuries. It is an interesting example of how Newman can turn an argument apparently against the Church into evidence in its favour — in this case an argument which had been of his own making only six years previously.

In one sense then, this article may show Newman somewhat grasping at straws to bolster his faith in the Anglican Church. There is a very great deal of narrative in the article, quoted at length from the books under review, presumably to provide evidence of the American church's life. In fact there was even more of this in the 1839 original text, as the Textual Appendix shows. There were lengthy - one has to say tedious - details of church architecture, and even of one particular organ, and of the experiences of Anglican churchmen in the wilds, especially the adventures of a lay-reader by the name of Samuel Gunn, which made this long article even longer. We can be grateful that the Newman of 1871 trimmed these out, though readers may still find even this edited version something of a strain on their patience at times.

However, there is entertainment too. Newman himself said of this article, 'I have written what I fear is a somewhat flippant one on the American Church, though I respect her members too much to mean to be so.'[173] Newman writes of 'the excesses of Sectarianism in the North American States' with a certain

---

[172] pp.[382-3]
[173] *Letters and Diaries*, VII, p.138.

English detachment and amusement. We hear of the 'Seed and Snake Baptists', the 'Dunkers, who ... wear a peculiar dress', the camp meetings where 'The people become powerfully excited; they shout 'Glory' and 'Amen'; they scream, jump, roar, and clap their hands, and even fall into swoons, convulsions, and death-like trances', the Quakers, a third of whom 'have lately declared themselves Unitarians', the Universalists, the followers of Ann Lee 'whom they consider the woman mentioned in Revelation', and the 'Mormonites ... the only sect of pure American origin'.[174] Such a list has a cumulative effect - we get a picture of American religion as anarchic but also as ridiculous. He then presents the American Anglican Church as the haven of apostolic truth amidst this chaos.

But after praising the 'remarkable birth of this Church out of the ashes; its instinctive appreciation of the [Apostolic] Succession; ... its sudden and vigorous development',[175] Newman starts to express concerns about the American church. He first has an interesting passage beginning 'All systems ... which live and are substantive, depend on some or other inward principle or doctrine, of which they are the development'[176] in which he outlines a theory of development for the American church. But he says that 'no Church is fully and simply developed into its full proportions'.[177] He thinks that the American church has got in her 'that rudimental truth on which all true Churches rest',[178] but he sees various factors having a deleterious effect on her, especially the influence of so many of the church's members having recently been Dissenters, i.e. non-Anglican Christians of a more Protestant belief. He notes with alarm attempts to revise the American Prayer Book to remove references to the Holy Trinity. This showed 'the influence of a refined and covert Socinianism'[179], i.e. denial of the divinity of Christ. He notes that it appealed particularly to the well off and makes an interesting analysis of the connection between Socinian belief and 'a trading country', such as the

---

[174] pp.[325-6]
[175] p.[332]
[176] p.[333]
[177] p.[335]
[178] p.[336]
[179] p.[347]

United States, or, as we would put it today, a free market or consumerist economy:

> Commerce is free as air; ... Exclusiveness, separations, rules of life, observance of days, nice scruples of conscience, are odious to it. ... A religion which neither irritates their reason nor interferes with their comfort will be all in all in such a society.[180]

Of the whole passage, Edward Short comments, 'No better description of nominal Christianity has ever been penned'.[181] It worries Newman that the Episcopal church is principally having success among 'the opulent merchants and traders in towns'; there are apparently 'few, if any, poor persons' in the Episcopalian churches. He continues in a passage where the satire works, as Ian Ker has noted,[182] through exposing the incongruous:

> If this view of things is allowed a footing, a sleek gentlemanlike religion will grow up within the sacred pale, with well-warmed chapels, softly cushioned pews, and eloquent preachers ... we think we may say without fear of mistake, that pews, carpets, cushions, and fine speaking are not developments of the Apostolical Succession ... who would ever recognize in a large double cube, with bare walls, wide windows, high pulpit, capacious reading-desk, galleries projecting, and altar obscured, an outward emblem of the heavenly Jerusalem, the fount of grace, the resort of Angels?[183]

This is part of an interesting piece of socio-cultural analysis by Newman in this part of the Essay, identifying the connection between a consumerist lifestyle and liberal religious belief and practices. It is not just a matter of style — it has theological implications. He notes the lack of the celebration of the Eucharist in Episcopal Church gatherings; and he also expresses concern about the bad effects of the elections of bishops as producing 'intrigue, party feeling, and dispute among the

---

[180] p.[349]
[181] Short, E., *Newman and his Contemporaries*, London, 2011, p.294.
[182] Cf. Ker, Ian, 'Newman the Satirist' in *Newman After a Hundred Years*, Oxford, 1990, p.8.
[183] pp.[350-1]

clergy'. He has noted the problems of the financing of the clergy through the voluntary contributions of the laity:

> Nothing is more Christian than that the people of the Church, who are benefited by her ordinances, should "willingly offer" for her support: nothing more unchristian than that individual clergymen should be at the mercy of the people, and be under the temptation of "preaching smooth things" to get bread, clothes, and lodging.[184]

He traces in detail 'the element of lay interference through the various functions of American ecclesiastical government at the present time'[185] by lay participation in synods, for instance. We rightly see Newman as the champion of the laity in the church, but this essay reminds us that, as always, his view was a nuanced one.

He is also concerned about the way that some American churchmen write of the episcopacy as if it were merely some preferred form of governance in the church or even an addition to it, rather than the essence of the church. An American bishop had written that Presbyterian bodies have simply an 'imperfect' form. Newman is aghast:

> Imperfect! is a mouse an imperfect kind of bat? is it a bat all but the wings? Could we sew wings on it and make it a bat? Did all the swelling of an ambitious heart develop the frog into the bull? Could it "perfect its defective organization"? So it is with Independency or Presbyterianism viewed in themselves: as forms they are as distinct from the Church as "one kind of flesh" from another.[186]

Finally, Newman even makes a certain fun of the Episcopalian enthusiasm about 'the liturgy', i.e. the Book of Common Prayer, as a panacea for all situations.

By the end of the article, Newman seems to have as many doubts about the American church as hopes. As Edward Short puts it, 'we can see Newman extolling the putative vitality of

---

[184] p.[312]
[185] p.[360]
[186] p.[370]

the American church with strenuous resolve, even as he sharply calls it into question.' And when Newman has praised the American church as 'a living principle,'[187] Short remarks 'one wonders whether Newman truly believed what he was saying.'[188] Certainly, there is a tension within this 'flippant' essay - it is an uneasy mixture of affirmation, hope, satire and worry.

IX. Selina, Countess of Huntingdon

This volume ends with a very readable essay which contains some of Newman's sharpest satirical writing and which expresses his greatest doubts yet about the Church of England. Its subject, Selina Hastings, *née* Shirley, (1707–91), underwent an evangelical conversion experience and from then on threw the power of her remarkable personality and her considerable financial resources into the Methodist movement, ultimately creating her own denomination, 'The Countess of Huntingdon's Connexion', which had ministers and chapels throughout the country. It still has twenty-one churches in the U.K. today. Newman deplored both her theology and the sectarian outcome of her work, but he greatly respected the woman herself:

> She devoted herself, her name, her means, her time, her thoughts, to the cause of Christ. ... She acted as one ought to act who considered this life a pilgrimage, not a home,—like some holy nun, or professed ascetic, who had neither hopes nor fears of anything but what was divine and unseen.[189]

However, the Countess, as Ronald Knox was later to remark, 'has not been fortunate in her official biographer',[190] and it was this biography, *The Life and Times of Selina, Countess of Huntingdon, by a Member of the Houses of Shirley and Hastings*, that Newman reviewed in *The British Critic* in October 1840. Knox summarises the book as 'a monument of pietism, and pietism disfigured by unremitting snobbishness'.[191] It is this unattractive mixture that attracts Newman's satirical

---

[187] p.[334]
[188] Op.cit., p.293.
[189] pp.[388-9]
[190] Knox, R., *Enthusiasm* (1950), p.484.
[191] Ibid.

eye. He remarks on the three appearances of Lady Huntingdon's crest even before the first page of text and the way the author, with evident pride, describes himself as 'a *cadet of her illustrious family*'.[192] Later in the book, recounting how a Methodist clergyman was deprived of his curacy by his bishop, the author is particularly outraged because the clergyman '*was of a good family*'.[193] The author quotes the Methodist leader George Whitfield writing to the Countess in sycophantic terms about '"her ladyship's condescension, *and* the unmerited super-abounding grace and goodness of Him who has loved me," etc'.[194] Here aristocratic favour is apparently valued on an equal footing with God's grace.

Much of this may be seen as trivial, merely an unfortunately unctuous expression of traditional English class deference, but Newman has more serious issues with Methodism which he describes frankly as 'a heresy'.[195] The author of the *Life* claims that before her conversion Lady Huntingdon, despite her evidently Christian way of life, was filled with complacency and was 'an absolute stranger to the inward and universal change of heart, wrought by the gracious operations of the Spirit of God'.[196] Newman points out that the author presents no evidence for this astonishing criticism which amounts to a charge of Pelagianism. In fact 'all this is the mere illusion of persons who will not inquire into facts'.[197] What Newman is getting at here is that the author's assumption about Lady Huntingdon's spiritual state at this stage of her life is based on the Calvinist doctrines of the natural depravity of human nature and the division of humanity into the saved and the damned. Newman had himself originally held such beliefs, but he had found in his pastoral work as a clergyman that such a theoretical division was simply unreal. As he puts it here, 'we do not argue against doctrines or facts, when really such, we only are jealous of theories'.[198]

---

[192] p.[390]
[193] p.[392]
[194] p.[394]
[195] p.[387]
[196] p.[395]
[197] p.[396-7]
[198] p.[398]

Newman's technique in this essay involves a frequent modulation of his tone. One moment he is serious, paying generous tribute to 'the bold and energetic preaching' of Wesley and Whitfield who 'spoke to the consciences of rich as well as poor' as 'preachers of repentance to those who needed repentance'.[199] But a few lines later he cannot resist the satirical opportunity given him by the Prince of Wales' reported remark that, 'when I am dying, I shall be happy to *seize the skirt* of Lady Huntingdon's mantle *to lift me up* with her to Heaven'. Newman comments with mock Protestant outrage:

> the Calvinistic biographer of Lady Huntingdon ... must feel in his heart, that, under the language of Scripture, it [the remark] savours of what he considers the leaven of Popery, that it interferes with the doctrine of justification by faith only, ascribes to Lady Huntingdon works of supererogation, tends to saint-worship, and encourages the notion that the intervention of one man can be of service to the soul of another.[200]

Again, writing about the non-believing Lord Bolingbroke, whom Lady Huntingdon attempted to influence, Newman first remarks that Bolinbroke's status as a religious outsider gave him a certain impartiality in judging a movement like Methodism. But when Newman says that such sceptics 'will often admire and defend extreme thinkers of whatever cast of opinion, while they despise those who move forward, or rather sideways or crossways, on two or three principles at once'[201] he is having a dig at the contradictions of mainstream Anglicanism which he had criticised in Essay VII.

For Newman has another target in this essay, besides Calvinistic Methodism and its social snobbery. Bolingbroke had told Lady Huntingdon that the King had recommended that '"Mr. Whitfield should be advanced to the bench [of bishops], as the only means of putting an end to his preaching."'[202] This wittily expressed the Church of England's 'imbecile policy'[203]

---

[199] p.[400]
[200] pp.[400-1]
[201] p.[402]
[202] p.[403]
[203] Ibid.

towards this new religious movement. The Church should have been able to find 'places in her economy'[204] for Methodism, but the Anglican establishment could not work out its attitude to it: 'it gave out no authoritative judgment on it … it had no line of policy towards it—it could but speak of it negatively, as going *too far*, or vaguely, as wanting in *discretion* and *temper*'; whereas Methodism, by contrast, 'was a living, acting thing, which spoke and did, and made progress, amid the scattered, unconnected, and inconsistent notions of religion which feebly resisted it'.[205] Newman obviously has a parallel with the Oxford Movement in mind. In both cases, the Church of England hierarchy is incapable of responding coherently to something new and vital. He quotes from the *Life* accounts of a series of Anglican bishops' contradictory dealings with various Methodists, including an occasion when a bishop and several of his clergy stood mutely watching Whitfield's powerful effect on a crowd of ten thousand people — a situation which Newman archly remarks was 'a type of the conduct of the Established Church during the whole movement'.[206] He summarises the situation: the Methodists 'had a message to deliver, a position to defend, and that one and the same to all', whereas their Anglican opponents 'had none. [They] did not maintain any definite, or aggressive, or opposite doctrine, such as the sacramental power of the Church, or the Catholic character of their own creed.'[207]

There follows an interesting analysis by Newman of the effect of the Church of England's incoherent attitude on all such Evangelicals. It creates among them, he says, 'a great notion of their own superiority'. They have no interest in the views of other churchmen unless they coincide with or approach their own. What is particularly striking, given that Newman is writing about Evangelicals, is that he now goes on to make explicit the parallel with the Oxford Movement. He says that in this approach, 'we see the meaning of the style of certain publications, to which the last seven years have given birth',[208] i.e. the

---

[204] p.[404]
[205] p.[405]
[206] p.[406]
[207] p.[410]

Tracts for the Times. With an air of detachment, he says that these writers (of whom of course he himself was the foremost)

> thought that the very first point to be secured in the contro-versy, was the inflicting upon all readers that theirs was a whole positive consistent objective system, which had to be mastered, … one which they had to approach, study, enter upon, and receive or reject, according to their best judgment. They wished it to be recognized as a creed, and to gain from others the attention due to one. … They knew that comprehension or compromise was simply beside the mark.[209]

The force of this extraordinary yoking together of Evangelicals and Tractarians is to warn the Church of England about what is likely to happen if the Church cannot find a coherent response to the Oxford Movement. It's not clear exactly what response Newman wants; it's almost as if he is taunting the Establishment to react in some way - any way - to the Oxford Movement, rather than have the dithering incoherence of its response to Method-ism. Can we feel here the late Anglican Newman spoiling for the crisis which Tract 90 was to precipitate?

It is significant that Newman moves next to the key question of authority. The Anglican bishops had failed to exert theirs, and so, Newman argues, the Methodists evolved an authority of their own: 'Lady Huntingdon became acting bishop instead of them'.[210] He quotes, with evident glee, the description by Whitfield of how her ladyship is *'like a good archbishop, with his chaplains around him'*. Introducing a letter in which Lady Huntingdon magisterially reproves one of her clergymen, Henry Venn, Newman comments: 'Thus she speaks *ex cathedrâ,*— Selina Episcopa, dilecto filio Henrico Venn'.[211] One hostile critic of Newman, Frank Turner, claims that Newman 'commended'[212] Whitfield's description of Lady Huntingdon, but he has com-pletely missed the satire here. *Pace* modern proponents of

---

[208] p.[411]
[209] Ibid.
[210] p.[412]
[211] p.[413]
[212] Turner, F.M, *John Henry Newman: The Challenge to Evangelical Religion* (2002), p.346.

female ordination, for Newman it was self-evidently absurd for a woman, whether aristocratic or not, to assume the powers of a bishop. Turner goes on to claim that Lady Huntingdon's role in her 'Bethel' was to be paralleled by Newman's role in the community at Littlemore, but this is a false analogy. Newman's role there, albeit an informal one, was closer to that of a religious superior - the role he was subsequently to play at the Oratory. But he scrupulously refrained from giving orders to those who joined him at Littlemore and constantly insisted on the authority of his bishop, to whom indeed he was always obedient. By contrast, Lady Huntingdon's assumption of authority resulted in the founding of a new sect named after her.

Newman turns next to the scandalous case of the affair of Rev. Haweis who acquired a parish living in dubious circumstances and refused, with the support of another leading Methodist, the Rev. Madan, to give it up. The situation was solved by Lady Huntingdon throwing money at the problem—£1,000, equivalent to about £167,000 today— to buy the living. This part of the article was much longer in the original 1840 text (see the Textual Appendix), and we can be grateful that Newman shortened it. Why does he go into such detail on this affair? Because of the way the sordid business did no harm at all to both clergymen's standing as leading Methodists. 'Dr. Haweis does not particularly shine' in the affair,' says Newman, with some understatement; but, he continues:

> if faith, such as he was considered to have, blots out all, even the most enormous sins, it is not wonderful if Lady Huntingdon and her friends considered it a sovereign prophylactic against any prospective mischief happening to his soul from mere peccadillos against the law whether of charity, generosity, equity, or honour.[213]

Once again, Newman is pointing out, in this essay's characteristic sardonic tone, the deleterious results of the Methodists' Calvinist theology, in this case of the perfection of the 'elect' which lets these clergymen off serious charges against them.

---

[213] p.[417]

And as for Mr. Madan, Newman adds with further irony that 'this gentleman ... baptized with fire and enlightened in the nature of regeneration',[214] went on to write a book advocating polygamy. Finally, Newman highlights another leading Methodist minister, the Rev. Berridge, whom Whitfield had praised as 'an Angel of the Church' but who seems to have been an eccentric buffoon.

The conclusion to the article has a distinctly uneasy tone. Newman now makes the claim that the Methodist revival owed everything to the Church of England itself, since Wesley and Whitfield, as her ordained ministers, had obtained their graces through her. And so

> The English Church *could not but* have had a revival, if it be a branch of the true Church; that Wesley and Whitfield were the instruments of that revival (as far as they were such), was what may be called an accident of Providence'.[215]

This awkward *a priori* argument is part of his strategy to bolster faith in the Anglican Church on the basis that it has demonstrable life. But Newman goes on to make the extraordinary statement, for an Anglican, that:

> The Church Established, if so be, may not be a true branch; the English people, if so be, may have forfeited the gift; and surely we are all most unworthy of it, and have abundant cause for thankfulness, *so far as we have reason to suppose that we still have it.* [my emphasis][216]

- which leaves the reader wondering whether it does indeed still have that divine gift of being a true branch of the Church. Clearly, Newman has come a long way from the 'supreme confidence' in the cause of the Church of England that he had when he wrote the earlier articles. And it is on this note of considerable doubt that Volume I of *Essays Critical and Historical* closes.

Andrew Nash

---

[214] p.[419]
[215] p.[424]
[216] Ibid.

A NOTE ON THE TEXT

The first edition of these collected essays was published by Basil Montagu Pickering in 1871. The text used for this Gracewing edition is the sixth edition published by Longmans, Green and Co. in 1885 which was Newman's final revised version (subsequent editions published in his lifetime being reprints of this). Other works by Newman, except the *Letters and Diaries*, are also cited in the uniform Longmans editions.

Footnotes

The page layout and headings in this Gracewing edition exactly copy the Longmans edition, except for the addition of the Editor's footnotes. Newman's own footnotes are followed by [N] to distinguish them from the Editor's footnotes. Where Newman's footnotes are in square brackets, they are the ones he added to his original texts for the 1871 and 1885 editions. Some of Newman's notes need further explanation, so the [N] is sometimes followed by an Editor's Note. All other footnotes are by the Editor.

Page numbering

It is the practice of Newman scholars to cite his works using the uniform Longmans editions. To facilitate this in the present volume the page numbers of the Longmans edition are placed in square brackets at the appropriate places in the margins of the text. All references in the Editor's Introduction and the Textual Appendix are to these page numbers.

ESSAYS CRITICAL AND HISTORICAL

VOLUME I

TO

WILLIAM FROUDE, ESQ., F.R.S.[1]

To you, my dear William, I dedicate these miscellaneous compositions, old and new, as to a true friend, dear to me in your own person, and in your family, and in the special claim which your brother Hurrell[2] has upon my memory;—as one, who, amid unusual trials of friendship, has always been fair to me, never unkind;—as one, who has followed the long course of controversy, of which these Volumes are a result and record, with a large sympathy for those engaged in it, and a deep sense of the responsibilities of religious inquiry, and the sacredness of religious truth.

Whatever may be your judgment of portions of their contents,[3] which are not always in agreement with each other,

---

[1] *WILLIAM FROUDE*: (1810-79); an undergraduate at Oriel while Newman was a Tutor, he became close to Newman but did not follow him into the Catholic Church, becoming increasingly sceptical and ultimately agnostic. He had a distinguished career as a nautical engineer. Newman remained friends with him and his wife throughout his life.

[2] *your brother Hurrell*: Richard Hurrell Froude (1803-36), Fellow of Oriel and a disciple of John Keble, was a major influence on Newman, and they became close friends. He developed tuberculosis, and in search of improvement to his health he travelled to Italy with his father and Newman. He was a key founder of the Oxford Movement, contributing four of the *Tracts for the Times*. After his death, the publication of his *Remains* in 1838, edited by Newman, shocked the protestant public with Froude's praise for the mediaeval church and his dislike of the Reformers.

[3] *Whatever may be your judgment . . .* : When Newman initially proposed dedicating

3

you will, I know, give them a ready welcome, when offered to your acceptance as the expression, such as it is, of the author's wish, in the best way he can, of connecting his name with yours.

I am, my dear William Froude,

Most affectionately yours,

JOHN HENRY NEWMAN.

August 1, 1871.

Essays Critical and Historical to him, Froude was hesitant in case it gave a false impression that he still had more Christian faith than was now the case; cf. *Letters and Diaries*, Vol. XXV, p.365. Newman's wording here reflects that, and Froude was happy to accept the dedication

ADVERTISEMENT

THESE Essays, with the exception of the last,[1] were written while their author was Fellow of Oriel, and a member of the Established Church. They are now after many years republished, mainly for the following reason:—

He does not hold now, on certain important points, the opinions to which he gave expression then; yet he cannot destroy what he has once put into print: "Litera scripta manet."[2] He might suppress it for a time; but, sooner or later, his power over it will cease. And then, if either in its matter or its drift, it is adapted to benefit the cause, which it was intended to support when it was given to the world, it will be republished in spite of his later disavowal of it. In order to anticipate the chance of its being thus used after his death, the only way open to him is, while living, without making alterations, which would destroy its original character and force, to accompany it with additions calculated to explain why it has ceased to approve itself to his own judgment. If he does as much as this, he may reasonably hope, that either no reprint of it will be made

---

[1] *the last*: in Volume II.
[2] *"Litera scripta manet."*: "the written word endures"

hereafter, or that the reprint of his first thoughts will in fairness be allowed to carry with it a reprint of his second. This, accordingly, has been his attempt in the present edition of these Essays, as far as they demand it of him; and he is sanguine that he has been able to reduce what is uncatholic in them, whether in argument or statement, to the position of those "Difficultates"[3] which figure in dogmatic treatises of theology, which by their incisiveness court the favourable attention of the Protestant reader, and are elaborately drawn out, and set forth to the best advantage, in order that they may be the more carefully and satisfactorily answered.

A further "difficulty," he is well aware, remains behind. With the run of men, the mere fact that a doctrine is disputed, is a sufficient reason for considering it disputable; and the spectacle of two sides of a great ecclesiastical question advocated with equal earnestness by one and the same author, tends necessarily to create in them a despondent, or liberalistic, or sceptical habit of mind on the subject of religious truth altogether. He is sorrowfully conscious that his course in life, and the writings with which he has all along accompanied it, are open to this reproach. He can but say for himself that such a misfortune has been a necessity of his position; the position of a man, who, from various circumstances, has been obliged through

---

[3] *"Difficultates"*: 'difficulties', objections to the Catholic faith.

so many years to think aloud. Who is there of us all, who would be pleased, or could bear, to have all his thoughts, as current events elicited them, contemporaneously put upon paper? Yet this has been the author's lot. However, he has touched upon the subject, not to excuse himself, but in order that these volumes should go out to the world with such an express recognition on his part of an evil, which he deeply feels to be incidental to them, as may serve as a caution, and, if so be, a safeguard against it.

The first Essay was written in 1828, for the *London Review*; the second in 1835, for the *Tracts for the Times*; the last in 1846, for the *Dublin Review*; the rest for the *British Critic*, between 1837 and 1842. They are arranged chronologically, except that, for the convenience of the volumes, Essays IX. and X. have changed places.

In this Edition the Note upon St. Ignatius' Epistles is no longer to be found, being transposed to a more suitable place in "Tracts Theological and Ecclesiastical;" and in its stead is inserted an Article from the *British Critic*, which has not till now been reprinted.

I.

POETRY, WITH REFERENCE TO ARISTOTLE'S
POETICS.

WE propose to offer some speculations of our own on Greek Tragedy, and on Poetry in general, as suggested by the doctrine of Aristotle[1] on the subject.

1.

Aristotle considers the excellence of a tragedy to depend upon its plot[2]—and, since a tragedy, as such, is obviously the exhibition of an action, no one can deny his statement to be abstractedly true. Accordingly, he directs his principal attention to the economy of the fable; determines its range of subjects, delineates its proportions, traces its progress from a complication of incidents to their just and satisfactory settlement, investigates the means of making a train of events striking or affecting, and shows how the exhibition of character may be made subservient to the purpose of the action. His treatise is throughout interesting and valuable. It is one thing, however, to form the *beau ideal* of a tragedy on scientific principles; another to point out the actual beauty of a particular school of dramatic composition. The Greek tragedians are not generally felicitous in the construction of their plots. Aristotle, then, rather tells us what Tragedy should be, than what Greek Tragedy really [2]

---

[1] *Aristotle*: (384-322 B.C.), pupil of Plato, tutor of Alexander the Great, taught at the Lyceum in Athens; his writings cover a huge number of subjects. The *Poetics* is thought to be a late work and may be the record of his lecture notes rather than a formal treatise.
[2] *plot*: Cf. *Poetics* VI: 'Of these elements the most important is the plot, the ordering of the incidents; for tragedy is a representation, not of men, but of action and life, of happiness and unhappiness—and happiness and unhappiness are bound up with action' (trans. T.S.Dorsch, *Classical Literary Criticism*, Penguin, 1965, p.39)

was. And this doubtless was the intention of the philosopher. Since, however, the Greek drama has obtained so extended and lasting a celebrity, and yet its excellence does not fall under the strict rules of the critical art, we have to inquire in what it consists.

That the charm of Greek Tragedy does not ordinarily arise from scientific correctness of plot, is certain as a matter of fact. Seldom does any great interest arise from the action; which, instead of being progressive and sustained, is commonly either a mere necessary condition of the drama, or a convenience for the introduction of matter more important than itself. It is often stationary—often irregular—sometimes either wants or outlives the catastrophe. In the plays of Æschylus[3] it is always simple and inartificial; in four out of the seven there is hardly any plot at all;[4] and, though it is of more prominent importance in those of Sophocles,[5] yet even here the Œdipus at Colonus is a mere series of incidents,[6] and the Ajax a union of two separate subjects;[7] while in the Philoctetes, which is apparently busy, the circumstances of the action are but slightly connected with the *dénouement*.[8] The carelessness of Euripides in the construction

[3] *Æschylus*: (525-465 B.C.) the first Greek tragedian; seven of his plays are extant. Newman first read him at Oxford in 1820, writing to his sister Jemima, 'Never I think have I read an author with whom I have been so much struck; I am lost in astonishment, I am stupefied, I am out of breath'. *Letters and Diaries*, Vol.I, p.84.

[4] *four . . . hardly any plot at all*: presumably *The Persians*, *Seven Against Thebes*, *Prometheus Bound* and *The Suppliants*. The other three are the *Agamemnon*, the *Choephorœ* and the *Eumenides*.

[5] *Sophocles*: (496-406 B.C.); seven of his plays are extant.

[6] *a mere series of incidents*: *Oedipus at Colonus* is the sequel to *Oedipus Tyrannus* in which Oedipus, who had been separated from his parents since birth, unwittingly killed his father Laius, the king of Thebes, and then married his mother, Jocasta, the queen. These crimes, albeit not Oedipus' fault, had been followed by a plague at Thebes which had only ceased on Oedipus' discovery of what he had done. In despair he blinded himself and went into exile. In *Oedipus at Colonus* he arrives at the village of Colonus, near Athens, where, in accordance with a prophecy, he wishes to die. During the play Creon, the ruler of Thebes, arrives and tries to take Oedipus back to his city but is prevented by Theseus, the ruler of Athens, who at the end of the play accompanies Oedipus to the site of his death.

[7] *the Ajax . . . a union of two separate subjects*: Ajax commits suicide in shame at his insane slaughtering of the Greeks' cattle after he was not awarded the arms of Achilles. The second half of the play consists of debates as to whether his body should be buried.

[8] *the Philoctetes . . . but slightly connected with the* dénouement: The play takes place during the Trojan war. The action concerns the attempt by Odysseus, by means of his fellow warrior Neoptolemos, to get the wounded Philoctetes to return to the Trojan war from the island where he has been marooned by the Greeks. The play concludes with

of his plots is well known.[9] The action then will be more justly viewed as the vehicle for introducing the personages of the drama, than as the principal object of the poet's art; it is not in the plot, but in the characters, sentiments, and diction, that the actual merit and poetry of the composition are found. To show this to the satisfaction of the reader, would require a minuter investigation of details than our present purpose admits; yet a few instances in point may suggest others to the memory.

For instance, in neither the Œdipus Coloneus nor the [3] Philoctetes, the two most beautiful plays of Sophocles, is the plot striking; but how exquisite is the delineation of the characters of Antigone[10] and Œdipus, in the former tragedy, particularly in their interview with Polynices,[11] and the various descriptions of the scene itself which the Chorus furnishes! In the Philoctetes, again, it is the contrast between the worldly wisdom of Ulysses,[12] the inexperienced frankness of Neoptolemus,[13] and the simplicity of the afflicted Philoctetes, which constitutes the principal charm of the drama. Or we may instance the spirit and nature displayed in the grouping of the characters in the Prometheus, which is almost without action;[14] the stubborn enemy of the new dynasty of gods;[15] Oceanus[16] trimming, as an accomplished politician, with the change of affairs; the single-hearted and generous Nereids;[17] and Hermes,[18]

---

the sudden appearance of the god Heracles telling Philoctetes about his future cure and glory at Troy, and Philoctetes agrees to return.
[9] *the carelessness of Euripides . . . :* Euripides (480-406 B.C.) made frequent use of the *deus ex machina* device whereby at the end of the drama a god suddenly descends to resolve the plot.
[10] *Antigone*: Oedipus's daughter. She supports her father in his desire not to return to Thebes.
[11] *Polynices*: one of Oedipus's two sons who were cursed by him for failing to support him.
[12] *Ulysses*: the Latin name for Odysseus
[13] *frankness of Neoptolemus*: Neoptolemos is reluctant to trick Philoctetes in the way Odysseus wants him to and eventually is honest with him.
[14] *the Prometheus . . . almost without action*: For the whole of the play Prometheus is bound to the rock to which Zeus has condemned him for having given human beings the gift of fire. The other characters debate with and about him.
[15] *the new dynasty of gods*: The Olympian gods overthrew the previous deities, the Titans.
[16] *Oceanus*: one of the Titans, son of Uranus and Gaia, god of the great sea which encircled the earth.
[17] *Nereids*: goddess nymphs of the sea

the favourite and instrument of the usurping potentate.[19] So again, the beauties of the Thebæ[20] are almost independent of the plot; it is the Chorus which imparts grace and interest to the actionless scene;[21] and the speech of Antigone at the end, one of the most simply striking in any play, has, scientifically speaking, no place in the tragedy, which should already have been brought to its conclusion.[22] Then again, amid the multitude of the beauties of the irregular Euripides, it would be obvious to notice the character of Alcestis,[23] and of Clytemnestra in the Electra;[24] the soliloquies of Medea;[25] the picturesque situation of Ion, the minister of the Pythian temple;[26] the opening scene of the Orestes;[27] and the dialogues between Phædra and her attendant in the Hippolytus,[28] and the old man and Antigone in

---

[18] *Hermes*: the messenger god

[19] *the usurping potentate*: Zeus the principal god who led the other Olympians in their overthrow of the Titans.

[20] *Thebæ*: *Seven Against Thebes* by Aeschylus.

[21] *the actionless scene*: The play consists mostly of dialogues between the citizens of Thebes and their king Eteocles about the attacking Argive army led by seven captains.

[22] *the speech of Antigone at the end* . . . : It has been suggested that this speech was not part of Aeschylus' original play but was added by a later writer after the popularity of Sophocles' *Antigone*.

[23] *Alcestis*: the eponymous heroine of Euripides' play. She agrees to die in place of her husband Admetus who has been given a long life by the gods on condition that he finds such a substitute.

[24] *Clytemnestra in the Electra*: Clytemnestra was the wife of King Agamemnon but became the lover of Aegisthus during her husband's absence at the Trojan war. In Euripides' *Electra,* she and Aegisthus are killed in revenge by her son Orestes, supported by his sister Electra, who is then pursued by the Furies for having committed matricide.

[25] *Medea*: the eponymous protagonist of Euripides' play. She is married to Jason, the leader of the Argonauts, but kills their children in revenge when he abandons her for the princess Glauce.

[26] *Ion*: the eponymous protagonist of Euripides' play. His mother Creusa, a noble Athenian maiden, was raped by the god Apollo and when a baby was born left him in a cave. He later became a servant in Apollo's shrine. Years later Ion and his mother are reunited, and the goddess Athena confirms the identity of his father with a message from Apollo; mother and son return to Athens in happiness.

[27] *the Orestes*: by Euripides. It covers the events following Orestes' killing of Clytemnestra and Aegisthus. The opening scene contains a lengthy soliloquy by Electra recounting the previous events.

[28] *the Hippolytus*: by Euripides. Hippolytus, the son of Theseus following his rape of the Amazon, Hippolyta, is dedicated to chastity. Theseus's wife Phaedra falls in love with him, but Hippolytus refuses her advances. When she commits suicide, Hippolytus keeps her guilty secret and is blamed by his father who exiles him. Following an intervention by the goddess Artemis, father and son are eventually reconciled before Hippolytus dies. The Attendant is Phaedra's nurse with whom she has a long conversation in an early scene when Phaedra is pining for love of Hippolytus.

the Phœnissæ;[29]—passages nevertheless which are either unconnected with the development of the plot, or of an importance
superior to it.

Thus the Greek drama, as a fact, was modelled on no [4]
scientific principle. It was a pure recreation of the imagination,
revelling without object or meaning beyond its own exhibition.
Gods, heroes, kings, and dames, enter and retire: they may have
a good reason for appearing,—they may have a very poor one;
whatever it is, still we have no right to ask for it; the question
is impertinent. Let us listen to their harmonious and majestic
language, to the voices of sorrow, joy, compassion, or religious
emotion,—to the animated odes of the chorus. Why interrupt
so transcendent a display of poetical genius by inquiries
degrading it to the level of every-day events, and implying
incompleteness in the action till a catastrophe arrives? The very
spirit of beauty breathes through every part of the composition.
We may liken the Greek drama to the music of the Italian
school;[30] in which the wonder is, how so much richness of
invention in detail can be accommodated to a style so simple
and uniform. Each is the development of grace, fancy, pathos,
and taste, in the respective media of representation and sound.

However true then it may be, that one or two of the most
celebrated dramas answer to the requisitions of Aristotle's
doctrine, still, for the most part, Greek Tragedy has its own
distinct and peculiar praise, which must not be lessened by a
criticism conducted on principles, whether correct or not, still
leading to excellence of another character. This being as we
hope shown, we shall be still bolder, and proceed to question

[29] *the Phœnissæ*: *The Phoenician Women* by Euripides, covering the same events as
Seven Against Thebes. Antigone and Jocasta (see above) try unsuccessfully to stop the
battle between Jocasta's brothers Polyneices and Eteocles. The brothers kill each other,
and Antigone opposes the decree of Creon, the ruler of Thebes, that Polyneices' body
may not be buried. She goes into exile in Athens. The 'old man' is Antigone's tutor;
they have a conversation up on the city walls, describing the battle and the various
combatants.
[30] *music of the Italian school*: Newman associated Aeschylus with music, telling
Jemima in 1820 that he wanted to set some of his Choruses to music (cf. *Letters and
Diaries*, Vol.I, p.97), and he particularly enjoyed Italian music. A book of violin music
which belonged to him in 1817 contains music by Viotti (1755-1874), Vaccari
(1775-1824) and Spagnoletti (1768-1838) (cf. *Letters and Diaries*, Vol.XXV, pp.351-2).

even the sufficiency of the rules of Aristotle for the production of dramas of the highest order. These rules, it would appear, require a fable not merely natural and unaffected, as a vehicle of more poetical matter, but one laboured and complicated, as the sole legitimate channel of tragic effect; and thus tend to [5] withdraw the mind of the poet from the spontaneous exhibition of pathos or imagination to a minute diligence in the formation of a plot.

2.

To explain our views on the subject, we will institute a short comparison between three tragedies, the Agamemnon, the Œdipus, and the Bacchæ,[31] one of each of the tragic poets, as to which, by reference to Aristotle's principles, we think it will be found that the most perfect in plot is not the most poetical.

1. Of these, the action of the Œdipus Tyrannus is frequently instanced by the critic as a specimen of judgment and skill in the selection and combination of the incidents; and in this point of view it is truly a masterly composition. The clearness, precision, certainty, and vigour with which the line of the action moves on to its termination is admirable. The character of Œdipus, too, is finely drawn, and identified with the development of the action.

2. The Agamemnon of Æschylus presents us with the slow and difficult birth of a portentous secret—an event of old written in the resolves of destiny, a crime long meditated in the bosom of the human agents.[32] The Chorus here has an importance

---

[31] *the Bacchae*: by Euripides.

[32] *The Agamemnon . . .* : The family of Agamemnon had long been cursed, and the gods or destiny had played a part in its various tragedies which occurred years before the action of Aeschylus' play. The 'portentous secret' concerned the brothers Thyestes and Atreus who were joint rulers of Mycenae. In revenge for Thyestes' adultery with Atreus' wife, Aerope, Atreus killed Thyestes' sons and tricked him into eating their flesh at a banquet. Thyestes fled to Delphi where the oracle decreed that the only way he could get revenge on Atreus was by having a child by his own daughter, Pelopia. He then came across a girl in the dark and raped her, not recognising that it was Pelopia or she recognising him, but accidentally left his sword behind. Pelopia was later found by Atreus who married her, and she subsequently gave birth to a boy, Aegisthus, who had actually been fathered by Thyestes in the rape. Years later Atreus' own sons, Agamemnon and Menelaus, captured Thyestes and brought him to Atreus who ordered

altogether wanting in the Chorus of the Œdipus. They throw a pall of ancestral honour over the bier of the hereditary monarch, which would have been unbecoming in the case of the upstart king of Thebes. [33] Till the arrival of Agamemnon, they occupy our attention, as the prophetic organ, not commissioned indeed, but employed by heaven, to proclaim the impending horrors. Succeeding to the brief intimation of the watcher who opens the play, they seem oppressed with forebodings of woe and crime which they can neither justify nor analyze. The expression [6] of their anxiety forms the stream in which the plot flows— everything, even news of joy, takes a colouring from the depth of their gloom. On the arrival of the king, they retire before Cassandra,[34] a more regularly commissioned prophetess; who, speaking first in figure, then in plain terms, only ceases that we may hear the voice of the betrayed monarch himself, informing us of the striking of the fatal blow. [35] Here, then, the very simplicity of the fable constitutes its especial beauty. The death of Agamemnon is intimated at first—it is accomplished at last;

Aegisthus, by now grown up, to execute him with the sword left with Pelopia. About to die, Thyestes recognised the sword, and so Pelopia realised that her unknown rapist had been her own father and at this revelation killed herself. Aegisthus, realising that Thyestes was his real father, now killed Atreus, and Thyestes became ruler of Mycenae. Agamemnon fled to Argos where he became king and married Clytemnestra, while his brother Menelaus became king of Sparta and married Helen. She was seduced by, or seduced, the Trojan prince Paris who took her to Troy, and Menelaus asked his brother Agamemnon for help getting her back. Before setting out with the Greek army for Troy, Agamemnon sacrificed his daughter Iphigenia to the gods in order to get a favourable wind for the fleet, in response to a command of the goddess Artemis whom he had offended. The *Agamemnon* opens with the Greeks having finally conquered Troy, after ten years of war, and Agamemnon being apparently welcomed home by his wife Clytemnestra. She and her lover Aegisthus, the 'human agents' Newman is referring to, have thus both 'long meditated' the crime by which they now take their revenge on Agamemnon, Clytemnestra for Iphigenia's death, and Aegisthus for the killing and cannibalistic banquet of his brothers by Agamemnon's father, Atreus. With Aegisthus' help, Clytemnestra murders Agamemnon in his bath.

[33] *the hereditary monarch . . . the upstart king of Thebes*: Agamemnon inherited the throne of Mycenae from his father Atreus, whereas Oedipus had only come to the throne of Thebes by killing his father. 'Upstart' seems a harsh judgment on Oedipus who was the hapless victim of a prophecy.

[34] *Cassandra*: a captured Trojan princess whom Agamemnon has brought with him as his concubine. She has been given the gift of prophecy, foretelling Agamemnon's death; she is subsequently murdered by Clytemnestra.

[35] *the voice of the betrayed monarch himself . . .* : the cry of Agamemnon is heard as he is murdered offstage.

throughout we find but the growing in volume and intensity of one and the same note—it is a working up of one musical ground, by figure and imitation, into the richness of combined harmony. But we look in vain for the progressive and thickening incidents of the Œdipus.

3. The action of the Bacchæ is also simple.[36] It is the history of the reception of the worship of Bacchus in Thebes; who, first depriving Pentheus of his reason, and thereby drawing him on to his ruin, reveals his own divinity. The interest of the scene arises from the gradual process by which the derangement of the Theban king is effected, which is powerfully and originally described. It would be comic, were it unconnected with religion. As it is, it exhibits the grave irony of a god triumphing over the impotent presumption of man, the sport and terrible mischievousness of an insulted deity. It is an exemplification of the adage, "Quem deus vult perdere, prius dementat."[37] So delicately balanced is the action along the verge of the sublime and grotesque, that it is both solemn and humorous, without violence to the propriety of the composition: the mad fire of the Chorus, the imbecile mirth of old Cadmus and Tiresias,[38] and the infatuation of Pentheus, who is ultimately induced to dress himself in female garb to gain admittance among the Bacchæ, are made to harmonize with the terrible catastrophe which concludes the life of the intruder. Perhaps the victim's first

[7]

---

[36] *the action of the Bacchae . . . :* The play concerns the visit to Thebes by the god Dionysius (Bacchus). He is the son of Zeus by his human mother Semele, daughter of Cadmus, the founder of the city. Semele's family doubt his divine fatherhood, and he now wants to take revenge on them for this. He has recruited women of the city to join his female followers, the Bacchae, but Pentheus, the current king of Thebes, has tried to forbid their drunken and savage rites. Dionysus, disguised as a priest of this new religion, allows himself to be captured but cannot be harmed by Pentheus. He tempts Pentheus to watch the Bacchae's orgiastic rites in the mountains, disguised as a woman. Pentheus begins to go mad, and by a trick of Dionysus he is delivered into the Bacchae's hands. The drunken and wild women include Pentheus' mother, Agave, who tears her own son to pieces.

[37] *"Quem deus vult perdere, prius dementat":* "Whom the god wishes to destroy, he first makes mad."

[38] *Cadmus and Tiresias:* Cadmus, the former king of Thebes is an old man by the time of the play. He and Tiresias, a blind seer, originally plan to join the revelry of the Bacchae but are forbidden to do so by Pentheus. At the end of the play Cadmus and his wife are condemned by Dionysius to be turned into snakes.

discovery of the disguised deity is the finest conception in this splendid drama. His madness enables him to discern the emblematic horns[39] on the head of Bacchus, which were hid from him when in his sound mind; yet this discovery, instead of leading him to an acknowledgment of the divinity, provides him only with matter for a stupid and perplexed astonishment:

> A Bull, thou seem'st to lead us; on thy head
> Horns have grown forth: wast heretofore a beast?
> For such thy semblance now.[40]

This play is on the whole the most favourable specimen of the genius of Euripides—not breathing the sweet composure, the melodious fulness, the majesty and grace of Sophocles; nor rudely and overpoweringly tragic as Æschylus; but brilliant, versatile, imaginative, as well as deeply pathetic. Here then are two dramas of extreme poetical power, but deficient in skilfulness of plot. Are they on that account to be rated below the Œdipus, which, in spite of its many beauties, has not even a share of the richness and sublimity of either?

3.

Aristotle, then, it must be allowed, treats dramatic composition more as an exhibition of ingenious workmanship, than as a free and unfettered effusion of genius. The inferior poem may, on his principle, be the better tragedy. He may indeed have intended solely to delineate the outward framework most suitable to the reception of the spirit of poetry, not to discuss the nature of poetry itself. If so, it cannot be denied that, the poetry being given equal in the two cases, the more perfect plot will merit the greater share of praise. And it may seem to agree with this view of his meaning, that he pronounces Euripides, in spite of the irregularity of his plots, to be, after all, the most tragic of the Greek dramatists, that is, inasmuch as he excels in his appeal to those passions which the outward form of the

[8]

---

[39] *horns*: Bacchus/Dionysus was sometimes depicted with the horns of either a bull or ram on his head.
[40] *A bull thou seem'st . . . thy semblance now*: *Bacchae*, ll. 917-919.

drama merely subserves. Still there is surely too much stress laid by the philosopher upon the artificial part; which, after all, leads to negative, more than to positive excellence; and should rather be the natural and, so to say, unintentional result of the poet's feeling and imagination, than be separated from them as the direct object of his care. Perhaps it is hardly fair to judge of Aristotle's sentiments by the fragment of his work which has come down to us. Yet as his natural taste led him to delight in the explication of systems, and in those absolute decisions which came of his vigorous talent for thinking through large subjects, we may be allowed to suspect him of entertaining too cold and formal conceptions of the nature of poetical composition, as if its beauties were less subtle and delicate than they really are. A word has power to convey a world of information to the imagination, and to act as a spell upon the feelings; there is no need of sustained fiction,—often no room for it. The sudden inspiration, surely, of the blind Œdipus, in the second play bearing his name, by which he is enabled, "without a guide," to lead the way to his place of death, in our judgment, produces more poetical effect than all the skilful intricacy of the plot of the Tyrannus. The latter excites an interest which scarcely lasts beyond the first reading—the former "decies repetita placebit."[41]

[9]   Some confirmation of the judgment we have ventured to pass on the greatest of analytical philosophers, is the account he gives of the source of poetical pleasure; which he almost identifies with a gratification of the reasoning faculty, placing it in the satisfaction derived from recognizing in fiction a resemblance to the realities of life—"The spectators are led to recognize and to syllogize what each thing is."[42]

But as we have treated, rather unceremoniously, a deservedly high authority, we will try to compensate for our rudeness by illustrating his general doctrine of the nature of Poetry, which we hold to be most true and philosophical.

---

[41] *"decies repetita placebit."*: "though ten times repeated, will continue to please", Horace, *Ars Poetica*, 365.
[42] *"The spectators are led . . . ."*: *Poetics* IV.

4.

Poetry, according to Aristotle, is a representation of the ideal. Biography and history represent individual characters and actual facts; poetry, on the contrary, generalizing from the phenomenon of nature and life, supplies us with pictures drawn, not after an existing pattern, but after a creation of the mind. Fidelity is the primary merit of biography and history; the essence of poetry is fiction. "Poesis nihil aliud est," says Bacon,[43] "quam historiæ imitatio ad placitum."[44] It delineates that perfection which the imagination suggests, and to which as a limit the present system of Divine Providence actually tends. Moreover, by confining the attention to one series of events and scene of action, it bounds and finishes off the confused luxuriance of real nature; while, by a skilful adjustment of circumstances, it brings into sight the connexion of cause and effect, completes the dependence of the parts one on another, and harmonizes the proportions of the whole. It is then but the type and model of history or biography, if we may be allowed the comparison, bearing some resemblance to the abstract mathematical formulæ [10] of physics, before they are modified by the contingencies of atmosphere and friction. Hence, while it recreates the imagination by the superhuman loveliness of its views, it provides a solace for the mind broken by the disappointments and sufferings of actual life; and becomes, moreover, the utterance of the inward emotions of a right moral feeling, seeking a purity and a truth which this world will not give.

It follows that the poetical mind is one full of the eternal forms of beauty and perfection; these are its material of thought, its instrument and medium of observation,—these colour each object to which it directs its view. It is called imaginative or creative, from the originality and independence of its modes of thinking, compared with the commonplace and matter-of-fact conceptions of ordinary minds, which are fettered down to the

---

[43] *Bacon*: Francis Bacon (1561–1626), first Baron Verulam and Viscount of Saint Albans; politician, writer and philosopher.
[44] *"Poesis nihil . . . ad placitum."*: "Poesy [...] is nothing else but feigned history", *The Advancement of Learning*, IV, 1.

particular and individual. At the same time it feels a natural sympathy with everything great and splendid in the physical and moral world; and selecting such from the mass of common phenomena, incorporates them, as it were, into the substance of its own creations. From living thus in a world of its own, it speaks the language of dignity, emotion, and refinement. Figure[45] is its necessary medium of communication with man; for in the feebleness of ordinary words to express its ideas, and in the absence of terms of abstract perfection, the adoption of metaphorical language is the only poor means allowed it for imparting to others its intense feelings. A metrical garb has, in all languages, been appropriated to poetry—it is but the outward development of the music and harmony within. The verse, far from being a restraint on the true poet, is the suitable index of his sense, and is adopted by his free and deliberate choice. We [11] shall presently show the applicability of our doctrine to the various departments of poetical composition; first, however, it will be right to volunteer an explanation which may save it from much misconception and objection. Let not our notion be thought arbitrarily to limit the number of poets, generally considered such. It will be found to lower particular works, or parts of works, rather than the authors themselves; sometimes to disparage only the vehicle in which the poetry is conveyed. There is an ambiguity in the word "poetry," which is taken to signify both the gift itself, and the written composition which is the result of it. Thus there is an apparent, but no real contradiction, in saying a poem may be but partially poetical; in some passages more so than in others; and sometimes not poetical at all. We only maintain, not that the writers forfeit the name of poet who fail at times to answer to our requisitions, but that they are poets only so far forth, and inasmuch as they do answer to them. We may grant, for instance, that the vulgarities of old Phœnix in the ninth Iliad,[46] or of the nurse of Orestes in

---

[45] *Figure*: imagery such as metaphor, simile and personification.
[46] *the vulgarities of old Phoenix in the ninth Iliad*: Phoenix is one of the Myrmidons, the followers of Achilles. Along with Ajax and Odysseus, he urges Achilles to return to the battle, in a very passionate speech during which he reminds Achilles that he had helped bring him up. Some critics have suggested that this speech is a later interpolation

the Choephorœ,[47] are in themselves unworthy of their respective authors, and refer them to the wantonness of exuberant genius; and yet maintain that the scenes in question contain much incidental poetry. Now and then the lustre of the true metal catches the eye, redeeming whatever is unseemly and worthless in the rude ore; still the ore is not the metal. Nay, sometimes, and not unfrequently in Shakspeare, the introduction of unpoetical matter may be necessary for the sake of relief, or as a vivid expression of recondite conceptions, and, as it were, to make friends with the reader's imagination. This necessity, however, cannot make the additions in themselves beautiful and pleasing. Sometimes, on the other hand, while we do not deny the incidental beauty of a poem, we are ashamed and indignant on witnessing the unworthy substance in which that beauty is   [12] imbedded. This remark applies strongly to the immoral compositions to which Lord Byron devoted his last years.[48]

5.

Now to proceed with our proposed investigation.

1. We will notice *descriptive poetry* first. Empedocles[49] wrote his physics in verse, and Oppian[50] his history of animals. Neither were poets—the one was an historian of nature, the other a sort of biographer of brutes. Yet a poet may make natural history or philosophy the material of his composition. But under his hands they are no longer a bare collection of facts or principles, but

---

in the text of the Iliad.

[47] *the nurse of Orestes in the Choephorœ*:   In her monologue about Orestes whom she had nursed as a baby, the Nurse refers to how he dirtied his nappy without her noticing: 'Children's young insides are a law to themselves. I needed second sight for this, and many a time I think I missed, and had to change the baby's clothes.' (trans. R.Lattimore, University of Chicago Press, 1953, lines 757-759)

[48] *immoral compositions . . . his last years*:   The later works of Lord George Gordon Byron (1788-1824) include his drama *Cain*, which re-tells the Biblical narrative from the murderer's point of view as a victim of God's decrees, and his poem *Don Juan* which is cynical about traditional sexual morality.

[49] *Empedocles*:   (flourished c.444 B.C.), philosopher; he wrote two works, *On Nature* and *Purifications*, but they survive only in fragments.

[50] *Oppian*:   There are now thought to be two writers of this name, both of whom wrote about animals. Oppian of Corycus (flourished c.169 A.D.) wrote a work about fishing, the *Halieutica*. Oppian of Appamea (flourished c.211 A.D.) wrote a work on hunting, the *Cynegetica*.

are painted with a meaning, beauty, and harmonious order not their own. Thomson[51] has sometimes been commended for the novelty and minuteness of his remarks upon nature. This is not the praise of a poet; whose office rather is to represent known phenomena in a new connection or medium. In L'Allegro and Il Penseroso[52] the poetical magician invests the commonest scenes of a country life with the hues, first of a cheerful, then of a pensive imagination. It is the charm of the descriptive poetry of a religious mind, that nature is viewed in a moral connexion. Ordinary writers, for instance, compare aged men to trees in autumn—a gifted poet will in the fading trees discern the fading men.[53] Pastoral poetry is a description of rustics, agriculture, and cattle, softened off and corrected from the rude health of nature. Virgil,[54] and much more Pope[55] and others, have

[13] run into the fault of colouring too highly; instead of drawing generalized and ideal forms of shepherds, they have given us pictures of gentlemen and beaux.

Their composition may be poetry, but it is not pastoral poetry.[56]

2. The difference between poetical and historical *narrative* may be illustrated by the Tales Founded on Facts,[57] generally of a religious character, so common in the present day, which we must not be thought to approve, because we use them for our purpose. The author finds in the circumstances of the case many particulars too trivial for public notice, or irrelevant to the main

---

[51] *Thomson*: James Thomson (1700-48) wrote four poems on the seasons.

[52] *L'Allegro and Il Penseroso*: by John Milton (1608-74).

[53] Thus:—"How quiet shows the woodland scene! Each flower and tree, its duty done, Reposing in decay serene, Like weary men when age is won," etc. [N] John Keble, 'All Saints Day', ll.1-4. Keble (1792-1866), a Fellow of Oriel with Newman, was to become one of his closest allies in the Oxford Movement; see Editor's Introduction above p.xiii.

[54] *Virgil*: Publius Virgilius Maro (70-19 B.C.), famous for his *Aeneid*; Newman is referring to his pastoral poem, the *Eclogues*, with its idealised shepherds and shepherdesses.

[55] *Pope*: Alexander Pope (1688-1744). Newman is referring to his *Pastorals*.

[56] *not pastoral poetry*: Both poets were writing in an established genre of 'pastoral' which dated back to Theocritus in the 3rd century B.C., but Newman shows his Romantic sensibility in wanting a new, more 'natural' version of pastoral.

[57] *Tales Founded on Facts*: by M.A.Grant, published in 1820. The author explains in his Introduction that his chief aim is 'to inculcate religious and moral sentiments.' The work was aimed at children.

story, or partaking perhaps too much of the peculiarity of individual minds: these he omits. He finds connected events separated from each other by time or place, or a course of action distributed among a multitude of agents; he limits the scene or duration of the tale, and dispenses with his host of characters by condensing the mass of incident and action in the history of a few. He compresses long controversies into a concise argument, and exhibits characters by dialogue, and (if such be his object) brings prominently forward the course of Divine Providence by a fit disposition of his materials. Thus he selects, combines, refines, colours,—in fact, poetizes. His facts are no longer actual, but ideal; a tale founded on facts is a tale generalized from facts. The authors of Peveril of the Peak,[58] and of Brambletye House,[59] have given us their respective descriptions of the profligate times of Charles II. Both accounts are interesting, but for different reasons. That of the latter writer has the fidelity of history; Walter Scott's picture is the hideous reality, unintentionally softened and decorated by the poetry of his own mind. Miss Edgeworth[60] sometimes apologizes for [14] certain incident in her tales, by stating they took place "by one of those strange chances which occur in life, but seem incredible when found in writing."[61] Such an excuse evinces a misconception of the principle of fiction, which, being the perfection of the actual, prohibits the introduction of any such anomalies of experience. It is by a similar impropriety that painters sometimes introduce unusual sunsets, or other singular phenomena of lights and forms. Yet some of Miss Edgeworth's works contain much poetry of narrative. Manœuvring[62] is perfect in its

---

[58] *Peveril of the Peak*: a novel by Walter Scott (1771-1832).

[59] *Brambletye House*: a novel by Horace Smith (1779-1849)

[60] *Miss Edgeworth*: Maria Edgeworth (1767-1849), novelist.

[61] . . . *incredible when found in writing"*: This sentence does not occur in Maria Edgeworth's novels. Newman's use of the plural - 'sometimes apologises for certain incident[s?] in her tales' - suggests that what follows is not an actual quotation but merely the sort of thing she wrote. One of her characters does say that 'nothing is more unlike a novel than real life' (*Belinda*, Ch.3).

[62] *Manœuvring*: One of five stories in the first series of Edgeworth's *Tales of Fashionable Life* (1809). It concerns the manoeuvring of Mrs.Beaumont to marry her children off for money and status, while they wish to marry for love.

way,—the plot and characters are natural, without being too real to be pleasing.

3. *Character* is made poetical by a like process. The writer draws indeed from experience; but unnatural peculiarities are laid aside, and harsh contrasts reconciled. If it be said, the fidelity of the imitation is often its greatest merit, we have only to reply, that in such cases the pleasure is not poetical, but consists in the mere recognition. All novels and tales which introduce real characters, are in the same degree unpoetical. Portrait-painting, to be poetical, should furnish an abstract representation of an individual; the abstraction being more rigid, inasmuch as the painting is confined to one point of time. The artist should draw independently of the accidents of attitude, dress, occasional feeling, and transient action. He should depict the general spirit of his subject—as if he were copying from memory, not from a few particular sittings. An ordinary painter will delineate with rigid fidelity, and will make a caricature; but the learned artist contrives so to temper his composition, as to sink all offensive peculiarities and hardnesses of individuality, [15] without diminishing the striking effect of the likeness, or acquainting the casual spectator with the secret of his art. Miss Edgeworth's representations of the Irish character[63] are actual, and not poetical—nor were they intended to be so. They are interesting, because they are faithful. If there is poetry about them, it exists in the personages themselves, not in her representation of them. She is only the accurate reporter in word of what was poetical in fact. Hence, moreover, when a deed or incident is striking in itself, a judicious writer is led to describe it in the most simple and colourless terms, his own being unnecessary; for instance, if the greatness of the action itself excites the imagination, or the depth of the suffering interests the feelings. In the usual phrase, the circumstances are left "to speak for themselves."

Let it not be said that our doctrine is adverse to that individuality in the delineation of character, which is a principal

---

[63] *representations of the Irish character*: e.g. in her novels *Castle Rackrent* and *Belinda*.

charm of fiction. It is not necessary for the ideality of a composition to avoid those minuter shades of difference between man and man, which give to poetry its plausibility and life; but merely such violation of general nature, such improbabilities, wanderings, or coarsenesses, as interfere with the refined and delicate enjoyment of the imagination; which would have the elements of beauty extracted out of the confused multitude of ordinary actions and habits, and combined with consistency and ease. Nor does it exclude the introduction of imperfect or odious characters. The original conception of a weak or guilty mind may have its intrinsic beauty; and much more so, when it is connected with a tale which finally adjusts whatever is reprehensible in the personages themselves. Richard[64] and Iago[65] are subservient to the plot. Moral excellence in some characters may become even a fault. The Clytemnestra [16] of Euripides is so interesting, that the divine vengeance, which is the main subject of the drama, seems almost unjust. Lady Macbeth, on the contrary, is the conception of one deeply learned in the poetical art. She is polluted with the most heinous crimes, and meets the fate she deserves.[66] Yet there is nothing in the picture to offend the taste, and much to feed the imagination. Romeo and Juliet are too good for the termination to which the plot leads; so are Ophelia[67] and the Bride of Lammermoor.[68] In these cases there is something inconsistent with correct beauty, and therefore unpoetical. We do not say the fault could be avoided without sacrificing more than would be gained; still it is a fault. It is scarcely possible for a poet satisfactorily to

---

[64] *Richard*: King Richard III in Shakespeare's play of that name.
[65] *Iago*: In *Othello* Iago gives various motives for his destruction of Othello and Desdemona, but none of them seems sufficient for the scale of his evil actions. Newman's comment that such characters are 'subservient to the plot' contrasts with other Romantic critics' attempts to treat them as real people.
[66] . . . *the fate she deserves*: Lady Macbeth's guilt drives her mad and she commits suicide.
[67] *Ophelia*: In *Hamlet*, Hamlet's apparent rejection of her and his killing of her father drive her insane, and she drowns in circumstances suggesting suicide.
[68] *the Bride of Lammermoor*: Lucy Ashton, the eponymous heroine of Walter Scott's novel (1819), is the victim of Lady Ashworth's various schemes to prevent her marrying her true love, Edgar. Eventually tricked and forced into another marriage, she stabs her hated bridegroom on their wedding night, goes mad and dies.

connect innocence with ultimate unhappiness, when the notion of a future life is excluded. Honours paid to the memory of the dead are some alleviation of the harshness. In his use of the doctrine of a future life, Southey[69] is admirable. Other writers are content to conduct their heroes to temporal happiness;— Southey refuses present comfort to his Ladurlad, Thalaba, and Roderick,[70] but carries them on through suffering to another world. The death of his hero is the termination of the action; yet so little in two of them, at least, does this catastrophe excite sorrowful feelings, that some readers may be startled to be reminded of the fact. If a melancholy is thrown over the conclusion of the Roderick,[71] it is from the peculiarities of the hero's previous history.

4. Opinions, feelings, manners, and customs, are made poetical by the delicacy or splendour with which they are expressed. This is seen in the *ode, elegy, sonnet,* and *ballad*; in which a single idea, perhaps, or familiar occurrence, is invested by the poet with pathos or dignity. The ballad of Old Robin Gray[72] will serve for an instance, out of a multitude; again, Lord Byron's Hebrew Melody, beginning, "Were my bosom as false,"[73] etc.; or Cowper's Lines on his Mother's Picture;[74] or

[17]

---

[69] *Southey*: Robert Southey (1774-1843); Poet Laureate at the time Newman was writing.

[70] *Ladurlad, Thalaba and Roderick*: Southey's epic romances which Newman had admired from his youth. 'The mysterious quests and journeys in these romances, their relentless movement through time, and their vision of the life of dedication and faith, seemed to offer Newman a foretaste of his own spiritual odyssey. It was *Thalaba* which inspired him with a sense of mission at the opening of the Oxford Movement, and as late as 1850, five years after his conversion to Roman Catholicism, he could still remember the work as 'the most sublime of English poems—I mean *morally* sublime.' Hill. A.G., 'Three Visions of Judgement: Southey, Byron and Newman', 1990.

[71] *the conclusion of the Roderick*: In *Roderick the Last of the Goths* (1814), set during the 8th century Moorish invasion of Visigothic Spain, the protagonist King Roderick rapes Florinda, the daughter of an ally, Julian. In remorse, and after a victory by the Moors, Roderick becomes a hermit. Julian goes over to the Moors. By the end the Moors are defeated, Julian repents, and Florinda has confessed that the rape was as much a seduction on her part. However, there is no happy ending, as Roderick returns to his hermit's life.

[72] *the ballad of Old Robin Gray*: *Auld Robin Gray* by Lady Anne Barnard (1750-1825).

[73] *Hebrew Melody* . . . : This collection of verses by Byron was published in 1815, preceded by a musical version set to Jewish tunes by Isaac Nathan. In 'Were My Bosom as False as Thou Deem'st It To Be', the speaker is a Jew lamenting his exile from Israel and implicitly reproaching the Christian reader for what he has lost. Newman's

26

Milman's Funeral Hymn in the Martyr of Antioch;[75] or Milton's Sonnet on his Blindness;[76] or Bernard Barton's Dream.[77] As picturesque specimens, we may name Campbell's Battle of the Baltic;[78] or Joanna Baillie's Chough and Crow;[79] and for the more exalted and splendid style, Gray's Bard;[80] or Milton's Hymn on the Nativity;[81] in which facts, with which every one is familiar, are made new by the colouring of a poetical imagination. It must all along be observed, that we are not adducing instances for their own sake; but in order to illustrate our general doctrine, and to show its applicability to those compositions which are, by universal consent, acknowledged to be poetical.

The department of poetry we are now speaking of is of much wider extent than might at first sight appear. It will include such moralizing and philosophical poems as Young's Night Thoughts,[82] and Byron's Childe Harold.[83] There is much bad taste, at present, in the judgment passed on compositions of this kind. It is the fault of the day to mistake mere eloquence for

---

appreciation of the pathos of the poem shows his sympathy for this 'outcast'.
[74] *Cowper . . . : On Receipt of His Mother's Picture* (1798), William Cowper (1731-1800).
[75] *The Martyr of Antioch*: epic poem by Rev. Henry Hart Milman (1791-1868) about the martyrdom of the possibly apocryphal 3rd century St. Margaret of Antioch. Milman was Professor of Poetry at Oxford when Newman was writing.
[76] *Milton's Sonnet on his Blindness*: in his *Poems etc. on Several Occasions* (1674).
[77] *Bernard Barton's Dream*: Bernard Barton (1784-1849), Quaker poet and hymn-writer; friend of Southey. 'The Dream' is based on an actual dream the poet had about his dead wife.
[78] *Campbell's Battle of the Baltic*: Thomas Campbell (1777-1844), Scottish poet, best known for his war-songs. 'The Battle of the Baltic', about Nelson's victory at the Battle of Copnhagen, was published in 1801.
[79] *Joanna Baillie's Chough and Crow*: Joanna Baillie (1762-1851), Scottish poet and dramatist; friend of Walter Scott. In 'The Chough and the Crow' the two birds revel in freedom of the night time when everyone is asleep.
[80] *Gray's Bard*: Thomas Gray (1716-71), poet, best known for his 'Elegy in a Country Churchyard'. 'The Bard', an influential poem in the Romantic Movement, features a Welsh bard who meets King Edward I, curses him and predicts a future Welsh influence on English literature.
[81] *Milton's Hymn on the Nativity*: 'On the Morning of Christ's Nativity' (1692), an ode on the Incarnation of Christ and the Redemption.
[82] *Young's Night Thoughts*: Edward Young (1683-1765); his long 'The Complaint, or Night Thoughts on Immortality', published 1742-5, contains various meditations on death and the transitory nature of life.
[83] *Byron's Childe Harold*: 'Childe Harold's Pilgrimage', published 1812-18, concerns the lengthy wanderings of a disillusioned young man. Newman does not share the widespread popular admiration of this and Young's poem.

poetry; whereas, in direct opposition to the conciseness and simplicity of the poet, the talent of the orator consists in making much of a single idea. "Sic dicet ille ut verset sæpe multis modis eandem et unam rem, ut hæreat in eâdem commoreturque sententiâ."[84] This is the great art of Cicero[85] himself, who, whether he is engaged in statement, argument, or raillery, never ceases till he has exhausted the subject; going round about it, and placing it in every different light, yet without repetition to

[18] offend or weary the reader. This faculty seems to consist in the power of throwing off harmonious verses, which, while they have a respectable portion of meaning, yet are especially intended to charm the ear. In popular poems, common ideas are unfolded with copiousness, and set off in polished verse—and this is called poetry. Such is the character of Campbell's Pleasures of Hope;[86] it is in his minor poems that the author's poetical genius rises to its natural elevation. In Childe Harold, too, the writer is carried through his Spenserian stanza[87] with the unweariness and equable fulness of accomplished eloquence; opening, illustrating, and heightening one idea, before he passes on to another. His composition is an extended funeral sermon over buried joys and pleasures. His laments over Greece, Rome, and the fallen in various engagements, have quite the character of panegyrical orations; while by the very attempt to describe the celebrated buildings and sculptures of antiquity, he seems to confess that *they* are the poetical text, his the rhetorical comment. Still it is a work of splendid talent, though, as a whole, not of the highest poetical excellence.

---

[84] *"Sic dicet . . . commoreturque sententia"*: "He will speak about one and the same thing, turning it over and expressing it in so many ways, that he may cling to that one idea and the thought of it may remain." Cicero, *Orator ad M. Brutum*, 40.
[85] *Cicero*: Marcus Tullius Cicero (106-43 BC), Roman statesman, writer and philosopher. Newman greatly admired his prose style: 'They [other Roman authors] write Latin; Cicero writes Roman' (*Idea of a University*, p. 282).
[86] *Campbell's Pleasures of Hope*: another lengthy philosophical poem, widely popular in its day; it ranges over historical and political events in different countries.
[87] *Spenserian stanza*: the verse form invented by Edmund Spenser (1552-99) for his immense epic poem *The Faerie Queen*. Each nine-line rhyming stanza contains eight lines of iambic pentameter and a concluding ninth of iambic hexameter.

Juvenal[88] is perhaps the only ancient author who habitually substitutes declamation for poetry.

5. The *philosophy of mind* may equally be made subservient to poetry, as the philosophy of nature. It is a common fault to mistake a mere knowledge of the heart for poetical talent. Our greatest masters have known better;—they have subjected metaphysics to their art. In Hamlet, Macbeth, Richard, and Othello, the philosophy of mind is but the material of the poet. These personages are ideal; they are effects of the contact of a given internal character with given outward circumstances, the results of combined conditions determining (so to say) a moral [19] curve of original and inimitable properties. Philosophy is exhibited in the same subserviency to poetry in many parts of Crabbe's Tales of the Hall.[89] In the writings of this author there is much to offend a refined taste; but, at least in the work in question, there is much of a highly poetical cast. It is a representation of the action and reaction of two minds upon each other and upon the world around them. Two brothers of different characters and fortunes, and strangers to each other, meet. Their habits of mind, the formation of those habits by external circumstances, their respective media of judgment, their points of mutual attraction and repulsion, the mental position of each in relation to a variety of trifling phenomena of everyday nature and life, are beautifully developed in a series of tales moulded into a connected narrative. We are tempted to single out the fourth book, which gives an account of the childhood and education of the younger brother, and which for variety of thought as well as fidelity of description is in our judgment beyond praise. The Waverley Novels[90] would afford us specimens of a similar excellence. One striking peculiarity

---

[88] *Juvenal*: Decimus Junius Juvenalis (60-c.130), Roman satirist.
[89] *Crabbe's Tales of the Hall*: George Crabbe (1754-1832), poet who wrote realistically about the lives of ordinary people; 'Tales of the Hall', his last collection of poems, was published in 1817.
[90] *Waverley Novels*: by Walter Scott, so called because Scott initially did not put his name as author on them and so the first few appeared as 'By the Author of Waverley' (his first novel). They eventually ran to forty-eight volumes, including *Kenilworth*, *Ivanhoe* and *Old Mortality*, mentioned by Newman here; they were enormously popular and were translated into many languages.

of these tales is the author's practice of describing a group of characters bearing the same general features of mind, and placed in the same general circumstances; yet so contrasted with each other in minute differences of mental constitution, that each diverges from the common starting-point into a path peculiar to himself. The brotherhood of villains in Kenilworth, of knights in Ivanhoe, and of enthusiasts in Old Mortality, are instances of this. This bearing of character and plot on each other is not often found in Byron's poems. The Corsair[91] is intended for a remarkable personage. We pass by the inconsistencies of his character, considered by itself. The grand fault is, that whether it be natural or not, we are obliged to accept the author's word for the fidelity of his portrait. We are told, not shown, what the hero was. There is nothing in the plot which results from his peculiar formation of mind. An everyday bravo[92] might equally well have satisfied the requirements of the action. Childe Harold, again, if he is anything, is a being professedly isolated from the world, and uninfluenced by it. One might as well draw Tityrus's stags grazing in the air,[93] as a character of this kind; which yet, with more or less alteration, passes through successive editions in his other poems. Byron had very little versatility or elasticity of genius; he did not know how to make poetry out of existing materials. He declaims in his own way, and has the upperhand as long as he is allowed to go on; but, if interrogated on principles of nature and good sense, he is at once put out and brought to a stand.

[20]

Yet his conception of Sardanapalus and Myrrha[94] is fine and ideal, and in the style of excellence which we have just been admiring in Shakspeare and Scott.

---

[91] *The Corsair*: A narrative poem published in 1814 about a privateer—a sailor licensed by the government to attack enemy shipping. Byron's protagonist is presented as an outcast with a grudge against the world. The book was a best-seller.

[92] *bravo*: a brigand

[93] *Tityrus's stags . . .*: In Virgil's *Eclogue* I, Tityrus in a dialogue with Meliboeus says that 'sooner will light stags . . . feed on air' than that he will forget. Tityrus's stags are therefore creatures who are impossibilities.

[94] *Sardanapalus and Myrrha*: Sardanapalus is the King of Assyria in Byron's historical drama of that name; Myrrha is his mistress.

6.

These illustrations of Aristotle's doctrine may suffice.

Now let us proceed to a fresh position; which, as before, shall first be broadly stated, then modified and explained. How does originality differ from the poetical talent? Without affecting the accuracy of a definition, we may call the latter the originality of right moral feeling.

Originality may perhaps be defined the power of abstracting for one's self, and is in thought what strength of mind is in action. Our opinions are commonly derived from education and society. Common minds transmit as they receive, good and bad, true and false; minds of original talent feel a continual propen- [21] sity to investigate subjects, and strike out views for themselves;—so that even old and established truths do not escape modification and accidental change when subjected to this process of mental digestion. Even the style of original writers is stamped with the peculiarities of their minds. When originality is found apart from good sense, which more or less is frequently the case, it shows itself in paradox and rashness of sentiment, and eccentricity of outward conduct. Poetry, on the other hand, cannot be separated from its good sense, or taste, as it is called; which is one of its elements. It is originality energizing in the world of beauty; the originality of grace, purity, refinement, and good feeling. We do not hesitate to say, that poetry is ultimately founded on correct moral perception; that where there is no sound principle in exercise there will be no poetry; and that on the whole (originality being granted) in proportion to the standard of a writer's moral character will his compositions vary in poetical excellence. This position, how-ever, requires some explanation.

Of course, then, we do not mean to imply that a poet must necessarily display virtuous and religious feeling; we are not speaking of the actual material of poetry, but of its sources. A right moral state of heart is the formal and scientific condition of a poetical mind. Nor does it follow from our position that every poet must in fact be a man of consistent and practical principle; except so far as good feeling commonly produces or results from good practice. Burns[95] was a man of inconsistent life; still, it is known, of much really sound principle at bottom. Thus his acknowledged poetical talent is in nowise inconsistent with the truth of our doctrine, which will refer the beauty which exists in his compositions to the remains of a virtuous and [22] diviner nature within him. Nay, further than this, our theory holds good, even though it be shown that a depraved man may write a poem. As motives short of the purest lead to actions intrinsically good, so frames of mind short of virtuous will produce a partial and limited poetry. But even where this is instanced, the poetry of a vicious mind will be inconsistent and debased; that is, so far only poetry as the traces and shadows of holy truth still remain upon it. On the other hand, a right moral feeling places the mind in the very centre of that circle from which all the rays have their origin and range; whereas minds otherwise placed command but a portion of the whole circuit of poetry. Allowing for human infirmity and the varieties of opinion, Milton, Spenser, Cowper, Wordsworth,[96] and Southey, may be considered, as far as their writings go, to approximate to this moral centre. The following are added as further illustrations of our meaning. Walter Scott's centre is chivalrous honour; Shakspeare exhibits the characteristics of an unlearned and undisciplined piety; Homer the religion of nature and conscience, at times debased by polytheism. All these poets are religious. The occasional irreligion of Virgil's poetry is painful to the admirers of his general taste and delicacy. Dryden's Alexander's Feast[97] is a magnificent composition, and has high poetical beauties; but to a refined judgment there is something intrinsically unpoetical in the end to which it is devoted, the praises of revel and sensuality. It corresponds to a process of clever reasoning erected on an untrue foundation—the one is a fallacy, the other is out of taste. Lord Byron's Manfred[98] is in

---

[95] *Burns*: Robert Burns (1759-96), Scotland's national poet; he was known for his dissipated lifestyle.
[96] *Wordsworth*: William Wordsworth (1770-1850), the celebrated Lakes poet.
[97] *Dryden*: John Dryden (1631-1700), poet and dramatist. 'Alexander's Feast' is an ode for St. Cecilia's Day.
[98] *Byron's Manfred*: a dramatic poem with supernatural elements. Its eponymous hero

parts intensely poetical; yet the delicate mind naturally shrinks from the spirit which here and there reveals itself, and the basis on which the drama is built. From a perusal of it we should infer, [23] according to the above theory, that there was right and fine feeling in the poet's mind, but that the central and consistent character was wanting. From the history of his life[99] we know this to be the fact. The connexion between want of the religious principle and want of poetical feeling, is seen in the instances of Hume[100] and Gibbon,[101] who had radically unpoetical minds. Rousseau,[102] it may be supposed, is an exception to our doctrine. Lucretius,[103] too, had great poetical genius; but his work evinces that his miserable philosophy was rather the result of a bewildered judgment than a corrupt heart.

According to the above theory, Revealed Religion should be especially poetical—and it is so in fact. While its disclosures have an originality in them to engage the intellect, they have a beauty to satisfy the moral nature. It presents us with those ideal forms of excellence in which a poetical mind delights, and with which all grace and harmony are associated. It brings us into a new world—a world of overpowering interest, of the sublimest views, and the tenderest and purest feelings. The peculiar grace of mind of the New Testament writers is as striking as the actual effect produced upon the hearts of those who have imbibed their spirit. At present we are not concerned with the practical, but the poetical nature of revealed truth. With Christians, a poetical view of things is a duty,—we are bid to colour all things with hues of faith, to see a Divine meaning in every event, and a

---

is wracked with guilt for some mysterious offence.

[99] *from the history of his life*: Byron wrote *Manfred* shortly after he had fled England following the break-up of his marriage and rumours of his having had an affair with his half-sister.

[100] *Hume*: David Hume (1711-76), philosopher and political economist; he was sceptical in his religious views.

[101] *Gibbon*: Edward Gibbon (1737-94), historian, known for his religious scepticism as shown in his scoffing treatment of Christianity in his *History of the Decline and Fall of the Roman Empire*. Despite his scepticism, he was one of Newman's favourite writers.

[102] *Rousseau*: Jean-Jacques Rousseau (1712-78), political philosopher; his religious views were unorthodox.

[103] *Lucretius*: Titus Lucretius Carus (c.99-55 B.C.), author of the lengthy philosophical poem *De Rerum Natura* in which he argued that the gods had no influence on the world and that the soul was not immortal.

superhuman tendency. Even our friends around are invested with unearthly brightness—no longer imperfect men, but beings taken into Divine favour, stamped with His seal, and in training for future happiness. It may be added, that the virtues peculiarly Christian are especially poetical—meekness, gentleness, compassion, contentment, modesty, not to mention the devotional [24] virtues; whereas the ruder and more ordinary feelings are the instruments of rhetoric more justly than of poetry—anger, indignation, emulation, martial spirit, and love of independence.

7.

A few remarks on poetical composition, and we have done. The art of composition is merely accessory to the poetical talent. But where that talent exists, it necessarily gives its own character to the style, and renders it perfectly different from all others. As the poet's habits of mind lead to contemplation rather than to communication with others, he is more or less obscure, according to the particular style of poetry he has adopted; less so in epic, or narrative and dramatic representation,—more so in odes and choruses. He will be obscure, moreover, from the depth of his feelings, which require a congenial reader to enter into them—and from their acuteness, which shrinks from any formal accuracy in the expression of them. And he will be obscure, not only from the carelessness of genius, and from the originality of his conceptions, but it may be from natural deficiency in the power of clear and eloquent expression, which, we must repeat, is a talent distinct from poetry, though often mistaken for it.

However, dexterity in composition, or *eloquence* as it may be called in a contracted sense of the word, is manifestly more or less necessary in every branch of literature, though its elements may be different in each. Poetical eloquence consists, first, in the power of illustration; which the poet uses, not as the orator, voluntarily, for the sake of clearness or ornament, but almost by constraint, as the sole outlet and expression of intense [25] inward feeling. This spontaneous power of comparison may, in some poetical minds, be very feeble; these of course cannot show to advantage as poets. Another talent necessary to composition is the power of unfolding the meaning in an orderly manner. A poetical mind is often too impatient to explain itself justly; it is overpowered by a rush of emotions, which sometimes want of power, sometimes the indolence of inward enjoyment, prevents it from describing. Nothing is more difficult than to analyse the feelings of our own minds; and the power of doing so, whether natural or acquired, is clearly distinct from experiencing them. Yet, though distinct from the poetical talent, it is obviously necessary to its exhibition. Hence it is a common praise bestowed upon writers, that they express what we have often felt, but could never describe. The power of arrangement, which is necessary for an extended poem, is a modification of the same talent, being to poetry what method is to logic. Besides these qualifications, poetical composition requires that command of language which is the mere effect of practice. The poet is a compositor; words are his types; he must have them within reach, and in unlimited abundance. Hence the need of careful labour to the accomplished poet,—not in order that his diction may attract, but that the language may be subjected to him. He studies the art of composition as we might learn dancing or elocution; not that we may move or speak according to rule, but that, by the very exercise our voice and carriage may become so unembarrassed as to allow of our doing what we will with them.

A talent for composition, then, is no essential part of poetry, though indispensable to its exhibition. Hence it would seem that attention to the language, for its own sake, evidences not the [26] true poet, but the mere artist. Pope[104] is said to have tuned our tongue. We certainly owe much to him—his diction is rich, musical, and expressive: still he is not on this account a poet; he elaborated his composition for its own sake. If we give him poetical praise on this account, we may as appropriately bestow it on a tasteful cabinet-maker. This does not forbid us to ascribe the grace of his verse to an inward principle of poetry, which

---

[104] *Pope*: Pope (see above p.[12]n) was best known for his witty, satirical poems such as *The Rape of the Lock*; he has no Romantic sensibility of the sort Newman admired.

supplied him with archetypes of the beautiful and splendid to work by. But a similar gift must direct the skill of every fancy-artist who subserves the luxuries and elegances of life. On the other hand, though Virgil is celebrated as a master of composition, yet his style is so identified with his conceptions, as their outward development, as to preclude the possibility of our viewing the one apart from the other. In Milton, again, the harmony of the verse is but the echo of the inward music which the thoughts of the poet breathe. In Moore's[105] style, the ornament continually outstrips the sense. Cowper and Walter Scott, on the other hand, are slovenly in their versification. Sophocles writes, on the whole, without studied attention to the style; but Euripides frequently affected a simplicity and prettiness which exposed him to the ridicule of the comic poets. Lastly, the style of Homer's[106] poems is perfect in their particular department. It is free, manly, simple, perspicuous, energetic, and varied. It is the style of one who rhapsodized without deference to hearer or judge, in an age prior to the temptations which more or less prevailed over succeeding writers—before the theatre had degraded poetry into an exhibition, and criticism narrowed it into an art.

January, 1829.

---

[105] *Moore*: Thomas Moore (1779-1852), poet and songwriter, known for such lyrics as 'The Minstrel Boy'.
[106] *Homer*: (?9th century B.C.), the great Greek epic poet, author of the *Iliad* and the *Odyssey*.

27

NOTE ON ESSAY I.[107]

THE *London Review*, in the first number of which the foregoing Essay appeared, was started in 1829, under the editorship of Mr. Blanco White. Its history is given in his Life by Mr. Thom[108] (vol. i., p. 448, etc.): "On Sunday, 27th July, 1828," (Mr. White says in his Journal,) "Dr. Mayo, who came to see Senior and myself from Tunbridge Wells to Hastings, where I was for the benefit of my health, made me the proposal of editing a new Review. The project of this Quarterly had originated in Senior, who, having engaged the support of Dr. Whately[109] and many others, had now only to procure an editor. Dr. Mayo urged me to accept the offer, both as a literary friend and as my medical adviser ... The unexpected opening thus made for useful occupation, and the chance of a better provision for my old age than I could make by taking pupils at Oxford, roused me into all the energy of revived hope: I accepted the charge with alacrity."

The time was favourable for a new Quarterly, so far as this, that the long-established Quarterly[110] (if my memory is correct) was in the crisis of a change, or a succession, of editors, and was not at the moment altogether satisfactory to the great political and religious party, which it has ever represented. And

---

[107] *NOTE ON ESSAY I.*: added by Newman for the 1871 edition.
[108] *Life by Mr. Thom*: *The Life of the Rev. Joseph Blanco White : written by himself; with portions of his correspondence*, ed. John Hamilton Thom, 1845.
[109] *Dr. Whately*: Richard Whately (1787-1863), Fellow of Oriel, one of the leading 'Noetics' (rationalist Anglicans). He was an early mentor of Newman, but they diverged as Newman adopted more High Church views, leading to a 'formal break' in 1829; cf. *Apologia Pro Vita Sua*, p.8.
[110] *the long-established Quarterly*: The *Quarterly Review*, founded in 1809 as a rival to the *Edinburgh Review*.

[28] in fact its publisher entered into correspondence with Mr. White with a view to an arrangement, which would supersede the projected Review. However, the former had no real cause of apprehension; the new publication required an editor of more vigorous health and enterprising mind, of more cheerful spirits, and greater power of working, and with larger knowledge of the English public, than Mr. White possessed; and writers, less bookish and academical than those, able as they were, on whom its fate depended. Southey, by anticipation, hit the blot. As a whole, the Review was dull. "Be of good heart in your new undertaking," he says in a letter to Mr. White, November 11th, 1828, "and it cannot fail. My advice is, that you should have always a considerable proportion of *attractive matter*, for which current literature may always supply abundant subjects. A *good* journal I know you will make it; *get for it the character of an entertaining one*, and you have hit your own mark as well as the publisher's. Rely upon this, that you have my best word, my best wishes, and shall not want my best aid, when I can with propriety give it."

Also it happened unfortunately for Mr. White, that, having been brought to Oxford mainly by the Tory party on account of his "seasonable," as they called it, witness against Catholicism, during the contest about the Catholic claims,[111] he formed, when settled there, so close a friendship with Dr. Whately and others of opposite political opinions, as to be led in February, 1829, to vote for the re-election of Mr. Peel, on his change in Parliament in favour of the Catholics. This step, which gave great umbrage to the majority of residents, had a proportionate effect upon his wearied and troubled mind. His editorial duties and the Review itself ended with its second number. He writes to a friend, May 20, 1829, "My compact with the evil spirit, the demon of the book-market is almost at an end … I hope very

---

[111] *the contest about the Catholic claims*: the controversy over the Roman Catholic Relief Act of 1829 which gave British Catholics basic political rights after centuries of exclusion and persecution, brought in by the Home Secretary Sir Robert Peel after previously opposing such reform.

soon to be entirely free from the nightmare of the *London Review*."

As to my own article, the following reference is made to it [29] in my "*Apologia*" (2nd edition), p. 11: "I recollect how dissatisfied Dr. Whately was with an article of mine in the *London Review*, which Blanco White good-humouredly only called 'Platonic';" and indeed it certainly omits one of the essential conditions of the idea of Poetry, its relation to the affections,— and that, in consequence, as it would seem, of confusing the function and aim of Poetry with its formal object. As the aim of civil government is the well-being of the governed, and its object is expediency; as the aim of oratory is to persuade, and its object is the probable; as the function of philosophy is to view all things in their mutual relations, and its object is truth; and as virtue consists in the observance of the moral law, and its object is the right; so Poetry may be considered to be the gift of moving the affections through the imagination, and its object to be the beautiful.

I should observe that several sentences of this Essay, which in passing through the press were, by virtue of an editor's just prerogative, altered or changed, now stand as I sent them to him.

II.

ON THE INTRODUCTION OF RATIONALISTIC
PRINCIPLES INTO REVEALED RELIGION.

IT is not intended in the following pages to enter into any general view of so large a subject as Rationalism, nor to attempt any philosophical account of it; but, after defining it sufficiently for the purpose in hand, to direct attention to a very peculiar and subtle form of it existing covertly in the popular religion of this day. With this view two writers, not of our own Church, though of British origin, shall pass under review,—Mr. Erskine[1] and Mr. Jacob Abbott.[2]

This is the first time that a discussion of (what may be called) a personal nature has appeared in this series of Tracts,[3] which has been confined to the delineation and enforcement of principles and doctrines. However, in this case, I have found that, if it was important to protest against certain views of the day, it was necessary, in order to do this intelligibly, to refer to the individuals who have inculcated them. Of these the two Authors above mentioned seemed at once the most influential and the most original; and Mr. Abbott being a foreigner, and Mr. Erskine having written sixteen years since, there seemed a possibility of introducing their names without assuming to exercise the functions of a Review.

---

[1] *Mr. Erskine*: Thomas Erskine (1788-1870), Scots Episcopalian, author of *Remarks on the Internal Evidence for the Truth of Revealed Religion* (1820) and *Essay on Faith* (1822).

[2] *Mr. Jacob Abbott*: Jacob Abbott (1803-1879), American Congregational minister and author of *The Corner-Stone, A Familiar Illustration of the Principles of Christian Truth*, Boston (1835). He was enormously prolific, writing many books for children and popular histories.

[3] Tracts for the Times. [N]

It will be my business first to explain what I mean by [31] Rationalism, and then to illustrate the description given of it from the writings of the two Authors in question.

§ I.

THE RATIONALISTIC AND THE CATHOLIC TEMPERS CONTRASTED.

RATIONALISM is a certain abuse of Reason; that is, a use of it for purposes for which it never was intended, and is unfitted. To rationalize in matters of Revelation is to make our reason the standard and measure of the doctrines revealed; to stipulate that those doctrines should be such as to carry with them their own justification; to reject them, if they come in collision with our existing opinions or habits of thought, or are with difficulty harmonized with our existing stock of knowledge. And thus a rationalistic spirit is the antagonist of Faith; for Faith is, in its very nature, the acceptance of what our reason cannot reach, simply and absolutely upon testimony.

There is, of course, a multitude of cases in which we allowably and rightly accept statements as true, partly on reason, and partly on testimony. We supplement the information of others by our own knowledge, by our own judgment of probabilities; and, if it be very strange or extravagant, we suspend our assent. This is undeniable; still, after all, there are truths which are incapable of reaching us except on testimony, and there is testimony, which by and in itself, has an imperative claim on our acceptance.

As regards Revealed Truth, it is not Rationalism to set about [32] to ascertain, by the exercise of reason, what things are attainable by reason, and what are not; nor, in the absence of an express Revelation, to inquire into the truths of Religion, as they come to us by nature; nor to determine what proofs are necessary for the acceptance of a Revelation, if it be given; nor to reject a Revelation on the plea of insufficient proof; nor, after recognizing it as divine, to investigate the meaning of its declarations, and to interpret its language; nor to use its doctrines, as far as they can be fairly used, in inquiring into its divinity; nor to compare and connect them with our previous knowledge, with a view of making them parts of a whole; nor to bring them into dependence on each other, to trace their mutual relations, and to pursue them to their legitimate issues. This is not Rationalism; but it is Rationalism to accept the Revelation, and then to explain it away; to speak of it as the Word of God, and to treat it as the word of man; to refuse to let it speak for itself; to claim to be told the *why* and the *how* of God's dealings with us, as therein described, and to assign to Him a motive and a scope of our own; to stumble at the partial knowledge which He may give us of them; to put aside what is obscure, as if it had not been said at all; to accept one half of what has been told us, and not the other half; to assume that the contents of Revelation are also its proof; to frame some gratuitous hypothesis about them, and then to garble, gloss, and colour them, to trim, clip, pare away, and twist them, in order to bring them into conformity with the idea to which we have subjected them.

[33]   When the rich lord in Samaria said, "Though God shall make windows in heaven, shall this thing be?"[4] he rationalized, as professing his inability to discover *how* Elisha's prophecy was to be fulfilled, and thinking in this way to excuse his unbelief. When Naaman, after acknowledging the prophet's supernatural power, objected to bathe in Jordan, it was on the ground of his not seeing the *means* by which Jordan was to cure his leprosy above the rivers of Damascus.[5] "*How* can these things be?" was the objection of Nicodemus to the doctrine of regeneration;[6] and when the doctrine of the Holy Communion was first announced, "the Jews strove among themselves," in answer to their Divine Informant, saying, "*How* can this man give us His flesh to eat?"[7]

---

[4] *When the rich lord . . . shall this thing be?"*: 2 Kings 7:2. Elisha had prophesied that 'tomorrow about this time shall a measure of fine flour be sold for a shekel, and two measures of barley for a shekel, in the gate of Samaria', i.e such food would become very expensive. When the rich lord doubted this prophecy, Elisha replied 'Behold, thou shalt see it with thine eyes, but shalt not eat thereof'. Newman sees the rich lord as a type of the rationalist doubter who will not accept a revelation he does not understand.

[5] *When Naaman . . . the rivers of Damascus*: 2 Kings 5:12.

[6] *"How can . . . doctrine of regeneration*: John 3:4: 'How can a man be born when he is old?'

When St. Thomas, believing in our Lord, doubted of our Lord's resurrection,[8] though his reason for so doing is not given, it plainly lay in the astonishing, unaccountable nature of such an event. A like desire of judging for one's self is discernible in the original fall of man. Eve did not believe the Tempter, any more than God's word, till she perceived that "the fruit was good for food."[9]

So again, when men who profess Christianity ask *how* prayer can really influence the course of God's providence, or *how* everlasting punishment, as such, consists with God's infinite mercy, they rationalize.

The same spirit shows itself in the restlessness of others to decide *how* the sun was stopped at Joshua's word,[10] *how* the manna was provided,[11] and the like; forgetting what our Saviour suggests to the Sadducees,—"*the power* of God."[12]

2.

Conduct such as this, on so momentous a matter, is, generally speaking, traceable to one obvious cause. The Rationalist makes himself his own centre, not his Maker; he does not go to God, but he implies that God must come to him. And this, it is to be feared, is the spirit in which multitudes of us act at the present day. Instead of looking out of ourselves, and trying to catch glimpses of God's workings, from any quarter,—throwing ourselves forward upon Him and waiting on Him, we sit at home bringing everything to ourselves, enthroning ourselves in our own views, and refusing to believe anything that does not force itself upon us as true. Our private judgment is made everything to us,—is contemplated, recognized, and consulted as the arbiter of all questions, and as independent of everything external to us. Nothing is considered to have an existence except so far

[34]

---

[7] *"How can . . . flesh to eat?"*: John 6:52.

[8] *When St. Thomas . . . doubted our Lord's resurrection*: Cf. John 20:25.

[9] *"the fruit was good for food."*: Genesis 3:6.

[10] *the sun stopped at Joshua's word*: Cf. Joshua 10:12-14.

[11] *how the manna was provided*: Cf. Exodus 16:1-35.

[12] "the power *of God.*": In answer to the question about the woman who had had seven husbands, all of whom had died, so in the resurrection (in which the Sadducees did not believe) 'whose wife shall she be of the seven?' Jesus replied, 'Ye do err, not knowing the scriptures, nor the power of God.' Matthew 22:29.

forth as our minds discern it. The notion of half views and partial knowledge, of guesses, surmises, hopes and fears, of truths faintly apprehended and not understood, of isolated facts in the great scheme of Providence, in a word, the idea of Mystery, is discarded.

Hence a distinction is drawn between what is called Objective and Subjective Truth, and Religion is said to consist in a reception of the latter. By Objective Truth is meant the Religious System considered as existing in itself, external to this or that particular mind: by Subjective, is meant that which each mind receives in particular, and considers to be such. To believe in Objective Truth is to throw ourselves forward upon that which we have but partially mastered or made subjective; to embrace, maintain, and use general propositions which are larger than our own capacity, of which we cannot see the bottom, which we cannot follow out into their multiform details; to come before and bow before the import of such propositions, as if we were contemplating what is real and independent of human judgment. Such a belief, implicit, and symbolized as it [35] is in the use of creeds, seems to the Rationalist superstitious and unmeaning, and he consequently confines Faith to the province of Subjective Truth, or to the reception of doctrine, as, and so far as, it is met and apprehended by the mind, which will be differently, as he considers, in different persons, in the shape of orthodoxy in one, heterodoxy in another. That is, he professes to *believe* in that which he *opines*;[13] and he avoids the obvious extravagance of such an avowal by maintaining that the moral trial involved in Faith does not lie in the submission of the reason to external realities partially disclosed, but in what he calls that candid pursuit of truth which ensures the eventual adoption of that opinion on the subject, which is best for us individually, which is most natural according to the constitution of our own minds, and, therefore, divinely intended for us. I repeat, he owns that Faith, viewed with reference to its objects, is never more than an opinion, and is pleasing to God, not as an active principle apprehending definite doctrines, but as a result and fruit, and therefore an evidence of past diligence,

---

[13] opines: holds as an opinion which he has thought out for himself

independent inquiry, dispassionateness, and the like. Rationalism takes the words of Scripture as signs of Ideas; Faith, of Things or Realities.

For an illustration of Faith, considered as the reaching forth after and embracing what is beyond the mind, or Objective, we may refer to St. Paul's description of it in the ancient Saints; "These all died in Faith, *not having received* the promises, but *having seen them afar off*, and were persuaded of them, and embraced them, and confessed that they were strangers and pilgrims on the earth:"[14] or to St. Peter's; "Of which salvation the Prophets have inquired and searched diligently, who *prophesied* of the grace that should come *unto you, searching what, or what manner of time* the Spirit of Christ which was in [36] them did signify, when it testified beforehand the sufferings of Christ, and the glory that should follow; unto whom it was revealed, that *not unto themselves*, but unto us they did minister the things *which are now reported unto you* by them that have evangelized you."[15] Here the faith of the ancient Saints is described as employed, not merely on truths so far as mastered by the mind, but on truths beyond it, and even to the end withheld from its perfect apprehension.

On the other hand, if we would know the narrow and egotistic temper of mind to which the Rationalistic Theory of Subjective Truth really tends, we find an illustration of it in the following passage of a popular Review.[16] Without apparently any intention of denying that the wonders of nature "declare the glory of God and show His handiwork,"[17] the writer[18] seems to feel that there is one thing better and higher than the witness which they bear to a mere point in metaphysics; viz., the exact mathematical knowledge to which they can be subjected. He thus descants:—

---

[14] *"These all died in Faith . . . pilgrims on the earth"*: Hebrews 10:13-14.

[15] *"Of which salvation . . . have evangelized you."*: I Peter 1: 10-13.

[16] *a popular Review*: The Edinburgh Review, No. CXXIII, April – July 1835. The article is a book review of *Observations on Bielas' Comet* by Sir J.F.W.Herschel.

[17] *. . . show His handiwork."*: Psalm 19:1.

[18] *the writer*: Dionysius Lardner (1793-1859), a populariser of science. The article in the Edinburgh Review is unsigned, but Lardner later incorporated the review in a lecture he gave in America and published under his own name.

"To the historian of science it is permitted to penetrate the depths of past and future with equal clearness and certainty; facts to come are to him as present, and not unfrequently more assured than facts which are past. Although this clear perception of causes and consequences characterizes the whole domain of physical science, and clothes the natural philosopher with powers denied to the political and moral inquirer, yet Foreknowledge is eminently the privilege of the Astronomer. Nature has raised the curtain of futurity, and displayed before him the succession of her decrees, so far as they affect the physical universe, for countless ages to come; and the Revelations of which she has made him the instrument, are supported and verified by a never-ceasing train of predictions fulfilled. He [the Astronomer] shows us the things which will be hereafter;[19] not obscurely shadowed out in figures and in parables, as must necessarily be the case with *other* Revelations, but attended with the most minute precision of time, place, and circumstance. He [the Astronomer] converts the hours as they roll into an ever-present miracle, in attestation of those Laws which the Creator through him has unfolded; the sun cannot rise, the moon cannot wane, a star cannot twinkle in the firmament, without bearing testimony to the truth of his [the Astronomer's] Prophetic Records. How nobly is the darkness which envelopes metaphysical inquiries compensated by the flood of light which is shed upon the physical creation! *There* all is harmony, and order, and majesty, and beauty. How soothing and yet how elevating it is to turn to the splendid spectacle which offers itself to the habitual contemplation of the Astronomer! How favourable to the development of all the best and highest feelings of the soul are such objects! The only passion they inspire being the Love of Truth, and the chiefest pleasure of their votaries arising from Excursions through the imposing scenery of the universe: scenery on a scale of grandeur and magnificence, compared with which whatever we are accustomed to call sublimity on our planet, dwindles into ridiculous insignificancy. Most justly has it been said, that nature has implanted in our bosoms a craving after the Discovery of Truth, and assuredly that glorious instinct is never more irresistibly awakened than when our notice is directed to what is going on in the heavens," etc. etc. (*abridged.*)

[37]

The writer of these sentences cannot be said exactly to rationalize, because he neither professes belief in Revelation,

---

[19] *the things which will be hereafter*: Cf. Revelation 1:19. This allusion to scriptural prophecies makes the Astronomer a surer prophet than the biblical author of '*other* Revelations'.

nor dresses up any portion of its contents into a scientific, intelligible shape. But he lays down the principle on which rationalists proceed, and shows how superior, that principle being assumed, astronomy is to the Gospel. He tells us that knowledge, or what he calls truth, elicits "the best and highest feelings of the soul;" that the "love" and "craving" for such knowledge is the most noble of "passions," and a "glorious instinct;" that the attainments of such knowledge, say for instance, about the Milky Way[20] or the Lost Pleïad[21] (supposing it were possible), is emphatically "Revelation," not a mere inkling, conveyed in figures and parables, like "other" Revelations, but "soothing, and yet how elevating!" opening [38] upon the scientific "excursionist" the most splendid "scenery," a "compensation" for "metaphysical darkness;"—moreover, that the "physical universe" "eminently" gifts the astronomer with "the privilege of foreknowledge," and is converted for his use into a "prophetic record." No partial knowledge, he implies, can be so transporting as this unclouded light,—the subject-matter of our contemplations, of course, never having any bearing at all upon the transport which the contemplations create. To know the God of nature in part is a poor thing in comparison of knowing the laws of nature in full. To meditate on His power or skill, on His illimitable being and existence, on His unity in immensity, is a mere nothing compared with the ecstasy which follows on the infallible certitude of the physical philosopher, that particles of matter are attracted towards each other by a force varying inversely as the square of their distance.[22] I do not say that the writer in question would thus express himself, when brought to book; but it is the legitimate sense of his words, and the secret thought of his heart, unless he has but enunciated a succession of magniloquent periods.

---

[20] *the Milky Way*: The astronomer William Herschel (1738-1822) had studied the structure of the Milky Way.
[21] *the Lost Pleïad*: The Pleiads (more usually Pleiades) are a constellation of seven stars, only six of which are visible to the naked eye. According to Greek mythology, they were the seven daughters of Atlas and Pleione. The 'lost' one was variously identified as Electra, Merowe or Celæno.
[22] *particles of matter . . . the square of their distance*: Newton's Law of Universal Gravitation.

3.

I have said he is not a rationalist; I do not call him so, because he does not own to a belief in Revealed Religion, or tamper with its contents. Rather he tends, how little soever he may realize it, to discard even Theism itself from his list of *credenda*.[23] The only truth which he seems to think it worth while pursuing, is the knowledge of the universe; for a system can be more easily and thoroughly mastered than an Infinite Mind. Laws are stable; but persons are strange, uncertain, inexplicable. "Ex pede Herculem;"[24] if I know one fact about the physical world, I know a million others; but one divine act and no more carries me but a little way in my knowledge of "Summum illud et æternum, neque mutabile, neque interiturum."[25] There is some chance of our analyzing nature, none of our comprehending God.

[39]

Such is the philosophy of the writer whom I have quoted; and such is Rationalism in its action upon Scripture and the Creed. It considers faith to consist rather in the knowledge of a system or scheme, than of an agent; it is concerned, not so much with the Divine Being, as with His work. Mr. Erskine is one of the writers who are presently to engage my attention; here I will anticipate my mention of him by citing a passage from his Essay on Faith,[26] in illustration of the parallelism, as I read him, between him and the Reviewer. He assumes the very principle of the latter, viz., that clear knowledge is the one thing needful for the human mind, and by consequence that Christian faith does not really consist in the direct contemplation of the Supreme Being, in a submission to His authority, and a resignation to such disclosures about Himself and His will, be they many or few, distinct or obscure, as it is His pleasure to make to us, but in a luminous, well-adjusted view of the scheme of salvation, of the economy of grace, of the carrying out of the

---

[23] credenda: things which ought to be believed

[24] *"Ex pede Herculem"*: "[You may judge] Hercules by his foot".

[25] *"Summum illud et æternum, neque mutabile neque interiturum"*: "the most high and eternal, neither changeable nor destructible"; from *De Deis Gentium* (1565) by Lilio Gregorio Giraldi. Perhaps Newman read the phrase in Joseph De Maistre's *Les Soirées de Saint-Petersbourg* (1822) where it is quoted.

[26] *his Essay on Faith*: published in 1822. The extract quoted is pp.31-32.

Divine Attributes into a series of providential and remedial appointments. He writes as follows:—

"I may understand many things which I do not believe; but I cannot believe anything which I do not understand, unless it be something addressed merely to my senses, and not to my thinking faculty. A man may with great propriety say, I understand the Cartesian System of Vortices,[27] though I do not believe in it. But it is absolutely impossible for him to believe in that system without knowing what it is. A man may believe in the ability of the maker of a system without understanding it; but he cannot believe in the *system itself* without understanding it. Now there is a meaning in the Gospel, and there is declared in it the system of God's dealings with men. This meaning, and this system, must be understood, before we can believe the Gospel. We are not called on to believe the Bible, merely that we may give a proof of our willingness to submit in all things to God's authority, but that we may be influenced by the objects of our belief," etc. [40]

That is, I cannot believe anything which I do not understand; therefore, true Christianity consists, not in "submitting in all things to God's authority," His written Word, whether it be obscure or not, but in understanding His acts. I must understand a scheme, if the Gospel is to do me any good; and such a scheme is the scheme of salvation. Such is the object of faith, the history of a series of divine actions, and nothing more; nothing more, for everything else is obscure; but this is clear, simple, compact. To preach this, is to preach the Gospel; not to apprehend it, is to be destitute of living faith.

Of course I do not deny that Revelation contains a history of God's mercy to us; who can doubt it? I only say, that while it is this, it is something more also. Again, if by speaking of the Gospel as clear and intelligible, a man means to imply that this is the whole of it, then I answer, No; for it is also deep, and therefore necessarily mysterious. This is too often forgotten. Let me refer to a very characteristic word, familiarly used by Mr. Erskine, among others, to designate his view of the Gospel Dispensation. It is said to be a *manifestation*, as if the system

---

[27] *the Cartesian system of Vortices*: René Descartes (1596-1650) devised a Theory of Vortices which postulated that space was entirely filled with matter in various states, moving about the sun.

presented to us were such as we could trace and connect into one whole, complete and definite. Let me use this word "Manifestation" as a symbol of the philosophy under review; and let me contrast it with the word "Mystery," which on the other hand may be regarded as the badge or emblem of orthodoxy. Revelation, as a Manifestation, is a doctrine variously received by various minds, but nothing more to each than that which each mind comprehends it to be. Considered as a Mystery, it is a doctrine enunciated by inspiration, in human language, as the only possible medium of it, and suitably, according to the capacity of language; a doctrine *lying hid* in language, to be received in that language from the first by every mind, whatever be its separate power of understanding it; entered into more or less by this or that mind, as it may be; and admitting of being apprehended more and more perfectly according to the diligence of this mind and that. It is one and the same, independent and real, of depth unfathomable, and illimitable in its extent.

[41]

4.

This is a fit place to make some remarks on the Scripture sense of the word Mystery. It may seem a contradiction in terms to call Revelation a Mystery; but is not the book of the Revelation of St. John as great a mystery from beginning to end as the most abstruse doctrine the mind ever imagined? yet it is even called a *Revelation*. How is this? The answer is simple. No revelation can be complete and systematic, from the weakness of the human intellect; *so far as* it is not such, it is mysterious. When nothing is revealed, nothing is known, and there is nothing to contemplate or marvel at; but when something is revealed, and only something, for all cannot be, there are forthwith difficulties and perplexities. A Revelation is religious doctrine viewed on its illuminated side; a Mystery is the selfsame doctrine viewed on the side unilluminated. Thus Religious Truth is neither light nor darkness, but both together; it is like the dim view of a country seen in the twilight, with forms half extricated from the darkness, with broken lines, and isolated masses. Revelation, in this way of considering it, is not a revealed *system*, but consists of a number of detached and

[42]

incomplete truths belonging to a vast system unrevealed, of doctrines and injunctions mysteriously connected together; that is, connected by unknown media, and bearing upon unknown portions of the system. And in this sense we see the propriety of calling St. John's prophecies, though highly mysterious, yet a revelation.

And such seems to be the meaning of the word Mystery in Scripture, a point which is sometimes disputed. Campbell, in his work on the Gospels,[28] maintains that the word means a *secret*, and that, whatever be the subject of it in the New Testament, it is always, when mentioned, associated with the notion of its being now revealed. Thus, in his view, it is a word belonging solely to the Law, which was a system of types and shadows, and is utterly foreign to the Gospel, which has brought light instead of darkness. This sense might seem to be supported by our Lord's announcement (for instance) to His disciples, that to them was given to know the mysteries of His kingdom;[29] and by His command to them at another time to speak abroad what they had heard from Him in secret.[30] And St. Paul in like manner glories in the revelation of mysteries hid from the foundation of the world.[31]

But the passages of Scripture admit, as I have suggested, of another interpretation. What was hidden altogether before Christ came, could not be a mystery; it became a Mystery, then for the first time, by being disclosed at His coming. What had never been dreamed of by "righteous men,"[32] before Him, when revealed, as *being* unexpected, if for no other reason, would be [43] strange and startling. And such unquestionably is the meaning of St. Paul, when he uses the word; for he applies it, not to what was passed and over, but to what was the then state of the doctrine revealed. Thus in the text, 1 Cor. xv. 51, 52, "Behold I show you a Mystery; we shall not all sleep, but we shall all be

---

[28] *Campbell . . . :* George Campbell (1719-1796), Scottish Professor of Divinity. He published *The Four Gospels* in 1789.

[29] *our Lord's announcement . . . the mysteries of His kingdom.:* Cf. Matthew 13:11.

[30] *His command to them . . . heard from Him in secret:* Cf. Luke 8:17.

[31] *St. Paul . . . the foundation of the world.:* Cf. Romans 16:25.

[32] *"righteous men":* Matthew 13:17: "Many prophets and righteous men have longed to see what you see."

changed, in a moment, in the twinkling of an eye, at the last trump." The resurrection and consequent spiritualizing of the human body, was not dreamed of by the philosophy of the world till Christ came, and, when revealed, was "mocked,"[33] as then first becoming a mystery. Reason is just where it was; and, as it could not discover it beforehand, so now it cannot account for it, or reconcile it to experience, or explain the manner of it: the utmost it does is by some faint analogies to show that it is not inconceivable. Again, St. Paul, speaking of marriage says, "This is a great Mystery, I mean, in its reference to Christ and the Church;"[34] that is, the ordinance of marriage has an inward and spiritual meaning, contained in it and revealed through it, a certain bearing, undefined and therefore mysterious, towards the heavenly communion existing between Christ and the Church:—as if for persons to place themselves in that human relation interested them in some secret way in the divine relation of which it is a figure. Again: "Great is the Mystery of piety; God was manifested in the flesh, justified in the Spirit, seen of Angels, preached unto the Gentiles, believed on in the world, received up into glory" (1 Tim. iii. 16). Now is the revelation of these truths a Manifestation (as above explained) or a Mystery? Surely the great secret has, by being revealed, only got so far as to be a Mystery, nothing more; nor could become a Manifestation, (that is, a system comprehended as such by the human mind,) without ceasing to be anything great at all. It must ever be small and superficial, viewed only as received by man; and is vast only when considered as that external truth into which each Christian may grow continually, and ever find fresh food for his soul.

[44]

As to the unknown, marvellous system of things spoken of in the text just quoted, it is described again, in an almost parallel passage, as regards the subject, though differently worded, in the Epistle to the Hebrews: "Ye are come unto Mount Zion, and unto the city of the living God, the heavenly Jerusalem, and to an innumerable company of Angels, to the full concourse and

---

[33] *"mocked"*: Acts 17:32, when St. Paul preached to the philosophers at Athens: "Now when they heard of the resurrection of the dead, some mocked; but others said, 'We will hear you again about this.'"

[34] *"This is . . . and the Church."*: Ephesians 5:32.

assembly of the first-born enrolled in heaven, and to God the Judge of all, and to the spirits of the perfected just, and to Jesus the Mediator of the New Covenant, and to the blood of sprinkling, that speaketh better things than that of Abel" (xii. 22-24). In like manner when St. Paul speaks of the election of the Gentiles as a Mystery revealed,[35] the facts of the case show that it was still a mystery, and therefore but revealed to be a mystery, not a secret explained. We know that the Jews did stumble at it:[36] why, if it was clear and obvious to reason? Certainly it was still a Mystery to them. Will it be objected that it had been plainly predicted? Surely not. The calling indeed of the Gentiles had been predicted, but not their equal participation with the Jews in all the treasures of the Covenant of grace, not the destruction of the Mosaic system. The prophets everywhere speak of the Jews as the head of the Gentiles; it was a new doctrine altogether (at least to the existing generation) that the election henceforth was to have no reference whatever to the Jews as a distinct people. This had hitherto been utterly hidden and unexpected; it emerged into a stumbling-block, or Mystery, when the Gospel was preached, as on the other hand it became to all humble minds a marvel or mystery of mercy. Hence St. Paul speaks of the Mystery "which in other ages was not made known to the sons of men, that the Gentiles should be *fellow-heirs*, and of the *same body*, and *partakers of His promise in Christ* by the Gospel."[37]

[45]

5.

In these remarks on the meaning of the word Mystery, some of the chief doctrines of the Gospel Revelation have been already enumerated; before entering, however, into the discussion which I have proposed to myself, it may be right briefly to enumerate the revealed doctrines in order, according to the Catholic, that is, the anti-rationalistic, notion of them. They are these: the Holy Trinity; the Incarnation of the Eternal Son; His atonement and merits; the Church as His medium and

---

[35] *St. Paul speaks . . . a Mystery revealed*: Cf. Ephesians 3:6, quoted at the end of this paragraph.

[36] *the Jews did stumble at it*: Cf. I Corinthians 1:23: "We preach Christ crucified, a stumbling block to Jews and folly to Gentiles."

[37] *"which in other ages . . . by the gospel."*: Ephesians 3:6.

instrument through which He is converting and teaching mankind; the Sacraments, and Sacramentals (as Bishop Taylor[38] calls them), as the definite channels through which His merits are applied to individuals; Regeneration, the Communion of Saints, the Resurrection of the body, consequent upon the administration of them; and lastly, our faith and works, as a condition of the availableness and efficacy of these divine appointments. Each of these doctrines is a Mystery; that is, each stands in a certain degree isolated from the rest, unsystematic, connected with the rest by unknown intermediate truths, and bearing upon subjects unknown. Thus the Atonement:—*why* it was necessary, *how* it operates, is a Mystery; that is, the heavenly truth which is revealed, extends on each side of it into an unknown world. We see but the skirts of God's glory in it.

[46] The virtue of the Holy Communion; how it conveys to us the body and blood of the Incarnate Son crucified, and how by partaking it body and soul are made spiritual. The Communion of Saints; in what sense they are knit together into one body, of which Christ is the head. Good works; how they, and how prayers again, influence our eternal destiny. In like manner what our relation is to the "innumerable company of Angels,"[39] some of whom, as we are told, minister to us;[40] what to the dead in Christ, to the "spirits of the just perfected,"[41] who are ever joined to us in a heavenly communion; what bearing the Church has upon the fortunes of the world, or, it may be, of the universe.

That there are some such mysterious bearings, not only the incomplete character of the Revelation, but even its documents assure us. For instance. The Christian dispensation was ordained, "to the intent that now unto *the principalities and powers* in heavenly places might be known by *the Church* the

---

[38] *Bishop Taylor*: Jeremy Taylor (1613-67), Anglican divine, Bishop of Down and Connnor; author of *The Rule and Exercises of Holy Living*. Newman deliberately mentions Bishop Taylor as an authoritative Anglican author using this term as protestants restricted the word 'sacraments' to Baptism and the Eucharist only, and Newman wishes to stress the wider sacramental life of the church through other rites also.

[39] *"innumerable company of Angels,"*: Hebrews 12:22.

[40] *some of whom, as we are told, minister to us*: Cf. Hebrews 1:14: "Are they not all ministering spirits, sent forth to minister for them who shall be heirs of salvation?"

[41] *"spirits of the just perfected"*: Hebrews 12:23.

manifold wisdom of God" (Eph. iii. 10). Such is its relation to the Angels. Again to lost spirits; "We wrestle not against flesh and blood, but against principalities, against powers, against the rulers of darkness in this world, against spiritual wickedness in heavenly places" (Eph. vi. 12). In like manner our Lord says, "the gates of hell shall not prevail against" the Church (Matt. xvi. 18); implying thereby a contest. Again, in writing the following passage, had not St. Paul thoughts in his mind, suggested by the unutterable sights of the third heaven,[42] but to us unrevealed and unintelligible? "I am persuaded that neither death, nor life, nor Angels, nor principalities, nor powers, not things present, nor things to come, nor height, nor depth, nor any other creature, shall be able to separate us" (that is, the Church,) "from the love of God which is in Christ Jesus our Lord" (Rom. viii. 38, 39).

The practical inference to be drawn from this view is, first, [47] that we should be very reverent in dealing with Revealed Truth; next, that we should avoid all rash theorizing and systematizing as relates to it, which is pretty much what looking into the Ark[43] was under the Law: further, that we should be solicitous to hold it safely and entirely; moreover, that we should be zealous and pertinacious in guarding it; and lastly, which is implied in all these, that we should religiously adhere to the form of words and the ordinances under which it comes to us, through which it is revealed to us, and apart from which the Revelation does not exist, there being nothing else given us by which to ascertain or enter into it.

Striking indeed is the contrast presented to this view of the Gospel by the popular theology of the day! That theology is as follows: that the Atonement is the chief doctrine of the Gospel; again, that it is chiefly to be regarded, not as a wonder in heaven, and in its relation to the attributes of God and to the unseen world, but in its experienced effects on our minds, in the change

---

[42] *unutterable sights of the third heaven*: Cf. II Corinthians 12:2: 'I knew a man in Christ' i.e. himself, 'above fourteen years ago, (whether in the body, I cannot tell; or whether out of the body, I cannot tell: God knoweth;) such an one caught up to the third heaven.'

[43] *looking into the Ark*: Cf. 1 Samuel 6:19: "And he slew some of the men of Bethshemesh, because they looked into the ark of the Lord."

it effects when it is believed. To this, as if to the point of sight in a picture, all the portions of the Gospel system are directed and made to converge; as if this doctrine were so fully understood, that it might fearlessly be used to regulate, adjust, correct, complete, everything else. Thus, the doctrine of the Incarnation is viewed as necessary and important to the Gospel, *because* it gives virtue to the Atonement; of the Trinity, *because* it includes the revelation, not only of the Redeemer, but also of the Sanctifier, by whose aid and influence the Gospel message is to be blessed to us. It follows that faith is nearly the whole of religious service, for through it the message or Manifestation is received; on the other hand, the scientific language of [48] Catholicism, concerning the Trinity and Incarnation, is disparaged, as having no tendency to enforce the effect upon our minds of the doctrine of the Atonement, while the Sacraments are limited to the office of representing, and promising, and impressing on us the promise of divine influences, in no measure of conveying them. Thus the Dispensation, in its length, depth, and height, is practically identified with its Revelation, or rather its necessarily superficial Manifestation. Not that the reality of the Atonement, in itself, is formally denied, but it is cast in the background, except so far as it can be discovered to be influential, viz., to show God's hatred of sin, the love of Christ, and the like; and there is an evident tendency to consider it as a *mere* Manifestation of the love of Christ, to the denial of all real virtue in it as an expiation for sin; as if His death took place merely to show His love for us as a sign of God's infinite mercy, to calm and assure us, without any real connexion existing between it and God's forgiveness of our sins. And the Dispensation thus being hewn and chiselled into an intelligible human system, is represented, when thus mutilated, as affording a remarkable evidence of the truth of the Bible, an evidence level to the reason, and superseding the testimony of the Apostles. That is, according to the above observations, that Rationalism, or want of faith, which has in the first place invented a spurious gospel, next looks complacently on its own off-spring, and pronounces it to be the very image of that notion of the Divine Providence, according to which it was originally modelled; a procedure, which, besides more serious objections, incurs the logical absurdity of arguing in a circle.

49

§ 2.

MR. ERSKINE'S "INTERNAL EVIDENCE."

AND this is in fact pretty nearly Mr. Erskine's argument in his Internal Evidence:[44] an author, concerning whom personally I have no wish to use one harsh word, not doubting that in his theory he is unjust to himself, and is only the organ, eloquent and ingenious, of unfolding a theory, which it has been his unhappiness to mistake for that Catholic faith which is revealed in the Gospel. Let us now turn to the Essay in question.

1.

Mr. Erskine begins in the following words:

"There is a principle in our nature, which make us dissatisfied with unexplained and unconnected facts; which leads us to theorize all the particulars of our knowledge, or to form in our minds some system of causes sufficient to explain or produce the effects which we see; and which teaches us to believe or disbelieve in the truth of any system which may be presented to us, *just as* it appears adequate or inadequate to afford that *explanation* of which we are in pursuit."

After speaking of two processes of reasoning which the mind uses in discovering truth, viz., one, "by ascending from effects to a cause," and the other, when we "descend from a cause to effects," he observes:

50

"In these processes of reasoning we have examples of conviction upon an evidence which is, most strictly speaking, internal—an

---

[44] *his Internal Evidence*: See above note on p.[30].

evidence altogether independent of our *confidence in the veracity* of the narrator of the facts."—P. 8.

Observe, he starts with this general proposition, viz., that we naturally "believe or disbelieve in the truth of any system which may be presented to us," according as it contains in it, or not, a satisfactory adjustment of causes to effects, the question of testimony being altogether superseded. Accordingly, he expressly says a little further on of the Apostles: "Their system is true in the nature of things, even were they proved to be impostors," p. 17; that is, the Scripture scheme of salvation is true in the nature of things; and self-evident, so that it needs nothing besides its intrinsic verisimilitude to compel our assent to it.

He explains himself thus:

"*The first faint outline of Christianity*," he says, "presents to us a view of God operating on the characters of men through a manifestation of His own character, in order that by leading them to participate in some measure of His moral likeness, they may also in some measure participate of His happiness."—P. 12.

"If the actions attributed to GOD, by any system of religion, be really such objects as, when present to the mind, do *not* stir the affections at all, that religion cannot influence the character, and is *therefore* utterly useless."—P. 23.

"The *object* of Christianity is to bring the character of man into harmony with that of God."—P. 49.

"The *reasonableness* of a religion seems to me to consist in there being a *direct and natural* connexion between a believing the doctrines which it inculcates, *and* a being formed by these to the character which it recommends. If the belief of the doctrines has *no* tendency to train the disciple in a more exact and more willing discharge of its moral obligations, *there is evidently a very strong probability against the truth of that religion* ... What is the history of another world to me, unless it have some *intelligible relation* to my duties or happiness?"— P. 59.

Now in these passages there is, first, this great assumption, [51] that the object of the Christian Revelation is ascertainable by us. It is asserted that its object is "to bring the character of man into harmony with that of God." That this is *an* object, is plain from Scripture, but that it is *the* object is nowhere told us; nowhere is it represented as the object in such sense, that we may take it as a key or rule, whereby to arrange and harmonize the various parts of the Revelation,—which is the use to which the author puts it. God's works look many ways; they have objects (to use that mere human word) innumerable; they are full of eyes before and behind, and, like the cherubim in the Prophet's vision,[45] advance forward to diverse points at once. But it is plainly unlawful and presumptuous to make one of those points, which happen to be revealed to us, the end of ends[46] of His providence, and to subject everything else to it. It plainly savours of that Rationalism above condemned; for what is it but to be resolved, that what is revealed to us, is and shall be a complete system; to reject everything but what is so complete; and to disallow the notion of Revelation as a collection of fragments of a great scheme, the notion under which the most profound human philosophy is accustomed to regard it?

"Christianity," says Bishop Butler,[47] "is a scheme quite beyond our comprehension. The moral government of God is exercised by gradually conducting things so in the course of His providence, that every one at length and upon the whole shall receive according to his deserts; and neither fraud nor violence, but *truth and right shall finally prevail*. Christianity is a particular scheme under this general plan of Providence, and a part of it, conducive to its completion, with regard to mankind; consisting itself also of various parts and a mysterious economy, which has been carrying on from the time the world came into its present wretched state, and is still carrying on for its recovery by a divine person, the Messiah, who is to 'gather together in one the [52] children of God, that are scattered abroad,'[48] and establish 'an everlasting kingdom, wherein dwelleth righteousness.'[49] ... Parts likewise of this economy, are the miraculous mission of the Holy Ghost, and His ordinary assistance as given to good men; the invisible government which Christ exercises over His Church ... and His future

---

[45] *like the cherubim in the Prophet's vision*: Cf. Ezekiel 9:11 ff.

[46] *the end of ends*: Cf. Aristotle, *Nicomachean Ethics*, 1097.a31. It is evident that Newman is referring to Aristotle here since in the 1836 text he quoted this phrase in the original Greek; see the Textual Appendix.

[47] *Bishop Butler*: Joseph Butler (1692-1752), Bishop of Durham.

[48] *'gather together . . . scattered abroad'*: John 11:52.

[49] *'an everlasting . . . dwelleth righteousness.'*: Daniel 9:24.

return to judge the world in righteousness, and completely re-establish the kingdom of God ... Now little, surely, need be said to show, that *this system or scheme of things is but imperfectly comprehended by us*. The Scripture expressly asserts it to be so. And, indeed, *one cannot read a passage relating to this great mystery of godliness, but what immediately runs up into something which shows us our ignorance in it*, as everything in nature shows us our ignorance in the constitution of nature."[50]

In this passage the great philosopher, though led by his line of argument to speak of the Dispensation entirely in its reference to man, still declares that even then its object is not identical with man's happiness, but that it is justice and truth; while viewed in itself, every part of it runs up into mystery.

Right reason, then, and faith combine to lead us, instead of measuring a divine revelation by human standards, or systematizing, except so far as it does so itself, to take what is given as we find it, to use it and be content. For instance, Scripture says that Christ died for sinners; that He rose for our justification, that He went that the Spirit might come; *so far* we may systematize. Such and such-like portions of a scheme are revealed, and we may use them, but no farther. On the other hand, the Catholic doctrine of the Trinity is a mere juxtaposition of separate truths, which to our minds involves inconsistency, when viewed together; nothing more being attempted by theologians, for nothing more is told us. Arrange and contrast them we may and do; systematize (that is, reduce them into an intelligible dependence on each other, or harmony with each other) we may not; unless indeed any such oversight of Revelation, such right of subjecting it to our understandings, is committed to us by Revelation itself. What then must be thought of the confident assumption, without proof attempted, contained in the following sentence, already quoted? [53]

"The first faint *outline* of Christianity presents to us a view of God operating on the characters of men through a manifestation of His own character, in order that, by leading them to participate in some measure

---

[50] Anal. ii. 4. [N]: Butler's *Analogy of Religion* (1736). Newman records in the *Apologia*, pp.102-3, the great influence that this book had on him.

in His moral likeness, they may also in some measure participate in His happiness."

That God intends us to partake in His moral likeness, that He has revealed to us His own moral character, that He has done the latter in order to accomplish the former (to speak as a man), I will grant, for it is in Scripture; but that it is the *leading idea* of Christianity, the chief and sovereign principle of it, this I altogether deny. I ask for proof of what seems to me an assumption, and (if an assumption) surely an unwarranted and presumptuous one.

Again: he says that "the reasonableness of a religion seems to him to consist in there being a *direct and natural* connexion between a believing the doctrines which it inculcates, and a being formed by these to the character which it recommends." But surely it is conceivable that reasons may exist in the vast scheme of the Dispensation (of the bearings of which we know nothing perfectly), for doctrines being revealed, which do not directly and naturally tend to influence the formation of our characters, or at least which we cannot see to do so. Here again we have the authority of Bishop Butler to support us, in considering that,

[54] "we are *wholly ignorant what degree of new knowledge* it were to be expected God would give mankind by Revelation, upon supposition of His affording one; or how far, or in what way, He would interpose miraculously, to qualify them to whom He should originally make the Revelation, *for communicating the knowledge given by it*; and to secure their doing it to the age in which they should live, and to secure its being transmitted to posterity."[51]

Next, notice was above taken of the selfishness of that philosophy, which resolves to sit at home and make everything subordinate to the individual. Is not this instanced in one of the foregoing passages? "What is the history of another world *to me*, unless it have some intelligible relation to my duties and happiness?" Was this Moses' temper, when he turned aside to see the great sight of the fiery bush?[52] What was the burning

---

[51] Anal. ii. 3. [N]

bush to Moses? The Almighty indeed so displayed Himself with a view to the deliverance of His people from Egypt; but Moses did not know that, when he went to see it; that was not his motive for going.

Further, be it observed, the above theory has undeniably a tendency to disparage, if not supersede, the mysteries of religion, such as the doctrine of the Trinity. It lays exclusive stress upon the *character* of God, as the substance of the Revelation. It considers the Scripture disclosures as a *Manifestation* of God's character, a formal representation of that character in an intelligible shape to our minds, and nothing more. The author says:

> "These terms, 'manifestation' and 'exhibition,' suit best with the *leading idea* which I wish to explain, viz., that the facts of Revelation are developments of the moral principles of the Deity, and carry an influential address to the feelings of man."—P. 26.

Now, is the theological doctrine of the Trinity such a development? Is it influentially addressed to our feelings? Is it "an act of the divine government," as the author elsewhere expresses himself? [55]

The immediate and inevitable result, or rather the operation of Mr. Erskine's "leading idea," when applied to the matter of the Scripture Revelation, is surely a refutation of it. It will be found to mean nothing, or to lead pretty nearly to Socinianism.[53] Let us take an instance: he says, that the reasonableness of a religion, and therefore its claim on our acceptance, consists in there being a direct and natural tendency in belief in its doctrines to form that moral character which it recommends. Now, I would ask,—do we never hear it asked,—have we never been tempted ourselves to ask,—"What is the *harm* of being, for instance, a Sabellian?"[54] And is not the habit of thought, from which such questionings proceed, owing to the silent influence

---

[52] *Moses . . . the fiery bush?*: Cf. Exodus 3:3
[53] *Socinianism*: The teaching of Fausto Sozzini (Latinised as Socinus) (1539-1604) who denied the divinity of Christ.
[54] *Sabellian*: Someone who holds the views of Sabellius, a third century heretic who taught that that the Son and the Holy Spirit were not divine Persons but different manifestations or 'masks' of God the Father, thus denying the Incarnation.

of such books as this of Mr. Erskine's? Further, do we not hear persons say, "As to the Athanasian doctrine,[55] I do not deny there is a Mystery about the Manifestations of the Divine Nature in Scripture, but this Mystery, whatever it is, as it does not interfere with the practical view of the doctrine, so, on the other hand, it cannot subserve it. It is among the secret things of God, and must be left among them;"—as if we might unthankfully throw back again into the infinite abyss, any of the jewels which God has vouchsafed to bring us thence.

2.

The reader may at first sight be tempted to say, "This is surely a violent handling of Mr. Erskine's words. What he does mean, is, not that the *want* of connexion between doctrine and precept is an objection, (though his words strictly taken *may* say this,) but, that where such a connexion does exist, as we see it does in Christianity, *there* is a strong argument in behalf of the divinity of a professed Revelation." Probably this was his original meaning, and it would have been well, had he kept to it. But it is the way with men, particularly in this day, to generalize freely, to be impatient of such concrete truth as existing appointments contain, to attempt to disengage it, to hazard sweeping assertions, to lay down principles, to mount up above God's visible doings, and to subject them to tests derived from our own speculations. Doubtless He, in some cases, vouchsafes to us the knowledge of truths more general than those works of His which He has set before us; and when He does so, let us thankfully use the gift. This is not the case in the present instance. Mr. Erskine has been led on, from the plain fact, that in Christianity there is a certain general bearing of faith in doctrine upon character, and so far a proof of its *consistency*, which is a token of divine working,—led on, to the general proposition, that in a genuine Revelation all doctrines revealed must have a direct bearing upon the moral character enjoined by it; and next to the use of this proposition as a test

[56]

---

[55] *the Athanasian doctrine*: The teaching of St. Athanasius (296-372), the great opponent of Arianism and defender of the divinity of Christ. Newman was particularly well-versed in this subject, cf. his *Arians of the Fourth Century* (1833); he was later to publish *Select Treatises of St. Athanasius* (1842).

for rejecting such alleged doctrines of the Gospel, for instance, the Catholic doctrine of the Trinity, as do not manifestly satisfy it.

That I am not unfair upon Mr. Erskine will appear from the following passages:

> "*The abstract fact* that there is a plurality in the unity of the Godhead, really makes *no address either to our understandings, or our feelings, or our consciences.* But the *obscurity* of the doctrine, as far as *moral* purposes are concerned, is dispelled, when it comes in such a form as this 'God so loved the world,' etc.; or this, 'But the Comforter which is,' etc.—Our *metaphysical* ignorance of the Divine Essence is not indeed in the slightest degree removed by this mode of stating the subject; but our moral ignorance of the Divine Character is enlightened, and *that is the thing with which we have to do.*"—P. 96. [57]

Now I do not say that such a passage as this is a denial of the doctrine of the Athanasian Creed;[56] but I ask, should a man be disposed to deny it, *how* would the writer refute him? Has he not, if a Trinitarian, cut away the ground from under him? Might not a Socinian or Sabellian convince him of the truth of their doctrines, by his own arguments? Unquestionably. He has laid down the principle, that a Revelation is *only so far* reasonable as it exhibits a direct and natural connexion between belief in its doctrines and conformity to its precepts. He then says, that in matter of fact the doctrine of the Trinity is only influential as it exhibits the moral character of God; that is, that so far as it does not, so far as it is abstract (as he calls it) and in scientific form, that is, as it is a Catholic Dogma, it is not influential, or reasonable, or by consequence important, or even credible. He has cut out the *Doctrine* by its roots, and has preserved only that superficial part of it which he denominates a "*Manifestation*,"—only so much as bears visibly upon another

---

[56] *the Athanasian Creed*: This creed, which in the Anglican *Book of Common Prayer* was appointed to be read at certain times, expresses the orthodox belief in the Holy Trinity in a lengthy series of detailed statements. However, many churches omitted its recitation, and it was particularly disliked by liberals. Although a classic statement of the Catholic Faith, it is now no longer believed to have been written by St. Athanasius himself.

part of the system, our moral character,—so much as is perceptibly connected with it,—so much as may be comprehended.

But he speaks so clearly on this subject that comment is perhaps needless.

"In the Bible," he says, "the Christian doctrines ... stand as indications of the character of God, and as the exciting motives of a corresponding character in man."

Before proceeding, there is an assumption here: often the doctrines so stand, not always, as he would imply. When St. Paul bids Timothy hold fast the form of sound words,[57] or St. Jude exhorts his brethren to contend earnestly for the faith,[58] these Apostles are evidently anxious about the faith for its own sake, not for any ulterior reason. When St. John requires us to reject any one who brings not the true doctrine,[59] nothing is said of that doctrine as an "exciting motive" to a certain character of mind, though viewed on one side of it, it certainly is such. St. Paul glories in the doctrine of Christ crucified, as being a *strange* doctrine and a *stumbling-block*.[60] St. John states the doctrine of the Incarnation, in the first chapter of his Gospel, as a heavenly truth, which was too glorious for men, and believed in only by the few, and by which the Father, indeed, was manifested, but which *shone in darkness*.[61] But to return to the passage which I commenced:

[58]

"In the Bible, the Christian doctrines are always stated in this connexion, they stand as indications of the character of God, and as the exciting motives of a corresponding character in man. Forming thus the connecting link between the character of the Creator and the creature, they possess a majesty which it is impossible to despise, and exhibit a form of consistency and truth which it is difficult to disbelieve. Such is Christianity in the Bible; *but in creeds and Church articles it is far otherwise*. These tests and summaries originated from

---

[57] *St. Paul bids Timothy . . .* : Cf. 2 Timothy 1:13.
[58] *St. Jude exhorts his brethren . . .*: Cf. Jude 3.
[59] *St. John requires us . . .* : Cf. 2 John 10.
[60] *St. Paul glories in the doctrine of Christ crucified . . .* : Cf. I Corinthians 1:23.
[61] shone in darkness: Cf. John 1:5.

the introduction of doctrinal errors and metaphysical speculations into religion; and in consequence of this, they are not so much intended to be the repositories of the truth, as barriers against the encroachment of erroneous opinions. The doctrines contained in them, therefore, are not stated with any reference to their *great object* in the Bible,—the regeneration of the human heart by the knowledge of the Divine character. *They appear as detached propositions*, indicating no *moral* cause, and pointing to no *moral* effect. They do not look to God on the one hand as their source; nor to man on the other as the object of their moral urgency. *They appear like links severed from the chain to which they belonged*; and *thus* they lose all that evidence which arises from their consistency, and all that dignity which is connected with their high design. I do not talk of the propriety or impropriety of having Church Articles, but the evils which spring from receiving impressions of religion exclusively or chiefly from this source."—Pp. 93, 94.   [59]

It is always a point gained to be able to come to issue in controversy, as I am able to do here with the writer under consideration. He finds fault with that disjoined and isolated character of the doctrines in the old Catholic creed, that want of system, which to the more philosophical mind of Bishop Butler would seem an especial recommendation from its analogy to the course of nature. He continues:

"I may instance the ordinary statements of the doctrine of the Trinity, as an illustration of what I mean. It seems difficult to conceive that any man should read through the New Testament candidly and attentively, without being convinced that this doctrine is essential to, and implied in, every part of the system: but it is not so difficult to conceive, that although his mind is perfectly satisfied on this point, he may yet, if his religious knowledge is exclusively derived from the Bible, feel a little surprised and staggered, when he for the first time reads the terms in which it is announced in the articles and confessions of all Protestant Churches. In these summaries, the doctrine in question is stated by itself divested of all its Scriptural accompaniments, and is made to bear simply on *the nature of the* Divine Essence, and the *Mysterious fact* of the existence of Three in One. *It is evident that this fact, taken by itself, cannot in the smallest degree tend to develop the Divine Character*, and therefore cannot make any moral impression on our minds."—Pp. 94, 95.

Another assumption; it is as incorrect to say that dogmas do not impress and influence our minds, as to say they are not stated in Scripture as dogmas. The doctrine of the Trinity *does* "tend to develop the Divine Character," *does* "make a moral impression on our minds;" for does not the notion of a Mystery lead to awe and wonder? and are these not moral impressions? He proceeds:

[60]

"In the Bible it assumes quite a different shape; it is there *subservient to the manifestation* of the moral character of God. The doctrine of God's combined justice and mercy, in the redemption of sinners, and of His continued spiritual watchfulness over the progress of truth through the world, and in each particular heart, could not have been communicated without it, so as to have been distinctly and vividly apprehended; but it is never mentioned, except in connexion with these objects; nor is it ever taught as a separate subject of belief. There is a great and important difference between these two modes of statement. In the first, *the doctrine stands as an isolated fact of a strange and unintelligible nature*, and is apt even to suggest the idea, that *Christianity holds out a premium for believing improbabilities*. In the other, it stands indissolubly united with an act of Divine holiness and compassion, which radiates to the heart an appeal of tenderness most intelligible in its nature and object, and most constraining in its influence."—Pp. 95, 96.

Here, at length, Rationalism stands confessed; doctrines, it seems, are not true, if they are not explicable. Again:

"The hallowed purpose of restoring men to the lost image of their Creator, is in fact the very soul and spirit of the Bible; and *whenever this object does not distinctly appear, the whole system becomes dead and useless*."

If so, what judgment are we to pass upon such texts as the following? "We are unto God a *sweet savour of Christ*, in them that are saved, *and in them that perish; to the one we are the savour of death unto death*: and to the other, the savour of life unto life." "What if God, *willing to show His wrath and to make His power known*, endured with much long-suffering the vessels of wrath fitted to destruction, and that He might make known the riches of His glory on the vessels of mercy, which He had afore prepared unto glory?" "He hath appointed a day in which He will judge the world in righteousness, by that Man whom he hath ordained." "*Behold, I come quickly,* and My reward is with Me, *to give every man according as his work shall be.*"[62]   [61] The glory of God, according to Mr. Erskine, and the maintenance of truth and righteousness, are *not* objects sufficient, were there no other, to prevent "the whole system" of revealed truth from "becoming dead and useless." Does not this philosophy tend to Universalism?[63] can its upholders maintain for any long while the eternity of future punishment? Surely they speak at random, and have no notion what they are saying. He proceeds:

"In Creeds and Confessions this great purpose is not made to stand forth with its real prominency; its intimate *connexion* with the different articles of faith is not adverted to; the *point* of the whole argument is thus lost, *and Christianity is misapprehended to be a mere list of mysterious facts.* One who understands the Bible may read them with profit, *because his own mind may fill up the deficiencies,* and when their statements are correct, they may assist inquirers in certain stages, by bringing under their eye a concentrated view of all the points of Christian doctrine; and they may serve, according to their contents, either as public invitations to their communion, or as public warnings against it; ... but they are not calculated to impress on the mind of a learner a vivid and *useful* apprehension of Christianity."—P. 139.

It is not the design of this Paper to refute Mr. Erskine's principles, so much as to delineate and contrast them with those of the Church Catholic. Since, however, he has already, in several of these extracts, *assumed* that Scripture ever speaks of revealed doctrines in a directly practical way,—not as objects of faith merely, but as motives to conduct,—I would call attention to the following passage, in addition to those which have been above pointed out. "Jesus answered and said unto him, Verily, verily, I say unto thee, *Except a man be born again, he cannot see the kingdom of* God. Nicodemus saith unto Him,

---

[62] 2 Cor. ii. 15, 16. Rom. x. 22, 23. Acts xvii. 31. Rev. xxii. 12. [N]

[63] *Universalism*: the belief that all will be saved because Hell is temporary.

[62]   *How* can a man be born when he is old? can he enter the second time into his mother's womb and be born? Jesus answered, Verily, verily, I say unto thee, *Except a man be born of water and of the Spirit, he cannot enter into the kingdom of God.* That which is born of the flesh is flesh, and that which is born of the Spirit is spirit. *Marvel not* that I said unto thee, Ye must be born again. The wind bloweth where it listeth, and thou hearest the sound thereof, but *canst not tell* whence it cometh and whither it goeth: so is every one that is born of the Spirit. Nicodemus answered and said unto Him, How can these things be? Jesus answered and said unto him, Art thou a master in Israel, and knowest not these things? Verily, verily, I say unto thee, We speak that We do know, and testify that We have seen; and *ye receive not Our witness.* If I have told you earthly things, and ye *believe not, how shall ye believe* if I tell you of heavenly things? And *no man ascendeth up to heaven, but He that came down from heaven, even the Son of man which is in heaven.*" [John iii. 3-13.]

Some persons, doubtless, are so imbued with modern glosses and the traditions of men, that they will discern in all this but a practical exhortation to conversion, change of heart, and the like; but any one who gets himself fairly to look at the passage in itself, will, I am persuaded, see nothing more or less than this,—that Christ enunciates a solemn *Mystery* for Nicodemus to receive in *faith*; that Nicodemus so understands His words, and hesitates at it; that our Lord reproves him for hesitating, tells him that there are even higher Mysteries than that He had set forth, and proceeds to instance that of the Incarnation. In what conceivable way would a supporter of Mr. Erskine's views make the last remarkable verse "subservient to the manifestation [63] of the moral character of God," or directly influential upon practice? The latter part, particularly the conclusion, of the sixth chapter of the same Gospel, would afford another instance in point.

3.

Now let us hear what Mr. Erskine says in like manner on the doctrine of the Atonement, which he would exalt, indeed, into the substance of the Gospel, but in his account of which, as well as of the other Mysteries of Revelation, he will, I fear, be found wanting.

"The doctrine of the Atonement through Jesus Christ, which is the corner-stone of Christianity, and to which *all the other doctrines of Revelation are subservient,*"—

(Here is the same most gratuitous assumption,—)

—"has had to encounter the misapprehension of the understanding as well as the pride of the heart."—

(Now observe, he is going to show how the understanding of the Church Catholic has *misapprehended* the doctrine,—)

"This pride is natural to man, and can only be overcome by the power of truth; but the misapprehension might be removed by the simple process of reading the Bible with attention; because it has arisen from neglecting the record itself, and taking our information from the discourses or the *systems of men* who have engrafted the metaphysical subtilties of the schools upon the unperplexed statement of the word of God. In order to understand the facts of Revelation, we must form a system to ourselves; but if any subtilty, *of which the application is unintelligible to common sense,* or *uninfluential on conduct,* enters into our system, *we may be sure that it is a wrong one.*"

"Systems of men!" he means by this Catholic teaching, indeed it has been fashionable of late so to speak of it; but let me ask, which teaching has the more of system in it, that which [64] regards the doctrines of Revelation as isolated truths, so far as they are not connected in Scripture itself, or that which pares away part, and forcibly deals with the rest, till they are all brought down to an end cognizable by the human mind? Let him speak for himself; he, at least, expressly sanctions the formation of a *system,* whatever be the case with Catholic believers. He proceeds:

"The *common-sense* system of religion consists in two connexions,—first, the connexion between the doctrines and the character of God which they exhibit; and secondly, the connexion between the same doctrines and the character which they are intended to impress on the mind of man. When, therefore, we are considering a religious doctrine, our questions ought to be, first, What view does this doctrine give of the character of God in relation to sinners? And secondly, What influence is the belief of it calculated to exercise on the character of man? ... There is something very striking and wonderful in this adaptation, and the deeper we search into it, the stronger reason shall we discover for admiration and gratitude, and the more thoroughly shall we be convinced that it is not a lucky coincidence," etc.—P. 97.

These last remarks are true of course in their place; so far as we think we see an adaptation, even though Scripture does not expressly mention it, let us praise God and be thankful;—but it is one thing to trace humbly and thankfully what we surmise to be God's handiwork, and so far as we think we see it, and quite another thing to propound our surmises dogmatically, not only as true, but as the substance of the Revelation, the test of what is important in it, and what is not; nay, of what is really part of it, and what not. Presently he says as follows:

[65] "The doctrine of the Atonement is the great subject of Revelation. God is represented as delighting in it, as being glorified by it, and as being most fully manifested by it. *All the other doctrines radiate from this as their centre*. In *subservience to it*, the distinction in the unity of the Godhead has been revealed. It is described as the everlasting theme of praise and song amongst the blessed who surround the throne of God."—Pp. 101, 102.

Now that the doctrine of the Atonement is so essential a doctrine that none other is more so, (true as it is,) does not at all hinder other doctrines in their own place being so essential that they may not be moved one inch from it, or made to converge towards that doctrine ever so little, beyond the sanction of Scripture. There is surely a difference between being prominent and being paramount. To take the illustration of the human body: the brain is the noblest organ, but have not the heart and the lungs their own essential rights (so to express myself), their own independent claims upon the regard of the physician? Will not he be justly called a theorist who resolves all diseases into one, and refers general healthiness to one organ as its seat and cause?

One additional observation is to be made on Mr. Erskine's view of the Atonement. He considers, in common with many other writers of his general way of thinking, that in that most solemn and wonderful event, we have a Manifestation, not only of God's love, but of His justice. For instance:

"The distinction of persons in the Divine nature we cannot comprehend, but we can easily comprehend the high and engaging morality of that character of God, which is developed in the history of the New Testament. God gave His equal and well-beloved Son to suffer in the stead of an apostate world; *and through this exhibition of awful justice*, He publishes the fullest and freest pardon. He thus teaches us that it forms no part of His scheme of mercy to dissolve the eternal connexion between sin and misery. No; this connexion stands sure, and one of the chief objects of Divine Revelation is to convince men of this truth; and *Justice* does the work of mercy, when it alarms us to a sense of danger," etc.—P. 74.

The view maintained in this and other extracts, and by others [66] besides Mr. Erskine, is remarkable for several reasons. First, for the *determination* it evinces not to leave us anything in the Gospel system unknown, unaccounted for. One might have thought that here at least somewhat of awful Mystery would have been allowed to hang over it; here at least some "depth" of God's counsels would have been acknowledged and accepted on *faith*. For though the death of Christ manifests God's *hatred of sin*, as well as His love for man, (inasmuch as it was sin that made His death necessary, and the greater the sacrifice the greater must have been the evil that caused it,) yet *how* His death expiated our sins, and what satisfaction it was to God's *justice*, are surely subjects quite above us. It is in no way a great and glorious *Manifestation* of His *justice*, as men speak nowadays;[64]

---

[64] This passage has been misunderstood from the word *manifestation* not being taken in the sense intended by the writer. The word may either mean the making a *fact evident*, or making the *reason* of it *intelligible*; it is used above in the latter sense. Christ's atoning death does indeed proclaim the fact that God's justice *is* satisfied, but it does not contain in it an explanation *how* it came to be a satisfaction. In the former sense then it may properly be called a manifestation of God's justice; not in the latter, though it is often

it is an event ever *mysterious* on account of its necessity, while it is *fearful* from the hatred of sin implied in it, and most *transporting and elevating* from its display of God's love to man. But Rationalism would account for everything.

[67] Next it must be observed, as to Mr. Erskine himself, that he is of necessity forced by his hypothesis to speak of God's justice as if manifested to our comprehension in the Atonement, if he speaks of it at all, however extravagant it may be to do so. For unless this were the case, the Dispensation would not be a "Manifestation," the revealed scheme would be imperfect, doctrines would stand apart from those elementary ideas which we have of the Divine Character from nature and Scripture—a result which Mr. Erskine pronounces in the outset to be contrary to reason, and fatal to the claims of a professed Revelation.

Mr. Erskine attempts to explain away this remaining Mystery of the Dispensation, as others have done before him: they have suggested that the vicarious satisfaction of Christ acts as a salutary lesson, how severe God might be to those who sin, did they receive their deserts, a lesson to all races of intellectual beings, present and to come, in order to the stability of His moral government:

"The design of the Atonement was to make mercy towards this offcast race *consistent with the honour and the holiness of the Divine Government*. To accomplish this gracious purpose, the Eternal Word, who was God, took on Himself the nature of man, and as the elder brother and representative and champion of the guilty family, He solemnly acknowledged the justice of the sentence pronounced against sin, and submitted Himself to its full weight of woe, in the stead of His adopted kindred. *God's justice found rest here*; His law was magnified and made honourable," etc.—Pp. 102, 103.

---

said to be so. The Atonement is a satisfaction to God's justice, in that His just anger was in matter of fact averted thereby from us sinners; but we do not know in what way it satisfied His justice to afflict Christ instead of us. This is a mystery, though many persons speak as if they *saw* the fitness of it. It *manifests* to our *comprehension* the love and holiness of God; it is a *proof* of love towards man, and of hatred of sin; it is not a *proof* to us that He is just; but must be taken *on faith* as a *result* of His being so. (Ed. 1838.) [On this point vide the Author's Discourse to Mixed Congregations, No. 15, *init.*, p. 306, etc., ed. 4.] [N] Discourse 15 on 'The Infinite of the Divine Attributes' is about why 'our Lord Jesus Christ, the Son of God, died on the Cross in satisfaction for our sins'.

Thus justice comes to be almost a modification of benevolence, or of sanctity, or the carrying out of a transcendent expediency. To such conjectures it is sufficient, as against Mr. Erskine, to answer, that a human hypothesis is not a divine manifestation.

An illustration, somewhat to the same effect, is used in the Essays of Mr. Scott,[65] of Aston Sandford.

[68]

"The story of Zaleucus,[66] prince of the Locrians, is well known: to show his abhorrence of adultery, and his determination to execute the law he had enacted, condemning the adulterer to the loss of both his eyes, and at the same time to evince his love to his son who had committed that crime, he willingly submitted to lose one of his own eyes, and ordered at the same time one of his son's to be put out. Now what adulterer could *hope to escape*, when *power was vested in* a man whom neither *self-love*, nor *natural affection* in its greatest force, could induce to dispense with the law, or relax the rigour of its sentence?"— Essay ix.

True, this act would show intense energy of determination to uphold the existing laws, clearly enough; and so did Mucius Scævola[67] show intense energy in burning off his hand; but what is this illustration to the question of *justice*? The mystery remains, that the Innocent satisfied for the guilty.

5.

One more subject of examination, and that not the least important, is suggested by the foregoing passages. Mention has been made in them once or twice of the *facts* of Revelation; the doctrines are said to be facts, and such facts to be all in all. Now according to Catholic teaching, doctrines are divine truths, which are the objects of faith, not of sight; we may call them facts, if we will, so that we recollect that they are sometimes facts or realities of the unseen world, and that they are not

---

[65] *Mr. Scott*: Thomas Scott (1745-1821), Anglican divine, Rector of Aston Sandford, best known for his *Commentary On The Whole Bible* (1788-1792).

[66] *The story of Zaleucas*: Cf. Polybius, *History*, Book II.

[67] *Mucius Scaevola*: Arrested by the Etrucan army, attempting to kill Porsenna and threatened with torture, he showed by courage by putting his left hand in the fire; cf. Pindar, *Olympian Odes* 10, 17-18.

synonymous with actions or works. But Mr. Erskine, by a remarkable assumption, rules it, that doctrines are facts of the revealed divine *governance*, so that a doctrine is made the same as a divine action or work. As Providence has given us a series of moral facts by nature, as in the history of nations or of the individual, from which we deduce the doctrines of natural religion, so Scripture is supposed to reveal a second series of [69] facts, or works, in the course of the three Dispensations,[68] especially the Christian, which are the *doctrines* of religion, or at least, which together with the principles involved in them, are the doctrines. Thus Christ's death upon the cross is an historical fact; and the meaning of it is that which illustrates and quickens it, and adapts it for influencing the soul. Now if we ask, how on this theory the doctrine of the Trinity is a fact in the divine governance, we are answered that it must be thrown into another shape, if I may so express myself; it must be made subordinate, and separated into parts. The series of Christian facts is supposed to pass from the birth to the death of Christ, and thence to the mission of the Holy Ghost. We must view the divinity of Christ in His death, the divinity of the Spirit in His mission. That they are therein exhibited, I grant; but the theory requires us to consider this the scriptural and only mode of their exhibition.

This theory is supposed by some of its upholders to be sanctioned by Butler; for they seem to argue, that as the course of nature is a collection of manifested facts, so is the course of grace.[69] But that great divine knew better than to infer, from what he saw, what was to be expected in a Revelation, were it to be granted. He asserts plainly the contrary; his whole argument is merely negative, defending Christianity as far as nature enables him to do so,—not limiting the course of the Revelation to the analogy of nature. Accordingly, the Church Catholic has ever taught (as in her Creeds) that there are facts revealed to us, not of this world, not of time, but of eternity, and that absolutely and independently; not merely embodied and

---

[68] *the three Dispensations*: the Patriarchal, the Mosaic and the Christian.
[69] *as the course of nature . . . so is the course of grace*: The full title of Butler's work is *The Analogy of Religion Natural and Revealed to the Constitution and the Course of Nature*.

indirectly conveyed in a certain historical course, not subordinate to the display of the Divine Character, not revealed merely relatively to us, but primary objects of our faith, and essential in themselves, whatever dependence or influence they [70] may have upon other doctrines, or upon the course of the Dispensation. In a word, it has taught the existence of *Mysteries* in religion, for such emphatically must truths ever be which are external to this world, and existing in eternity;—whereas this narrow-minded, jejune, officious, and presumptuous human system teaches nothing but a *Manifestation, i.e.* a series of historical works conveying a representation of the moral character of God; and it dishonours our holy faith by the unmeaning reproach of its being metaphysical, abstract, and the like,—a reproach, unmeaning and irreverent, just as much so as it would be on the other hand to call the historical facts earthly or carnal.

I will quote some passages from Mr. Erskine's work, to justify this account of his view, and then shall be able, at length, to take leave of him. He says:

"It may be proper to remark that the acts attributed to the Divine Government are usually termed 'doctrines,' to distinguish them from the moral precepts of a religion."—P. 25.

Thus the doctrine of the Trinity, *as such*, is not a doctrine of the Gospel. Again:

"It is not enough to show, in proof of its authenticity, that the facts which it affirms concerning the dealings of God with His creatures, do exhibit His moral perfections in the highest degree; it must also be shown that these facts, when present to the mind of man, do naturally, according to the constitution of his being, tend to excite and suggest that combination of feelings which constitutes his moral perfection. But when we read a *history* which authoritatively claims to be an *exhibition* of the character of God in His dealings with men, if we find in it that which fills and overflows our most dilated conceptions of moral worth, etc.; ... and if our reason farther discovers a system of powerful moral stimulants, embodied *in the facts* of this *history*; ... if we discern that the spirit of this history gives peace to the conscience, etc.; ... we may then well believe that God has been pleased in pity,

[71] etc. ... to clothe the eternal laws which regulate His spiritual government, in such a form as may be palpable to our conceptions, and adapted to the urgency of our necessities."—Pp. 18, 19.

"I mean to show that there is an intelligible and necessary connexion between the *doctrinal facts* of revelation and the character of God; ... and farther, that the belief of these *doctrinal* facts has an intelligible and necessary tendency to produce the Christian character," etc.—Pp. 20, 21.

"The object of this dissertation is to analyse the component parts of the Christian scheme of doctrine with reference to its bearings both on the character of God and on the character of man; and to demonstrate that *its facts* not only present an expressive *exhibition* of all the moral qualities which can be conceived to reside in the divine mind, but also contain all those objects which have a natural tendency to excite and suggest in the human mind that combination of moral feelings which has been termed moral perfection."—P. 16.

"God has been pleased to present to us a most interesting *series of actions*, in which His moral character, *as far as we are concerned*, is fully and perspicuously embodied. In this *narration*," etc.—P. 55.

"It [the Gospel] addresses the learned and unlearned, the savage and the civilized, the decent and the profligate; and to all it speaks precisely the same language! What then is this universal language? It cannot be the language of metaphysical discussion, or what is called abstract moral reasoning; ... its argument consists in a relation of *facts*."—P. 55.

Now that in these passages, the doctrines of the Gospel are resolved into facts which took place in God's governance, and that its mysteries are admitted, only so far as they are qualities or illustrations of these historical facts, seems to me, not only the true but the only interpretation to be put upon their wording. If they do not mean this, let this at least be proposed, as an approximation to the real meaning; I do not see what else they can mean; however, let it be observed, that the principles which have been laid down in this discussion are not at all affected by any failing, if there be failing, in the illustration of them which I have been drawing by contrast, on this or any other point, from the work of Mr. Erskine.

72

§ 3.

MR. ABBOTT'S "CORNER STONE."

HERE then we have arrived at a point where we part company with Mr. Erskine, and join Mr. Abbott,[70] who advances further in a most perilous career. The principle with which Mr. Erskine began has been above discovered to issue in a view or theory of the Gospel, which may be contemplated apart from that principle. That the human mind may criticize and systematize the Divine Revelation, that it may identify it with the Dispensation, that it may limit the uses of the latter to its workings through our own reason and affections, and such workings as we can ascertain and comprehend,—in a word, that the Gospel is a *manifestation*, this is the fundamental principle of Mr. Erskine's Essay. Mr. Jacob Abbott seems so fully to take this principle for granted, that it would be idle to do more than notice his doing so; it will be more to the purpose to direct attention to his treatment of the Theory, in which Mr. Erskine's principle seems to issue, viz., that the Gospel is a *collection of facts*. I am now referring to Mr. Abbott's work called "The Corner Stone," which I do not hesitate to say approaches within a hair's breadth of Socinianism: a charge which I would by no means urge against Mr. Erskine, whatever be the tendency of his speculations.

1.

73

In the work in question, Mr. Abbott disclaims entering into theological questions, properly so called (Preface, p. vi.); nor is there any necessity for his entering into them, so that the line of discussion which he does take, does not intrude upon them or provoke them.

---

[70] *Mr. Abbott*: see above, Editor's Introduction, p.xvii.

"I have made this *exhibition* of the Gospel," he says, "with reference to its *moral* effect on human hearts, and not for the purpose of taking sides in a controversy between different parties of Christians."

Again:

"A system of theology is a map or plan, in which every feature of the country must be laid down in its proper place and proportion; this work is, on the other hand, a series of views, as a traveller sees them in passing over a certain road. In this case, the road which I have taken leads indeed through the heart of the country, but it does not by any means bring to view all which is interesting or important. The reader will perceive that the *history* of Jesus Christ is the clue which I have endeavoured to follow; that is, the work is intended to exhibit religious truth, as it is connected with the various events in the life of our Saviour. In first introducing Him to the scene, I consider His exalted nature as the *great moral Manifestation of the Divinity to us.* Then follows a view *of His personal character, and of His views of religious duty*," etc.—Pp. vi. vii.

Let us observe here the similarity of language between the two writers I am speaking of. They are evidently of the same school. They both direct their view to the Gospel *history* as a Manifestation of the Divine Character; and though, in the above extracts, Mr. Abbott uses language more guarded than Mr. Erskine, there will be found to be little or no practical difference between them. But there seems this most important distinction in their respective applications of their Theory, though not very distinct or observable at first sight; that Mr. Erskine admits into [74] the range of his Divine facts such as are not of this world, as the voluntary descent of Christ from heaven to earth, and His Incarnation, whereas Mr. Abbott virtually limits it to the witnessed history of Christ upon earth. This, so far as it exists, is all the difference between orthodoxy and Socinianism.

For this encroachment Mr. Erskine indeed had prepared the way; for he certainly throws the high doctrines of religion into the background; and the word "Manifestation" far more naturally fits on to a history witnessed by human beings, than to dispositions made in the unseen world. But Mr. Erskine certainly has not *taught* this explicitly.

If we wish to express the sacred Mystery of the Incarnation accurately, we should rather say that God is man, than that man is God. Not that the latter proposition is not altogether Catholic in its wording, but the former expresses the *history* of the Economy, (if I may so call it,) and confines our Lord's personality to His divine nature, making His manhood an adjunct; whereas to say that man is God, does the contrary of both of these,—leads us to consider Him a man primarily and personally, with some vast and unknown dignity superadded, and that acquired of course after His coming into existence as man. The difference between these two modes of speaking is well illustrated by a recent Unitarian author, whom on account of the truth and importance of his remarks, I am led, with whatever pain, to quote:

"A quick child, though not acquainted with logic, ... will perceive the absurdity of saying that Edward is John ... As the young pupil must be prepared to infer from the New Testament that a perfect man is perfect God, he ... must be imperceptibly led to consider the word God as expressing a quality, or an aggregate of qualities, which may be [75] predicated of more than one, as the name of a species; just as when we say John is man, Peter is man, Andrew is man ... And so it is, with the exception of a few who, in this country, are still acquainted with that ingeniously perverse system of words by means of which the truly scholastic Trinitarians (such as Bishop Bull[71] and Waterland,[72] who had accurately studied the fathers and the schoolmen,) appear to evade the logical contradictions with which the doctrine of the Trinity abounds; all, as I have observed for many years, take the word God, in regard to Christ, as the name of a species, and more frequently of a dignity."—*Heresy and Orthodoxy*, p. 91.[73]

It will be observed of this passage, that the writer[74] implies that the Catholic mode of speaking of the Incarnation is not

---

[71] *Bishop Bull:* George Bull (1634-1710), Anglican divine, theologian and controversialist, later Bishop of St David's, author of *Defensio Fidei Nicaenae* (1685).
[72] *Waterland:* Daniel Waterland (1683-1740), Anglican theologian, wrote *A Vindication of Christ's Divinity* (1719) and took a middle course between Socinianism and the orthodox position of the Nonjurors.
[73] Heresy and Orthodoxy: *Observations on Heresy and Orthodoxy* (1835) by Joseph Blanco White.
[74] Mr. Blanco White. [N] See above note on p.[27].

exposed to a certain consequence, to which the mode at present popular is exposed, viz., the tendency to explain away Christ's divinity. Man is God, is the popular mode of speech; God is man, is the Catholic.

2.

To return. It seems then that Mr. Erskine proceeds in the orthodox way, illustrating the doctrine that God became man; Mr. Abbott, starting with the earthly existence of our Lord, does but enlarge upon the doctrine that a man is God. Mr. Erskine enforces the Atonement, as a Manifestation of God's moral character; Mr. Abbott the life of Christ with the same purpose,— with but slight reference to the doctrine of the Expiation, for of course he whose life began with his birth from Mary, had given up nothing, and died merely because other men die. Here then is something very like Socinianism at first sight.

But again, let us see how he conducts his argument. Here again he differs from Mr. Erskine. The latter considers the incarnation of the Son of God to be a manifestation of God's [76] mercy. Here then in his view, which so far is correct, there is a double Manifestation—of the Son of God personally in human nature, and of God morally in the history and circumstances of His incarnation; though Mr. Erskine's argument leads him to insist on the latter. Mr. Abbott assumes the latter as the sole Manifestation, thus bringing out the tendency of Mr. Erskine's argument. In other words, he considers our Lord Jesus Christ as a man primarily, not indeed a mere man, any more than the conversion of the world was a mere human work, but not more than a man aided by God, just as the conversion of the world was a human work aided and blessed by God; a man in intimate union, nay in mysterious union with God, as Moses might be on the Mount, but not more than Moses except in degree. He considers that certain attributes of the Godhead were manifested in Jesus Christ, in the sense in which the solar system manifests His power, or the animal economy His wisdom; which is a poorly concealed Socinianism.—So this, it appears, is what really comes of declaiming against "metaphysical" notions of the Revelation, and enlarging on its moral character!

That I may not be unfair to Mr. Abbott, I proceed to cite his words:

"In the first place, let us take a survey of the *visible universe*, that we may see what *manifestations* of God appear in *it*. Let us imagine that we can see with the naked eye all that the telescope would show us; and then, in order that we may obtain an uninterrupted view, let us leave this earth, and, ascending from its surface, take a station where we can look, without obstruction, upon all around. As we rise above the summits of the loftiest mountains, the bright and verdant regions of the earth begin to grow dim. City after city, etc. ... Our globe itself cuts off one-half of the visible universe at all times, and the air spreads over us a deep canopy of blue, which during the day shuts out entirely the other half. But were the field open we should see in every direction the endless perspective of suns and stars as I have described them ... [77] God is everywhere ... The Deity is the *All-pervading Power* which lives and acts throughout the whole. He is not a separate existence, having a special habitation in a part of it ... God is a Spirit. A Spirit; that is, He has no form, no place, no throne. Where He acts, there only can we see Him. He is the wide-spread omnipresent power which is everywhere employed, but which we can never see, and never know, except so far as He shall manifest Himself by His doings.

"If we thus succeed in obtaining just conceptions of the Deity as the invisible and universal *power*, pervading all space, and existing in all time, we shall at once perceive that the only way by which He can make Himself known to His creatures is by *acting Himself out*, as it were, in His works; *and of course the nature of the Manifestation which is made will depend upon the nature of the works*. In the structure of a solar system, with its blazing centre and revolving worlds, the Deity, invisible itself, acts out its mighty power, and the unerring perfection of its intellectual *skill*. At the same time, while it is carrying on these mighty movements, it is exercising, in a very different scene, its untiring *industry*, and unrivalled *taste*, in clothing a mighty forest with verdure, etc., etc. ... And so everywhere this unseen and universal essence *acts out its various attributes by its different works*. We can learn its nature only by the character of the effects which spring from it.

"This universal essence, then, must display to us its nature, by acting itself out in a thousand places *by such manifestations* of itself as it wishes us to understand. Does God desire to impress us with the idea of His *power*? He darts the lightning, etc. etc. Does He wish to beam upon us in *love*? What can be more expressive than the sweet summer sunset, etc.? … How can He make us acquainted with His *benevolence and skill*? Why, by acting them out in some mechanism which exhibits them. He may construct an eye or a hand for man, etc. How can He give us some conception of His *intellectual powers*? He can plan the motions of the planets, etc. etc. … But the great question, after all, is to come. It is the one to which we have meant that all we have been saying should ultimately tend. *How can such a Being exhibit the moral principle by which His mighty energies are all controlled?*"—Pp. 6-14.

[78]   This is eloquent writing; but this is not the place for dwelling on this quality of it; as to its doctrine, to speak plainly, it savours unpleasantly of pantheism.[75] It treats the Almighty, not as the great God, but as some vast physical and psychological phenomenon. However, we are immediately concerned with the author's views, not on Natural, but on Revealed Religion. He continues thus:

"He is an unseen, universal power, utterly invisible to us, and imperceptible, except so far as He shall act out His attributes in what He does. *How shall He act out moral principle?* It is easy, by His material creation, to make any impression upon us which material objects can make; but how shall He exhibit to us the moral beauty of justice and benevolence and mercy between man and man? … He might declare His moral attributes, as He might have declared His power; but if He would bring home to us the one as vividly and distinctly as the other, He must act out His moral principles by a moral *Manifestation*, in a moral scene; *and the great beauty of Christianity* is, that it represents Him as doing so. He brings out the purity, and spotlessness, and moral glory of the Divinity, through the workings of the human mind called into existence for this purpose, and stationed in a most conspicuous attitude among men … Thus the moral perfections of Divinity show themselves to us in the only way by which, so far as we can see, it is possible directly to show them, by coming out in action, in the very field of human duty, by a mysterious union with a human intellect and human powers. It is God manifest in the flesh—*the visible moral image of an all-pervading moral Deity*, Himself for ever invisible."—Pp. 14, 15.

On this explanation of the Incarnation, now, alas! not unpopular even in our own Church, viz., that "God manifest in

---

[75] *pantheism*: the belief that there is no distinction between God and the universe.

the flesh" is "the *visible moral* image" of God, let us hear the judgment of one who was a Trinitarian, and has lately avowed himself a convert to Unitarianism.[76] He thus relates the change in his own religious profession:

"In my anxiety to avoid a separation from the Church by the deliberate surrender of my mind to my old Unitarian convictions, I took refuge in a modification of the Sabellian theory, and availed [79] myself of the moral unity which I believe to exist between God the Father and Christ, joined to the consideration that Christ is called in the New Testament the *Image* of God, and addressed my prayers to God *as appearing in that image.* I left nothing untried to cultivate and encourage this feeling by devotional means. But such efforts of mere feeling (and I confess with shame their frequency on my part for the sake of what seemed most religious) were always vain and fruitless. *Sooner or later my reason has not only frustrated but punished them.* In the last-mentioned instance the devout contrivance would not bear examination. *Sabellianism is only Unitarianism disguised in words*: and as for the worship of an image in its absence, the idea is most unsatisfactory. In this state, however, I passed five or six years; but the return to the clear and definite Unitarianism in which I had formerly been, was as easy as it was natural."—*Heresy and Orthodoxy*, p. viii.

This passage proves thus much, not perhaps, that the philosophising in question *leads* to Socinianism, but that it is a philosophy under which Socinianism may *lie hid*, even from a man's own consciousness; and this is just the use I wish to make of it against Mr. Abbott. He ends as follows:

"The substance of the view which I have been wishing to impress upon your minds is, that we are to expect to see Him solely through the *Manifestation He makes of Himself in His works.* We have seen in what way some of the traits of His character are displayed in the visible creation, and how at last He determined to *manifest His moral character*, by bringing it into action *through the medium of a human soul.* The plan was carried into effect, and the mysterious person thus formed appears for the first time to our view in the extraordinary boy," etc.—Pp. 15, 16.

---

[76] *one who has lately avowed himself a convert to Unitarianism*: Blanco White again.

In these passages it seems to be clearly maintained that our Lord is a Manifestation of God in precisely that way in which His creatures are, though in a different respect, viz., as regards His moral attributes,—a Manifestation, not having anything in it essentially peculiar and incommunicable, and therefore "*a* Manifestation," as he in one passage expresses himself, not *the* Manifestation of the Father.

[80]

Further, he expressly disclaims any opinion concerning the essential and superhuman relation, or (as he calls it) the "metaphysical" relation of the Son to the Father, in a passage which involves a slight upon other doctrines of a most important, though not of such a sacred character:

"Another source of endless and fruitless discussion is disputing about questions *which can be of no practical consequence*, however they may be decided; such as the *origin* of sin, the state of the soul between death and the resurrection, the salvation of infants, the *precise metaphysical relationship* of the Son to the Father."—P. 323.[77]

Why called *metaphysical*, I do not understand. Is Almighty God Himself then, in Mr. Abbott's view, *physical*? But we have been already introduced to this word by Mr. Erskine, whose original fallacy also, be it observed, is faithfully preserved in this passage;—"questions which can be of no practical consequence," as if we have any warrant thus to limit, or to decide upon, the gracious revelations of God. He continues:

"We have said they are of no practical consequence; *of course* an ingenious reasoner *can contrive* to connect practical consequences with *any subject whatever*, and in his zeal he will exaggerate the importance of the connection;"

I interrupt the reader, to remind him that the subjects spoken of in this careless, self-satisfied way, are those which from the first have been preserved in Creeds and Confessions as the most necessary, most solemn truths;—

---

[77] Vide also p. 197. [N]

"in fact *every subject in the moral world is more or less connected with every other one*; nothing stands out entirely detached and isolated, and *consequently* a question which its arguers will admit to be merely a theoretical one, will never be found."—P. 324.

But if so, who shall draw the line between truths practical [81] and theoretical? Shall we trust the work to such as Mr. Abbott? Surely this passage refutes his own doctrine. *We* also say that there are no two subjects in religion but may be connected by our minds, and therefore, for what we know, perchance are connected in fact. All we maintain in addition, is, that evidence of the fact of that connexion is not necessary for the proof of their importance to us, and further, that we have no right to pronounce that they are revealed merely with a view to their importance to us.

He disposes of the Catholic doctrine of Christ's eternal Sonship by calling it metaphysical; how he escapes from the Catholic doctrine of the Incarnation we have already seen,—he resolves it into a moral Manifestation of God in the person of Christ. But his view requires a few more words of explanation. First, as I have already had occasion to notice, he speaks of God in pantheistic language, as an Anima Mundi,[78] or universal essence, who has no known existence except in His works, as an all-pervading power or principle, not external to the created world, but in it, and developed through it. He goes on to say that this Almighty, who is thus illimitable and incomprehensible, is exhibited in *personal* attributes in Christ, as if all the laws and provisions, in which he energizes in nature impersonally, were condensed and exemplified in a real personal being. Hence he calls our Lord by a strange term, the *personification* of God, *i.e.* (I suppose) the personal image, or the manifestation in a person. In other words, God, whose Person is unknown in nature, in spite of His works, is revealed in Christ, who is the express image of His Person; and just in this, and (as I conceive) nothing more, would he conceive there was a difference between the manifestation of God in Christ, [82]

---

[78] *Anima Mundi*: world soul. Originating with Plato: 'We may consequently say that this world is indeed a living being endowed with a soul and intelligence' (*Timaeus* n, 29). Cf. also Friedrich. Schelling (1775-1854) *Von der Weltseeele* (1798).

and the manifestation of Him in a plant or flower. Christ is a *personal* Manifestation. Whether there be any elements of truth in this theory, I do not concern myself to decide; thus much is evident, that he so *applies* it as utterly to explain away the real divinity of our Lord. The passages are as follow:

"It is by Jesus Christ that we have access to the Father. This vivid exhibition of His character, this *personification of His moral attributes*, opens to us the way. Here we see a manifestation of divinity, an image of the invisible God, which comes as it were down to us; it meets our feeble faculties with a personification." etc.—P. 40.

"We accordingly commenced with His childhood, and were led at once into a train of reflection on the nature and the character of that eternal and invisible Essence *whose attributes were personified in Him*."—P. 192.

"The human mind ... reaches forward for some vision of the Divinity, the great unseen and inconceivable Essence. Jesus Christ is the *personification of the divinity for us*, the brightness of His glory and the express image of His person."—P. 200.

3.

Next, as to his opinions concerning the doctrine of the Atonement. I will not deny, I am glad to perceive, that some of his general expressions are correct, and taken by themselves, would be satisfactory; but they are invalidated altogether by what he has at other times advanced. It may be recollected that Mr. Erskine in his treatise on Internal Evidence, lays such a stress upon the use of the Atonement *as a Manifestation*, as to throw the real doctrine itself into the shade. Viewed in itself, Christ's death is, we believe, a sacrifice acting in some unknown way for the expiation of human sin; but Mr. Erskine views it (as indeed it may well be viewed, but as exclusively it should [83] not be viewed,) as a mark and pledge of God's love to us, which it would be, though it were not an Expiation. Even though Christ's incarnation issued in nothing more than His preaching to the world and sealing His doctrine with His blood, it would be a great sign of His love, and a *pledge* now of our receiving blessings through Him; for why should He die except He meant to be merciful to us? but this would not involve the necessity of an expiation. St. Paul died for the Church, and showed his love for it in this sense. When then the view of the Christian is limited, as Mr. Erskine would almost wish it to be, to the *Manifestation* of the Atonement, or the effect of the Atonement on our minds, no higher doctrine is *of necessity* elicited than that of its being a sign of God's mercy, as the rainbow might be, and a way is laid, by obscuring, to obliterate the true doctrine concerning it. So far Mr. Erskine proceeds, not denying it (far from it), but putting it aside in his philosophical Evidence: Mr. Abbott, upon the very same basis, is bolder in his language, and almost, if not altogether, gets rid of it.

In the following passage he applies Mr. Erskine's doctrine of the moral lesson, taught in Christ's death, of the justice and mercy of God: and he will be found distinctly to assert that the virtue of it lay in this, viz., that it was a *declaration* of God's hatred of sin, the same in kind as the punishment of the sinner would have been, only more perfect, as a means of impressing *on us* His hatred of sin: not as if it really reconciled us to an offended Creator.

"The balm for your wounded spirit is this, that the moral impression in respect to the nature and tendencies of sin, which *is the only possible reason* God can have in leaving you to suffer its penalties,"

(one should think the reason might be that "the wages of sin is death,"[79])

"is accomplished *far better* by the life and death of His Son;"—   [84]

(surely it is a greater balm to know that Christ has put away the wrath of God,[80] as Scripture says, than to theorize about "moral impressions" beyond the word of Scripture. Observe too, he says, "the *life* and death," excluding the proper idea of Atonement, which lies in the death of Christ, and so tending to resolve it into a Manifestation,)

---

[79] *"the wages of sin is death"*: Romans 6:23.
[80] *Christ has put away the wrath of God*: Cf. Romans 3:25.

"God never could have wished to punish you for the sake of doing evil;"—

(God punishes the sinner, not indeed for the sake of evil, but as a just and holy God,)

"and all the good which He could have accomplished by it is already effected in another and a better way."—P. 179.[81]

Here is the same assumption which was just now instanced from Mr. Erskine, viz., that God cannot inflict punishment except in order to effect a greater good, or (as Mr. Abbott himself has expressed it just before) "because the welfare of His government requires" it, which is a mere hypothesis.

Again:

"A knowledge of the death of Christ, with the explanation of it given in the Scriptures, touches men's hearts, it shows the nature and tendencies of sin, it produces fear of God's displeasure, and resolution to return to duty; and thus *produces effects by which* justice is satisfied,"—

(observe, not by an expiation, but by the repentance of the offender in consequence of the "moral impression" made on him by the "Manifestation" of Christ's death,—)

"and the authority of the law sustained far better in fact than it would be by the severest punishment of the guilty sinner."—P. 174.

[85]   "Look at the *moral effect* of this great sacrifice, and feel that it takes off all the necessity of punishment, and all the burden of your guilt."—P. 190.

The necessity of punishment is (according to Mr. Abbott) the well-being of the Universe: and the virtue of the great sacrifice is, not expiation, atonement in God's sight, but the *moral effect* of Christ's death on those who believe in it. So again, in a passage lately quoted for another purpose, he says:

---

[81] Vide also p. 173. [N]

"It is by Jesus Christ that we have access to the Father. *This vivid exhibition of His character*, this personification of His moral attributes, *opens to us the way*."—P. 40.

Lastly, we have the same stress laid upon the facts of the Gospel as in Mr. Erskine's work, with this difference, that Mr. Erskine supposes the orthodox doctrine, or what he considers such, to be conveyed in the facts; Mr. Abbott, with the liberalism to which his predecessor leads, but which is more characteristic of this day than of fifteen years ago, seems to think that various theories may be raised about the facts, whether orthodox or otherwise, but that the facts alone are of consequence to us.

"Such are the three great *Manifestations* of Himself to man which the one Unseen All-pervading Essence has made and exhibited to us in the Bible, and in our own experience and observation."—

(—This sentence, be it observed in passing, savours strongly of Sabellianism; he has spoken of what he calls three Manifestations of Almighty God, as our natural Governor, as influencing the heart, and as in Jesus Christ, without there being anything in his way of speaking to show that he attributed these Manifestations respectively to Three Persons. He proceeds:)

"Though there have been interminable disputes in the Christian Church about the language which has been employed to describe these [86] *facts*, there has been comparatively little dispute among even nominal Christians[82] about the *facts themselves*."—P. 39.

Such is the theology to which Mr. Erskine's principle is found to lead in the hands of Mr. Abbott; a theology (so to name it) which violently robs the Christian Creed of all it contains, except those outward historical facts through which its divine truths were fulfilled and revealed to man.

---

[82] *nominal Christians:* This phrase perhaps echoes the Calvinist distinction between the converted (real) and the unconverted (nominal) Christian.

4.

This brief explanation of Mr. Abbott's theological system may be fitly followed up by some specimens of the temper and tone of his religious sentiments. In this way we shall be able to ascertain the character of mind which such speculations presuppose and foster.

"Jesus Christ had a *taste* for beauty, both of nature and art; He admired the magnificent *architecture* of the Temple, and *deeply lamented* the necessity of its overthrow, and His *dress* was at least of such a character that the disposal of it was a subject of importance to the well-paid soldiers who crucified Him."—Pp. 50, 51.

Let us think seriously, is Christ God, or is He not? if so, can we dare talk of Him as having "a taste for nature"? It is true Mr. Abbott does speak in this way of the Almighty Father also; so that it may be said rather to prove that he has a low conception of God than of Christ. Perhaps it will be more truly said that his want of reverence towards the Saviour, has led on to the other more direct profaneness. Yet a "taste for beauty of *art*," for "architecture"! This of the Eternal Son of God, the Creator; will it be said that He is man also? true;—but His personality is in His Godhead, if I may express myself in theological language. He did not undo what He was before, He did not cease to be the infinite God, but He added to Him the substance of a man, and thus participated in human thoughts and feelings, yet without impairing (God forbid) His divine perfection. The Incarnation was not "a conversion of the Godhead into flesh, but a taking of the manhood into God."[83] It seems there is *need* of the Athanasian Creed in these dangerous times. A mystery, indeed, results from this view, for certain attributes of Divinity and of manhood seem incompatible; and there may be instances in our Lord's history on earth of less than divine thought and operation: but *because* of all this we never must speak, we have utterly no warrant to speak, of the Person of the Eternal Word

[87]

---

[83] *not "a conversion . . . the Manhood into God."*: A quotation from the Athanasian Creed, hence Newman's comment that there is a need for this to be recited in services. He is thus justifying his own practice of including it, when it was prescribed, in the church of St. Mary the Virgin where he was Vicar at this time. Other Oxford Movement divines also had this creed recited in their churches.

as thinking and feeling like a mere man, like a child, or a boy, as simply ignorant, imperfect, and dependent on the creature, which is Mr. Abbott's way. To proceed:

"Jesus Christ was in some respects *the most* bold, energetic, decided, and courageous man *that ever lived*; but in others he was the most flexible, submissive, and yielding."—P. 51.

The Son of God made flesh, though a man, is beyond comparison with other men; His person is not human; but to say "most of all men" is to compare.

"There never was a mission, or an enterprise of any kind, conducted with a more bold, energetic, fearless spirit, than the Saviour's mission."—P. 52.

This sentence may not seem objectionable to many people, and as it is similar to many others in the work, it may be right to remark upon it. The truth is, we have got into a way of, what may be called, panegyrizing our Lord's conduct, from our familiarity with treatises on External Evidence. It has been the fashion of the day to speak as to unbelievers, and, therefore, to level the sacred history to the rank of a human record, by way of argument. Hence we have learned to view the truth merely [88] externally, that is, as an unbeliever would view it; and so to view and treat it even when we are not arguing; which involves, of course, an habitual disrespect towards what we hold to be divine, and ought to treat as such. This will in part account for the tone in which the History of the Jews is sometimes set forth. And it is remarkably illustrated in the work before us, which, though pointedly addressed only to those who "have confessed their sins and asked forgiveness," who "strive against temptation, and seek help from above," (vid. p. 1,) yet is continually wandering into the external view of Christ's conduct, and assumes in a didactic treatise, what is only accidentally allowable in controversy. To return:—

"There is something very bold and energetic in the measures He adopted in accomplishing His work ... In fact, there perhaps never was so great a moral effect produced in three years, on any community so extensive, if we consider at all the disadvantages incident to the customs of those days. There was no press, no modes of extensive written communication, no regularly organized channels of intercourse whatever between the different portions of the community. He acted under every disadvantage."—Pp. 53, 54.

Under no disadvantage, if He were God. But this is only part of one great error under which this writer lies. "There was no press"! What notions does this imply concerning the nature, the strength, and the propagation of moral truth!

"He sought solitude, He shrunk from observation: in fact, almost the only *enjoyment* which He seemed really to love, was His *lonely ramble* at midnight, for rest and prayer ... It is not surprising, that *after the healed crowds and exhausting labours of the day*, He should love to retire to silence and seclusion, to enjoy the cool and balmy air, the refreshing stillness, and all the beauties and glories of midnight among the solitudes of the Galilean hills, to find there happy communion with His Father," etc.—P, 55.

[89]   The more ordinary and commonplace, the more like vulgar life, the more carnal the history of the Eternal Son of God is made, the more does this writer exult in it. He exults in sinking the higher notion of Christ, and in making the flesh the *hegemonic*[84] of a Divine Essence. Even a prophet or apostle might be conceived to subdue the innocent enjoyments of His lower nature to the sovereignty of faith, and enjoy this world only as an emblem and instrument of the unseen. But it is the triumph of Rationalism to level everything to the lowest and most tangible form into which it can be cast, and to view our Lord Himself, not in His mysterious greatness, acting by means of human nature, and ministered unto by Angels[85] in it, but as what I dare not draw out, lest profane words be necessary,—as akin to those lower natures which have but an animal existence.

"Another thing which exhibits the *boldness and enterprise* that characterized His plans for making an impression on the community,

---

[84] hegemonic: the seat of the soul or controlling part, in Stoic philosophy
[85] *ministered unto by Angels*: Cf. Matthew 4:11; Luke 22.43.

was the *peculiarly new and original style of public speaking* He adopted."—P. 55.

"This, then, is the key to the character of Jesus Christ in respect to *spirit and decision*."—P. 57.

"For the real sublimity of courage, the spectacle of this deserted and defenceless sufferer coming at midnight to meet the betrayer and his band, *far exceeds that of Napoleon* urging on his columns over the bridge of Lodi,[86] or even that of Regulus returning to his chains."[87]— Pp. 59, 60.

Who could have conceived that there was any possible category under which the image of our Lord could be associated with that of Napoleon?

"He *evidently observed and enjoyed* nature. There are many allusions to His solitary walks in the fields, and on the mountains, and by the seaside; but the greatest evidence of His *love for nature* is to be seen in the manner in which he speaks of its beauties. *A man's metaphors* are drawn from the sources with which he is most familiar, or which interest him most."—P. 60.

"We learn in the same manner how distinct were the *impressions of beauty or sublimity*, which the works of nature made upon the Saviour, by the manner in which He alluded to them ... Look at the lilies of the field,[88] says He ... *A cold heartless man*, without *taste or sensibility*, would not have said such a thing as that. He could not; and we may be as sure, that Jesus Christ *had stopped to examine and admire* the grace and beauty of the plant," etc.—Pp. 61, 62.

[90]

"Now Jesus Christ noticed these things. He *perceived* their beauty and enjoyed it."—P. 62.

Surely such passages as these are simply inconsistent with faith in the Son of God. Does any one feel curiosity or wonder, does any one search and examine, in the case of things fully

---

[86] *Napoleon urging his columns over the bridge of Lodi*: On May 10 1796 Napoleon led his armies victoriously against the Austrians. He wrote later, "It was on the evening of Lodi that I believed myself a superior man."

[87] *Regulus returning to his chains*: Marcus Regulus, the Roman general and consul, was taken prisoner by the Carthaginians in 255 BC. He was released and sent to Rome on condition that he urge terms unfavourable to Rome. However, once at Rome he urged the Senate not to accept the terms and voluntarily returned to Carthage where he was put to death. He was often quoted as an exemplar of the Stoic ideal.

[88] *Look at the lilies of the field*: Cf. Matthew 6:28.

known to him? Could the Creator of nature "stop to *examine*" and "enjoy the grace and beauty" of His own work? Were indeed this said of Him in Scripture, we should say, "Here is one of the Mysteries which attend on the Incarnation;" but since we cannot suspect such writers as Mr. Abbott of inventing a Mystery for the sake of it, we must take it as evidence of an earthly and Socinian bias in his view of the Saviour of mankind.

"He observed everything, and His *imagination was stored* with an inexhaustible supply of images, drawn from every source, and with these He illustrated and enforced His principles in a manner altogether unparalleled by any writings, sacred or profane."—P. 63.

So this is the ashes to be given as children's meat, to those who "confess" and repent, and try to know God's will in the Gospel!

"Even His disciples, till they came to see Him die, had no conception of His love. They learned it at last, however. They saw Him suffer and die; and inspiration from above explained to them something about the influence of His death ...

[91]   "It is hard to tell which touches our gratitude most sensibly; the ardent love which led Him to do what he did, or the *delicacy with which He refrained from speaking of it* to those who were to reap its fruits."—P. 94.

—that is, the delicacy towards sinners of an injured Creator, coming to atone in some mysterious way by His own sufferings for their sins in the sight of His God and Father.

"There is, in fact, no moral or spiritual safety without these feelings, *and our Saviour knew this full well*."—P. 204.

"Jesus Christ *understood human nature better* ... He was *wiser* than the builders of the Pyramids ... The Saviour did the work, and *did it better*, by a few parting words."—P. 217.

5.

Such are the feelings which this author ventures to express concerning Him, who is his Lord and his God. In reprobating them, however, I have neither wish nor occasion to speak against him as an individual. For we have no concern with him.

We know nothing of his opportunities of knowing better, nor how far what appears in his writings is a true index of his mind. We need only consider him as the organ, involuntary (if you will) or unwitting, but still the organ, of the spirit of the age, the voice of that scornful, arrogant, and self-trusting spirit, which has been unchained during these latter ages, and waxes stronger in power day by day, till it is fain to stamp under foot all the host of heaven. This spirit we may steadily contemplate to our great edification; but to do more than denounce it *as such*, to judge or revile its instruments would involve another sin besides uncharitableness. For surely, this is a spirit which has tempted others besides those who have yielded to its influences; and, like an infection of the air,[89] it has perchance ere now, in some degree, not perhaps as regards the high doctrines of the Gospel, but in some way or other, breathed upon those who, at the present crisis of things, feel themselves called upon solemnly to resist it. The books of the day are so full of its evil doctrine in a modified shape, if not in its grosser forms,—the principles (I may say) of the nation are so instinct with it or based on it,—that the best perhaps that can be said of any of us, or at most of all but a few, is, that they have escaped from it, "so as by fire,"[90] and that the loudness of their warning is but a consequence of past danger, terror, and flight.

I would view, then, works such as this, whether in their publication, or in their general reception, as signs of the religious temper of this Age. What shall be said of the *praise* that has been lavished on them? the *popularity* they have acquired? Granting that there are many things in them, from which a religious mind may gain some good (for no one accuses Mr. Abbott of being deficient in quickness and intelligence, and he evidently has had opportunities of studying human nature, whatever success has attended him in it,—and it must be confessed that his first work published here[91] was of a less objectionable character, and might well interest at first sight those who "thought no evil,"[92]) but, allowing all this, yet it may

[92]

---

[89] *an infection of the air*: A number of diseases, such as cholera, were thought in the early nineteenth century to be air-borne.
[90] *"so as by fire"*: Cf. I Corinthians 3:15.
[91] *his first work published here*: The Young Christian, published in 1832.

be fairly asked, is the book from which I have cited, one which can come very near to Christian minds without frightening them? How is it then that so many men professing strict religion, have embraced and dwelt on its statements without smelling the taint of death which is in them? And is there not something of a self-convicted mischief in that view of religion which its upholders (independent of each other, and disagreeing with each other materially in other points of doctrine and discipline) attempt to support by editing a book, as conducive to it, which [903 turns out to be all but Socinian? The reason (I believe) why many pious persons tolerate teaching such as this, is, that they have so fully identified spirituality of mind with the use of certain phrases and professions, that they cannot believe that any one whatever can use them freely without the teaching of the Holy Spirit: to believe it otherwise, would be unsettling their minds from the very foundation,—which indeed must take place sooner or later, whether they will or not.

With some quotations from the preface of one of Mr. Abbott's editors,[93] one of the most learned, orthodox, and moderate of the Dissenters of the day, I will bring this discussion to an end.

"Mr. Abbott has so much of originality in his manner of thinking, and of *unguarded simplicity* in his style of expression," [as render a friendly editor useful,] "there might be peril that without such a precaution some readers would take a premature alarm, when they found some essential doctrines of Christianity conveyed *in terms of simplicity*, and elucidated by very familiar analogies, which appear considerably removed from our accredited phraseology ... *Whatever use we make of the language of the theological schools, we should never go beyond our ability to translate it into the plain speech of common life.*"[94]

As far as the words go, this means, when duly explained, though the writer could not of course intend it, that Mr. Abbott's merit consists in having translated Trinitarianism into

---

[92] *"thought no evil"*: Cf. 1 Corinthians 13:5.
[93] *one of Mr. Abbott's editors*: Dr. John Pye Smith (1775-1851), leading Congregationalist theologian.
[94] *"Mr. Abbott has ... of common life."*: *The Cornerstone*, Preface, p. xiv.

Socinianism. And that this is no unfair interpretation of the words, is plain from what presently follows, in which he speaks of the prejudice which the orthodox language and doctrine of divinity create against orthodoxy in the minds of those who are orthodox, *all but* receiving these orthodox statements. In other words, expressly specifying the Unitarians, he requires us to adopt Mr. Abbott's language in order to reconcile them to us. I quote his words:

"But there is one department in the inseparable domain of theology [94] and religion upon Mr. Abbott's treatment of which I should be very blameable were I to withhold my convictions. Among us, as well as in the New England States, there is a body, large and respectable if considered absolutely, but far from large when viewed in comparison with the numbers of other professed Christians. It consists of those who disbelieve the doctrines held, as to their essential principles, by all other Christian denominations, with respect to the way in which sinful, guilty, degraded mankind may regain the favour of God and the pure felicity of the world to come; the doctrines of a divine Saviour, His assumption of our nature, His propitiation and righteousness, and the restoration of holiness and happiness by His all-gracious Spirit. This class of persons is treated by some public men, and in some influential writings, chiefly periodical, with scorn and contumely, and are held up to hatred, not to say persecution; they are continually represented as blasphemers and infidels, alike dangerous to the State and inimical to all vital religion. Hence thousands of excellent persons, deriving their only knowledge from the source to which I have alluded, regard this portion of their neighbours with horror, never think of treating them with tenderness, never attempt to obtain a lodgment for truth and holy affections in their hearts. Ah! little think these well-meaning persons, etc. This is a state of things full of mischief and danger. Surely it is a pressing duty to do all that we can for clearing away the clouds of ignorance and misrepresentation which, with so dire effect, discolour and distort the objects seen through them.

"For this purpose it is to me an heartfelt pleasure to say that Mr. Abbott's 'Corner Stone' is admirably adapted. Notions producing feelings, and those feelings of deep and wide activity in the formation of religious sentiments, have been derived from Pelagius,[95] Socinus,[96]

---

[95] *Pelagius*: (c.354-420/440) British born monk and theologian who taught that concupiscence and death were natural, thus denying Original Sin, and also that salvation

99

and Episcopius,[97] from Clarke,[98] Law,[99] and Watson,[100] from Lardner,[101] Priestley,[102] and Channing;[103] and it is the thoroughly pervading influence on the mind of those mutually acting feelings and sentiments which produces all that is formidable in the theoretical objections, and much of that which is effective in the practical repugnance, which are entertained by many against the doctrines of grace and holiness through the Atonement and the Spirit of Christ. How desirable to meet those feelings in their germinating principle; to anticipate those sentiments, by the dissolution of the causes which would form them!

[95] This is what our author has done. His *reasonings and illustrations upon the personal and official attributes* of our Lord and Saviour are such as may be compared to *the correctness of anatomical knowledge, the delicacy of touch, and the astonishing preciseness of applying the probe and the knife, which we admire in the first surgeons of the age.*"[104]

A correct and memorable witness, indeed, to the kind of treatment offered by these religionists to Him, whom, after His exposure on the cross, His true disciples reverently "took

---

could be attained by the will alone. Pelagianism was opposed by Augustine and condemned by Pope Innocent I in 417, by the Council of Carthage and then by Pope Zosimos in 418.

[96] *Socinus*: See above note on p.[57].

[97] *Episcopius*: Simon Bischop (1583-1643), Professor of Theology at Leyden, condemned for Arminian teaching by the Synod of Dort

[98] *Clarke*: Samuel Clarke (1675-1729), Rector of St James, Piccadilly; his *Scripture-Doctrine of the Trinity* (1712) had Unitarian overtones.

[99] *Law*: William Law (1686-1761), nonjuring Anglican divine and spiritual writer; his *A Serious call to a Devout and Holy Life* (1728) was widely influential and played a role in Newman's own conversion to Christianity at the age of 15.

[100] *Watson*: Richard Watson (1737-1816), Bishop of Llandaff, Fellow of the Royal Society and Regius Professor of Divinity.

[101] *Lardner*: Nathaniel Lardner (1684-1768), nonconformist minister who wrote *The Credibility of the Gospel History; or the Principal Facts of the New Testament confirmed by Passages of Ancient Authors, who were contemporary with our Saviour or his Apostles, or lived near their time* (Part 1, 1727; Part 2, 1733-55). (1727-1757).

[102] *Priestley*: Joseph Priestley (1733-1804), Presbyterian minister who embraced Socinianism and published the *Theological Repository*. In his *A History of the Corruptions of Christianity* he denied the Divinity of Christ and hence the Trinity. He became one of the founders of the Unitarian Society.

[103] *Channing:* William Ellery Channing (1780-1842), American Unitarian pastor of the Congregational Church in Federal Street, Boston, who adopted Unitarian views from 1820.

[104] *"But there is one department . . . the first surgeons of the age.":* The Cornerstone, pp.xxii – xxiii.

down," and "wrapped in fine linen," and "laid in a sepulchre wherein never man before was laid."[105]

I will conclude by summing up in one sentence, which must be pardoned me if in appearance harsh, what the foregoing discussion is intended to show. There is a widely, though irregularly spread School of doctrine among us, within and without the Church, which aims at and professes peculiar piety as directing its attention to the heart itself, not to anything external to us, whether creed, actions, or ritual. I do not hesitate to assert that this doctrine is based upon error, that it is really a specious form of trusting man rather than God, that it is in its nature Rationalistic, and that it tends to Socinianism. How the individual supporters of it will act as time goes on is another matter,—the good will be separated from the bad; but the School, as such, will pass through Sabellianism, to that "God-denying Apostasy,"[106] to use the ancient phrase, to which in the beginning of its career it professed to be especially opposed.

---

[105] ... *before was laid.* ": Luke 23:25.
[106] *"God-denying apostasy" to use the ancient phrase*: According to Eusebius (*Ecclesiastical History*, Book V, Ch. 28, 6) this phrase was used by Pope St. Victor I (d.189) when he excommunicated Theodotus the cobbler, founder of the "god-denying apostasy" of Paul of Samosata (200-275), Bishop of Antioch, who taught that Christ was a man inspired by God, rather than God himself incarnate.

POSTSCRIPT.

Since the above Essay was in type, an American periodical,[107] has been put into the writer's hands, containing an account of Dr. Schleiermacher's[108] view of the doctrine of the Holy Trinity.

It seems, indeed, impossible to doubt that a serious doctrinal error is coming as a snare over the whole of the Protestant division of Christendom, (every part, at least, which is not fallen into worse and more avowed heterodoxy,) being the result of an attempt of the intellect to delineate, philosophise, and justify that religion (so called) of the heart and feelings, which has long prevailed. All over the Protestant world,—among ourselves, in Ireland, in Scotland, in Germany, in British America,[109]—the revival of religious feeling during the last century took a peculiar form, difficult indeed to describe or denote by any distinct appellation, but familiarly known to all who ever so little attend to what is going on in the general Church. It spread, not by talents or learning in its upholders, but by their piety, zeal, and sincerity, and its own incidental and partial truth. At length, as was natural, its professors have been led to a direct contemplation of it, to a reflection upon their own feelings and [97] belief and the genius of their system; and thence has issued that philosophy of which Mr. Erskine and Mr. Abbott have in the foregoing pages afforded specimens.

---

[107] The Biblical Repository, Nos. 18 and 19; in which is translated and reviewed "Schleiermacher's Comparison of the Athanasian and Sabellian Views of the Trinity." [N] The translator/reviewer was Moses Stuart (1780–1852), American Congregationalist biblical scholar.

[108] *Dr. Schleiermacher*: Friedrich Daniel Ernst Schleiermacher (1768-1834), German protestant theologian, highly influential exponent of liberal theology. He emphasised feeling as the basis for religion and advocated a Sabellian interpretation of the Holy Trinity.

[109] *British America*: The term used for Canada in the 1830s.

The American publication above alluded to is a melancholy evidence that the theologians of the United States are bringing the learning and genius of Germany to bear in favour of this same (as the writer must call it) spurious Christianity. Some passages from it shall be here extracted, which will be found to tend to one or other of these three objects, all of them more or less professed in the two works above analysed.

1. That the one object of the Christian Revelation, or Dispensation, is to stir the affections, and soothe the heart.

2. That it really contains nothing which is unintelligible to the intellect.

3. That misbelievers, such as Unitarians, etc., are made so, for the most part, by Creeds; which are to be considered as the great impediments to the spread of the Gospel, both as being stumbling-blocks to the reason, and shackles and weights on the affections.

1. "With regard to Schleiermacher's views as a Trinitarian, I can truly say that I have met with scarcely any writer, ancient or modern, who appears to have a deeper conviction of, or more hearty belief in, the doctrine of the real Godhead of the Father, Son, and Holy Spirit ... 'God manifest in the flesh,' seems to be inscribed, in his view, on every great truth of the Gospel, and to enter as a necessary ingredient into the composition of its essential nature. Yet Schleiermacher was not made a Trinitarian by creeds and confessions. Neither the Nicene nor Athanasian symbol, nor any succeeding formula of Trinitarian doctrine, built on this, appears to have had any influence in the formation of his views. From the Scriptures, and from arguments flowing, as he believed, out of Scriptural premises, he became, and lived, and died, a hearty and constant believer in the One Living and True God, *revealed to us as* Father, Son, and Holy Ghost ... He ventured to inquire whether, in the vehemence of dispute, and in the [98] *midst of philosophical mists*, the former survey had been in all respects made with thorough and exact skill and care, and whether a report of it *in all respects intelligible and consistent* had been made out."— Translator, No. 18, pp. 268, 269.

2. "After defending in various places, in the most explicit manner, and with great ability, the doctrine of the Godhead of the Son and Spirit, and *showing that such a development of the Deity is demanded by our moral wants, as sinners, in order that we may obtain peace and sanctification*; he concludes," etc.—*Ibid.*

3. "Of his view of the Trinity, we may at least say that *it is intelligible*. But who will venture to say, that any of the definitions heretofore given of personality in the Godhead in itself considered, I mean such definitions as have their basis in the Nicene or Athanasian Creeds, are *intelligible and satisfactory* to the mind?"—P. 277.

4. "The sum of Schleiermacher's opinions ... is that ... the Unity ... is God *in se ipso*;[110] ... but as to the Trinity, the Father is God as revealed in the works of creation, providence, and legislation; the Son is God in human flesh, the divine Logos incarnate; the Holy Ghost is God the Sanctifier, who renovates the hearts of sinners, and dwells in the hearts of believers. The personality of the Godhead consists in these developments, made in time, and made to intelligent and rational beings. Strictly speaking, personality is not in his view eternal; and from the nature of the case as thus viewed, it could not be, because it consists in developments of the Godhead to intelligent beings," etc.—P. 317.

5. "That God has developed Himself in these three different ways, is what they [Sabellius and Schleiermacher] believe to be taught in the Scriptures, and to be commended to our spiritual consciences by the nature of our wants, woes, and sins."—No. 19, p. 81.

6. "Dr. Schleiermacher asks, with deep emotion, what more is *demanded*? what more is *necessary*? what more can *further the interest of practical piety*?"—P. 82.

7. "I can see no *contradiction*, no *absurdity*, nothing even *incongruous* in the supposition that the Divine nature has *manifested* itself as Father," etc.—P. 88.

8. "Why should it ever have any more been overlooked that the names Father, etc., are names that have a *relative* sense ... than that such names as Creator," etc.—P. 110.

[99] 9. "It may be proper for me to say, that the results of this reexamination of the doctrine of the Trinity are, in their essential parts, the same which I some years since advocated in my letters addressed to the Rev. Dr. Channing,"[111] etc.—P. 115.

---

[110] in se ipso: in himself

[111] *Rev.Dr. Channing*: In his letters addressed to Dr. Channing, Stuart had actually argued against Channing's Unitarianism which he saw as leading to infidelity (as Newman did). Stephen Thomas (*Newman and Heresy. The Anglican Years*, Cambridge, 2003) argues that Stuart was not in fact Sabellian in his views and that Newman's reading 'must have been careless, skimming through Stuart's pages to find quotations to fit a preconceived view formed during the analysis of Erskine and Abbott' (p.138). However, Stuart clearly endorses Schleiermacher's views, and Newman thought that such a 're-examination' of the doctrine of the Trinity was in fact Sabellian and that such an approach ultimately led to Unitarianism, as it had in the case of Blanco White.

These extracts are perhaps sufficient to justify the apprehensions above expressed, as far as the more religious part of Protestant America is concerned. It is believed that Protestant France also would afford similar evidence of the Sabellian tendencies of the day.

February 2, 1836.

Note on Essay II.

[The author of the second of the works criticised in the foregoing Essay met my strictures with a Christian forbearance and a generosity which I never can forget. He went out of his way, when in England, in 1843, to find me out at Littlemore, and to give me the assurance, both by that act and by word of mouth, that he did not take offence at what many a man would have thought justified serious displeasure. I think he felt what really was the case, that I had no unkind feelings towards him, but spoke of his works simply in illustration of a widely-spread sentiment in religious circles, then as now, which seemed to me dangerous to gospel faith.

I have no other record of the incident, than the following two paragraphs in a well-known newspaper of the day.

(From "The English Churchman.")

"A few Sundays ago, a stranger, who had been observed joining very attentively both in the morning and afternoon services at Littlemore, begged permission in the evening to introduce himself to Mr. Newman. It proved to be none other than the well-known author of the 'Corner Stone,' and the 'Young Christian,' and the object of his call was to express his deep and sincere obligations to Mr. Newman for the severe strictures which had been made upon his work some time since in the 'Tracts for the Times.' He confessed that they had the greatest effect upon his mind, and that he should write very differently now. Mr. Newman asked if there were anything he would wish altered in a subsequent edition of [the Tract, but Mr. Abbott admitted the entire fairness of the review, and wished nothing to be withdrawn or altered."

To the Editor of "The English Churchman."

"Sir,—I am very sorry to observe a paragraph in your paper of yesterday on the subject of the call with which I was favoured in this place, some time since, by Mr. Abbott. It has been evidently sent to you with a friendly feeling towards myself, to which I am not at all insensible, but it is kinder to me than it is respectful towards Mr. Abbott. What I saw of him impressed me with such feelings in his favour, that it would grieve me indeed did he think, from anything that has got abroad, that he had reason to charge me (in my report of our conversation) with rudeness, or want of consideration towards himself. I will add what I stated to him, that if in my remarks in the 'Tracts for the Times' upon one of his publications, I was betrayed into any expressions which might be considered personal, instead of confining myself to the work itself which I was criticising, I am sorry for them, and wish them unsaid. I saw him but for half an hour in his rapid passage across the country; but wherever he is, and whether I shall see him again or no, he has my good wishes and my kind remembrances.—I am, etc.,

"JOHN H. NEWMAN.

"Littlemore, Oct. 6."

I should add, that the exciting cause of my writing the above criticisms on works of Mr. Erskine and Mr. Abbott was my deep and increasing apprehension, that the religious philosophy, on which they are based, was making its way into Oxford, and through Oxford among the clergy, by the writings of Dr. Whately, Dr. Hampden's Bampton Lectures,[112] and Mr. Blanco White's (then) recent publications. This explains, for instance, supr. pp. 69, 85, and 91. Vid. "*Apologia*," pp. 57, 385-6.

---

[112] *Dr. Hampden's Bampton Lectures*: Renn Dickson Hampden (1793-1868), Anglican divine, former Fellow of Oriel. Newman attacked his Bampton Lectures of 1832 for their Arian doctrine, and a fierce controversy ensued. In 1836, the year of Tract 73's publication, Bampton was appointed Regius Professor of Divinity, despite strong opposition from the Tractarians.

III.

APOSTOLICAL TRADITION.

1.

A SMALL volume[1] has just now made its appearance which well deserves notice, as being the record of what the title-page styles a "Brothers' Controversy"—that is, an interchange of letters between a clergyman and his Unitarian brother-in-law on the subject of the cardinal doctrine which separates them in religion.

The disputants are men of education and ability: the clergyman orthodox, serious, amiable; his opponent a man of candour and good sense; and "the whole" correspondence professes to be sent to the press "faithfully, without comment, without altering a word or syllable" on one side or on the other.

If men are to argue with each other, they must, of course, find some common ground to argue upon. What gives this controversy to us a painful interest is that this common ground, accepted on either side in this case, is nothing short of a common error, so that in the event the combatants leave off pretty much where they were when they began. It is better, certainly, to hold the truth on wrong grounds than not to hold it at all; but it is better still to hold it on grounds which, not being erroneous, cannot be made a starting-point for distinct religious error in the long run. If the principles on which a controversy is [103] conducted are false or uncertain, it is likely to be little more than a trial of strength between the parties engaged in it, and is doomed to failure from the first.

---

[1] *A SMALL volume*: *The Brothers' Controversy, being a genuine correspondence between a Clergyman of the Church of England and a Layman of Unitarian Opinions* (London, 1835).

Such is the judgment that we are obliged to pass on the assumptions on which these friends are content to place their issue. They take it for granted, as beyond all question, that, if we would ascertain the truths which Revelation has brought us, we have nothing else to do but to consult Scripture on the point, with the aid of our own private judgment, and that no doctrine is of importance which the Christian cannot find for himself in large letters there. Not, of course, that, in calling this a mere assumption and a mistake, we would for an instant deny that Scripture has one, and but one, teaching, one direct and definite sense, on the sacred matters of which it treats, and that it is the test of revealed truth; but, as Anglicans,[2] we maintain that it is not its own interpreter, and that, as an historical fact, it has ever been furnished for individuals with an interpreter which is external to its readers and infallible, that is, with an ecclesiastical Tradition, derived in the first instance from the Apostles—a Tradition illuminating Scripture and protecting it; moreover, that this Tradition, and not Scripture itself, is our immediate and practical authority for such high doctrines as these friends discuss. To attempt to prove against adversaries our Lord's Divinity and Incarnation by Scripture without Tradition, seems to us a mistake as great as that of attempting to speak a living language by studying its classics, or to ascertain physical facts by pure mathematics without experiment or observation.

We have said that the common ground, on which these disputants erect their arguments, admits of being used in behalf of error; but we must go further. Their first principle really is [104] inconsistent with there being any certainties in Revelation whatever; for, if nothing is to be held as revealed but what every one perceives to be in Scripture, there is nothing that can be so held, considering that in matter of fact there is no universal agreement as to what Scripture teaches and what it does not teach: and why are one man's opinions to be ruled by the readings of another? The right which each man has of judging for himself *ipso facto* deprives him of the right of judging for

---

[2] *as Anglicans*: This phrase is not in the original 1836 text. See the Textual Appendix and the Editor's Introduction p.xxv.

other inquirers. He is bound to tolerate all other creeds by virtue of the very principle on which he claims to choose his own. Thus ultra-Protestantism infallibly leads to Latitudinarianism.

2.

However, our proper business here is not to prove what is so very much of a truism, but to fulfil an intention which we expressed some time since, of attempting an exposition and an explanation of the Anglican doctrine on the subject. First, however, by way of introduction, we mean to devote a few pages to the volume which has given us the opportunity of redeeming our pledge.

The Unitarian, then, as we have said, claims the right of private judgment, and the clergyman grants it to him. Says the former,—

"The Protestant Church says that the Gospel is addressed *to every individual*; and I say that he, who does not use his most serious and powerful understanding in endeavouring rightly to comprehend it, hides his best talent, instead of improving it."—P. 32.

Says the clergyman in response,—

[105] "As to the duty of free inquiry, it is impossible for any one to advocate it more entirely than I do; only let Scripture authority be paramount. But, if any one tampers with Scripture, ... then, be he friend or foe, I will join in reprobating such conduct."—P. 51.

Manifestos such as these profess to enunciate some large principle, maxim, or law, of axiomatic or enthymematic[3] force, carrying its proof in its very wording; yet how evident an assumption is involved both in the former of these two statements and in the latter! If by "the Gospel" the Unitarian means the written document of Matthew or of Mark, of Luke or of John, then he has to prove, what he takes for granted, that that document is addressed to every individual inquirer of all times and places as a summary of the Christian religion; but, if he uses the word in its primary sense of "good tidings," then his "understanding," whether "powerful" or not, need in no sense be taxed by what is in its very idea nothing else than an oral

---

[3] *enthymematic*:   based on an unstated premise.

message of peace, requiring on his part no sagacity, labour of thought, perseverance, or learning,—in short, no intellectual effort at all beyond that of faith. And in like manner, the clergyman must be asked on his part why it is that he advocates "the duty of free inquiry," and yet withdraws the "authority of Scripture" from its action? If inquiry is a healthy exercise as regards the creed, why not as regards the canon? but if we may not "tamper with" the authority of "Scripture," why with the authority of Tradition?

Of course both disputants will maintain that in fact no authoritative Tradition now exists, so as to admit of any such appeal to it as we have supposed; but they ought to bear in mind that others believe in its existence, if they do not, whereas the layman is so supremely unsuspicious that Anglicans hold it, as to bring it against us, as a *reductio ad absurdum*, that we grant St. Paul never to have taught the orthodox creed in his catechiz- [106] ings and preachings, but solely in certain *obiter dicta* of his extant Epistles. He asks with reference to the Book of Acts,—

"Can I believe that concerning Jesus, whom the Apostles so preached" [*i.e.*, as a mere man] "year after year to Jews and Gentiles, professing their own inspiration and express commission to teach, saying that they had taught all the gospel, it was afterwards *for the first time* revealed *in a letter* written by one of them to a church he had established in a heathen country" [*vide* Rom. ix. 5[4]], "and in this letter, not by direct declaration of the writer, but incidentally, by way of allusion, in a parenthesis, that He was the very and eternal God?"—P. 70.

Strange that a grave controversialist should impute to a school so sober as the Anglican so unnatural and poor a view of the process by which the Catholic truths were first presented to the world! Yet he reiterates,—

"It is to me inconceivable that the Apostle could possibly, in the winding up of a sentence in an Epistle, *intend to reveal* the astonishing doctrine that Christ was God ... that the Apostle, having preached

---

[4] *Rom. ix. 5*: '. . . of whom as concerning the flesh Christ came, who is over all, God blessed for ever. Amen.' This was frequently used as a 'proof-text' of the Divinity of Christ.

Christ crucified and risen, should, *after years* of such preaching, *bring out* this revelation in so cursory and elliptical a manner."—P. 129.

An additional remark is in place here. Our disputant in this passage insists on the *silence* of the Apostles, year after year, on the subject of our Lord's Divinity, while protesting nevertheless that they had "taught *all* the gospel." Let it be observed, then, that in that very address delivered at Miletus, to which the Unitarian specially refers, as being that in which St. Paul declares that he has preached "the whole counsel of God,"[5] far from being silent as to our Lord's Divine nature, he even declares it with startling explicitness. He exhorts the elders whom he had called around him to "feed the flock of God, whom He hath purchased with His own blood."[6]

[107]   3.

But let us observe how the clergyman, a sensible and well-instructed man, replies to his opponent. We do not find that he anywhere expresses surprise at his brother-in-law's unwarrantable assumption, but, in handling the argument founded upon it, he curiously flutters about what we deem the real answer to it, without ever lighting upon or touching it. He leaves the ground of Biblical criticism, and appeals to the belief of the early Church. So far good; and he quotes from Irenæus and Tertullian, whose testimonies are of some authority, "as showing" the layman's "notion to be erroneous" (pp. 95, 96). Presently he says, "I have shown by quotations from Irenæus and Tertullian that the primitive Christians understood it in the sense we attach to it" (p. 107). This is promising; he is now in the right track: alas! he raises our hopes only to disappoint them. One would think, before he appealed to the primitive Church, that he ought to have ascertained *why* the fact of its testimony tells in favour of the interpretation of Scripture, whatever that turns out to be, to which it testifies. The plain reason is this—that that testimony comes close upon the Apostles, and thereby is more likely to convey to us their sense of a Scripture

---

[5] *"the whole counsel of God,"*: Acts 20:27.
[6] *... His own blood."*: Acts 20:28.

112

passage; in other words, it has a certain Apostolical authority in explaining Scripture; and, in consequence, it is a source of Christian truth in some sense independent of Scripture—a guide to a certain extent superseding the need of private judgment. If it have not this authority, and on this account, it is no more than the opinion of any other generation of men, and quite irrelevant in a question in controversy. Almost as reasonably might the clergyman require his brother-in-law to yield to his own [108] interpretation as to Irenæus's, if that Father's proximity to the Apostles has no weight in the dispute, except indeed that a second opinion corroborates a first.

Nevertheless, in spite of his wishing to avail himself of the Fathers, he does not fully understand why he quoted Irenæus. The layman boldly says,—

"Your quotations from Irenæus and Tertullian prove that the now received construction existed in their time, and was received by them; in other words, that they were Trinitarians, *and this is all*."—P. 130.

In his reply to this plain speaking, the clergyman not only misses the true force of his own argument, but suggests a novel basis for it—viz., that, *since creeds did not exist in the primitive Church* (a position running counter both to fact and to the necessities of his argument), the primitive belief in the doctrine of the Trinity is an evidence of what is the true sense of Scripture, as witnessed by unbiassed and unprejudiced judgments. He says,—

"It is difficult to find persons in these times who have never heard of creeds before they read the Bible; but it appears to me that the most satisfactory way of ascertaining the truth of your remark will be to observe what doctrines those minds found in the Bible who certainly *could have their minds prejudiced by no creed*, save that which they received from the mouth of the Apostles, or which they learned from the inspired writings."—P. 195.

In this extract let us observe carefully the clause, "save that which they received from the mouth of the Apostles." The writer

113

not only *burns*, he has the truth in his hands; yet, as his whole argument shows undeniably, he scarcely has caught hold of it but he lets it go again. It is a game of Blind-man's Buff.[7] The notion of an Apostolical creed authoritatively interpreting Scripture is, after all, quite beyond him. He continues:—

[109]   "Let us next see what Clement of Rome believed, *while as yet unschooled by creeds and articles*, etc. ... Trying Ignatius[8] by the same test, we find him, etc. ... As to the *object* I had in view in quoting these passages, since I find that Barnabas, Clement and Ignatius, *without creed preceding*, arrived at the same *conclusion* that I have—namely, that Christ was God, and also Creator of the world—I am little inclined to distrust that 'orthodox education' to which you seem to attribute the *inferences* I draw from the study of the Scriptures."—P. 196.

Elsewhere he enlarges on this view in a genuine Protestant tone:—

"We say, reason from Scripture, and expound Scripture by comparing it with itself, instead of with the dogmas of men; and this is the appeal I wish everywhere to be made."—P. 115.

Again,—

"I assert that neither the Church of England, nor I, have ever required persons to take their creeds for granted, or forbidden the unbiassed comparison of them with the words of Scripture ... The eighth Article of our Church says, 'The three creeds ought thoroughly to be received and believed.' And why? Because the Church says so? No; but because 'they may be proved by most certain warrant of Holy Scripture.' The word of God is the test by which we pronounce they are to be tried."—Pp. 185-7.

---

[7] *Blind-man's Buff*: a game in which one blindfolded person tries to catch hold of the other, non-blindfolded, participants. When a person is caught, he or she becomes the blindfolded one.

[8] *Ignatius*: St. Ignatius (c.50–98/117), Bishop of Antioch, Church Father; well known for his Epistles which stress the authority of the bishop in the Christian community; cf. Essay VI.

All this is true, but not the whole truth. The reason of the clergyman's misapprehension is obvious: he is hampered by the ultra-Protestant sense in which he reads our Articles. At the time they were drawn up, the rights of Scripture, as the test of Tradition, were disparaged; and therefore they contain a protest in behalf of the former. Were they drawn up now, it would be necessary to introduce a protest in behalf of Tradition, as indeed incidentally occurs, even as it is, in the famous clause of the Twentieth Article, which declares that "the Church" (*i.e.* the Church Catholic) "has *authority* in controversies of faith"—viz., as being the steward of Apostolical teaching. However, the circumstance that the direct statements of the Articles are mainly [110] in defence of the authority of Scripture has given specious ground for the school of ultra-Protestants to assert that Scripture is a sufficient guide in matters of faith to the private Christian, who may put on it whatever sense he thinks the true sense, instead of submitting to that one sense which the writers intended, and to which the Church, in matter of fact, has testified from the first. We see in the controversy before us the consequences of this mistake. Our orthodox disputant has to argue points which have been ruled in his favour centuries upon centuries ago, as if inquiry were never to have an answer and an end. He is obliged to have recourse to grammatical criticism, to consult Dr. Elmsley[9] in the Bodleian about the meaning of particles (p. 48), and, after all his toil, is met with the candid and perplexing avowal on the part of his opponent, that for himself he does not think it necessary to rest his faith on any one "certain sentence in a letter written by an Apostle" (p. 65). The clergyman, in consequence, is obliged to look about for philosophical evidence, and fortifies his scheme of doctrine by the shallow and dangerous argumentations of Mr. Erskine. After all, he takes the desperate step of referring the personal reception of the orthodox truth to a supernatural influence—a

---

[9] *Dr. Elmsley:* Peter Elmsley (1773-1825), classical scholar; Principal of St. Alban Hall, Oxford (where Newman was Vice-Principal 1825-6), and Camden Professor of Ancient History. He produced editions of the ancient Greek tragedians and had a wide reputation for his scholarship.

resolution of his difficulty which of course dispenses with the necessity of arguing altogether.

At length his unlucky first principle is after all too strong for him; and, in spite of his appeal to Heaven and its inscrutable grace, overcome by the logic of his adversary, he allows himself to accept, however hesitatingly, those latitudinarian views which are the legitimate issue of the ultra-Protestantism with which he started. He condemns, though reluctantly, the anath-[111] emas of the Athanasian Creed: why, except as investing with undue sanctions mere deductions made by the private human intellect from the text of Scripture?

> "Nothing that I have advanced upon the subject of the Athanasian Creed is, as I conceive, in the least degree inconsistent with my joining in the sentiment of Tillotson,[10] and wishing it removed from our Church service. If I were called upon to give my vote on the subject, it would be for its omission; but this would not at all imply that I felt less uneasiness as to the future salvation of those who deny the Lord that bought them; nor do I see how the entertaining such fears necessarily leads to any breach of charity."—P. 108.

We do not set much by this salvo, which seems to us but the protest of true Christian feeling against the latitudinarian conclusions of an inexorable logic. Is it indeed possible for the run of men, if they are bound to hold that the high doctrines about our Lord are only the private, uninspired inferences of individuals from the Scripture text, to hold also that they are necessary to be believed in order to salvation? Does not, then, as we have said, the theory that Scripture only is to be the guide of Protestants, lead them to a certainty, when it is mastered, to become liberals? We do not for an instant suppose that the Catholic doctrine is not in Scripture, and that clear and unprej-udiced readers will not find it there; still, while belief in the document—"the Bible and the Bible only"—is made the first thing, and belief in the doctrine is only the second, and is considered nothing more than an inference of the private

---

[10] *Tillotson*: John Tillotson (1630 – 1694), Anglican divine, controversialist and latterly Archbishop of Canterbury.

student, it inevitably follows in the case of the multitude, who are not clear-headed or unprejudiced, that the definition of a Christian will be made to turn, not on faith in the doctrine, but on faith in the document, and Unitarianism will come to be thought, not indeed true, but not unreasonable, not unchristian, not perilous.

4.   [112]

Leaving, then, this halfway house to latitudinarianism, which this anxious clergyman has in all good faith done his best, on a Protestant basis, to put into habitable condition, let us go on to our proper subject—that is, to try whether, as regards such sacred dogmas as relate to our Lord's Person, a better stand against the liberalism of the day cannot be made by the Anglican theology. This theology teaches the existence, the uninterrupted continuance from the time of the Apostles, of a tradition of our Lord's Divinity—a tradition interpretative of what is also said of Him in Scripture, and dispensing, as far as its subject-matter extends, with the need of private judgment on the sacred text, as being the voice of Christendom in every time and place. This is the hypothesis which, *apropos* of Mr. Blanco White's recent work,[11] we pledged ourselves some months back[12] to consider; and, though our most careful treatment of it must be worse than imperfect, yet we shall gain as much as we aim at, if we succeed in any measure in directing the attention of our readers to an important subject, especially important in this day.

Much as we differ from Mr. White in the main conclusions to which he has come, he fully bears out what we have been saying above; he denies an Apostolical tradition of doctrine, and therefore he is consistently a Unitarian. He thinks that Scripture has no authorized interpreter, and that dogmatic statements are no part of Revelation. Chillingworth[13] and Locke[14]

---

[11] *Mr. Blanco White's recent work*: See above note on p.[27].
[12] *some months back*: 'in our January number' in the original 1837 version. See Textual Appendix.
[13] *Chillingworth*: William Chillingworth (1602–44), Anglican controversialist. His *The Religion of Protestants* was published in 1637.
[14] *Locke*: John Locke (1632 – 1704), philosopher. His *A Letter Concerning Toleration* was published in 1689.

thus spoke before him, nor would he consider that we paid him a bad compliment in saying so. Every clear-headed thinker, he would say, must so determine. Bible religion, so called, and a creed with anathemas[15] never can stand together, except at the

[113] bidding of the law of the land, or under the prejudices of education, or with the inducements of self-interest. Men in general, it is true, are ruled by habit, by authority, by prejudice, by associations, and against these ordinary motives of action philosophers indeed may strive in vain; but still there is no doubt what will ever be the result, when an age or a people begins to think.

"Certainly," says Chillingworth, "if Protestants be faulty" [in playing the Pope], "it is for doing it too much, and not too little. This presumptuous imposing of the senses of men upon the general words of God, and laying them upon men's consciences together, under the equal penalty of death and damnation—this vain conceit that we can speak of the things of God better than in the words of God—this deifying of our own interpretations, and tyrannous enforcing them upon others—this restraining of the Word of God from that latitude and generality, and the understandings of men from that liberty wherein Christ and the Apostles left them—is and hath been the only fountain of all the schisms of the Church, and that which makes them immortal: the common incendiary of Christendom, and that which tears into pieces, not the coat, but the bowels and members of Christ. Take away these walls of separation, and all will quickly be one."— *Rel. of Prot.*, iv. 17.

In like manner Locke:—

"When they have determined the Holy Scriptures to be the only foundation of faith, they nevertheless lay down certain propositions as fundamental which are not in the Scripture; and because others will not acknowledge these additional opinions of theirs, nor build upon them, as if they were necessary and fundamental, they therefore make a separation in the Church, either by withdrawing themselves from

---

[15] *a creed with anathemas*: i.e. the Catholic faith; the dogmatic decrees of Councils, such as the Council of Trent, have anathemas attached to them, condemning those who do not believe the articles of faith defined in them.

others or expelling the others from them. Nor does it signify anything for them to say that their confessions and symbols are agreeable to Scripture, and to the analogy of faith. For if they be conceived in the express words of Scripture, there can be no question about them ... but if they say that the articles which they require to be professed are consequences deduced from the Scripture, it is undoubtedly well done of them who believe and profess such things as seem unto them so agreeable to the rule of faith. But it would be very ill done to obtrude those things upon others, unto whom they do not seem to be the [114] indubitable doctrines of the Scripture. This only I say—that, however clearly we may think this or the other doctrine to be deduced from Scripture, we ought not therefore to impose it upon others, as a necessary article of faith, because we believe it to be agreeable to the rule of faith. I cannot but wonder at the extravagant arrogance of those men, who think that they themselves can explain things necessary to salvation more clearly than the Holy Ghost, the eternal and infinite Wisdom of God."—*Letter on Toler., fin.*

And Hoadley,[16] in his life of the semi-Arian, Dr. S. Clarke,[17] speaking of him and his opponents in the Trinitarian question:—

"Let me add this one word more, that, since men of such thought and such learning have shown the world in their own example how widely the most honest inquirers after truth may differ on such subjects, this, methinks, should a little abate our mutual censures, and a little take off from our positiveness about the necessity of explaining in this or that one determinate sense, the ancient passages relating to points of so sublime a nature."

And lastly, Dr. Hampden, to whose lot it has fallen to state objections to Catholic Truth in a more distinct shape than they have been found in the works of Churchmen for some time. He says:—

---

[16] *Hoadley*: Benjamin Hoadly (1676-1761), low church Anglican bishop and controversialist. In 1749 he produced an eleven-volume edition of Clarke's sermons, with a preface on Clarke's life and opinions. In his sermon before George I, *The Nature of the Kingdom of Christ*, he taught that Christ had not established any form of church government.
[17] *the semi-Arian, Dr. S. Clarke*: See above note on p.[94].

"The real causes of separation are to be found in that confusion of theological and moral truth with religion, which is evidenced in the profession of different sects. Opinions on religious matters are regarded as identical with the objects of faith, and the zeal which belongs to dissentients in the latter is transferred to the guiltless differences of fallible judgments. Whilst we agree in the canon of Scripture, in the very words, for the most part, from which we learn what are the objects of faith, we suffer disunion to spread among us through the various interpretations suggested by our own reasonings on the admitted facts of Scripture. We introduce *theories of the Divine Being* and His attributes, theories of human nature and of the universe, principles drawn from the various branches of human philosophy, into the body itself of revealed wisdom. And we then proceed to contend for these unrevealed representations of the Wisdom of God, as if it

[115] were that very Wisdom as it stands forth confessed in His own living oracles. The Wisdom that is from above is at once 'pure' and 'gentle'; surely it has no resemblance to that dogmatical and sententious wisdom which theological controversy has created."—*Observ. on Rel. Diss.*, pp. 7, 8.[18]

5.

We agree then with these writers in their strong protests against the assumption that private judgment is compatible with dogmatic certainty; but a man need not be a liberal because he is not a Protestant. Granting that Scripture does not force on us its full dogmatic meaning, that cannot hinder us looking for that meaning elsewhere. Perhaps Tradition is able to supply both interpretation and dogma. For that there should really be no definite, no dogmatic meaning at all in Scripture in its sacred revelations, is, to say the least, a very paradoxical position.

This is what these authors forget when they write so magisterially and fluently. They agree in ignoring the existence, in fact—nay, the probability, or the very possibility—of an Apostolical Tradition, supplementary to and interpretative of Scripture. The idea of such an aid to Christian teaching does not seem even to enter into their comprehension. They take for granted that the accumulated knowledge about our Lord and His religion which must have flowed from the lips of the

---

[18] Observ. On Rel. Diss.: *Observations on Religious Dissent*, published in 1834.

Apostles upon their converts, in their familiar conversations, catechizings, preachings, ecclesiastical determinations, prayers, was clean swept away and perished with the closing of the canon and the death of St. John. All the information of the great forty days came to nought, except so far as it accidentally strayed into one or other passage of the Apostolic Epistles. No one had ever any curiosity to ask the Apostles, during the remnant of their lives, any point of faith; no one had felt interest enough to [116] ascertain from them who their Master was, why He died, and with what results. No one retained any memory of their teaching concerning God, or the human soul, or the unseen state, or the world of saints and angels, or the Church on earth; no one had sought for explanation of any verse in St. Matthew or St. Luke, of the doctrine contained in the first or in the sixth chapters of St. John, or of the symbol of "the Lamb," or of the nature of "the Spirit"; or, anyhow, nothing had been asked, nothing answered, but what already was recorded by a singular chance in the books of the New Testament, or at least nothing that was of the slightest importance and worth preserving. The great Churches of the day, at Corinth, Rome, Antioch, and Ephesus, the learned school of Alexandria, knew in the year A.D. 100 and onwards as much of all these matters as we do now, and no more. Their interpretations of the sacred writings were just on a par with the private judgments of clever commentators, orthodox or heterodox, now—one as good as another, conjectural, personal, inferential, unauthoritative. "Pious opinions," as they have been called, "theories upon facts," "dogmatical and sententious wisdom," "hieroglyphics, casting shadows," "metaphors explanatory of metaphors," "vain conceits," "presumptuous impositions,"—it seems nothing better than these remains to us, these are all the leavings, if we are to credit Chillingworth, Locke, Hoadley and the rest, of the contemporaries and the disciples of our Lord.

6.

Dr. Hampden, however, is bolder still, and goes farther: in order to deprive us of the barest dream of enjoying an Apostol-

ical voice in illustration and confirmation of an Apostolical
[117]   writing, he assures us that the very idea of Tradition is a mistake,
that there is no such thing as a succession of preaching and
hearing, that what is called Tradition teaches us—nay, professes
to teach us—nothing more than Scripture, nothing at all, true
or false; that it has nothing to do with the transmission of
knowledge, and for this plain reason—because it is but the
judgment of ecclesiastics exercised on Scripture. He says,
"Tradition is *nothing more* than expositions of Scripture,
reasoned out by the Church, and embodied in a code of
doctrine" (p. 4). It is but the gold and silver of inspired writers
taken out in coppers.

This surely is a most startling and paradoxical statement. We
had fancied that St. Paul "*delivered*" to his converts "that which
he also *received*;"[19] we had fancied that St. Irenæus[20] enumerated
the succession of Bishops, through whom the tradition of gospel
doctrine had come down to his day, and that Tertullian[21] testified
to a like tradition, and that Vincent of Lérins[22] had even gained
a name in theological history by appealing to the testimony, not
of Scripture, but of antiquity and catholicity, as the warrant for
the creed of his day. But it seems, after all, that the celebrated
"Quod semper, quod ubique, quod ab omnibus," means nothing
more than "The Bible, and the Bible only, is the religion of
Protestants."[23] Nor shall we surely be singular in being thus
surprised at such an issue of this great controversy. It will sound
strange, we think, to the hosts of Protestant controversialists,
especially to Hales[24] and to Chillingworth, to Tillotson and
Newton,[25] who have in good faith taunted the Pope and his

---

[19] *St. Paul* "delivered*" to his converts "that which he also* received;*"*: Cf. I Corinthians
15:3
[20] *St. Irenæus*: 2nd century Church Father, bishop; his *Adversus Haereses* includes an
account of the episcopal office.
[21] *Tertullian*: 2nd-3rd century Church Father, layman; his *De Praescriptione Haereti-
corum* defends the apostolic succession.
[22] *Vincent of Lérins*: 5th century Church Father; his *Commonitorium* contains his
famous dictum that the Church's true doctrine is '*quod ubique, quod semper, quod ab
omnibus creditum est*' ('what has been believed everywhere, always, and by all').
[23] *"The Bible, and the Bible only . . . "*: Famous dictum first enunciated by Chillingworth.
[24] *Hales*: John Hales (1584–1656), Anglican divine and scholar.
[25] *Newton*: Thomas Newton (1704-82), Anglican divine, later a bishop; a biblical

Bishops for so long a time as determining their creed by traditions of men and lying legends. Nor will it be a less surprise to the theologians of Rome themselves, whose very profession and boast it is that their Church has ever preserved inviolate, [118] and is ever transmitting to posterity, not merely by the canon of Scripture, but by a living observance, that very religion of which the Apostles commenced the delivery, and which, they would say, Protestant doctors have supplanted by that process of deduction which after all is, according to Dr. Hampden, simply identical with Tradition itself.

Had Scripture never been written, Tradition would have existed still; it has an intrinsic, substantive authority, and a use collateral to Scripture. This surely, and nothing else, is the doctrine of Bellarmine[26] and his co-religionists. "Totalis regula fidei," he says (*De V. D. non Scr.* 12[27]), "est Verbum Dei, sive Revelatio Dei ecclesiæ facta, quæ *dividitur* in duas regulas partiales, Scripturam et Traditionem."[28] And he has a chapter on the tests by which we ascertain what traditions are Apostolical; and among the uses of Tradition he places that of interpreting Scripture doctrine. He says, "It happens very often that Scripture is ambiguous and perplexed, so that, unless there be an interpreter who cannot err, it cannot be understood. Examples abound: the equality of the Divine Persons, the Procession of the Holy Ghost, etc. ... and many similar points admit, indeed, of being *deduced* from the sacred writings; but with such difficulty that, if Scripture testimonies were the sole weapon, the controversy with heady men would never come to an end." And Bossuet[29] in like manner (*Expos.*,[30] ch. xvii., xviii.): "Jesus

---

scholar, his *Dissertation on the Prophecies* was an influential source for the idea that the Pope was the Antichrist. Newman was shortly to write a witty critique of Newton's worldly and careerist life in an article in *The British Critic* in 1840, later republished as 'The Protestant Idea of Antichrist' in *Essays Critical and Historical*, II, pp. 112-185.
[26] *Bellarmine*: St. Robert Bellarmine (1542–1621), Jesuit theologian, bishop and Doctor of the Church.
[27] De V.D. non Scr. 12: *De Verbo Dei non Scripto*, 12.
[28] *"Totalis regula fidei . . . Scripturam et Traditionem"*: "The entire rule of faith is God's Word, or the Revelation of God made to the whole Church, which is divided into two partial rules, Scripture and Tradition."
[29] *Bossuet*: Jacques-Benigne Bossuet (1627-1704), French bishop, preacher, scholar and controversialist.

Christ, having laid the foundation of the Church by preaching, the unwritten word was consequently the first rule of Christianity; and, when the writings of the New Testament were added to it, its *authority was not forfeited on that account*; which makes us receive with *equal veneration* all that has been taught [119] by the Apostles, whether in writing or by word of mouth." Yet Dr. Hampden rules it absolutely in half a sentence, that "Tradition is *nothing more* than expositions of Scripture *reasoned out* by the Church."

Nor will Anglican writers be less surprised at a statement which, if it can be maintained, is fatal to the authority of Vincent of Lérins, and to the corner-stone of our theology. Certainly, if Tradition is but a subtle mode of arguing and deducing from the Bible, the interference of critics of our theological school in "the Brothers'" controversy is a simple blunder, as we shall have no case as against the combatants and the first principle which they hold in common. But what would Bishop Jebb[31] say to the doctrine that Tradition was nothing else than Scripture inference? Jebb considers that the Church of Rome has erred, not certainly in fancying Tradition to be all one with Scripture, but in considering the former as so separate from the latter, and so independent of it, that it may be true and authoritative, though it says what Scripture is silent upon. "The Church of Rome," he says, "maintains, not only that there are two rules of belief, but that these two rules are co-ordinate; that there is an unwritten, no less than a written Word of God, and that the authority of the former is alike definitive with the authority of the latter."[32] What, again, must the present Bishop of Lincoln[33] think of this same doctrine, who is still more explicit than Jebb in enunciating Jebb's principle, and whose language is so strong

---

[30] Expos.: *Exposition de la Doctrine de L'Église catholique sur les Matières de Controverse* (1671).
[31] *Bishop Jebb*: John Jebb (1775–1833), Church of Ireland divine.
[32] *"The Church of Rome . . . the authority of the latter."*: *Sermons on Subjects Chiefly Practical; with illustrative notes and an appendix, relating to the character of the Church of England, as distinguished both from other branches of the Reformation, and from the modern Church of Rome*, London, 1824, p.370-1.
[33] *the present Bishop of Lincoln*: John Kaye (1783-1853).

and so apposite to the course of thought which we are pursuing, that we cannot refrain from setting it before the reader?

"If we mistake not the signs of the times," says Dr. Kaye, in his work upon Tertullian,[34] "the period is not far distant when [120] the whole controversy between the English and Romish Churches will be revived, and all the points in dispute again brought under review. Of those none is more important than the question respecting Tradition; and it is therefore most essential that they who would stand forth as the defenders of the Church of England should take a *correct and rational view* of the subject—the view, in short, *which was taken by our divines at the Reformation. Nothing was more remote from their intention than indiscriminately* to condemn all Tradition. . . . What our Reformers opposed was the notion that men must, upon the mere authority of Tradition, receive as necessary to salvation doctrines not contained in Scripture. . . . In this, as in other instances, they wisely adopted a middle course: they neither bowed submissively to the authority of Tradition, nor yet rejected it altogether."—P. 297, ed. 1826.

In another place he speaks still more distinctly. "Tertullian," he says, "appeals to Apostolical Tradition, to a rule of faith, not *originally* deduced from Scripture, but delivered by the Apostles orally to the Churches which they founded, and regularly transmitted from them to his own time. How, I would ask, is this appeal inconsistent with the principles of the Church of England, which declares *only* that Holy Scripture *contains* all things necessary to salvation? Respecting the *source* from which the rule of faith was *originally* deduced, our Church is silent."—P. 587.

7.

This is the doctrine of genuine Anglicanism; and surely it embodies a principle as consonant to the considerateness of Revealed Mercy, as it is welcome to those who would profit by that Revelation to the full. Certainly there are strong reasons, prior to evidence for weak human nature to desire, nay, almost [121]

---

[34] *work upon Tertullian*: *The Ecclesiastical History of the Second and Third Centuries, Illustrated from the Writings of Tertullian*, Cambridge, 1826.

to expect such an informant as we are supposing, to help them in determining the meaning of Scripture where the clearness of its teaching is not on a level with its importance. Such a guide is not a superfluity. Scripture is not written in a dogmatic form, though there are dogmatic passages in it; it contains portions and tokens, nay, the promise, of a boon, which nature so intimately desiderates that it betakes itself to false teachings if it cannot get true. To the millions for whom Redemption has been wrought, creeds and catechisms, liturgies and a theological system, the multitudinous ever-sounding voice, the categorical, peremptory incisiveness, the (so to say) full chime, of ecclesiastical authority, is a first necessity, if they are to realize the world unseen. Yet, strange to say, this need is denied by writers, because they cannot have it supplied just in the way they wish. Dr. Hampden here again distinguishes himself by paradox. He "asks," in his *Bampton Lectures* with the Unitarian above quoted, "whether it is *likely* that an Apostle would have adopted the form of an epistolary communication for imparting *mysterious propositions* to disciples with whom he enjoyed the opportunity of personal intercourse, and to whom he had already 'declared the whole counsel of God'" (p. 375). This argument, let it be observed, is intended to prove that Christianity is not dogmatic, because Scripture is not dogmatic in its form or its profession. Let us suppose that there was not one dogmatic sentence in the New Testament—let the argument be, Christianity is not dogmatic, because its Scriptures are not dogmatic,— is it not far more reasonable to argue that, considering the need, if Christianity is not dogmatic in its books, we must look for its dogmas elsewhere?

[122]   We shall think it safe to assume the latter proposition as a sound one, and under its controversial force and the countenance of the learned Prelate whose words are given above, we now proceed to apply the doctrine of Apostolical Tradition to the purposes of that controversy which "the Brothers" attempted to settle on the ground of private judgment.

8.

First, then, every one knows that a definite doctrine concerning our Lord's origin and nature is taught at this day all over the Church, and that this doctrine, in matter of fact, was, strictly speaking, *taught* to the present generation—not learned by it so much as taught it—*taught* it by the generation immediately before it, not gathered in the first instance by its own inferences from Scripture. This was the fact; and there is as little doubt that that previous generation of men was in like manner taught in the same matters by their own predecessors; and further, that this process of transmission and acceptance—that is, of tradition—has gone on for many centuries: nay, we might say, up to the very first or Apostolic century; but (not arbitrarily to place it so high), at least to the fourth century of our era—that is, up to little more than 200 years from the death of St. John. We will stop, then, at the year 325, being sure that no one will deny that our Lord's Divinity has ever since the fourth century been an article of the Christian creed, and has ever since been acknowledged through the whole extent of Christendom as a fundamental, or rather as the cardinal, doctrine of revealed religion. The question is, whether the events of A.D. 325 and the following years do not bear conclusive testimony to the fact that this great article of faith, then publicly acknowledged, was also taught [123] 200 or 250 years before by St. John and St. Paul—whether the year 325 does not transmit to 1800 what it had received from A.D. 60 or 90. We answer this question in the affirmative, and our reasons are as follows:—

In the second decade of the fourth century a controversy arose in Alexandria about our Lord's proper Divinity. It was brought before the Bishop, and, when his authority was unequal to the settlement of it, it led to the summoning of the first Ecumenical Council at Nicæa, in A.D. 325, which was attended by 318 bishops from all parts of the world, as representatives of the whole Church Catholic. Out of this number so collected more than 300 at once pronounced that that doctrine concerning our Lord, such as we hold it now—viz., that He was "God of God"—was the doctrine taught by the Apostles in the beginning.

This was their concurrent and energetic testimony, as history records it; and now, was or was not that testimony practically decisive on the question what it was that after our Lord's departure the Apostles had taught about our Lord in Jerusalem, Antioch, Ephesus, Alexandria, and Rome?

Here, then, first let it be observed that no external authority interfered to incline them to the doctrine to which they subscribed. Constantine had originally considered the dispute which led to their meeting as little better than a question of words, and had written to Alexandria to order both parties engaged in it to tolerate each other and keep quiet. On finding, however, both before and at the Council, the general opinion to be against Arius, the originator of the disturbance, he changed his course in favour of orthodoxy, at the cost of abandoning [124] thereby his personal friends, and zealously defended the side professed by the majority. After a few years he changed back again, and exposed the Bishops and populations of the Church to the revenge of an exasperated faction. Constantius, who succeeded him, also sided with the heretics, and far more decidedly. He fiercely persecuted the orthodox, assembled Council after Council to destroy the authority of the Nicene, and at the end of his reign dragooned 400 bishops in the West and 150 in the East into giving an indirect denial to the doctrine witnessed to and solemnly professed in 325. Thus political influences told strongly against, not for, the triumph throughout Christendom of the tradition of orthodoxy. The creed of Nicæa was not the imposition of secular power.

Nor did it proceed from a powerful coalition of mutually sympathizing and allied hierarchies. On the contrary, there were long-existing rivalries between those several Churches which took part in the Council. There had been at an earlier date serious disputes between Rome and Ephesus, Rome and Carthage, Rome and Antioch, Rome and Alexandria; and, if it be said that the Bishop of Rome himself was not at Nicæa—only delegates from him—in the same degree as his influence would not be felt there, is it remarkable that he should have so zealously co-operated in the West in carrying out the determinations of the East. Moreover, whatever local influence there was of a theological character at Nicæa was in favour of the heresy, for a member of the original Arian party, and a friend of Arius, was in possession of its see. Further, there was an old jealousy between Alexandria and Antioch, which, as far as it was allowed to act, would tell powerfully in the direction of blunting or thwarting any such keen assertion of the orthodox doctrine as the Council carried out. Moreover, there was at that [125] time a schismatical communion called the Novatian,[35] of about seventy years' standing, spreading through Asia Minor and Africa as well as Italy, bitterly opposed to the Catholics and the see of Rome, and representing at the Council the theology of A.D. 250. This communion is known to have held the dogmatic symbol adopted at the Council as zealously as its Fathers, and afterwards suffered persecution from the Arians.

9.

Again, it must be borne in mind that the great Council at Nicæa was summoned, not to decide for the first time what was to be held concerning our Lord's nature, but, as far as inquiry came into its work, to determine the fact whether Arius did or did not contradict the Church's teaching, and, if he did, by what sufficient *tessera*[36] he and his party could be excluded from the communion of the faithful. That authoritative and formal interpretation of the written word, which we have above treated as a probability, is in truth a matter of history in the early Church. The fact of a tradition of revealed truth was an elementary principle of Christianity. A body of doctrine had been delivered by the Apostles to their first successors, and by them in turn to the next generation, and then to the next, as we have said above. "The things that thou hast heard from me through many witnesses," says St. Paul to Timothy, "the same commit thou to faithful men, who shall be able to teach others

---

[35] *Novatian*: Novatian (200-258) took a rigorist approach towards those who had lapsed from the faith under persecution. His supporters refused to accept the election of Pope Cornelius and made Novatian anti-pope in opposition to him.

[36] tessera: token or voucher, meaning in this context the standard to judge by.

also."[37] This body of truth was in consequence called the "depositum," as being a substantive teaching, not a mere accidental deduction from Scripture. Thus St. Paul says to his [126] disciple and successor Timothy, "Keep the deposit,"[38] "hold fast the form of sound words,"[39] "guard the noble deposit."[40] This important principle is forcibly insisted on by Irenæus and Tertullian before the Nicene era, and by Vincent after it. "'O Timothy,'" says Vincent, "'guard the *depositum,* avoiding profane novelties of words.' Who is Timothy today? Who but the universal Church, or, in particular, the whole body of prelates, whose duty it is both themselves to have the full knowledge of religion, and to instruct others in it? What means 'guard'? Guard the deposit because of enemies, lest, while men sleep, they sow tares upon the good seed, which the Son of Man has sowed in His field. What is 'the deposit'? That which hath been intrusted to you, not that which thou hast discovered; what thou hast received, not what thou hast thought out; a matter, not of cleverness, but of teaching, not of private handling, but of public tradition."[41]

This doctrine of a deposit leads to another remark. It involves in its idea a teaching which had no natural limit or circuit. Such teaching, carried on as it might be in the lifelong contact of master and scholar, was too vast, too minute, too complicated, too implicit, too fertile, to be put into writing, at least in times of persecution; it was for the most part conveyed orally, and the safeguard against its corruption was the number and the unanimity of its witnesses. The canon of Scripture was an additional safeguard—not, however, as limiting it, but as verifying it. Also it was kept in position, and from drifting, by the Creed: that is, by a fixed form of words, the articles of which were the heads and main points, and memoranda for the catechist and preacher, and which were rehearsed and accepted

---

[37] *"The things that thou . . . teach others also.":* II Timothy 2:2.
[38] *"Keep the deposit":* a literal translation of I Timothy 6:20: τὴν παραθήκην φύλαξον.
[39] *"hold fast the form of sound words,":* II Timothy 1:13.
[40] *"guard the noble deposit":* a literal translation of II Timothy 1:14: τὴν καλὴν παραθήκην φύλαξον.
[41] *"'O Timothy'" says Vincent . . . but of public tradition.":* Vincent of Lérins, *Commonitorium* 22.53.

by every candidate for baptism, by way of avowing his adherence to that entire doctrine which the Church was appointed to [127] dispense.[42] The Divinity, then, of our Lord could not have been asserted and recorded at Nicæa, unless the separate Churches there represented had severally found it in their *depositum fidei*.

A further remark is in point. It followed from the very Catholicity of the Church that its tradition, as now described, while one and the same in its matter everywhere, or at least in its substance, was manifold, various and independent in its local manifestation. Each Branch of the extended body had its own distinct line of traditional teaching from the Apostles; and each branch was loyally, nay, obstinately, attached to its own traditions, whatever their peculiarities might be, and reluctant, on grounds of conscience, to yield any portion of them in favour of the traditions of other churches, even when they related to what was indifferent or of minor moment, or at least only of expedience. Thus the dispute between Ephesus and Rome related to the time of keeping Easter.[43] Thus there was a question of the authority of the Apocalypse and other books of Scripture,[44]

---

[42] Here we have light cast on a question which may, for what we know perplex us before many years are over. It is notorious that there are persons in the Church who wish its recognition of baptismal regeneration removed. Now, inasmuch as one of the articles of the Nicene Creed witnesses to the "one baptism for the remission of sins," and since, anyhow, the doctors of the early Church would so explain the less complete form of words which occurs in the Apostles' Creed, "the forgiveness of sins," it follows, if the above view is correct, that to deny baptismal regeneration is *heresy*, and that a Church which indulged its members in such denial would have forfeited its trust, and would have done much to deprive it of any claim upon our allegiance. [N]

This comment, which was part of the 1836 text, turned out to be a prescient one. In 1850 there occurred the controversy of the Gorham Judgment, when the Bishop of Exeter refused to appoint Rev. George Gorham to a parish because the latter rejected the doctrine of baptismal regeneration. The case went to the Privy Council where the bishop was over-ruled. Tractarians were deeply disturbed by this evident subjection of the Church of England to the state on a doctrinal matter, and some, such as Henry Manning, became Catholics as a result.

[43] ... *the time of keeping Easter*: The churches of Asia Minor, following a practice probably dating to the time of the apostles, kept Easter on the 14th day of the Jewish month of Nisan, whereas the Roman practice was to keep it on the following Sunday. Pope Victor I held a synod in 193 which ruled that the Roman practice should be followed everywhere. Bishop Polycrates of Ephesus held a rival synod which rejected this ruling, and Pope Victor excommunicated him.

[44] ... *the Apocalypse and other books of scripture*: The Apocalypse (Revelation) was rejected as canonical by many Eastern churches for a long time, though accepted in the

and a more serious question relative to the baptism of heretics.[45]
In such controversies the one party religiously refused to yield
to the other. The unanimity at Nicæa, then, was not a mutual
[128] sacrifice of views between separate churches for the sake of
peace; not merely the decision of a majority; but simply and
plainly the joint testimony of many local bodies, as independent
witnesses to the separate existence in each of them, from time
immemorial, of that great dogma in which they found each other
to agree. Indeed, it is hard to suppose that they could be found
to disagree in what was obviously so primary and elementary
a question in the revealed system.

And there is evidence in the history of the Council that this
duty of faithfulness to a *depositum* was directly before the minds
of the assembled Fathers. On the contrary, it is observable that
the handful of Bishops who supported Arius did not make any
appeal to any uninterrupted tradition in their favour. They did
but profess to argue from Scripture and from the nature of the
case; if they went further, it was but to profess that they had
been taught their doctrine by a certain presbyter of Antioch,
whose disciples they avowed themselves to be, and that with a
sort of *esprit de corps*;[46] they did not commit themselves to
immemorial tradition. Athanasius[47] takes advantage of their
dating one of their numerous confessions of faith, to insist upon
this contrast. "Having composed," he says, "a creed according
to their tastes, they headed it with mention of the consul, and
the month, and the day, as if to suggest to all men of understanding, that now from the time of Constantius,[48] not before, their
faith dates its rise. . . . They say, 'We publish the Catholic Faith,'
and then they add consulate, month, and day, that, as prophets

West. During the first two centuries there were disputes about the canonicity of
Hebrews, James, 2 Peter, and 2 and 3 John, though they were accepted as part of the
canon by the end of the 4th century.
[45] *the baptism of heretics*: The practice of re-baptising heretics who were becoming
Catholics was initiated in North Africa by St. Cyprian (c.200-258). It was condemned
by Pope St. Stephen I (d.257). The Church recognises any baptism which uses the
Trinitarian formula as valid, no matter who performs it.
[46] *esprit de corps*: group spirit, feeling of loyalty among comrades
[47] *Athanasius*: St. Athanasius (296–373), bishop and Doctor of the Church; the great
champion of orthodoxy against Arianism.
[48] *Constantius*: The Emperor Constantius II (317 – 361).

marked the period of their histories and their ministries by dates, so they might be accurate in the date of their faith. Nay, I wish they had confined themselves to speak of their own private faith, (for in fact it did then begin,) and had let alone the Catholic [129] faith; whereas they wrote, not 'Thus we believe,' but 'We publish the Catholic faith.' ... On the other hand [the Nicene Fathers], many as they were, ventured nothing such as these men ventured; but, whereas about the Easter Feast they said, 'This is our decree,' they did not use the word 'decree' when speaking of the faith, but said, 'Thus believes the Catholic Church;' for what they set down was no discovery of theirs, but the doctrine which was taught by the Apostles."—*De Syn.* 3-5.[49]

Nor can it be successfully maintained that an identity of doctrine, such as is found in A.D. 325, in such various quarters of Christendom, was the gradual, silent, insensible, homogeneous growth of the intermediate period, during which the vague statements of Apostles, parallel to those in Scripture, were adjusted and completed. This theory of a development into a higher view of our Lord's Person is not tenable. For, not to mention the existence of the Novatians, who had split off from the Church within 150 years of St. John's death, and yet were as determined in upholding the Nicene doctrine as the Catholics, it so happens that in the very age of the Apostles a sect arose external to the Church,[50] which opened upon theologians all those more subtle questions concerning the nature of Christ which were agitated within the Church during the fourth and fifth centuries. "What think ye of Christ? whose Son is He?"[51] had been the question from the first; it was, as was natural, the first and direct question before the minds of preachers, catechists, hearers, and converts, in the propagation of the Gospel. Wherever the truth was taught, there was the probability of an heretical opposition to it; and such opposition brought out in

---

[49] De Syn.: Athanasius, *De Synodis.*
[50] *a sect arose external to the Church*: the Gnostics, who held complex mystical beliefs about the evil nature of the universe and claimed to reveal esoteric knowledge ('gnosis'). Gnosticism pre-dated Christianity, though it was quick to adopt a quasi-Christian form and produced apocryphal gospels.
[51] *"What think ye of Christ? whose Son is He?"*: Matthew 22:42.

[130] the earlier centuries, as well as the later, the protest of Catholic theologians. We confidently affirm that there is not an article in the Athanasian Creed concerning the Incarnation which is not anticipated in the controversy with the Gnostics; not a question which the Apollinarian[52] or the Nestorian[53] heresy raised, which may not be decided in the words of Ignatius, Irenæus, and Tertullian. If, then, our Lord after all was by the Apostles accounted and preached as a mere man, are we to believe in the phenomenon of this one and the same substitution everywhere of a new doctrine about Him, in the course of 220 years (nay, perhaps of only 70), in times of persecution, among peoples of different languages, characters, attachments, and religious attainments, and in spite of the safeguard of episcopal transmission? All this, moreover, without record of the change, or assignable reason why it should be made anywhere, or what brought it about:—lastly, with the unaccountable belief on the part of the Fathers in the Council that the view which they enforced was that which the Apostles had bequeathed them.

We have been viewing the argument on its hierarchical side; the witness of the Christian people for the orthodox truth is not less striking—nay, more so—than that of the Bishops. One or two of the great cities were corrupted as time went on, but the mass of the laity was decided and fervent in its maintenance of the sacred truth that was in jeopardy. The population of Alexandria, Antioch, Edessa, Cæsarea, Rome, and Milan, were even patterns in their profession of the dogma to the distressed, menaced, and hardly-used ecclesiastics.[54]

---

[52] *Apollinarian*: Apollinaris (d.392), Bishop of Laodicea, taught that Christ did not have a human rational mind but that this was replaced by the Logos. The heresy was condemned by the Council of Chalcedon in 451.

[53] *Nestorian heresy*: Nestorius (386-450), Patriarch of Constantinople, taught that there were two persons in Christ, the divine and the human and so denied the title of 'Theotokos' (God-bearer, Mother of God) to the Virgin Mary. His teaching was condemned at the Council of Ephesus in 431 and the Council of Chalcedon in 451. Nestorian Christians went into schism; they became established in Persia, and Nestorian missionaries later reached India and China.

[54] *Vide* "History of the Arians," Ed. 4, and Note V., p. 445. [N] Newman's own *Arians of the Fourth Century*, published in 1833. Note V is on 'The Orthodoxy of the Body of the Faithful during the Supremacy of Arianism' was added in the Fourth Edition; it had first appeared as an article in *The Rambler*, July 1859.

10.   [131]

So much, then, on the argument in behalf of our Lord's Divinity from Apostolical Tradition; and perhaps the reader may consider that enough has now been said upon the subject: but, before dismissing it, he must be prevailed upon to attend to one or two collateral illustrations of it, by way of showing, in corroboration of what was observed above, how natural and reasonable this argument from Tradition must be considered.

First, we take a passage from "The Brothers' Controversy" itself. The clergyman objects to his Unitarian brother-in-law, that the mass of men, as being unlearned, cannot safely decide about the doctrine of the Trinity by means of reasonings from the text of Scripture, since the original is to them an unknown tongue. He is answered as follows:—

"I have never crossed the Atlantic, and cannot know, but by reading voyages and histories, or by oral communications, that any land exists there; voyagers and historians have often lied or erred; yet I am as much convinced of the existence of a continent there as I am of the field now before my eyes. Do I, then, rely upon the testimony of men, who may be deceivers? No, it is not in the nature of things, it is absolutely impossible, that such concurrence should take place in the relation of falsehoods. The history of the death and resurrection of Christ was written in a language as unknown to me as are opposite shores of the ocean I have never traversed; *yet the concurrence of translators is as convincing to me as if the account were in my native language, and I do not rely on human authority.*"—P. 155.

What is this but a statement of the argument from Tradition? Why will not such a disputant consider the Fathers interpreters of Scripture as regards Catholic doctrine?

Again, let us refer to Paley's[55] argument for the truth of the received Christian history, as contained in the seventh chapter of the first part of his "Evidences." It will be found that what [132] he there advances for the facts of the Religion may be transferred, with little alteration, in proof of its doctrines. He begins

---

[55] *Paley*: William Paley (1743–1805), Anglican divine. His *View of the Evidences of Christianity* was published in 1794.

by asking "Whether the story which Christians have now be the story which Christians had then?" which has been our very question as regards the doctrines of our Religion. He answers in the affirmative, upon these four considerations. First, because "there exists no trace or vestige of any other story." "There is not a document or scrap of account, either contemporary with the commencement of Christianity, or extant within many ages after that commencement, which assigns a history substantially different from ours." Now, this is clearly fulfilled as regards doctrine also. It is true there were some few who taught differently from the Catholic Faith; but even they did so, not as witnessing an historical fact, or from Tradition, but as claiming to interpret Scripture for themselves—a ground of argument which does not interfere with the argument from Tradition. Or again, if they appealed to Tradition, as the Gnostics did, it was to a secret Tradition, known and delivered only by a few of the Apostles, and professedly contrary to the public teaching of those Apostles—a pretence which was evidently adopted to evade the difficulty of their discordance from Catholic teaching, and which grants, in the very form of it, that Apostolical Tradition was against them. The only real exception which we remember is the same heretical party at Rome, in the beginning of the third century, which boldly pronounced their heresy to be Apostolical; and even these soon abandoned their claim.

Paley proceeds: "The remote, brief, and incidental notices of the affair, which are found in heathen writers, so far as they [133] do go, go along with us." The same may be said of the theological doctrine also. Pliny[56] witnesses to the worship of Christ as a God by His disciples, and Celsus[57] objects against them the same observance.

Then Paley says: "The whole series of Christian writers, from the first age of the institution down to the present, in their

---

[56] *Pliny*: Gaius Plinius Caecilius Secundus (61–c.112), known as Pliny the Younger. When he was Governor of Bythinia he wrote to the Emperor Trajan asking advice about how to deal with Christians in his area and reported that two Christian women whom he had had tortured had said that in their meetings they 'sang a hymn to Christ as a god'(*Epistulae* X. 96).
[57] *Celsus*: 2nd century Greek philosopher who wrote a polemic against Christianity.

discussions, apologies, arguments, and controversies, proceed upon the general story which the Scriptures contain, and upon no other. This argument will appear to be of great force, when it is known that we are able to trace back the series of writers to a contact with the historical books of the New Testament, and to the age of the first emissaries of the Religion, and to deduce it, by an unbroken continuation, from that end of the train to the present." This surely applies word for word to the received doctrine also.

Next,—"Now, that the original story, the story delivered by the first preachers of the institution, should have died away so entirely as to have left no record or memorial of its existence, although so many records and memorials of the time and its transactions remain, and that another story should have stept into its place and gained exclusive possession of the belief of all who professed themselves disciples of the institution, is beyond any example of the corruption of even oral tradition, and still less consistent with the experience of written history; and this improbability, which is very great, is rendered still greater by the reflection that no such change as the oblivion of one story and the substitution of another took place in any future period of the Christian era." Here Paley even adds a consideration which we had passed over: "If the catholicity of the fourth century is not in substance the catholicity of the first, can we feel sure that our present MSS. of the New Testament in substance agree with the MSS. of St. Jerome?"[58]

Further,—"The religious rites and usages that prevailed [134] amongst the early disciples of Christianity were such as belonged to and sprang out of the narrative now in our hands; which accordancy shows that it was the narrative upon which these persons acted, and which they had received from their teachers." The same holds good as regards the doctrines also: Baptism witnesses to the doctrine of the Trinity, and the Eucharistic Rite grows out of and teaches the doctrines of the Incarnation and Atonement—that is, these two rites are contin-

---

[58] *St. Jerome*: (347-420), Father of the Church; he translated the Bible into Latin (the 'Vulgate' version) from original Greek texts.

uous mementos of doctrines such as those which we at this day believe to be Apostolic.

Lastly,—"The story was public at the time" when the Gospels were written; "the Christian community was already in possession of the substance and principal parts of the narrative. The Gospels were not the original cause of the Christian history being believed, but were themselves among the consequences of that belief." Paley says this to show that the story, coinciding though it did in its details with the Scripture narrative, yet rested on authority wider and other than it. The same may be said of Catholic doctrine also. While no one can deny that at least it is reconcilable with the sacred text, we find even our opponents contending that it was not the object of the text to enforce it, nor the result of the text to construct it.

Paley concludes by maintaining that "these four circumstances are sufficient to support our assurance that the story which we have now is in general the story which Christians had at the beginning"; meaning by *in general* "in its texture and in its principal facts"; and we can desire nothing more to be granted to us as regards the received teaching concerning our Lord's Divinity and Incarnation.

[135]   Illustrations might be multiplied on this subject without limit; one more shall be added from the universal practice of infant baptism. "Since the proofs drawn by consequences from some places of Scripture for any side of this question," says Wall,[59] in his preface to his well-known work, "are not so plain as to hinder the arguments drawn from other places for the other side from seeming considerable ... it is no wonder that the readers of Scripture, at this distance from the Apostles' times, have fallen into contrary sentiments about the meaning of our Saviour's command, and the practice of the Apostles in reference to this baptizing of infants. When there is in Scripture a plain command to proselytize or make disciples all nations, baptizing them ... there is nobody that will doubt but that the Apostles knew what was to be done in this case, and, conse-

---

[59] *Wall*: William Wall (1647-1728), Vicar of Shoreham. His 'well-known work' was *A History of Infant Baptism*, first published in 1705 and widely influential.

quently, that the Christian Churches in their time did as they should do in this matter. And since the Apostles lived, some of them, to near the end of the first century, ... it can never sink into the head of any considering man, but that such Christians as were ancient men about 100 or 150 years after ... the Apostles' death, which is A.D. 200 or 250, must easily know whether infant-baptism were in use at the time of the Apostles' death or not, etc." It seems, then, that those who deny the force of the argument from Catholic Tradition discard the true and sufficient interpreter of Scripture, not only according to the Roman Bellarmine, but according to the Anglican Wall.

11.

Our discussion has run to an exorbitant length. However, before parting with us, let the reader do us the favour to observe [136] how the Fathers are accustomed to speak of those private and self-authorized interpretations of the sacred volume, which writers of this day, accepting some of them and rejecting others, view one and all benignantly, calling them, (heretical and orthodox alike,) "pious opinions," "guiltless differences," "theories of the Divine Being and attributes," and so on. "Perhaps some one will ask," says Vincent of Lérins, "whether the heretics also do not make use of testimonies from Holy Scripture? Yes, indeed, they do use them, and lay great stress on them; for you may see them ready quoters of each book of God's sacred law—the books of Moses, of Kings, the Psalms, the Apostles, the Evangelists, the Prophets. Whether they are among their own people or among strangers, in private or in public, discoursing or writing, at convivial meetings or in the open ways, scarcely anything do they advance of their own notions without attempting to present them in the words of Scripture ... If one of them be asked whence he proves, whence he teaches that I ought to abandon the universal and ancient faith of the Catholic Church, he promptly replies, 'Because it is written;' and on the spot is ready with a thousand texts, instances, authorities, from Law and Psalms and Apostles and Prophets, precipitating the unhappy soul, by a new and perverse interpretation of them, from the citadel of Catholicity into the abyss of heresy."—*Comm.* 35-38.[60]

Tertullian, in like manner, two centuries earlier:—"Thy faith hath saved thee, not thy practice in the Scriptures. Faith rests in the Rule [*i.e.*, the Creed]. You have a law, and in the keeping of it is salvation ... To know nothing in opposition to the Rule is to know all things ... As for that person, if there be such, for [137] whose sake you enter upon the discussion of the Scriptures, to confirm him when in doubt, will he in consequence incline to truth or rather to heresies? ... Therefore I do not advise appeal to the Scriptures. It is a ground on which there can be either no victory, or a doubtful one, or at least not a certain."—*De Præscr.*, 14-19.[61]

It would seem as if Tertullian and Vincent had little more respect for mere deductions from Scripture in matters of faith than the modern writers above quoted: differing from them, however, in calling such deductions not "pious," but "impious opinions." What they would have called Dr. Hampden's own opinions, it is neither difficult nor to our purpose to determine.

July, 1836.

---

[60] Comm.: *Commonitorium*
[61] *De Præscr.*: *De praescriptione hereticorum.*

NOTE ON ESSAY III.

THE doctrine of the foregoing Essay is, on the whole, so consonant with what I should write upon its subject now, that the reasons which are given above in the Advertisement, for preserving the original text in these volumes generally, do not apply here. Accordingly I have availed myself of the liberty thus allowed me to make large alterations in it of a literary kind.

In consequence of imputations which were freely cast on my friends and myself[62] at the time of its first publication, and from circumstances have never been retracted, I repeat here what I stated in a footnote then, that it was written before Dr. Hampden's appointment to the Regius Professorship of Divinity in February, 1836, being a continuation of a series of protests conscientiously made against his theology by the author and others from the date of November, 1834.—Vide *Apologia*, p. 57, 2nd Ed.

---

[62] *imputations which were freely cast on my friends and myself*: This article had appeared during the controversy over Hampden's appointment as Regius Professor of Divinity, and its publication was attacked as part of a continuing 'persecution' of Hampden by the Tractarians. However, a footnote by Newman in the original text (see the Textual Appendix) made clear that the article had been in written and set in type before Hampden's appointment.

IV.

FALL OF DE LA MENNAIS.

M. F. DE LA MENNAIS has given us an account of what passed between him and the Papal See in 1831-1832, in a small volume entitled "Affaires de Rome."[1] It is a curious and instructive work; and, though coming from the pen of an acknowledged partisan, and therefore not implicitly to be trusted, it deals too largely in facts, and has too much the air of truth, not to demand the attention of all Churchmen. That great and ancient power, the Church Catholic, which dates her origin from the first preaching of the Gospel, which was founded by the Apostles, and which claims to be indissolubly connected with its fortunes, has been taken captive by her enemies, blinded, and set to servile employments—to make men good citizens, and to promote the enlightenment and comfort of the world; except when she is brought out of the prison-house on some great pageant, "to make sport," to invest the institutions of earth with something of a religious character, and to pay homage to its mighty men, as her creators and governors. Such at least is M. de la Mennais' opinion; and this is the curious circumstance, that the Roman Church, so high and apostolic, as her champions in these parts would represent her, so voluntary, so law-less, so unshackled, is after all, according to this foreign witness, but an established thing, up and down the countries in which she ought only to sojourn, not less or much more of a Law Church, practically, than our own. Indeed, the main difference between

---

[1] *Affaires de Rome: Memoires Adressés au Pape; des maux de l'église et de la société, et des Moyens d'y Remédier* [Roman Business. Reflections Addressed to the Pope, concerning the evils of the church and of society], 1837.

her and ourselves, taking him for our informant, seems to be this; that we have hitherto been well-treated, and Romanists ill-treated by the civil power;—that we have received bread, and have obeyed through gratitude; and they have been robbed and beaten, till they fawned upon their oppressors out of sheer exhaustion. Certainly, of the two, ours has been the better bargain. The consequences are natural; two parties at present wish our downfall; our ill-starred foreign brethren, in order to level us to themselves, and our own masters, to rival foreign spoliations. Whigs and Papists, the high and the low, combine, the one from ambition, the other from envy; the one cry out, "I will ascend into heaven; I will exalt my throne above the stars of God: I will sit upon the mount of the congregation:"[2] and the others begin to say, "Art thou also become weak as we? Art thou become like unto us?"[3]

M. de la Mennais's book then is curious and instructive, as setting before us the actual state of the Roman Communion, both ecclesiastically and morally; and, in consequence, as holding out to us some warning of what may come on ourselves. It is curious, moreover, as indicating the existence of a party within it, at variance with the present policy of its rulers, living upon historical recollections and ancient principles, and ripe for insurrection. Moreover, it is curious as exhibiting the principles of this insurgent party, which is faithful to the same mixture of truth and error, right and bad feeling, which has been the inheritance of its church for many centuries. It will be our endeavour to put the Abbé's volume before the reader in some of these various lights.

1.   [140]

When good churchmen in England have of late years, in our presence, exclaimed against the various successful encroachments of the State upon that liberty which was their birthright, it has been our wont to counsel them patience, by referring to the state of the Greek Church, in which the Great Turk,[4] a mere

---

[2] *"I will ascend into heaven . . . the mount of the congregation:"*: Isaiah 14:13.
[3] *"Art thou also . . . like unto us?"*: Isaiah 14:10.

heathen, or rather an antichrist, appoints the patriarch;[5] under the feeling that we had no right to complain as yet, when our rulers were appointed, not by pagans, but only by schismatics, latitudinarians, profligates, socinians, and infidels. But the work before us suggests comfort nearer home; the poor Gallican Church is in a captivity, not only doctrinal, which we all know, but ecclesiastical, far greater than ours. M. de la Mennais mentions the following instances of it.

In 1801, Buonaparte, as Consul, negotiated a concordat with the Pope,[6] by which the government had secured to it the right of presenting to the French sees, on the condition of its "professing the Catholic religion."[7] It was stipulated, at the same time, that if the Consuls[8] or their successors ever ceased such profession, a new concordat should settle the mode of nomination. This arrangement was acknowledged and acted on under the Restoration,[9] the kings being, by profession, "most Christian," and guardians of Catholicism. But after the events of the Three Days,[10] the State could no longer fulfil its own part of the compact. Louis Philippe was king "by the grace of the people;" and was obliged, according to one of the fundamental principles of the Revolution, whatever he might be in his own person, to become, at least in profession, of no particular religion. It [141] follows, in our author's words,—that "the government had no longer the right to present to the sees; and the danger was obvious of allowing ministers, who might be Deists,[11] Protes-

---

[4] *the Great Turk*: the Ottoman Emperor

[5] *the Patriarch*: of Constantinople

[6] *a concordat with the Pope: I*n 1801 Pope Pius VII and Napoleon signed an agreement which allowed the Church in France to operate (after the years of persecution following the Revolution) but gave the state wide powers over it, including the appointment of bishops. The Pope later regretted signing the concordat..

[7] P. 3. [N]

[8] *the Consuls*: The Consulate was the form of French government from 1799 until 1804. It provided for three Consuls as rulers of France, of whom Napoleon was First Consul. In reality he alone held real power, becoming First Consul for life in 1802 and Emperor in 1804.

[9] *the Restoration*: the return of the Bourbon monarchy to power, in the person of Louis XVIII, in 1814.

[10] *the events of the Three Days*: 27th, 28th and 29th July 1830, during which French King Charles X abdicated in the face of a popular revolution, and the Duke of Orleans, Louis Philippe, became king.

[11] *Deists*: rationalists who believe in a God but deny Revelation.

tants, Jews, or Infidels, to choose the successors of the Apostles of Jesus Christ."[12] However, *the government continues to appoint the bishops as before*; and has availed itself of its privilege, to introduce into the hierarchy persons who have justified the fears, with which such a prerogative naturally inspired all pious men.[13]

An attempt has been made to encroach upon the rights of the Church in her inferior, as well as her highest appointments. The government has interfered in the appointment of parish priests. On a vacancy in a living the bishop of the diocese nominates the new incumbent; he has been expected by the new government to take his choice out of persons named to the Minister of Religion by the local magistracy. In the diocese of Nimes, instances have occurred of the government's taking the absolute nomination into their hands. One parish went without a clergyman for many months, because the bishop's nominee was opposed by the nominee of a colonel. In another, the appointment was given to the nominee of a Protestant mayor. M. de la Mennais adds: "Since the nomination of canons and vicars-general required the approval of the government, it followed, that the whole hierarchy fell directly or indirectly into the hands of enemies of the Church, *who, after having all their life had the vision of her ruin before their eyes, found themselves all at once in a position to give her pastors as many as they chose*."[14] It is an edifying comment on this fact that M. Montalivet,[15] [142] when, as Minister of Religion, he had the disposal of all the government Church patronage, avowed it to be his wish so to manage the education of the people as to destroy *superstition*.

The following acts are instances of interference, with still less regard to law or usage; political necessity being of course in part their excuse. A circular from the Minister of Religion to the bishops, enjoined them to add the name of Louis Philippe in the sentences in the service where "the king" is prayed for,

---

[12] P. 64. [N]
[13] The Abbé mentions M. l'Abbé G., bishop of B.; M. l'Abbé R., of D.; and M. l'Abbé H., of M. [N] Lammenais' original text gives only the initials in this same way.
[14] P. 66. [N]
[15] *M. Montalivet*: Jean-Pierre Bachasson, Comte de Montalivet (1766-1823).

"contrary," says our author, "to the immemorial usage of the Church of France, respected even under Napoleon."[16] By another circular they were ordered to interdict the observance of certain festivals, declared not obligatory by the concordat; with a view of hindering the attendance at church on those days. Another circular ordered the clergy to warm the water used in baptism during the winter. In the dioceses of Lyons and Grenoble, the names of children are demanded for registration before baptism.

On the Abbé Gregoire's[17] death, though he died in separation from the Catholic Church, the government took possession of a parish church, in Paris, and caused a solemn service to be performed over the body by some separatist priests. A like outrage occurred on the death of the Abbé Berthier,[18] who died in schism; and the government intimated its intention, as a matter of right and duty, always so to act in parallel circumstances. Aristotle, if we mistake not, has been represented as inclining to the notion that pity is the long-scented presage of one's own participation in another's misfortunes. We sincerely pity the French Church.

[143] The clergy are paid by the State, by a yearly budget. This salary was originally an indemnity in part of the immense spoliations of the Church at the first Revolution, and was settled by the concordat of 1801. It has ceased to be considered a debt, as might easily be anticipated; and is increased or diminished at pleasure by the government, who claim the right of suppressing it altogether.

Instances have occurred of clergy being refused the bills due to them on the treasury, for their salaries, because the underlings of government have been dissatisfied with their mode of going on.[19] What sets off this proceeding is the circumstance, that according to French law, government cannot withhold a public

---

[16] P. 67. [N]

[17] *the Abbé Gregoire*: Henri Grégoire (1750–1831) was a priest of radical republican political views who supported the Revolution. He was elected a Constitutional bishop and was therefore excommunicated since he had been appointed without the Pope's consent.

[18] *the Abbé Berthier*: another Constitutional bishop, also excommunicated.

[19] P. 75. [N]

functionary's pay, without proceeding to displace him: and if he cannot be displaced, without action in a court of law.

Lastly, the parish priests are under the immediate *surveil-lance* of the mayors, and for every day's non-residence are fined a portion of their stipend.[20]

Such is the condition of the Church under a government which *professes* no religion; it is paid by the State, enslaved and insulted. No wonder; one is only surprised that it has fared no worse from those who would get religion out of the world altogether, if they could. But what is surprising is, the hard treatment which religion has received from those who are commonly considered its best friends—the Bourbons of the Restoration, and the great Conservative party who attached themselves to them. They retained Buonaparte's concordat of 1801, though formed on those principles of tyranny which he exercised towards all over whom he extended his patronage. The bishops were not permitted a freedom of intercourse with each other, or with Rome; and punishments, up to banishment, were assigned to any priest for corresponding with what is to [144] them the centre of Christendom. In spite of provincial and diocesan synods, and ecclesiastical courts, the Council of State was the sole judge of all disputes relative to religion and conscience.[21] Education was entrusted to a lay body, to the exclusion of the clergy; the religious management, and even teaching in schools, subjected to civil authority; religious fraternities legally permitted, only under a license revocable at pleasure. Much of this might be excused, on the plea that the Bourbon Monarchy did but take what it found established; nay, even might be justified, on the plea of its Christian profession. But what shall we say to the two celebrated ordinances of June 16, 1828, which, though forced upon the reigning prince,[22] attest

---

[20] P. 68. [N]

[21] Pp. 46, 47. [N]

[22] *forced on the reigning Prince*: Charles X (1757-1836) was persuaded by his chief Minister, the Viscount de Martignac, a moderate, to approve these anti-Church laws in an attempt to placate the King's Republican opponents. Charles never believed in this policy of compromise and later attempted to assert his absolutist rule, provoking the 1830 Revolution in which he was overthrown.

thereby so much the more strikingly the slavery of the Church, under the system over which he nominally presided? By these all colleges were suppressed which remained in the hands of the clergy, and all ecclesiastical schools were put under the civil authority; the number of candidates for Orders was limited, they were obliged to wear a particular dress, and their masters, having been previously approved by government, took an oath not to belong to any religious society not recognized by the State. Such was the legislative patronage extended by the Bourbons to the Church, in spite of their attachment to it. They did what they could,—did favours, that is, which for the most part were personal only, and came to an end with themselves; or political favours which would come to an end with the civil power. They increased the number of the bishops, gave them seats in the Chamber, increased their stipends, encouraged the ceremonies of religion, favoured its missions (as they were called); they did all but restore to the Church its own proper power—power over itself, over its members, or what, in the case of individuals, is liberty of person.

[145]

There is not much to choose, then, for the French Church, between friends and foes; except that friends are better behaved:—but how to account for this unanimity between them? At first sight, it seems obvious to attribute it to the present miserably irreligious state of France, which makes it impossible for its rulers, however well inclined, to do any real service to the Church. But M. de la Mennais has no difficulty in showing that the phenomenon is independent of the age and the place in which it has occurred. In France, it is as old at least as the reign of Louis XIV.,[23] and is, as he maintains, the working, not of infidelity, but of Gallicanism;[24] which is, as it would really appear, only the surrender to the king of that illegal power over the Church, which had heretofore been possessed by the Pope. The Gallican principle is the vindication of the Church, not into

---

[23] *Louis XIV*: (1638-1715), an absolutist who centralised all power in the monarchy, including power over the church.
[24] *Gallicanism*: the view held by many French churchmen that the Pope's authority was subject to General Councils and that the Crown had authority over virtually all aspects of the French church.

independence, but into State patronage. The liberties of the Gallican Church are its *establishment*, its becoming, in Scripture language, "the servant of men."[25] These liberties were solemnly recognized in the articles of the famous council held in Paris in 1682, in which was confirmed the king's claim to exercise in all churches within his kingdom, a right which he possessed but in portions of it, viz., that on a vacancy in a see, he should enjoy its revenues and its patronage till it was filled up. On the Pope's resisting the innovation, and refusing to confirm the bishops nominated by Louis, the latter, zealous of course for his Church's liberty, caused them to be consecrated and inducted into their sees on his own authority. Next, he summoned the council in question, in which it was decreed,—1. That the Pope could not interfere with the temporal concerns of princes, [146] directly or indirectly; 2. That in spiritual matters, he was subject to a general council; 3. That the rules and usages of the Gallican Church were inviolable; and 4. That the Pope's decision in points of faith was not infallible, unless attended by the consent of the Church. It matters little what is the wording of such resolutions, or what their precise doctrinal signification: they were aimed at the assistance afforded to religion by an external power against the pressure of the temporal power within, and they succeeded in making the king the head of the French Church, in much the same sense in which he is its supreme governor among ourselves. On the restoration of the Bourbons, Gallicanism returned with them, and its four articles were made the rule of the government schools. At first the clergy were little disposed to co-operate with the Court; but, a judicial decree in 1826 having declared the articles to be part of the fundamental laws of the kingdom, they were gradually persuaded that resistance was hopeless, and looked about how they might admit them, without committing the Church to the practical conse-quences.

Such was the cautious course adopted by the Episcopal Bench, tending, however, according to M. de la Mennais, to

---

[25] *"servant of men"*: Cf. Galatians 1:10: 'For do I now persuade men, or God? or do I seek to please men? for if I yet pleased men, I should not be the servant of Christ.'

commit the Church to a position essentially schismatical, and thereby ruinous to its highest interests. It was under these circumstances that he made what seems to have been his first appearance as an ecclesiastical writer; he took up the defence of the Papal claims against the Gallicanism of the higher clergy; and fell forthwith under the animadversion of the police, (indulgent as it then was towards political publications,) for advocating, not any political measure, but certain theological [147] doctrines which had formerly displeased Louis XIV. Thus we see that it is not infidelity, but Gallicanism, which is the real enslaver of the French Church.

Yet even this fails of being the full and sufficient explanation of its captivity; as is plain from the circumstance that the same calamity has fallen upon Italy and Austria, countries apparently far removed from the contagion of Cisalpine[26] opinions. In Tuscany the police exercises a censorship on the pastoral letters and other writings of the bishops; and till lately, if not at present, in Piedmont also. In Venice and Lombardy the Austrian government has the sole control of the promulgation of the Pope's circulars and other acts. At Milan, publications against Roman rights and doctrines are freely permitted; while political works are strictly forbidden. Even in Spain, the crown had the power and the will, during the rebellion of its colonies, to hinder the Holy See for seven years from filling up the South American bishoprics as they fell.

Some deeper cause then exists, according to M. de la Mennais, for the slavery of religion throughout the Roman Communion; and he ascribes it to the fact of the temporal establishment of religion. If the Church is to be free in each of the countries through which it is spread, it must, he considers, have some *point d'appui*[27] to depend on. Rome, he considers, is this resting-point and centre of Catholicism. Catholics are one everywhere, while they concur and determine in Rome; they

---

[26] *Cisalpine*: Literally, 'this side of the Alps', i.e. non-Italian. Originally, the Cisalpine Club was formed by some aristocratic English Catholic laymen who aimed to make Catholicism acceptable to the British government of the day. By extension, the term means an attitude which lessens Papal authority in the Church.

[27] *point d'appui*: rallying point (for soldiers)

become schismatical wherever they set up a separate interest from it. Rome is, in this point of view, the guardian and security of the religious liberties of the whole world, being a court of final appeal between the Church and the local civil government. Hence it is the interest of the civil government, if it would subject its own Church to itself to break it off from its centre of power, or to make it schismatical,—in other words, to *establish* [148] it. Formal schism is the ultimate state of civil protection. It was realized in England, he says, at the time of the Reformation; it has since been gradually, and is still, maturing in the various countries which remain nominally attached to Rome. Such is, it would appear, the philosophy of M. de la Mennais; a few remarks upon it shall be made presently, but first let us complete our sketch of it.

This dislocation of the Church Catholic has been effected, he considers, by the evil influence exerted upon it by its temporalities. Her local rulers have been bribed or terrified into siding with the crown. In England she bartered her birthright for pottage.[28] The case was, in some measure, the same in France, under the Restoration. The Court party attempted to prove that religion could not exist healthily except under the protection of the State; and liberally offered that protection in return for its submission. "The cry then was," says M. de la Mennais, "'All goes well; there is nothing to fear for God: the king protects Him.' The king, in fact, condescended to allow Him to choose for Himself a certain fixed number of young persons for the service of the altars,[29] always on condition of his own superintendence of their education. His object was to relieve the Episcopate of this charge, *fatigued, as it was besides, by its civil functions*; for these functions, too, were a mode of making himself sure of it. The bishops laid down their mitres at the door of the chamber of peers; their crosiers at that of the council of state. Gold was lavished in exchange for an uncon-

---

[28] *she bartered her birthright for pottage*: Cf. Genesis 25:29-34 where Esau gives his birthright to Jacob in exchange for a pottage of lentils.
[29] *a fixed number of young persons . . .* : The number of seminarians was limited by the government.

[149]

ditional obedience."[30] And a satisfactory exchange it was, compared with what it has been the fate of their Church to undergo, where rulers were not so conservatively or so religiously minded. Bribery is out of date now; and the violences in France, since the revolution of 1830, and in Spain and Portugal during the last year or two,[31] show us that fear rather than hope is now the approved instrument of the civil power in its warfare with religion.

Violence, however, eventually defeats its own purpose; when men have nothing to lose, they have nothing to fear; and recollections and desires of the forgotten spiritual dominion of the Church arise out of the destruction of its temporal. Such might already be the case with the communion of Rome, but for the present state of "the centre of unity" itself which, having been bribed long ago in common with its dependencies, has not yet been called upon to part with its portion of the "consideration." "Quis custodiet ipsos custodes?"[32] Hence, M. de la Mennais has no hopes for Christendom while the Pope is a temporal prince. To the great disgust, as it would seem, of the Court of Rome, he maintains this to be the root of all the existing evil in the Church. He considers the See of St. Peter as the $\pi \ddot{v} \sigma \tau \acute{\omega}$, the fulcrum by which he is to move the world;[33] and he finds it removed from the rock on which it was originally built,[34] and based upon the low and marshy ground which lies beside it.[35] Here, then, two points lie before us for examination, to which we shall apply ourselves, the supposed true position, according to our author's theory of the Papacy in the Church Catholic, and its actual condition at the present day.

---

[30] P. 301. [N]

[31] *in Spain and Portugal during the last year or two*: In Spain there was a civil war between the Carlists, who were Catholic and conservative, and the supporters of the regent Maria Cristina, who were more liberal. In Portugal, there was a civil war between absolutists, supporting Miguel I, and liberals, supporting Pedro I, who enacted measures against the religious orders.

[32] *"Quis custodiet ipsos custodes?"*: *"Who will guard the guardians?"*

[33] $\pi \ddot{v} \sigma \tau \acute{\omega}$, *the fulcrum by which* . . . : Archimedes (c.287 – c.212 B.C.) said that if there was a fixed point on which to stand, he could move the earth with a fulcrum.

[34] *the rock on which it was originally built*: Cf. Matthew 16:18.

[35] *marshy ground*: The Pontine Marshes to the south-east of Rome were still undrained at this time.

2.

It is impossible to determine, and it is useless to speculate, what designs Providence proposed to fulfil by means of the Church, which have not been answered. In the Mosaic law we [150] find an anticipation of a time when the government of Israel should be kingly, yet the actual adoption of that form of polity was, under the circumstances, a sin in the people. In like manner the Papacy, too, may be a human and a rebellious work, and yet, in the divine counsels, a centre of unity may have been intended for the Church in process of time.[36] Such speculations are only admissible as tending to account for the mingled and apparently inconsistent strain in which one is forced in this day to speak of the Papal power as an evil, yet not a pure evil, as in itself human, yet, relatively to the world, divine. Providence carries on His mysterious work by instruments which are not simply His own; as He is now effecting great good in the world by the British power, in spite of its great religious errors, so surely He may, in a dark age also, be represented by a light short of the brightest and purest. And, in like manner, at this day also, in an irreligious State like France, the Romanizing Church there existing may, relatively, be God's minister, as if it were as pure as the primitive. Moreover, we of this generation may be quite unequal to the task of discriminating accurately between what is human and what divine in the system under review, and, except in greater matters, of saying this is Apostolic, this is Popish. This remark must be borne in mind in the following account of M. de la Mennais' system. We do not simply assent to what he advances, yet there is much in it which demands attention. Often we admit his facts and principles, not his conclusions and applications.

It is matter of history, then, that the Latin Church rose to power, not by the favour of princes, but of people. Of course, when the barbarian leaders poured down upon the Roman

---

[36] *a centre of unity . . . in process of time*: In this phraseology, we may see a glimmer of Newman's later concept, in his *Essay on the Development of Christian Doctrine* (pp.148ff) of the development of Papal authority which first lay latent but then became more fully developed as the growth and needs of the Church required it.

[151] empire, she made alliance with them, and so far made use of them. In like manner she afterwards availed herself of the Normans. But if we look at the elementary foundation of her power, and the great steps by which she built it up, we seem to discern the acts, not of a parasite, but of a rival of imperial greatness, appealing to the people, maintaining the freedom and equality of all men in the Gospel. The Church, indeed, would have been a specimen of a singular sort of constitution, such as the world has never seen, had it been developed upon its original idea:—an indefinite number of sovereigns[37] elected at a mature age, from and by this respective people, yet not without the necessary approbation and assistance of each other, bound together in districts, absolute within their respective limits, regulated without by fixed laws, and converging to more and more distant points of union, till they terminated in a few, or even a single centre. The waters of this world were not still enough, to allow such a system duly to crystallize; but what we do see from the first, and what actually was fulfilled with whatever divergence from the original direction is, religion throwing itself upon the people, resorting to passive obedience as its legitimate defence, in collision with the temporal powers, and again, victorious over them. The martyrdom of St. Laurence[38] is a singular illustration of what, perhaps, in the Apostolic plan, was intended to be the Church's course of action always in like circumstances. As Archdeacon of Rome, he was in possession of the Church's treasure; the civil power demanded it. Here was the problem of which we are in this day reminded daily. How is the Church to have property, yet not be dependent on the State? If the State guarantees its security, it has a right to interfere. This is instanced at the present time, even as to the miscellaneous and liberty-loving sects of the

[152] American Union. There, an Independent or Baptist communion, we believe, *cannot* expel one of its members without showing cause to the State that the proceeding is equitable. Why? Because the religious body being chartered for the legal

---

[37] *sovereigns*: i.e. bishops
[38] *the martyrdom of St. Laurence*: in 258.

possession of property, excommunication is a civil injury to the ejected party, unless he has violated the fundamental rules of the corporation. Profession of certain doctrines may, of course, be made one of the conditions of membership, and, when the case turns upon points of doctrine, the State does not interfere; but the previous question, whether or not it is a point of doctrine that is in dispute, falls, as we understand, under the cognizance of the civil courts. Such is the consequence of accepting the protection of the State; what is the consequence of refusing it? Does it imply the necessity of surrendering or being robbed of the Church's property, when it is demanded by the civil power? St. Laurence answers in the negative.[39] He refuses to give it up, and is burned for refusing. Doubtless, in the long run, the gridiron of St. Laurence would be found a more effectual guarantee of Church property than a coronation oath or an act of parliament. A broiling here and there, once or twice a century, would, on the whole, have ensured to the Church the unmolested enjoyment of her property throughout her dominions down to this day. Public opinion and long precedent would have ultimately protected the persecuted without law.

The opposition made by St. Ambrose[40] to the Empress Justina,[41] affords a second illustration of the successful employment, on the part of the Church, of non-resistance and passive maintenance of the truth, in her dealings with the princes of this world. Such conduct brought the multitude on his side, as by a natural law; and that illustrious bishop, by merely doing nothing, was able to overcome the imperial court, just as the [153] Apostles may be supposed in some cases to have incited the

---

[39] *St. Laurence answers in the negative*: When the Roman authorities demanded that Laurence hand over the Church's treasure of which he had charge as one of the deacons, he asked for three days, during which time he distributed it among the poor. He then gathered the poor and infirm and presented them to the Prefect, saying 'Here is the Church's treasure.' For this he was martyred by being burnt alive on a gridiron.
[40] *St. Ambrose*: c.337-397, Bishop of Milan and Doctor of the Church.
[41] *the Empress Justina*: Justina, mother of the western emperor Valentinian II, was, like him, an Arian. In 385 she and Valentinian demanded that Ambrose hand over one of the churches in Milan for Arian worship. Ambrose refused, barricading himself and the congregation inside the church, and Justina and Valentinian did not dare to use force against him.

enthusiasm of spectators by their miracles, and to have effected cures involuntarily, over and above their supernatural powers, by the sympathetic influence of the imagination.

Such is the basis on which the Papacy, with whatever corruptions, has been reared. The second and third Gregories[42] appealed to the people against the emperor, in order to establish image-worship. Upon the same basis, as is notorious, was built the ecclesiastical monarchy. It was not the breath of princes or the smiles of a court which fostered the stern and lofty spirit of Hildebrand[43] and Innocent.[44] It was the neglect of self, the renunciation of worldly pomp and ease, the appeal to the people. "The scandals of the tenth century," says Gibbon,[45] "were obliterated by the *austere and more dangerous virtues* of Gregory the Seventh and his successors; and in the ambitious contests which they maintained for the rights of the Church, their sufferings or their success must equally tend to increase the popular veneration. They sometimes wandered in poverty and exile, the victims of persecution; and the apostolic zeal with which they offered themselves to martyrdom, must engage the favour and sympathy of every Catholic breast. And sometimes thundering from the Vatican, they created, judged, and deposed the kings of the world; nor could the proudest Roman be disgraced by submitting to a priest, whose feet were kissed, or whose stirrup was held by the successors of Charlemagne"[46] (chap. 69). With this great spectacle of the middle ages before his eyes, M. de la Mennais asks, How has this power come to an end? what is the proximate cause of its loss? what was it the power *consisted* in? History answers him in the spirit of the [154] foregoing passage:—that the power consisted in asceticism; it

---

[42] *the second and third Gregories*: Pope Saint Gregory II (reigned 715-31) and his successor Pope Saint Gregory III (reigned 731-41) both opposed the iconoclasm of the Byzantine emperor Leo III.

[43] *Hildebrand*: Pope Saint Gregory VII (c.1025-85); a reforming Pope, he vigorously promoted the rights of the Church, and specifically of the Papacy, against the Holy Roman Empire.

[44] *Innocent*: Pope Innocent II (reigned 1130-43); also a reforming Pope, he called the Second Council of the Lateran.

[45] *Gibbon*: See above note on p.[23].

[46] *Charlemagne*: (c.742-814), King of the Franks, was crowned Roman Emperor by Pope Leo III.

fell when the Popes condescended to take part in the intrigues of the Italian states as mere temporal princes, instead of ruling by a pure spiritual sway, as might have been, the "luctantes ventos tempestatesque sonoras"[47] of the European world. The temporal splendour of the Popedom has been the ruin of its spiritual empire; M. de la Mennais' scheme accordingly is this, that the present Pontiff should utterly neglect his temporalities, take a high line, exert his spiritual powers, throw off the absolute courts who are his present supporters, and place himself at the head of the democratic movement throughout Europe. He writes most eloquently on this subject.

"What strikes one at first sight in Rome, as it is, is the almost entire absence of action, and her humiliating dependence on temporal sovereignties. Immense questions have been mooted in the world; they take possession of all minds, are agitating all hearts, are fermenting through society, and disquiet it as a raging fever; what has Rome said? Not a word. A deep revolution is in process in the bosom of Christendom, the insurgent people shatter in pieces their old laws, their ancient institutions, call loudly for a new order of things, and, being resolved to establish it, violently overturn the obstacles which are put in their way; what has Rome done? Not a thing. Her power is attacked and defended, her doctrine is questioned, from all quarters voices are raised, suppliant voices, Catholic voices. 'Speak,' they say, 'speak[48] that your children may learn from your mouth what to believe; that they may know what to hold by concerning the faith, concerning their duties, nay, concerning your own rights; what has been Rome's answer, what her sentence? Nothing at all. Her authority is ignored, her jurisdiction encroached on by the powers of the world, who shackle, nay break the intercourse of pastors with people, and by force or fraud commit whole populations to schism; what battles has she fought in behalf of her independence, by way of saving from spiritual death these unfortunate portions of Christ's flock? Not one . . .

"The Vicar of Jesus Christ, in the exercise of his divine functions, [155] is dependent on the engagements and interests of the temporal prince:

---

[47] *"luctantes ventos tempestatesque sonoras"*: "the struggling winds and howling tempests", Virgil, *Aeneid*, Book I, line 53.

[48] *'speak* . . . : Newman has inserted quotation marks which are not in the original French text, but he forgets to close them—indeed it is not clear in the French where they should do so.

obliged, in consequence of his relative weakness in the line of pure politics, to temporize with the most dangerous enemies of the Church, in spite of himself he is carried away into a system of concessions which is ever enlarging and must end in the ruin of Catholicism; concessions in the choice of bishops, concessions on points of discipline;—what shall I say? 'He stretches out his hands, and another binds him, and leadeth him whither he would not.'[49] His children are in fear about every one of his acts, and above all about his speaking. How anxiously do they watch his lips, divinely destined to teach the nations, lips from which could proceed at every instant truth in all its power! He whose voice ought to resound through the whole world with an energy all heavenly, is not free for aught but the silent prayer at the foot of the cross. Have we here, then, the Supreme Pastor, the head of the universal society instituted by Jesus Christ? What, then, is our position in it? O Father, whom God has given to guide us in our exile, to show us the way home, if the expression of our grief has in appearance aught of bitterness or rudeness, it is that our affection for you knows no bounds, and that our whole soul is in suffering on seeing that extreme humiliation to which they have reduced you! . . . To justify these condescensions, this deplorable subjection of the Eternal See to the thrones which rise in the morning and fall at evening, the interests of Religion itself are alleged. But what interests can she have apart from the liberty of the ministry, the liberty of preaching, of discipline, and of sacraments? forsooth, she will be persecuted, she will be kept down. What! has she not been persecuted from her first start? Was it not in the bosom of persecution, at the stake and on the scaffold, amid the furious cries of the populace and the crafty shackles of edict-makers, that she made her greatest and most rapid advance? Has she not promises which will not pass away, a force which nothing can overcome?"—Pp. 243-246.[50]

This extract is enough as a specimen of the line of argument taken by M. de la Mennais, and his mode of defending it; and

---

[49] *'He stretches out his hands . . . whither he would not.'*: Cf. John 21:18: 'Verily, verily, I say unto thee, When thou wast young, thou girdedst thyself, and walkedst whither thou wouldest: but when thou shalt be old, thou shalt stretch forth thy hands, and another shall gird thee, and carry thee whither thou wouldest not.'

[50] *. . . nothing can overcome?"*: In this 1871 text Newman makes a number of emendations to the 1837 translation of de Lammenais' text (see the Textual Appendix); presumably he has the original French text in front of him again in 1871. He also does so on p.[159] and p.[170].

whatever be thought of the duty of the Pope under his circumstances, which is another matter, no one can doubt that his temporal power is in fact the immediate cause of his pusillani- [156] mous conduct. We do not mean that he would forthwith start up a Gregory or Innocent if he gave it up, or that his people to the extremities of the Roman Church would at once recognize in him their rightful sovereign and master. That he is at this day a temporal prince, and that he is on the other hand enslaved in spirituals, are rather joint effects of some deeper and more real causes; still it is true that the Papal monarchy proper so depends upon the renunciation of mere temporal dominion, that while the Pope has the latter, he cannot aspire to the former. And if, as our author considers, a universal empire is an object to be desired, the fashions of the world, the pomp of a temporal court, worldly alliances and engagements, wealth, rank, and ease, certainly must be laid aside.

3.

Full of these ideas, M. de la Mennais wished on the Revolution of the Three Days to have established in France what he would consider a purer ecclesiastical system than the existing one. Believing that the Church Catholic was equal to any emergence or variety of human society, he desired her to throw herself upon the onward course of democracy, and to lead a revolutionary movement, which in her first ages she had created. She had risen originally as the champion of suffering humanity; let her now return to her first position. Times indeed far different had intervened; in the last three centuries especially she had ruled by means of secular influences, and her instruments were of a secular character. The order of Jesuits especially, which had fought her battle, was well suited to the circumstances in which through that period she found herself. They were as well fitted for a smooth, polished, learned, and luxurious era, as the [157] begging friars for the centuries before them. But now that their season is over, they are out of place; and nothing is more to be deprecated for the Church than their not understanding this. A time of revolution is at hand; rougher deeds, more sifting and subtle inquiries, more recondite principles, a stronger mode of action, have to be encountered than suit the Jesuits. The Jesuits have been too much men of the world, have had too little depth, too little originality of mind, and independence of conduct, and romance and grandeur of character, to serve the present exigencies of the Church. They have succeeded, not by immediately acting on the people, but by acting upon rulers and great men. "Under a popular government," asks our author, "what would they be? deprived of their peculiar advantage of secular force, reduced to the influence which mind exerts on mind, they will soon disappear in the crowd." The Church must have instruments according to her need. Liberty is the cry of the day; Christian liberty is the idea which the Church must develop, and on which the society which lies before us is to be built. The cry for liberty he considers to be no irreligious or inordinate feeling; it is the voice of truth, of our best nature; it is a religious sentiment, which acts irregularly and extravagantly only because in the existing system it is not allowed legitimate vent. The popular disorders and violences are but perversions of what is in itself holy and divine.

Now here we seem to see the elementary error of M. de la Mennais, an error fruitful in many others, and which betokens him the true disciple of the Gregories or Innocents of past times. He does not seem to recognize, nay, to contemplate the idea, [158] that rebellion is a sin.[51] He seems to believe in the existence of certain indefeasible rights of man, which certain forms of government encroach upon, and against which a rising is at any time justifiable. Accordingly what we, in our English theology, should call the lawless and proud lusts of corrupt nature, he almost sanctifies as the instinctive aspirations of the heart after its unknown good. Such were the cravings of Eve after the forbidden fruit; some such vision of a *summum bonum*,[52] unpossessed but attainable, did the tempter suggest to her. But the promise, "Ye shall be as gods,"[53] seems in M. de la Mennais'

---

[51] *rebellion is a sin*: Cf. The Second Book of Homilies, 21, *An Homily Against Disobedience and Willful Rebellion* (1571).
[52] summum bonum: highest good
[53] *"Ye shall be as gods,"*: Genesis 3:5

system to be a sufficient justification of rebellion. Hence he is able to draw close to the democratical party of the day, in that very point in which they most resemble antichrist; and by a strange combination takes for the motto of his *L'Avenir*, "Dieu et la Liberté."[54]

Starting from this beginning, it is not surprising he should practically quite discard the doctrine, that the "many are always bad;" he seems to consider them only mistaken. The excesses, tumults, and waywardness of popular feeling, all that is evidently sinful and irreligious in what are called "the masses," he lays at the door of their rulers; who, by damming or obstructing the current of their instinctive and most laudable desires after something they have not, have caused it to overflow, or to be furious. We almost could fancy he held that the multitude of men were at bottom actually good Christians: certainly he speaks of them with compassion and tenderness, as mistaken children, who mean only to pursue their own good, but know not how. Here again is a clear connexion between his theology and the popular philosophy of the day. He is a believer in the gradual and constant advance of the species, on the whole, in knowledge and virtue, and here he does but faithfully represent [159] the feeling, nay, the teaching of his own Church. They who look at Antiquity as supplying the rule of faith,[55] do not believe in the possibility of any substantial increase of religious knowledge; but the Romanist believes in a standing organ of Revelation, like the series of Jewish prophets, unfolding from time to time fresh and fresh truths from the abyss of the divine counsels.

"Whether one looks without, or retires into one's own soul," our author eloquently says, "to inquire about this mysterious instinct of the future inherent in every creature, everything warns us that a great transformation is in preparation. Life, withdrawing itself into its recesses, palpitates there with vigour; the outward dress which it has worn is withered by the breath of time. A twofold throe of destruction and regeneration, but the latter scarcely apparent yet to those who do not penetrate beneath the surface, is in operation throughout society.

---

[54] *"Dieu et la Liberté"*: "God and Liberty"
[55] *They who look at Antiquity . . .* : i.e. Anglicans.

Society rejects her old institutions, henceforth dead; she rejects the ideas which animated them, *before reason was raised to a more enlarged notion of right, more exact and pure. New sentiments, new views, announce a new era.* The voices which issue from the ruins of the past, convey to the ears of the young generation strange sounds which astonish them, vague words which they understand not. Full of ardour and confidence, they make for that point in the heavens where they see the light, leaving behind them the ghosts of what is no more, to creep away and utter their wailings in the night. Go back or stop they cannot, if they would. An irresistible power forces them ever onwards. What matter the perils, the fatigues of their march! They say, like the Crusaders, 'It is the will of God.'[56] Genius too is a prophet. From the mountain height she has descried the land far away, where the people shall repose on getting quit of the wilderness; and our posterity, one day possessed of that happy land, shall repeat from age to age the name of him whose voice cheered their fathers during their journey."—Pp. 209, 210.

In consequence, he has very little sympathy with those who, on principle, resist innovations, whether as thinking the changes proposed intrinsically wrong, or, though right in themselves or desirable, yet forbidden to them, and, therefore, if made, to be made by Providence Himself, not by man's taking the first step. He has a keen perception of the truth that Almighty power has promised empire to the Church; but, like Jeroboam,[57] he cannot bear to wait God's time. He is not content with cherishing the promise and making much of it, but he goes about to fulfil it by his own devices. The Pope may, for him, be acting the part of David under Saul,[58] but gets no credit from M. de la Mennais: or, again, he considers the voice of nations and the visible course of things to be God's voice, and a sufficient warrant for our moving according to them,—the fact that things change and

[160]

---

[56] *'It is the will of God.'*: The Crusaders' battle-cry was 'Deus vult!' or 'Deus le volt!'
[57] *Jeroboam*: Cf. I Kings 11:29ff. The prophet Ahijah told Jeroboam that he would become king of ten of the twelve tribes of Israel. Jeroboam later led a rebellion against Solomon's successor Rehoboam.
[58] *David under Saul*: Cf 1 Samuel 16-31. The prophet Samuel tells King Saul that God has removed his Spirit from him; he anoints David as king instead. As David's prowess as a warrior against the Philistines makes him popular, his relationship with Saul becomes increasingly fraught, culminating in his victory over Saul on the battlefield, after which Saul commits suicide.

revolutions take place to be a command to take part in change and revolution. It is not wonderful that, with these principles, he cordially approves of what the Roman Church and Mr. O'Connell[59] are doing in Ireland, sympathizes in their struggle, and holds them up for the edification of the Pope and Papal world.

With such sentiments M. de la Mennais ought to profess utilitarianism to be the true philosophy of political action;[60] and he certainly seems to do so, as much so as if he professed himself an infidel. He almost seems to consider that politics do not admit of being made the subject-matter of duty. The French clergy returned with the Bourbons;—one might suppose there were some old recollections of loyalty, or even vows of allegiance, to attach them, and to excuse their attachment, to the sons of St. Louis.[61] Far from it; he measures the unfortunate family only according to their power of advancing the interests of the Church; and considers they may be cast off without pity, if he does but succeed in proving that it is inexpedient to hold by them. The Church is always free and unshackled with pledge or promise; able to take up or put down any power of the earth [161] at pleasure, as if the duty of self-protection dispensed, not merely with the obligation of forming engagements, but of keeping them when formed. "In a country," he says, "where the sovereignty is in dispute, or civil war is threatening, neutrality is the first interest of the Church, unless it be its first duty."[62] This he applies as a guiding principle to the French Church at the present moment. Doubtless it is sage advice; and it *may* be also honourable; but whether it be honourable or not seems, in his view, an irrelevant question. In like manner, he is not very

---

[59] *Mr. O'Connell . . . Ireland*: Daniel O'Connell (1775-1847), supported by the Irish Catholic Church, led a successful campaign for Catholic Emancipation, giving Catholics the right to serve as members of Parliament and removing other legal restrictions on Catholics. He also campaigned against the Act of Union.

[60] *utilitarianism to be the true philosophy of political action*: Newman has here hardened his criticism from the 1837 text (see the Textual Appendix). Utilitarianism—based on the principle of 'the greatest happiness of the greatest number'—was associated with the political philosopher Jeremy Bentham (1748-1832) whose secular ('infidel') outlook was hostile to orthodox Christian religious belief.

[61] *St .Louis*: St. Louis IX (1215-70), the saintly French king.

[62] P. 59. [N]

scrupulous by what means the Church is supported, provided it thrives and has its way. He will allow the clergy to receive their bread from aliens.[63] "It is an error," he says, "to suppose that Catholics only would support the Catholic clergy. In a country where a religion is universally spread, it draws into its service those even who are strangers to it."[64]

In a word, he is thoroughly political in his views and feelings. Quiet, repose, an invariable course of obedience, without object beyond itself, is, to all appearance, in his eyes a slavery. He sympathizes with the feeling of the day in thinking that energy, activity, bustle, extraordinary developments of intellect, are parts of the high and perfect state of the human mind; and that to be a freeman, is to have the power and will to encroach upon others. He divides modes of life into the ambitious and the selfish, as if thereby exhausting the subject.

"Deprived of political rights, of which the very name is unknown, the Roman population has no part, direct or indirect, either in government or administration. Self is the sole object of every one; [162] and, consequently, putting religion out of the question, gain is all in all with some, present enjoyment with others. Repose, laziness, slumber, interrupted from time to time by spectacles which excite the senses, this is the idea of happiness entertained by men who, notwithstanding, possess still a germ of elevated and energetic sentiments. No public life, nothing in consequence to rouse a noble activity, nothing social:—the established *regime* has a universal influence in the shape of unworthy private interest."—P. 108.

Such is M. de la Mennais' view of the interests and duties of the Roman Church, and we candidly confess we take him to understand it better than the Pope. He lays down, with great truth, the maxim, that of every institution a certain idea is the vital principle, on losing which it dies; and then he proceeds to declare, that popular influence is the life of the papacy. That wonderful power has, indeed, been like some Grecian demagogue, some Dionysius of Syracuse;[65] it has been a tyranny

[63] *aliens*: i.e. non-Catholics
[64] P. 78. [N]

based on democratic institutions. Its aristocratical influences have arisen, not from the framework of its polity so much as from the spirit of its worship, which retains, in great measure, the reverence, sanctity, and highmindedness of the real Gospel. Religious awe has refined and ennobled what else would have been rude and popular. But, while its carriage is aristocratic, the true basis of its power is the multitude; and de la Mennais, like a keen-sighted man, has discovered and zealously inculcates this truth. And of this truth he has been the confessor, and, as far as a man can be in these times, the martyr. He has fallen, as might be expected, under the displeasure of the Pope, is in consequence thrown out of all his means of usefulness, and is shunned by his former associates. Such are the consequences of being wiser than one's generation.

4. [163]

The history of this transaction, from first to last, is the direct object of his writing the work, from which we have been making extracts, and gives life to the speculations of which it is made up; and there is so much curious matter introduced into it as to be worth dwelling on for its own sake. It seems, then, that in 1830, on the Revolution of the Three Days, M. de la Mennais, and his friends, who had already taken the Pope's side against the Gallicanism of the Bourbons, (yet without any intention whatever of exalting thereby the Pope as they found him, but of imposing on him duties,) availed themselves of the unsettled state of the relations between the Church and the new government, to advocate the independence of the former in a periodical which they called *L'Avenir*.[66] They perceived that the dependence of the Church on the State, or its establishment, was the one thing on which the new French government was set; and they thence argued, independent of their own particular theory and the recollections of history, that independence was the one thing which it needed.

---

[65] *Dionysius of Syracuse*: Either Dionysius I (c.432-367 B.C.) or his son and successor Dionysius II (c.397-343 B.C.), both of whom were tyrants.
[66] L'Avenir: The Future

"Though the Catholics," he observes, "had not seen by themselves the evil which had accrued to them, and was accruing, from the union of Church and State, they might have divined it from the language of their adversaries. There was, indeed, but one thing they all desired and sought, the maintenance of that union. Read the government journals, follow the debates in the Chambers, listen to the orators in their hostile remarks upon religion and the Clergy; you will find at the bottom of what they urge but this one view,—the State must name the bishops, and superintend the choice of parish Clergy; it must have a hold over the parties intervening between the bishops and the Pope; it must examine the bulls issued by the Holy See before allowing them to be executed; it must hinder the spread of bad, that is, Roman doctrines; in short, it must preserve the supreme direction of spiritual matters, and, in consequence, it must pay the Clergy, since every Clergy which is not paid in one form or other, becomes sooner or later independent, and places the government under the necessity of respecting such independence, or of destroying itself while persecuting religion by fire and sword."—P. 71.

[164]

Here we may observe, by way of corollary upon the doctrine of this passage, that in England the party now in power[67] will ever act towards the Church in the spirit of the policy here explained. We have nothing to fear for the *Establishment* from them. If any party will fight sincerely and stoutly for it, it is that party. They fear the Church too much to let her go; at present they are but weakening her, as they hope, while they retain her. It is the kind and considerate office you perform to birds when you clip their wings, that they may hop about on a lawn, and pick up worms and grubs. Liberals do but want a *tame* Church.

But to proceed:—the *Avenir* commenced in October, 1830, and was continued daily. A month had hardly elapsed when it attracted the attention of government, on occasion of its protesting against the appointment of a liberal bishop. An action was commenced against the editors; and interest was excited in their behalf. A subscription was opened to defray the expenses of the prosecution. When the trial came on, a bold avowal was made of anti-Gallican Romanism on the part of the defendants,

---

[67] *the party now in power*: the Whigs (Liberals)

and an acquittal followed. This was a promising beginning; the *Avenir's* fame spread; its circulation extended; it converted liberals and Protestants; the Roman bishops of Ireland, assembled in council, pronounced it to be, as de la Mennais says, "un journal véritablement Chrétien;"[68] "its words found an echo" in England, Belgium, and the New World, from New Orleans to [165] Boston. A society called "L'Agence Générale"[69] seconded its efforts. Similar journals and similar societies began to rise in other cities of France; when, alas! the authors of the movement found that that Power was against them, whose true interests they were desirous most to subserve. The names "heretics" and "schismatics" began to be applied to them. The reading of their journal was forbidden in many dioceses; on the suspicion of being concerned in it, professors were deprived of their chairs, and parish priests of their livings. "Une inexorable et vaste persécution,"[70] as M. de la Mennais, somewhat rhetorically perhaps, calls it, was projected against these champions of Romanism in its purest and most primitive form. They were attacked in religious publications; injurious motives assigned to their proceedings; their views misrepresented; even their words misquoted. They were accused, most unjustly surely, of being innovators like Luther.[71] But the remarkable thing was, that amid this disturbance the bishops kept still as the grave; no statements were fixed upon for condemnation; all was vague suspicion, surprise, and uneasiness at what seemed so novel and so chimerical.[72] Next the notion spread, not unreasonable certainly, that not clergy, or bishops, or government, or royal-

---

[68] *"un journal véritablement Chrétien;"*: "a genuinely Christian journal;"
[69] *"L'Agence Générale"*: L'Agence Générale pour la Défense de la Liberté Religieuse [The General Agency for the Defence of Religious Liberty] was founded by De La Mennais and his companions in December 1830 and quickly became popular among the younger clergy. It particularly championed the creation of Catholic schools free of state control.
[70] *"Une inexorable et vaste persécution,"*: "an inexorable and wide persecution"
[71] M. de la Mennais's account of Protestantism is as follows, being almost terse and descriptive enough for a Dictionary: "Système bâtard, inconsequent, étroit, qui, sous une apparence trompeuse de liberté, se résout pour les nations dans le despotisme brutal de la force, et pour les individus dans l'égoïsme."—P. 342. [N] "A bastard system, inconsistent and narrow, which, under a misleading appearance of liberty, turns into brutal coercive despotism for nations, and into egoism for individuals."
[72] *chimerical*: wildly fanciful

167

ists, alone were displeased at their proceedings; but that the new Pope himself had to be convinced of the expediency and propriety of them. Gregory XVI., the present Pontiff, had just ascended the papal throne; and in the winter of 1831-1832 the [166] conductors of *L'Avenir* found it necessary to suspend the publication of their journal, after a run of thirteen months, and to repair to Rome for the purpose of vindicating their proceedings.

When they set out, they professed they were only going to ask and to accept the doctrine of truth from the Pope's mouth. "O, father!" they exclaim in their journal, "deign to cast your eyes on some of the lowest of your children, who are accused of being rebels to your infallible and gentle authority. Behold them before you, read their soul; there is nothing there they would conceal. *If one of their views, one only differs from yours, they disavow it, they abjure it. You are the Rule of their doctrines*; never have they held others, never."

Meanwhile the successor of St. Leo and St. Gregory[73] was engaged in certain diplomatic transactions with the schismatical court of St. Petersburg,[74] which indisposed, if not incapacitated him for exercising impartially the high spiritual functions to which his children made appeal. He was providing for the safety of his temporalities imperilled by the seizure of Ancona by the French,[75] and had no heart for authoritatively deciding any new and delicate question in doctrine. M. de la Mennais came to him as an oracle of doctrine, and found him only disposed to give political directions. Nothing can be more discordant, less capable of a common measure, than a question of abstract

---

[73] *St. Leo and St. Gregory*: Pope St. Leo the Great (reigned 440-61) and Pope St. Gregory the Great (reigned 590-604), both examples of saintly popes who defended the interests of the Church with zeal and wisdom. Newman is implicitly comparing Gregory XVI with them unfavourably.

[74] *the schismatical court of St. Petersburg*: i.e. the Russian government which was Orthodox, not Catholic.

[75] *the seizure of Ancona by the French*: The city of Ancona in northern Italy was part of the Papal States. When it was seized by insurgents in February 1831, Pope Gregory XVI's legate negotiated an armistice with the insurgents, but the Pope later changed his mind. Austrian troops and a Papal army ruthlessly suppressed the insurgents in January 1832. France protested at this and on 23rd February occupied the city.

religious truth, and a question of practice and matter of fact, in relation to the measures to be pursued by one secular power towards another; as discordant was the position of the Pope with that of the conductors of the *Avenir*.

The French Revolution in July, 1830, had been followed in no long time by insurrection within the papal territories; Austria intervened to reduce the revolting cities; and France took [167] possession of Ancona to keep Austria in check. These events placed the Sovereign Pontiff between two opposite dangers; his fears from France are intelligible enough; Austria, on the other hand, had always been supposed to covet the portion of the pontifical states on the north of the Apennines; and the suspicion had been so strong in Rome, in 1821, that the government had not allowed the Austrian forces to pass through the city on their way to Naples. Whilst then the Pope was in this unpleasant dilemma, Russia, according to M. de la Mennais, stepped in and offered her aid. She alleged that she could not possibly have any interested views as regards the Italian peninsula, either revolutionary or ambitious, and she offered to place a force at the Pope's disposal to defend him against all emergencies. In return she did but ask, that the Pope would take the part of the Autocrat against Poland,[76] and instruct the Polish Roman bishops accordingly. The offer was accepted on the specified condition.

Such were the matters which occupied the mind of the Supreme Pontiff, during the visit of de la Mennais and his friends. He and they continued there from January to July, and with difficulty obtained an interview with him; the condition being exacted of them, that they would not in the course of it say a word about the matters which brought them to Rome. They then addressed a memorial to him, explaining their views and principles; after some weeks an answer came, in a short note from the Cardinal who had presented it (Pacca[77]), that the Pope's

---

[76] *the part of the Autocrat against Poland*: At this time Poland was partitioned between Prussia, Austria and Russia. In 1830 there was a Polish rebellion against Russia, the November Uprising, which led to the Polish-Russian War, eventually won by Russia. The Pope subsequently wrote an Encyclical Letter to the Polish Bishops, *Cum Primum*, on civil disobedience, stressing submission to the Russian Emperor.

[77] *Pacca*: Cardinal Bartolomeo Pacca (1756-1844).

disapprobation of their proceedings continued, but that the inquiry they had asked was in progress. Finding nothing more could be done, at length they determined to depart; and in their way back they received from Cardinal Pacca, together with a [168] copy of the Pope's Encyclical Letter[78] on his accession, which had just been published, his formal decision concerning themselves. The Cardinal was instructed to express the Pope's satisfaction at their dutiful conduct in submitting their doctrines to his judgment; that he undertook the more readily the examination of them, as having been addressed by bishops from all quarters, who desired the solemn decision of the Infallible See on the doctrines of the *Avenir*, doctrines which had excited so much attention, and occasioned so much division among the clergy; that accordingly he had made mention of them in his Encyclical Letter; that it pained him to see that they brought before the public delicate matters, which belonged to himself to determine; that he condemned their doctrines relative to civil liberty, toleration, and the liberty of the press; that "though, *under certain circumstances, prudence tolerates error as the less evil, these things should never be represented by a Catholic as good or desirable in themselves*;" lastly, that he was relieved by recollecting the solemn and commendable promise they had made and published, that they would accord "an unqualified submission to the Vicar of Jesus Christ."[79]

Now, at first sight, one might think the whole matter settled; here are Catholics asking the Pope's commands, and they receive them; they represent themselves as his dear and devoted and most afflicted sons, and entreat him to rescue them from the painful state of suspense and indecision which his silence occasions. The Pope at length opens "his oracular mouth;" what remains but to obey? nothing less: a new and large question arises, viz., to decide in what cases and about what things obedience is due to the Pope; and M. de la Mennais, in spite of [169] his contempt for Protestantism, likes his private judgment, and,

---

[78] *the Pope's Encyclical Letter: Mirari Vos*, which condemned many of the libertarian principles which Lammenais held, though without mentioning him by name.
[79] Pp. 155, 156. [N]

in spite of his fear of National Religion, almost relapses into Gallicanism, when he finds he must give way, if the Pope does not.

A Roman Catholic is bound to believe the Pope's decision as true in matters of doctrine, and to submit to it as imperative in matters of discipline; but the critical question is, what are matters of doctrine? The Church is supposed to declare "the word of God"—but she cannot declare more than she has received; what are the limits of the revelation, and of her message? Are the questions of civil liberty, the liberty of the press, and the like, included in it? can they in consequence be turned into points of faith? is the Pope's decision concerning them to be *believed* or *obeyed*? The Pope says, believed; M. de la Mennais says, obeyed. He offers, that is, to *yield in his conduct*, he puts an end to his journal, and breaks up his Association. Is not this enough? No; he must receive the Pope's decision with an "interior assent;" he must profess his *belief* that it is *true*. He asks, What is the *medium* by which its truth is recommended to me? if it *be* doctrine, then indeed I do believe it sincerely; for I know fully well that, in spite of all errors in other matters, in spite of corruption of system, of temporalities, political engagements, and whatever else is wrong in the state of Rome, the Pope is assuredly infallible in points of doctrine. He has the whole message of Divine Truth latent in him; this I believe as piously as the Protestant believes that it is all written in Scripture. I assent to it on the same ground on which he assents to what is Scriptural; but after all, is there not a real distinction, such as no one can mistake, between politics and religion, and am I bound to believe the Pope in the former? am I obliged to denounce, for instance, the Polish revolt, as if in obedience to an article of faith? "Such an engagement," he [170] actually says, "is supremely repugnant *to my* conscience. If the profession of Catholicism involved the principle of it, I never should have been a Catholic; for never should I have admitted it, never should I have been able. In every case, to subscribe to it without an inward conviction, without belief, would have been a cowardly and odious lie; not the whole world would have persuaded me to it."[80]

M. de la Mennais then, as is very evident, finds himself brought into a worse dilemma than he describes the Pope to lie in between the French and Austrians. Matters which he maintains are purely political, and which he considers to be so declared by previous ecclesiastical decisions, are forced upon him by Rome as if matters of faith. Which way is he to turn? he refuses to accept them, and defends his refusal, as far as we are able to follow him, in the following simple but very observable manner; viz., he thinks that he has the right of *interpreting* the Pope's words in *accordance* with *his own* interpretations of the previous decisions of the Church. This is worthy of attention, because it shows that objections brought by Protestants in controversy against the Roman theory of infallibility, are not so unreal and subtle as Romanists would represent them; who are apt to reply, that the doctrine *works well*, is easy and intelligible in practice, in spite of abstract difficulties. Now, here we have M. de la Mennais on our side, as an instance in fact, as well as an authority. He seems almost to maintain, that is, as far as he allows himself to think on the subject, that the true sense of previous decisions of the Church may be so clear to the apprehension of men in general, that when [171] a new Encyclical issues from Rome, opposing their interpretation of those decisions in its letter, they are bound to explain it away, rather than to renounce the view of doctrine they have already gained from them. If this be the case, the Romanist is abandoned to his private judgment as well as the Protestant. But let us hear his own words; he thus describes the various feelings of Roman Catholics on the present political position of the Pope:

"One portion of Catholics, in my opinion the most considerable, have hushed their thoughts, repressed the beating of their hearts, shut their eyes, and journey on in silence as moving statues, along the path pointed out to them by the supreme guide. Others comment on his words, and by way of reconciling them with their own views, put on

---

[80] Page 167. [N]

them forced interpretations, inconsistent with each other, and with the simple and clear sense which those words carry with them. They have denied that this sense can be that which the Pope had intended to express; and why? because it appeared to them contrary to doctrines expressly authorized, and shocked their most profound convictions. *They said, not the Pope is mistaken in so teaching, but the Pope cannot so teach, for else he would be mistaken.* Now is it not really to annul a judgment, to assume the right, in any degree whatever, of forming a judgment on it? In matter of Catholic faith, from an interpretation to a judgment is but one step, and an immediate one. Many have thought to escape from the embarrassment in a more simple manner. We are subject, they have said, to the authority of Rome, but only in things spiritual; else we do not recognize it. Good; but who shall determine what is spiritual and what not? If Rome herself, evidently you obey altogether and always; if yourselves, you only obey as far as you please. In the former case, what becomes of your distinction, founded, as it is, on one of the most solemn maxims of Catholic doctrine? in the latter, what becomes of the authority of Rome?

"When such questions are proposed, it is clear there exists a secret struggle in the conscience itself, leading a man on the one hand to bow before an authority which he reveres, but on the other, succumbing to a view which is sovereign within, and of sentiments which master him."—P. 319.

M. de la Mennais says in this extract that Rome has taken [172] up a position which goes far towards involving a *reductio ad absurdum* of her claim to infallibility. We agree with him, and should congratulate him on a discovery which is no news to Protestants, did we not fear that he has too unsubdued a mind to take the discovery religiously. He is a powerful, original, and instructive writer; but there is just that ill flavour in his doctrine, which, in spite of all that is excellent in it, reminds one that it is drugged and unwholesome; and the conviction of this makes one tremble lest the same spirit, which would lead him to throw off civil authority, may urge him under disappointment to deny the authority of Religion itself.

October, 1837.

173

NOTE ON ESSAY IV[81]

THE foregoing article commences with the remark that the "Affaires de Rome," as "coming from the pen of an acknowledged partizan," is not "implicitly to be trusted;" and it ends by determining that "powerful" as is the writer, "there is just that ill flavour in his doctrine as to make one tremble, lest, under disappointment, he should be led to deny the authority of religion." This apprehension, as is well known, was fulfilled in the event. M. de la Mennais lost his faith and withdrew from Catholic communion; his two travelling companions, celebrated men, Montalembert[82] and Lacordaire,[83] happier and more consistent than he, accepted the Pontifical decision, which they had themselves invoked, and kept their promise of unconditional submission, to which they had by anticipation bound themselves.

To put the matter in its true light, I think it well to make an extract from Montalembert's Life of Lacordaire.

"The checkered career of the *Avenir* was drawing to a close. The ardent and generous sympathy called forth by it, was more than counterbalanced by the violent repugnance evinced towards it both by the partizans of democratic absolutism and the tried friends of monarchical authority. The ever-growing distrust of the Episcopate was a much more serious obstacle. To new and fair practical notions, honest in themselves, which have for the last twenty years been the daily bread of Catholic

---

[81] This Note was added by Newman in 1871.

[82] *Montalembert*: Charles-Forbes-René, Comte de Montalembert (1810-70), layman. After breaking with Lammenais, he continued to play a leading role in French ecclesiastical and political affairs.

[83] *Lacordaire*: Jean-Baptiste-Henri Dominique Lacordaire (1802-61), priest, journalist and noted preacher; he subsequently joined the Dominican order.

polemics, we had been foolish enough to add extreme and rash   [174]
theories; and to defend both with that absolute logic, which
loses, even when it does not dishonour, every cause.

"The giving up of the pecuniary indemnity stipulated for the
clergy by the Concordat between Pius VII. and Napoleon, was
one of the vagaries of this logic, precisely similar to that which
today urges certain men to cry for the abolition of the Pope's
temporal power, out of love for his personal freedom.

"Our task was further compromised in the eyes of the clergy,
on the one hand, by M. de la Mennais' philosophical system on
Certitude,[84] which he pretended to make the basis of his politics,
as well as of his theology; and, on the other, by the excessive
Ultramontanism[85] of that great writer, and his first disciples; for
it is well to add, for the information of those who have not
sounded the depths of French fickleness, that at that time
Ultramontane ideas were quite as unpopular with the large
majority of the clergy as Gallicanism is today.

"Finally, our material resources, exhausted not only by a daily
paper, but by so many different lawsuits and publications, ran
short.

"We were consequently condemned to silence, at least for a
time. But at the same time that we announced the discontinuance
of the paper (November 15, 1831, thirteen months after its first
appearance,) we announced the departure of its three chief
editors for Rome, for the purpose of submitting to the Sovereign
Pontiff, questions debated between our adversaries and ourselves, promising beforehand absolute submission to the papal
decision. This idea originated, I believe, with Lacordaire . . .

"No one evinced the least desire to stop them; and it was really
a pity, for this journey was a mistake. To force Rome to   [175]

---

[84] *philosophical system on Certitude*: This was expressed in the second volume of his
Essai sur l'indifférence en matière de religion (1822). 'In the main, his theory is that
certitude cannot be given by the individual reason; it belongs only to the general reason,
that is to the universal consent of mankind, the *common* sense; it is derived from the
unanimous testimony of the human race. Certitude, therefore, is not created by evidence,
but by the authority of mankind; it is a matter of faith in the testimony of the human
race, not the result of free enquiry.' (*Catholic Encyclopedia*)
[85] *Ultramontanism*: literally, 'beyond the mountains–ism' (i.e. the Alps); support for
extreme claims for the authority of the Pope; opposed to Gallicanism or Cisalpinism.

175

pronounce upon questions which she had allowed to be discussed freely for more than a year, was, to say the least, a
singular pretension.

"To be other than infinitely grateful to her for her silence, was
to mistake all the exigencies and all the advantages of our
position.

"Such a mistake can be accounted for in young men without
any experience of the things of the world, and of the Church;
but how account for it, and above all excuse it, in an illustrious
priest, already formed by age, as was the Abbé de la Mennais,
who was at that time over fifty, and who had already lived in
Rome, where Leo XII. had received him with great marks of
distinction?

"From the moment of our arrival at Rome, the cautious
reception everywhere given us showed us plainly that we should
not get the answer we were expecting. After having been asked
for an explanatory memorial, which was drawn up by
Lacordaire, we remained two months without hearing anything.
Then Cardinal Pacca wrote to M. de la Mennais, that the Pope,
whilst mindful of his services and his good intentions, had been
pained to see us moot questions and put forth opinions at least
dangerous; that he would submit our doctrines to examination,
and that, as the examination might be long, we could return to
our country. Pope Gregory XVI. then consented to receive us;
he treated us with that kind familiarity which was natural to
him; he did not reprove us in the slightest; but he did not allude,
even remotely, to the business which had brought us to Rome.

"The solution was certainly anything but brilliant and flatter-
ing, but it was undoubtedly the most favourable we had a right
to expect.

[176]   "Lacordaire was quite prepared for it. He rightly looked upon
it as nothing but a paternal warning, the most delicate imagina-
ble, one that left the least trace, which decided nothing and
compromised no one. During this residence of two months and
a half in the Eternal City, a great peace and light had risen upon
his soul . . . With the penetration that accompanies faith and
humility, he pronounced upon our pretensions the verdict, since

borne out by time, that great auxiliary of the Church and of truth
. . .

"In the meantime, the great writer, who had been called in the tribune the last of the Fathers of the Church, the eloquent and renowned doctor, the aged priest crowned for the last twenty years by the admiration and confidence of the Catholic world, was struggling with all his might against good sense and evidence, as well as against his duty as a Catholic and a priest. The youth had understood all; the formed man, the man of genius, wanted to ignore everything. Prudence, clearsightedness, dignity, and good faith, were all on the side of the disciple, and they became in his mouth so many solemn and pathetic warnings addressed to his cherished master. Vain and powerless attempt! Far from listening to the tender and respectful, but withal firm and honest voice of his young follower, the master foolishly gave way to his temper, and daily broke away further from his antecedents, from everything which ought to have restrained and enlightened him. He listened to none but two or three covert enemies of the pontifical authority; he was already meditating the unnatural alliances which lost him. Faith began to make way for sorry fancies in his soul. After Cardinal Pacca's letter, and the papal audience, Lacordaire resolutely put the following dilemma to him: 'Either we ought not to have come, or we must submit and keep silence.' M. de la Mennais would [177] not agree to this, and answered, 'I will push matters, and urge for an immediate decision; I will wait at Rome, and then make up my mind.' The real priest then took his determination: without overstepping the bounds of the most respectful deference, and distracted, as he himself told me, 'by the agonies of conscience battling against genius,' he announced his resolution of returning to France, and awaiting there in silence, without remaining inactive, the decision of authority:—'Next to speech,' he said, 'silence is the greatest power in the world.' ...

"Before, as well as after his departure, this faithful friend made the most persevering efforts to deliver me as he had himself. Scarcely had he returned to France, when he wrote to me . . . 'If he carries out his plan, remember that all his oldest friends and his most attached colleagues will abandon him, and that, driven by the false liberals into a course in which success is out of the question, there is no language sad enough to tell what will happen ... Let us not yoke our ideas and our hearts together, for the ideas of man, like the clouds which flit across the sun, are bright and fugitive like them.' . . .

"The sequel is well known. M. de la Mennais, after waiting four months, blind to the fact that this long delay was, at the same time, the safeguard of his honour and of his future, lost patience, and left Rome, publicly announcing his intention of returning to France, in order to continue, without any further formality, the *Avenir*.

"Upon hearing this, Lacordaire determined to go into Germany, and spend some time there in studious seclusion.

[178]   "We too took in Germany on our way back to France. Providence threw all three of us together at Munich where we were overtaken by the famous encyclical letter of the 15th of August, 1832, which had been directly evoked by the last threat of the Abbé de la Mennais, and in which, although he was not named, his new doctrines were, for the most part, manifestly condemned."—(Pp. 54-64, Trenor's translation.)

As to de la Mennais, "no one but an Angel or a Priest," said Madame Swetchine,[86] "could have fallen so low." "Prayers," says Montalembert, "went forth during twenty years from a multitude of souls, who hoped against hope, but in vain. No token of reconciliation, no sign of repentance, came to the consolation of those who would have given a thousand lives for the life of that soul. No other shelter has remained for their trust, but the impenetrable immensity of Divine Mercy. Still M. de la Mennais, in plunging deeper and deeper into the abyss, did not drag down with him a single individual. Unless I mistake, he is the only example in the history of Christianity, of a man, who,

---

[86] *Madame Swetchine*: Sophie-Jeanne Soymonof Swetchine (1782–1857), Russian who converted to Catholicism and went to live in Paris where she presided over a salon which attracted leading Catholic intellectuals. She influenced both Montalembert and Lacordaire; her correspondence with the latter was published posthumously.

possessed of everything that goes to the formation of the most formidable heresiarch, did not succeed in tearing away from the centre of unity the humblest of her children."

V.

PALMER ON FAITH AND UNITY.

It has been long observed, and lamented, that rich as our theology is, both in writers and in works, we have very few large systematic treatises for the use of our clergy and of divinity students, such as abound in other religious communities. We have no ecclesiastical historian as Fleury[1] or Mosheim,[2] no fully furnished polemic as Bellarmine,[3] and no dogmatic writer whom we can compare to Petavius[4] or Vasquez. Pearson's work indeed on the Apostles' Creed[5] is a methodical treatise, but not even the lapse of nearly three centuries has given us a standard expositor of the Thirty-nine Articles.[6] Our theology has proceeded in another direction. As a living writer has observed, it has been called forth by the pressure of external and occasional circumstances. For the most part it has not been the production of men detached from secular connexions, or blessed with the solitude of the cloister,—men who lived for the completion of

---

[1] *Fleury*: Claude Fleury (1640-1723), French Catholic church historian, best known for his 20-volume *Histoire ecclésiastique*.
[2] *Mosheim*: Johann von Mosheim (1693–1755), German Lutheran church historian; his works include the *Institutionum historiae ecclesiasticae* and *De rebus christianorum ante Constantinum commentarii*.
[3] *Bellarmine*: St. Robert Bellarmine (1542–1621). A Jesuit, he wrote numerous dogmatic and controversial works, including the *Disputationes de controversiis christianae fidei* and a lengthy controversial exchange with King James I. He was created a Cardinal by Pope Clement VIII and became Archbishop of Capua, known for his reforming zeal. He was declared a Doctor of the Church in 1931.
[4] *Petavius*: Denis Pétau (1583-1652), French theologian. His many works include the *Dogmata theologica* and a number of polemical writings.
[5] *Pearson's work . . .* : John Pearson (1612–86), Anglican theologian and bishop. His *Exposition of the Creed* was published in 1659.
[6] *the Thirty-nine Articles*: statement of the belief of the Church of England adopted in 1563, directed against Catholic doctrines rejected by Protestants.

great works, and whose employments were determined from within; but of those who had the charge of parishes or dioceses, or were confronted with opposition, or stimulated by contemporaneous events. There are indeed some great exceptions, such as Pearson's Comment, already mentioned, Bingham's Antiquities,[7] and Taylor's Ductor Dubitantium;[8]—but on the whole our divines have written, because they were obliged to [180] write, and so far as they were obliged. They have written answers to particular assailants, have grown out of pamphlets into folios, and, like great musicians, have worked out profound movements from subjects which the chance of the moment offered. Thus the works of Jewell,[9] Bramhall,[10] Horsley,[11] and Waterland,[12] are in great measure the gradual increase of controversy with a disputant, developing itself in fresh and fresh replies, handling and elaborating the same matter again and again. Hooker[13] is almost all through his writings engaged with Travers,[14] Cartwright,[15] or their fellows; Bull[16] in his more

---

[7] *Bingham's Antiquities*: Joseph Bingham (1668-1723), Anglican divine, published his *Origines Ecclesiasticae or Antiquities of the Christian Church* from 1708 to 1722.

[8] *Taylor's Ductor Dubitantium*: See above note on p.[45]. Taylor's *Ductor Dubitantium or the Rule of Conscience was published in 1660.

[9] *Jewell*: John Jewel (1522–71), Anglican divine, later a bishop; his *Apology of the Church of England* (1562) argues the case for the Church of England against the Catholic Church and was influential on subsequent Anglican polemic.

[10] *Bramhall*: John Bramhall (1594-1663) Anglican divine, later an Archbishop; his writings defend the Church of England against both the Catholic and extreme Protestant positions.

[11] *Horsley*: Samuel Horsley (1733-1806), Anglican divine, later a bishop; his numerous works include the polemical *Tracts*.

[12] *Waterland*: See above note on p.[75]. Waterland's works include a *History of the Athanasian Creed*.

[13] *Hooker*: Richard Hooker (1554–1600), Anglican divine and influential theologian; his *Of the Lawes of Ecclesiastical Politie* is his best known work. He espoused the 'via media' position of the Church of England.

[14] *Travers*: Walter Travers (1548–1635), English Puritan divine and theologian, was Hooker's Deputy at the Temple Church in London but bitterly opposed to him. Hooker and he had controversial exchanges on the subjects of Scripture and salvation, Hooker adopting a moderate position which included the view that even Roman Catholics could be saved.

[15] *Cartwright*: Thomas Cartwright (1535–1603), English Puritan divine; Hooker opposed his Calvinist views and his extreme Presbyterian criticism of the Church of England.

[16] *Bull*: See above note on p.[75]. Bull's *Defensio Fidei Nicaenae* (1685) argued against Petavius (q.v.) and the Dutch theologian Simon Episcopus (1583–1643) that the ante-nicene Fathers had held the same doctrine of the Trinity that was defined at the

considerable works with Petavius, Episcopius,[17] or Luther. Stillingfleet[18] often requires a comment in the words of adversaries for his illustration. Leslie[19] is controversial from first to last.

This peculiarity of English divinity has its advantages and its evils. There is in consequence vastly more character and life in it than in the divinity of other schools. Men wrote because they felt,—when their feelings were excited, and their hearts thrown open. About Hooker there is the charm of nature and reality; he discourses, not as a theologian, but as a man; and we see in him what otherwise might have been hidden, poetry and philosophy informing his ecclesiastical matter. In spite of his method and exactness, he preaches as well as proves, and his discussions are almost sermons. Bull, again, is, beyond his other traits, remarkable for discursiveness. He is full of digressions, which can only be excused because they are so instructive and beautiful. If he is often rhetorical, he is never dry; and never tires, except from the abundance of his matter. The same remark applies *mutatis mutandis* to Pearson's Vindiciæ[20] and Wall's Infant Baptism.[21] These are certainly advantages, and yet the advantages are not less. Works which have been called forth by particular circumstances require a knowledge of those circumstances to understand them. The late Bishop Lloyd[22] used to say with much truth, that if we did but know the respective occasions which led St. Paul to write his Epistles, we should at

[181]

Council of Nicæa. His *Harmonia Apostolica* (1669-70) argued against the Lutheran view of justification by faith alone.

[17] *Episcopius*: Simon Episcopius (1583–1643), Dutch protestant theologian of Remonstrant or Arminian views (disagreeing with a number of the doctrines of Calvinism).

[18] *Stillingfleet*: Edward Stillingfleet (1635–99), Anglican divine and theologian, later bishop; he took a latitudinarian (i.e. theologically liberal) position, and his works include controversies with both Presbyterians and Roman Catholics.

[19] *Leslie*: Charles Leslie (1650–1722), Anglican divine and controversialist; he published polemical works against the Quakers, Jews, Socinians and Catholics. A 'non-juror', he supported the Jacobite cause.

[20] *Pearson's Vindiciae*: His *Vindiciae epistolarum S. Ignatii* (1672) defended the authenticity of the letters of St. Ignatius of Antioch in answer to the French Hugenot controversialist Jean Daillé.

[21] *Wall's Infant Baptism*: See above note on p.[135].

[22] *Bishop Lloyd:* Charles Lloyd (1784-1829), Anglican divine, Regius Professor of Divinity at Oxford in 182; he was bishop of Oxford 1827-29.

once have the best of comments upon them. The case is much the same as regards our theological writers. A knowledge of the history of their times is one main step towards understanding them. This is a considerable difficulty in the way of making use of them. They are uninviting on first taking up, as requiring some effort of mind in the reader, as alluding to matters of which perhaps he knows little, or as plunging at once into a subject of which he has to learn the rudiments. Again, it is difficult to find in them any particular point which we may want to see discussed. We cannot be sure that the subject will be exhausted, or if so, in what order; before we can make them books of reference, we must have mastered them from beginning to end. And then moreover the most important parts often come in by the bye, where one would least expect it, like the treasures of nature, lying in veins and clefts of the rock, not sorted and set out to advantage as in a market. All this has a tendency to perplex the mind of the student; and in fact nothing is more common than to hear it asked by clergymen, when urged to give attention to theology, "Where am I to begin? how am I to get into the subject? I open a book, and read some pages, and shut it in despair of making anything of my experiment." And even when a student has mastered some great work of our theology, the idea of its subject left upon his mind is often not more complete and adequate than that (to use a familiar illustration) which a ride across country gives of the relative position and [182] importance of the tracts passed over, or which a stroll along green lanes affords of the *lie* of the neighbouring fields and villages. An experienced eye will be instructed, but a stranger will be at once enchanted and perplexed, and will either recollect little of what has passed before him, or will regard it as a picture rather than a reality.

And, moreover, if an inquirer be ill-disposed to receive what he reads, this absence of method and order will greatly strengthen his prejudice against it. Harmony of parts is the external test of a view being real. When one thing fits into another, when all the parts mutually support and are supported, when a theory is capable of accounting for all questions, and thus is, in a certain sense, self-balanced and self-sustained and entire, we have a *phantasia*[23] of truth forced upon our minds, even against our will. In this lies the attraction whether of the Roman or the Calvinistic theology, that, at first sight at least, each theory has no flaws. Now when this appearance is gained by exceeding the limits of the revealed word, (as we conceive it is in the case of those theologies,) it is a mere substitution of reason for faith; but as far as Revelation has joined truths together, and has made one depend and throw light on another, it is not for us to put asunder, what, when viewed as one, enlists the reason, or at least the imagination on its side. Facts are improbable only so far as they are isolated; what is called giving causes to them is in truth only giving them a connexion with other facts. They are said to be accounted for, when they are made parallel with each other, when marshalled in line, and reduced in theory to one common principle. Such is the rhetorical effect of order upon the beholder, whether we call it

[183] consistency as in conduct, or law as in physics, or design as in religion, or system as in theology. And its persuasiveness seems to proceed on the latent principle, that, since nothing can really exist that is self-destructive, or that contains in it the seeds of self-destruction, or, in other words, since the results of any one thing must, as proceeding from one, harmonize and duly adjust with each other, and whereas in consequence things which are discordant cannot result from one principle, therefore there is a probability at first sight that various phenomena, found together, and withal consistent and uniform, do belong, and therefore do witness, to some one real principle existing as the cause of them. Now English[24] theology and English treatises are deficient in this internal presumption of truth, and in consequence are at a disadvantage when an inquirer is suspicious or hostile. Not only are our best writers but partially systematic, but one writer can often, fairly or unfairly, be brought to oppose another, till our edifice seems, from foundation to summit, to be rather a random heap of stones cast together from without,

---

[23] phantasia: imaginary reality; illusory appearance.
[24] *English*: i.e. Anglican.

than a living body developing and expanding itself from within. Hasty reasoners, then, instead of viewing it as a theology, or separating what really belongs to it from what is adventitious or accidental, refer its actual parts to distinct sources, Roman, Lutheran, or Calvinistic, and refuse to consider Anglicanism as anything more than a name for a certain assemblage, in time and place, of heterogeneous materials.

2.

These thoughts are suggested to us by a recent "Treatise on the Church of Christ, designed chiefly for the use of students of theology," by Mr. Palmer, of Worcester College, a work which, not only from the name of its author, but in connexion [184] with the line of thought which we have been pursuing, deserves the attentive consideration of all who have at heart our Church's well-being. It does, in fact, as far as it goes, profess to provide a remedy for the fortuitous origin and personal characteristics of our classical works on theology, being a careful mapping out of its province, as regards some of its most important departments. It is divided into four parts,—on the Notes of the Church as applied to existing Christian communities, on the theological aspect of the British Reformation, on Scripture and Tradition, and on the Church's Authority; and, though this division does not pretend to be very scientific, the separate heads give promise of the methodical treatment of great matters, and the discussions which respectively follow them amply fulfil it.

This work, on which we shall now offer some remarks, will also be found of service, as directed against a distinct class of misapprehensions from those of which we have hitherto spoken. It does the Church a service, not only of a remedial nature, with reference to the unmethodical divinity of the seventeenth, but also as regards the meagre and attenuated divinity of the eighteenth century, though we suppose the author did not intend it. There are at this day, as in the last century, a vast number of religious persons, who think that there is no such science as theology, or, to speak more correctly, that though there be, yet

it has no concern with religion, but rather is prejudicial to it. This opinion must necessarily follow from the ultra-Protestant theory, that every man is his own divine; that divinity, of which every man is capable, being in fact nothing at all. Accordingly it is not unusual, in certain quarters, to speak as if vital truth lay,
[185] as it is sometimes expressed, "in a nutshell," as if there was nothing to learn, nothing to determine. Because Scripture speaks of faith being all in all, and the Apostles say "repent," or "believe in Christ," or "obey," persons consider, sometimes that religion is a certain apprehension of the merits of Christ, and nothing more,—sometimes that it is sincerity and morality, and nothing more. Now it is evidently a great assistance to such speculators, to remove from public view all appearance of a theological system. If persons can be got to forget the fact that there is such a thing as a science professing to be divine in origin as well as in matter, then they will be more easily persuaded that each man can be his own teacher. There is on the face of the case no reason why they should not be. Those who maintain the necessity of teachers, are met with the previous question, whether there is anything to teach. The unlearned condition, then, of our Church during the last century, has favoured the growth of ultra-Protestantism, not only as letting slip the means by which it was to be refuted in detail, but as confirming its main position concerning Private Judgment, by tacitly allowing, as a point confessed on all hands, that there was nothing which individuals might not find out for themselves, that in fact there was no real body of doctrine, no matter of instruction forthcoming, that faith had no objective character, but was either an internal feeling on the one hand, or a good life on the other. This benefit then, if no other, and a great one it is, results from works such as that before us, that the author has claimed for us, or rather reclaimed, a territory, where none was before suspected,—that he has opened the windows which were blocked up, and let in light upon our prison-house, and showed us the fair and rich country which is our portion by inheritance.
[186] He has pointed out large and great questions, more or less bearing upon our personal interests, our most sacred duties, and

our future prospects, which individuals cannot settle for themselves, in which they must depend on others, in which, from the
nature of the case, it must surely be the Divine Will, that they
should accept such guidance as promises fairest, and should
abandon both extremes, whether of seeking an infallible
assurance of their spiritual safety, or of acquiescing in a worldly
security. This is the true exercise of Private Judgment, and to
this Mr. Palmer's book leads,—not the taking up as truth what
comes first, or what we like,—but the patiently guiding ourselves amid the obscurities of our actual position, by those helps
which seem most probably to come from the Father of Lights,[25]
and in using which we shall best approve ourselves to Him.

There is another reflection which suggests itself from an
inspection of Mr. Palmer's work, as compared with those of
some other living writers of our Church. In all important
matters, as being of the same communion, he cannot but agree
with them; yet he so far differs from them in detail, as to show
he cannot be called, in any true sense, of one school or party
with them. No one can be ignorant that in the last few years
there has been a remarkable return in our Church to sounder
principles than have been for many years in fashion. It is not
wonderful that the phenomenon should be attributed, by those
who did not share in it, to the influence of certain places or
persons.[26] They were obliged to do so, by their own disagree-
ment with them; it was a position almost necessary to be
assumed, in order to prove that the opinions in question were
not true. It accounted for the rise and extension of those opinions
which otherwise might have to be referred to their intrinsic
claims upon attention. Now this theory, for it is merely such, is
exposed, as soon as examination is made into the writings of [187]
the different persons who are the subjects of this criticism. The
characteristic of a party theology is a sameness of view in minor
matters; whereas it is undeniable, that in the disquisitions of Mr.
Hook,[27] Mr. Keble,[28] Mr. Woodgate,[29] and our present author,

[25] *the Father of Lights*: Cf. James 1:17.
[26] *certain places or persons*: i.e. Oxford and the Tractarians.
[27] *Mr. Hook*: Walter Hook (1798–1875), Anglican divine and supporter of the Oxford
Movement. He published a volume of sermons in 1837.

we have traces of schools of thought as distinct from each other as is the history of the respective writers themselves. Mr. Palmer, if we are not mistaken, came to Oxford from Dublin; and his work is as independent of the other divines mentioned, as has been his theological education.

And this variety in minor matters between writers, who one and all are upholding the great principles of the English Church, leads to a still further reflection,—that her teaching, as a scientific system, is not yet sufficiently cleared and adjusted. In all the great questions of faith and practice, her voice has ever been plain and decisive; always sufficient for the guidance and comfort of her members. But it is not to be denied, that as regards the intellectual expression of certain truths, or the due development of them, or their bearings upon each other, or their relative importance, much remains to be done. Many difficulties remain to be sifted and settled; the points of mutual agreement, the limits of fair compromise, the line between open and close questions, the generalized forms of parallel views, the best modes of teaching, and the best modes of attacking, and the best modes of receiving an attack, are still to be ascertained in a variety of matters. The view to be taken of history and prophecy, of the world and of the civil power, of the other branches of the Church, of outlying bodies, the rules of Scripture interpretation,—these and other most important matters, have, [188] we do not say, to be determined, for some of them never will be, but to be thoroughly examined, that we may know just where we are, and where others are. And at present each fresh writer is, in some sense of the word, an experimentalist, endeavouring, by his researches into Antiquity, and the exercise of a calm and subtle judgment, to develop justly and accurately, under present circumstances, and in our existing medium of thought and expression, that Truth which the Apostles left behind them.

---

[28] *Mr. Keble*: John Keble;see note on p.[12].

[29] *Mr. Woodgate*: Henry Woodgate (1801-74), Anglican divine and supporter of the Oxford Movement; a Tutor and Fellow of St John's, he became a friend of Newman in 1825 and was present when Mary Newman was taken fatally ill in 1828. He resigned his fellowship in 1837 and became rector of Belbroughton near Birmingham. He dedicated his Bampton Lectures to Newman in 1839.

3.

To this work Mr. Palmer has brought very remarkable powers of mind. We use the word "remarkable" with a definite meaning. No one indeed is a good critic about the ability of a writer to whom he has to come as to a teacher; this is our position towards Mr. Palmer, and this is our disadvantage; but in spite of it, let us be allowed to say what has struck us concerning this author, as a hint to other readers. If then, any one takes up Mr. Palmer's work with the expectation of having the evidence of originality or power forced upon him by it, he will be much disappointed. Though Mr. Palmer often warms with his subject, and writes eloquently, yet we doubt whether there is one sentence in it which men far inferior to Mr. Palmer might not have written. Persons might take it up and lay it down, and wonder what the author was aiming at, accuse it of indecision or inconsistency, or pronounce it to be a feeble production of a very learned man. Its learning, indeed, and its great value as a learned work, no one could doubt; but those who dip into it will most probably resign themselves to the conclusion that it is a useful book of reference for facts, and nothing more. A closer study of it, however, on the part of such [189] persons, would probably change their opinion; and they would gradually discover that underneath the unpretending exterior which it assumes, it is the subtle working out of a system upon a few great principles, which sometimes come to the surface, but are generally hidden. It is an attempt, well weighed and wrought out with great patience and caution, to form, out of the phenomena before our eyes which are presented by the different parts of Christendom, a theory of the Church, which shall be at once conformable to ancient doctrine on the subject, and to the necessities of the modern English communion; an attempt to place us in a position in which we can defend ourselves against both Romanists and sectaries;[30] an attempt to which, as far as we can judge, facts throughout the work are made subservient from beginning to end, though of course we cannot pretend to

---

[30] *sectaries*: other Protestant denominations; Newman uses this term deliberately in order to show that such bodies are not part of the Church.

have actually studied it, except in parts, or with equal exactness everywhere even in these, or have mastered the drift and bearings of other portions of it. And we conceive that Mr. Palmer's view is as original in itself, as it is subtly carried out; by which epithets we neither express praise nor blame, but merely mean to state the fact that, while defending many Catholic truths, he has placed them in a light which has not commonly been adopted by other writers. Without further preface we shall now attempt to draw out some portions of his view, passing, as it does, from positions in which all Churchmen are pretty nearly agreed, to others about which they may fairly differ.

Men find themselves then, he seems to say, (though we are constituting ourselves his interpreters,) with many spiritual wants, with a consciousness that they need a Revelation and a [190] desire to receive it. For a long while Providence left them in this unhappy state, with no certain communications from Him; nay, to this day such is the state of the greater part of the world. But us He has blessed with a message from Him, the Gospel, to teach us how to please Him and attain to heaven; He has given us *directions* what to do. So far all parties, Roman-Catholic, Sectarian, and Anglo-Catholic, agree; but now comes the turning question, *where* those directions are, and *what*? The ultra-Protestant says they are in the Bible, in such sort that any individual taking it up for himself, in a proper spirit, may, by divine blessing, learn thence, without external help, "what he must do to be saved."[31] On the other hand, Mr. Palmer (without of course infringing upon his reverence for the Bible, as God's gracious gift to us, as inspired, and as the record of the whole revealed faith), maintains that not the Bible, but the Church is, in matter of fact, our great divinely-appointed guide into saving truth under divine grace, whatever be the *abstract* power or sufficiency of the Bible. As the ultra-Protestant would say to an inquirer,—"Read the Bible for yourself," so we conceive Mr. Palmer would make the inquirer reply,—"How can I, except

---

[31] *"what he must do to be saved.":* Cf .Acts 16:30.

some man should guide me?"[32] He would consider the Church to be practically "the pillar and ground of the truth;"[33] an informant given to all people, high and low, that they might not have to wander up and down and grope in darkness, as they do in a state of nature.

Then comes the question at once, *where* is the Church? We all know where the Bible is; it is a printed book, translated into English; we can buy it and use it; but where are we to find the Church, and what constitutes consulting and hearing it? Thus we are brought to the first subject which engages Mr. Palmer's attention, viz. the Notes of the Church, the criteria by which she [191] is discriminated and known to be God's appointed messenger or prophet. And here, at very first sight, it is plain that, if the Church is to be an available guide to poor as well as rich, unlearned as well as learned, its notes and tokens must be very simple, obvious, and intelligible. They must not depend on education, or be brought out by abstruse reasoning; but must at once affect the imagination and interest the feelings. They must bear with them a sort of internal evidence, which supersedes further discussion and makes their truth *self*-evident. This is the way in which, as it would appear, the Bible does affect us. It carries with it, in its style, matter, and claims, internal marks of something unearthly and awful. Such evidence may of course be disparaged by sophistry, or the Bible itself may be put out of sight; still these possible contingencies are no disparagement to the innate and practical influence of the Bible in convincing men of its own divinity. And similar evidences of course we are bound to find of the Church's divinity; not such as cannot possibly be explained away or put out of sight, but such as, if allowed room to display themselves, will persuade the many that she is what she professes to be, God's ordained teacher in attaining heaven.

Mr. Palmer is fully sensible of the necessity of plainness and simplicity in the Notes of the Church. Indeed he takes this

---

[32] *"How can I . . . guide me?"*: Acts 8:31. The question put by the Ethiopian eunuch to the apostle Philip, after Philip asked him if he understood the Scripture he was reading.
[33] *"the pillar and ground of the truth;"*: 1 Timothy 3:15.

necessity for granted as an axiom, and uses it freely as an argument for or against particular points in debate. Thence he goes on to assume as an axiom that there can be no real difficulty in finding the true Church. We notice this because it will serve as an instance to illustrate what we have said above, that his [192] work is at first but partially intelligible to readers, from their not understanding the principles on which it is conducted. For instance, the following passages might easily be criticized on this score by persons who opened the book at random, though they are really but simple and natural exhibitions of his main position.

He says:

"The Churches[34] of England *did not necessarily change* their religion because in one age certain opinions and practices were introduced, and in another were corrected or removed. To prove that the Church of England differs, in articles of faith, from her belief in any former age, *it would be necessary to go into a very long examination* of particular doctrines, and of the mode and degree in which they have been held by the Church in different ages, *which would obviously lead to great inconvenience*; *for* the great body of mankind are totally incapable of instituting such a comparison. *Therefore* this objection cannot afford any excuse for being separate from our branch of the Catholic Church."—Vol. i., pp. 245, 246.

That is, Consistency in doctrine is not a Note of the Church: therefore the less the inquirer thinks about her changes, the better. Again:

"As to the other Western synods which were previously held, and which are said to contradict our doctrine, we are prepared to show that they were merely particular synods, not confirmed by Catholic authority; and, moreover, that several of those objected in no degree differ from our doctrine. *This is the position we maintain*; but to enter" [that is, for the *inquirer* to enter] "into a particular examination whether it is well or ill-founded, *cannot be requisite* to determine

[34] *Churches*: Throughout these passages Newman has capitalised 'Churches', 'Church' and 'Catholic', though Palmer did not. He has italicised some phrases, for his own emphasis, and omitted some of Palmer's original italics.

whether the Church of England is a portion of the Catholic Church; *because* it would lead to lengthened investigations *which must be impossible to the great majority of men.* Suffice it to say, that we are *prepared* to prove that the Catholic Church has never condemned any doctrine which we maintain. *This being the case*, there can be *no presumption of our heresy* in any point."—Vol. i., p. 230.

That is, It ought to be enough for the inquirer to know that we are *prepared* to prove our point, and have a case; for how [193] can he be supposed able actually to enter into the proof? And again: "The English and other Churches—

"which differ in some points from her, may yet all be connected by this unity of the Catholic Faith. To prove that either of them is separated from this unity, *we must enter into a most extensive examination* of doctrines in controversy, with a view not merely to ascertain what the truth of Revelation really is, but to determine whether it is believed or denied by particular Churches; or whether the difference is apparent rather than real; whether it is a difference between individuals or Churches; and, finally, whether it is obstinately maintained. The *inconvenience* of such a process, and its *unsuitableness* to the great mass of mankind for the discovery of the true Church, is sufficiently obvious."—Vol. i., p. 231.

Such are Mr. Palmer's initial principles, viz., that the Gospel is to be learned by the individual from the Church; and that the Church is to be known by certain Notes or tokens; and that these Notes are of an obvious and popular character. He comes next to the question what these Notes are; and, taking the Creed for his guide, he has no difficulty in answering. Thence he learns that the Church must be *One*, must be *Holy*, must be *Catholic*, and must be *Apostolic*. These characters he sets down as her Notes. That existing body in any country which bears these marks, he would determine to be that Church once for all set up from the beginning, from which Christ has willed that individuals should learn the words of eternal life.

It is not to our purpose here to enter into the meaning of these characteristics, or to show that they are practically sufficient for the purpose for which they are assigned. We believe them so to be, but we are quite aware that the general opinion of the day will be against both Mr. Palmer and ourselves. This, however, [194] we regard very lightly, and recommend Mr. Palmer to do the same. We disregard it, because it is merely the opinion of the day; a long day perhaps, above a hundred years past, still a day which had a beginning, and assuredly will have an end.

> "The darkest day,
> Live till tomorrow, will have passed away."[35]

So says the poet, and we trust we shall see it fulfilled in the present instance. The English people have had all along the privilege of the Church's presence among them, but their governors have done their best to hide her characteristic badges. At no time, indeed, could they really rob her of what was part of herself, the stamp of features and the royal stature which her Maker gave her; but they have kept her out of the light that she might not be seen, or have put tawdry or homely attire upon her that she might not attract attention. They have shut her up within walls, that, if so be, she might cease to be "Catholic;" have made her eat and drink with sectaries that she might forget her "Apostolic" birth: and, as she could not appear "Holy" while she suffered the latter indignity, neither could she seem "One" while she suffered the former. Indignity, however, has seldom been added; they knew she was too dear to the nation to admit safely of such experiments upon her; so they gave her golden chains, and fed her, not with bread and water of affliction, but in kings' palaces and at kings' tables. However, anyhow, they hid her divine Notes, and in their stead they gave her some of their own special devising. For One, Holy, Catholic, and Apostolic, they have substituted political and civil watchwords, and with such spells they have thought, nay even still think, to work for her those miracles which her divine gifts accomplished of yore. She is, it seems, in the judgment of the day, not "the [195] Catholic Church," but the mere "Church of England," or "the

---

[35] *"The darkest day . . . have passed away"*: From 'The Needless Alarm' by William Cowper (1731-1800).

National Religion," or "the Religion of the majority;" not Apostolic, but "by law established," so that even divines, who really held the doctrine of the Apostolical Succession, have deemed fit to hold it only in their closets, as true indeed but not an influential or practical truth,—a truth which little concerned the multitude, which had no charm in it, which the many could not understand, which was no topic for the pulpit; in short, not as a "Note of the Church:" while in place of Unity and Sanctity they have been full of "our venerable establishment," "part and parcel of the law of the land," "the Episcopal Church," "Protestantism," "the glorious memory," "Martin Luther," and "civil and religious liberty all over the world." In short, they have taken tavern toasts for the Notes of the Church.

4.

Leaving, however, Mr. Palmer and the age to settle it between themselves concerning the respective influence of the old and the modern tokens of the Church's authority, we come to consider certain very serious objections which weigh against the reality of the former in this period of the world. Protestants of course will say that there are no Notes at all, for the Church is invisible; and, even if we suppose that Notes exist at this day, sufficient to determine for us the particular communion which is the very Church set up by the Apostles in the beginning, still what is the use of ascertaining it, considering that our object in ascertaining is to learn thereby the one true teaching, and she, the one true teacher, teaches one thing in this place, and another thing in that? Granting that in each country there is a dominant Christian body, a body such that there can be no mistake as to [196] its superior importance to the rest, and no question of its power of drawing men to join it from the fact of that superiority, still this dominant body (1) teaches different doctrines in different countries; nay, (2) is at enmity with itself, excommunicating itself as found on its right hand or left. Either then there is no longer any Church remaining, or else religious truth is of a variable nature, dependent on time and place, and it matters not what a man believes, so that he conforms to the state of things under which he finds himself. In other words, to attempt in the present state of things to be a Catholic, is (it may be urged) to be in heart a latitudinarian and a liberal; and the only escape from this conclusion is to take refuge in Romanism, which certainly does provide a Church one and the same in many places, as in form so in doctrine.

(I.) The most formidable aspect of the objection is the latter, viz., that the Church itself does not even *profess* to be one; not only differs from itself, but is aware that it differs, being separated into parts, each of which almost denounces, certainly shuns the rest. The Roman, Greek, and English, are its three great portions; and if the English does not reprobate the Roman or despise the Greek, at any rate the Greek and Roman denounce each other, and agree, to say the least, in keeping aloof from the English. Of the three it is obvious that the Roman communion is the least open to the objection, because it is the widest spread and the best organized; it seems to be universal, yet one. Accordingly it professes to dispense with both Greek and Anglican branches, and in many instances has actually carried its own succession into their sees. The Greek Catholics have no pretensions at all to universality; but Anglo-Catholicism might certainly have equalled Romanism in territory, if our Protestant [197] governors had felt any sufficient zeal in its cause. Considering the colonies of England in all parts of the world, it is not easy to estimate what the strength of the English Church at this day might have been, had not ministers been too jealous, and commerce been too avaricious and democratical.[36] However, she has hitherto most honourably refrained from imitation of "the Roman Obedience," as Mr. Palmer calls it, in disowning her sister Churches and identifying her communion with Catholicism. She has accepted their Orders, and respected their territory; though, by the way, it is remarkable that at this very moment a grasping and domineering spirit is at work among us

---

[36] *Considering the colonies of England . . .* : The Church of England had been relatively slow in sending missionaries to British colonies. The first Anglican mission to Africa did not take place until 1759. Newman is suggesting that British governments were more concerned with greedily trading with anyone, whatever their religion ('democratical'), than in spreading Christianity.

in some directions, very unlike that which we have hitherto cherished,—a spirit, which would imitate one of the worst features of the Papacy in past centuries, and tends to interfere with Rome in France[37] and with Constantinople in the Archipelago[38]—which seems bent, after the precedent of Hildebrand,[39] on reducing the whole of Christendom to the model of the reformed Prayer Book[40] and the Thirty-nine Articles.

But to return to Mr. Palmer; he, as might be expected, acknowledges both Greece and Rome in their respective places to be parts of the Church Catholic, though of course only parts; but then comes the anxious question, which must be satisfied before we can safely settle ourselves down in such a theory, viz., whether local bodies which have separated from each other can possibly be part of one and the same body; for if they cannot, we shall be driven perforce either to deny that there is a Catholic Church, or else to deny either the Roman Communion or our own to be part of it. Here, indeed, lies the common stratagem of Roman controversialists. They prove, what is plain enough, that there is one, and can be but one, Church; and then assuming that Rome and England cannot be part of one, they [198] argue, that if one must be taken in preference to the other, surely the Roman Church (allowing ever so much for its shortcomings in point of universality) is far nearer Catholic than the English. Mr. Palmer, however, denies the assumption on which this

---

[37] *to interfere with Rome in France*: In 1825 Matthew Luscombe (1776-1846) was consecrated a Scottish Episcopalian bishop and sent to Paris with continental jurisdiction over Protestants in France.

[38] . . . *Constantinople in the Archipelago*: In 1825 the Consular Advances Act empowered British Consuls to set up Anglican chaplaincies for British citizens, following the dissolution of the Levant Company which had previously been responsible for such arrangements in the Near East. This meant that the British Government was now formally appointing Anglican clergymen in areas such as the Greek Archipelago which geographically were under the jurisdiction of the Patriarch of Constantinople. Newman sees this, and the Paris appointment, as examples of the Church of England infringing on the rights of the Roman and Greek branches of the Church.

[39] *Hildebrand*: See above note on p.[153]. Newman's comparison of Anglican policy to this most notable promoter of the Papacy is deliberately provocative since Hildebrand was a *bête noire* for Protestants.

[40] *the reformed Prayer Book*: the Anglican *Book of Common Prayer*. Newman is implying the absurdity of trying to conform 'the whole of Christendom' to such a specifically English (and Protestant) standard.

conclusion is based; and, heading a chapter with the question "Whether the external Communion of the Universal Church can ever be interrupted," answers it in the affirmative.

This question, indeed, is one of the critical points of the controversy between us and Romanists; Mr. Palmer argues in defence of the English determination of it as follows:—He allows to the Romanist, that, even though different religious societies should agree together in fundamental doctrines, (whatever those doctrines are,) still if they have gone so far as to excommunicate and anathematize each other, they cannot be branches of one and the same Church Catholic; but he denies that breaches short of this extreme character are fatal to unity, or that those which exist between the Roman, Greek, and English communions bear that character. He argues that misunderstandings and quarrels were certain to arise in the Church in the course of years, and, as it extended, quarrels such as could not be settled without a centre of unity which does not exist; that where bishops and churches were free and equal, there was no possible arbiter; that both parties, to a certain extent, would be right, and both wrong; that in consequence they would be so circumstanced that either both parties ought to be reckoned as schismatical, or neither,—both cut off from the Church, or neither; and that while it is impossible to suppose both parties severed from the Living Vine without denying the present existence of the Church and holding that the prophecies [199] respecting her have failed, so it is more accordant to God's known mercies to suppose that He will bear with those human infirmities which are discernible both on the one side and the other. He grants, then, that acts of schism do separate from the Church, but denies that mere estrangement, though a sin somewhere, necessarily involves a schism, in that it is no act of rebellion against a constituted authority; and while Romanists argue *antecedently* in behalf of a centre of unity from the necessary occurrence of estrangements without it, Mr. Palmer argues, from the *fact* that there is no centre of unity, that therefore such estrangements are not schisms.

Again, unity cannot be more strictly a condition of the Christian Church than absence of idolatry of the Jewish; now the Jews did not cease to be God's people *ipso facto*[41] on their idolatry, though they were punished for it; nor do Christian communities cease to be part of the Christian Church, though they break communion, not denying that heavy judgments may be the consequence. Moreover, Mr. Palmer admits that the Fathers sometimes say strong things against the possibility of divisions really existing in the Church Catholic, as when St. Cyprian[42] says, "Unity cannot be severed, nor the one body by laceration be divided;" but he answers that they were not competent judges of a state of things not actually before their eyes. They used statements which were not realized to their minds, except in that form in which we accept them as fully as the Romanists. The Novatians,[43] for instance, in Cyprian's time, were establishing a *rival* communion to the Church in Rome and elsewhere. The point virtually in debate then was, whether *two* true Churches could be rivals in *one* place; but the question whether *two* Churches in *two* places could be in a state of *estrangement*, had never fairly been contemplated at that time, [200] and the words of the Fathers are but words and not ideas, which seem to bear, and do not bear, upon a state of things existing now, but not then.

Further, he argues in favour of his position from the fact that branches of the ancient Church were divided at times from each other, yet neither was considered *ipso facto* cut off from Christ. Thus

"Innocentius of Rome,[44] with whom St. Augustine[45] communicated, was himself not in communion with the eastern Churches."— Vol. i., p. 79.

---

[41] *ipso facto*: by that very fact
[42] *St. Cyprian*: (d.258), bishop of Carthage; he was martyred under Valerian I. The quotation is from his *De Ecclesiae Catholicae Unitate*, 23.
[43] *Novatians*: See above note on p.[129].
[44] *Innocentius of Rome*: Pope Saint Innocent I (reigned 401–17). An energetic defender of the primacy of the Roman see, he was in dispute with some of the Eastern churches over the deposition of St. John Chrysostom whom he supported.
[45] *St. Augustine*: (354-430), bishop of Hippo, Doctor of the Church; he wrote to Pope Innocent about the Pelagian heresy.

"I need not dwell," he proceeds, "on the excommunication of the Asiatic Churches by Victor[46] and the Roman Church; nor on that of Cyprian and the Africans by Stephen,[47] who, when some African bishops came to Rome, forbade the people to communicate with them, or even to receive them into their houses; nor on the excommunication of Hilary of Arles[48] by Leo. In all these cases, different parts of one and the same Catholic Church were separated from external communion. But we may observe instances in which this division was carried to a greater extent, and involved the whole Church. Fleury[49] (himself of the Roman communion) says, with reference to the death of Chrysostom, 'His death did not terminate the divisions of the Churches of the East and West; and while the Orientals refused to re-establish his memory, the Roman Church, followed by all the West, held firm to the resolution she had taken not to communicate with the oriental bishops, especially with Theophilus of Alexandria,[50] until an ecclesiastical[51] council should be held to remedy the evils of the Church."—Vol. i., p. 80.

He then proceeds to mention the division in the time of Acacius of Constantinople,[52] when communion between East and West was suspended. This state of things lasted thirty-five years. And, next, he alludes to the great schism of the West, A.D. 1379-1414, when the Latin Church was divided into two or three Obediences, subject to as many rival Popes, and in great degree estranged from mutual communion.[53] But if division in

[46] *Victor*: Pope St. Victor I (reigned c.189-99); he excommunicated some Eastern churches in the controversy over the date of Easter.
[47] *Stephen*: Pope St Stephen I (reigned 254-57); he was in dispute with African bishops over two Spanish bishops who had been deposed for denying the faith under persecution.
[48] *Hilary of Arles*: Saint Hilary of Arles (c. 403-49); he was excommunicated by Pope Leo I for his attempt to claim primacy over the church in south Gaul.
[49] *Fleury*: See above p.[179]. The quotation is from his *Histoire ecclésiastique,* I, xxii, 13.
[50] *Theophilus of Alexandria*: Patriarch of Alexandria, 385-412; he was involved in various violent controversies, especially the one over St. John Chrysostom.
[51] *ecclesiastical*: Palmer's text has 'œcumenical'.
[52] *Acacius of Constantinople*: Patriarch of Constantinople, 471-89; he was excommunicated by Pope Felix III in the dispute over Acacius's *Henotikon* which attempted to enforce unity among the Eastern churches while ignoring the decision of the Council of Chalcedon. This produced a split between East and West which lasted until after Acacius's death.
[53] *the great schism of the West . . .* : This began in 1378 when the cardinals who had elected Pope Urban VI in Rome changed their minds and subsequently elected another candidate who took up residence in Avignon where the popes had had their court for

the branches of the Church, where there is no rebellion against [201] constituted authority, is not *ipso facto* formal schism, length of time cannot make it such. If thirty-five years do not deprive a secluded branch of its Catholicity, neither does a hundred. The best answer, as Mr. Palmer observes, that Roman controversialists have made to such historical facts, has been to maintain that the estranged parties had right *motives*, and communicated all along with some *third party*. But it may be replied, if so, then that third party, and not the Pope, was the centre of unity. Again, Mr. Palmer disputes the matter of fact, there being no third party, with whom East and West were in communion, in the time of Acacius. Besides, he says that such a circumstance is at best only an alleviation, and does not tend to destroy the fact that there *is* a breach of communion between the parties at variance. Moreover, he acutely remarks that, if good motives, and the internal union kept up by *present* communion with a third party, are sufficient to retain all parties in a state of grace, then the same good motives, and the internal union resulting from *past* derivation from the universal Church, may do the same. And, further, he takes the definition of schism provided by Romanists themselves, and shows that it does not apply to the case under consideration. Schism is said to consist in "a separation from the communion of the Universal Church, which happens *either* when the Church excludes any one from its body, *or* when any one leaves its communion." There is evidently a supposable case, unprovided for by this definition, which is the very case in point; viz., that of the Church's being divided on some question, and each portion simply keeping to itself and discontinuing its intercourse with the other, yet without anathema. Lastly, he shows that Roman theologians allow what he contends for. "We do not pretend," says Nicole,[54] "that the actual [202]

---

some years previously. The two rival popes and their successors were supported by different parts of the church; later a Council at Pisa elected a third pope. The situation was eventually resolved by the Council of Constance in 1414. The Roman popes are regarded as the authentic ones, and the others as anti-popes.

[54] *Nicole*: Pierre Nicole (1625-95), French theologian and controversialist. Palmer's text footnoted the quotations from Nicole as 'Cited by Jurieu, *Unité de l'Église*, p.360, 361.' Pierre Jurieu (1637-1713) was a French protestant who had been in controversy with Nicole.

unity which consists in the *effective union* of all the Church is *essential* to the Church, because this union may be troubled by divisions and contests which God permits." He even lays down two conditions, on observance of which the parties at variance are not to be accounted schismatics,—the first, that "all those who are divided in good faith by some controversy which is not ruled or decided, *tend sincerely to unity*;" and the second, that they must "acknowledge a common judge, to which they refer their differences, which is a *General Council*."

This is an abstract of Mr. Palmer's observations on this important point; and it affords a specimen of the pains and completeness with which his work is executed. And in the same careful way he goes into the Greek and English histories, and shows that, whatever unhappy quarrels exist, no formal excommunications are pending between them and Rome, or between each other. Nor is this mode of treating the subject any evasion of the real difficulty. If, indeed, the question were a moral one, there is no doubt that we are as far separated from Rome as any formal excommunication could make us. Our opinions, habits, and feelings, as a nation, have very little in common with the Roman Church and system. But it is a question of positive religion; the Church Catholic is a positive institution, and its essence, as being such, lies in formal observances; and the same mode of arguing which would infer that the Church had failed, because its portions are *virtually* in schism, would avail to prove that the registration of infants among certain Dissenters is baptism, because, though water is not used, a religious dedication is *intended*.

[203]   5.

(2.) Now let us proceed to the other branch of the difficulty above mentioned, and observe how Mr. Palmer disposes of it. Granting that the Church has not committed suicide in the unnatural warfare of member against member, still the question remains, whether the differences of doctrine within it are not themselves such,—whether Rome, Greece, and England, are not so far opposed in their notions as to what the Gospel is,—that either religious truth is of a variable nature, or it is an absurdity to call the Church of England practically one with the Church of Rome. This is what may be objected; and "what," it may be asked, "becomes of the Notes of the Church, what purpose do they serve, what relief and guidance is afforded to the inquiring mind, if the Church thus indicated preaches Popery in Rome, and Zwingli-Lutheranism[55] in England?" The difficulty is certainly considerable; apparently insurmountable by those who hold that the Roman communion is the communion of Antichrist; for they either contract the Catholic Church into a few countries, with the Donatists[56] of old; or, if they allow Rome to be part of the Church still, in spite of its teaching heresy, they seem to go against the prophecies which speak of the Church's teachers never being removed, nor the Divine Word in her mouth failing.

Mr. Palmer does not seem to consider that the *formal* doctrine of the Roman Church is of so erroneous a nature as it is often considered, though of course he is quite alive to the pernicious characters of the existing Roman system viewed in action; nor does he pursue the mode which most of our divines have taken, when they would rescue her from the extreme sentence which ultra-Protestants would pass upon her. It has [204] been usual with them to contend, that, with all her errors, she "holds the foundation," as they express it, and therefore is to be accounted a branch of Christ's institution, though a corrupt branch. Accordingly, they have employed themselves in determining what the foundation is, or laying down those Fundamentals of faith which are sufficient for the being of a Church, in spite of the wood, hay, and stubble heaped upon them. Now the advantage of this view in the controversy is obvious. If it be once certain what the general range of doctrines is, which

---

[55] *Zwingli-Lutheranism*: the doctrines of Ulrich Zwingli (1484-1531) and Martin Luther (1483-1546).
[56] *Donatists*: A sect, named after its leader Donatus, which arose in the church in North Africa in the fourth century, following the persecution by the Emperor Diocletian. Christians who during the persecution had handed over the Scriptures were known as 'traditores', and the Donatists subsequently claimed that, if clergy, their sacraments were invalid. Only the Donatists themselves, the 'pure', were the true Church. They became widespread in North Africa and had their own bishops. They were condemned by the pope of the day and were the subject of detailed refutation by St. Augustine.

constitutes "the Faith," it is certain what are *not* those doctrines, that is, what are additions to it; and thus we are so far released from the discordant teaching of antagonist Christian bodies, and may throw ourselves on historical evidence, being thereby provided not only with means for opposing such Churches as have added to the primitive faith, but with the satisfaction, while opposing them, of knowing that, while they hold the original deposit or foundation, as well as their own additions, they enjoy the rights and privileges of the Christian Church. We may grant or maintain without inconvenience that those additions are great and serious; and, on the other hand, we may grant without embarrassment the existence of defects in our own system. This is the theory of the *Via Media*. However, Mr. Palmer does not adopt it: he thinks that Fundamentals of faith cannot be assigned; and consequently, since the Catholic Church is promised general unanimity and freedom from error in some sense or other, and since Fundamentals do not exist thus absolutely true and universally received, he is led to consider that she does even at this day preach everywhere, in Rome, London, Constantinople, and St. Petersburg, one and the same

[205]   doctrine, and that, the true doctrine,—except in very minor and secondary points,[57] or except as popular errors interfere with it. This will appear from the following passages.

He observes, for instance, that "it is *very probable* that in reality she," the English Church, "agrees in *all* matters of faith with other Churches, for she admits the same rule,—Catholic Tradition."—Vol. i., p. 226. Speaking of the Oriental Churches, he says, "It does not appear that they differ, in articles of faith, from the rest of the Church. The Roman Churches claim them as agreeing with *themselves* on almost every point; *and* if we may judge by their published sentiments, we should conclude that the Oriental Church, as a body, denies no article of faith

---

[57] *one and the same doctrine . . . minor and secondary points*: Palmer subsequently denied that he had ever said this. See Newman's Postscript to Volume II of *Essays Critical and Historical*, p.[454]. He added that 'in my opinion, several of the errors and abuses of the Roman Church are of a very important nature, and very detrimental to Christian piety, though they be not, strictly speaking, contrary to the article of faith' (ibid).

which we *ourselves* maintain."—P. 182. As to the great Western Councils in the middle ages, "several of those objected to in no degree differ from our doctrine."—P. 230. "We account for the absence of communion between ourselves and other Churches *without imputing heresy, schism, or apostasy* to them or to ourselves."—Pp. 251, 252. Speaking of the Archbishop of Moscow's summary of Christian Divinity (1765),[58] he says, "The doctrine of this work in all matters of faith and morality *appears generally unexceptionable. It only differs from ours* in defending certain practices which we have judged it more wise and pious to remove, and in the verbal dispute about the Procession,[59]" etc.—Vol. i., p. 181. Again: "It is confessed that *some doctrinal errors*, and *some superstitious practices*, prevailed in them [the Western Churches] in latter ages; but,[60] as no article of the faith appears to have been denied or corrupted by these Churches in general, there seems no reason whatever to dispute their Christianity."—P. 277.

Elsewhere he has the following very observable passage:

"Our adversaries, however reluctantly, are obliged to bear witness [206] to the general orthodoxy of our faith. The very points on which we are assailed by some Romanists, are relinquished by others. The points of difference are acknowledged to be but few, by some of their most noted and learned writers; and the Church of England is triumphantly cleared of heresy on every point by their confessions. Are we charged by Bossuet[61] with denying the authority of the Church, and rendering

---

[58] *the Archbishop of Moscow's summary of Christian Divinity*: Metropolitan Platon Levshin (1737-1812) had published *Orthodox Doctrine: or, A Short Compend of Christian Theology* in 1765 before he became Archbishop. It was translated into German and English (by Robert Pinkerton in 1814 as *The Present State of the Greek Church in Russia*) and gained him an international reputation.
[59] *the verbal dispute about the Procession*: The Eastern churches teach that the Holy Spirit proceeds from the Father, whereas the Western church says from the Father 'and the Son'—the famous 'filioque' clause added to the Nicene Creed. Modern theologians would agree with Newman that this does not amount to a substantive theological difference of view on the Trinity.
[60] *ages; but, as no article*: At this point Newman has silently omitted a further sentence in Palmer's text which he had originally quoted (see the Textual Appendix).
[61] *Bossuet*: Jacques-Bénigne Lignel Bossuet (1627–1704), celebrated preacher, prolific controversialist and theologian; later a bishop.

it subservient to the civil power? Milner[62] replies to him, that the Church of England holds on these points the principles of the Catholic Church. Are we accused of denying the Real Presence? Milner and Hornyold[63] acknowledge our perfect belief of that doctrine. I will not here dwell at length on these things; it is sufficient to add, that the Articles of the Church of England have been approved in almost all points by Davenport[64] and Du Pin;[65] and that various Romanists of note have held the difference between us to be so small, as to render a reunion of the Churches by no means impossible."—Vol. i., pp. 231, 232.

He adds in a note the confession of "Dr. Charles O'Conor,[66] by far the most learned writer who has arisen among the Papists of these countries, in modern times;" who says:

"I am confident that above three parts of those debates which separate Protestants from Catholics might be laid aside; that they serve only to exasperate and alienate us from each other; and that if our Church were heard canonically, she would not only reject with horror the false doctrines and notorious abominations so often imputed to

---

[62] *Milner*: John Milner (1752–1826) Catholic bishop and controversialist. Palmer footnoted this reference to Milner's *Letters to a Prebendary*, Letter II.

[63] *Hornyold* : John Hornyold (1706–1778) Catholic bishop and author of several works explaining the Catholic faith. Palmer footnoted this reference to Hornyold's *Real Principles of Catholics*, p.243.

[64] *Davenport*: Christopher Davenport (1598-1680), religious name *Franciscus a Sancta Clara*, Franciscan priest and theologian. Palmer footnoted to his *Paraphrastica Expositio Articulorum Confessionis Anglicanae* (which was published as an appendix to his *Deus, Nature, Gratia* in 1634) but without a page reference. This appendix argued that the Thirty-nine Articles could be interpreted more in accordance with Catholic teaching than was usually supposed. Palmer's footnote also referred to 'Barnes, Catholico-Romanus Pacificus', but again without a page reference. John Barnes (d.1661) was a Benedictine monk of controversial views who ended up confined by the Inquisition; his *Catholico-Romanus Pacificus*, was published in Oxford postumously in 1680.

[65] *Du Pin*: Louis Ellies du Pin (1657–1719), church historian. Gallican in his views, he was accused of unorthodoxy by Bossuet. Palmer footnoted this reference to 'Mosheim, Eccl. Hist. vol. vi. where the heads of Du Pin's Commonitorium are stated in the correspondence relative to Archbishop Wake.' Du Pin had a correspondence in 1718 with the Archbishop of Canterbury, William Wake, about reunion.

[66] *Dr. Charles O'Connor*: Charles O'Connor (1764–1828), Catholic divine. In 1810 he published his controversial *Columbanus ad Hibernos, or Seven Letters on the Present Mode of Appointing Catholic Bishops in Ireland; with an Historical Address on the Calamities occasioned by Foreign Influence in the Nomination of Bishops to Irish Sees.* This took an anti-ultramontanist approach, and he was subsequently excommunicated.

her, but she would also smooth many other difficulties which lie in the way of reconciliation and peace."—*Columbanus*, Letter 3, p. 130.

Such, on the whole, is Mr. Palmer's judgment of the state of Christendom generally. And, speaking in particular of the English and foreign Churches, he says: "Our communion is interrupted by accidental circumstances, misunderstandings, faults, etc., which do not, strictly speaking, involve either party in schism or heresy."—Vol. i., p. 237. "It is true that their [207] Church [the Roman] is in error on several points, and even perhaps in matters of faith, but it seems that they were prevented by so many excusable circumstances from seeing the right way, that we ought not to judge too harshly, and exclude from the Church of Christ so vast a multitude of believers, so many nations, and such a crowd of ancient Churches. . . . Nor is there evidence that any of their doctrines have been ever formally and clearly condemned by the Catholic Church. No one pretends that they have been so; and the truth is, that many of their theologians so explain and teach the doctrines in dispute, that the difference, as represented by them, is in most points not considerable."—P. 286-7. "There is scarcely a point in debate between us, in which our doctrines might not be proved simply from Romish theologians. I have observed a thousand proofs of this."—*Ibid*. "The opinions and practices common to the Western Churches, which were objected to, were not contrary to faith, according to the opinion of the Reformation, evidenced by the Confession of Augsburgh.[67]"—Vol. ii., p. 130.

And on the character of the differences between parties in our own Church at the time of the Reformation he speaks as follows:

"We deny that any new important truth unknown for ages to the Catholic Church, or never heard of before, was promulgated at [the] time [of the Reformation] in the Church of England. We by no means admit that the Royal Supremacy then acknowledged by the Church of

---

[67] *the Confession of Augsberg*: the statement of Lutheran beliefs, presented to the Holy Roman Emperor Charles V at the meeting of the Imperial Diet at Augsberg in 1530.

England was novel. We suppose that some superstitious opinions, commonly received by abuse in some Churches, *e.g.*, the Papal Infallibility and Universal Jurisdiction, Purgatory, Transubstantiation, were suppressed; some doctrines were defined more accurately which had been vaguely and imperfectly held; the Scriptures were more freely circulated; several superfluous and absurd rites were removed, and others were corrected. There was nothing in all this which required any extraordinary mission or superlative sanctity. . . . The Lutherans always, as we know, asserted that they did not differ in any article of faith from the Catholic or even the Roman Church, but only as to certain abuses and erroneous opinions."—Vol. i., p. 429.

[208]

Thus Mr. Palmer seems to hold that the existing Church in every age, in spite of and allowing for the clouds of popular or scholastic error which are upon her, though not of her, is one and the same, sufficient teacher of her children; and, being an ordinance of God so visible, so distinctly marked, so incommunicable in her attributes, can always be found by those who seek for her.

6.

Now we doubt not that many persons fresh from the study of Burnet[68] and Tomline[69] will be moved by some of the above statements;—whom we request to respect the liberty of the English Protestant. The Revolution[70] did not change Articles or Liturgy,[71] though it brought in another mode of thinking; what divines said before it, they may, if they please, say now. We do not indeed concur, as far as we are able to form an opinion, in the particular theory which seems to have led Mr. Palmer to the statements above quoted, but we do vindicate for him in this matter, and for any one who agrees with him, a freedom of

---

[68] *Burnet*: Gilbert Burnet (1643–1715), Anglican divine, strong supporter of William of Orange, later Bishop of Salisbury. A theologian and historian, he wrote a *History of the Reformation of the Church of England.*

[69] *Tomline*: Sir George Pretyman Tomline (1750–1827), Baronet and Anglican divine, later Bishop of Lincoln and then of Winchester. His writings include *Elements of Christian Theology.* Both Tomline and Burnet were strongly anti-Catholic.

[70] *the Revolution*: the so-called 'Glorious Revolution' of 1689, in reality a foreign-backed *coup d'etat* to depose James II because of his Catholicism and replace him with the Dutch protestant William of Orange who invaded with a large Dutch fleet and army.

[71] *Liturgy*: the Book of Common Prayer.

judgment which our Church has never taken from us, and which many of our most revered divines have exercised. For instance, Hammond,[72] as quoted by Mr. Palmer, makes a suggestion, which, if breathed now, would in some quarters create a panic or rouse a persecution:

"As we exclude no Christian," he says "from our communion that will either filially or fraternally embrace it with us, being ready to [209] admit any to our assemblies that acknowledge the foundation laid by Christ and His Apostles, *so we as earnestly desire to be admitted to like freedom of external communion* with *all* the members of *all* other Christian Churches, and would *most willingly*, by the use of the ancient method of *Litteræ Communicatoriæ*,[73] maintain this communion with those with whom we cannot corporally assemble, and *particularly with those who live in obedience to the Church of Rome*."—Of Schism, ch. ix., sec. 3.

Mr. Palmer then has a full right, if he thinks fit, to hold the doctrine which is contained in the foregoing passages of his work; and that, whether the arguments for its truth, which approve themselves to him, are satisfactory to others or not. We shall not here attempt to call them in question; all we profess to do is to draw attention to the state of the case, and show to what his doctrine leads and what it accomplishes.

The received notion in the English school seems to be, as has already been observed, that the faith which the Apostles delivered, has ever existed in the Church whole and entire, ever recognized as the faith, ascertainable as such, and separable (to speak generally) from the mass of opinions, which with it have obtained a footing among Christians. It is considered definite in its outline, though its details admit of more or less perfection; and in consequence it is the property of each individual, so that he may battle for it in his day, how great soever the party

---

[72] *Hammond*: Henry Hammond (1605–1660), Anglican divine; chaplain to Charles I. His writings were influential in the Anglo-Catholic tradition.
[73] *Litteræ Communicatoriæ*: in patristic times, letters of communion signed by their bishop carried by Christians when travelling abroad which vouched for them as genuine members of the Church so that they could receive communion in Catholic churches in other countries.

attacking it; nay, as not receiving it simply from the Church of the day, but through other sources besides, historical and scriptural, he may defend it, if needs be, against the Church, should the Church depart from it; the faith being the foundation of the Church as well as of the individual, and the individual being bound to obey the Church, only so far as the Church holds to the faith. This is the doctrine of Fundamentals,[74] and its peculiarity is this; that it supposes the Truth to be entirely objective and detached, not lying hid in the bosom of the Church as if one with her, clinging to her and (as it were) lost in her embrace, but as being sole and unapproachable as on the Cross or at the Resurrection, with the Church close by, but in the background.

[210]

Now what the advantages of this doctrine are, will be seen by observing the disadvantages of the opposite, which Mr. Palmer adopts; but at the same time it is confessedly a less simple and a more difficult doctrine than his. The chief difficulty obviously lies in determining what *is* the fundamental faith. A number of our most considerable divines have said that it is the Creed; but others take a different view of it. Waterland[75] enumerates no less than eight distinct opinions, besides his own. Mr. Palmer urges this objection with great force, insisting upon the apparent absurdity of laying down, as if to settle controversies, what is more difficult to settle than anything else, and raises more disputes than it even professes to extinguish. In this opinion he agrees with a writer, who has attracted some notice of late, and whose thoughts are not the less deep because they happen to be ardent. "Your trumpery principle," observes Mr. Froude,[76] in a letter to a friend,[77] "about Scripture being the sole rule of faith in *fundamentals* (I nauseate the word), is but a mutilated edition" of the Protestant principle of the Bible and

---

[74] *Fundamentals*: an attempt by some Protestant theologians to state the basic doctrines of Christianity, common to various denominations, belief in which would constitute membership of the Church.
[75] *Waterland*: See above note on p.[75]. Waterland's *Discourse on Fundamentals* was published in 1734-5.
[76] *Mr. Froude*: See above note on p.[v].
[77] *a friend*: Newman; 2nd July 1835.

the Bible only, etc., "without the breadth and axiomatic character of the original."—*Remains*, vol. i., p. 415. It is not the habit
of Mr. Palmer's mind to speak thus absolutely, and he is writing
a formal treatise; yet the following sentences contain as decisive
an opinion on the subject, if less frankly expressed. Of Fundamentals he says, "As an ambiguous term, as conveying no one
definite notion, it seems unqualified to be of any practical utility
in questions of controversy."—Vol. i., p. 122. "It can only cause [211]
confusion and perplexity, while it affords the most perfect
facility to sophistical reasoners to escape from cogent arguments
by changing imperceptibly the sense of the propositions."—P.
127. Thus argues our author; yet surely it is unfair to represent
the question as one about the use of a *word*. With whatever
variations it has been used, still in the mouths of opponents of
Romanism it denotes an idea as well; viz., the idea of a doctrine
fully distinguished from other religious opinions, and already
disengaged from its witnesses, and once for all recorded,
whether this was done in the apostolic or in the primitive age;
and, as being such, it is opposed to the Roman theory of the
faith, as being even down to this hour partially latent in the
Church, and capable of growing into new definitions and being
developed into new members any day. It is indeed as fair to urge
the difficulty of determining *what* the Fundamentals of Faith
are, as, on the other hand, to urge the difficulty of determining
what the Church's formal decision is, whether in the Pope, or
in General Council, or in the Church diffusive; but it might as
truly be said, that the Church's "judgment" was an ambiguous
word, because divines differed in what it consists, as to ridicule
the question of Fundamentals as a verbal dispute, because
Protestants differ one with another what to call fundamental.

We have already said, it is not our intention here to enter
into the question itself; but it should be clearly understood that
it is no trifling point which is in debate,—that, while its decision
this way or that is very important, so again it is one of
considerable difficulty. It appears to us, very plain that the
primitive ages held the existence of a fundamental faith, and
also very hard to determine what that faith was. On the other [212]

hand, the theory that the Church is absolutely our informant in divine truth, is most simple and unembarrassed certainly; but then, if we assume as a principle, we fight to disadvantage against the Romanists, for unless we can appeal to the past, how can we condemn the present? and how can we detect additions unless we know what it is which is added to? Accordingly, Mr. Palmer seems to be led on to hold, that the faith of the Church *admits* of addition; again, that there is no test of apostolic doctrine beyond universal consent, and that any doctrine which has once been generally received must be apostolic, or, in other words, that the majority cannot be wrong.[78] For instance, in answer to the objection of Romanists against the Greeks, that the latter have not received the definitions of faith concerning papal primacy, purgatory, etc., made in the Councils of Lyons, Florence, and others, he does not contend that such subjects are not part of the faith once delivered, and therefore the denial of them cannot be heresy, but "the Western Churches, at the time of such definitions, were not evidently *greater* and more numerous than the Eastern, and therefore their acceptance of the above synods was not a sufficient proof of the approbation of the majority of the Catholic Church."—Vol. i., p. 203. He adds, "This position is of so much importance that it deserves a more particular notice." And after analyzing the state of East and West in this respect, and comparing the number of dioceses in each at various times, with the respective losses of the former

---

[78] *the faith of the church . . . majority cannot be wrong*: Palmer denied that he had said this. 'I have expressly argued against the latter position, vol. ii, p. 136, etc. As to the former, I have distinctly stated that the articles of our faith were but once revealed and admit of no addition, vol. i., p. 89. Perhaps it may be supposed that, in admitting that, before the universal Church has decided some question of controversy, different opinions may be held without heresy, while I hold, that, after the judgment of the Church, there should be no more diversity, I may seem to admit the articles of faith to be capable of addition. This was not my intention; I only mean, that, in the heat of controversy when different opinions are supported by men of learning, it may for a time be doubtful what the revealed truth is, and therefore persons may for a time not receive that truth, may even hold what is contrary to it; and yet, until the authority of the universal Church has decided the question, and left them without excuse, they may be free from the guilt of formal heresy. I only speak here of controversies which the Church had not decided in former ages; or in which the testimony of tradition as well as Scripture is disputed.' (Appendix, *Essays Critical and Historical*, Volume II, p.[455-6])

from the Saracens[79] and the Nestorian[80] and Eutychian[81] heresies, and of the latter in Africa, and again the gains of the former in Russia and of the latter in Germany, Denmark, etc., he concludes:

"There is therefore no probability that the Eastern Church in the [213] middle of the eleventh century, and even long afterwards, *fell short* of the Western, either in the number of its bishops, the extent of its jurisdiction, or the number and variety of the nations it embraced. It is impossible to determine precisely the number of bishops on each side; but there is neither proof nor presumption that the *majority* of the Church took part with the Roman Pontiff against the Greeks; and it is impossible to affirm with any certainty that the Western Churches were greater than the Eastern, up to the period of the Reformation."

Accordingly he takes one by one the Councils of the Middle Ages, and shows that, for one reason or another, they were not really ecumenical, or their decrees consequently binding on our faith. Whether or not we think this necessary, (for some will think that the mere fact that they went beyond the creed or fundamental faith, is a sufficient disproof of their Catholicity,) at any rate it is interesting to see the argument worked out historically, and this Mr. Palmer has done in a very masterly way. Thus against the Fourth Lateran,[82] which is commonly held to have established the doctrine of Transubstantiation, he urges, among other considerations, the following:

"This synod consisting only of Latin bishops, and, having never been received by the Oriental Churches, cannot be considered as invested with the authority of the Catholic Church. It was not acknowledged as ecumenical by the first edition of the Synod of Florence,[83] nor in the licence of Pope Clement VII. for publishing that synod,[84] nor by Cardinal Contarenus,[85] nor by the historians Platina,[86]

---

[79] *Saracens*: i.e. the Islamic invaders.
[80] *Nestorian*: See above note on p.[130].
[81] *Eutychian*: The Monophysite heresy was associated with Eutyches (*c.*380—*c.*456), an archimandrite in Constantinople, who said that Christ did not have both human and divine natures but one fused nature. This teaching was condemned at the Council of Chalcedon in 451. Newman was later to write about the Monophysite crisis in *An Essay on the Development of Christian Doctrine*.
[82] *Fourth Lateran*: Council held in 1215
[83] *the synod of Florence*: the Council of Basel-Ferrara-Florence (1431–45).

Nauclerus,[87] Trithemius,[88] or Albertus Stadensis.[89] The general doctrine of the decree on faith was directed against heretics who denied all that was most sacred in Christianity. But this decree has not the authority which might have been expected, because it appears not to have been made *concilialiter*,[90] with synodical deliberation, discussion, and giving of suffrages; but Innocentius[91] caused it to be read with many others in the presence of the synod, and the bishops seem to have remained silent ...

[214]   "This objection alone would render the authority of such decrees very dubious, according to Bellarmine, Bossuet, Delahogue,[92] etc., for the promises of Christ to aid His Church in determining the truth always suppose the use of ordinary means. These decrees were indeed known in the Western Church afterwards, rather under the name of Pope Innocentius, than of the Lateran synod. Hence, if we admitted that it was the intention of this synod to define the modern Roman opinion of Transubstantiation as 'de fide,' it would not follow that its definition was binding on the Church. ...

"That the whole Western Church believed the common opinion of Transubstantiation not to be a matter of faith, may be inferred absolutely and conclusively from the fact, that while this opinion was held by the majority of scholastic theologians till the period of the Reformation, several other opinions, entirely inconsistent with it, were openly held and taught by writers of eminence, without any condemnation or censure. Durandus a S. Porciano,[93] about 1320, taught that

---

[84] *the licence of . . . that synod*: Palmer footnoted this reference: 'Lauonii Epistolæ, liv. viii. ep. xi. This edition styled the synod of *Florence* the *eighth* synod.'

[85] *Cardinal Contarenus*: Gaspar Contarenus (d.1542). Palmer footnoted this reference: 'Opera Contareni p.563'.

[86] *Platina*: Bartolomeo Platina (1421–81), humanist and historian; his works include *Lives of the Popes* (*Vitæ Pontificum*) published in 1479.

[87] *Nauclerus*: Johannes Nauclerus (c1425-1510), humanist and historian; his *World Chronicle* (*Memorabilium omnis aetatis et omnium gentium chronici commentarii*) was published posthumously in 1516.

[88] *Trithemius*: Johannes Trithemius (1462–1516), abbot, historian, astrologer and occultist; his major historical work was *The Annales of Hirsau* (*Annales Hirsaugiensis*), published in 1514.

[89] *Albertus Stadensis*: Albert of Stade (fl. 13th century), historian; he wrote a *Chronicle* of history from the creation to 1256.

[90] *concilialiter*: in a conciliar manner

[91] *Innocentius*: Pope Innocent III (1160-1261).

[92] *Delahogue*: Abbé Louis Delahogue (d.1830); French refugee theologian who taught at Maynooth College, Ireland; his works include *Tractatus De Ecclesia Christi* (1807) to which Palmer footnoted in a reference to pp.212, 278.

[93] *Durandus a S. Porciano*: Durandus of Saint-Porçain (c.1275-1334), scholastic philosopher and theologian; he wrote a *Commentary on the Sentences* of Peter Lombard

the matter of bread and wine *remain* after consecration. Nevertheless he was so far from being censured, that the Pope made him Bishop of Annecy, and afterwards of Meaux; and he is praised by Trithemius and Gerson,[94] the latter of whom recommended his writings to students in the University of Paris. Cardinal d'Ailly,[95] who presided at the Council of Constance, A.D. 1415, says, that 'although Catholics agree that the body of Christ is in the Sacrament, there are different opinions as to the *mode*. The first is,' etc. ... Thus we see that the common opinion of Transubstantiation was only an '*opinion*,' and that different opinions were held by 'Catholics.' In fine, the scholastic theologians generally mention the different opinions, without imputing heresy to those that receive them."—Vol. ii., pp. 219-225.

Our limits will not allow us to say more on the subject of Mr. Palmer's book, or we should be tempted to set before the reader other specimens of its most instructive contents. It must not be supposed, because we have been led to discuss the main principle of his Treatise, that the work is mainly engaged in laying down principles, and is of an abstract or merely rudimental character. This indeed would be misrepresenting one of the most various, comprehensive, and elaborate works which the [215] present day has produced. But the discussions it contains would at best be but defectively exhibited in a Review, whereas it is both practicable and may prove useful to describe the basis on which the Treatise rests. For till Anglo-Catholics get a clear view of their elementary principles, not merely of the general character of their theology, as to which Mr. Palmer has no

to which Palmer referred in a footnote: 'Durand. Commentar. in Sent. lib. iv. dist. xi. qu. 3. He says, "praedictus autem modus conversionis substantiae panis in corpus Christi constat quod est possibilis. Alius autem modus qui communius tenetur est intelligibilis, nec unus istorum est magis per ecclesiam approbatus vel reprobatus quam alius."' ['It is agreed that the aforesaid mode of the conversion of the substance of the bread into the body of Christ is possible. But there is another mode, more commonly held, which is intelligible, nor is one of these modes more approved or reproved throughout the Church than the other.']

[94] *Gerson . . . University of Paris*: Jean de Charlier de Gerson (1363-1429), French divine, known for his conciliarist theology. Palmer footnoted: 'See the Preface to Durandi Comment, in Sent. Pet. Lombard. Antwerp. 1567.'

[95] *Cardinal d'Ailly*: Pierre d'Ailly (1350-1420), French divine, also conciliarist in his theology. Palmer footnoted: 'Cardinalis de Aliaco in 4 dist. 6, art. 11. cited by Tournely, De Eucharistia, t. i. p. 265. See also Field, Of the Church, Appendix to Part iii. c. 17; Bull's Works by Burton, vol. ii. P.257.'

difference with other Anglican divines, they cannot hope to make a satisfactory fight against the enemies which surround them. Our author's theory of the revealed system issues, of course, in the same opinions and doctrines as that of other English divines; the only question is, as to what is the elementary formula, or key, to which the phenomena of that system may best be referred.

October, 1838.

NOTE ON ESSAY V.[96]

THERE is very little that I feel called on, as a Catholic, to add to the account which I have given above of Mr. Palmer's theory. Of course Catholics will differ from Anglicans in their respective views of the value of historical facts, such as those which Mr. Palmer adduces; for these rarely have in themselves so determinate a direction towards this and not that conclusion, as to be able to resist the stress of the personal tendencies of the controversialist who is handling them. "The Pope made Durandus, who had views of his own about the Eucharistic Presence, Bishop of Annecy;" what is the polemical value of this fact? is it decisive in favour of Mr. Palmer's thesis? or of some little worth? or of no worth at all? and so of all such small facts as are contained in pp. 164, etc. Of course details must be entered into, and facts may turn up which are really "stubborn things;" but, as regards Rome and England, the historical dispute "labitur et labetur,"[97] for neither party can oblige the other to see facts from its own point of view.

Putting aside, then, Mr. Palmer's facts, and turning to his principles, Catholics will not have much to complain of in him. Not only is he, in the work before us, one of the gravest and most temperate of writers, as well as one of the best furnished and most careful, as becomes a theologian, but he goes much farther than most—I may rather say than any—Anglican divines, in his recognition of the basis of argument on which the Catholic system rests. He disowns the *Via Media*, as Anglicans generally understand it; he seems to allow that the [217] Rule of Faith has not been fixed once for all from the beginning;

---

[96] Added by Newman in 1871.
[97] *"labitur et labetur"*: "It glides on and will glide on"; cf. Horace, *Epistles* 1.2.41-4.

he holds that the dogmatic teaching of the Church is capable of increase; that Councils have authority and power to make additions to it; nay, strange to say, that a mere majority of votes in a Council is the voice of the Infallible Church. No wonder that Fr. Perrone[98] says of such a man, in comparison with the other Oxford writers, "Inter eos Palmer doctrinâ et moderatione cæteris præstari nobis visus est;"[99] and, in another place, uses of him, in spite of his many errors, the often-quoted words, "Cum talis sis, utinam noster esses."[100]

Such is the teaching of Mr. Palmer on the Rule of Faith; on the Unity of the Church he is not equally satisfactory. He maintains what is called the "Branch theory;" that is, that the Roman, Greek, and Anglican communions make up the one visible, indivisible Church of God, which the Apostles founded, to which the promise of perseverance was made; a view which is as paradoxical, when regarded as a fact, as it is heterodox, when regarded as a doctrine. Such surely is the judgment which must be pronounced upon it in itself, and as considered apart from the motives which have led Anglicans to its adoption; for these, when charitably examined, whether in Mr. Palmer or in his friends, are far from reprehensible; on the contrary, they betoken a goodwill towards Catholics, a Christian spirit, and a religious earnestness, which Catholics ought to be the last to treat with slight or unkindness.

Let it once be admitted that in certain minds misconceptions and prejudices may exist, such as to make it their duty in conscience (though it be a false conscience) to remain in Anglicanism, and then this paradoxical view of the Catholic [218] Church is, in them, better, nearer the truth, and more hopeful than any other erroneous view of it. First, because it is precept

---

[98] *Fr. Perrone*: Giovanni Perrone (1794-1876), Italian Jesuit priest and theologian; he was influential at Rome, and his many works were widely translated. Newman later got to know him during his period of study in Rome after his reception into the Church. Perrone wrote a reply to Palmer's *Treatise*.

[99] *"Inter eos Palmer . . . nobis visus est;"*: "Among them Palmer seems to us to surpass the others in doctrine and moderation."

[100] *"Cum talis sis, utinam noster esses."*: "While you are thus, I wish that you were ours." Newman himself had quoted this saying in Tract 20, *Of the Visible Church*, applying it to Rome.

of Unity. Such men cannot bear to think of the enormous scandal,—the loss of faith, the triumph to infidels, the obstacle to heathen conversion,—resulting from the quarrels of Christians with each other; and they cannot rest till they can form some theory by which they can alleviate it to their imagination. They recollect our Lord's most touching words,[101] just before His passion, in which He made unity the great note and badge of His religion; and they wish to be provided with some explanation of this apparent broad reversal of it, both for their own sake and for that of others. As there are Protestants whose expedient for this purpose is to ignore all creeds and all forms of worship, and to make unity consist in a mere union of hearts, an intercourse of sentiment and work, and an agreeing to differ on theological points, so the persons in question attempt to discern the homogeneity of the Christian name in a paradoxical, compulsory resolution of the doctrines and rites of Rome, Greece, and Canterbury into some general form common to all three.

Nor is this all; the kindliness of their theory is shown by the strong contrast which it presents to a persuasion, very strong and widely prevalent in the English Establishment, in regard to the Catholic Church. The palmary,[102] the most effective argument of the Reformers against us, was that Rome is Antichrist. It was Mr. Keble's idea, that without this tenet the Reformers would have found it impossible to make head against the *prestige*, the imposing greatness, the establishment, the momentum of Catholicism. There was no medium; it was either from God or from the evil one. Is it too much to say, that, wherever Protestantism has been earnest and (what is called) spiritual, [219] there this odious imagination has been vigorous? Is it too much to say, that it is the received teaching of Anglican bishops and divines from Latimer[103] down to Dr. Wordsworth?[104] Have

---

[101] *Our Lord's most touching words*: Cf. John 17:20-23.

[102] *palmary*: deserving the palm of victory; likely to be successful.

[103] *Latimer*: Bishop Hugh Latimer (c. 1487-1555); burnt at the stake under Mary I for his Protestantism.

[104] *Dr. Wordsworth*: Christopher Wordsworth (1807–85), Anglican divine, Bishop of Worcester and author of a number of theological works.

Catholics then no bowels of compassion for Mr. Palmer, when he, a Pharisee of the Pharisees,[105] by birth and education of the strictest sect of zealots, an Irish Protestant, adopts such a *Via media* towards the Church as I have been describing? He, I know full well, can play the zealot too on an occasion,—as by token, in his Letters to Dr. Wiseman;[106] still these are the writing of Mr. Palmer, the controversialist, not the theologian, and as a theologian I am considering him; and surely, whatever be the personalities in which he thinks it becoming to indulge in the former capacity, and however rightly we protest against him, he may fairly claim our admiration and praise on finding that, in his theological teaching, he is inconsistent enough to show us a goodwill, of which at first sight he seems to be incapable. It is gratifying that, though he will not be a Catholic, he should give it as his opinion that "*some* doctrinal errors and *some* superstitions prevailed among the Churches of our communion, but that no article of faith appears to have been denied or corrupted,"[107] and that men "ought not to judge too harshly or exclude from the Church of Christ so vast a multitude of believers, so many nations, such a crowd of ancient Churches."[108] This is a great improvement on the ordinary language spouted forth against us by Irish Protestants at public meetings, amid "shudders and cheers."[109]

The third motive which leads religious Anglicans to hold the doctrine in question is one of a personal nature, but of no unworthy sort. Though they think it a duty to hold off from us,

---

[105] *a Pharisee of the Pharisees*: Cf. Acts 23:6.

[106] *his Letters to Dr. Wiseman*: *Letters to N.Wiseman, D.D., on the errors of Romanism in respect to the worship of saints, satisfactions, purgatory, indulgences, and the worship of images and relics*, London, 1843.

[107] "some *doctrinal errors . . . denied or corrupted.*": Palmer, *Treatise*, p.276-7. Newman has contracted this quotation, as well as adding the emphasis; the original passage reads: 'It is confessed that some doctrinal errors, and some superstitious practices, prevailed in them in latter ages; but it has already been observed, that the existence of some faults and imperfections by no means annuls the character of a church; and, as in the present case, it arose from want of information and discussion, and besides *no article of the faith* appears to have been denied or corrupted by these churches in general, there seems no reason in general to dispute their Christianity.'

[108] "*ought not to judge . . . of ancient Churches.*": Ibid., p.286.

[109] "*shudders and jeers*": Nineteenth century newspaper reports of meetings gave the audience reactions in such phrases.

they cannot be easy at their own separation from the *orbis terrarum*[110] and from the Apostolic See,[111] which is the conse- [220] quence of it; and the pain it causes them, and the expedient they take to get relieved of it, should interest us in their favour, since these are the measures of the real hold which, in spite of their still shrinking from the Church, Catholic principles and ideas have upon the intellects and affections.

These remarks, however, in favour of the advocates of what may be called the Anglican paradox, are quite consistent with a serious apprehension, that there are those among them, known of course only to God, who make that paradox the excuse for stifling an inquiry which conscience tells them they ought to pursue, and turning away from the light which otherwise would lead them to the Church. And next, as to this paradox itself, all the learning, all the argumentative skill of its ablest champions, would fail in proving that two sovereign states were numerically one state, even though they happened to have the same parentage, the same language, the same form of government; and yet the gulf between Rome and England, which is greater than this demarcation between state and state, men like Mr. Palmer merely call "an interruption of external union."

On this subject, many years ago I wrote as follows:

"It may be possibly suggested that the universality, which the Fathers ascribe to the Catholic Church, lay in its Apostolical descent, or again in its Episcopacy; and that it was one, not as being one kingdom or *civitas*[112] at unity with itself, with one and the same intelligence in every part, one sympathy, one ruling principle, one organization, one communion, but because, though consisting of a number of independent communions, at variance (if so be) with each other even to a breach of intercourse, nevertheless all these were possessed of a legitimate succession of clergy, or all governed by bishops, priests, and [221] deacons. But who will in seriousness maintain that relationship, or that resemblance, makes two bodies one? England and

---

[110] *orbis terrarium*: lit. the world; the whole church throughout the world.
[111] *the Apostolic See*: Rome
[112] civitas: state

Prussia are two monarchies; are they therefore one kingdom? England and the United States are from one stock; can they therefore be called one state? England and Ireland are peopled by different races; yet do not they form one kingdom notwithstanding? If unity lies in the Apostolical Succession, an act of schism is from the nature of the case impossible; for, as no one can reverse his parentage, so no Church can undo the fact, that its clergy have come by lineal descent from the Apostles. Either there is no such sin as schism, or unity does not lie in the episcopal form or in episcopal ordination. And this is felt by the controversialists to whom I am referring, for they are in consequence obliged to invent a sin, and to consider not division of Church from Church, but the interference of Church with Church to be the sin of schism, as if local dioceses and bishops with restraint were more than ecclesiastical arrangements and bye-laws of the Church, however sacred, while schism is a sin against her essence," etc., etc.—*Developm. of Doctrine*, chap. iv., Sec. 2, [chap. vi., sec. 2, ed. 1878]; (vid. also *Loss and Gain*, part ii., chap. 17, 18; *Angl. Difficult.*, Lecture 6.)

VI.

THE THEOLOGY OF ST. IGNATIUS.

THE undertaking which we are proposing to ourselves in the following pages, is one of no small delicacy, but of proportionally great importance; and if we only succeed in making some suggestions for its satisfactory accomplishment, which others may pursue for themselves, we shall deem it worth while to have attempted it.

That a certain system, called Catholicism, was the religion of the whole of Christendom, not many centuries after the Christian era, and continued to be mainly identified with the Gospel, whether with or without certain additions, at least down to the Reformation, is confessed by all parties. The point debated between them has reference to the origin of this system,—when it began, and who began it. Those who maintain its Apostolic origin, are obliged to grant that it is not directly and explicitly inculcated in the Apostolic writings themselves. When they turn for aid to the generation next to the Apostles, they find but few Christian writers at all, and the information to be derived from them to be partial and meagre. This is their difficulty, and the difficulty which we purpose here to meet, by considering how the text of those writers who have come down [223] to us—the Apostolic Fathers as they are called—is legitimately to be treated, and what light, thus treated, it throws upon the question which is in dispute between Catholics and their opponents.

The works of the Apostolical Fathers, we repeat, are short, and their doctrinal declarations, of whatever kind, brief and almost sententious. If, then, they bear witness to what in the following centuries is taught diffusely, they must witness, from the nature of the case, in words which, as being few, admit of a various interpretation more readily than if they were more numerous and explicit. Accordingly, the controversy between those who appeal to them for and against the Catholic system of doctrine, or any portions of it, turns upon this issue—whether the Catholic and later statements are due developments, or but ingenious perversions of those passages from St. Clement or St. Ignatius, which are brought forward as proofs of them. For instance, Clement uses the word προσφορὰ, *sacrifice*, and λειτουργία, or *liturgy*; and Ignatius θυσιατήριον, *altar*; and αἵρεσις, *heresy*. Are the Greek words adequately represented by the English, which convey the more modern or Catholic ideas? Or are these English words but comments, and unfair, untrue comments,—glosses—upon the language of an era anterior to the system of which those words form part? This is the question now to be considered.

1.

It will be seen at once, then, that the state of the case is one in which every reader is likely to make up his mind according to his previous modes of thinking. Men have ever a tendency to explain phenomena of whatever sort on the principles familiar to their own minds, or by their own bias. Thus witnesses in a [224] court of justice unconsciously colour, according to their party feelings, the particulars of a fray, and give very precise and very sincere contradictions to each other on the points of detail, whether of time, of language used, or of conduct, on which the rights of the transaction turn. In like manner, historians explain events their own way, and the followers of opposing religions interpret them on conflicting views of divine Providence. The case is the same as regards the reasons for and against some particular proposition; it is not that each party allows those of the other, and strikes a balance in order to arrive at a practical conclusion; but to the one or the other its own side of the question shines out in the light of unclouded demonstration, and the other appears absolutely weak and contemptible. Each side is unable to feel the force of the case opposed to it, and drops all considerations but those which make for itself. So are we constituted; and in the instance before us, in like manner, unless a document speaks out with extraordinary clearness, it will not impress its own sense, whatever it be, on a reader; but he will consider his own in particular to be the one natural sense, and every other to be strained and perverse. The one party will take it, for instance, as a self-evident truth that θυσιατήριον in Ignatius cannot but mean altar in the modern sense; and the other, that this is a refinement put upon the free inartificial language of a primitive document.

Now how this question is to be settled, what principle is to be adopted in order to assay these conflicting explanations of the state of the case, by what test we are to discriminate a sophistical from a genuine interpretation of a given text, shall be considered presently; here, in the first place, we would insist on this, that, whereas explanations look strange or not, according to our previous bias, therefore their looking strange to us is [225] no reason that they are not true. Accordingly, when a modern controversialist speaks of taking Scripture in a "natural" way, he really means in *his own* way; when he exhorts us to take the words "keep the deposit,"[1] or "we have an altar,"[2] or "the husband of one wife,"[3] "simply and plainly," without reference to the "disputes" and "fancies" by which men have obscured the intelligible meaning of the sacred text, he is only begging us to take the truth of his previous view for granted, and to rule the question on his side; and when he censures the "wildness," or "perverseness," or "subtlety of mind," or "illogical reasoning," which would explain "illumination"[4] of baptism, or "whosesoever sins ye remit,"[5] etc., of sacerdotal power, or any other still more sacred text or phrase of the sacred truth with which the Church has ever identified it, he really does but

---

[1] *"keep the deposit"*: See note on pp.[125-6].
[2] *"we have an altar"*: Hebrews 13:10.
[3] *"the husband of one wife"*: I Timothy 3:2.
[4] *"illumination"*: Cf. Hebrews 10:32.
[5] *"whosesoever sins ye remit"*: John 20:23.

express surprise that he never heard that interpretation before. Prepossession has imposed, and habit has fixed for him, a certain meaning on the words of Scripture; and, as we all know, a man's will is the best of all possible reason; and habit is confessedly a second nature.

We can conceive persons carrying this process of private interpretation to any extent; indeed, whoever takes the trouble to watch what goes on in those around him, or in himself, will have instances at command stronger than he would dare to indulge his fancy in inventing. One remarkable illustration, to which many will bear witness, has occurred in the case of a certain well-known book of religious poems, which need not be more particularly specified.[6] This book, for eight or ten years, was cherished by persons of a great variety of opinions, who [226] saw in it their own doctrines, or at least had very little suspicion, commensurate with the fact, of the unbending churchmanship of the author. The last year or two has discovered what his real views are; and now at length they are detected in his work, and exposed to reprobation in the public prints. A more remarkable instance still is one to which we can bear witness ourselves, though certainly it is one which is not likely to occur every day, of a person of great ability having read the first half dozen of the Tracts for the Times on their original publication, and rising from their perusal without any notion at all, first *what* the doctrine of the Apostolical Succession was; next, that any member of the English Church, nay further, that the said Tracts, maintained it. This seems marvellous; but the explanation, if we may attempt one, was as follows: the individual in question read them with this one view, to see if there was anything "*spiritual*," as he would call it, in them; it was not his object to throw his mind upon them and ascertain what *was* there, but to determine whether something else was not there, or how far it was there; and his *idea* of the Tracts, as of every other subject, was framed upon this artificial division of things in his mind,— not what their real opinions were, or whether they were of any

---

[6] The Christian Year. [N] by John Keble, published in 1827.

opinion at all, but whether they had in them one certain doctrine, which was as distinct from their subject-matter as the types they were printed in, or the paper which they covered.

In like manner, we believe it to be possible, nay and not uncommon, for a student to employ himself laboriously in the Fathers, and yet to attain to as little idea of the rich mines of thought, or the battle-fields which he is passing over, as if he was visiting the coasts of the Mediterranean without a knowledge of history or geology. There is a popular story called "Eyes and No Eyes,"[7] which we need hardly do more than recall to the [227] reader's recollection:—two boys take a walk together, and return the one full and the other empty of intelligence gained in the course of it. Thus students rise from the Fathers, some profited by them, others disappointed, complaining that there is nothing or little in them, or much that is very fanciful; and all because they do not know what to look for, or are possessed with one or more ideas which they in vain seek to find in them. Their notion of the matter of divinity is so different from what prevailed in primitive times, that the surface of their minds does not come into contact with what they read; the points on which they themselves would insist slip on one side, or pass between those of the Fathers; their own divisions of the subject are cross-divisions, or in some way or other inconsistent with theirs. Thus they are ever at cross-purposes with the author they are studying; they do not discern his drift; and then, according as their minds are more or less of a reverent character, they despise or excuse him. At best they call him "venerable," which means out of date and useless. We have known one whom all would have acknowledged to be at the time deeply versed in the Fathers, yet taken by surprise by the question whether bishops and priests were the same or distinct orders in the early Church? as not having even contemplated the question. Again, we know a person[8] who, when he entered on them, read and analyzed

---

[7] *"Eyes and No Eyes"*: 'Eyes and No Eyes; or, The Art of Seeing' appeared in *Evenings at Home,* a book of stories for children by the brother and sister John Aikin and Anna Barbauld, published in 1799.
[8] *a person*: Newman himself.

Ignatius, Barnabas,[9] Clement,[10] Polycarp,[11] and Justin,[12] with
exceeding care, but who now considers his labour to have been
all thrown away, from the strange modern divisions under which
he threw the matter he found in them. Indeed, with our modern
notions and modern ignorance, it will be well if we think the
[228] Fathers no worse than unprofitable reading, and not rather
heretical, Arian or Papistical, as the case may be. Readers of
Justin, for instance, who are unversed in Bull's *Defensio*,[13] are
likely to consider Justin the former;[14] and readers of Cyprian,[15]
who are versed in Milner's Church History,[16] will pronounce
Cyprian the latter. Inconsistency, again, and contrariety form
another class of charges which modern minds will not be slow
to urge against the Fathers: they pronounce that to be unintelligible or self-contradictory which they have not the depth to
reconcile with itself, or the key to explain. It is much more
comfortable to suppose a book to be absurd, than one's self to
be dull; and, as in the fable of the Lion and the Man,[17] moderns

---

[9] *Barnabas*: mentioned in the Acts of the Apostles as one of the early Christians in
Antioch (13:1); he later worked with St. Paul (11:25ff). The *Epistle of Barnabas* was
ascribed to him but is now thought to be of later date.

[10] *Clement*: Pope St. Clement (1st century), second or third bishop of Rome after St.
Peter. His *Letter to the Corinthians* is the first documentary evidence of the Roman
church intervening in the affairs of another church.

[11] *Polycarp*: St. Polycarp (68-155), bishop of Smyrna; he had been a disciple of St.
John the apostle. His *Letter to the Philippians* is extant, as is an account of his martyrdom.

[12] *Justin*: St. Justin Martyr (103-165), layman, author of numerous works of apologetics.

[13] *Bull's* Defensio: see note on p.75. In his *Defensio Fidei Nicaenae*, Bull argued that
the ante-nicene Fathers, such as Justin, held the same faith in the divinity of Christ as
was defined by the Council of Nicaea.

[14] *consider Justin the former*: In his writings the Son appears to be subordinate to God
the Father which would make Justin appear Arian.

[15] *Cyprian*: see note on p.[119]. His view of the Roman See as being the centre of the
Church's unity would make Cyprian appear to Protestants 'Papistical'.

[16] *Milner's Church History*: Joseph Milner (1744-97), *History of the Church of
Christ* (1794–1809) in three volumes, two more being added by his brother Isaac Milner
(1750-1820).

[17] *the fable of the Lion and the Man*: Newman was later to re-tell this fable in his
Lectures on the Present Position of Catholics in England (1851), pp.2-4: 'The Man
once invited the Lion to be his guest, and received him with princely hospitality. The
Lion had the run of a magnificent palace, in which there were a vast many things to
admire. There were large saloons and long corridors, richly furnished and decorated,
and filled with a profusion of fine specimens of sculpture and painting, the works of
the first masters in either art. The subjects represented were various; but the most
prominent of them had an especial interest for the noble animal who stalked by them.
It was that of the Lion himself; and as the owner of the mansion led him from one

have the decision all their own way. The ancient Church cannot speak for herself.

Whatever then be the true way of interpreting the Fathers, and in particular the Apostolical Fathers, if a man begins by summoning them before him, instead of betaking himself to them,—by seeking to make them evidence for modern dogmas, instead of throwing his mind upon their text, and drawing from them their own doctrines,—he will to a certainty miss their sense. We are grieved to see a controversialist go to Irenæus or Cyprian with the so-called "Articulus stantis vel cadentis Ecclesiæ"[18] in his hand, to measure them by; we are grieved for his own sake at his selecting a doctrine, which, though true in itself, and essential in its implicit form, is as unnecessary as an avowed proposition, and as inadequate as an elementary

---

apartment into another, he did not fail to direct his attention to the indirect homage which these various groups and tableaux paid to the importance of the lion tribe. There was, however, one remarkable feature in all of them, to which the host, silent as he was from politeness, seemed not at all insensible; that diverse as were these representations, in one point they all agreed, that the man was always victorious, and the lion was always overcome. The man had it all his own way, and the lion was but a fool, and served to make him sport. There were exquisite works in marble, of Samson rending the lion like a kid, and young David taking the lion by the beard and choking him. There was the man who ran his arm down the lion's throat, and held him fast by the tongue; and there was that other who, when carried off in his teeth, contrived to pull a penknife from his pocket, and lodge it in the monster's heart. Then there was a lion hunt, or what had been such, for the brute was rolling round in the agonies of death, and his conqueror on his bleeding horse was surveying these from a distance. There was a gladiator from the Roman amphitheatre in mortal struggle with his tawny foe, and it was plain who was getting the mastery. There was a lion in a net; a lion in a trap; four lions, yoked in harness, were drawing the car of a Roman emperor; and elsewhere stood Hercules, clad in the lion's skin, and with the club which demolished him. Nor was this all: the lion was not only triumphed over, mocked, spurned; but he was tortured into extravagant forms, as if he were not only the slave and creature, but the very creation of man. He became an artistic decoration, and an heraldic emblazonment. The feet of alabaster tables fell away into lions' paws. Lions' faces grinned on each side the shining mantel-piece; and lions' mouths held tight the handles of the doors. There were sphinxes, too, half lion half woman; there were lions rampant holding flags, lions couchant, lions passant, lions regardant; lions and unicorns; there were lions white, black and red: in short, there was no misconception or excess of indignity which was thought too great for the lord of the forest and the king of brutes. After he had gone over the mansion, his entertainer asked him what he thought of the splendours it contained; and he in reply did full justice to the riches of its owner and the skill of its decorators, but he added, "Lions would have fared better, had lions been the artists.'

[18] *"Articulus stantis vel cadentis Ecclesiae,"*: "the article [of faith] of a standing or falling Church"; originally used by Luther about the doctrine of justification by faith.

formula, and as preposterous as a standard of either Father's works, as if one were to criticise Gothic architecture by the proportions of Italian,[19] or to attempt the mysterious strains of Beethoven on the flute or guitar; and much more, when the modern doctrine which is introduced is actually untenable, such [229] as "assurance,"[20] or as post-baptismal regeneration.[21] Such then is one serious truth which should be kept in view in judging of the Fathers,—that they who come with modern notions will find in them no notions at all; for they are not willing to discern that their writings are Catholic, and they will not be able to find what they are else. And another important position is this,—that they who are versed in their writings are more fitted to have a judgment concerning them, and duly to interpret particular passages in them, than they who are not; and, as this too is very much forgotten at the present day, it will be right here to speak of it distinctly.

Nothing then is more common than a supercilious way of dealing with the writings of the Fathers, as if it were enough to measure the nature and value of their contents by antecedent reasoning, without having the trouble of a personal inspection of them. It is the fashion of the day to consider the plausibility of a theory about them as a warrant for its truth, the question of fact being altogether superseded. For instance, it is common to say that Pagan, Jewish, or philosophical notions came into the Church and corrupted it; now what are the grounds for this assertion? First, because Pagans, Jews, and philosophers were converted; and, next, because there are doctrines and practices in the Church parallel to those which existed among Pagans, Jews, and philosophers; but how far the *actual history* of Christianity substantiates such an hypothesis, is not examined. What abstractedly *may be*, this, it seems, in the given case, *must be*. Again, we may hear it objected to the received account of

---

[19] *Italian*: i.e. classical.
[20] *"assurance"*: the Protestant doctrine that the true believer has a subjective inner certainty that he or she has been saved.
[21] *post-baptismal regeneration*: the Protestant doctrine that the regenerating grace of salvation is given not, as in Catholic, Orthodox and most Anglican teaching, at baptism but in some later conversion event.

this or that early heresy, that our information about it comes merely from opponents, and that it holds good as a general proposition, that the statements of a theological opponent are never to be trusted. Certainly, this is a general truth, but what [230] is that to the purpose in a particular case? Is the evidence of testimony to be peremptorily put aside, as it is by Hume in his celebrated dictum about miracles?[22] Who denies that opponents are often prejudiced, and not to be trusted? and that their testimony therefore is, in all cases, to be narrowly watched? But how does that acquit a critic, in a given case, who will not take that case as it stands? Yet a great many men do make some such grand general sentiment as we have specified an excuse for not inquiring, and yet deciding; not merely for suspending their judgment, as not having time to inquire, but for magisterially absolving this or that heretic, as if they could possibly tell, before going into the case, how far the dictum in question applied, and how far it did not. It is very strange that, while in other sciences the maxim "cuique credendum in arte suâ"[23] is accepted, yet that, in theological knowledge, any one, however ignorant, conceives he can judge for himself, as if the common voice of mankind acknowledged such judgment in theology as a natural faculty. Persons fancy that without reading, or at least by mere dipping into the Fathers, they can describe their characters, enumerate their points of faith, and decide on the interpretation of particular passages and expressions. They conceive that they take luminous views of history, because they confine themselves to their own circle of thought and opinion.

A man says, "I want to write a book upon the Fathers; I know exactly what to think of them, and pretty well what I mean my work to be. I want it to convey to the general reader what I have already in my own mind, a lucid idea of the position they held in the Universal Church, their place in the Divine Dispensation, what they are, and what they are not. They have their excel- [231]

---

[22] *Hume in his celebrated dictum about miracles* David Hume (1711-76), Scottish philosopher and historian. He argued that our experience of the unvarying processes of nature always outweighs any testimony we may hear of an alleged miracle (cf. *An Enquiry Concerning Human Understanding* (1748), Section 10).

[23] *"cuique credendum in arte sua"*: "each man should be believed in his own expertise"

lences and defects, and I mean to be candid towards them. I reverence them, and shall show it; I will point out also where they failed, and show that this was the fault of their age, not of them. I will refute also those who at this moment cry them up in so exaggerated a way; and will set them an example of a calm dispassionate judgment, neither saying too much nor too little. For this purpose, it is necessary that I should read both what the Fathers have written, and what their recent upholders say. This I mean to do; I have got or can command a good library, and the best editions. But first I shall put down my ideas on paper; and to do this, it will be sufficient to make use of Gibbon's Roman Empire,[24] Mosheim's smaller Church History, '*Ante Constantinum*,' his Ecclesiastical Dissertations,[25] Dallæus *De Usu Patrum*,[26] Beausobre on Manicheism,[27] Lardner's Credibility,[28] Jones on the Canon,[29] Basnage's Annals,[30] and parts of Osburn's Errors of the Primitive Fathers.[31] When I have got my ideas into shape, I will consult and pursue the references of these authors, and illustrate my main positions from the Fathers. So much for the ancients; as to their inordinate admirers of this day, I know their views tolerably well already; any one can see through what is a mere revival of Laud's[32] or the non-juring

---

[24] *Gibbon's Roman Empire*: See above note on p.[23].

[25] *Mosheim's* . . . : Johann Lorenz von Mosheim (1693–1755), German Lutheran ecclesiastical historian; author of *Institutionum historiae ecclesiasticae libri IV* (1726), *De rebus christianorum ante Constantinum commentarii* (1753). Mosheim adopted the Protestant view that the Catholic Church had corrupted primitive Christianity.

[26] *Dallæus* De Usu Patrum: Jean Daillé (Latin, Dallæus) (1594–1670), French Hugenot scripture scholar; his *A Treatise concerning the right use of the Fathers* (1651) argued against the Fathers as sources of authentic Christian teaching.

[27] *Beausobre on Manicheism*: Isaac de Beausobre (1659–1738), French Protestant ecclesiastical historian; author of *Histoire Critique de Manichée et du Manichéisme* (1734–39).

[28] *Lardner's Credbility*: See above note on p.[94].

[29] *Jones on the Canon*: Jeremiah Jones (1693-1724), non-conformist preacher, best known for his *A new and full method of settling the canonical authority of the New Testament: To which is subjoined A vindication of the former part of St. Matthew's gospel* (1798).

[30] *Basnage's Annals*: Jacques Basnage De Beauval (1653–1723), Protestant divine, historian and polemicist; author of *Histoire de l'église depuis Jésus-Christ jusqu'à présent* (1699).

[31] *Osburn's Errors of the Primitive Fathers*: William Osburn, *Doctrinal Errors of the Apostolical and Early Fathers* (1835).

[32] *Laud*: William Laud (1573-1645), Anglican High Church divine. As Archbishop of

theology.[33] However, I will be candid to them also, for doubtless they are pious, excellent men, and they advocate what has truth in it, though in an exaggerated form; and they have certainly got some things from the Fathers, good or bad, though they have distorted them." Such is the history of the conception of a great theological work. Our divine then sets about it; he dips into the Fathers, and they confirm his anticipations; he writes rapidly; he sketches off his characters; exhibits the lights and shades of Augustine[34] or Jerome,[35] the leading idea of the Nicene Council,[36] [232] or of the Theodosian Code.[37] He condemns the Fathers for some things; applauds them in other cases; explains away their language in other. He interprets them upon his own modern notions, and calls it vindicating them. He warms with his subject, and becomes eloquent. His book is now written, and the Fathers still are to be read in course;—this is dry work, and time presses; his prospective range of reading contracts; his sense of its obligation fades; he is much more certain that he is right, than when he entered on his subject; what then is the use of reading? He publishes; he is cried up; his name carries weight. He says one thing; Bull or Beveridge[38] says another. Of his readers, one man prefers a writer of the nineteenth century to one of the seventeenth; another thinks his views so sensible and probable as to carry conviction with them; a third rejoices

Canterbury under Charles I he attempted to enforce a more Catholic style of worship and theology in the Church of England. He was eventually outmanoeuvred by his Puritan opponents, charged with high treason and executed.

[33] *non-juring theology*: The non-jurors were those Anglican divines who refused to take the oath of allegiance to King William of Orange, when he came to power in 1688, because it would break their previous oath to James II. They were mostly High Churchmen.

[34] *Augustine*: See above note on p.[200].

[35] *Jerome*: St. Jerome (c. 347–420), priest and Doctor of the Church; author of the Vulgate translation of the Bible.

[36] *the Nicene Council*: The first ecumenical council, held in 325 at Nicæa; it defined the Catholic belief in the divinity of Christ against Arianism.

[37] *the Theodosian Code*: the codification of Roman laws carried out at the command of the Emperor Theodosius and completed in 438. It covered all the laws passed from the time of Constantine and included the legalization of Christianity and various laws against heretics such as the Arians.

[38] *Beveridge*: William Beveridge (1637–1708), Anglican divine, later Bishop of St. Asaph; author of various works drawing on the writings of the Fathers, including *Codex Canonum Ecclesiæ Primitivæ Vindicatus ac Illustratus* (1678).

to be able to argue that since great divines differ, there is no getting at the truth, that anything can be proved from the Fathers, and anything asserted of the history and tenets of primitive Christianity; and a fourth, for the same reason, is really perplexed. Anyhow, *he* has gained his point; he has shown that the arguments of his adversaries admit of question, has thrown the whole subject into the gulf of controversy, and given a specimen how the age of railroads should behave towards the age of martyrs.

Now the elementary fallacy in this process is the notion, that persons who are not familiar with the Fathers are as good judges of their motives, aims, and meaning as those who are. Men fancy, for instance, that though they have never seen Clement or Ignatius, or any other Father before, they are quite as well qualified to interpret the words *liturgia*,[39] or *prosphora*,[40] as if they knew them all well. How different is their judgment in other matters! Who will not grant, except in the case of theology, that an experienced eye is an important qualification for understanding the distinction of things, or detecting their force and tendency? In politics, the sagacious statesman puts his finger on some apparently small or not confessedly great event, promptly declares it to be "no little matter," and is believed. Why? because he is conceived to be a scholar in the language of political history, and to be well read in the world's events. In the same way the comparative anatomist falls in with a little bone, and confidently declares from it the make, habits, and age of the animal to which it belonged. What should we say to the unscientific hearer who disputed his accuracy, and attempted to argue against him? Yet, is not this just the case of those sciolists,[41] or less than sciolists in theology, who, when persons who have given time to the Fathers recognize in some phrase or word in Clement or Ignatius a Catholic doctrine, object that the connexion between the phrase and the doctrine is not clear *to them*, and allow nothing to the judgment of the

[233]

---

[39] *liturgia*: λειτουργία, liturgy

[40] *prosphora*: προσφορὰ, sacrifice

[41] *sciolists*: those who claim to be knowledgeable but in fact have only superficial learning

experienced, over that of ordinary men? Or again, surely it needs not be formally proved, that sympathy and congeniality of mind have a place in enabling us to enter into another's meaning. His single words or tones are nothing to one man; they tell a story to another; the one man passes them over; the other is arrested by them, and never forgets them. Such is the difference between reading an Apostolical Father with or without a knowledge of theological language.

To read then a particular Father to advantage, we must, as a preliminary, do these two things—divest ourselves of modern ideas and prejudices, and study theology. The work of Bull, for instance, above mentioned, or the Fifth Book of the Ecclesiastical Polity,[42] or Laud on Tradition,[43] will give quite a new [234] character to our studies; it will impart to them a reality, and thereby an interest, which cannot otherwise be gained, and will give an ancient document a use by giving it a meaning. Such seems the state of the case; and now some instances shall be given by way of illustration.

2.

We feel, indeed, a difficulty in entering upon the subject, both from the impossibility of doing justice to it in a few words, and on account of the especially sacred character of the doctrines which it will introduce. On both accounts it is unsuitable to a Review; nevertheless, we trust that some useful hints may be practicable in spite of the opposite dangers of saying too much and too little. We begin, then, thus:—When it is said that of two persons,—one who comes to an ancient theological document with modern or ultra-Protestant notions, and another with ecclesiastical notions (that is, the notions, for instance, of the fourth or fifth century, or of our divines, such as Bull, Bramhall,[44] or Beveridge,)—and who in consequence

---

[42] *the Ecclesiastical Polity*: by Richard Hooker; see above note on p.[180].

[43] *Laud on Tradition*: not a specific work; Laud gave a role to Tradition which more Protestant writes did not allow; e.g. 'Now it is *traditio universalis*, the constant and universal tradition of the whole Church of Christ, which is of greatest authority next to Scripture itself ...', *A Speech in Answer to the Right Honourable Lord Say* (1641).

[44] *Bramhall*: John Bramhall (1594–1663), Anglican divine, Archbishop of Armagh;

interpret the words, phrases, and dicta (say) of Ignatius or Clement in opposite ways,—that of these the latter is right and the former wrong; of course a connexion is assumed between the received system of theology in the Church and of these early Fathers, as if that system was their legitimate comment. This assumption is plainly involved; and its justification rests upon the truth of a circumstance, which has been already touched upon, viz., that the ecclesiastical sense is the only real *key* to their writings; it alone fits into their wards; it alone makes much of and gives a sufficient sense to those points on which they lay stress. As when we say a person better understands another who

[235] discerns and gives an interpretation to his hints, looks, and gestures, than he who either does not see them, or passes them over;—as we say that a construer or translator enters into the spirit of an author who brings more out of him than the many see in him: so, to say the least, the Church system has greater claims to be considered Ignatian or Clementine than the ultra-Protestant, in that it comes at least with the profession of being an interpretation of documents in which the other discerns little or nothing. This is the point to be illustrated; and to keep within compass we shall confine our remarks to Ignatius.

Mr. Jacobson[45] has found an admirable motto for his recent edition of the Apostolical Fathers, in a passage of Cicero,[46] which deposes to the value of Antiquity on the ground of its greater proximity to the divine origin of the things which it witnesses—"quæ, quo proprius aberat ab ortu et divina progenie, hoc melius ea fortasse, quæ erant vera, cernebat."[47] We do not assume for Ignatius more than this, that his witness comes immediately after the inspired sources of truth, that he was the friend of Apostles, and that, therefore, he was more likely to

---

apologist for the Church of England who wrote against Puritans, Catholics and the philosopher Hobbes.
[45] *Jacobson*: see above Editor's Introduction, p.xxxvi.
[46] *Cicero*: see above note on p.[17].
[47] *"quae, quo proprius . . . erant vera, cernebat."*: "[antiquity] which, the nearer it was in time from its origin and from divine generation, so much the better, perhaps, was able to discern what was true." The quotation is from Cicero's Tusculan Disputations I: XII, 26, but 'proprius' has been wrongly transcribed for the original 'propius'. It was correct in the 1839 text.

know their views of Gospel truth, and consequently their meaning in their extant writings, than a modern. This being taken for granted, the following remarks are made in proof of this point, that St. Ignatius' view of Gospel truth was very much the same as that taken in "the Catholic religion," and not that of ultra-Protestantism.

Ignatius writes in various Epistles as follows:

"There is one physician, both fleshly and spiritual, born and unborn; God incarnate, true life in death; both of Mary and of God; first passible, then impassible."—*Eph.* § 7.[48] Our God, even Jesus the Christ, was borne in the womb by Mary according to the dispensation[49] [236] of God, of the seed of David, and of the Holy Ghost."— § 18. "Suffer me to copy the passion of my God."—*Rom.* § 6.[50] "I endure all things, as He who became perfect man enables me."—*Smyrn.* § 4.[51] "Study the seasons, await Him who is above all seasons, independent of time; the Invisible, who for us became visible; the Impalpable, the Impassible, who for us became passible, who for us endured in every way."—*Pol.* § 3.[52] "What availeth it me, if any one praiseth me, but blasphemeth my Lord, not confessing that He bore flesh."—*Smyrn.* § 5.

In these extracts there are a number of remarkable expressions, which the student in Catholic theology alone will recognize, and he at once, as belonging to that theology, and having a special reference to the heretical perversions of it. He will enter into, and another might pass over, such words and phrases as γεννητός καὶ ἀγέννητος,[53] —ἐν σαρκὶ γενόμενος θεός.[54] —ἐκ Μαρίας καὶ ἐκ θεοῦ,[55] —παθητὸς καὶ ἀπαθὴς,[56] —ἄχρονος,[57] —ἀόρατος, δι᾽ἡμᾶς ὁρατός,[58] —τέλειος

---

[48] Eph.: *Letter to the Ephesians.*
[49] κατ᾽ οἰκονομίαν. Here is an additional word, which afterwards is known to have a technical meaning. [N]
[50] Rom.: *Letter to the Romans*
[51] Smyrn.: *Letter to the Smyrnaeans*
[52] Pol.: *Letter to Polycarp Bishop of Smyrna*
[53] γεννητὸς καὶ ἀγεννητος: born and unborn
[54] ἐν σαρκὶ γενόμενος θεὸς: God incarnate
[55] ἐκ Μαρίας καὶ ἐκ θεοῦ: of Mary and of God
[56] παθητὸς καὶ απαθὴς: passible and impassible
[57] ἄχρονος: independent of time
[58] ἀόρατος, δὶ ἡμᾶς ορατός: invisible, for us invisible

ἄνθρωπος γενόμενος,[59] —σαρκόφορος,[60] —πάθος τοῦ θεο.[61] He will perceive such expressions to be dogmatic, and will be at home in them.

1. For instance, take the words τέλειος ἄνθρωπος, *perfect man*. A heresy existed in the beginning of the fourth century, which was in fact a revival of the Docetæ,[62] in St. John's times, viz., that our Lord was not really a man as other men are, that He had no intellectual soul, and, as they went on to say, not even a real body. Such was the tenet of Apollinarianism;[63] and the Catholics protested against it by maintaining that Christ was "*perfect man.*" This was their special symbol against the heresy, as we find it in the Athanasian Creed,[64] "*perfect man*, subsisting of a reasonable soul and human flesh.*" The Apollinarians joined issue on this point; they contended that it was impossible for [237] one and the same person to contain in him δύο τέλεια[65] and that since our Lord was perfect God, He could not be perfect man. In consequence, this became a turning-point of the controversy, and is treated as such, among other authors, by Athanasius, Nazianzen,[66] Epiphanius,[67] Leontius,[68] and Maximus.[69]

The importance of the word is most readily shown by its occurrence in the Creeds. The Athanasian has already been mentioned; in like manner a confession ascribed by Theodoret[70] to St. Ambrose,[71] speaks of our Lord Jesus Christ, "who in the

---

[59] τέλειος ἄνθρωπος γενόμενος: became perfect man
[60] σαρκοφόρος: flesh-bearing; bore flesh
[61] πάθος τοῦ θεοῦ: the suffering of God
[62] *Docetæ*: lit. 'illusionists', a heretical sect which taught that Christ only 'seemed' to have a human body or human nature, thus denying the Incarnation. I and II John are directed against them.
[63] *Apollinarianism*: See above note on p.[130].
[64] *Athanasian Creed*: See above note on p. [57].
[65] δύο τέλεια: two perfects
[66] *Nazianzen*: Gregory of Nazianzus (c.329–389), Archbishop of Constantinople, Doctor of the Church.
[67] *Epiphanius*: Epiphanius of Salamis (c.310-403), Bishop of Constantia and author of numerous theological works.
[68] *Leontius*: Leontius Byzantinus (c. 485–c. 543), theologian.
[69] Athan. in Apollin., i. 16; Naz. Orat., li. p. 741; Epiph. Ancor., 77; Leont. frand. Apollin., p. 489; Max. Dial., iv. 5. [N] St. Athanasius *De Incarnatione Domini Nostri Jesu Christi contra Apollinarium*. St .Gregory Nazianzus *Orations*. Epiphanius' *Ancoratus*. Leontius *Adversus fraudes Apollinaristarum* (it is now not thought to be by Leontius). Maximus the Confessor, c. 580–662, monk and theologian, *Dialogue with Pirron*.
[70] *Theodoret*: (393-457), Bishop of Cyrus and theologian.
[71] *St. Ambrose*: See above note on p.[151].

last days became incarnate, and took on Him a *perfect* manhood of rational soul and body;" so that "of two *perfect* natures an union has been made ineffably," etc. In a Creed of Pelagius,[72] who was orthodox on this point, we are told that "they who own in the Son an imperfect God and *imperfect* man, are to be accounted not to hold truly either God or man." And John of Antioch,[73] in his explanation to St. Cyril,[74] confesses that our Lord is "perfect God and *perfect* man, of a reasonable soul and body."[75] The expression, then, "perfect man," was a portion of the dogmatic Catholic view existing in the fourth and fifth centuries. Now, as we have above quoted, it belongs also to Ignatius: "I endure all," he says, "as He, who became *perfect* man, enables me." Here, then, on the one hand we find a word in Ignatius which is scarcely taken from Scripture, which is uncongenial to modern sentiments, which is uncalled-for by the context, which has the air of a dogmatic expression, which was well adapted to expose existing errors, and which is found in a work which does actually oppose heresies of various sorts. On [238] the other hand, we find this word undeniably and prominently a dogmatic term in the fourth century; can we doubt that it is dogmatic in Ignatius? or, in other words, that Ignatius' tone of writing is inconsistent with the modern theory, whether that pious feelings, or again that good lives, are the whole of religion, and formal creeds are superfluous or burdens?

2. Take another instance. He speaks of those who "blaspheme" Christ, "not confessing that He bore flesh" (σαρκόφορον).[76] This word is of a dogmatic character on the very

---

[72] *Pelagius*: See above note on p.[94].

[73] *John of Antioch*: (d.441), Patriarch of Antioch; he initially supported the heretical Nestorius against St. Cyril but was later reconciled with the latter.

[74] *St. Cyril*: Cyril of Alexandria (c. 376 – 444), Patriarch of Alexandria, Doctor of the Church; opponent of Nestorianism.

[75] Vide also Epiph. Ancor., 121; Theod. Hist., v. 9; and Confessions in Fourth, Fifth, and Sixth General Councils. In like manner, our second Article speaks of "two whole and *perfect* natures." [N] Theodoret's *Historia Ecclesiastica. Fourth, Fifth, and Sixth General Councils*: the Councils of Chalcedon (451), Constantinople II (553) and Constantinople III (680-1). *our second Article*: of the Thirty-Nine Articles; see note on p.[179].

[76] *"blaspheme" Christ, "not confessing that he bore flesh"*: Letter to the Smyrnaeans, 5.

face of the passage; and it is notoriously such in after-contro-versy. It is so used by Clement of Alexandria,[77] Athanasius, and in the Confessions of the Emperors Valentinian,[78] Valens,[79] and Gratian.[80] It was used both in the Apollinarian and Nestorian controversies; by the Catholics against Nestorius, who asserted that our Lord was not θεὸς σαρκοφόρος, but ἄνθρωπος θεοφόρος,[81] and by the Apollinarians as imputing to the Catho-lics what was the Nestorian tenet.

3. Again: Nestorius holding, after the Cerinthians[82] and other early Gnostics, that the Son of God was distinct from Christ, a man, as if Christ had a separate existence or personality, the Catholics met the heresy, among other strong statements, by the phrases that "God was born, and suffered on the cross," and that the Blessed Virgin was θεοτόκος, "the Mother of God." On the other hand, such phrases, it is scarcely necessary to say, are considered, in the judgment of this day's religion, at once incorrect and unbecoming. This is not the place to go into the history of the controversy, and to show their propriety and necessity. The latter of the two is found in Origen,[83] who, moreover, employed himself in an inquiry into its real [239] meaning,[84] which is remarkable as showing that it was at that time a received word; for we do not investigate what we have

---

[77] *Clement of Alexandria*: Titus Flavius Clemens (c.150-c.215), theologian, author of numerous writings.

[78] *Valentinian*: *Valentinian I* (321–375), Roman Emperor from 364 to 375. He restored the freedom of worship to Christianity after his predecessor Julian had attempted to revive paganism.

[79] *Valens*: (328–78), Emperor of the eastern Roman empire from 364 to 378; brother of Valentinian I. He was Arian in his belief and persecuted Catholics, so it is unclear why Newman is citing him.

[80] *Gratian*: (359–83), Emperor from 375 to 383; son of Valentinian I. He suppressed pagan worship and issued an edict that all were to obey the decrees of the Council of Nicaea, thus outlawing heresies such as Arianism.

[81] *not* θεὸς σαρκοφόρος *but* ἄνθρωπος θεοφόρος: 'not God bearing flesh but man bearing God'

[82] *Cerinthians*: followers of Cerinthus (1st century) who taught, amongst other things, that Jesus the man was distinct from Christ.

[83] *Origen*: Origen of Alexandria (c.185-c.254), widely influential theologian.

[84] Vide Socr. Hist., viii. 32; Gailand, Bibl. P., t. 14, Append., p. 87. [N] The *Historia Ecclesiastica of* Socrates of Constantinople (b. c.380). This cites Origen using the term *Theotokos* in his Commentary on Romans (though the genuineness of this text has now been questioned). Andrea Gallandi (1709-79), Oratorian priest, author of *Bibliotheca veterum patrum antiquorum scriptorum ecclesiasticorum Graecorum* (14 vols 1765-81).

invented. It is used by Alexander,[85] Nazianzen, and Athanasius, and, as many think, by Dionysius.[86] As to the former phrase, Irenæus speaks of our Lord's "descensio in Mariam;"[87] Tertullian of His descending "in vulvam, de vulvâ carnem participaturus;"[88] of "Dei passiones;"[89] "Dei interemptores;"[90] and Athanasius of the "σῶμα θεῦ,"[91] and of the consequent duty of worshipping It. Athanasius, indeed, as is well known, objected to the phrase that God suffered, *as used* by Apollinaris, understanding him by θεὸς[92] to mean θεότης;[93] but that it was a usual and received phrase in the Catholic Church cannot be doubted. Now turning to Ignatius, we find it in a passage above quoted from his Epistles; he speaks of being "a follower of the πάθος τοῦ θεοῦ."[94] In like manner he says that "our God, Jesus the Christ, was borne in the womb ἐκνοφορηθη,[95] by Mary." Is this the language of the modern school, and not rather of the Catholic Church?

4. Another expression commonly insisted on by the Fathers, in their dogmatic teaching, is that of the "one" Christ; and that for various doctrinal reasons which need not be dwelt on here. Not to mention Scripture, we find it in the Nicene Creed, and still more emphatically in the Athanasian, "who, although He is God and man, yet He is not two, but *one* Christ; *one*, not by, etc. ... *one* altogether, not by, etc. ... God and man is *one* Christ." There are numberless passages in the Fathers to the same effect; we will cite two only. Irenæus[96] says that St. John "acknowl-

---

[85] *Alexander*: St. Alexander (d.326), Patriarch of Alexandria; author of, amongst other writings, two *Epistles* on Arianism.

[86] *Dionysius*: St. Dionysius of Alexandria (d.265); he uses the term *Theotokos* in his epistle to Paul of Samosata.

[87] *"descensio in Mariam"*: "the descent into Mary"

[88] *"in vulvam, de vulvâ carnem participaturus"*: "into the womb, receiving flesh from the womb"

[89] *"Dei passiones"*: "the sufferings of God"

[90] *"Dei interemptores"*: "the killers of God"

[91] "σῶμα θεῦ": "the flesh of God"

[92] θεὸς: *God*

[93] θεότης: divine nature

[94] πάθος τοῦ θεοῦ: suffering of God

[95] ἐκνοφορήθη: conceived

[96] *Irenæus*: St. Irenæus Bishop of Lyons (d.c.202), Church Father; he is an important witness to the Apostolic tradition, having seen and heard St. Polycarp who was a disciple of St. John the Evangelist.

edges *one and the same* Word of God; and Him Only-begotten, and Him incarnate for our salvation," and that St Matthew knows "*one and the same* Jesus Christ," and that St. Paul [240] "plainly intimates that there is one God who promised His Son through the prophets, and *one* Jesus Christ our Lord" ... and that St. Mark "announces *one* and the same Son of God, Jesus Christ, who was announced by the prophets ... All the aforesaid (heretics)," he adds, "though they confess with the tongue that Jesus Christ is *one*, trifle with themselves."—*Hær.* iii. 16, §§ 2, 3, 6.[97] And Nazianzen, "God came forth from the Virgin with the assumption (of humanity), being from two contraries, flesh and spirit, *one*; of which the one was made God, and the other made it God" (ὧν τὸ μὲν ἐθίωσε τὸ δὲ ἐθεώθη). Now let it be observed, this is the very mode of speaking which Ignatius adopts: "There is one physician, *both* fleshly *and* spiritual," etc. "One faith, and *one* Jesus Christ." It surely cannot be doubted that Ignatius in this passage, and Scripture before him, is dogmatic; that is, that the phrase in question is not accidental and transitory, but has a definite and permanent force, or is an article of faith.

5. Again: One especial sign of dogmatic statements is, that the words and phrases contained in them are contrasted with one another. Where the particular terms in which the sense is conveyed are not to be insisted on, in such a document apparent inconsistency in their use is not considered to matter; they are smoothed over and reconciled. For instance, when it is said, upon St. Paul's conversion, first, that his companions "heard a voice, but saw no man,"[98] and afterwards that they "saw the light, but heard not the voice,"[99] we think little of the verbal contradiction, from an understanding that the sense is not confined within the words themselves, but that an appeal is made to the intelligence of the reader as their interpreter. When, however, an author seems aware of this apparent inconsistency, [241] yet does not retract, but even insists on it, we rightly conceive

---

[97] Hær: St. Ireneaeus, *Adversus haereses*, 'Against Heresies', directed against Gnosticism.
[98] *"heard a voice but saw no man,"*: Acts 9:7
[99] *"saw the light but heard not the voice,"*: Acts 22:9

that he has a purpose in so doing, that there is something in his expressions which is above us, something which we cannot master or make subjective, and may not attempt to reconcile at our private discretion. Such, before the event, were the two prophecies, one of which said that Zedekiah should go to Babylon,[100] the other that he should not see it;[101] which were reconciled in the event by his losing his eyes before he was taken thither.[102] The Athanasian Creed aptly exemplifies what is here meant; almost its whole dogmatic force lying not in any peculiarity of phrase, but in antithetical structure. In like manner, Irenæus:

"Being *Invisible*, He was made *visible*; being *Infinite*, He was made *finite*; being *Impassible*, He was made *passible*; being the *Word*, He was made *man*," etc.—*Ibid.* § 6.

Again, Vincent of Lerins:[103]

"In one and the same Christ are two substances; *one* divine, the *other* human; *one* from God the Father, the *other* from the Virgin Mother; *one* co-eternal and co-equal with the Father, the *other* of one substance with His Mother; yet one and the same Christ in either substance. There is one and the same Christ, God and man; the same *not created* and *created*; the same *unchangeable and impassible*, and *changed and suffering*; the same *equal*, and *inferior*, to the Father; the same *begotten of the Father* before the world, and *born* in the world of *His Mother; perfect God* and *perfect man*."—Commonit. § 19.[104]

And Athanasius:

"He was born before the worlds *from the Father*; He was also in these last days *from the Virgin*; before *Invisible*, even to the holy powers of heaven, *visible* now by reason of His union with the manhood which was seen; seen, I say, *not* in His invisible divinity, *but* by the action of the divinity through man's body and entire

---

[100] *Zedekiah should go to Babylon*: Cf. Jeremiah 32:5; 34:3
[101] *he should not see it*: Cf. Ezekiel 12:13
[102] *losing his eyes before he was taken thither*: Cf. 2 Kings 25:7
[103] *Vincent of Lerins*: see note on page [117].
[104] *Commonit.*: *Commonitorium.*

humanity (ὅλου ἀνθρώπου), which He renewed by making it His own."—*Orat. in Arian*, iv. fin.[105]

[242]   Every one would feel these to be dogmatic passages, and to belong to what may be called Church divinity, yet let it be observed, there is scarcely one word in them which bears on it the signs of a theology, such as ὁμοῦσιον,[106] περιχώρησις,[107] or προέλευσις,[108]—not one word which we might not find in Ignatius. The dogmatical character of each depends entirely on the contra-position of words in themselves common; that is to say, there is no reason why we should call Athanasius in such a passage dogmatic (as we do, and rightly), which will not much more apply to such passages as the following in Ignatius: "There is one physician, both *fleshly* and *spiritual*, *with* and *without* beginning, God become *flesh*, true *life* in death, both *of Mary* and *of God*; first *passible*, then *impassible*;" or again, "the Invisible who for us became *visible*; the Impassible who for us became *passible*"—*Pol.* 3; or again, as some read, "One Jesus Christ, who was of the race of David according to the flesh, the *Son of Man*, and *Son of God*."—*Eph.* § 20.

These are various specimens of passages on which we may rely in proof of the theological or dogmatical character of St. Ignatius' Christianity, and the drift of that theology. The only further question which can be asked is, whether our argument does not prove too much; whether the remarkable coincidence thus resulting between him and the writers of later times is not greater than can be real; and therefore whether it is more than a mere coincidence ingeniously brought to light, and a gratuitous gloss upon his meaning? But this is easily answered by appealing to the historical fact already alluded to, that heresies beset the Church of the first century, which did but re-appear, substantially the same, but in more subtle forms, in the fourth and fifth. It is not wonderful that the mysteries of the faith irritated the reason of unhumbled minds from the beginning;

---

[105] Orat. in Arian.: *Discourse 4 Against the Arians.*
[106] ὁμοῦσιον: consubstantial
[107] περιχώρησις: the mutual indwelling of the three Divine Persons of the Holy Trinity
[108] προέλευσις: going forth

nor to those who have studied the subject will it seem wonderful [243] that it should strive to escape from them by the same methods. There are, in fact, but a few modes of denying the truth, and these were adopted by various sects of the Gnostics in the time of Ignatius, as by Apollinaris and Nestorius in the time of Athanasius and Vincent. That the minute questions debated by later heretics existed before their times, is sufficiently proved even if we confine ourselves to the treatises of Tertullian against Praxeas, and De Carne Christi;[109] but the great work of Irenæus[110] *contra Hæreses* is also evidence to the same effect, not to speak of the various passages to be found in Origen, and the fragments of Hippolytus.[111] However, perhaps the general tone of the Epistles themselves will be considered a most satisfactory proof, if we believe that in any sense they are his,[112] that Ignatius had an eye to heretics in what he wrote, and of his judgment upon them.

"Be not dismayed at those who *seem worthy of trust*, and yet teach *strange doctrine. Stand firm*, as the anvil under the stroke; for it is like a great combatant, to be smitten and to conquer."—*Pol.* § 3.

It is maintained by some persons nowadays, that the early heretics were always of immoral lives, and condemned as such, not for their opinions; to such disputants we recommend the following passage:

"Be not deceived, brethren; those who *corrupt families* shall not inherit the kingdom of God. If, therefore, they who do this *according to the flesh*, have suffered death, *how much more*, if by evil doctrine

---

[109] *Tertullian . . . : Quintus Septimius Florens Tertullianus*, (c.155 – c. 240), layman, author of many works of apologetics; latterly he became a Montanist, but his earlier works are orthodox. *Praxeas* was a Monarchian, i.e. non-Trinitarian; he revised his views in response to Tertullian's criticism. The *De Carne Christi* [Concerning the Flesh of Christ] was directed against Docetic denial of the reality of the Incarnation.
[110] *Irenæus*: See above note on p.[117].
[111] *Hippolytus*: St. Hippolytus of Rome (170-235); theologian and Father of the Church; anti-pope and martyr.
[112] *if we believe that in any sense they are his*: The genuineness of the texts of some of St. Ignatius' letters was disputed. See Newman's Note [p.262], added in the 1871 edition.

he *corrupt the faith of God*," (we have already heard from Ignatius *what* that faith is,) "for which Jesus Christ was crucified? Such a one has become polluted, and shall go into the fire unquenchable, and so shall he who hearkens to him."—*Eph.* § 16.[113]

[244]   Again, the following passages would in this day certainly be said to be "uncharitable to the persons" of the heretics designated:

"I beseech you, yet not I, but the love of Jesus Christ, to use only the Christian nourishment, and to abstain from strange herbs, which is heresy (ἥτις ἐστὶν αἵρεσις) . . . they administer their *deadly drug*, as it were, in a sweet potion, which whoso is ignorant takes with pleasure, and in it death."—*Trall.* § 6.[114] "I warn you against *wild beasts in human form*, whom you ought not only not to receive, but, if possible *not even to fall in with; only to pray for them*, if peradventure they may repent, which is difficult; but the power is with Jesus Christ, our true life."—*Smyrn.* § 4.

So speaks a bishop of the first century,—"wild beasts in human form;" have not such terms been somewhere done into English in the nineteenth by the words of "venerable men," men of "inoffensive," "uncontroversial" dispositions?[115]

3.

We have now to proceed to ground, not more sacred indeed than what has formed our subject hitherto, for that cannot be, but which, requiring to be examined more minutely, and in its details, cannot be entered upon without greater risk of unsuitable language. We earnestly hope we shall not transgress the bounds of propriety in our introduction of solemn topics, or forget that we are writing as reviewers, not as divines; yet the line of argument in which we are engaged seems to require that we

---

[113] [St. Ignatius speaks of those who had known the truth and left it (as St. Peter, about the immoral sects, in the terrible words, "It had been better for them not to have known," etc.), not of those who are born and educated in error, and never had reason to doubt about what they had received.] [N] *"It had been better. . .* : 2 Peter 2:21.
[114] Trall.: *Letter to the Trallians*
[115] *somewhere done into English . . .* : Newman is being ironic; these are the epithets given, by their supporters, to Anglican writers of liberal, unorthodox, opinions.

should allude to a doctrine, which yet we are loth to approach from its peculiar character.

Let then the following expressions of St. Ignatius be [245] observed:

"Being followers of God, and rekindling in the blood of God, (ἀναζωπυρήσαντες ἐν αἴματι θεοῦ,) ye have perfectly accomplished the work connatural to you (συγγενικὸν ἔργον)."—*Eph.* § 1. "These are not the planting of the Father: if they were, they would have appeared to be branches of the Cross, and their fruit would have been incorruptible; by which, in His passion, He invites you His members. The Head then cannot be born without the members, God promising a *union* (ἕνωσιν), *which is* Himself."—*Trall.* § 11. "In which (the Churches) I pray there may be a union (ἕνωσιν) of *flesh* and spirit with Jesus Christ, who is our Life evermore, in faith and in love which surpasseth all things, but, in the first place, in Jesus and the Father."— *Magn.* § 1.[116] "Fare ye well in an unanimity of God, possessing a *Spirit Indivisible, which is Jesus Christ.*"—*Ibid.* § 15. "For this cause did the Lord accept ointment upon His head, that He might *breathe incorruption* into His Church … Why do we waste away (ἀπολλύμεθα) in folly, not considering *the gift* (χάρισμα) which the Lord hath sent *in truth*?"—*Eph.* § 17. "(Christ) was born and baptized, that by *His passion* (τῷ πάθει) He might *purify water.*"—*Ibid.* § 18. "If any one is able to remain in chastity, *to the honour of the flesh of the Lord*, let him remain also in humbleness."—*Pol.* § 5. "I have no pleasure in corruptible food, nor in the pleasures of this life; I would have *God's bread*, heavenly bread, bread of life, *which is flesh of Jesus Christ*, the Son of God, who was born afterwards of the seed of David and Abraham: and I would have *God's draught, His blood*, which is love incorruptible, and ever-springing life."—*Rom.* § 7.

Now it is very remarkable how modern readers receive such passages. They come to them with low notions, they never suspect that they allude to anything which *they* cannot reach, and being unable to discern any high objects to which such language is appropriate, they pronounce it hyperbolical, or, as sometimes, a corrupt reading. They seem to put it as a dilemma, "either we are blind or St. Ignatius speaks beyond his sense."

---

[116] *Magn.*: *Letter to the Magnesians*

[246] For instance, a late writer says of some of his statements: "No consideration, either of reason or Scripture, seems to have power for a moment to check the mad career of his turgid and bloated, but often eloquent, declamation; or to deter him from working up his exhortations to the highest pitch of hyperbole."[117] Such a mode of speaking is of course extreme, and argues a want of mere common refinement, to say nothing of modesty and reverence; but even persons who have these qualifications, if possessed of modern ideas, will be disposed to conclude that St. Ignatius was turgid and Asiatic in his diction. Now we cannot deny that he was an Asiatic, and spoke like an Asiatic; so were, and so spoke, Isaiah, St. Paul, and St. John. St John, St. Paul, and Isaiah, have also been supposed to use words without definite meaning, merely because their meaning was beyond the reach of their unscrupulous critics; perhaps the case is the same with Ignatius. Perchance the holy martyr had a range of conceptions which are as remote from the philosophy of this age, as from the mental vision of savages. Perchance his words stood for ideas perfectly well known to him, and recognized by his brethren. If so, it is unjust to him, and unkind to ourselves, for us, modern divines, to reconcile his words to our own ignorance, by imputing to him bombast. This consideration, by the way, may be profitably suggested to all who are in the habit of censuring Church writers of whatever age, as circuitous, wordy, confused, cloudy, and fanciful. They may, doubtless, be all this; perhaps in this particular passage or work they are. Still, the question will arise in the breast of modest inquirers, whether, if one or other party must be in fault, the reader may not possibly be shallow rather than the writer unreal. Now, in the case of St.

[247] Ignatius, one remarkable thing is, that, while to a modern Protestant he is so unmeaning, a disciple of Irenæus, Athanasius, or Cyril of Alexandria, will be in no perplexity at all as to what his words mean, but will see at once a sense, and a deep and sufficient one, in them. If so, thus much would seem to follow: that, whichever party is the more scriptural, anyhow St. Ignatius,

---

[117] Osburn, *Errors*, p. 191. [N]

the disciple and friend of the sacred writers, is on the side of the Catholics, not of the moderns.

Let us be persuaded to take his words literally, and not think the literal interpretation too strange to be the true one, and we shall come very nearly to a great and sacred doctrine, which, while it exculpates our author from all appearance of turgidity or declamation, has ever been held in the Church Catholic. It would seem then to be certain, that Ignatius considers our life and salvation to lie, not in the Atonement by itself, but in the Incarnation; but neither in the Incarnation nor Atonement as past events, but, as present facts, in an existing mode, in which our Saviour comes to us; or, to speak more plainly, in our Saviour Himself who is God in our flesh, and not only so, but in flesh which has been offered up on the Cross in sacrifice, which has died and has risen. The being made man, the being crucified in atonement, the being raised again, are the three past events to which the Eternal Son has vouchsafed to become to us what He is, a Saviour; and those who omit the Resurrection in their view of the divine economy, are as really defective in faith as if they omitted the Crucifixion. On the Cross He paid the debt of the world, but as He could not have been crucified without first taking flesh, so again He could not, as it would seem, apply His atonement without first rising again. Accordingly, St. Ignatius speaks of our being saved and living not simply in the Atonement, but, as the passages already quoted signify, in the flesh and blood of the risen Lord, first sacrificed [248] for us, then communicated to us. More definite passages than these might be quoted from his Epistles, but let us at first be contented with these. To take the first of them: "rekindling in the blood of God." If this merely means that we are raised to a new life by the Atonement, or merely by the moral effect of the knowledge of the doctrine, it is certainly strained and inflated language; but if it be taken literally, the idea will rise, and the language will sink. If it means what the Church Catholic teaches, that the *body* and *blood* of the Word Incarnate is in some real, though unknown way, communicated to our souls and bodies, and thus becomes the principle of a new life, then no words can reach what is intended. So again, when he speaks of a "*union with the flesh and spirit of Jesus Christ*," and of our "possessing an *Indivisible Spirit*, which is Jesus Christ," he surely speaks of a union with Christ's *flesh*, which is *spirit*. Again, when he says, "I would have God's bread, heavenly bread, bread of life, *which is flesh of Jesus Christ*, I would have God's draught, *His blood*," if he merely means, I long for the *benefits* of Christ's death, one could not defend him from the charge of an extravagant use of words. And again, when he says that Christ has "breathed incorruption into His Church," and that the pouring out of the ointment was a sort of preparation or figure for this, unless he is to be taken literally, that there is a real gift or communication, he makes a *fact* the symbol of a *metaphor*, which is the very objection commonly and soundly brought against the Socinian comments on the Epistle to the Hebrews. When again he speaks of remaining in chastity "to the honour of our Lord's flesh," if he means, what the words literally imply, that chastity is a reverence paid to the holy and divinely virginal nature which Christ imparts to us from Himself, the sentiment is plain and very awful; otherwise it surely would seem to be a rude and indecorous phrase.[118]

[249]

If it be objected to a literal interpretation of the phrases in question, that Ignatius, far from so intending, sometimes explains them of moral virtues or graces, as when he speaks of "*faith*, which is the flesh of the Lord, and *love*, which is His blood;" of "fleeing to the *Gospel*, as to the flesh of Jesus Christ," and of His blood, which is *love* incorruptible," we would answer, that such passages only imply that the supernatural gift *includes* the moral virtue, or that the virtue or grace consists in

---

[118] εἰς τιμὴν τοῦ κυρίου τῆς σαρκός. Commentators confess themselves perplexed. Voss asks, "Quid sibi vult, rogo, *in castitate in honorem carnis dominicæ*? otiosis hæc interpretanda relinquo." He proceeds to say, that he is certain that the word σαρκός has got transposed, and that we ought to read ἐν ἁγνείᾳ τῆς σαρκός μένειν εἰς τιμὴν τοῦ κυρίου. Mr. Jacobson assents. Mr. Chevallier translates, "to the honour of Him who is the Lord of *all* flesh:" omit the "all," which is not in the Greek, and the sense which we have expressed above is substantially conveyed whether by "the flesh of the Lord," or by "the Lord of the flesh." [N] "*Quid sibi vult . . . .*": "I ask, what does he mean by *in castitate in honorem carnis dominicæ*? I leave this to those who have the leisure to interpret it."

the supernatural gift. If, for instance, one says that "a house is a shelter against the weather," or of "our shelter being a house," no one would have any right thence to argue that "house" had no literal sense, and was only a metaphor standing for protection or shelter; the proposition meaning no more than this, that the house is to us shelter, or that shelter lies in having a house.

So far then on the sense of Ignatius as drawn from the literal import of the words themselves; but now let us see what light is thrown on this interpretation by one or two passages from later writers. The phrases, let it be observed, in Ignatius, to be illustrated, are such as these: "breathing incorruption into His Church;" "by His passion purifying water;" "union of flesh and [250] spirit with Christ," and the like; which we conceive to allude to a mysterious communication of our Lord's humanity to Christians, as a principle which renews and purifies the stock of fallen Adam. Let us even suppose that these phrases are in themselves obscure; yet when an author is hard to be understood, it is fair to adduce other authors to illustrate his meaning: is not this what we always do in critical or antiquarian researches? Let us see then whether Athanasius, Gregory, and Cyril, are not thus adducible for Ignatius. For instance, the first-mentioned of the three says:

"When [Adam] disobeyed the commandments of God, he fell under sinful imaginations; not that God created these imaginations which led him captive, but that the devil sowed them by deceit upon man's reason, when in transgression and in alienation from God: so that the devil set up the law of sin in man's nature, and death, which reigns through the work of sin. For this cause, then, came the Son of God, to undo the works of the devil. But you say: He undid them by *abstaining from sin Himself.* But this is not an undoing of sin, for it was not in *Him* that the devil originally wrought sin, as if His coming into the world, and not sinning, should undo sin. But the devil wrought sin by *sowing it* in the reason and intellect of man. Wherefore it became impossible for nature, being possessed of reason, and having sinned of free-will, and being under sentence of death, to reclaim itself into freedom; as the Apostle says, 'This was what the law could not do, in that it was weak through the flesh.' Wherefore the Son of God

251

came, by means of Himself, to *set* it *up* (the flesh) *in* His own (divine) nature, from a new beginning and a marvellous generation."—*Apoll.* ii. § 6.

Or we may take the following passages from Gregory Nazianzen:

"Let us see what the reason is, which [the Apollinarians] assign for Christ's becoming man, or (as they prefer to say) flesh. If it be, that [251] God might be contained in place, being otherwise infinite, and might hold converse with men by the flesh, as by a veil, clever is their mask, and the plot which they enact ... But if He came to undo the condemnation of sin, *cleansing each nature by itself*, then, as He *needed flesh*, because flesh had been condemned, and soul, because soul had been condemned, so also He *needed* the rational principle," (which Apollinaris denied,) "*for the sake of the rational principle*, which in Adam had not only fallen, but, as physicians speak, was the seat of the disease (προπαθήσαντα)."—*Orat.* 51, pp. 742, 743.[119]

The argument urged in these passages against Apollinaris is this: unless the divine nature of the Word was joined to a rational soul, as well as to a human body, our rational soul was not *cleansed* and *renovated* as well as our body. Now let attention be paid to this argument; for it is just one of those which are called fanciful and mystical, merely because readers will not take it literally, and mistake the reverence with which a writer words it for indistinctness or confusion of thought. A modern reasoner[120] is tempted to ask, "*How* does Christ's divine nature, being joined to that particular soul which He vouchsafed to create and make His own, cleanse *all* human souls? is not this a mere poetical or cloudy way of talking? When it is said that He suffered in soul and body *instead* of man, that His divine nature gave efficacy to that suffering, and that the Christian's soul and body are pardoned and gifted in consequence, such a statement I can understand, provided that this cleansing means no more than putting away guilt.[121] And "I suppose" (a reasoner

---

[119] *Orat.*: Orations

[120] *A modern reasoner*: not a real person - Newman is imagining such a 'reasoner'.

[121] ... *guilt.*: Newman has forgotten to close his quotation marks here before opening

may proceed), "I suppose that this is all the Fathers really do mean; only they were not clear-headed, and loved the appearance of mystery and contrivance. They were pious men, but were not above their age; and they encumbered Christian truth with a play of words, because words were their food. They delighted in inventing unreal antitheses, and in pursuing [252] metaphors unfairly, and in discovering causes in mere connexions or coincidences, and in spinning out theories and systems, and in interpreting the words of Prophets and Apostles into pretended allusions to the trivial accidents or remote events of which they themselves were witnesses. Thus because the Eternal Word assumed soul and body, and offered them up in sacrifice, a theory is built up as if that assumption literally hallowed all souls and bodies, not one only. But how can what is done to one, be done to another, except by a figure of speech? and what profit is there in propounding and using against heretics a system of words which have no corresponding realities?" Such is the judgment commonly formed of the Fathers, in consequence of the deep prejudice of this age, which thinks it absolutely impossible that they can literally mean what they say, which is, that, as Adam not only introduced but *diffuses* death, so Christ diffuses life.

However, one should think that there might be found passages strong enough even to overcome the prejudice, and break through the slumbers, of this generation. Let us see whether St. Cyril of Alexandria is not equal to it. He speaks as follows:

"Christ gave His own body for the life of all, and next He implants (ἐνοικίζει) into us life by means of it; how, I will say as I can. Since then the life-giving Word of God has inhabited the flesh, He has refashioned it unto His own perfection, which is life; and altogether, being joined to it by an ineffable mode of union (ἕνωσις), He has set it forth as life-giving, just as He is Himself by nature. Wherefore the body of Christ is life-giving to *all who partake*; for it expels death, when it is present in those who are dying, and it rids them of

---

them again at "I suppose".

corruption, as travailing in itself with that Word which perfectly annuls corruption."—*in Joan.* iv. p. 354.[122] "In no other way could the nations be rid of the blindness which lay upon them, and behold the divine [253] and holy light, that is, receive the knowledge of the Holy and Consubstantial Trinity, than by partaking His holy flesh, and washing away ingrained sin, and putting off the rule of the devil; viz., through Holy Baptism. And when the Saviour marked upon the blind man" (viz, in John ix.) "the type of the mystery in anticipation, He at the same time imparted to him the virtue of the participation by the anointing of the spittle. As a figure of Holy Baptism, He bids him to run and wash in Siloam. As then we believe the body of Christ to be life-giving, since it is the temple and dwelling-place of the living God the Word, possessing all His operations, so we say also that it is the supply of illumination. For it is the body of light naturally and really such; and as when He raised the dead man, the only-begotten son of the widow, He did not hold it enough to command alone, and say, 'Young man, I say unto thee arise,' though accustomed to conduct all things which He wishes by a word, but put His hand too upon the bier, showing that His body also has the life-giving energy, so here also" (in John ix.) "He anoints with the spittle, teaching us that His body, even by the merest contact, supplies (πρόξενόν εστι) illumination."—*in Joan.* vi. p. 602.

In the above remarks no allusion has been made to any external means or ordained instrument by which the Fathers considered this most sacred and mysterious gift to be imparted, though there was one passage of Ignatius which contained a sufficiently clear allusion to that Rite which the Church has ever accounted the repository of the gift—not to mention other texts which refer to baptism. That passage was where he says, "I would have God's *bread*, which is flesh of Jesus Christ; I would have God's *draught*, which is His blood." The following passages are of a still more definite character:

"That ye obey the bishop and the presbytery with an entire mind; breaking one bread, which is the *medicine of immortality*, our antidote against death."—*Eph.* § 20. "What availeth it me, if any one praiseth me, but blasphemeth my Lord, denying that He bore the flesh. . . .

---

[122] *in Joan.: Commentary on the Gospel of John*

Even heavenly things and the glory of Angels, and the powers visible and invisible, are condemned if they believe not in the blood of Christ. [254] ... These abstain from the Eucharist and from prayer, because they confess not that the Eucharist is flesh of our Saviour Jesus Christ, which suffered for our sins, which the Father in His mercy raised again. They then, denying the gift of God, perish in their disputings. Well had it been for them to make much of it, that they might rise again."—*Smyrn.* §§ 5-7. "Endeavour to use one Eucharist; for there is one flesh of our Lord Jesus Christ, and one cup, that His blood may make us one, *εἰς ἕνωσιν τοῦ αἵματος αὐτοῦ.*"—*Phil.* § 4. "The Gospel hath a special gift; the presence of our Lord Jesus Christ, His passion and resurrection. For the beloved prophets brought tidings of Him; but the Gospel is the accomplishment of incorruption."—*Ibid.* § 9.

In some of these passages a connexion is mentioned as existing between the Eucharist and the gift of the Resurrection or immortality. May not the following passage from Irenæus,[123] the disciple of Polycarp, who was Ignatius' friend, and (as we now speak) editor of his Epistles, be considered to throw light on his meaning?

"Altogether in error are they who despise the entire dispensation of God in the incarnation of Christ, and deny the salvation of the flesh, and reject its regeneration, saying that it does not admit of being *incorruptible.* But if the flesh be not saved, then did not the Lord redeem us with His own blood; then is not the cup of the Eucharist the communication of His blood; then is not the bread which we break the communication of His body. For blood is not, except from veins and flesh, and the other parts of man's substance, which the Word of God was truly made. .... As the blessed Paul says in his Epistle to the Ephesians, 'We are members of His body, from His flesh and His bones,'[124] not saying this of any spiritual and invisible man," (that is, as the heretics, who explained away the passage,) "but of the constitution of man as he really is, which is made of flesh, and nerves, and bones, which is nourished by His cup, which is His blood, and increased by the bread, which is His body."—*Hær.* v. 2, §§ 2, 3.

---

[123] *Irenæus*: See above note on p.[117].
[124] *'We are members . . .* : Eph. 5:30.

4.

We have now said perhaps enough. To draw out fully the case for Catholic doctrine, which this Apostolical Father supplies, would lead us beyond both the literal and moral bounds of a Review. It would be a great service if some divine would put out the text of these Epistles, with a running comment from the Fathers who come after them. It is hardly too much to say that almost the whole system of Catholic doctrine may be discovered, at least in outline, not to say in parts filled up, in the course of them. There are indeed one or two omissions, as if on purpose to prove to us their genuineness; for in a later age these certainly would have been supplied; the chief of which is the scanty notice they contain of the Catholic doctrine of the Trinity, and of baptismal regeneration, which in Ignatius' time were not subjects of controversy. But after all deductions from the completeness of his theological system, let us see what we possess in the course of these seven short compositions. We have, first, the principle of dogmatic faith; next, the doctrine of the Incarnation, almost as theologically laid down as it is in the fourth and fifth centuries; then, that of the dissemination of a new and divine nature in the fallen stock of Adam, and that by means of the Eucharist. So far has been shown above; further we read in them of the divine origin and obligation of the Episcopal regimen; as when he says, "He for whom I am bound is my witness that I have not learned this doctrine from flesh of man; the Spirit proclaimed these words, 'Apart from the bishop do nothing.'"—*Phil.* § 7.[125] The divine authority of the bishop, as the representative of our unseen Maker and Redeemer, in such words as—"In any delusion of his visible bishop, a man trifles rather with the Bishop invisible; and so, the question is not with flesh, but with God who seeth the secrets."—*Magn.* § 3.[126] The doctrine of the three orders: as, for instance, "Do all things in a unanimity of God, the bishop holding precedency over you in the place of God, and the presbyters in the place of the council of Apostles, and the deacons, my dearest, entrusted

[255]

[256]

---

[125] *Phil.: Letter to the Philadelphians*
[126] *Magn.: Letter to the Magnesians.*

with the ministry of Jesus Christ."—*Ibid.* § 6. The doctrine of unity, as when he says, "All that are of God, and Jesus Christ, these are with the bishop; and all that shall repent and turn to the unity of the Church, these also shall be of God."—*Phil.* § 3. The doctrine of the Church's Catholicity: "The bishops who are stationed at the ends of the earth, are after the mind of Jesus Christ."—*Eph.* § 3. The diocesan system: "Maintain the honour of thy post," he says to Polycarp, "with all earnestness fleshly and spiritual."—*Pol.* § 1. The sin of going by individual judgment in matters of faith: "Be not deceived, brethren; whosoever followeth one that creates schism, he inherits not the kingdom of God; whosoever walks by some foreign opinion, he consents not to the passion of Christ."—*Phil.* § 3. What may be called the sacramental character of unity: "There is one Jesus Christ, who surpasses all things: together therefore haste ye all, as to a temple of God, as to one altar, as to one Jesus Christ, who proceeded from one Father, and is in one and to one returned."—*Magn.* § 7. The consecrating power and authority of bishops over all Church appointments: "Let no one do anything pertaining to the Church apart from the bishop; let that be esteemed a sure Eucharist, which is administered either by the bishop or by those to whom he has committed it. Where the bishop is seen, there let the body of believers be; even as where Christ Jesus is, there is the Catholic Church. Apart from the bishop, it is lawful neither to baptize, nor to make an agape;[127] but whatever he judges right, that also is well pleasing unto God, that all which is done be safe and sure."—*Smyrn.* § 8. Again: "It is fitting for parties, who purpose matrimony, to [257] accomplish their union with the sanction of the bishop."—*Pol.* § 5. And the importance of united prayer.—*Trall.* § 12.[128] "When ye meet often together in the same place, the powers of Satan are destroyed, and his deadliness is dissolved by the unanimity of your faith."—*Eph.* § 13.

---

[127] *agape*: The meal eaten by the Christian community together, originally associated with the Eucharist.
[128] *Trall.: Letter to the Trallians*

To these might be added his implied praise of virginity, and his implied countenance of formal resolves for that purpose, when he says, "If he boasts, he is perishing."—*Pol.* § 5; see also *Smyrn.* § 13. Apparently, too, his recognition of what has since been called the *disciplina arcani.*[129]—*Trall.* § 5; of what has also been called the *Limbus Patrum*[130]—*Magn.* § 9; of the Lord's Day—*ib.*; of the acceptableness of good works—*Pol.* § 6; of grace as inherent, not merely external—*Eph. title*; of ecclesiastical councils—*Pol.* § 7; of departed saints remembering or at least benefiting us—*Trall.* § 13;[131] and of communion with them in life and death.—*Eph.* § 12: and not least important, as throwing a light on all that has been said by the contrast, his hatred and condemnation of Judaism[132]—*Magn.* § 10; *Phil.* § 6. However, it requires no great sagacity to anticipate that some readers, before they get to the end of this list, may accuse, not us, for we are but stating apparent facts, but our venerable author, of "popery;"—such suspicion we shall leave to die away, as it assuredly will, when theological science is better understood. "Popery," it cannot be too often repeated, is the corruption of these and other true or probable doctrines; and so unnecessary and headstrong has been our opposition during the last hundred and fifty years to the corruption, that we have mistaken, and given "Popery" the advantage of our mistaking, what are Catholic doctrines or opinions for it.

[258]

5.

Dismissing this misapprehension, against which we are not bound to do more here than to protest, we invite attention to the remarkable phenomenon which these celebrated Epistles present. Are they genuine? Are they but genuine on the whole? Are they genuine all but certain incidental corruptions which

---

[129] *the* disciplina arcani: the practice of not speaking, or writing, about the most sacred doctrines or rituals of the Church to catechumens or to non-Christians.

[130] *the* Limbus Patrum: The "Limbo of the Fathers", the place where the Old Testament patriarchs went after death and from which they were led to heaven by Christ after his death and his 'descent into hell' before his resurrection.

[131] Vide Pearson's note *in loco*. [N] See above notes on pp.[179] and [180].

[132] *hatred and condemnation of Judaism*: See above, Editor's Introduction, pp.xl-xli.

cannot now be detected? Let it be granted only as far as this, that the substance of them is what Ignatius wrote,—and those who deny this may wrestle, as they best can, with the greater difficulties in which they will find themselves,—and is any further witness wanting to prove that the Catholic system, not in an inchoate state, not in doubtful dawnings, not in mere tendencies, or in implicit teaching, or in temper, or in surmises, but in a definite, complete, and dogmatic form, was the religion of St. Ignatius; and if so, where in the world did he come by it? How came he to lose, to blot out from his mind, the true Gospel, if this was not it? How came he to possess this, except it be apostolic? One does not know which, of the two, to be most struck with,—his precise unhesitating tone, or the compass of doctrine he goes through; the latter, however, has this peculiar force, which the former has not, that it quite cuts off the suspicion, if any lingers on the mind, that the conciseness with which his sentiments are conveyed has given opportunity for their being practised on by theologians, and tortured into Church meanings which they really have not. Granting that, by a mere coincidence, some one form of words in his Epistles might have been misinterpreted into an apparent countenance of some later doctrine, or that some one word like θυσιαστήριον[133] or εὐχαριστία[134] might be laden with a sense which came in later, it is quite impossible, surely, that so great a number of coinci- [259] dences should have occurred, that so many distinct doctrines, afterwards existing in the Church, should accidentally find a place, find form of words capable of denoting them, and used afterwards to denote them, in so short a document. Either the Epistles of St. Ignatius have been the document from which the Church system has been historically developed, which no one maintains, or the Church system is the basis on which St. Ignatius wrote his Epistles. No other alternative presents itself except that of denying their genuineness. It is a curious speculation, whether, in the progress of controversy, divines

---

[133] θυσιαστήριον: altar
[134] εὐχαριστία: eucharist

The Theology of the

who are determined at all risks not to admit the Church system, will not fall back upon it. Stranger things have happened.

A representation of another kind has lately been attempted,[135] which even if it were true as a statement, would be impotent as an argument. Efforts have been made to disparage the personal qualifications of the writer. We cannot congratulate the parties engaged on the happiness of their attempt. They have indeed undertaken an odious work without any possible remuneration. What can it profit them, though they were ever so able to show, what is the utmost that is attempted, that St. Ignatius had an inflated style, or that he was excited in the immediate prospect of martyrdom? Does bad taste in writing make a person incapable of receiving and holding Gospel truth? Or could the expectation of torments and death make him forget what he had heard from the Apostles, suggest to him a new Gospel, open upon him an original range of ideas, stamp them on his memory, make him think that his brethren held them, and make them also cherish and preserve this new doctrine as if that which the Apostles had taught both him and them, and persuade Polycarp also to edit the record of it? nay, moreover (supposing all these marvels), make him prophetic, so that he should anticipate, in almost all its parts, a system which, on the hypothesis of these objectors, came into the Church in the lapse of after centuries, from Jewish, Pagan, and philosophical sources? That from these sources the doctrines and practices of Catholics were afterwards in a measure corrupted, no one denies; and the correspondence in many cases between the heathen rite or philosophical dogma and the Christian, favoured the corruption. Thus Platonism[136] might corrupt the doctrine of the Trinity in the fourth century into Arianism, and Paganism the love-feasts[137] in the fifth; but it is quite another thing to say, with Faustus the Manichean,[138]

[260]

---

[135] *A representation ... attempted*: This was evidently some criticism of Ignatius from an ultra-protestant source, but it has not proved possible to trace the precise reference.
[136] *Platonism*: philosophical thought deriving ultimately from Plato (429-347 B.C.)
[137] *the love-feasts*: the *agape*; see above.
[138] *Faustus the Manichean*: Faustus of Mileve (4th century), Manichean bishop who wrote attacks on Christianity. St. Augustine met him in Carthage in 383 while he was himself a Manichean and later wrote his *Contra Faustum* against him.

that therefore Paganism brought in the Agape, or, with Dr. Priestley,[139] that philosophy brought in the doctrine of the Trinity; and what is not true in the case of this usage and this doctrine, need not be true either, and at least must not be assumed as true, of other doctrines and rites, which nevertheless may have been corrupted. Now the great value of St. Ignatius' Epistles in the controversy is, that their date is prior to the earliest date which can be alleged with any plausibility for the rise of these supposed corruptions. Justin Martyr[140] certainly had been instructed in the Greek philosophy; but what had Ignatius to do with Aristotle or Plato? Does any one pretend that there is any connexion, however remote, between him and the schools of Athens? Does his history, parentage, language, or style, betray it? Granting, for argument's sake, that the springs of truth were poisoned at Alexandria by Clement and Origen, nay, poisoned everywhere, at once, in one and the same way, and without historical traces of the catastrophe, yet who shall venture to assert, in the fullest licence or rather tyranny of [261] conjecture, that St. Ignatius, the contemporary and disciple of Apostles, and an Asiatic, was perverted, by causes unknown, to teach as apostolic a false doctrine, and, when travelling to martyrdom, to confess it repeatedly and consistently to churches which had not lost St. John's guidance above half a dozen years? Surely it is impossible. Give us, then, but St. Ignatius, and we want nothing more to prove the substantial truth of the Catholic system; the proof of the genuineness and authenticity of the Bible is not stronger; he who rejects the one, ought in consistency to reject the other.

And if the Catholic system, as a system, is brought so near to the Apostles; if it is proved to have existed as a paramount thought and a practical principle in the minds of their immediate disciples and associates, it becomes a very grave question, on this ground alone, waving altogether the consideration of uninterrupted Catholic consent, and the significant structure and indirect teaching of Scripture, whether the New Testament is

---

[139] *Dr. Priestley*: See above note on p.[94].
[140] *Justin Martyr*: See above note on p.[227].

not to be interpreted in accordance with that system. If indeed Scripture actually refuses to be so interpreted, then indeed we may be called on to suspend our judgment; but if only its text is *not inconsistent* with the Church system, there is surely greater reason for interpreting it in accordance with it than not; for it is surely more unaccountable that a new Gospel should have possessed the Church, and that, in the persons of its highest authorities, and almost in the lifetime and presence of Apostles, than that their extant writings should not have upon their surface the whole of Scripture truth. And thus we take our leave of St. Ignatius.

January, 1839.

NOTE ON ESSAY VI.

IN the foregoing Essay it was assumed that the controversy of the seventeenth century, on the subject of St. Ignatius' Epistles, in which Pearson bore so distinguished a part, had issued in a plain proof of the substantial genuineness of the text of the Medicean and Colbertine MSS. And it was inferred from this as a premiss, that apostolic Christianity was of a distinctly dogmatic character, it being impossible for those who resisted this inference to succeed in explaining away the text of Ignatius, as those MSS. contain it, and only open to them to take refuge in a denial of the premiss, that is, of the genuineness of that text. Then it was added as to such denial, "It is a curious speculation whether, in the progress of controversy, divines, who are determined at all risks not to admit the Church system, will not fall back upon it;—stranger things have happened."

So I wrote in 1838, and what I then anticipated has actually taken place since, though not in the way that I anticipated it. I did not fancy that the controversy would have been revived[141] on grounds both new, and certainly at first sight plausible, as has been the case. Those new grounds do not change my own judgment on the matter in dispute; but they have a real claim to be taken into consideration.

---

[141] *the controversy would have been revived*: In 1845 William Cureton (1808-64) published a translation of three of the Letters of Ignatius from a Syriac manuscript which had been discovered in an Egyptian monastery. These versions were longer than the received Greek texts but also omitted some of the passages that Newman had quoted in this article. Cureton maintained that these were the authentic original versions of the Letters. In 'On the text of the Epistles of St. Ignatius' in *Tracts Theological and Ecclesiastical* (1870), Newman refuted Cureton's view; and subsequent criticism has agreed with Newman that the shorter Greek texts are the genuine ones.

Note on Essay V

[This was done in a paper, which in former editions was placed here, but has now been transposed to "Theological Tracts."]

VII.

PROSPECTS OF THE ANGLICAN CHURCH.

THE existing state of parties in the Church is remarkable enough to justify some notice of it at the present moment, when a controversy is in progress, which has so powerfully arrested the attention, and excited the feelings, of its members. It is indeed melancholy to be called to such a task; for it is melancholy that there should be parties at all in a body which its Divine Founder intended to be one. However, that there are such is undeniable as a matter of fact; and with this fact we are principally concerned at present. What the cause of it is, and with whom the blame lies, of having brought things to such a pass, is another question, which shall not here be discussed.

1.

The controversy in question began, it need scarcely be said, in the publication of certain Tracts, several years since, by certain members of the University of Oxford, which thereupon were accused in various quarters of tending to Popery. And it as little requires to be proved that there is at the present moment a reaction in the Church, and a growing reaction towards the views which it has been their endeavour, and, as it seemed on [264] their commencement, almost hopeless endeavour, to advocate. The fairness of their prospects at the present moment is proved by the attack which has been made upon them by the public journals, and is confessed both by the more candid and the more violent of their opponents. For instance, the amiable Mr.

Bickersteth[1] speaks of it as having manifested itself "with the *most rapid growth* of the hotbed of these evil days." The scoffing author of the Via Media[2] says—"At this moment the Via is *crowded with young enthusiasts* who never presume to argue, except against the propriety of arguing at all;" and the candid Mr. Baden Powell,[3] who sees more of the difficulties of the controversy than the rest of their antagonists put together, admits that, "however mistaken some of the notions, or exaggerated reports, which prevail on the subject, it is not the less certain that there does exist considerable ground for some such statement; and certainly an ample reason for making a close inquiry into the facts of the case. It is clear," he proceeds, "from published authorities, that opinions and views of theology (of at least a very marked and peculiar kind, applying more especially to the subject of Church authority and others dependent on it,) have been *extensively adopted and strenuously* upheld, and are *daily gaining ground* among a considerable and influential portion *of the members*, as well as ministers, of the Established Church." And the author of the Natural History of Enthusiasm,[4] in a work the first part of which has appeared since these sheets were sent to press, speaks still more strongly: "The spread of these doctrines," he says, "is in fact now having the effect of rendering all other distinctions obsolete, and of severing the religious community into two portions, fundamentally and vehemently opposed one to the other. *Soon there will* [265] *be no middle ground left*; and every man, and especially every

---

[1] *Mr. Bickersteth*: Edward Bickersteth (1786–1850), Anglican clergyman of fiercely evangelical opinions. The quotation that follows is from his *Remarks on the Dangers of the Church of Christ* (1839); this is not among the publications listed by Newman at the head of his original 1839 article (see the Textual Appendix).
[2] *the scoffing author of the Via Media*: Not a reference to Newman's own *Via Media* but possibly a review of it. However, the words have not proved traceable (nor do they appear in the publications listed by Newman), so the identity of the 'scoffing author' is unknown. Perhaps it was an anonymous reviewer—the usual practice at this time.
[3] *the candid Mr. Baden Powell*: Baden Powell (1796-1860), liberal Anglican divine. The quotation that follows is from his *Tradition Unveiled* (1839), pp.3-4.
[4] *the author of the Natural History of Enthusiasm*: Isaac Taylor (1787-1865), historical and religious writer and noted anti-Tractarian. The quotation is from his *Ancient Christianity and the Doctrines of the Oxford Tracts* (1839-40), p.xix.

clergyman, will be compelled to make his choice between the two."

In order to show how widely the testimony to the fact extends, we will but add, out of many, two testimonies taken from the very extremes of educated society. The first is the grave witness of a bishop,[5] speaking (as the title-page of his publication implies) *ex cathedrâ* to his clergy, publishing at their request, and furnished with ample means of knowledge, at least of the external fact, if not of the works, which he condemns. He speaks of a "subject" which "is *daily assuming a more serious and alarming aspect*, and threatens a revival of the worst evils of the Romish system. Under the specious pretence of deference to antiquity, and respect for primitive models, the *foundations* of our Protestant Church are *undermined* by men who dwell within her walls, and those who sit in the Reformers' seat are traducing the Reformation." The other authority we allude to, is the amusing writer[6] of Random Recollections of the Lords and Commons, who, in a new publication, called "Travels in Town," thus speaks of the spread of the doctrines of the Church:

"They have, indeed, already made fearful progress in different parts of the country, and, as before stated, are now making rapid progress where they were before unknown. One of the largest churches in Brighton is crowded every Sunday to hear those doctrines preached by the Rev. Mr. Anderson; so is the church of Dr. Hook, in Leeds. In fact, there are few towns of note to which they have not extended; nay, they have even reached obscure and insignificant places in the remotest parts of the kingdom. They are preached in small towns in Scotland. They obtain in Elginshire, which is 600 miles north of London; and I found them myself in the heart of the Highlands of Scotland, when travelling there three months ago . . . Nor are they confined to mere churches and chapels of ease. As before remarked, [266] they are advocated in the newspaper and periodical press. The

---

[5] Dr. Sumner, Bishop of Chester. [N] John Bird Sumner (1780-1862), Anglican divine, later Archbishop of Canterbury. The quotation is from his *Charge of the Bishop of Chester* (1838), p.2.

[6] *the amusing writer*: James Grant (1802-1879), newspaper editor; his *Random Recollections of the Lords and Commons* was published in 1836. The quotation is from his *Travels in Town* (1839), vol.ii. p.127.

Morning Post sustains the character of their apologist in London; and the Liverpool Mail, the Coventry Herald, and other journals identify themselves with them in the country. The Oxford Tract doctrines have *even* insinuated themselves into the House of Commons. There is, at least, one county member in the centre of England, who cherishes them with more than a parental affection, and who is most zealous in his efforts to inoculate others with them."

This being then the state of the case, no wonder a well-known Scotch Magazine,[7] alluding to certain "unfortunate and deeply regretted publications"[8] in behalf of these doctrines, feelingly observes, "The time is gone by when those works can be passed over without notice, and *the hope that their influence would fail is now dead.*"

Mr. Hunter Gordon,[9] assuming the fact, proceeds to assign it to a *reaction* of religious sentiment; in which we agree with him, though differing from him in the particular light in which he views it.

"Protestantism," he says, "whose just boast it is to have set reason free from the fetters of ecclesiastical authority, *is not a fixed or stationary principle.* On the contrary, it is in *a state of rapid and irresistible progression*; nor did it stop short or rest content with that measure of liberty of conscience which the Reformation established. Each age still carried the right of private judgment further than the preceding; and it is only within the memory of the present age that the minds of men, both here and on the Continent, *have begun to pause* in their career of discursive reasoning and speculation, and *to revert towards faith and authority.* Symptoms have even appeared of a disposition to revert to the other extreme."

---

[7] *a well-known Scotch Magazine*: *Blackwood's Edinburgh Magazine*, vol.44, July-December 1838, p.505.

[8] *deeply regretted publications*: The writer listed these as "'Tracts for the Times,' "Froude's Remains," and Palmer's "Church of Christ," "Newman's Sermons," &c. &c.'

[9] *Mr. Hunter Gordon*: (1799/1800-55), barrister and writer. The quotation is from his *The Present State of the Controversy between the Protestant and Roman Catholic Churches* (1837), p.43-44.

All this is certainly very remarkable at first sight, considering the long time that these views have been withdrawn from our public teaching, and how gradually and certainly they seemed to be tending toward utter extinction. These very circumstances, however, have been, under God's good providence, the chief causes of their revival. The truth is, that while our Church is [267] bound as she is to her present Prayer Book, Services, and Homilies, there must ever be a point beyond which she cannot fall away from her professed principles without exciting the scruples and alarms of tender consciences. However silently and determinately the change may go on, this salutary check will be felt at last, and prevent matters from progressing further, at any rate within the Church. And when this takes place, and men at length begin to reflect on their existing state of belief, and turn back to survey that view of religion from which they have drifted, then the very novelty of it, and (as many an opponent of it will even confess) the touching beauty, loftiness of idea, and earnestness of character which it evidences or requires, take possession of their minds, and they proceed to advocate from affection what they took up as a duty.

This, it may be presumed, is a fairly correct account of the immediate circumstances under which the reaction to the true principles of the Church is at this time taking place. But other causes, collateral and disposing, may be enumerated in addition. One has been the plain tokens, which have appeared of late on the part of our civil governors, of an intention to withdraw the protection which Protestant England has as yet ever extended to the Church.[10] In the defection which threatens her from this quarter, her members naturally look about for other means of sustaining her present hold upon the popular mind; and, being deprived of "the arm of flesh," are thankful to find that they

---

[10] *withdraw the protection which Protestant England has as yet ever extended to the Church*: e.g. the Irish Church Temporalities Act (1833) which reduced the number of sees of the Church of Ireland (1833); the Poor Law Amendment Act (1834) which took the provision of assistance for the poor away from church vestries; the Marriage Act (1837) which abolished the Anglican monopoly on performing marriages, allowing other religious bodies to do so and also instituting civil marriages.

have in their armoury spiritual weapons, long disused indeed, but, through God's mercy, not forfeited, and of untold efficacy.

[268] Again, the violence of the acting parties among the sectarians has both opened men's minds to the serious moral evils latent in sectarianism, and also removed or diminished the reluctance, which would otherwise have been felt, to recur to principles indirectly condemnatory of persons, with whom they had hitherto been living in habits of intimacy or intercourse.

But besides these, and similar causes of the moment, there has been for some years, from whatever cause, a growing tendency towards the character of mind and feeling of which Catholic doctrines are the just expression. This manifested itself long before men entered into the truth intellectually, or knew what they ought to believe, and what they ought not; and what the practical duties were, to which a matured knowledge would lead them. During the first quarter of this century a great poet[11] was raised up in the North, who, whatever were his defects, has contributed by his works, in prose and verse, to prepare men for some closer and more practical approximation to Catholic truth. The general need of something deeper and more attractive than what had offered itself elsewhere, may be considered to have led to his popularity; and by means of his popularity he re-acted on his readers, stimulating their mental thirst, feeding their hopes, setting before them visions, which, when once seen, are not easily forgotten, and silently indoctrinating them with nobler ideas, which might afterwards be appealed to as first principles. Doubtless there are things in the poems and romances in question, of which a correct judgment is forced to disapprove; and which must be ever a matter of regret; but contrasted with the popular writers of the last century, with its novelists, and some of its most admired poets, as Pope,[12] they stand almost as oracles of Truth confronting the ministers of error and sin.

---

[11] *a great poet*: Sir Walter Scott (1771-1832) first made his name as a poet, though today he is better known for his novels.
[12] *Pope*: Alexander Pope (1688-1744). Although he was a Catholic, there is virtually no reflection of his faith in his writing; his *Essay on Man* expresses a broadly fatalist philosophy.

And while history in prose and verse was thus made the [269] instrument of Church feelings and opinions, a philosophical basis for the same was under formation in England by a very original thinker,[13] who, while he indulged a liberty of specula-tion which no Christian can tolerate, and advocated conclusions which were often heathen rather than Christian, yet after all instilled a higher philosophy into inquiring minds, than they had hitherto been accustomed to accept. In this way he made trial of his age, and found it respond to him, and succeeded in interesting its genius in the cause of Catholic truth. It has indeed been only since the death of Coleridge that these results of his writings have fully shown themselves; but they were very evident when they were once seen, and discovered the tenden-cies which had been working in his mind from the first. Two living poets[14] may be added, one of whom in the department of fantastic fiction, the other in that of philosophical meditation, have addressed themselves to the same high principles and feelings, and carried forward their readers in the same direction.

These writers, however, are to be noticed far more as indications of what was secretly going on in the minds of men, than as causes of it. The reaction in the Church, or whatever other name we may give it, was long ago anticipated; that is, long before it showed itself in any distinct tokens which would be obvious to the multitude. Twenty-three years since a saga-cious observer,[15] withdrawn from the world, and surveying its movements at a distance, writes as follows:

"No Church on earth," he says, "has more intrinsic excellence [than the English Church], yet no Church, probably, has less practical influence. Her excellence then, I conceive, gives ground for confiding that Providence never will abandon her; but her want of influence would seem no less clearly to indicate, that divine wisdom will not [270] always suffer her to go on without measures for her improvement.

---

[13] *a very original thinker*: Samuel Taylor Coleridge (1772–1834), poet, critic and philosopher.
[14] *two living poets*: Robert Southey (1774-1843) and William Wordsworth (1770-1850); see above note on p.[16].
[15] *a sagacious observer*: Alexander Knox 1757–1831), Church of Ireland lay theologian; his *Remains* were published in 1834.

271

"Temporary adversity is that to which, in all such cases, as far as we know, the providence of God has hitherto resorted; and we can form a clear idea of the manner in which a temporary depression of the English Church might exalt its moral qualities.... But I conjecture that other valuable results, perhaps not otherwise to be arrived at, are to be hoped for from the apprehended reverse. Hitherto the Church of England, though more temperate in her measures than any other portion of the reformed body, has manifested no sentiment with such unremitting intensity as dread of whatever could be deemed Popery. I deny not the expediency, perhaps the necessity, of this feeling, in such circumstances as have hitherto existed. But it has given safety to the Church of England at the expense of perfection, which last can be attained only by proving all things, and holding fast what is good; and this discrimination can be practised only in the absence of prejudice. As matters are, dread of transubstantiation has made the sacrament a ceremony; and to ward off infallibility, every man has been encouraged to shape a creed for himself. The next certain cure for this extreme will be to experience its fruits. Another fall by dissenterism will make it be felt, that if Popery can be a Charybdis, there is a Scylla on the other side no less dangerous. But it will be still more useful to learn, that, in the mixed mass of the Roman Catholic religion, there is gold and silver and precious stones, as well as wood, hay, and stubble; and that everything of the former nature is to be as carefully preserved, as everything of the latter nature is to be wisely rejected.

"Such are the considerations with which I comfort myself against events which I think I see approaching.... Shall the present negligence and insensibility always prevail? This cannot be: the rich provision made by the grace and providence of God, for habits of a noble kind, is evidence that men shall arise fitted both by nature and ability, to discover for themselves, and to display to others, whatever yet remains undiscovered, whether in the words or works of God. But if it be asked how shall fit instruments be prepared for this divine purpose, it can only be answered that, in the most signal instances, times of severe trial have been chosen for divine communications. . . . My persuasion of the radical excellence of the Church of England does not suffer me to doubt that she is to be an illustrious agent in bringing the mystical kingdom of Christ to its ultimate perfection."—*Knox's Remains*, vol. i., p. 51, *et seq.*

[271]

272

Such is the prophecy of a calm and sagacious mind, whose writings are themselves no slight evidence of the intellectual and moral movement under consideration. In this respect he outstrips Scott and Coleridge, that he realizes his own position, and is an instance in rudiment of those great restorations which he foresaw in development. And while he shares with those eminent writers of his day the work of furthering what he anticipated, others doubtless, in a similar seclusion from passing events, shared with him anticipations which they were not led to further, or even to record. It was impossible for serious-minded men, ever so little versed in Antiquity, and in the history of the Reformation, not to see that, for a century and more past, primitive truth had either been forgotten, or looked down upon, and our own engagements to it tacitly loosened. Indeed, opinions which were openly acquiesced in by free-thinkers, and noticed with satisfaction by the world's philosophers and historians, could not but excite strange impressions in the minds of true Churchmen, partly melancholy, partly by way of contrast, leading them to look forward into the future, and to anticipate change and improvement in the public mind. A much venerated clergyman[16] of the last generation, one of the most strenuous maintainers of ancient doctrines, and an energetic opponent of those who wished to carry our Church further than it had hitherto gone in the career of Protestantism, said shortly before his death to a friend of our own, "Depend on it, the day will come, when those great doctrines now buried," those connected with the Church, "will be brought out to the light of day, and then the effect will be quite fearful." If there be any [272] who now blame the impetuosity of the current, let them rather turn their reflections upon those who have dammed up our majestic river till it has become a flood.

---

[16] *a much venerated clergyman*: Thomas Sikes (d. 1834), Rector of Guilsborough. His remarks were made in conversation with W. J. Copeland; cf. Liddon's *Life of Pusey*, Vol 1, pp 257-8.

2.

Now if there be any truth in these remarks, it is plainly idle and perverse to refer the change of opinions which is now going on to the acts of two or three individuals, as is sometimes done. Of course every event in human affairs has a beginning; and a beginning implies a when, and a where, and a by whom, and a how. But except in these necessary circumstances, the phenomenon in question is in a manner quite independent of things visible and historical. It is not here or there; really it has no progress, no causes, no fortunes; it is not a movement, it is a spirit, it is a spirit afloat, neither "in the secret chambers" nor "in the desert,"[17] but everywhere. It is within us, rising up in the heart where it was least expected, and working its way, though not in secret, yet so subtly and impalpably, as hardly to admit of precaution or encounter, on any ordinary human rules of opposition. It is an adversary in the air, a something one and entire, a whole wherever it is, unapproachable and incapable of being grasped, as being the result of causes far deeper than political or other visible agencies,—the spiritual awakening of spiritual wants.

Nothing can show more strikingly the truth of this representation, than to refer to what may be called the theological history of the individuals who, whatever be their differences from each other on important or unimportant points, yet are associated together in the advocacy of the doctrines in question. Dr. Hook[18] and Mr. Churton[19] represent the High Church dignitaries of the [273] last generation; Mr. Perceval[20] the Tory aristocracy; Mr. Keble[21] is of the country clergy, and comes from valleys and woods, far removed both from notoriety and noise; Mr. Palmer[22] and Mr. Todd[23] are of Ireland; Dr. Pusey[24] became what he is from among

[17] *neither "in the secret chambers . . .* : Cf. Matthew 24:26: 'Wherefore if they shall say unto you, Behold, he is in the desert; go not forth: behold, he is in the secret chambers; believe it not.'

[18] *Dr. Hook*: Walter Farquhar Hook (1798–1875), Anglican divine; vicar of Leeds and later Dean of Chichester.

[19] *Mr. Churton*: Edward Churton (1800–74), Anglican divine, Rector of Crayke; he was sympathetic to the Tractarians.

[20] *Mr. Perceval*: Arthur Philip Perceval (1799–1853), Anglican divine; royal chaplain.

[21] *Mr. Keble*: See above note on p.[12].

[22] *Mr. Palmer*: see the Editor's Introduction, p. xxxii.

the Universities of Germany, and after a severe and tedious analysis of Arabic MSS. Mr. Dodsworth[25] is said to have begun in the study of Prophecy; Mr. Newman[26] to have been much indebted to the friendship of Archbishop Whately;[27] Mr. Froude,[28] if any one, gained his views from his own mind. Others have passed over from Calvinism[29] and kindred religions.

While we write, a fresh instance of this independence and individuality meets our eye; which is so beautifully expressed that we must be allowed to set it before the reader.

"For the view contained in this Preface," says Mr. Oakeley[30] in the remarks prefixed to his Whitehall Sermons, "such as it is, the author is alone responsible. . . . It has been developed (so far as it can be said to be developed) in his mind *partly by study, partly by reflection, partly by conversation with one or two friends, inquirers like himself.* Neither does he by any means wish to disclaim (far otherwise) the influence of the teaching and example of certain members of his own University, who have for some time past been actively engaged in calling the attention of the Church in this nation to the theology of primitive times, and of her own earlier age; and thus are very commonly, but very erroneously, represented as the founders of a system, *to which they are after all but some, among many, witnesses.* With those persons the present writer, though indebted to them for many acts of kindness, and far more indebted to them for benefits which, unconsciously to themselves, they have, as he humbly trusts,

---

[23] *Mr. Todd*: James Henthorn Todd (1805–69), Church of Ireland divine; biblical scholar and later Librarian of Trinity College, Dublin.
[24] *Dr. Pusey*: Edward Bouverie Pusey (1800–82), Anglican divine, biblical scholar, close friend of Newman and one of the leaders of the Tractarians who were often called 'Puseyites'.
[25] *Mr. Dodsworth*: William Dodsworth (1798-1861), Anglican divine; he became a Catholic in 1850.
[26] *Mr. Newman*: Newman refers to himself in this way as the original *British Critic* article was unsigned (as was the usual practice).
[27] *Archbishop Whateley*: Joseph Whately (1730-97), Anglican divine, later Archbishop of Dublin; at Oriel he became Newman's mentor when the latter first became a Fellow. Newman describes his influence on him and their subsequent divergence in the *Apologia*, pp.114-118.
[28] *Mr. Froude*: See above note on p.[v].
[29] *Calvinism*: the teaching of John Calvin (1509-64), French Protestant theologian, more extreme than Luther; he taught a strict doctrine of predestination.
[30] *Mr. Oakeley*: Frederick Oakeley (1802-80), Anglican divine; he followed Newman into the Catholic Church in 1845 and subsequently became a Catholic priest. His *Whitehall Sermons* were published 1837-9.

been instrumental in conveying to him, has yet never enjoyed the happiness and privilege of constant and familiar intercourse. From this circumstance *his testimony to the truths*, which they have long been engaged in upholding, *may possibly have gained in independence* what it has certainly lost in completeness."—Pp. lv. lvi.

[274] Mr. Oakeley has but expressed in this extract what many could repeat after him. Where, then, is the common origin to which may be referred the present movement? What head of a sect is there? What march of opinions can be traced from mind to mind? They are one and all in their degree the organs of One Sentiment, which has risen up simultaneous in many places very mysteriously.

We consider then this to be a truer view of the recent rise of Catholic opinions, than the one ordinarily given. Its progress, for example, has been lately referred, by a candid looker-on,[31] to the confident tone of its visible organs, and the tendency of the human mind, in certain states, to accept whatever is forcibly urged upon its acceptance; and it is accordingly anticipated, that, when the excitement is over which such a mode of conversion implies, and the mind is turned calmly to examine the grounds of its new opinions, there will be a corresponding, though not perhaps so sudden a relapse from them. Now this, though an intelligible, and what is called sensible view of the matter, is surely deficient in depth; deficient for this reason, if for no other, that it does not contemplate and provide against the chance of deep moral causes being in operation, which are not seen. It may be frankly confessed that an excitement of the feelings, of whatever kind, *has* much to do with what is taking place, and perhaps will have still more,—and so again has the influence of authority, respect for character, and the like; so has sentiment, imagination, or fancy; and lastly, though the writer, to whom we refer, would perhaps deny it, so has discussion, argument, investigation. But neither one, nor all of them together have been the real operating *cause*; rather they had

---

[31] *a candid looker-on*: It has not proved possible to identify this writer; the comment does not appear to be in any of the texts Newman listed at the head of the original article.

been the means only, through which that cause has acted. Men who feel in themselves a moral need, which certain doctrines supply, may be right or wrong in their feeling, as the case may [275] be; and the doctrines may supply it more or less genuinely; but anyhow they embrace the doctrines because they need them; and if they give tokens of being moved by argument, or feeling, or fancy, or by sympathetic excitement, or by influence and authority, it is merely that they are moved *through* these means, not by them. Minds contented with what they are and what they have, easily resist solicitations whether of imagination or argument; but they who wish for things which they have not, start and look about them with beating hearts and troubled eyes, when a whisper, from whatever source, tells them that their yearnings perchance may find somewhat to satisfy them. Such feelings, if of earth, are merely enthusiastic, and often argue impatience and want of discipline:—thus youths of high spirit indulge ambitious views, or allow themselves in other ways to idolize the creature; but when those feelings are true and right, they are the motions of a divine love, and the disposition to confide which they involve, whithersoever tending, is of the nature of faith. As to what *are* earthly, what heavenly feelings, and who is to discriminate between them, this is quite another question, on which men of different sentiments will decide differently. All we insist on is, that religious opinion in general is the result of something deeper than mere caprice or than syllogistic conviction, and more enduring than excitement or passion.

3.

We have been led on from considering the history of the present reaction in religious opinion, to discuss the moral causes to which religious opinion is to be referred; and we say that, in a given case, argument, novelty, influence of others, imaginative beauty, these and the like appeals which address themselves to [276] the mind from without, are but touchstones or tests, bringing out the hidden dispositions of one man, not of another. They are but the occasions, not the causes, of a man's changing his mind, and any other view of them is a very shallow one. But at the same time we have no intention of disputing that, besides this moral orthodoxy, as it may be called, there are a great number of persons of unformed characters and opinions, who have not definite basis enough within them, good or bad, to respond to or revolt from the real substance of the various *phantasiæ*[32] offered to them; and they certainly are arrested and accidentally persuaded one way or the other by those visible exhibitions, which to the former class of minds are but means and channels of something deeper. As some men are converted or repulsed by the hidden sympathy or antipathy of their hearts toward the objects presented to them, many more, being incapable of either, are what is called "convinced," that is by *argument*, or "taken," that is by mere *fancy*, or "persuaded," that is by mere *external influence*. Such persons, while they remain in this state, without root in themselves, are ever liable to be "convinced," "taken," or "persuaded" back again, and then they are rightly called *inconsistent*; though very often, nay in a measure always, in spite of the superficial character of such alternations, their hearts are unconsciously operated upon, for good or bad, by that doctrine, which they at first took up, not from its congeniality to their own minds, but from the shape in which it addresses them. And again some are called inconsistent by the world, whose changes are really owing to the keenness of their cravings after true spiritual nourishment. Persons thus earnestly on the look-out for something higher in the way of religion, than they at present possess, naturally close at once with whatever promises best. Then as their tone of mind rises, they become dissatisfied with their first choice; and on something better offering itself, quit it; not of course from light or capricious motives, but from the ordinary development of their own character and perceptions.

[277]

All these things being considered, it would not be at all surprising if, in spite of the earnestness of the principal advocates of the views in question, for which every one seems to give them credit, there should be among their followers much

---

[32] *phantasiæ*: notions, ideas.

that is enthusiastic, extravagant, or excessive. All these aberrations will be and are imputed to the doctrines from which they proceed; not unnaturally, but hardly fairly, for aberrations there must ever be, whatever the doctrine is, while the human heart is sensitive, capricious, and wayward. It must be so in the nature of things; it cannot be helped; a mixed multitude went out of Egypt with the Israelites.[33] Truth and falsehood do not meet each other here by harsh lines; there are ten thousand varieties of intermixture between them. There will ever be a number of persons professing the opinions of a movement party, who talk loudly and strangely, do odd or fierce things, display themselves unnecessarily, and disgust other people; there will be ever those who are too young to be wise, too generous to be cautious, too warm to be sober, or too intellectual to be humble;—of whom human sagacity cannot determine, only the event, and perhaps not even that, whether they feel what they say, or how far: whether they are to be encouraged or discountenanced. Such persons will be very apt to attach themselves to particular persons, to use particular names, to say things merely because others say them, and to act in a party-spirited way; and in what has been above said, about the invisible and spiritual character [278] of the present reaction, there was no intention of denying that of necessity it will be invested externally, from the circumstances just mentioned, in the dress and attributes of a school.

There is no warrant, however, for supposing that the agents themselves in the present revolution of religious sentiment partake in the fault we have been specifying; though, as is natural, it is the fashion to lay it at their door. It has been the fashion; though, in spite of a certain learned dignitary in the North,[34] we hope it is a fashion going out, to accuse them of being simple Dominics,[35] or men who contract their notion of

---

[33] *a mixed multitude went out of Egypt . . .* : Cf. Exodus 12:38
[34] *a certain learned dignitary in the North*: As the 1839 text reveals, this was George Townsend (1788-1857), low church Anglican divine, extremely hostile to the Oxford Movement; at the time of Newman's article, he was vicar of North Allerton. Strongly anti-Catholic, in 1850 he had an audience with Pope Pius IX and attempted to convert him to Protestantism.
[35] *Dominics*: i.e. like St. Dominic (1170-1221), founder of the Order of Preachers (Dominicans), seen by Protestants as a fanatical heresy-hunter.

religious truth to a narrow range of words, and would fain burn every one who scruples to accept it. Now it is certainly true, that they attach the deepest importance to Catholic principles in themselves; but as certainly they do not consider any opinion to be *per se* the salvation or the condemnation of the individual holding it, but a real, congenial, hearty belief, which, whether it exist or not, an Omniscient Eye only can discern. They seem to believe that certain doctrines are the rightful property of certain minds, and true doctrines of true minds; that many minds are neither true nor untrue, but in a transition or intermediate state; moreover that true and untrue doctrines exert an influence upon all minds which admit them, whether of the formed or unformed class. In their judgments of individuals then they go as far as this, that the holding a true doctrine is in itself a right thing; the denying a true doctrine in itself an act of sin, as any other sinful act; and this they would say is quite sufficient, without going further, to influence our impressions of the persons holding the one and the other. If it be said that error, though of the nature of sin in itself, is not necessarily so in the [279] person holding it, they are willing to admit this; but they think at the same time that it is *primâ facie* evidence of a very cogent sort against that person. Lastly, they consider it a duty to act towards such persons, *as if* they were really what they appeared to be; for they are *in the place* of heretics, they profess themselves such: they stand in a hostile position to the Church, and the Church is bound, by her discipline and (as it were) her ceremonial, to withdraw her protection from them.

All this is by the way; and we will not interrupt the course of our remarks to notice an extreme misconception of the writer, to whom we have above referred, on this head;[36] but we may be

---

[36] Yet we may mention it in a note. This gentleman says: "Who does not lament to read in the pages of the learned Author of the History of the Arians, the defence of some of the worst principles on which the Church of Rome established all its usurpations? Who would believe that in the present day, . . . when he is relating in very just language the evil consequences of the conduct of the heretics, who opposed, in the fourth century, the doctrine of the Divinity of Christ, he declares, that it is 'but equitable to anticipate those consequences in the persons of the heresiarchs, rather than to suffer them gradually to unfold, and spread far and wide after their day, sapping the faith of their deluded and less guilty followers.' That is, it is better to inflict punishment upon the persons of the

allowed, perhaps, in proof of what we have said, to cite the [280]
Preface to the series of "Plain Sermons," which writers[37] in the
Tracts for the Times have lately commenced. Of these Sermons
we will but say, that, if they continue as they have begun, they
will do as much to calm and reassure religious persons, and to
root Catholic doctrines into the hearts of their upholders, as any
publication to which the last five years have given birth. The
Editors say:

"If therefore, as time goes on, there shall be found persons, who,
admiring the innate beauty and majesty of the fuller system of
Primitive Christianity, and seeing the transcendent strength of its
principles, shall become loud and voluble advocates in their behalf,
speaking the more freely because they do not feel them deeply as
founded in divine and eternal truth, of such persons it is our duty to
declare plainly, that as we should contemplate their condition with

---

heresiarchs, than to wait to confute their opinions because those opinions are
injurious."The fact is simply this. Mr. Newman is speaking of the duty of cross-
examining, pressing hard in argument, and forcing into consequences, the originator
of an heretical opinion, as the Fathers at Nicæa did Arius. He says this is charitable to
all parties, as tending to open their eyes; and equitable withal, since a heresiarch, instead
of hiding his heresy from himself under ambiguous phrases, should have its full
consequences, its fullest developed malignity, wrought out in his own instance, instead
of its running its course through other minds, and growing by degrees into its full
proportions after perhaps his death. There is not any allusion of any kind in the passage
or context to persecution at all; and we entirely believe that the author himself had not
the most distant intention of alluding to it. If Mr. T. will look again, he will see that by
"person" Mr. Newman does not mean the heresiarch's actual body, as he strangely
supposes. But Mr. T. seems to have no idea of any castigation but a physical one. Let
us assure him there are such things as moral force, and victories in argument.A person
who has written on the "idolatrous tendency" of the Tracts for the Times, repeats this
mistake apparently on Mr. T.'s authority; and we have lately heard a still further
improved version of it, viz., "that there was no amount of physical suffering which Mr.
Newman did not profess himself ready to inflict in order to put down his
opponent."[This note reminds me that I have been unfair to myself in my Apologia,
p.47, ed. 2, in saying, in answer to Mr. T.'s charge, "Arius was banished, not burned;"
for there is nothing whatever, as above observed, about civil punishment in the passage
in question. The notice of Arius's banishment occurs in a subsequent part of my volume,
which throughout discountenances civil penalties for religious opinions as leading to
hypocritical conformity.] [N]
[37] [Mr. Thomas Keble and Mr. Isaac Williams.] [N] Thomas Keble (1793-1875),
Anglican divine, was the younger brother of John Keble (see above note on p.[12]);
author of four of the *Tracts for the Times* and forty-eight of the *Plain Sermons* that
Newman is referring to. Isaac Williams (1801-65), a Tractarian Anglican divine, was
a friend of Thomas Keble and the author of numerous poems and hymns.

much serious misgiving, so would they be the last persons from whom we should seek support.

"But if, on the other hand, there shall be any, who, in the silent humility of their lives, and in their unaffected reverence for holy things, show that they in truth accept these principles as real and substantial, and by habitual purity of heart and serenity of temper, give proof of their deep veneration for sacraments and sacramental ordinances, those persons, whether our professed adherents or not, best exemplify the kind of character which the writers of the Tracts for the Times have wished to form."[38]

[281]   Nothing, as it appears to us, can be more wise and religious than the temper which these remarks breathe. What more can be required of the preachers of neglected truth, than that they should caution persons against being carried away by it into the opposite extreme, and should admit that some who do not assent to their preaching, are holier and better men than some who do? Whether those peculiar doctrines which they are reviving, be true or not, is another question, into which we do not now enter; though no reader of the British Critic can doubt what our answer would be. We only say that the truth of their doctrine is the only point which lies open for discussion. It is not the mode of enforcing it, which is in fault. While they hold the sentiments of the above extract, their opponents will "not find any occasion against" them, except they "find it concerning the law of" their "God."[39] They are not answerable for the dust and din which attends every great moral movement. The truer doctrines are, the more liable they are to be perverted.

But to return. We allow, then, as those writers themselves confess, that the present widely spread change of opinion is by no means clear of moral extravagance in the case of individuals, which its promoters would fain see away, if they had their will. Nor again is it at all certain, that their influence will never recede where it has once gained a footing. Again, it may often happen, as the Editors of the Sermons contemplate, that persons rightly

---

[38] *"If therefore . . . wished to form.":* Plain Sermons by Contributors to the *"Tracts for the Times."* Vol.I., London, 1839, pp.1-2.
[39] *"not find any occasion . . . their "God":* Cf. Daniel 6:5

disposed in the main, but of less keen sensibilities, will be discouraged or perplexed by the appearances which the movement presents at the very outset, and prevented from embracing the truth, though offered to their acceptance, by the force of "logical conviction," or "imagination," or "external influence," having already acted upon them the other way. These are the [282] instruments by which our ideas of religion become impressed upon us, whatever they are; and as the heart shows itself tender and alive to truth when brought home to us through them, so it is almost of necessity dull and impenetrable when such natural avenues are closed. However, in spite of the extravagances, misapprehensions, and inconsistencies to which we have alluded, in men both on the right and on the wrong side of ecclesiastical questions, there will after all be a general coincidence between a certain set of opinions and a certain character. The one will attend upon the other, and be a sort of type of it, correct in the main, though not to be depended on in every particular case. It is surely reasonable to judge in this way. We expect of a person who has adopted a set of opinions, whatever it may be, a character and tone of mind to correspond; and if we fail to see it in him, we note down the inconsistency. And in the present instance there is nothing to prevent this general expectation from holding good. The views of Catholic truth which are now brought out are deficient in many of those suspicious attractions which other systems hold out to the pride of intellect and originality of mind, to powers of eloquence, to susceptibility of emotion, to impatience of restraint. These views elevate the Church, but they sink the individual: and therefore those who take up with them are the more to be depended on, as far as this goes, for the sincerity and consistency of their profession. It is easy indeed to talk of mere sentiment, romance, and the perception of the beautiful, acting powerfully upon such persons, and being the cause of the present revolution in religious opinion. Of course, if the doctrines in question do give scope for the exercise of these feelings, their advocates are not to blame for this: they cannot [283] help the Church system being beautiful in idea: it is so, whether

283

they would have it so, or whether they would not. But at the same time, the sense of the beautiful, we would beg to suggest, as cherished and elicited by the Catholic doctrines, is, after all, no syren to beguile the unstable, to "take the prison'd soul and lap it in Elysium:"[40] no need here for men to summon up fortitude, to be inflexible, to tie themselves hand and foot, for fear the winning sounds should lure them on to their own undoing. A very moderate foresight of the consequences of indulging it, would, we apprehend, be sufficient to make such precaution against its fascinations quite unnecessary. There are interests and motives which make a more pressing appeal on us than the sense of the beautiful. Yet, if this quality in Catholicism, which is so very much suspected by the prudent and reasoning among us, does carry men away, we do not see that any permanent mischief can come of it, where men are aware what they are doing. We see no harm in persons obeying the higher perceptions and impulses of their minds for the time being, whatever they may be, whether of the contemplative, or what is called the romantic, or again, of a more active and businesslike character,—provided always that they are ready to go on with what they have begun; to acquiesce in consequences when they come upon them; to take up with a course as a whole.

This influence of accidental causes, as instruments by which the catholicly-disposed mind is introduced to the objective catholic truth, is fully acknowledged and defended by Dr. Pusey in his recent Letter to the Bishop of Oxford.[41] He says:

[284] "One has begun probably by one portion of the system, another by another, as Providence guided his disposition or his circumstances; yet as he took up, one by one, increasing duties, he found himself but filling up voids in himself; his unevenness or inequalities softened; inconsistencies subdued, and himself by each such approximation only rendered less out of harmony with the system in which he was placed; not thinking himself 'some great one,' but rather 'an unprofitable

---

[40] *"take the prison'd . . . in Elysium"*: John Milton (1608-74), *Comus*, l. 256.
[41] *recent Letter to the Bishop of Oxford*: *Letter to the Bishop of Oxford on the Tendency to Romanism imputed to Doctrines held of old as now in the English Church*. By E. P. Pusey, D.D. Parker, Oxford. 1839.

servant,'[42] who was slowly learning to 'do that which was his duty to do.'"—P. 236.

4.

We have been making admissions as to the operation of accidental causes in the present extension of Church principles, over and above the mere force of those principles themselves, and we make them without scruple or apprehension. Nor should we much object to carrying on such admissions farther; to admitting that certain accidental causes, such as the tendencies of the age, the national character, the character of the persons more especially engaged in the work, and the like, may be giving a tone and a bias to the rising Church spirit itself, and that of a nature to adhere to it even throughout its future progress. Accidental causes are indeed found to work both ways; they both influence the mind in embracing certain doctrines, and they permanently fix the expression and development of those doctrines afterwards. Thus truth in every age is marked by hues and touches, not its own strictly, however they may harmonize with it; and these become its historical distinctions in future time. This is unavoidable, and moreover it can hardly be doubted that much is gained by it; provided, of course, the true foundation is preserved throughout. Variety, to a certain extent, seems to be a prevailing law in the systems both of nature and of grace, and to be a great source of beauty and richness in both. Indeed, just as we say in physics, that nature "abhors a vacuum," in the same way, it would almost seem, in moral subjects, that she abhorred identity; that is, [285] identity of the narrow, absolute, formal kind, which is not content with that oneness of principle, which corresponds to the unity of physical laws, but would shape everything into one mould. It is a great characteristic in fact of the true system, that it can afford to be thus free and spontaneous, to vary its aspect, to modify, enlarge, and accommodate itself to times and places without loss of principle. Why should not the different ages of the Church, with their different characters, make up a whole,

---

[42] *an unprofitable servant . . . duty to do'*: Luke 17:10.

just as the Church itself in every age is, as St. Paul says, "many members, yet but one body"?[43]

We mention this, because some persons are apt to think when Antiquity is talked about, that it implies an actual return to the exact forms of opinion and modes of feeling which are known to have prevailed in those earlier times; and they forthwith begin to talk about the nineteenth century, and the impossibility of our retrograding, and the folly and disadvantage of too narrow a standard, and the fallacy of thinking that whatever is ancient is, as such, an object of imitation. Simeon on his pillar,[44] Antony in the mountain,[45] Councils in full debate, and popular elections,[46] incense and oil, insufflations[47] and stoles with crosses on them,[48] complete their notion of the Ancient Religion, when they hear it recommended. But all this is surely out of place at the present time. Nothing has been said by those whose writings have been so severely animadverted on lately, to show that they are antiquarian fanatics, urging the ancient doctrine and discipline upon the present age in any other except essential points, and not allowing fully that many things are unessential, even if abstractedly desirable. As to these points, let the age acknowledge and submit itself to them in proportion as it can enter into them with heart and reality; in proportion as the reception of them would be, in its case, the natural development of Church principles. There are such things as indifferent points of character, all will admit, in which every age and every individual may be idiosyncratic without blame; and these surely may

[286]

---

[43] *"many members, yet but one body"*: I Corinthians 12:20

[44] *Simeon on his pillar*: St. Simon Stylites (c.390-459), an ascetic who lived on top of a column for thirty-seven years, becoming famous and influential for his spiritual advice.

[45] *Antony in the mountains*: St. Antony (d. 356-7), Abbot; he was initially a hermit, but eventually disciples gathered around him whom he formed into a community. He is seen as the founder of monasticism.

[46] *popular elections*: In the early centuries bishops were often elected by a vote of the faithful or even by popular acclamation, as in the case of St.Ambrose in 374.

[47] *insufflations*: the practice of breathing into or onto something or someone in a liturgical rite. It was used in various ceremonies in patristic times and was part of the rite of baptism before the changes after the Second Vatican Council. In contemporary Catholic liturgy it is used in the rite of consecration of chrism by the bishop in the Maundy Thursday Chrism Mass. It had been abolished in all Protestant services.

[48] *stoles with crosses on them*: Stoles are usually adorned with a crosses at either end; all such decoration was absent from the equivalent 'scarf' worn in Anglican worship.

and often do produce theological differences of rite, usage, opinion, and argument, which fairly admit of a mutual toleration. We readily allow that the writer of the Homily on Alms-deeds[49] scarcely keeps step when he would walk in company with St. Cyprian; and that Tertullian, on the other hand, feels uncomfortable when thrust by a venerated living prelate[50] into the Thirty-nine Articles; or again, that even Bishop Bull in his Harmonia[51] has not effected more than an armistice between the early Church and the German Protestants, on the subject which he treats.

Again, this age is a practical age: the age of the Fathers was more contemplative; their theology, consequently, had a deeper, more mystical, more subtle character about it, than we with our present habits of thought can readily enter into. We lay greater stress than they on proofs from definite verses of Scripture, or what are familiarly called texts, and we build up a system upon them; they rather recognized a certain truth lying hid under the tenor of the sacred text as a whole, and showing itself more or less in this verse or that as it might be. We look on the letter of Scripture more as a foundation, they as an organ of the truth. Such a difference is quite allowable, or rather natural or even necessary. The Fathers might have traditionary information of the general drift of the inspired text which we have not. Moderns argue from what alone remains to them; they are able to move more freely. Moreover, a certain high moral state of mind, [287] which times of persecution alone create, may be necessary for

---

[49] *the Homily on Almsdeeds*: The Books of Homilies were authorized sermons issued in two books (in 1547 and 1562-3) for use in the Church of England. The Homily on Almsdeeds says 'that holy father Cyprian taketh good occasion to exhort earnestly to the mercifull worke of giving almes and helping the poore, and there he admonisheth to consider how wholsome and profitable it is to releeve the needy, and helpe the afflicted, by the which wee may purge our sinnes, and heale our wounded soules' which contradicts the Protestant doctrine of justification by faith alone.

[50] Dr. Kaye, Bishop of Lincoln. [N] Bishop John Kaye (1783–1853) published *Ecclesiastical History of the Second and Third Centuries, Illustrated from the Writings of Tertullian* (1826), based on lectures he had given as Regius Professor of divinity at Cambridge. He structured the work on the plan of the Thirty-Nine Articles, quoting Tertullian in support of the doctrines of each of them. This unusual arrangement was commented on unfavourably by critics.

[51] *Bishop Bull in his Harmonia*: See above note on p.[180].

a due exercise of mystical interpretation. To attempt it otherwise than from the heart, would be a profanation; better not attempt it at all.

This should be understood; if persons, in this day, do not feel "sufficient for such things"[52] spontaneously, we are not going to force such things upon them as a piece of imitation. No good could come of merely imitating the Fathers for imitation's sake; rather, such servility is likely to prevent the age from developing Church principles so freely as it might otherwise do. Even the Fathers were of different schools. The respective characters of the Alexandrian, Antiochene, Roman, and African are distinctly marked. Again, it is hardly possible to deny that Augustine's theology is in a certain sense what may be called a second edition of the Catholic Tradition, the transmission of the primitive stream through an acute, rich, and powerful mind. Another change took place in point of tone and view (for it does not fall into our subject to allude to positive errors) in the theology of the schoolmen. And there have been other great changes since, involving changes in the moral state and (what may be called) mind of the Church, and that over and above the silent progress which society has been making, the revolutions of civil government, the march of civilization, and, what has necessarily attended upon it, a far more active and excited state of the public mind. These causes must have produced and must be still producing their several effects, greater or less, upon us, such as would extend at last to our theology. Indeed we cannot suppose any set of events of this nature to leave the world exactly where they found it; they [288] would influence, or alarm, or develop, or direct the minds of divines, as the case might be.

In this way, then, it is that we stand with respect to Antiquity. We cannot, if we would, move ourselves literally back into the times of the Fathers: we must, in spite of ourselves, be church-men of our own era, not of any other, were it only for this

---

[52] *"sufficient for such things"*: Cf. 2 Corinthians 2:16

reason, that we are born in the nineteenth century, not in the fourth.[53]

5.

We are tempted to illustrate this matter a little more fully. Every one knows that in mathematics the same truths may be thrown into the language of geometry or algebra, the same conclusions worked out by distinct processes in this or that medium or *calculus*. The same thing takes place in all sciences. A problem which continually meets us is, how to express the truths of one province of knowledge in the terms of another. To take the stock illustration, red may be called the sound of a trumpet when thrown into the *calculus* of sound. Again, the great difficulty of translating is to find the equivalent expressions in the *calculus* of a fresh language. What, again, is the art of rhetoric but the reduction of reasonings, in themselves sound, into the *calculus* of the tastes, opinions, passions, and aims of [289] a particular audience. A parallel task frequently occurs in law; namely, the problem of bringing an existing case under established precedents, and expressing it in the formula which are received.

"Very accurate definitions," says De Lolme,[54] "as well as distinct branches of cases and actions, were contrived by the first Roman jurist consults: and when a man had once made his election of that peculiar kind of action by which he chose to pursue his claim, it became out of his power to alter it. Settled forms of words, called *actiones legis*,

---

[53] [Of course it is true that the past never returns, and that reactions are always in one sense innovations. But what is said above goes further than this, further than I habitually went myself as an Anglican, and in my deliberate judgment. The hypothesis about the *depositum fidei* in which I gradually acquiesced was that of doctrinal development, or the evolution of doctrines out of certain original and fixed *dogmatic truths*, which were held inviolate from first to last, and the more firmly established and illustrated by the very process of enlargement; whereas here I have given utterance to a theory, not mine, of a certain *metamorphosis* and recasting of doctrines into new shapes,—"in nova mutatas corpora formas,"—those old and new shapes being foreign to each other, and connected only as symbolizing or realizing certain immutable but nebulous *principles*.] [N] *"in nova mutatas corpora formas"*: This is an adaptation by Newman of the opening of Ovid's *Metamorphoses*. The full line is: 'In nova fert animus mutatas dicere formas corpora' - '[my] mind inclines to speak about forms changed into new bodies.'
[54] *De Lolme*: Jean-Louis de Lolme (1741–1804), political philosopher. The quotation is from his *The Constitution of England* (1771), p.108.

were moreover contrived, which men *must absolutely use* to set forth their demands . . . Extremely like the above *actiones legis* are the *writs* used in the English courts of law. Those writs are framed for and adapted to every branch or denomination of action, such as *detinue,*[55] *trespass*, etc."

He proceeds:

"Of so much weight in the English law are these original delineations of cases, that no cause is suffered to be proceeded upon, unless they first appear as legal introductions to it. However important or interesting the case, the judge, *till he sees the writ he is used to*, or at least a writ issued from the right manufacturer, is both deaf and dumb. *He is without eyes to see, or ears to hear* . . . To remedy the above inconvenience, or rather in some degree to palliate it, *law fictions* have been resorted to in the English law, by which writs, being warped from their actual meaning, *are made* to extend to cases to which they in no shape belong. Law fictions of the kind we mention were not unknown to the Roman jurisconsults; and, as an instance of their ingenuity in that respect, may be mentioned that kind of action in which a daughter was called a son. Several instances might also be quoted of the fictitious use of writs in the English courts of common law. A very remarkable expedient of that sort occurs in the method generally used to sue for the payment of certain kind of debt before the Court of Common Pleas; such (if I mistake not) as a salary for work done, indemnity for fulfilled orders received, etc. The writ issued in these cases is grounded on the supposition that the person sued has trespassed on the ground of the plaintiff, and broken by force of arms through his fences and enclosures, etc."

[290]   If another illustration of these economies (as they may be called) is wanted, it will be found in the House of Commons, where no matter of principle can be introduced till it is thrown into the *calculus* of expediency.

Such in its origin and nature, though not such in its magnitude, is the change which the adjuncts of Christian teaching, its opinions, feelings, objects, and temper, may undergo in different

---

[55] detinue: 'A form of action which lies for the recovery, in specie, of personal chattels from one who acquired possession of them lawfully, but retains it without right, together with damages for the detention.' (Black's Law Dictionary)

Prospects of the Anglican Church

eras. For instance, the doctrine of justification by faith only is the form in which the Reformation cast that eternal truth catholicly implied in the act of baptism, of which it is the equivalent. The Augustinian doctrine of predestination is the mode in which minds of a peculiar formation have, in a corrupt state of the Church, expressed the eternal truth, that the way of life is narrow. Or to take an instance of a different kind; this age, as we said above, is more practical, the primitive more contemplative; that age adopted a mystical religion, ours a more literal. How, then, in our age are those wants and feelings of our common nature satisfied, which were formerly supplied by symbols, now that symbolical language and symbolical rites have almost perished? Were we disposed to theorize, we might perhaps say, that the taste for poetry of a religious kind has in modern times in a certain sense taken the place of the deep contemplative spirit of the early Church. At any rate it is a curious circumstance, considering how much our active and businesslike habits take us the other way, that the taste for poetry should have been developed so much more strongly amongst ourselves than it seems to have been in the earlier times of the Church; as if our character required such an element to counterbalance the firmer and more dominant properties in it. We only mention this by way of instancing (if it is allowable to interpret it so) the power which seems to exist in altered states [291] of society and of the human intellect, and much more, with reverence be it spoken, of the divinely gifted Church, of working out for themselves channels of their own, to certain moral ends, when former ones have been lost sight of, or have become uncongenial to the public taste. It may appear to some far-fetched, of course, to draw any comparison between the mysticism of the ancients, and the poetry or romance of the moderns, as to the religious tendencies of each; yet it can hardly be doubted, that, in matter of fact, poetry has been cultivated and cherished in our later times by the Cavaliers and Tories[56] in

---

[56] *by the Cavaliers and Tories*: There was a group of 'Cavalier' poets in the 17th century (most of whom wrote about the sensual pleasures of love in a way which would certainly earned the disapproval of Puritans but probably of Newman too), but Newman is using

a peculiar way, and looked coldly on by Puritans and their modern representatives. In like manner, a Romanist writer[57] observes of the "Christian Year," with a mixture of truth and error, that it is an attempt to collect and form into a crown the scattered jewels which the torrent of the sixteenth century has left to the English Church. Poetry then is our mysticism; and so far as any two characters of mind tend to penetrate below the surface of things, and to draw men away from the material to the invisible world, so far they may certainly be said to answer the same end; and that too a religious one.

Enough has now been said to explain what we consider the views of the present revivers of ancient truth. In going back to Antiquity, they do not wish to force men upon bare, literal, accurate Antiquity in points unessential; upon Antiquity exactly as it was when ancient times were modern. Identity of appearance is not the law on which the parts of the creation exist; and, as far as it shows itself, it has the most insipid associations connected with it. What happens in individuals, in countries, and in works, holds good also in times and eras. Let, then, party [292] spirit, cowardice, misapprehension, indolence, and secularity,

___

the term in a looser sense since he refers to poets of 'our later times'. Of the poets whom Newman praised in Essay I, Robert Southey, was appointed Poet Laureate by the Tory government of his day, and Wordsworth and Coleridge both had increasingly conservative views as they grew older. Byron could be termed 'Cavalier' in terms of his loose lifestyle, though he was certainly no Tory politically. The 'modern representatives' of the Puritans were the Evangelicals, who indeed generally regarded most poetry as worldly.

[57] *a Romanist writer*: This was Nicholas Wiseman (1802-65): 'We can conceive the inward regrets of one who has picked out with beautiful skill, and woven into a golden chain, the few grains of poetic feeling which the torrent of the Reformation tore from the ancient Church, and has preserved in the dry and sandy desolation of its "Christian Year;" upon seeing how much fit matter for a muse like his has been indiscriminately and unfeelingly swept away, how much nobler and moving themes he would have possessed, had that touch been gentler, which broke off the flowers, when it pretended but to prune the plant.' ('Tract Occasioned by the Controversy Respecting Dr. Hampden's Appointment to the Divinity Chair at Oxford in 1836', p.15, reprinted in *High-Church Claims: or A Series of Papers on The High-Church Theory, Anglican Claims to Apostolical Succession, etc.*, London, Catholic Institute of Great Britain, 1841). Wiseman, later the first Cardinal Archbishop of Westminster, took a close interest in the Oxford Movement. Newman had met him in Rome during his trip to Italy in 1833. Wiseman's article on Donatism in the *Dublin Review* in July 1839 made a major impact on Newman; see the Editor's Introduction, p.xlvii.

clamour as they will, we cannot but trust that a great work is going on. In spite of the dread of Antiquity, the calumny of "popery," the hatred of austerity, the reluctance to inquire, and the vast hubbub which is thereby caused on all sides of us—we have good hope meanwhile that a system will be rising up, superior to the age, yet harmonizing with and carrying out its higher points, which will attract to itself those who are willing to make a venture and face difficulties, for the sake of something higher in prospect. And for such minds it will be a reward, and one which they will have fully deserved, to discover at length that they have less sacrifices to make, less to give up of their natural tastes and wishes, by adopting the rule of Catholic tradition, than they could have anticipated beforehand. On this, as upon other subjects, the proverb will apply, "fortes fortuna juvat."[58] It is wrong, indeed, to have longings or schemes for being let off easily; and doubtless there are those with whom all duty is up-hill work: it is so in the affairs of life; it is no less so in religion; but, if serious people would but make up their minds to take what in the plain order of Providence is put before them, according to the amount of evidence for it, at all hazards, or, to use the language of the day, with a sounder meaning, to "march with the age," they would be surprised to see, when they *had* adopted the primitive system, how naturally and easily it fitted on to them, and how little it had of the galling nature of a yoke, a bondage, and a burden; names which are liberally bestowed upon it at present. As it is, however, the mere name of Antiquity seems to produce a sudden collapse of the intellect in many quarters, certain shudders, and spasms, and indescribable inward sensations. Of course, while such a condition of [293] mind lasts, nothing is left for those who happily are not infected by the epidemic but patience and activity; the causes which incapacitate the world for understanding them, happily incapacitating it also for opposing.

---

[58] *"fortes fortuna juvat"*: "fortune favours the brave"

6.

We may seem to have been speaking in a sanguine way about the spread of the opinions in question; but this is in reality far from our intention. About the future we have no prospect before our minds whatever, good or bad. Ever since that great luminary, Augustine, proved to be the last bishop of Hippo, and his labours for his own Africa were lost forthwith in its Vandalic, and finally in its Saracenic captivity, Christians have had a lesson against attempting to foretell *how* Providence will prosper and bring to an end what it begins. What is true of great things, is true of little also. Catholic principles *ought* to spread at the present time as far as there is any substratum, as it may be called, in the national mind to support and give reality to them; but what a question is this, not to go to others, even to guess at! or rather it belongs simply to that invisible world into which none of us are admitted. What lies before our highly-favoured but unfortunate Church we know not; the principles now on the rise may be destined to prevail; or some miserable schism may gradually fritter them away, and some more miserable compromise suffocate them. We will not enter into the question, or risk any anticipation. There is nothing rash, however, in venturing one prediction, which will lead to some further remarks, viz., that, whether they maintain their ground or not, the two principles antagonistic to them will not maintain theirs. Whether the English Church can keep a firm hold on Laud's divinity[59] or not, it is very certain that neither Puritanism or Liberalism has any permanent inheritance within her.

As to Liberalism, we think the formularies of the Church will ever, with the aid of a good Providence, keep it from making any serious inroads upon the clergy;[60] besides, it is too cold a principle to prevail with the multitude; so we shall say no more about it.

[294]

---

[59] *Laud's divinity*: William Laud; see above note on p.[231].

[60] [It must be confessed, however, these formularies have not excluded it from the Anglican Church; still it has no stay in Anglicanism, or in any other religious communion, for it is a transition state, and is running its sure course, and in a great number of minds has already resolved itself into that avowed scepticism or infidelity which is its issue.] [N]

We have called the other system of opinion Puritanism, because we cannot hit upon a fit name for it. It is a very peculiar creed, as being based on no one principle, but propping itself up upon several, and those not very concordant; and thus to give it a name is almost as desperate a task as to set about giving it a consistence. To call it Evangelical, would be an unlawful concession; to call it Puritan, were to lose sight of its establishment side; to call it Ultra-Protestant, would be to offend its upholders; and to call it Protestant, would not be respectful to Protestantism. Anti-Catholic is vague; Anti-Sacramentarian is lengthy. This, indeed, is its very advantage in controversy with the upholders of Catholic principles; that it has a short and glib word ready at hand, and may promptly call them "Papists," while they had no retort courteous to inflict upon it. However, be its name what it will, it stands for the largest, most compact, most prominent party in our Church at this moment. It has much power, much money, much influence; and would seem, from its position, to have the ability, as it has (consciously or unconsciously) the will, to effect sooner or later important [295] changes in our doctrine and discipline.

But in spite of these appearances in its favour, a closer examination will show us that it cannot remain in its present state much longer; inasmuch as an internal principle of union, permanence, and consistency is wanting; and where this is wanting, a principle of life is wanting, and all is outward show. Its adherents are already separating from each other, and it is not difficult to see that in due time they will melt away like a snowdrift. Indeed their very success would cause this result, if there were no other reason. The possession of power naturally tends to the dissolution of mutual trust and intimate fellowship; how much more so then in the case of a party, which is not only open to the wilfulnesses and rivalries of our frail nature, but which actually sanctifies them by propounding as a first principle, that in spirituals no man is really above another, but that each individual, from high to low, is both privileged and bound to make out his religious views for himself? But over and above this, the system in question, if so it may be called, is, as we have intimated, full of inconsistencies and anomalies; it is built, not on one principle, but on half a dozen; and thus contains within it the seeds of ruin, which time only is required to develop. At present not any one principle does it carry out logically; nor does it try to adjust and limit one by the other; but as the English language is partly Saxon, partly Latin, with some German, some French, some Dutch, and some Italian, so this religious creed is made up of the fragments of religion which the course of events has brought together and has imbedded in it, something of Lutheranism, and something of Calvinism, something of Erastianism,[61] and something of

[296]   Zuinglianism,[62] a little Judaism, and a little dogmatism, and not a little secularity, as if by hazard. It has no straightforward view on any one point on which it professes to teach; and to hide its poverty it has dressed itself out in a maze of words, which all inquirers feel and are perplexed with, yet few are able to penetrate. It cannot pronounce plainly what it holds about the sacraments, what it means by unity, what it thinks of Antiquity, what fundamentals are, what the Church; what again it means by faith. It has no intelligible rule for interpreting Scripture beyond that of submission to the arbitrary comments which have come down to it, though it knows it not, from Zuingle or Melancthon.[63] "Unstable as water, it cannot excel."[64] It is but the inchoate state or stage of a doctrine, and its final resolution is in Rationalism. This it has ever shown when suffered to work itself out without interruption; and among ourselves it is only kept from doing so by the influence of our received formularies. When then it is confronted, as now it is more and more likely to be, by more consistent views, it cannot maintain its present unscientific condition. It will either disappear on this side or

---

[61] *Erastianism*: the theory that the church should be subservient to the state, as the Church of England is; it is attributed to the Protestant theologian Thomas Erastus (1524-83), though it is a deduction from his principles rather than stated explicitly in his writing.

[62] *Zuinglianism*: (today Zwinglianism) the theology of Huldrych Zwingli (1484-1531), Swiss Protestant divine; he disagreed with Luther particularly about the Eucharist, seeing it as a purely symbolic rite.

[63] *Melancthon*: Thomas Melancthon (1497-1560), German Lutheran theologian.

[64] *"unstable as water, it cannot excel"*: Cf. Genesis 49:4

that, or be carried out. Some of its adherents will be startled and return to sounder views; others will develop themselves into avowed liberalism. Its many societies and institutions, however well organized and energetic, will avail it nothing in this crisis. They are but framework and machinery, and, while they presuppose a creed, they are available for one almost as much as another. As opinions change, these will be modified or destroyed. Imposing and flourishing as they are in appearance, they have as little power to stop the march of opinion as a man in a boat to act directly on its motion; they are the mere material or corporeal part of the system,—the instrument, not the living principle of its soul.

Thus the matter stands as regards the far-spread religious [297] confederacy of our days. We have no dread of it at all; we only fear what it may introduce. It does not stand on entrenched ground, or make any pretence to a position; it does but occupy the μεταίχμιον,[65] the space between contending powers, Catholic truth and Rationalism; neither of these owning it, or making account of it, or courting it; on the contrary, both feeling it to be a hindrance in the way of their engaging with each other, and impatiently waiting to be rid of it. Then, indeed, will be the stern encounter, when two real and living principles, simple, entire, and consistent, one in the Church, the other out of it, at length rush upon each other, contending not for names and words, or half views, but for elementary notions and distinctive moral characters. Meanwhile the advocates of the motley Protestantism we have been describing, as if aware of its intrinsic hollowness and imbecility, are at this moment trying to make the most of their accidental advantages while they last; and would fain clench matters in their favour by such organic changes, whether in our discipline or services, or such accidental implications or authoritative explanations of doctrine, as the meeting of Convocation,[66] or the erection of architectural

---

[65] μεταίχμιον: the No Man's Land between armies.
[66] *Convocation*: the assembly of bishops and higher clergy of the church, originally established in the seventh century as the Convocations of Canterbury and York, the latter eventually becoming wholly subordinate to the former. Following the establishment of the Church of England at the Reformation, the Convocations had lost most of

memorials,[67] or decisions in the law courts,[68] would give them an opportunity for effecting.

Let us hear the author of "Ancient Christianity"[69] on the prospective fortunes of this section of the religious world. He says:

"Nothing can be less desirable to the evangelical clergy than to be forced into any formal or particular argument with their accomplished and learned brethren, on the very points that have driven some of their most distinguished predecessors, and of themselves, to the edge of nonconformity, and which chafe many a sensitive conscience. They may, by the aid of peculiar considerations, drawn from the perils of the times, have brought themselves to believe that they seriously disaffect nothing in the ritual or constitution of the Church: and they may be satisfied with this or that elaborate explanation of certain difficulties; nevertheless the uneasiness, although assuaged, is not removed, for the difficulty is real, and its reality and its magnitude must be brought afresh before them, to the renewal of many painful conflicts of mind, whenever the genuine and original Church of England principle and discipline comes, as now, by the Oxford divines, to be insisted on, expounded, and carried on to its fair consequences. What the English Reformers had in view was, Ancient Christianity, or the doctrine, and discipline, and ritual of the Nicene age, and of the times nearly preceding that age. . . But how utterly

[298]

---

their power to Parliament and by the nineteenth century had effectively ceased to function. Some Anglicans began to call for the Convocations to be revived which they eventually were.

[67] *the erection of architectural monuments*: Newman has in mind the Martyrs Memorial in Oxford which had been proposed at this time by Charles Golightly (1807-1885), a vehement opponent of the Oxford Movement. Its intention was not only to make a strong public statement of Protestantism and anti-Catholicism in Oxford but also to embarrass Newman and other members of the Oxford movement by challenging them to declare their support or opposition to it.

[68] *decisions in the law courts*: A prophetic remark by Newman. In 1850 the Privy Council overruled the church courts which had decided that Henry Gorham, an Anglican clergyman who denied the doctrine of baptismal regeneration, should not be appointed to a parish. This demonstration of the civil courts' power over Anglican doctrine caused a number of Tractarian clerics to become Catholics, including Henry Manning, later Cardinal Archbishop of Westminster.

[69] *"Ancient Christianity"*: See above note on p.[264]. Taylor thought that even by the time of the Nicene period the Church had become corrupted in its doctrines, and he therefore rejected all the great fourth century Fathers of the Church such as those he contrasts with Protestant writers at the end of the passage quoted. It is a favourite tactic of Newman's to use quotations from hostile writers to make his point.

different a notion of Christianity was that which animated the zeal of the founders of Methodism, and which in the main was caught by the fathers of the evangelical clergy! Holding to the same orthodoxy, the same Nicene and Athanasian doctrine, everything else in the two systems stands out as a point of distinction. What parallels could be more incongruous, even to absurdity, than such as one might strive to institute, for instance, between Cyprian[70] and Romaine,[71] Tertullian[72] and Milner,[73] Chrysostom[74] and Cecil,[75] Augustine[76] and Scott,[77] Jerome[78] and Newton?"[79]—Pp. 8, 9.

7.

There is another consideration which should be dwelt upon. It was long objected to the clergy that they were not a reading body; and much has been said, especially in attacks upon the Universities, concerning the profound attainments of German theologians. Sectarians have said much about our incumbents being in the commission of the peace[80] or fox-hunters;[81] thoughtful men have shaken their heads and come to the conclusion that it cannot be helped, the English being an active, not a studious race; and divinity professors have for years been doing what they could to revive the taste for reading. Now it is strange that amid all this accusation, all this regret, all this endeavour, it seems to have been forgotten that reading implies *books*, as [299]

[70] *Cyprian*: See above note on p.[199].
[71] *Romaine*: William Romaine (1714–1795), Anglican divine of strongly evangelical and Calvinist opinions.
[72] *Tertullian*: See above note on p.[117].
[73] *Milner*: Joseph Milner (1744–1797) Anglican divine of evangelical views, best known for his *History of the Church of Christ* which influenced Newman when young.
[74] *Chrysostom*: St. John Chrysostom (c.307-407), Patriarch of Constantinople and Father of the Church.
[75] *Cecil*: Richard Cecil (1748–1810), Anglican divine of evangelical views, associated with the influential Clapham Sect.
[76] *Augustine*: See above note on p.[200].
[77] *Scott*: Thomas Scott (1747-1821), Anglican divine of Evangelical views; he was a founder of the Church Missionary Society, and his autobiographical *The Force of Truth* was widely popular.
[78] *Jerome*: See above note on p.[231].
[79] *Newton*: See above note on p.[117].
[80] *the commission of the peace*: i.e. Justices of the Peace, magistrates; at this time it was still frequently the case that Anglican clergymen held these civil judicial positions.
[81] *fox hunters*: There was a long tradition of fox-hunting Anglican clergymen, and they were frequently the subjects of satire as personifying theologically ignorant and worldly clergy. Before the Reformation, hunting had been forbidden to Catholic clergy.

its correlative; that the clergy cannot read without reading something, and that that something will be to a certainty the works of divines who are of authority, not of those who are not. It is no use reading, unless we read something that is of use. There is no sense in reading nonsense; and we may be sure, if men make up their minds to sacrifice society, and outdoor amusements, and active employments, that they will not do so for the drudgery of reading newspapers, periodicals, novels, annuals, Exeter Hall divinity,[82] *et id genus*,[83] unless they be very ascetically disposed. If men resign themselves to being students in theology, they will read theological works. They will not read Milner or Scott, whatever their merits; they will read Hooker,[84] Taylor,[85] Barrow,[86] Waterland,[87] Wall,[88] Bingham;[89] and that, not to take for granted every word of each of these writers, which would be impossible, but in order to gain general notions what theology is. At the same time, unless they set themselves altogether against them and reject them *in toto*, (as some extreme persons do,) their views of religion must be influenced by them,—must become very different from those which are now popular,—very much more primitive, very like what religionists of the day call Popery. No one of any party denies, for instance, that Hooker says many things strange to our present notions of divinity; all that ultra-Protestants say in explanation is, that the leaven of Popery was not at that day worked out of the Church. We hold it to be a matter of fact which no one can doubt, that if a man strictly confined himself to the very letter of Hooker or of Taylor, he would be as seriously accused of

---

[82] *Exeter Hall divinity*: Exeter Hall in London was the meeting place of the Evangelicals and particularly of the anti-Catholic societies. Newman had satirised such meetings in an article in *The British Critic* in 1838, a review of *Random Recollections of Exeter Hall in 1834-1837 By one of the Protestant Party*. It is to be regretted that he did not chose to republish this effective and amusing example of his satire in *Essays Critical and Historical* or elsewhere.

[83] et id genus: and this sort of thing

[84] *Hooker*: See above note on p.[180].

[85] *Taylor*: See above note on p.[45].

[86] *Barrow*: Isaac Barrow (1630-1677), Anglican divine and theologian; he was also a celebrated mathematician who taught Isaac Newton.

[87] *Waterland*: See above note on p.[75].

[88] *Wall*: See above note on p.[135].

[89] *Bingham*: See above note on p.[179].

Popery by the multitude, and as plausibly, as Mr. Palmer[90] or
Mr. Newman. These writers differ from Hooker and Taylor
perhaps in many details: but it is not those details which make [300]
them called Popish; it is the general strain of their doctrine, the
tenor of their thoughts, in which they are as really followers of
Hooker or Taylor as they are not followers of the religion of the
day. But to return to Hooker and Taylor; they must be studied,
it seems; and why, except because they are of name? and what
is the reason that they are so, except that they are men of great
intellect? Are they likely to turn out men of weak reasonings,
inaccurate statements, fanciful theories? Are they not likely to
say many things strongly and persuasively? Is it wonderful that
they who read them, should be moved and convinced by them?
Is it wonderful, then, that if their works are again opened to our
clergy and become text-books, that our clergy should become
much more Catholic and less Protestant in their religious views
than they were?

This consideration will show how unsuitable is the vexation
which seems in some quarters to be felt, that the present spread
of a taste for theological study should most unfortunately be
connected with opinions, as it is pretended, savouring of Popery.
But what if it turns out that this apparent accident is but a
necessary condition? Men will not study what they take no
interest in, and care not for. If they are to read our divines, they
must withal like them. Jackson's[91] works sold for waste paper
at the beginning of the century; they now bring seven guineas;
have the clergy many seven guineas to throw away on what is
not to influence or guide them? Are that great writer's views on
Catholic tradition, justification, and Christ's presence, to go for
as little, as when they sold for seven-and-sixpence, bound and
in good condition? And so again of the Fathers: if they are to
be read, are they to be read to no purpose or to some purpose? [301]
are they or are they not to inform and instruct? There is but one
other alternative, which we have already hinted at, that students

---

[90] *Palmer*: See the Editor's Introduction to Essay V, p.xxxii.
[91] *Jackson*: Thomas Jackson (1579–1640), Anglican divine and theologian; he was
strongly anti-Calvinist in his views.

should read to carp and oppose; which, we suppose, would not mend the matter, even in the judgment of those who are so cross at the present untoward burst of Catholicism.[92]

But these cross persons will answer, that of course divines modern and ancient are to be read for instruction, but they are not to be followed slavishly or hotly; that they are to be read with discrimination, with judgment; and that this is the thing so much to be regretted at the present time, that there is such a lack of sound discretion, of wisdom, of moderation, of tact; so much of what is extreme, so much of excitement, so much of party, so much to shock and offend, so much that is to be deprecated and ought never to have been done. Now such persons must be plainly asked, whether by moderate and judicious opinions they do not mean just those very opinions, neither more or less, which do not shock themselves? whether there are not persons, on the other hand, whom their own opinions are calculated to shock? or again, if they shock and offend no one, whether the plain reason of this be not, because they do not or cannot put their opinions, whatever they are, before the world? whether, in short, their *vagueness* is not their sole protection? This, indeed, we think will be found generally to hold; that what men in common mean by *strong* opinions really are *clear* and *distinct* opinions. You may hold the most fatal errors or the most insane extravagances, if you hold them in a misty, confused way. Numbers will persist in countenancing and defending even these. But ask yourself what you mean by your words, try to master your own thoughts, try to ascertain what you believe and [302] what you do not, avoid big professions, blustering epithets, and languid generalities; and lookers-on at once begin to wonder why you should so needlessly hurt people's feelings and damage your own cause. In the present day mistiness is the mother of wisdom. A man who can set down half a dozen general propositions, which escape from destroying one another only by being diluted into truisms, who can hold the balance between opposites so skilfully as to do without fulcrum or beam, who

---

[92] *Catholicism*: i.e. Anglo-Catholicism within the Church of England.

never enunciates a truth without guarding himself from being supposed to exclude the contradictory, who holds that Scripture is the only authority, yet that the Church is to be deferred to, that faith only justifies, yet that it does not justify without works, that grace does not depend on the sacraments, yet is not given without them, that bishops are a divine ordinance, yet those who have them not are in the same religious condition as those who have,—this is your safe man and the hope of the Church; this is what the Church is said to want, not party men, but sensible, temperate, sober, well-judging persons, to guide it through the channel of No-meaning, between the Scylla and Charybdis[93] of Aye and No.[94] But, alas! reading sets men thinking; shut up their books, if this is a mischief; but if you do not, count the cost, weigh and measure the consequences. They will not keep standing in that very attitude, which you please to call sound Church-of-Englandism or orthodox Protestantism. It tires them, it is so very awkward; and for the life of them they cannot continue in it long together, where there is neither article nor canon to lean against; they cannot go on for ever standing on one leg, or sitting without a chair, or walking with their legs tied, or grazing, like Tityrus's stags,[95] on the air. Premises imply conclusions; germs lead to developments; principles have issues; doctrines lead to action. As well might you invert a [303] pitcher of water, and expect the contents to eschew the ground and remain *jam jam ruitura*,[96] as fancy that men will not carry out the truths which they have gained, whether from their own minds, or from our divines, or from the Fathers. They may take one view or another of the English or the Primitive Church; but, whatever else it be, on the long run, it will be a consistent view.

---

[93] *Scylla and Charybdis*: in Greek mythology, two sea-monsters, the former like a gigantic whirlpool, between which sailors had to navigate to avoid being swallowed up by either.

[94] *Aye and No*: Cf. James 5:12

[95] *Tityrus's stags*: See above note on p.[20].

[96] jam jam ruitura: 'on the brink of collapsing'. The phrase is found in a poem by Claudius Claudianus (c.370-404) in a passage about the Emperor Honorius's father rescuing Rome from disaster, taking on himself the whole weight of everything on the brink of collapse. The image Newman draws from it (though it is not what Claudian says) is of the water jar held upside down and the water not coming out but always being on the verge of doing so.

It may be Rationalism, or Erastianism, or Popery, or Catholicity; but it will be real. It will not be a merely transition view; it will not be Lutheranism, or Presbyterianism, or Jewellism,[97] or Burnetism,[98] or Paleyism,[99] or Erskinism.[100] Effects will sooner or later be seen to presuppose causes; correlatives to imply each other; contradictions to exclude each other; the elephant will not for ever stand on the tortoise,[101] nor the Barmecide[102] fatten upon empty dishes. The most intense horror of Popery cannot undo facts or legitimatize fallacies. And the sooner certain zealous friends of Protestantism understand this, the better.

8.

What has been said suggests one remark in addition. The reaction which has been the subject of it is not confined to England. This is a fresh fact, and it does not require much proof. Look at the state of Germany, where the old Rationalism of the last century is succeeded by Pantheism, by the modified Lutheranism of Neander and Leo,[103] or by a return to Romanism. Look to Holland, where an attempt is now making to revive Calvinism on its strictest and most exclusive principles. Look to Denmark,[104] where, to say the least, men seem to be sighing in secret for something deeper and firmer than the creed in [304] which they have been brought up. Look at the Church of Rome

---

[97] *Jewellism*: See above note on p.[180].

[98] *Burnetism*: See above note on p.[208].

[99] *Paleyism*: See above note on p.[131].

[100] *Erskinism*: See above note on p.[30].

[101] *the elephant . . . on the tortoise*: There was said to be an Indian myth that the universe was supported on the back on an elephant which was standing on a tortoise, though no such story in fact appears in Hindu mythology. The idea is found in Locke's *Essay Concerning Human Understanding* which may be Newman's source for this.

[102] *the Barmecide*: In the *Tales of the Arabian Nights* one of the Barmecides, a rich Persian family, gives an imaginary banquet of empty plates to a hungry visitor; so, *pace* Newman, it is actually the guest, not the Barmecide, who cannot fatten on empty dishes.

[103] *Neander and Leo*: Johann Neander (1789-1850) was a German Protestant historian and theologian, much influenced by Schleiermacher; his thought emphasises the importance of Christian feeling. Heinrich Leo (1799-1878) was a German historian and theologian; his views have been described as pietist with some leanings towards Catholicism. Newman was kept informed of religious developments in Germany by Pusey who had studied there.

[104] *Denmark*: During the first half of the nineteenth century Denmark enjoyed a 'golden age' of Romanticism, including the writings of N. F. S. Grundtvig (1783–72) whose many hymns changed the character of Danish church worship.

itself, everywhere, in which discipline and zeal have succeeded to a long indifference. Consider that at the present moment, in the three great literary countries of Europe—Germany, France, and England—translations of the Fathers,[105] in series, are now in course of publication, by a simultaneous and apparently independent movement in each place. Consider that the Germans are beginning to study the schoolmen.[106] Look at the state of literature in London; the old Benthamism[107] shrivelling up, and a richer and warmer philosophy succeeding. Consider the state of our Universities; at Cambridge, Utilitarianism, Shelleyism, Coleridgism, edging forward and forward, no one knowing how, to a more Catholic theology;[108] at Dublin, no uncertain tokens of a great and happy change, and that among able and serious men of various characters of mind, and of schools of opinion;[109] Oxford again, the head-quarters of that special revolution of thought which has been our subject.

[105] *translations of the Fathers*: A Library of the Fathers in English translation, planned by Pusey and supported by Newman and Keble, had been begun to be published in 1838.

[106] *the schoolmen*: the scholastic theologians of the Middle Ages, pre-eminently Aquinas.

[107] *Benthamism*: See above note on p.[160].

[108] *at Cambridge . . .*: Newman's argument here—a somewhat optimistic one—is that opinion at Cambridge is moving in a Catholic direction, starting from the rationalist Utilitarianism of the philosopher Jeremy Bentham (1748-1832), through the atheism and radicalism of the Romantic poet Percy Bysshe Shelley (1792-1822), to the more conservative thought of Samuel Taylor Coleridge (see above p.[269]). Newman's fellow Tractarians Frederick William Faber and Frederick Rogers had been making visits to Cambridge at this time and bringing back favourable reports. However, Newman's comment in a letter of 27th January 1839 is more sceptical: 'Some junior Cambridge men are taking up Church principles, and, as they do every thing, too much in the way of a fashion, as a theory or literature. If so, it will run its course and come to an end. These Cambridge men have such a want of seriousness. They are Utilitarians, Shelleyans, Coleridgians, Mauricians by turns—and may be any thing else.' (*Letters and Diaries*, Vol. VI, p.20).

[109] *at Dublin ... able and serious men*: These men included William Palmer (see Esssay V); another Church of Ireland divine, James Henthorn Todd (1805–69), with whom Newman was in correspondence (cf. *Letters and Diaries*, Vol.VII, pp. 4, 61-3, 67, 69-70, 77, 82) and who gave a series of lectures on the Antichrist in which he criticised the traditional Protestant identification of the Antichrist with the Pope; and a Dublin solicitor called Graham with whom Newman was also in correspondence (cf. ibid., pp.5, 50, 63, 82). However, Newman is rather overstating his case about the 'great and happy change' at Dublin towards Tractarian opinions: Todd told him that 'I could not name more than three clergymen resident in Dublin, who are of my mind in Church matters' (ibid., p.62).

Consider the number of volumes which, in the course of a few years, the fervour of the movement has thrown out, and the hunger of the Church has absorbed.

"Were I to give you a full list of the works they have produced within the short space of five years," says Mr. Bird[110] to his friend, speaking of the Oxford school, "I should surprise you: you would see what a task it would be to make yourself complete master of their system, even in its present probably immature state. They commenced their labours, I believe, in 1833; .... and going on with a yearly birth of a thick volume of the Tracts for the Times, the fourth of which belongs to the present year, and of which an indefinite series may be expected, they send forth, at intervals, numerous large octavo volumes (some of them heavy in more respects than one, in spite of the acknowledged talent of the writers), accompanied by a light array of separate tracts, [305] sermons, letters, and poetry, and ably supported by Reviews and Articles ... The writers as a body have adopted, according to Dr. Pusey, the motto, 'In quietness and confidence shall be your strength.'[111] With regard to confidence, they have justified their adopting it; but as to quietness, it is not being very quiet to pour forth such a rapid succession of controversial publications in the compass of so few years."—*Letter*, p. 5.

Or again let us attend to the author of "Ancient Christianity":[112]

"The general scheme of principles and sentiments that has been embodied in the publications referred to, recommends itself by a still depth, a latent power, a momentum, and a consistency in its development, which are the very characteristics of those movements that are to go on, and are to bring with them great changes, whether for the better or the worse."—P. 2.

---

[110] *Mr. Bird*: Charles Smith Bird (1795-1862), Anglican divine of strongly evangelical and anti-Catholic and anti-Tractarian views. The quotation is from his *The Oxford Tract System Considered with Reference to the Principle of Reserve in Preaching, in a Letter to a Friend Abroad*, 1838.
[111] *'In quietness . . . your strength.'*: Pusey had taken this quotation (from Isaiah 30:15) as the title of a sermon preached before the University of Oxford on 5th November 1837.
[112] *"Ancient Christianity"*: See above notes on pp.[264] and [297].

All these are signs of change, not in this or that individual, but in the public mind. The reading public is coming under the influence of notions and convictions very different from those which have been fashionable of late. It exemplifies the march of the whole of educated Europe. The phenomenon, which has long been preparing in this country, is a European movement. This is the fact to which we would draw attention, and the inference is as plain as itself. To what does the current of opinion point? It points everywhere to Dogmatism, to Mysticism, or to Asceticism; it points on one side to Popery, on another to Pantheism, on another to Democracy; it does *not* point to the schools of the Reformation. England cannot any longer be Calvinistic, or Zuinglian, or Lutheran; does it wish to be democratic, or pantheistic, or popish? does it wish to be infected by the democratism of France, the pantheism of Germany, or the popery of Italy? Surely then our true wisdom [306] now is to look for some Via Media which will preserve us from what threatens, though it cannot restore the dead. The spirit of Luther is dead; but Hildebrand[113] and Loyola[114] are still alive. Is it sensible, sober, judicious, to be so very angry with those writers of the day, who point to the fact, that our divines of the seventeenth century have occupied a ground which is the true and intelligible mean between extremes? Is it wise to quarrel with this ground because it is not exactly what we should choose, had we had the power of choice? Is it true moderation, instead of trying to fortify a middle doctrine, to fling stones at those who do? On the other hand, is there not something natural and reasonable in what the latter parties are doing? they betake themselves to the old works, long neglected; they determine to put them in condition again. There is much to be mended; some additions necessary; some portions superseded by changes in

---

[113] *Hildebrand*: See above notes on pp.[153] and [197].
[114] *Loyola*: St. Ignatius Loyola (1491-1556), Spanish priest, founder of the Jesuits, a leading force in the Counter Reformation. Suppressed by Pope Clement XIV in 1773, the Jesuits had been restored by Pope Pius VII in 1814 and were now undergoing a revival. As with the reference to Hildebrand, the Anglican Newman is being deliberately provocative to his Anglican readership in contrasting the vigour of Roman Catholicism with the 'dead' spirit of Protestantism.

the art of war. Culverins and demi-sakers[115] are gone out of fashion. They may not, perhaps, draw their lines or make their trenches in the same direction to an inch, or so as to include the same number of square feet; yet, on the whole, they are taking up a position on the old sconce,[116] and are repairing the works.

If this be a true account of the present position of things, it is plainly idle to make the whole turn upon this man or that; as if the movement arose from individuals, not from the age. What do persons who speak as if it did, think to gain by so treating it? Can you stop the course of opinion now that it has begun, by stopping the mouths of one or two men, even supposing you could do so? Surely it will be better for you, ultra-Protestant as you are, instead of reproaching them with a storm, which is [307] none of their raising, to thank them for making the best of a bad matter, or not the worst, if not the best. The current of the age cannot be stopped, but it may be directed; and it is better that it should find its way into the Anglican port, than that it should be propelled into Popery, or drifted upon unbelief. You cannot make others think as you will, no, not even those who are nearest and dearest to you. And if you cannot do this, if principles will develop themselves, beyond the arbitrary points of which you are so fond, and by which they have hitherto been limited, like prisoners on parole; then it becomes a piece of practical wisdom to take what you can get, since you cannot have what you like, or, to use the common illustration, to cut your coat according to your cloth.

Would you rather have your sons and daughters members of the Church of England, or of the Church of Rome? That is the real alternative, if we follow things to their results; and the Romanists feel this. Anglo-Catholicism is a road leading off the beaten highway of Popery: it branches off at last, though for some time it seems one with it. Accordingly they look on the English Church as a fraudulent come-off, as a sort of *cul de sac*, a bye-path which brings persons indeed to what looks like a holy place, and a temple, but which is only so from an external

---

[115] *culverins and demi-sakers*: cannons used in the 15th and 16th centuries.
[116] *sconce*: a small fort

semblance of venerableness; like those modern specimens of architecture on which the plasterer's skill has been made to imitate the effects of time. They view ours, in short, as a Church which gratifies feelings apart from the proper objects of them; and thus they both envy her as a rival, and most unjustly feel irritation towards her, as an artful and unfair one. Do they not thus recognize in us their real and most formidable opponents?

April, 1839.

Note on Essay VII

The foregoing Essay is thus noticed in my "History of my Religious Opinions" (*Apologia*), p. 94: "It is not altogether mine; for my memory goes to this,—that I had asked a friend[117] to do the work; that then, the thought came on me, that I would do it myself; and that he was good enough to put into my hands what he had with great appositeness written, and that I embodied it in my Article. Every one, I think, will recognize the greater part of it as mine."

Now, on going through it carefully for re-publication, I am quite clear, first, that it is from first to last my writing; and secondly, that what I have borrowed from the papers of my friend is the topic, which I have worked out and illustrated between pp. 283 and 292, and on which I have appended a note at p. 287, pointing out the difference between it and the view of doctrine which was habitual to my own mind.

---

[117] *a friend*: This is most likely to be Henry Wilberforce (1807-1873), youngest son of William Wilberforce the abolitionist; he became an Anglican clergyman and a Tractarian and later a Catholic. In May 1838 Newman wrote to him asking him to write an article for the *British Critic* on a number of books including *Thoughts on the past and present State of the Religious Parties in England* by Robert Vaughan (London, 1838). A footnote in the *Letters and Diaries*, Vol.VI, p.252 states that Wilberforce never wrote the article, and Newman's article does not review Vaughan's book, but Wilberforce must in fact have provided some 'papers' which Newman later used.

VIII.

THE ANGLO-AMERICAN CHURCH.

1.

FEW passages in the history of the Church are better calculated to raise the Christian heart in admiration and gratitude to the Giver of all good, than her fortunes in the United States, fortunes which have a still greater promise in the future, than a present accomplishment. Her power in withstanding persecution, in overcoming heresy, in retaining her hold over nations, in absorbing into herself and exercising the functions of political bodies, nay, her mere continuance in the world, though always to appearance losing ground and breaking up,—all these signs of an ever-watchful Providence are most wonderful; yet not less than any is the spectacle of the mustard-seed cast upon the wilderness, finding a lodgment in the hard soil, and taking root, no one knows how, and promising to become a large tree.[1] In her first planting, and almost wherever she has been propagated, the Church went out as a whole, completely organized, fully furnished in all things, even though one or two individuals were the keepers of the treasure. A bishop issuing forth, to convert the heathen, evolves a Church from himself by his apostolical powers, and transmits to it the perfect creed which he has brought with him. Far otherwise was it with the Church's [310] planting in America—she found her way thither in the most feeble and destitute condition. She had no bishops, no visible form of government, churches but here and there, scanty ordinances, few teachers. She was overrun and overborne by other forms of Christianity, and, when the Revolution came, she lost the provisions which had been made for her support.

---

[1] *mustard seed* . . . : Cf. Matthew 13:31ff and parallels.

By that rough tempest the tender or rather sickly vine which the mother Church was rearing as she best might, was torn down from the props and lattices on which she had been trained; and lay along the ground to be trampled under foot by passers-by. How were those broken branches ever to bear fruit? How was that to grow which could not stand? Who would have prophesied anything hopeful of her, who thought it worth while to prophesy at all? Yet the principle of life was there; the holy stranger was for a while silent and was forgotten; but at length "the fire kindled, and at the last she spake with her tongue."[2]

Even then though we had no especial connexion or concern with the American Church, we should be led as Christians to dwell upon her history as a signal instance of Almighty God's faithfulness to His own appointed ordinances, so that what seemed "born out of due time"[3] lived and throve, and "out of the mouths of very babes and sucklings"[4] praise was perfected. But to us English Christians the sight has a nearer and deeper interest. The English Church, the glory of Christendom, where Bede[5] taught and whence Boniface[6] went forth, now sits solitary among the nations.[7] The Queen of the Isles, how has she suffered amid the passions of men! how straitened within her seas, who once had a continent for her range, and its bishops for her hosts or guests! It avails not to look at the past; what [311] was done is (as they say) "a matter of history," which means, we may entertain our own private opinion about it. The result is pretty clear; Christendom is broken up, and we have suffered not less than other nations from the convulsion. Rome, Greece, and England, all have suffered; but just at this moment we are speaking about ourselves. We then have lost the sympathy of the world; and those who deprived us of it have felt in duty

---

[2] *"the fire kindled . . . with her tongue."*: Cf. Psalm 39:3: 'the fire burned, then I spake with my tongue.'

[3] *"born out of time"*: Cf. I Corinthians 15:8

[4] *"out of the mouths . . . "*: Cf. Psalm 8:2

[5] *Bede:* St. Bede the Venerable (672-735), monk, Doctor of the Church; best known for his *Ecclesiastical History of the English People.*

[6] *Boniface*: St. Boniface (d.754), monk, missionary and martyr, known as the Apostle of Germany.

[7] *sits solitary among the nations*: an echo of Lamentations 1:1: 'How doth the city sit solitary, that was full of people! how is she become as a widow! she that was great among the nations, and princess among the provinces, how is she become tributary!'

bound to do what they could to make up to us our loss. The civil power, which has cut us off from Christendom, has done, it must be confessed, its utmost to reconcile us to our degradation. It has maintained, of course, our captivity as a first principle of the Constitution, but it has taken very great pains to keep us from fretting. If the Church was to exist at all in England, it was like a law of the Medes and Persians,[8] that she must exist for England alone; she must be a prisoner if she was to be an inmate; but, that being taken for granted, she has been accorded a most honourable captivity. Nothing has been denied her short of freedom; power, wealth, authority, rank, consideration, have been showered upon her, to make her as happy as the day is long. She has been like Rasselas[9] in a happy valley, or like the Crusader in Armida's garden;[10] what want was unsupplied? Yet even of our first parent it is said under far more blessed circumstances, "For Adam there was not found a help-meet for him."[11] "Aliquid desideravere oculi,"[12] which neither fawning beast nor painted bird could supply. He found a want in Paradise itself; and so upon this our poor Church of England, which is *not* in Paradise, this evil has fallen, in spite of "princes and other children of men,"[13] that she has been solitary. She has been among strangers; statesmen, lawyers, and soldiers frisked and prowled around; creatures wild or tame have held a parliament [312] over her, but still she has wanted some one to converse with, to repose on, to consult, to love. The State indeed, to judge by its acts, has thought it unreasonable in her, that she could not find in a lion and a unicorn[14] a sufficient object for her affections. It

---

[8] *law of the Medes and Persians*: Cf. Daniel 6:15: 'Know, O king, that the law of the Medes and Persians is, That no decree nor statute which the king establisheth may be changed.'

[9] *Rasselas*: The eponymous hero of Samuel Johnson's fable *The History of Rasselas, Prince of Abissinia* (1759), who escaped from the beautiful valley, in which he had been brought up, in order to see the world.

[10] *the Crusader in Armida's garden*: In *La Gerusalemme liberata* (1581), an epic poem by Torquato Tasso (1544-95) about the First Crusade, the Crusader Rinaldo falls in love with the sorceress Armida and is kept by her in a magic garden; he is eventually brought to realise his infatuation and escapes.

[11] *"For Adam . . . for him"*: Genesis 2:20

[12] *"Aliquid desideravere oculi"*: "the eyes longed for something else", *De Vita Iulii Agricolae*, Tacitus, 45, 5.

[13] *"princes and other children of men"*: Cf. Psalm 146:3: 'Put not your trust in princes nor in the son of man'.

has set her to keep order in the land, to restrain enthusiasm, and to rival and so discountenance "Popery;" and if she murmured, if she desired to place bishops in the colonies, or to take any other measure which tended to Catholicity, it has used expostulation and upbraiding. "Am I not," it has seemed to whisper, "am I not your own parliament? pour your griefs into my bosom. Have I not established you by law? Am not I your guide, philosopher, and friend? I am ready to meet all your desires. I will decide any theological point for you, or absolve vows and oaths for you,[15] as easily as I send soldiers to collect your tithes." And if this did not succeed, then in a gruffer tone, "Are not you my own Church? Have I not paid for you? Have I not cut you off from Christendom to have you all to myself? Is not this the very alliance, that you should take wages and do service? and where will you find service so light and wages so high?"

Under these circumstances, the rest of the Church, either caring nothing for us, or accounting it a point of charity to wish us dead, and the State intruding its well-meant but unamiable blandishments, it is pleasant to look across the western wave, and discern a friendly star breathing peace and shedding benison. This is our second reason for rejoicing in the American Church. It gives us some taste of Catholic feelings, and some enjoyment of Christian sympathy.

[313] There is yet a third reason for satisfaction more intimately important to ourselves. This friendly Church is a daughter of ours, and is our pride as well as our consolation. The daughter is the evidence of the mother's origin; that which lives is the true Church; that which is fruitful lives; the English Church, the desolate one, has children. There was a time when a satirist could say of her:

---

[14] *a lion and a unicorn*: the 'supporters' on the royal coat of arms; i.e. the Church of England has to 'love' the Crown as its Supreme Governor.

[15] *absolve vows and oaths for you*: Newman is referring to the oath of allegiance to the crown which had been sworn to James II. After he had been deposed in the 'Glorious Revolution', parliament then required that a new oath was sworn to the usurping William of Orange, thus absolving people of their previous oath to James. It was a standard part of Protestant polemic that Catholics could have their oath of allegiance to the crown absolved by the Pope (as was the case when Pius V excommunicated Elizabeth I). Newman shows that the Protestant State had done exactly the same thing.

"Thus, like a creature of a double kind,
In her own labyrinth she lives confined;
To foreign lands no sound of her is come,
Humbly content to be despised at home."[16]

That day of rebuke is passed. The English Church has fulfilled the law which evidences her vitality. So has it been from the beginning; stocks and stones do not increase and multiply, but all "grass and herb yielding seed after his kind, and the tree yielding fruit, whose seed is in itself, after its kind."[17] It is with the moral world as with the material. Genius is creative; truth and holiness draw disciples round them; the Church is a mother. This then is our own special rejoicing in our American relatives; we see our own faces reflected back to us in them, and we know that we live. We have the proof that the Church, of which we are, is not the mere creation of the State, but has an independent life, with a kind of her own, and fruit after her own kind. Men do not gather grapes of thorns or figs of thistles; the stream does not rise higher than the spring; if her daughter can exist, though the State does not protect, the mother would not cease to be, though she were protected by the State no longer.

For all these reasons, as Christian, as solitary, and as their mother, the English Church looks out with thankfulness and affection upon the churches which are springing up in North America, whether in our existing or our late colonies; on both [314] with affection, but with more of triumph on the latter. And on considering the vast extent of that continent, and its possible destinies in the divine counsels should the world continue, no anticipation seems too great for the office they are appointed to fill, and for the work they are to do in ages to come.

---

[16] *"Thus like a ... despised at home."*: John Dryden (1631-1700), *The Hind and the Panther*, ll.401-4.
[17] *"grass and herb ... after its kind."*: Genesis 1:12

2.

To Mr. Caswall,[18] an Englishman by birth, an American by his Orders, we are indebted for the most graphic and circumstantial, as well as the latest account[19] which has been published of the present state of the American Church. This gentleman is in all respects a man of note. He has the energy of a missionary, the curiosity of a traveller, and the sobriety of a man of letters. His special object, as he states in his Preface, has been that of "exhibiting to the British public *the vital energy* of the Episcopal system, and the real benefit of an adherence to its essential principles;" the very subject of which we have been speaking, and about which we shall presently say something more. "The view," he continues, "of a thousand republican clergymen, and five hundred thousand republican laymen, contending for a liturgy and for the sacred regimen of bishops, will be sufficient to prove that the system which has flourished under the tyranny of the Roman Empire, and the constitutional monarchy of England, contains in itself nothing repugnant to the principles of political self-government. At the same time, the wonderful progress and improvement of the American Church serve to confute the Romanist, who asserts, that the Church of England is sustained merely by the secular arm, and [315] that in the event of her losing that support, she must of necessity become extinct."—Pp. v., vi. Elsewhere he tells us, that this young Church "is increasing in numbers more rapidly than any other Protestant denomination in America. It has even gained on the fast-extending population of the United States, so that it has quadrupled itself during the last twenty-four years, while the population of the Union has little more than doubled. Should it continue to increase in the same ratio, it will outnumber the Church of England before fifty years have elapsed; and before the end of a century, it will embrace a majority of the population of the States."

---

[18] *Mr. Caswall*: Henry Caswall (1810-70), Episcopal divine and academic; born in Wiltshire, he migrated to America in 1828 and was ordained into the Protestant Episcopal Church but returned to England several times to serve as an Anglican minister.
[19] *the latest account*: *America and the American Church*, Rev. Henry Caswall, London, 1839, one of the books Newman listed at the head of his original 1839 review; see the Textual Appendix.

We shall not understand the full force of these statements, until we look back at the condition in which Episcopacy found itself at the end of the revolutionary war.

"When the colonies were actually separated from Great Britain," he says, "the destruction of the Church appeared almost inevitable, notwithstanding the fact that the great Washington himself was an Episcopalian. A few years nearly overthrew the work which had been slowly carried forward by the exertions of a century and a half. The Propagation Society[20] no longer rendered its accustomed aid. Many of the clergy were thus left entirely destitute, and some were obliged to betake themselves to secular employments for support. In the northern states the clergy generally declined officiating, 'on the ground of their ecclesiastical connexion with the liturgy of the Church of England.' In the south, many worthy ministers, conceiving themselves bound by oath to support the government of Great Britain, refused to enter upon a new allegiance, and quitted the country. By an unjust decision, the lands possessed by the Propagation Society in Vermont were confiscated, and applied to the purposes of education. An equally unconstitutional sentence, ultimately despoiled the clergy of Virginia of their glebes[21] and churches; while, in addition to all these calamities, Episcopalians in general became subject to unmerited political prejudices. Most of their churches were emptied; there was no centre of unity, no ecclesiastical government."—Pp. 173, 174.

This was the melancholy condition of the Church in 1783, [316] and from that date to the close of the century it was fully employed in organizing itself upon the Apostolical model. It obtained bishops from Scotland and England by 1787, and in the course of the thirteen years which followed, "its members had learned in some measure to rely on their own resources, and its ministers were supported in some instances comfortably by the voluntary contributions of their flocks."—P. 184. Yet the number of clergymen little exceeded two hundred; and these were widely scattered through the country bordering on the Atlantic. No great enterprises were undertaken, because a hard struggle was necessary to maintain the ground already occupied.

---

[20] *The Propagation Society*: The Society for the Propagation of the Gospel in Foreign Parts, founded in 1701 as a missionary society for the North Atlantic colonies.
[21] *glebes*: church lands

In 1790 the number of bishops was seven; and by 1811 only one or two dioceses had been added. The inferior clergy had scarcely increased at all, and little attention was paid to theological preparation. But at this time the energies of the Divine Kingdom began to show themselves. Mr. Caswall gives us this summary:

"Few colleges were under episcopal control, and even there, theological education was neglected. The candidates were, therefore, compelled to pursue their studies under the direction of clergymen encumbered with parochial duties, or to resort to the institutions of dissenting denominations. Accordingly, about the year 1814, Bishop Hobart[22] of New York issued proposals for the establishment of a divinity-school under the superintendence of himself and his successors. The deputies to the General Convention from South Carolina were also instructed by their constituents to propose a similar scheme. The subject was for some time under consideration; and finally, in 1817, it was resolved to establish a theological seminary at New York for the benefit of the entire Church, and under its control. In the same year the diocese of North Carolina was admitted into union with the General Convention, and measures were adopted to organize the Church in Ohio. The Rev. Philander Chase[23] was consecrated to the episcopate of the latter diocese in 1819, and the Rev. J. S. Ravenscroft[24] to that of the former in 1823. New Jersey had been provided with a bishop, the Rev. Dr. Croes,[25] as early as 1815; and from this period, the advancement of the Church proceeded with almost unexampled rapidity. In 1814, the number of clergy was little more than 240, but in the course of twenty-four years, it has quadrupled itself, and the increase of congregations has been in an equal proportion.

[317]

"The destitute state of the western country led to the formation of a missionary association in Pennsylvania about the year 1818. By this association several missionaries were sustained in Pennsylvania and Ohio, and some churches were planted. In a few years this Society assumed a more extended form, and, under the auspices of the General Convention, became known as the 'Domestic and Foreign Missionary Society of the Protestant Episcopal Church.' For many years its

---

[22] *Bishop Hobart*: John Henry Hobart (1775–1830), the third Episcopal bishop of New York (1816–1830); see above Editor's Introduction p.xlvii.
[23] *Rev. Philander Chase*: (1775-1852); also a founder of educational institutions.
[24] *Rev. J. S. Ravenscroft*: John Stark Ravenscroft (1772-1830).
[25] *Rev. Dr. Croes*: John Croes (1762-1832).

operations were extremely limited, and it was not until 1830 that it produced any considerable benefit. In the meantime, Washington College was instituted, the General Theological Seminary received a constant accession of students, and a second institution of the same kind was established at Alexandria, near Washington, designed especially to promote the interests of religion in Virginia and the other southern dioceses. Bishop Chase proceeded to England in 1824, in the hope of obtaining assistance towards the foundation of a similar institution in Ohio. His efforts, it is known, were successful, and in 1831 he had the satisfaction of beholding nearly 200 inmates of 'Kenyon College and Theological Seminary.' At this time the number of clergy in Ohio was between fifty and sixty."

In Kentucky and Tennessee, the increase of the Church has been as rapid as in Ohio. In 1825 there was but one officiating clergyman in the first-mentioned state. In 1832 it contained eight clergymen, and in the same year a bishop was consecrated. In 1834 the "Theological Seminary of the Diocese of Kentucky" was incorporated; in the following year it received great pecuniary assistance from eastern Episcopalians, and in 1836 contained eighteen students. The clergy in the diocese now amount to twenty-one. So late as 1832 there were but three clergymen in Tennessee. There are now in that diocese about twelve, with a Bishop Otey,[26] and a theological seminary in [318] connexion with a college is already in contemplation. In the eastern states the progress of the Church has also been rapid and steady. The Church in Vermont had become in 1832 sufficiently strong to separate from the eastern diocese of which it had formed a part, and to receive a bishop. It is highly probable, that before many years, Massachusetts, Rhode Island, New Hampshire, and Maine will be provided with their respective prelates.—Pp. 187, 191.

In the Journal of the Proceedings of the General Convention of last year, twenty-one dioceses are enumerated. In 1835 the Church formally took upon itself a most important step,—the conduct of its missions, dispensing with the aid of the Society which had hitherto been indirectly its organ. Since this "great and momentous measure," as Mr. Caswall justly calls it, has

---

[26] *a Bishop Otey:* James Hervey Otey (1800–63).

passed, the missionary income of the Church has greatly increased. In 1835 it was about £6,000, and in 1836 it became £12,431.[27]

3.

From these great steps in the development of Catholic principles one most important consequence will probably follow, which could not have been anticipated when they were taken,—the destruction of the voluntary system[28] in the bad sense of the word. Nothing is more Christian than that the people of the Church, who are benefited by her ordinances, should "willingly offer" for her support: nothing more unchristian than that individual clergymen should be at the mercy of the people, and be under the temptation of "preaching smooth things"[29] to get bread, clothes, and lodging. Such an evil threatens to arise when there is a less demand for clergy in

[319] America than at the present moment. It was obviated in the early Church by the offerings being made to the bishop of the diocese, who distributed them at his discretion among the parochial clergy; that is, in the way in which missionaries are actually paid at this day. When once then the Church has in its hands funds for the payment of missionaries, it may easily extend the system to the payment of clergy.

There seems to be no lack of liberality in contributions among the laity of the Church, at New York especially. If there is an infant parish established in the West, and unable to erect a place of worship, application is made to New York. If there is a new school to be instituted in any part of the country, if there is a church burnt down, if there is a professorship to be endowed, recourse is instantly had to New York as the place where substantial tokens of sympathy may certainly be expected. "Applicants after applicants," says Mr. Caswall, "come crowding in, and the fountain of benevolence still remains unexhausted, and even increasing in abundance. I have been credibly informed that many of the wealthiest merchants

---

[27] *£12,431*: equivalent to nearly £1 million today (2018).
[28] *the voluntary system*: clergy being financially supported wholly by the voluntary offerings of their congregations.
[29] *"preaching smooth things"*: Matthew 24:11

habitually devote a tenth part of their incomes, and sometimes much more, to religious purposes."—P. 155.

This munificence shows itself, as it should, in the erection and decoration of churches. At Hartford, in Connecticut, where lately was a wooden building, in which Bishop Chase officiated, "a splendid and substantial Episcopal church, of stone," he says, "has been erected in its stead, and presents the noblest specimen of Gothic architecture which I have seen in America. At the time of my visit the tower was not wholly completed; but when finished, I should think that the expense could not fall short of twenty thousand pounds.[30] The interior is in perfect keeping with [320] the exterior; all is rich and solid, without any superfluous or trifling decorations."—P. 145. Elsewhere he tells us that in one of the eastern cities, "The Protestant Episcopal church of St. Peter is a finished specimen of Gothic architecture. The walls, which rise forty feet above the ground, are built of hammered blue-stone trimmed with granite. The dimensions of the church are 65 feet in breadth by 120 feet in length, including the tower and vestry-room. The tower, which is at the north end, is 23 feet square and 138 feet high. The pulpit and reading-desk are in excellent keeping with the rest of the work, for beauty and richness of design. The ground-floor contains 138 pews, and the galleries 68. At the northern end of the building, in the gallery, stands the organ, a splendid instrument, in height 31 feet, in breadth 21 feet, and in depth 13 feet. The number of draw-stops is 34. The cost of this organ was 5,000 dollars (£1,125)[31]."—P. 283.

At Rochester, in New York, there is a Gothic church which cost £22,500.[32]—P. 113. In the west too, it appears, some very handsome places of worship have been erected. Even in Ohio, there are two which cost respectively £12,600[33] and £5,400[34] sterling. "Church architecture," our author informs us, "is rapidly improving, and a better taste is prevailing more and more. Cathedrals are still confined to the Roman Catholics; but

---

[30] *twenty thousand pounds*: equivalent to nearly £1.6 million today.

[31] *£1,125*: equivalent to nearly £90,000 today.

[32] *£22,500*: equivalent to nearly £1.8 million today.

[33] *£12,600*: equivalent to over £1,006,000 today.

[34] *£5,400*: equivalent to over £430,000 today.

the Roman Catholic buildings of that description are often greatly inferior to Episcopal churches." It is an interesting circumstance that, as of old time we were indebted for our cathedrals to our bishops, so in America the present Bishop of Vermont has begun to tread in the steps of Wykeham[35] and Wolsey,[36] by publishing a book of architectural plans.[37]

[321]   We are glad to add that other evidence of bountifulness in the worship of God are showing themselves. "Splendidly embroidered pulpit hangings, superb services of communion plate, and a profusion of silk and velvet, of gilding and of painting," are sometimes found; and though Mr. Caswall hints that these embellishments are not always of the severest and most reverential character, yet they show "the willing mind," and are pleasant to think upon.

The poorer districts seem to vie with the more wealthy in their voluntary care of an unendowed Church. "Not unfrequently," our author says, "[a clergyman] receives a waggon-load of substantial comforts, such as two or three barrels of flour, ten or twelve bushels of apples, a barrel of cider, and a sack of potatoes. Sometimes he is agreeably surprised by the receipt of a complete suit of clerical apparel, a hat, a pair of boots, or a variety of articles for his wife and children. I am acquainted with a young clergyman who, within a few weeks, received two or three fees for marriage of a hundred dollars each (£22).[38] I have known fifty dollars (not a fee) to be presented to a clergyman on a baptismal occasion, and an equal amount at a funeral, though gifts of this description are not frequent. Medical men and lawyers seldom charge a clergyman for their services, and quite recently the missionary bishop was conveyed on board a steamboat, without cost, from New Orleans to St. Louis, a voyage of more than a thousand miles."—Pp. 305, 306.

---

[35] *Wykeham*: William of Wykeham (1320–1404), Bishop of Winchester.

[36] *Wolsey*: Cardinal Thomas Wolsey (1473–1530), Archbishop of York and Lord Chancelllor of England under Henry VIII.

[37] *architectural plans*: Wykeham was responsible for a number of royal residences, including the reconstruction of Windsor Castle; Wolsey had Hampton Court Palace built for himself.

[38] *£22*: equivalent to nearly £1,800 today.

Mr. Caswall informs us of the consideration which was exercised on different occasions towards himself:

"A gentleman of the Episcopal Church, residing in Circleville, a connexion and namesake of the justly-celebrated Nonconformist Dr. Doddridge,[39] was part-owner of a commodious line of boats on the Ohio canal. Hearing of my indisposition, and of my arrangements for leaving Portsmouth, this worthy man, though almost a total stranger, [322] informed me that accommodations would be provided, at no expense, for myself and wife, on board one of his vessels. Such offers are made, in this country, with the intention that they should be accepted; and, accordingly, I did not hesitate to comply. The journey by canal was one of 330 miles, and would have cost us together about twenty dollars. "Instances of similar liberality to clergymen are by no means unfrequent in America. In travelling through Ohio, it has several times happened that after spending a night at an inn, and having taken supper and breakfast, the landlord has refused to accept any payment on hearing that I was a clergyman. For the same reason, a drayman, whom I once engaged to remove my furniture from one house to another, resisted all my efforts to induce him to receive a compensation. There are captains of steamboats who sometimes will carry clergymen at half-price, or without any charge."—Pp. 106, 107.

It should be observed, that this attention is paid to other ministers besides clergymen. "Medical men," the author adds, "also prescribe for the ministers of all denominations and for their families gratuitously."

In another place he observes of Albany, "Here we spent Sunday, and attended divine service at the two Episcopal Churches. The landlord of the comfortable hotel where we lodged was an Episcopalian. He treated us with the utmost hospitality, and refused to accept any compensation."—P. 115.

Mr. Caswall himself first belonged to the diocese of Ohio, whence he obtained his academical degree and his Orders; and he gives us an interesting description of a Sunday expedition in its vast and wild territory:

---

[39] *Dr. Doddridge*: Philip Doddridge D.D. (1702–51), English non-conformist divine, known for his many hymns.

"We rise early, and get a light breakfast an hour or two before the ordinary morning meal, and then sally forth with a few books, and some frugal provision for the day. The sun has risen about half an hour, and the dew is sparkling on the long grass. We proceed about half a mile through the noble aboriginal forest, the tall and straight trees appearing like pillars in a vast Gothic cathedral. The timber consists of oak, hickory, sugar-maple, sycamore, walnut, poplar, and chestnut; and the wild vine hangs from the branches in graceful festoons. Occasionally we hear the notes of singing-birds, but less frequently than in the groves of England. We soon arrive at a small clearing, where a cabin built of rough logs indicates the residence of a family. Upon the abundant grass, which has sprung up since the rays of the sun were thus admitted to the soil, a number of cattle, the property of the college, are feeding; and the tinkling of their bells is almost the only sound that strikes the ear. We climb over the fence constructed of split rails piled in a zigzag form; we traverse the pasture, and are again in the deep forest. The surface of the ground is neither flat, nor very hilly, but gently undulating. After an hour we arrive at a roughly constructed saw-mill, erected on a small stream of water. The miller is seated at the door of his cabin, clad in his Sunday suit, and reading a religious book lent him by us on a former occasion. We hold a short conversation with him; he expresses a growing interest in religion and the Church, and concludes by telling us that he wishes us hereafter to use his horse on our expeditions. We accept the offer as it is intended; my companion mounts the nag, and I walk by his side.

[323]

"We then pass through the woods along the banks of Vernon River; and in due time my companion descends from his seat, and I mount the quiet animal in his place. After another hour we arrive at a small village, or rather a collection of log-houses, the scene of our labours. At the further extremity of the street is a school-house, built of logs, with a huge chimney at one end, and a fireplace extending across one side of the apartment. Within it are a number of rough benches, and all around it is a kind of temporary arbour, covered with fresh boughs, for the accommodation of those who cannot find seats within. Having tied our horse to a tree, we enter the school-room and sit down to rest. Soon the children come flocking from the cabins and through the woods; and with them their parents and many grown-up people, attracted partly by curiosity, and partly by a sincere desire of religious instruction. In a short time the school-room is filled, and a number of persons are standing without in the shade of the arbour; I then give out one of the hymns in the Prayer Book, reading two lines at a time on account of the scarcity of books. The people join in singing it, and then all kneel down to prayer. I repeat a large portion of the service by memory, knowing that my hearers, although belonging to no sect whatever, have at present all the prejudices of sectarians[40] against 'praying by a book.' After prayer my companion adds a few words of exhortation, to which all listen with the deepest attention. We then instruct the children in the New Testament; and about midday we untie our horse, and set out on our journey homeward, intending to eat our cold refreshments on the way. [324]

"But scarcely have we left the village, when a blacksmith runs after us and requests us to stop. He wishes us always to dine with him on Sundays hereafter. We accordingly return to his cabin, and his wife sets before us a plentiful repast, consisting of chicken, potatoes, hot bread, apple-pies, and delicious milk. After some profitable conversation, we bid them farewell, and about three o'clock arrive at the miller's house, almost overcome by the excessive heat. When we have somewhat recovered from our fatigue, we proceed to a spot on the bank of the stream, where the grass is smooth, and where the thick foliage produces a comparative coolness. Here we find about a hundred persons collected, in hope of receiving from us some religious instruction. We conduct the service much in the same way as in the morning. The effect of the singing in the open air is striking and peculiar; and the admirable prayers of our Liturgy are no less sublime in the forests of Ohio than in the consecrated and time-honoured minsters of York or Canterbury.

"The service concluded, we return on foot, and as we approach the college with weary steps, the fire-flies glisten in the increasing darkness. We arrive at our rooms fatigued in body, but refreshed in mind, and encouraged to new efforts."—Pp. 35-39 (abridged).

4.

It is encouraging to find that the Church, though deprived of all external aids towards keeping up the appearance of unity, yet is recognized and joined, in those regions of religious extravagance, as the Catholic Church should be, on the ground of the consistency, definiteness, and stability of its creed. Persons of the most opposite sentiments, enthusiasts and (so called) Unitarians, seem in this respect to look upon her with interest and consideration, and to be drawn to her. However, we hardly know whether to regard the following as a pleasant specimen of it or not, but we give it in Mr. Caswall's words: [325]

---

[40] *sectarians*: i.e. non-Anglican Protestants, non-conformists.

"I took the steamboat from New York on Saturday, and had a delightful voyage down the Connecticut river. On the way I entered freely into conversation with a gentlemanly and intelligent passenger, who proved to be a Unitarian from Massachusetts. Pointing to the Episcopal churches which appeared on both sides of the stream, he remarked, 'Ah, if those churches had been in Massachusetts, there would have been few Unitarians.' He explained himself by expressing his conviction that Unitarians objected not so much to the doctrine of the Trinity taught by the Church, as to the unpalatable and, as he said, the revolting manner in which Christianity was presented by the orthodox congregational divines."—Pp. 149, 150.

Certainly the excesses of sectarianism in the North American States are such, that one need not be of a Socinian turn to be disgusted with them. Besides the old Calvinistic Baptists,[41] there are the Free-will,[42] the Seventh-day,[43] and the Six-principle Baptists;[44] the Christian Baptists,[45] who deny the proper Divinity of Christ; and the Campbellite Baptists,[46] many of whom are but in part believers in the Holy Trinity, and modify the doctrine of the Atonement. Besides these there are the Seed and Snake Baptists,[47] who, carrying out the Calvinistic system, divide mankind by a rigid line into the seed of the woman and the seed

---

[41] *Calvinistic Baptists*: those adhering to Calvin's doctrine of predestination, salvation being attained only by a small number of the elect.

[42] *Free-will*: Freewill Baptists, founded by Thomas Helwys (c.1575 – c.1616) and established in America by Paul Palmer (d. 1747), believed in General Atonement, i.e. that Christ died for all rather than only for the elect.

[43] *Seventh-day*: the Seventh-Day Baptists, originating in early 17th century England, kept Saturday, rather than Sunday, as the Sabbath. They are distinct from, though connected with, the better-known Seventh Day Adventists.

[44] *Six-principle Baptists*: founded in 1652 following a split within the first Baptist church in Rhode Island. Apart from their six theological principles (which were similar to those of many Baptist groups), their distinctive feature was the use of the laying-on of hands in some of their services.

[45] *Christian Baptists*: also known as the Disciples of Christ, founded by a merger in 1832 of followers of the former Presbyterian minister Barton Warren Stone (1772–1844) and followers of Alexander Campbell (1788–March 1866) (see below).

[46] *Campbellite Baptists*: Alexander Campbell, a Scotsman who emigrated to America, had been ordained by his father Thomas, the founder of the Brush Run church, a Baptist group in Pennsylvania.

[47] *Seed and Snake Baptists*: founded by Daniel Parker (1781–1844) who taught that the Serpent had mated with Eve to conceive Cain, whose descendants were therefore damned, whereas Abel, whose descendants were saved, was conceived by her union with Adam. The idea can also be found in ancient Gnostic sects. Parker's followers were known as 'anti-mission' Baptists because their beliefs, as Newman describes, meant that they saw all people as irrevocably divided into the saved and the damned, and therefore any attempt to convert people was wrong.

of the serpent; and lastly, the Dunkers,[48] who are principally German Baptists, and who wear a peculiar dress, a long robe with a girdle and hood, let their beards grow, feed on roots and vegetables, live men with men and women with women, not meeting even in their devotions, have each his own cell, a bench for a bed, a block of wood for a pillow, admit works of supererogation, and deny the eternity of future punishment. This strange mockery of Catholic Truth numbers as many as 30,000 adherents. As to the Calvinistic varieties, they go the lengths in [326] numerous instances of even considering the religious education of children as a sacrilegious interference with the work of divine grace. Among the Methodists the same disorders prevail which marked their first rise in England. In their camp meetings "sermons and exhortations succeed each other in quick succession; the most lively hymns are sung perhaps for an hour together, and extempore prayers are offered with extreme force of language and energy of action. The people become powerfully excited; they shout 'Glory' and 'Amen;' they scream, jump, roar, and clap their hands, and even fall into swoons, convulsions, and deathlike trances"—manifestations which are far more like the work of evil spirits than of Him who on earth "did not strive, nor cry," nor make "His voice heard in the streets."[49] Of the Quakers,[50] Mr. Caswall tells us, one-third have lately declared themselves Unitarians. Besides these, there are, among other sects, 600,000 Universalists, who teach the annihilation of the wicked; 6,000 Shakers, or followers of Ann Lee,[51] whom they consider the woman mentioned in Revelation, chapter xii., and who have all things common, lead a single life, and dance in divine worship; and the Mormonites, who, being

---

[48] *the Dunkers*: The popular name for the German Baptist Brethren who came to America in the early 18th century; they were so called because they practised baptism by total immersion ('dunking'), as opposed to sprinkling or pouring; they also had a foot-washing ritual.

[49] *"did not strive . . . in the streets."*: Isaiah 42:2

[50] *Quakers*: the Religious Society of Friends, nicknamed 'Quakers' in ridicule of their founder, George Fox (1624–91), having said that he had come to make people 'tremble at the word of the Lord'. Quakers arrived in America in 1656.

[51] *Ann Lee*: (1736-84), British-born visionary and founder of the United Society of Believers in Christ's Second Appearing, or Shaking Quakers; she taught complete celibacy for all, with shaking dancing as evidence of sin leaving the body. She was considered by her followers to be the female counterpart to Christ.

the only sect of pure American origin, shall be described in Mr. Caswall's words:

"Their delusion seems to be founded upon a prevailing and plausible opinion, which derives the descent of the American Indians from the ten lost tribes of Israel. The Mormonites assert that, in the time of the Jewish kings, an Israelite embarked on the Persian Gulf, and, after many adventures, crossed the Pacific, and arrived on the American coast. To this individual various revelations were committed, which were written on golden plates, and hidden under a stone in that part of the country now known as the state of New York. In process of time, viz., in the year 1829, an angel appeared to a man residing in [327] the vicinity, and directed his attention to the spot where the precious deposit was concealed. He searched and found the golden plates; but the language inscribed upon them was unknown. He was accordingly furnished with some talismanic power, by which he translated the original, word by word, and thus produced the 'Book of Mormon.' There are fifteen books, which fill a duodecimo volume of 588 pages, first published by Joseph Smith, of Ontario county, New York. It is needless, perhaps, to say that the original golden plates have never been produced. The Mormonites assert that the Land of Promise is beyond the Mississippi. They also declare that they possess the gift of working miracles. They consider the study of the Hebrew language to be a religious duty; and at one of their settlements, in Ohio, they recently engaged the son of a Jewish rabbi, a distinguished Hebrew teacher, to instruct the whole community. They already amount to 12,000."—Pp. 322, 323.

In reading such accounts, how are we thrown back into the times of early Church-history, and find ourselves among the Valentinians,[52] Marcionites,[53] Cataphrygians,[54] Ebionites,[55] Manichees,[56] and all the other prodigies to which the presence

---

[52] *Valentinians*: Followers of Valentinus (c.100-c.180), founder of a Gnostic heresy; his extremely complex system of thought bore little relation to orthodox Christianity.
[53] *Marcionites*: Followers of Marcion (c.85-c.160), a bishop, later excommunicated, who rejected the God of the Old Testament.
[54] *Cataphrygians*: 2nd century heretics, originating in Phrygia, who rejected St. John's Gospel and the Book of Revelation.
[55] *Ebionites*: a Jewish-Christian sect which insisted that the Jewish law must still be observed and who may have denied the divinity of Christ.
[56] *Manichees*: Followers of Manes (216-76/7), a Persian religious founder, who taught a dualist theology of two eternal principles of good and evil; St. Augustine was a Manichaean before his conversion to Christianity.

of the true Church gave rise, as the sun breeds reptiles;[57] and as the Church in those early times went forth conquering and to conquer amid them all, so we are prepared to believe that even in these fallen times she has so much of her ancient glory left her, as to eat them up like Aaron's rod,[58] and to grow and increase while they fall to pieces. Nay, under such circumstances, we are not sorry to be told, even of the Church of Rome, that by means of its numerous and well-conducted schools and colleges, it is daily acquiring a more powerful hold upon the public mind; for surely it is better to belong to any branch of the One True Church, than to sectaries, who, not to dwell on their tenets, do not even profess to belong to it.

But to return: Mr. Caswall informs us that in the towns and villages along the New York canal the "disorders and divisions among sectarian bodies have brought multitudes within the fold [328] of the Church."—P. 115. Elsewhere he tells us that a vast proportion of her members have originally belonged to one or other denomination of Christians, and "have united with her from a sincere and intelligent preference."—P. 332. And, what is still more remarkable, that "probably *more than half* of the parochial clergy, and *certainly almost half the bishops*, have been originally Presbyterians, Congregationalists, Methodists, or Baptists."

Mr. Caswall furnishes us with some instances of eminent individuals who have been converted from the sectarian communions. First may be mentioned Bishop Chase,[59] who is well known to many persons in England. He is a native of Cornish, a small town in the western part of the state of New Hampshire. His ancestors were English dissenters, and emigrated to America nearly a hundred years ago. "He was himself," as Mr. Caswall tells us, "educated in the Congregational or Independent persuasion, and continued his attachment to those principles until the year 1795, when nearly the whole of his father's family conformed to the Liturgy, and

---

[57] *as the sun breeds reptiles*: The spontaneous generation of some organisms by means of the 'vital heat' of the sun was an idea found in ancient times and believed in until disproved by the work of Louis Pasteur (1822-95).

[58] *Aaron's rod*: Cf. Exodus 7:12 where the rod of Aaron has turned into a serpent which consumes the rods of Pharaoh's magicians which have also turned into serpents.

[59] *Bishop Chase*: See above note on p.[316].

became members of the Episcopal Church. An examination of the Prayer Book, and of the important subject of an apostolical succession, were among the principal reasons which led to this remarkable change. Then in his nineteenth year he resolved to devote himself to the clerical office. Accordingly, after several years of close application to study, under the tuition of a member of the University of Oxford, then officiating as a parish minister in Albany, he received holy Orders in 1798, and was appointed a missionary to extend the blessings of religion in the new settlements in the western part of New York."—P. 22.

[329] Another, mentioned by Mr. Caswall, is the present rector of Bethel, in Vermont, "a venerable English gentleman, once a strong dissenter, and the minister of an Independent congregation in the mother country. Having arrived in America, he formed an acquaintance with the Episcopal Church, and became convinced that the chief grounds on which the dissenters originally seceded from the Church of England had been fully removed in this country. After due consideration, he was received as a candidate for the ministry, and was ultimately ordained to the priesthood, and elected rector of Christ Church, Bethel. He is a faithful and laborious pastor, and a zealous defender of the apostolic succession, and other distinctive principles of Episcopacy."—Pp. 140, 141.

Dr. Cooke,[60] who is the subject of the following extract, was a Professor in the Medical School at Lexington, and is known by a work on the Theory and Practice of Medicine.

"Educated in Virginia, and connected with some distinguished families in England, Dr. Cooke spent his youth among the best society, and in habitual intercourse with the most cultivated minds. Sceptical opinions were then unhappily prevalent, and he imbibed the poison which has destroyed so many of the inconsiderate and unreflecting. While still a young man, he was induced, by a happy curiosity, to purchase of an itinerant book-pedlar, a work on the evidences of Christianity. He took it home, shut himself up in his room, and applied his whole faculties to the study of the interesting subject. His naturally

---

[60] *Dr. Cooke:* John Esten Cooke (1783-1853), distinguished American physician. However, it was a different Dr. Charles John Cooke who was the co-editor of *Lectures on the Theory and Practice of Medicine* by John Elliotson which had just been published in 1839; Newman has evidently confused the two.

strong mind felt the entire force of the argument, and his native straightforwardness led him to an instant avowal of the change which took place in his sentiments.

"Knowing as yet nothing of Church history, he was not adequate to make a proper choice of a denomination, but immediately connected himself with the Methodists, partly on account of their local proximity, and partly through a just admiration of their energy and zeal. For many years he remained an active and influential member of that sect. At length Dr. Chapman's sermons on the Church[61] were published, and produced on his mind a strong apprehension that the American Methodists might be in a state of schism. He again shut himself up in his study, and applied himself closely to the perusal of such works on the subject as he could procure. [330]

"During this investigation, he attended no place of worship, and determined to attend none until he had succeeded in discovering the true Church. Finally, he came to the conclusion that Scripture as well as primitive Antiquity concurred in requiring an external commission derived from Christ through His Apostles, as the only warrant for the performance of the ministerial office. He became convinced, also, that the possession of such a ministry was a necessary mark of the true Church, and that all religious bodies destitute of that ministry are in a state of separation from the primitive fold. By the light of ecclesiastical history he now traced the Apostolic Succession through the early Church. He therefore connected himself with the American Episcopal Church; since here he found all that is best in Romanism, without its corruptions; all that is valuable among the dissenters, without their disorders.

"He afterwards imported from abroad, at a great expense, an admirable library, containing most of the primitive fathers, and the voluminous writings of former times on the subject of Church history. His convictions were complete, and he devoted his time and money, with unsparing liberality, to the diffusion of those important truths which he had so providentially acquired."—Pp. 226-228.

Dr. Chapman, who is mentioned in the last extract, is a vigorous and striking writer. No wonder that thoughtful men come over to the Church, when a powerful cause has such powerful advocates. We will quote a passage from one of his sermons, both for the view given in it of the religious state of

---

[61] *Dr. Chapman's sermons on the Church*: George Thomas Chapman (1786-1872), his *Sermons, upon the ministry, worship, and doctrines of the Protestant Episcopal church, and other subjects* was published in 1828.

331

the country, and for the force and liveliness with which it is given:

"On the supposition that the original Apostles were to re-appear for the purpose of converting the heathen to the knowledge of the true God and Jesus Christ whom He hath sent, what, I demand, would be the course adopted by them, the system they would deem it advisable to employ? If the Apostles, under such circumstances, were to pursue their previous course, it would be in strict conformity to the directions [331] Jesus gave them when 'speaking of the things pertaining to the kingdom of God.'[62] *He* was for one Church, and *they* would be for one, the same over which He presided as the Great Shepherd and Bishop of Souls.[63] He said nothing about Presbyterians, Congregationalists, Baptists, Methodists, or the other Dissenters, and the like silence would be preserved by them. [But] supposing them to be now engaged in evangelizing the pagan nations, on *your* multitudinous system of sects, each individual would be obliged to found some fifteen or twenty discordant churches, in order to include the two or three hundred which have contrived to make themselves acceptable to the Christian world. Not only must John advocate Episcopacy, and James, Presbyterianism; Peter, the theological unity of the Divine Nature, and Thomas, a Trinity in Unity; Philip, everlasting happiness to the righteous only, with the like duration of misery to the unrighteous, and Bartholomew, the more gratifying doctrine of universal salvation; Jude, the baptism of infants, and Matthew, its limitation to believers; Andrew, the perpetuity of the sacraments, and Simon, the Canaanite, their eventual disuse; James, the son of Alpheus, baptism by sprinkling, and Matthias, by immersion; Paul, the Supra, and Barnabas, the Sub-lapsarian dogma;[64] Timothy, an unlimited, and Titus, a limited atonement;[65] Silas, a personal, and Epaphroditus,[66] a spiritual reign of Christ upon the earth for the space of a thousand years;—but in addition to this, every one of the Apostles must prepare himself to bring forward at least twenty

[62] *'speaking of the things ... kingdom of God.'*: Acts 1:3.

[63] *the Great Shepherd and Bishop of Souls*: Cf. I Peter 2:25

[64] p 331. *the Supra . . . the Sub-lapsarian dogma*: Supralapsarianism is the view that God chose the elect and the damned even before the Fall, whereas Sublapsarianism holds that only God so chose after the Fall.

[65] *limited ... unlimited atonement*: Calvin taught that Christ's atonement was only efficacious for the elect, a limited number, and not for everyone, an unlimited number, as the Arminians taught.

[66] *Silas ... Epaphroditus*: Silas is mentioned in Acts as a companion of St. Paul; he is thought to be the same as Silvanus mentioned in II Corinthians, I and II Thessalonians and I Peter. Epaphroditus, St. Paul's scribe, is mentioned in Philippians.

different sects, and school his conscience to contend earnestly for the faith of as many opposing creeds. Instead of the prayer of Christ being strictly fulfilled, 'Holy Father, keep through Thine own name those whom Thou hast given me, that they may be one, as we are;'[67] instead of such fulfilment, principles must be embraced and carried out of this nature,—'Divide and subdivide, contradict each other and contradict your own selves, create this schism in one place and that in another, pronounce justification to be by faith in the morning, and by works in the afternoon.' So shall 'ye continue in my word,' and be 'my disciples indeed;' 'ye shall know the truth, and the truth shall make you free.'"[68]—Pp. 333, 334.

5.

And now, having said enough by way of introducing the reader to the American Church in its present state, we proceed to our main point, which is as follows:—We have been [332] surveying the remarkable birth of this Church out of the ashes; its instinctive appreciation of the Succession; its silent cherishing of it when obtained; and afterwards its sudden and vigorous development. Yet there is a very great deal to do still in America in the way of both the extension and the development of the Apostolical principle; extension through the body of Churchmen, development as regards its consequences. The former of these deficiencies is undeniable; many of its members do not yet hold the doctrine of the Succession, though the number of its maintainers is increasing. So far, however, everything is as we could wish; nothing substantial can be done in a hurry. "A great, and, it is believed, an increasing number of the clergy," says Mr. Caswall, "are strong in their assertion of the Apostolical Succession, and decline ecclesiastical intercourse with dissenting bodies."—P. 331. Again: "In every diocese there are very many, sometimes a great majority both among the clergy and the laity, who habitually consider their bishop as possessed of Apostolical authority, transmitted in an unbroken chain from the primitive ages. This opinion gives a dignity to the office in the estimation of the religious, such as no temporal wealth and no worldly titles could confer."—P. 86. All this is as well as it could be; but what we are anxious about,

---

[67] *'Holy Father . . . as we are;'*: John 17:11
[68] *'ye continue in my word . . . make you free'*: John 8:31-2

what meets with serious impediments, and is seldom even recognized as desirable, is the second of the above desiderata, the full and unreserved development of the Apostolical principle itself. American Christians possess and profess a high gift; but as yet they appear scarcely to understand, any more than ourselves, what that possession and profession involve. We shall devote the remainder of what we have to say to this point; [333] perhaps we may be somewhat free; but if we speak with good temper and a kind purpose, as we hope we shall, we have a right to some portion of that republican liberty which our brethren allow to each other and consider a virtue. To convey our meaning, we must begin some way back, at the risk of seeming ambitious.

All systems, then, which live and are substantive, depend on some or other inward principle or doctrine, of which they are the development. They are not a fortuitous assemblage of atoms from without, but the expansion of a moral element from within. They cannot die a natural death till this moral element dies, though, of course, they, as all things below, may be overcome by violence. But they are indestructible, considered internally, while their informing principle continues; for it is their life. Within they have nothing of a self-destructive nature; everything is evolved from one and the same formula; part cannot quarrel with part, both being results or transformations of that one. Their parts cohere, not from any immediate junction or direct association, but because they all spring from a principle, and into that principle resolve. While their inward life remains, they repair their losses; if existing portions are cut off, they put out fresh branches. But when that life goes, they are no more; they have no being, they dissolve. However fair they may look for a time, whether state, nation, society, church, university, moral agent, they are dead; and if they in appearance continue, still are they but phantoms, kept together by extraneous influences acting for extraneous purposes. Unity without is a result of unity within; but when there is nothing real within, what appears is as little real and substantive as a man's face in a glass, which is not the bodily development of a soul, but the result of certain external laws of matter. And, it [334] must be confessed, there are in the world a great number of these unreal beings and mockeries, whether in politics, religion, or morals; things like card-houses,[69] or scenes in a playhouse,[70] which make up an effect, but have no inside;—standing by the force of habit because no one meddles with them, and crumbling to bits directly they are touched,—or patched up and made decent by the interest of parties,—or recommended by the character or influence of individuals. Such a creature of time and chance many men have thought and think our own Church to be; and such she is proved not to be, as in ten thousand other ways, so especially as we noticed in the outset, by her vigorous offshoots growing up in the West. She scattered some of her seeds in the wilderness; and, while for a time they seemed to die, a spirit at length was found within them, which rose, throve, and at length took outward shape like her own. Thus she proved herself to be a living principle: she showed that her very dust is spiritual; that a soul is in her smallest portions; that when she imparts herself anywhere, be it in small or great measure, she gives herself whole and entire; she cannot give part of herself; she gives spirit, not matter, and by the energy of existence multiplies images of herself on every side. How unequal to great purposes, how shapeless and how unorganized were the companies which roamed from her bosom to the American continent! Without the look of a Church, and without the knowledge of their want. But a Church was in them, and when they came together in one, the spirit spake out. The word was in their hearts as a burning fire shut up in their bones, and they were weary of forbearing and could not stay. They had been without bishops, without ordinances, scattered among the mixed multitude of sectarianism and heresy; but they were different [335] from them within, though in outward respects alike. They had a creative principle in them, which the others had not. Others might tend to utter apostasy. Puritans might become Socinians; Baptists might form and reform, resolve and change like a calidoscope; Shakers, Dunkers, Swedenborgians,[71] Mormonites,

---

[69] *card-houses*: miniature buildings built up out of playing cards

[70] *scenes in a playhouse*: scenery in a theatre

[71] *Swedenborgians*: Followers of Emmanuel Swedenborg (1688-1772) who claimed to have a series of revelations or mystical experiences in which God revealed that Swedenborg was to reform Christianity.

might flit around them, but they, through God's mercy, were what they were and nothing else. They were ever tending upwards, not downwards, struggling upwards amid obstacles to the pure light of the Gospel, and, if let alone, then, by the power of the gift in them, ever developing into Churches, breaking forth into the Apostolic polity and the Catholic faith.

Still, it is true that obstacles might keep them down, and impede, or mutilate, or distort the development of the heavenly seed; and this, it would appear, is more or less the actual condition of every Church all over the world. No Church is fully and simply developed into its full proportions; all meet with external impediments, not the same everywhere, but some or other, which succeed in distorting and crippling them. One suffers from the influence of the temporal power, another from heathen masters, a third from the popular voice, a fourth from the schools of philosophy, a fifth from national progress, or civil institutions. One and all are tempted and more or less warped by fear of man, or covetousness, or sloth, or desire of rule, or present expediency, or the pride of reason. The inward principle develops in some degree, but partially and unequally, issuing in an inconsistent, or inchoate, or badly proportioned creed and polity. The American Church, if for no other reason, at least as being in her infancy, cannot hope to be free from this imperfection. In saying this we are bringing no heavy charge against her, since we as little arrogate such a good and perfect gift to any of ourselves, as to our American brethren.

[336]

But it is one thing to profess to have already attained, another to profess the necessity of attainment; one thing to pursue, another not to comprehend, unity of idea and action. And at this day, it is our habit, on both sides of the Atlantic, neither to desire nor understand real unity,—not to take-in the idea that effects follow from causes, and that a contradiction is self-destructive; but to call it moderation and judgment to sit down deliberately between two stools, or to leap into the ditch, and ultraism[72] to clear it; extravagance, to dare to be consistent and to endure the conclusions of our admitted premises. Instead of viewing the Gospel system as a living growth, like "some tall palm,"[73]

---

[72] *ultraism*: extreme opinions

[73] *"some tall palm"*: From the poem 'Palestine' by Reginald Heber (1783-1826): 'No

beautiful as being at once one and many, we build it up course by course, as we spread our layers of brick and mortar. Our architecture at the present day is a type, or rather an effect, of our state of mind. The lines of our buildings do not flow on, nor their arms expand, and return into themselves, as being the expansion of one whole idea, but we seem to be ever congratulating ourselves that we have got so far, and to be asking "What shall we do next?"—range rising above range, and pile placed aside of pile, without even the merit of being excrescences. And we make up for want of meaning in the whole by stress and earnestness in the parts; we lavish decorations on bit by bit, till what was at first unmeaning, ends by being self-contradictory.

Now as to the American Church, it has been her privilege to begin with so clear an announcement of that rudimental truth on which all true Churches rest, that we cannot but believe she is destined, in spite of obstacles, to advance onward to the measure of the stature of its perfect fullness. She has got that truth in her; and with gratitude we add, that the most [337] considerable of her bishops, living and dead, have developed it accurately no little way. They have gone forward from one truth to another; from the Apostolic Commission to the Succession, from the Succession to the Office,—in the office they have discerned the perpetual priesthood, in the priesthood the perpetual sacrifice, in the sacrifice the glory of the Christian Church, its power as a fount of grace, and its blessedness as a gate of heaven. They had felt and taught most persuasively the unearthly supernatural state in which all Christians stand, and their real communion in the invisible kingdom of God. You would not know whether you were in America or England while their books were before you, in Birmingham or New York, amid collieries or cotton-crops. The external world sinks to its due level; and universal suffrage is as little found there, as is the House of Commons. How much further these writers ought to have gone, what doctrines they left latent, and what they but half developed, we have neither purpose nor ability to say; but without determining what would be presumptuous, so much we

---

hammers fell, no ponderous axes rung; / Like some tall palm the mystic fabric sprung.'
This lengthy poem was very popular in Newman's time.

may safely maintain, that there is no conceivable point of opinion, or practice, or ritual, or usage, in the Church system, ever so minute,—no detail of faith and conduct ever so extreme, but what might be a legitimate and necessary result of that one idea or formula with which they started. Mammoths and megatheria[74] are known by their vertebræ; men's bodily temperaments have sometimes been discriminated by their nails;[75] and in like manner there is no development ever so ultimate but may be the true offspring of the Apostolical principle. A gesture, a posture, a tone, a word, a symbol, a season, a spot, may be its property and token, whatever be the real difficulty of ascertaining and discriminating such details; nay, and it is not fully developed till it reaches those ultimate points, whatever real danger there be of formality. However, let us see how far the American divines have proceeded, for that is the first point which comes into consideration.

[338]

First let us have recourse to Dr. Seabury of Connecticut,[76] the first who was consecrated diocesan bishop. What makes his sermons more interesting is that they seem to have been covertly controversial,—efforts, and successful efforts, at development, in spite of opposite influences which were assailing the nascent Church. He says:

"The authority under which the Apostles acted being derived from Christ, in the exercise of it they were His ministers, because the authority was originally and properly His, and they could act only in His name; and this authority being by successive ordinations continued down to this day, all duly authorized clergymen now act by it, and are therefore the 'ministers of Christ.'[77] On this commission is the

---

[74] *megatheria*: elephant-sized ground sloths that lived in South America from c.5 million BC to c.10,000 BC.

[75] *nails*: The state of the fingernails can indeed be an indication of medical problems.

[76] *Dr. Seabury of Connecticut*: Samuel Seabury (1729–96), the first American Episcopal bishop, second Presiding Bishop of the Episcopal Church and first Bishop of Connecticut. He had initially sought episcopal consecration by Anglican bishops in England, but they declined to ordain him unless he took the oath of supremacy to the British crown, which as a citizen of the new republic he was unable to do. He therefore went to Scotland where in 1784 he was consecrated by non-juring bishops (i.e. those who had refused to break their oath of loyalty to James II by swearing a new oath of loyalty to the usurping William II); these held High Church beliefs, as opposed to the mainstream Church of England's more Protestant theology.

[77] *'ministers of Christ'*: 1 Corinthians 4:1, 2 Corinthians 11:23.

authority of ministers in Christ's Church founded, and no man can justly claim any power in spiritual matters but as it is derived from it. No one will now pretend to have received his commission to preach the Gospel immediately from Christ, as the eleven Apostles had theirs, and none but enthusiasts will pretend to be empowered for that work by immediate revelation from heaven, as St. Paul was. It remains, then, that there is no other way left to obtain a valid commission to act as Christ's ministers in His Church, but *by an uninterupted succession of ordinations from the Apostles. Where this is wanting, all spiritual power in Christ's Church is wanting also*, while they who have any part of this original commission communicated to them are properly Christ's ministers, because they act in His name and by authority derived from Him."—Vol. i. p. 12.

He thus speaks in another sermon of the holy Eucharist:

"That there was, however, a *great and real change* made in the bread and the cup by our Saviour's blessing and thanksgiving and prayer, [339] cannot be doubted. Naturally they were only bread and wine, and not the body and blood of Christ. When He had blessed them, He declared them to be His body and blood. *They were, therefore, by His blessing and word, made to be, what by nature they were not*."—P. 149.

"The Eucharist is not only a sacrament, in which, under the symbols of bread and wine according to the institution of Christ, the faithful truly and spiritually receive the body and blood of Christ, but also, *a true and proper sacrifice*, commemorative of the original sacrifice and death of Christ, for our deliverance from sin and death—a memorial made before God to put Him in mind, that is, to plead with Him, the meritorious sacrifice and death of His dear Son, for the forgiveness of our sins, for the sanctification of His Church, for a happy resurrection from death, and a glorious immortality with Christ in heaven. From this account the priesthood of the Christian Church evidently appears."—P. 156.

To Bishop Seabury is owing the restoration to the consecration prayer in the American Communion Service,[78] of the oblatory words,[79] and the invocation of the Holy Spirit;[80]

[78] *the American Communion Service*: *The Communion-Office, or Order for the Administration of the Holy Eucharist or Supper of the Lord* published by Bishop Seabury in 1786. It was based on the Episcopal Church of Scotland's *Book of Common Prayer* which was similar to the original English 1549 version .

[79] *the oblatory words*: 'these thy holy gifts, which we now offer unto thee' referring to the consecrated elements as a sacrifice.

"which," as Bishop White[81] reminds us, "were left out of our own service at a subsequent review in King Edward's time, at the instance of two learned foreigners."[82]

He speaks of the state of the dead in the same forcible way:

"It was the belief of the primitive Christians, as well as of the old Jews, that at the departure of the soul from the body it went to a secret, invisible place, provided by God for its residence, there to remain till the general judgment; the wicked in uneasiness, remorse, and despair; the good in peace and refreshment, with an assured hope of God's favour, and a full acquittal at the final retribution. *On this ground stood the commemoration of the martyrs, and prayers for the faithful departed out of this life*, that God would grant them rest and peace in Christ, and free acquittal in the day of judgment."—P. 196.

[340]   Next, we will mention Bishop Hobart; he thus speaks of the Christian ministry in an ordination sermon:

"It is the distinguishing dignity of this office, and it will constitute also its tremendous responsibility, that it resembles in its origin, and in many of its important functions, the priesthood of Jesus Christ. As the Father sent Him in His human nature to be the Prophet, a Priest and a ruler of His people, so He sent His ministers to the end of the world to be the instructors, the *priests* and the governors of His Church. He received the anointing of the Spirit, and they receive *by the laying on of the hands of that apostolic succession in which the power of ordination is vested*, the gift of the Holy Ghost—that gift of office by which they became invested with *power* to minister in holy things."—P. 13.

---

[80] *the invocation of the Holy Spirit*: the words 'with thy Holy Spirit and Word vouchsafe to bless and sanctify these thy gifts and creatures of bread and wine' which, along with the 'oblatory' words, had appeared in the 1549 version of the *Book of Common Prayer* but had been removed in the 1552 version as they implied a more Catholic theology of the Eucharist.

[81] *White*: Bishop William White (1748–1836), first and fourth Presiding Bishop of the Protestant Episcopal Church.

[82] Memoirs, p. 154. [N] William White, *Memoirs of the Protestant Episcopal Church in the United States of America* (Philadelphia, 1820). The 'two learned foreigners' were the German Protestant Martin Bucer (1491-1551) and the Italian Protestant Peter Martyr (1499-1562), both of whom had come to England and had influenced Cranmer in his 1552 revision.

In one of his posthumous sermons, he gives the following precise account of the supernatural state of the Christian Church:

"It is indeed a truth, established by the whole tenour of the apostolic writings, that the blessings of salvation are ordinarily conveyed through the instrumentality of the Church, of which Christ is the Head and Saviour, and that *by union with this Church*, penitent believers are made partakers of all the benefits of His death and passion. 'The Lord added to the Church such as should be saved,'[83]—'Christ is the Head of the Church, the Saviour of the body,'[84]—'We are one body in Christ, members of His Body.'[85]—P. 308.

Thirdly, we will quote the glowing language of the eloquent Dehon:[86]

"What tokens shall we give Him of our love? We must espouse the cause which is dear to Him. We must promote the work which He desires to see accomplished. And especially upon *the Church, which He hath taken into so near a connection, as to make it one with Himself*, we may bestow tokens of our regard, which He will thus receive. The Church He loves. *With the Church He hath left the records of His truth, the representatives of His power, and the symbols of His presence.* For the Church, as His Body, He is constantly interceding in heaven, 'that He may present it unto Himself a glorious Church, not having spot or wrinkle, or any such thing.'[87]"—P. 266.

[341]

Again:

"Says the holy Chrysostom: 'When the Eucharist is celebrated, the angels stand by the priest, and the whole choir resounds with celestial powers, and the place about the altar is filled with them in honour of Him who is laid thereon.'[88] What sobriety should these considerations beget in us, when we come into God's house. How powerfully do they enforce that decency in worship, which the Apostle recommends, 'because of the angels.'[89] Especially with what pure hearts and clean hands, with what reverence and godly fear, should we come to the

---

[83] *'The Lord added ... '*: Acts 2:47

[84] *'Christ is the Head ... '* : Ephesians 5:23

[85] *'We are one body ... '*: Cf. 1 Corinthians 12:12, 12:27; Romans 12:5.

[86] *Dehon*: Theodore Dehon (1776–1817), second Protestant Episcopal Bishop of South Carolina.

[87] *... spot or wrinkle, or any such thing'*: Ephesians 5:27

[88] *'When the Eucharist ... '* : John Chrysostom, *On the Priesthood*, Book VI. 4.

[89] *'because of the angels. '*: 1 Corinthians 11:10

Holy Table. Consider with whom you there stand, who are the spectators of your conduct, yea! who are the associates of your devotion, when you 'laud and magnify God's glorious name.'[90]"—Pp. 133, 134.

One other short passage may be allowed us from a writer who would be found to be most eloquent, if we had room to quote him at length. Speaking of the necessity of an appointed ministry, he says:

"Look through the pagan world, and observe everywhere a priest, where you find an altar, a sacred office where you find a God. Would you know the divine counsel in this particular? Behold the Deity, in the dispensation to His chosen people, selecting a particular tribe for His service, and confining to them the right and the duty of ministering in holy things. Above all, it should satisfy our minds upon this topic, that our Saviour did ordain selected men, authorizing them to send others, as He sent them, to preach His Gospel, to administer His ordinances, and to guide and govern His visible Church. It is presumable, from the nature of the thing, that there would be found in the world an established priesthood, unto whom this ministry of reconciliation would be committed, for the edification of the Church. And blessed be our adorable Head, *such a priesthood there has been among His redeemed, from the first ministry of His Apostles unto the present day*, nor can we doubt His will, that, after the way of His appointment, it should be perpetuated in the world until His coming again."—P. 48, etc.

[342] It is pleasant to know that Bishop Dehon was as beautiful in his life and conversation as he is in his writings. He died in 1817, at the early age of forty-one, of the yellow fever; the personal tributes called forth by his death were of the warmest and deepest kind.

6.

Such are the principles of the American Church, legitimately resulting from her *idea*, as Catholic and Apostolic. Now let us consider the "extraneous influences," as Mr. Caswall justly calls

---

[90] *'laud and magnify God's glorious name'*: Preface, Order for the Administration of the Lord's Supper or Holy Communion, *Book of Common Prayer*.

them, which at present prevent their being duly understood, accepted, expanded, applied, by the large body of her members.

Now, it is obvious, one most potent and continual disturbing force in the development of Apostolical principles, is a circumstance above recorded, viz., the spread of the Church among Dissenters. Action and reaction are equal, except where a Church is as firm as a rock; and, in the present instance, while sectarians have gained from her, the Church has lost from them. Considering that half the existing hierarchy have had their baptism and education from dissent, it is truly marvellous that the Church is what she is; and it raises in the Christian mind admiration and thankfulness for the innate power of that system, which could effect so much, with so weak a subject-matter to work upon. A Church must have the iron grasp of Rome to be able to catch, without being caught; nor is it to be expected that our American brethren will be free from this infirmity for a long time to come. But here we are concerned with more definite illustrations and causes of the existing state of American theology.

Let not the friends, then, of the American Church be startled, if we say that in her first years she suffered seriously, and still suffers, from certain influences, which are too grievous to call by their right name, but of which she must be made fully aware, if she is ever to get clear of them. In saying this, we are speaking of what Mr. Caswall truly calls, "*extraneous* influences;" we are very far indeed from implying that the source of them is in the body itself, or that they penetrate into the body, but they act forcibly upon the body by external pressure, and have committed it to acts which have done much mischief ever since. Nor in this respect are we better circumstanced than they; we too in the time of the third William and the first Georges had certain impressions of the same kind made on us, which chilled, attenuated, and shrivelled up our faith and spirit. What, indeed, is that desire of Evidences,[91] that delight in objection and

[343]

---

[91] *Evidences*: Newman is thinking of *Natural Theology; or, Evidences of the Existence and Attributes of the Deity* (1802), William Paley (1743-1805). This argued that the design of nature showed evidence of a Creator, on the analogy of a watch implying a watchmaker. It was widely influential and was compulsory reading for Oxford undergraduates. Newman was wary of such an approach to apologetics: 'religious minds embrace the Gospel mainly on the great antecedent probability of a Revelation, and the

spontaneous incredulity, that pursuit of secular comfort, that contentment with mere decency and morality, which in its degree exist still among us all, but remains of the Socinian temper inflicted on us during that calamitous period? Nor have those malign influences ceased. They have worked their way unseen; and, whereas they are now more generally acknowledged than they were, they were detected years ago by one of the most keensighted men of his age, a name well known in America, Mr. Norris, of Hackney.[92] He thus writes to Bishop Hobart in 1822:

> "The American branch of Christ's Holy Catholic Church is filling at this time a most important station upon the earth. What our future fortunes are to be it would be presumptuous to calculate upon. There is amongst us a large measure of genuine Christian zeal and decided Church principle, and both are upon the increase; but then there is a tremendous confederation, topped by false brethren, and *bottomed by Socinians*, who are working incessantly and systematically upon all departments of the community. The specific object of it is, to make *schism catholic instead of unity*; unity therefore must fall, unless those who are its divinely appointed guardians cherish it with more than ordinary solicitude, and exercise an apostolic jealousy in maintaining *one* mind and *one* mouth among themselves."—*Hobart's Life*, p. 253.[93]

[344]

This extract is curious as bearing on our general subject; but to return to the American Church:—the presence of a Socinian influence among her members was a subject of apprehension

---

suitableness of the Gospel to their needs; on the other hand, ... on men of irreligious minds Evidences are thrown away. Further, ... to insist much on matters ... draws men away from the true view of Christianity, and leads them to think that Faith is mainly the result of argument, that religious Truth is a legitimate matter of disputation, and that they who reject it rather err in judgment than commit sin. [This tends] to betray the sacredness and dignity of Religion, when those who profess themselves its champions allow themselves to stand on the same ground as philosophers of the world, admit the same principles, and only aim at drawing different conclusions.' *University Sermons*, Sermon 10, pp.197-8. Newman's distrust of Paley's approach proved prescient when Darwin's *Origin of Species* (1859) provided arguments from the theory of natural selection which accounted plausibly for Paley's 'evidences' of design. This is not to say that Newman rejected the Argument from Design. See *Idea of a University* pp.449ff.
[92] *Mr. Norris of Hackney*: Henry Handley Norris (1771–1850), Anglican divine and theologian; leader of the 'Hackney Phalanx' group of High Churchmen.
[93] Hobart's Life: Berrian, William, *The Posthumous Works of the Late Reverend John Hobart, D.D. Bishop of the Protestant Episcopal Church in the State of New-York with A Memoir of his Life*, Vol.I (New York, 1833).

with some of the eminent persons in England who were interested or concerned in the question of their obtaining the Succession. Mr. Granville Sharp,[94] in a letter to Dr. Franklin, mentions the uneasiness occasioned at home, at reports which were circulated about the changes which the Americans intended to introduce into the Prayer Book. An "Episcopal congregation at Boston," he says, "adopted a liturgy formed after the manner of Dr. Clarke[95] and Mr. Lindsay"[96] (p. 315); and the Socinian party flattered themselves that the proceedings of the Convention indicated the same feeling. He adds that "the reports of Socinianism gave great offence to many worthy people" in England, "and more especially to the bishops, who had been sincerely disposed to promote the Church in America." The leaning which was thus evidenced in the East, was seconded from the South, for at that very Convention, concerning which the above-mentioned report had been circulated, so far was true, that Mr. Page[97] of Virginia, afterwards governor of the State, had moved to leave out the first four petitions of the Litany;[98] "and instead of them," says Bishop White, "to introduce a short petition, which *he* had drawn up, more agreeable to his ideas of the Divine Persons recognized in those petitions." He professed not to object to the invocation of our Lord, "which, he was of opinion, might be defended by Scripture;" but "the objection lay to the word Trinity, which he remarked to be unauthorized [345] by Scripture, and a foundation of much unnecessary disputation." But, since to admit only the fourth petition would leave the foregoing three liable to the charge of Tritheism,[99] he thought it best on the whole to strike out all four. Nay, the

---

[94] *Mr. Granville Sharp*: Granville Sharp (1735–1813), social reformer, best known for his tireless work against the slave trade; he was instrumental in arranging for American episcopal bishops to be consecrated by the Archbishop of Canterbury in 1787.
[95] *Dr. Clarke*: See above note on p.[94]. He planned a revised version of the *Book of Common Prayer* reflecting his Unitarian views.
[96] *Mr. Lindsay*: Theophilus Lindsey (1723–1808), Anglican divine and theologian, founder of the first Unitarian chapel in England, author of *The Book of Common Prayer reformed according to the plan of the late Dr Samuel Clarke* (1774).
[97] *Mr. Page*: John Page (1743-1808), thirteenth Governor of Virginia (1802-5).
[98] *the first four petitions of the Litany*: These begin, 'Of God the Father of Heaven', 'O God the Son, Redeemer of the World', 'O God the Holy Ghost, proceeding from the Father and the Son', 'O holy, blessed and glorious Trinity, three Persons and one God'.
[99] *Tritheism*: belief in three Gods

general impression concerning the strength of the Socinianizing party was so strong at the time, that even Bishop Provoost[100] of New York was believed, though, as it has since been shown, without foundation, to have advocated the omission of the fourth petition. This part of the Prayer Book, however, was saved; at the same time another portion of its contents, even more sacred, was sacrificed, the Nicene and Athanasian[101] Creeds; after mentioning which, it is little to add that the clause of the Apostles' concerning the descent of Christ into hell was struck out also. On the remonstrance of the English archbishops, the Nicene Creed was restored, and the article in the Apostles', but the Athanasian remains excluded to this day.

Even as much as this was not gained without a conflict. The Virginians instructed their deputies to the General Convention to be held at Philadelphia, to represent to the meeting that though "uniformity of doctrine would unquestionably contribute to the prosperity of the Church," yet they "earnestly wished that this might be pursued with *liberality and moderation*." "The obstacles," they continued, "which stand in the way of union among Christian societies are too often founded on *matters of mere* form. They are surmountable therefore by those who, breathing the spirit of Christianity, earnestly labour in this pious work. From the Holy Scriptures themselves, rather than the *comments of men*, must we learn the terms of salvation. Creeds therefore ought to be *simple*; and we are not anxious to retain [346] any other than that which is commonly called the Apostles' Creed." They proceed—"We will not now decide what ceremonies ought to be retained. We wish, however, that those which exist *may be estimated according to their utility*, and that such as may appear fit to be laid aside, may no longer be appendages of our Church."[102] In spite of them, the Nicene Creed, as we have said, was restored; but as to the Athanasian, Bishop White observes that, had the English archbishops insisted on its restoration, the pending negotiation for obtaining the Succession "was desperate, because, although there were

---

[100] *Bishop Provoost*: Samuel Provoost (1742–1815), third Presiding Bishop of the Protestant Episcopal Church and first Bishop of the Episcopal Diocese of New York.
[101] *Athanasian*: See above note on p.[57].
[102] White's Memoirs, p. 114. [N] See above note p.[339].

some who favoured a compliance, the majority were determined against it; among whom were two members present, *who had been chosen to the Episcopacy, and who voted against the restoration*, as appears on the journal."[103] Here then we have distinct evidence of the presence of Socinianism, not of course introducing itself *into* the acts of the Church, whether more or less, but exerting an influence *upon* them; and this serious circumstance led us above to view with jealousy, what at first sight might have been welcomed without suspicion, the opinion expressed to Mr. Caswall by the Unitarian of Boston as to the possibility at one time existing, of the Church becoming the religion of his party, instead of the heresy which in fact prevails there. Nor is the following account pleasant which belongs to a date later than that of Mr. Caswall's emigration.

"Here [at Andover] an opening for the Church had been made in a singular manner, and not the most desirable. The majority of the Congregational population having determined to remove their meeting-house to a more convenient situation, the minority were displeased, and withdrew from the congregation. For some time it was doubtful whether they would engage a Unitarian or a Universalist[104] [347] minister to preach to them; but ultimately they concluded on becoming Episcopalians, and having drawn up articles of association, they elected a vestry and wardens, and were admitted into union with the Church in Massachusetts. They assembled on Sunday in a school-house to the number of about forty or fifty; but although attentive to the sermon, they generally took slight interest in the worship, and made little use of the Prayer Book. There were many amiable and worthy people among them, and a few decided Episcopalians; but I soon perceived that nothing but time and perseverance, with Divine help, could succeed in establishing the principles of the Church upon so uncongenial a soil."—Pp. 135, 136.

7.

To tell the truth, we think one special enemy to which the American Church, as well as our own, at present lies open is the influence of a refined and covert Socinianism. Not that we

---

[103] P. 107. [N]

[104] *Universalist*: See above note on p.[61]. The first Universalist church in America was founded in Massachusetts in 1774.

fear any invasion of that heresy within her pale now, any more than fifty years ago, but it is difficult to be in the neighbourhood of icebergs without being chilled, and the United States is, morally speaking, just in the latitude of ice and snow. Here again, as our remarks will directly show, we mean nothing disrespectful towards our Transatlantic relatives. We allude, not to their national character, nor to their form of government, but to their *employments*, which in truth we share with them. A trading country is the *habitat* of Socinianism. Mr. Caswall in one place speaks of its "alluring doctrines:" this may seem a strange description of them, but it is perfectly true, as he uses it. There is no accounting for tastes; and there is a moral condition of mind to which this dismal creed *is* alluring. Mr. Caswall's words are as follows: "At Boston and Salem Unitarianism is very prevalent ... and great numbers of the *rich and fashionable* are attached to its alluring doctrines."—P. 134.

[348]   Not to the poor, the forlorn, the dejected, the afflicted, can the Unitarian doctrine be alluring, but to those who are rich and have need of nothing, and know not that they are "miserable and blind and naked;"[105]—to such men Unitarianism so-called is just fitted, suited to their need, fulfilling their anticipations of religion, counterpart to their inward temper and their modes of viewing things. Those who have nothing of this world to rely upon need a firm hold of the next, they need a deep religion; they are as if stripped of the body while here,—as if in the unseen state between death and judgment; and as they are even now in one sense what they then shall be, so they need to view God such as they then will view Him; they endure, or rather eagerly desire, the bare vision of Him stripped of disguise, as they are stripped of disguises too; they desire to know that He is eternal, since they feel that they are mortal.

Such is the benefit of poverty; as to wealth, its providential corrective is the relative duties which it involves, as in the case of a landlord; but these do not fall upon the trader. He has rank without tangible responsibilities; he has made himself what he is, and becomes self-dependent; he has laboured hard or gone through anxieties, and indulgence is his reward. In many cases

---

[105]   *"miserable, blind and naked"*: Revelation 3:17

he has had little leisure for cultivation of mind, accordingly luxury and splendour will be his *beau ideal* of refinement. If he thinks of religion at all, he will not like from being a great man to become a little one; he bargains for some or other compensation to his self-importance, some little power of judging or managing, some small permission to have his own way. Commerce is free as air; it knows no distinctions; mutual intercourse is its medium of operation. Exclusiveness, separations, rules of life, observance of days, nice scruples of [349] conscience, are odious to it. We are speaking of the general character of a trading community, not of individuals; and, so speaking, we shall hardly be contradicted. A religion which neither irritates their reason nor interferes with their comfort, will be all in all in such a society. Severity whether of creed or precept, high mysteries, corrective practices, subjection of whatever kind, whether to a doctrine or to a priest, will be offensive to them. They need nothing to fill the heart, to feed upon, or to live in; they despise enthusiasm, they abhor fanaticism, they persecute bigotry. They want only so much religion as will satisfy their natural perception of the propriety of being religious. Reason teaches them that utter disregard of their Maker is unbecoming, and they determine to be religious, not from love and fear, but from good sense.

Now it would be a miserable slander on the American Church to say that she was suited to such a form of mind as this; how can she, with her deep doctrines of the Apostolic Commission and the Eucharistic Sacrifice? but this is the very point; here we see around her the external influences which have a tendency to stifle her true development, and to make her inconsistent and unreal. If in the English Church the deep sea dried up more or less in the last century, why should it not in the American also? Let the latter dread her extension among the opulent merchants and traders in towns, where her success has principally been. Many undesirable persons will begin to see in the Church what they can find nowhere else; the Sectarian doctrines are more or less enthusiastic; the Roman Catholic despotic; in our Church there is (or may be) moderation, rationality, decency, and order, which are just the cardinal excellences, the highest "idea" of truth, the first and only fair, [350] to which their minds attain. If this view of things is allowed a footing, a sleek gentlemanlike religion will grow up within the sacred pale, with well-warmed chapels, softly cushioned pews, and eloquent preachers. The poor and needy, the jewels of the Church, will dwindle away; the clergy will sink in honour, and rich laymen will culminate. Already, Mr. Caswall informs us, "there are churches which rather resemble *splendid drawing-rooms* than houses of worship, and in which *the poor man could hardly feel himself at home.* Handsome *carpets* cover every part of the floor," and "the pews are luxuriously cushioned in a manner calculated to invite repose."—P. 289. Again: "At Chillicothe [in Ohio] the Episcopal Church contains many of the *wealthier and more refined families,* but *has not established itself in the preference of the great mass of the religious people,* who are principally, as in other parts of Ohio, Methodists, Presbyterians, and Baptists."—P. 55. Elsewhere he says, speaking *generally,* not of any particular place:

"*In the congregation there are few, if any, poor persons, so that it is often difficult to dispose of the communion-alms according to the regulations of the Rubric.*[106] The Episcopal congregations are generally composed of highly-intelligent and respectable people, many of whom have received an excellent education. Hence, intellectual sermons are held in great esteem, and elegant composition is duly appreciated. Commonplace discourses are disregarded, and old or borrowed ones are never tolerated. Some oratorical genius is always necessary to clerical success in republican America."—P. 296.

We are aware it is a bold thing to speak of a Church which is a hemisphere off us: we are speaking from books, not from practical knowledge; but we think we may say without fear of mistake, that pews, carpets, cushions, and fine speaking are not [351] developments of the Apostolical Succession. Fathers and brethren, we would say, if we might venture a word, dispense with this world when you enter the presence of another. Throw

---

[106] *the Rubric*: 'the Deacons, Churchwardens, or other fit person appointed for that purpose, shall receive the Alms for the Poor, and other devotions of the people, in a decent bason to be provided by the Parish for that purpose; and reverently bring it to the Priest, who shall humbly present and place it upon the holy Table.' Order for the Administration of the Lord's Supper or Holy Communion, *Book of Common Prayer.*

aside your pillows; set wide your closets; break down your partitions; tear away your carpets. Open a space whereon to worship freely, as those to whom worship was the first thing; who come to repent, not to repose; to give thanks, not to reason; to praise, not to enjoy yourselves. Dispense with your props and kneelers; learn to go down on the floor. What has possessed you and us to choose square boxes to pray in, while we despise Simeon upon his pillar?[107] Why squeeze and huddle together as you neither do, nor would dream of doing, at a dinner-table or in a drawing-room? Let the visible be a type of the invisible. You have dispensed with the clerk,[108] you are spared the royal arms;[109] but still who would ever recognize in a large double cube, with bare walls, wide windows, high pulpit, capacious reading-desk, galleries projecting, and altar obscured, an outward emblem of the heavenly Jerusalem, the fount of grace, the resort of Angels?

Having touched on the circumstances of worship, we may as well here notice some other points connected with it, in which the American Church has not yet carried out her elementary principle.

Mr. Caswall, for instance, tells us that "the communion-table seldom occupies its appropriate place, but is often little more than a narrow board placed in front of the reading-desk, in the situation usually occupied by the clerk in the Church of England."—P. 280. He adds, however, that in some churches of recent erection, the altar occupies a conspicuous and somewhat elevated position in a recess at the extremity of the building, opposite to the main entrance. This is a promising symptom of development going on in the Church, in spite of [352] "extraneous influences." At present, however, it marks the inconsistent state of things, that even so good a churchman as Mr. Caswall is but partially sensible of the position which the Holy Eucharist occupies in the Christian system. We hear

---

[107] *Simeon on his pillar*: See above note on p.[285].

[108] *the clerk*: In the Church of England the Parish Clerk was (and still is) a layman, appointed to assist the parish priest in various functions, especially during church services.

[109] *the royal arms*: From the time of the Reformation, the royal coat of arms was required to be displayed in Anglican churches to emphasise the royal supremacy over the Church of England, as opposed to the papal power.

nothing of its celebration in critical times, when we have a right to expect it; and no remark is made upon the omission. When that interesting man, Mr. Gunn, whose history Mr. Caswall gives at great length, at length fell in with a clergyman, Mr. Caswall thus speaks of the event: "Once more, after an interval of fifteen years, our lay-reader was permitted to *hear the word of life declared* by a commissioned ambassador of Christ."—P. 97. To hear? and not also to take and eat that Living Word, which a commissioned priest alone could give him? In Mr. Caswall's sketch of a diocesan convention, where he was present, he tells us, "The members assembled at 10 a.m. They took their seats in the front pews, the remainder of the building being occupied by a number of respectable persons attached to the Church. The Bishop entered in his episcopal robes, and took his seat within the rails of the communion-table. A clergyman appointed by the Bishop then read morning prayers; the Bishop performed the *ante-communion service*,[110] and a sermon was preached by another clergyman. *After divine service*, the Bishop called the convention to order."—P. 68. The business of the meeting follows; the meeting adjourns till the afternoon; it reassembles; the Bishop reads his annual address. He "urges upon the members the importance of *improving the occasion* by social prayer and *devotional fellowship*."—Committees make their reports, or are appointed; resolutions pass: so ends the first day. On the second prayers and a sermon—then business—reports from parishes—"such further accounts as appeared likely to *interest or edify*." It meets again the third day: divine worship—a canon passed—committee appointed—resolutions—"the members of the convention having been hospitably treated by the inhabitants of the place" (exceedingly proper),—a vote of thanks—a psalm sung—the episcopal benediction given—the convention "finally adjourned." Concerning the Holy Sacrament of the Eucharist, not a word. We speak of this as what happened in a particular case, without having any right or wish to suppose it a general rule. Indeed, in another place Mr. Caswall, speaking of the "regular Sunday services of a clergyman, says that the holy communion is

[353]

---

[110] the ante-communion service: i.e. readings from Scripture and prayers but not the Eucharist itself.

generally administered once a month."—P. 294. And elsewhere he expressly speaks of its celebration at the Convention of Massachusetts in 1833.—P. 121.

Again: the Gospel is a free gift, and in all its developments must take the shape of a free gift: it must not be bought; to the giver the receiver offers back of his best, but not as a bargain. What then are we to think of paying for seats in churches? or, if we have inherited the custom, what of extending it to the poor? yet we have the following uncomfortable account of what is taking place in the American Church: "There are but few free seats in Episcopal churches, and in fact there is not the same necessity. Few persons are so poor, and *still fewer would be willing* to accept it as a gratuity."—P. 282. Why not say at once "few persons are so poor as to accept the Gospel as a gratuity? Pride in things visible leads to pride in things unseen.

Again, he says, "The ancient practice of bowing at the name of Jesus is disused to a great extent."—P. 337. "The practice of turning to the east when the Creed is repeated has been entirely [354] forgotten."—P. 295. "The burial-grounds are generally remote from the churches, and are never consecrated."—P. 283. "In the Table of Vigils, etc. (in the Prayer Book), the Vigils are wholly omitted."—P. 243. "There is no place in America in which the service of a Church is performed daily, unless the General Theological Seminary at New York may be regarded an exception."—P. 595. "Some clergymen almost entirely neglect the observance of the feasts and fasts of the Church. I have known a few who have declined to celebrate Ash Wednesday and Good Friday, while they have united with other denominations in monthly meetings of prayer for missions, colleges, or other objects of interest."—P. 337. "The saints' days which occur during the week are very frequently left unnoticed, while weekly lectures on the nights of Wednesday or Thursday are very general."—*Ibid.* "The service for the churching of women is seldom used, except in the case of English people, who desire to conform to the practice of their ancestors."—P. 299.

All this suggests that there is abundance to do in the way of what we have called development. If persons neglect the ordinances of the Church, it is because they do not believe their virtue and efficacy. If they thought the Church had a gift of grace, they would be instant in the times and places in which she dispenses it. It is difficult to prove that it is a duty to come to church daily; it is easy for a Churchman to feel that it is a privilege.

Again: in the American Church bishops do not assume sees, but are named from their dioceses. In spite of whatever precedents may be urged in favour of this usage, we are clear that it is a piece of *purus putus Protestantismus*.[111] It is difficult [355] to analyze its *rationale*, but we have no doubt that so it is. The Church is *in* a country, not *of* it, and takes her seat in a centre. If a bishop has no throne or see, where is the one never-dying priest, without break, who is the living Apostle of the Church? Is a bishop a mere generalization of a diocese, or its foundation? a name or a person? Generalizations are everywhere, persons have a position. Does a bishop depend on his diocese, or his diocese on him? meanwhile the Roman Catholics have located their bishops, and though their succession in the country is later than ours,[112] they have thus given themselves the appearance of being the settlers, not strangers on a visit.

On the other hand, we are glad to learn from Mr. Caswall the following pleasing manifestations of a Catholic spirit in the details of worship;—at Christmas the churches are decorated with evergreens, tastefully hung in festoons. Since holly, box, and laurel cannot be obtained, "boughs of the cedar, pine, and hemlock are employed in their stead. These decorations are commonly arranged by the young ladies of the congregation."— P. 283. This is as it should be; the same interesting class should also employ themselves in working altar-cloths, and ornamenting service books, the *modicum* of embellishment which political revolutions have left us. Again:—

"The sign of the cross has lately made its appearance on many churches, agreeably with the early custom. Bishop Onderdonk,[113] of

---

[111] purus putus Protestantismus: the most utterly pure Protestantism

[112] *... later than ours*: Rev. John Carroll was ordained the first Catholic bishop in the United States in 1790.

[113] *Bishop Onderdonk*: Rev. Benjamin Treadwell Onderdonk (1791-1861), episcopal bishop of New York 1830-61. A supporter of the Oxford Movement, he was later suspended as bishop in 1845 after being found guilty of improper behaviour towards

New York, in a charge to his clergy, has commended the good taste displayed in this appropriate decoration; and has declared that only an anti-Protestant feeling can consider the sign of the cross as symbolizing the corruptions of Romanism."—P. 282.

Both infants and adults are sometimes baptized by immersion, according to the rubric. This, again, is cheering news. In one church in Kentucky the font is in the shape of a [356] large bath, six or seven feet in length. Several persons in Philadelphia have been baptized in the river (pp. 297, 298). Mr. Caswall observes, in another place:

"In Baptist neighbourhoods there are episcopal clergymen who greatly desire to see the old English rubric restored, by which all persons were required to be immersed at baptism, except when they were sick and unable to bear it. I am acquainted with a small episcopal congregation situated in the midst of Baptists, in which not a single infant has been presented for baptism during seven years, the parents being greatly influenced by the arguments of the sectarians."—P. 337.

This is a curious instance of "extraneous influences" working the right way.

7.[114]

But leaving these agreeable instances of the expansion of the Apostolical idea, which show that we have everything to hope of the American Church, we must go on to allude, for our space will hardly allow us to do more, to a much more systematic and overt deflexion from Church principles than any which we have yet mentioned, viz., the power usurped by the laity over the bishop's jurisdiction, which at present is an absolute bar to the due development of Catholicity. The Americans boast that their Church is not, like ours, enslaved to the civil power; true, not to the civil power by name and in form, but to the laity, and in a democracy what is that but the civil

women. However, his trial was controversial, as it was alleged by his supporters that he was being unjustly persecuted because of his Catholic views, and by his opponents that he was being unjustly defended for the same reason.

[114] *7.*: This should be no.8 This mis-numbering, whether by Newman or by the printer, continues for the remainder of the essay.

power in another shape? When Bishop Hobart returned from England, he preached and published a Sermon, in which, among other evils in our Church, he freely, but not at all unwarrantably, expressed his regret at what his biographer truly called "the extraordinary and inappropriate prerogative of the king, *through his ministers*, to designate the persons who shall be chosen for the episcopal office, whose authority is entirely divine, and the *absolute incapacity of the clergy* to exercise their ecclesiastical power independently of the State."—P. 333. He adds, "But here *no secular authority* can interfere with our high ecclesiastical assembly, nor control her legitimate powers." When this Sermon reached England it excited no little annoyance in certain quarters; and in the Quarterly Theological Review (before it became connected with the British Critic)[115] a very bitter attack appeared,[116] which called forth an answer from a generous friend of the Bishop's, the late Mr. Rose.[117] It is unnecessary to go into the details of his conclusive defence of Bishop Hobart from the uncomfortable reflections, which an apparently angry writer had thrown out against him. But it is to our purpose to observe the adroit and natural way in which, while defending a friend, he delicately retorts upon him and his the criticisms which the Bishop's Sermon had directed against us. The Bishop had been absurdly accused of ingratitude to his English hosts, merely for expressing opinions in America which in England he had frankly avowed to *them*! On this Mr. Rose observes:

"For myself I can only say, that if, after a sojourn in America, in speaking of American Episcopacy, I were to urge the strong tendency of an election for the high office of a bishop to produce intrigue, party feeling, and dispute among the clergy—if I were to state my exceeding dislike to make the clergy dependent on the voluntary contributions of the laity for support, and my

[357]

---

[115] ... *became connected with the British Critic*: *The Quarterly Theological Review and Ecclesiastical Record*, founded in 1793, was absorbed by *The British Critic* in 1828.

[116] *a very bitter attack appeared*: in the June 1826 issue.

[117] *Mr. Rose*: Hugh James Rose (1795-1838), Anglican divine, Rector of Hadleigh, Suffolk; founder of *The British Critic*. His defence of Bishop Hobart appeared in the *Christian Remembrancer*, September 1826. It was widely reproduced, including in American journals. Rose later invited Newman to write the book that was to become *The Arians of the Fourth Century*. The Oxford Movement was effectively founded at a meeting in his rectory in 1833.

belief that such a mode of provision would deprive them of that freedom of rebuke which I judge essential to the character of a Christian minister—if I were to object to the mixture of laymen [358] in their Lower House of Convention—if I were to state these things in the honesty of my heart, in a deep conviction that these *were* evils, and in an unaffected regret to see them in a Church, for the excellences of which, as a true Episcopalian, I had the strongest respect, and for whose continuance and extension I devoutly prayed; I should feel both surprised and grieved that any man could be found who would proclaim me an abuse hunter for thus expressing my honest belief."—*Hobart's Life*, pp. 348, 349.

Now, of the three evils specified in this passage Mr. Caswall acknowledges the voluntaryism[118] which obtains in his Church, and we have seen that there is a hope of its being in time removed. The evils existing in the elections of bishops he candidly confesses also, though he does not allow that they are necessary or unmixed. As to the third point, which is the one immediately before us, the introduction of the laity into the Conventions, it is implied by the venerable Bishop White, in his Memoirs of the American Church,[119] that that measure originated with himself. In the work in question, he admits, that as regards the early Church, there is no ground for saying that the laity was more than "occasionally present" at its synodical deliberations; but "he thinks it evident that in *very* early times, when every Church, that is, the Christian people in every city and convenient district round it, was an ecclesiastical commonwealth, with all the necessary power of self-government, the body of the people had a considerable share in its determinations."—P. 86. And he argues that "the same sanction which the people gave originally in a body, they might lawfully give by representation." He concludes, then, "that if the matter pleaded for be *lawful*, the question of the propriety of adopting it ought to be determined by expediency." And that [359]

---

[118] *voluntaryism*: in this context, the principle that the church is not supported by the state through taxation and has to rely entirely on the contributions of its members.

[119] *his Memoirs of the American Church*: *Memoirs of the Protestant Episcopal Church in the United States of America,* William White, D. D.. Bishop of Pensylvania, 1836, one of the books Newman was reviewing in the original *British Critic* article; see Appendix 1.

it is expedient, he determines first, because in the Church of England, which the American Church follows, the parliament has a most considerable synodical power; secondly, from the *difficulty* of introducing into America the Episcopal polity in any other way; and thirdly, from the *impossibility* of getting the laity to *submit* to ecclesiastical laws, (for instance, relating to admission or exclusion from the Lord's Supper,) enacted without their own concurrence. Here we see the operation of "extraneous influences." With all due respect to the memory of the venerable author of the "Memoirs," we must express our strong feeling that such views imply an insufficient appreciation of the "developments" of the Apostolical Succession. He advocated them in a pamphlet published without his name in 1783, and the principle of lay government was carried by the Convention. This was before the introduction of the Succession from England, or Dr. White's own consecration. The only bishop then in America was Dr. Seabury, of Connecticut; and he and his clergy strongly, though ineffectually, protested against it. He wrote to Dr. Smith, of Maryland,[120] with his characteristic clearness and cogency, sweeping away the doctrine of expediency, and joining issue on the question of historical facts. "The rights of the Christian Church," he said, "arise not from nature or compact, but from the institution of Christ; and we ought not to alter them, but to receive and maintain them, as the Holy Apostles left them. The government, sacraments, faith, and doctrine of the Church are fixed and settled. We have a right to examine what they are, but we must take them as they are. If we new model the government, why not the sacraments, creeds, and doctrines of the Church? But [360] then it would not be Christ's Church, but our Church, and would remain so, call it by what name we please."[121]

However, leaving the history of this important departure from primitive order, let us avail ourselves of Mr. Caswall's work to trace the element of lay interference through the various functions of American ecclesiastical government at the present

---

[120] *Dr. Smith of Maryland*: William Smith (1727–1803), Scottish Episcopalian divine who was invited to America by Benjamin Franklin. He was active in trying to persuade the British government to authorise a bishop for America.

[121] Memoirs, p. 291. [N]

time. And, first, as to the Diocesan Convention, which assembles once in the year. It consists of the bishop, all the clergy, and the lay delegates, of whom in some dioceses three, in others one, are sent by every parish. Thus the lay members of the synod are at least equal, and it may be treble the clerical, supposing, as appears to be the case, there is not more than one clergyman to a parish. In the convention at which Mr. Caswall was present, there were about thirty clerical, and about forty lay members. The committees, etc., appointed at the same meeting were constructed as follows: one clergyman and one layman to report on the unfinished business of the last convention; the standing committee of the diocese, three clergymen and three laymen; six clergymen and six laymen to be trustees of the diocesan college; four clergymen and four laymen as representatives of the diocese in the General Convention. Committees on missions and theological education, seem to have been appointed on the same principle. Moreover, the selection of members was not in the hands of the bishop, but made by ballot. Clergy and laity vote together in Convention, except there is a demand for what is called "a vote by orders." Then each class votes separately, and a majority of each is necessary for the proposed canon or resolution to pass. Thus the clergy, as Mr. Caswall observes (p. 72), can take no important step without the people, or the people without the [361] clergy. In some few dioceses the bishop has a veto upon the acts of the Convention, but its exercise would be so unpopular that it seldom takes place. It must be added, that among the matters which come before the Convention so constituted, are the conditions on which parishes should be admitted into the diocese, the qualifications of lay readers, the appointment of missionaries, the promotion of theological education, and the mode of trying clergy accused of heresy.

The Standing Committee of the Diocese requires a somewhat more distinct notice. It consists, according to the diocese, of five, three, or two, of each order, clergy and laity. It is the council of advice to the bishop; during a vacancy it issues dismissory letters,[122] institutes ecclesiastical trials, and acts, by

---

[122] *dismissory letters:* actually 'dimissory': formal permission from a bishop (letters dimissory) for a person from one diocese to be ordained in another, or (formerly) for

means of its clerical members, as superintendent of the deacons. No bishop can give ordination except to such as bring testimonials, signed by a majority of the standing committee. No bishop can be consecrated without the consent of the majority of the standing committees of all the dioceses in the Union, or of the General Convention.

When clergy are accused of any delinquency, the standing committee of the diocese prosecute; and a jury of five presbyters, chosen by the accused out of eight nominated by the bishop, try the cause, and a majority decides, and specifies the amount of punishment. The bishop may not exceed the sentence adjudged.

When a bishop needs a coadjutor, he is appointed, not by himself, but by his diocese.

The General Convention comes now to be considered. It is divided into two houses; the upper, consisting of the bishops, now seventeen in number; the lower, of clerics and laymen, not [362] exceeding four of each order from every diocese. When demanded by the deputies of any diocese, the voting is by dioceses, the lay representatives of each diocese having one vote, the clerics another. Sometimes the concurrence of both orders is necessary to constitute a vote. The General Convention thus formed enacts canons about public worship, makes alterations in the Prayer Book, defines the observance of the Lord's day, directs the publication of the Bible and Prayer Book, and gives leave to bishops to compose extraordinary forms of prayers. It defines, to a certain extent, the duties of bishops, priests, deacons, candidates for orders, and standing committees. It determines on what conditions a person may be admitted a candidate, how he shall conduct himself during his probation, the due age for consecration and ordination, the attainments requisite, the testimonials, and the times of ordination. It superintends the clergy in preparing their flocks for the bishops' visitation, in catechising, in registrations; it confines their labours within their own province, arbitrates in differences between pastor and flock, and lays down the law for clerical trial and punishment. It has the oversight of bishops'

---

an ordained person to leave one diocese for another. (*OED*)

charges, pastoral letters, visitations, and the yearly reports of their acts to their respective diocesan conventions. It arbitrates between dioceses, it provides missionary bishops, it legislates on the ordination of sectarian teachers,[123] it determines the relation of the American with foreign Churches, and it appoints the board of missions. These are the functions of a body constituted so largely of laymen.

Such is the serviceable sketch which Mr. Caswall gives us of the constitution of the American Church; according to which it would appear, without going to more Apostolical considerations, that those whose business or profession is not religious, are in matters theological and ecclesiastical put on a [363] level with bishop and clergy. We are quite sure such a constitution cannot work well; and if any one demurs, then we differ from him what is well and what is ill. It may throw light upon its practical working to quote a passage from another part of Mr. Caswall's work, which would seem to show that the laity, not to speak of the presbytery, would have no objection to the same high position in divine ministry, which they are allowed in Convention.

"In the reading of the Creed a disagreeable confusion sometimes arises when a stranger officiates. In my own parish, on one occasion, a bishop performed the services in the morning, and two priests in the afternoon and evening. The bishop read the article on the descent into hell, as it stands in the English Prayer Book; the first presbyter read the substitute permitted in America, 'He went into the place of departed spirits;' and the second omitted the article altogether. Very frequently the clergyman says one thing and the congregation another; and occasionally individuals, disapproving of their pastor's choice, repeat with marked emphasis the phrase which he rejects."—P. 295.

In making these remarks upon the system of lay interference, no disrespect is intended towards the venerated person in whom it originated. Every one has his place and his day in the purposes of Providence; and whatever these may be as regards the American Church, so far seems clear, that, if a more apostolical

---

[123] *sectarian teachers*: presumably, former non-conformist ministers who had applied to become Episcopalian priests.

constitution had been insisted on fifty years since, that Church at this day would not have been in numbers what she is. Mr. Caswell calls him "the Cranmer of the American Church;" comparisons are odious;[124] we hold him to be a great benefactor to his countrymen, and this is plain English, and has a better meaning than metaphors or metonymies.[125] He died within the last year or two, in the eighty-ninth year of his age, the sixty-sixth of his ministry, and the fiftieth of his episcopate; and in proportion as his actions have an essential place, so his death must necessarily be a memorable era in the history of his Church. The influence which he exercised so long must be succeeded by other influences, of whatever kind; may the bright day that is past be eclipsed by a brighter on the morrow!

[364]

At the General Convention following his death (1838), a resolution was passed, declaratory of their "cherished remembrance of his faithful and uninterrupted services," and of their gratitude to the Great Head of the Church for the long continuance" among them "of one, who by the beauty of his example, the purity of his designs, and the moderation of his counsels, contributed for more than half a century to advance the interests, both temporal and spiritual," of his communion.

8.

One other illustration we shall give of the deficiency of "development" at present observable in the American Church, and so bring these extended remarks to an end. It lies in a saying, we believe, of the excellent Bishop Hobart's, which has a very true and honest sense, but has been much and seriously misunderstood. To write encomiums here upon one whose praise is in all the churches, and whose memory is interesting personally to many around us who saw him when in England, would be beside the purpose; let us confine ourselves to the particular subject in which we consider that he has been misapprehended and his authority abused.

---

[124] *comparisons are odious*: a proverbial saying; in this case, Newman is subtly indicating his lack of enthusiasm for Cranmer because of his Protestant theology.

[125] *metonymies*: using the name of a thing or person to stand for another thing or person

The *celebre dictum*[126] to which we allude is this; that the true motto of a Church is "Evangelical Truth and Apostolical Order;"[127] and since these words have been adopted lately by deservedly influential persons among ourselves, there is still greater reason for pointing out what they ought to mean and what they ought not. Bishop Hobart seems to have found in America what we find here, a great deal of energy and warmth of feeling among dissenters and low churchmen, and a consequent and prevalent notion that Church principles were cold, formal, lifeless, external, and therefore unconducive, if not detrimental, to true piety and holiness. Accordingly he laboured, and successfully, to persuade persons so imagining, that true Catholicism did not exclude the exercise of the religious affections, and only trained them up to perfection in a right direction and upon a perfect model. The affections are the life of religion; but life does not exist except realized and made substantive in this or that subject; and if it is found to exist in an untoward subject, then it had better not be at all. Each creature has its own life; life is a principle of good or of evil, according as it is in this creature or in that; no one accounts highly the life of a tiger or a toad. And so with moral life; fanaticism implies life, so does bigotry, so does superstition; but none of these is true religion. And so again Evangelical Truth may be called the matter, and Apostolical Order the form which make up "the mind of Christ."[128] What is called a sense of sin, an insight into the divine purity, desire of pardon, a belief in the sacrifice provided, and so on, is the matter of religion; but it is not all that is necessary to make a religious man. According as these feelings and views are combined, directed, and used, they become fanaticism, enthusiasm, antinomianism[129], or Christian faith. All depends upon the

[365]

[126] celebre dictum: famous saying; from Erasmus' definition of a proverb: 'celebre dictum scita quapiam novitate insigne [a famous saying distinguished for some witty novelty]'.

[127] *"Evangelical Truth and Apostolical Order"*: Bishop Hobart was well-known for his adoption of this slogan. 'Dr. Hobart, unfurling the banner of evangelical truth and apostolical order, marched with fearless intrepidity to the front of the battle, and put the enemy to flight.' (Strachan, J., *A Letter to the Rev. Thomas Chalmers, D.D. Professor of Divinity in the University of Edinburgh On the Life and Character of the Right Reverend Dr. Hobart, Bishop of New-York, North-America.*)

[128] *"the mind of Christ"*: 1 Corinthians 2:16

informing principle: if this be short of the true, all will go to waste; if it be "Apostolical Order," it will be right. We are not speaking as if we liked the phrase ourselves, we are but explaining its real sense; we do think it liable to misconception; [366] it has actually met with it; and that misconception is as follows:—

Men speak as if "Apostolical Order" were (to use a homely illustration) like the roof of a house, or the top of a box, shutting in and making fast and tight "Evangelical Truth;" or like the "politeness," the charge for which in some dames' schools[130] used to be an extra two pence. Sectarians of all sorts, who profess the doctrine of Justification by Faith and its concomitants, are considered right as far as they go, only they do not go far enough. When will men learn that the true religious principle is one, and all its parts are parts of one? Apostolicity is not an *addition*, or a *completion*; it is *one side*, one whole *aspect* of Christian truth, and Evangelicity is another side. They are different modes of viewing one and the same thing; a man cannot have the Evangelic principle in purity without the Apostolic, nor the Apostolic without the Evangelical; they go together. If he believes the doctrine of Atonement, yet does not believe the doctrine of Baptism, he does not believe in the Atonement "in sincerity," to use St Paul's words;[131] his reception of that doctrine is not such as God claims of him. His faith is corrupt. It may be objected, that this excludes multitudes from having a right faith, who to all appearance are pious, excellent men. It does not exclude them; many a man holds *implicitly* what he has not learnt to put into words or had the opportunity of viewing objectively. Many a man is a believer in the Apostolical Succession who does not confess it, inasmuch as he *would* confess it, except for unavoidable accidents, such as ignorance and misapprehension. So much may be granted; but it never can be granted by any correct thinker that Evangelical Truth is so distinct from Apostolical, that a man may have one [367] without having the other, as he may know geometry without

---

[129] *antinomianism*: the belief that those who are saved do not have to obey the moral law revealed by God because they have already been justified.

[130] *dames' schools*: inexpensive private schools run by women in their own homes, providing simple elementary education before the days of provision by the state.

[131] *"in sincerity" ...* : Ephesians 6:24

knowing Greek; or that the rites of the Church are mere matter of external order or arrangement, independent of the substance of the Gospel, instead of being involved in its essential idea. As we know nothing of the Atonement except as wrought through Christ's natural body, so we know nothing of justification except as wrought through His mystical: and we may as well call a man orthodox who denies the truth of the Incarnation, though he professed to believe the Atonement, as one who preaches divine grace, yet denies the gifts and powers of the Church.

We are not entering into the question of *degrees* of unbelief; but there is no difference in principle between the two; both imply absence of faith. A man who has got to add "I believe in the Catholic Church" to his creed as not holding it in any sense before, has not merely to add, he has to reform the whole. He has to new-create and leaven his creed with a principle, which will affect it in all those other articles, which he already after a fashion holds. If Evangelical Truth (when opportunities have been granted) has not in his mind flowed out and developed into Apostolical Order, it is because he does not really hold Evangelical Truth. Till we master this view of religion, we shall (to use the poet's simile) be fastening the head of one creature on the body of another: we shall have a made-up, artificial being, not a nature, not a truth,—a mere dream of the fancy which never existed. A man who is *not only* Evangelical, *but also* Apostolical, is either in heart a mere Calvinist or Wesleyan,[132] and does not firmly hold anything about "order;" or he is a formalist, and has no real warmth in him. If he is both at once, he ceases to be either; he is something deeper; he is not a being made up of two separable things, order and warmth, but one thing, and order and warmth are but qualities of that one thing, which we view indeed under two aspects, but which exist together. [368]

9.

Now, assuming, as we shall do, that this representation is correct, we shall respectfully point out some errors which on both sides the water are the consequences of forgetting it.

---

[132] *Wesleyan*: a follower of John Wesley (1703-91), founder of Methodism.

It is supposed, for instance, that the two parties in the Church are each right, and have each half of the truth; and that to be quite right each must take the other half. Now that there is a sense in which such a statement is true cannot be doubted; but that, among ourselves for instance, a stiff dry establishment-man completes what is wanting in him by adopting what are called evangelical words and practices, or that a Lutheran or Calvinist "perfects his organization," as excellent men speak, by taking up the doctrine of Episcopacy as the best and most primitive form of Church government, we utterly deny. Such men become at best, as it has sometimes been expressed, "warm preachers of cold doctrines," or "cold preachers of warm ones," as it may be; yet how much of this sort of change is growing among us, and is hailed as an approximation between parties! And when other persons come and declaim against such union as a mere phantom and a deceit, and attempt to draw attention to the true Catholicism of the ancient Church, they are said to be frustrating one of the most favourable prospects of concord which our Church has ever had, and to be throwing back religion in Europe fifty years. Mr. Caswall seems to us to commit the same paralogism,[133] as far as his words go, (for we do not charge him with more than falling in with the current language of the day,) when he invites American Christians "to return to that pure Protestant Church from which they have generally seceded;" because "here is a form of worship *scriptural in doctrine and orderly in arrangement*, yet sufficiently diversified to meet that appetite for variety which is natural to man."—P. 326.

[369]

Hence, again, it is a favourite form of expression to speak of Presbyterians also and other sectarians[134] as "in an imperfect state," and, to use the phrase just above quoted, that their organization needs *completing*. For instance, speaking of the declension of the Puritans of New England into Socinianism, Mr. Caswall says that "the Episcopalian discovers its origin in the same causes which he thinks have produced the apostasies in the Protestant Churches of Geneva, France, and Germany, namely, *a defective form of Church government*; and the want of an evangelical liturgy."—P. 127. "The Church," he says,

---

[133] *paralogism*: false reasoning
[134] *sectarians*: non-Anglican Protestants

speaking of the time before the American Revolution, "was of necessity presented to the people in *an imperfect form*, the rite of confirmation being unpractised and almost unknown."—P. 170. Again, "at length an American bishop had been obtained, and the Church, in one State, appeared in a *complete form*."—P. 177. Perhaps this language is defensible when used of the Church; but "a parish," he tells us, "consists of all in any given place who *prefer the Episcopal form of worship and government to any other*," etc.—P. 65. And, "there being no Episcopal Church in Andover at the time, we often attended," he says, "the Seminary Chapel on Sundays, where the services were conducted according to the usual *plan* of the Independents:" (better to say in plain English, we attended the Independent chapel; to proceed:—) "while I could not but lament the *imperfect ecclesiastical organization* of these worthy people, I admired the energy of religious principle which developed itself [370] among them."—P. 130.

Now that they had religious energy, and the other excellent points of character which he details, we are most glad to hear, and to believe; but we never will violently take it to heart that they or any other people, having these excellent endowments, had not a certain *form* of government in addition. Either Church organization is far more than a form, or it does not call for a great deal of lamentation. There are no mere forms under the Gospel. Apostolic Order is an ethical principle, or it is not worth much. These worthy Independents were deficient in an inward element of truth, in a something mental, moral, spiritual, mystical, or they had no great loss, considering they were in unavoidable ignorance. They were not up to a certain point altogether right, and only wanted finishing. They were not dressed all but hat and shoes. Our author seems to consider that the Episcopal form is the *last* thing in the idea of a Church, and that therefore a Presbyterian or Independent body may be considered an imperfect sort of Episcopacy. Imperfect! is a mouse an imperfect kind of bat? is it a bat all but the wings? Could we sew wings on it and make it a bat? Did all the swelling of an ambitious heart develop the frog into the bull? Could it "perfect its defective organization"? So it is with Independency or Presbyterianism viewed in themselves: as forms they are as distinct from the Church as "one kind of flesh"[135] from another. We are not saying that they are without the privileges and grace of Christianity—that is another matter; we only say they are not the Church, they are not part of the Church, or all but the Church. And as to the individuals who profess them, they have already Church principles in their hearts, if they be real

[371] Christians; and if so, they certainly, as individuals, are imperfectly organized and imperfectly developed, and ought to be developed perfectly; but that cannot be looked for till stirrings manifest themselves within them which the Church alone can satisfy, a spiritual taste and a hunger of heart which the Church alone can feed, till they join the Church as the correlative of their minds, and gain the perfection of their nature by the gifts imparted through the Church.

The same unphilosophical view of things leads to misapprehension, of course, as regards the Church of Rome. As Sectarianism is thought to be all inside, so Romanism is thought to be all outside. Sectarianism is the man, and Romanism is his clothes,—of a particular make; the clothes indeed by themselves are of no use at all, but it is unbecoming for the man to go into public without them. "In the American Church," says Mr. Caswall, "the Church of Rome is acknowledged, though *corrupt*, to be a *true* Church."—P. 341. Nothing can be more exactly worded; but if it is a true Church, it must be living, and if living, it must have the gifts of grace, whatever its corruptions may be. It cannot be an outside only. It must have a real faith, and heart, and obedience. It must be in the main orthodox, as it is; for that Church which holds aright the doctrines of the Holy Trinity, Incarnation, Atonement, Original Sin, Regeneration, and the Last Judgment, we take to be in the main orthodox. However, to our surprise, Mr. Caswall, (whom, we repeat, we do not make personally responsible for every word he uses,) in his enumeration of the "orthodox" bodies in America, includes "most of the Quakers" and the "Dutch Reformed,"[136] and bestows upon the Church of Rome the boon of a most ominous silence.

---

[135] *"one kind of flesh"*: 1 Corinthians 15:39
[136] *Dutch Reformed*: dates from 1566; the first congregation in America was formed in 1628 in New Amsterdam.

"In regard to doctrine, I have already remarked that the great [372]
majority of American religionists are orthodox. This is most
emphatically the case; and affords a strong evidence that the Bible
alone is sufficient to impart a knowledge of all truth necessary to
salvation. It is a fact, which even a High Churchman can contemplate
with pleasure, that the Episcopalians, the Congregationalists,[137] the
Dutch Reformed, the German Reformed,[138] the Lutherans, the
Methodists, the Moravians,[139] the Presbyterians,[140] and most of the
Baptists and Quakers, agree in maintaining nearly all the truths
contained in the Apostles' Creed, the Nicene Creed, and the Thirty-
nine Articles. Among these denominations is found almost the whole
religious energy of the country, and from these the great philanthropic
institutions of America derive their prosperity and vigour."—Pp. 312,
313.

Now, even taking the Thirty-nine Articles as the strictest
form of Apostolic truth, still we must be allowed to consider
that the Quakers and Dutch Reformed deviate from them as far
as the Roman Catholics.

Another result of the same misconception is an incongruity
common with us as well as the Americans, of classing all sorts
of persons together as if of one and the same school of doctrine,
if they happen to have been prominent as religious writers,
whatever difference there be in their faith and temper of mind.
We have lately been so stunned with hearing of "our Basils and
our Baxters,[141] our Gregories and our Greggs,[142] our Jeromes,

---

[137] *Congregationalists*: radical Protestants who rejected episcopacy and believed that
each local congregation should govern itself; first established in American in the 1630s
in New England by Calvinist Puritan settlers.

[138] *German reformed*: initially the followers of Philip Melanchthon (1497-1560), but
later under Calvininst influence; it was formed in American in 1725 in Philadeplhia, at
first linked to the Dutch Reformed Church but independent after 1793.

[139] *Moravians*: Tracing their origins to the 14th century Bohemian Reformation
associated with Jan Huss (1369-1415), they acquired the name from being exiled to
Moravia (in the modern day Czech Republic) in the 18th century. A number of Moravian
missionaries arrived in America in the 1730s but they suffered various difficulties, and
the church was only successfully established in 1758 in Pennsylvania. They have
bishops and are not Calvinist in their beliefs.

[140] *Presbyterians*: Presbyterianism is a form of church government in which each local
church is governed by a group of presbyters or elders. There are no bishops. The Church
of Scotland was formed on this model, and most North American Presbyterian churches
originated from Scots immigrants.

[141] *our Basils and our Baxters*: St. Basil the Great (329-79), Bishop of Caesarea, Doctor
of the Church; Richard Baxter (1615-91), Puritan Anglican divine, theologian and
controversialist. Newman's point is that this list incongruously yokes together leading

our Jewels, and our Jays,"[143] that really it is with an effort we can appreciate the difference between one sound and another, or can say when notes are in tune together, and when not. It is said, that a man may go on sipping first white and then port, till he loses all perception which is which; and it is very great good fortune in this day if we manage to escape a parallel misery in theology. What false concords[144] are involved in passages like the following! "The Parish Library, printed at New York, by [373] the Episcopal press, contains the works of Leslie,[145] West,[146] Sherlock,[147] Cudworth,[148] Walton,[149] Bishops Jewell,[150] Gibson,[151] Sumner,[152] Jebb,[153] Burnett,[154] etc., with Chevalier's translation of Clement, Polycarp, Ignatius, and Justin Martyr."[155]—P. 330. Again, an eloquent and distinguished preacher, whose sermon is before us, at a late General Convention calls "for thousands of such preachers as Paul, and Barnabas, and Chrysostom,[156]

---

figures from the patristic age with later, and even contemporary, Protestant apologists.

[142] *our Gregories and our Greggs*: St Gregory the Great (540-604), Pope and Doctor of the Church; St. Gregory Nazianzen (see above note on p.[237]); St. Gregory of Nissa (d.385/6); St. Gregory Thaumaturgus (213-70/5); Tresham Dames Gregg (1800-81), Church of Ireland divine and controversialist.

[143] *our Jeromes, our Jewels and our Jays*: St. Jerome (see above note on p.[231]); Bishop John Jewel or Jewell (1522-71), Anglican divine and influential apologist for the Church of England; William Jay (1769-1853), non-conformist divine and writer.

[144] *false concords*: Again, Newman's point is that the list he quotes contains writers of diverse and incompatible doctrinal views.

[145] *Leslie*: Charles Leslie (1650-1722), non-juring Anglican divine; a vigorous polemicist who wrote against Quakers, Socinians, Jews and Catholics.

[146] *West*: Gilbert West (1703-56), poet, translator and apologist; author of *Observations on the Resurrection* (1747) which was widely popular.

[147] *Sherlock*: Bishop Thomas Sherlock (1678–1761), Anglican divine and apologist; his *The Tryal of the Witnesses of the Resurrection of Jesus* (1729) was reprinted many times.

[148] *Cudworth*: Ralph Cudworth (1617–88), Anglican divine and philosopher, one of the Cambridge Platonists and therefore liberal in his views.

[149] *Walton*: Brian Walton (1600–61), Anglican divine and scholar, best known for his Polyglot Bible (1652-7).

[150] *Jewell*: See above note on p.[372].

[151] *Gibson*: Bishop Edmund Gibson (1669–1748), Anglican divine; among his learned works was the *Codex juris ecclesiastici Anglicani* (1713).

[152] *Sumner*: See above note on p.[265]n.

[153] *Jebb*: Bishop John Jebb (1775–1833), Church of Ireland divine; his High Church writings make him a precursor of the Oxford Movement.

[154] *Burnett*: See above note on p.[208].

[155] *Chevalier's translation . . . .*: Temple Chevallier (1794-1873), Anglican divine, translator and astronomer. His *A Translation of the Epistles of Clement of Rome, Polycarp and Ignatius; and of the Apologies of Justin Martyr and Tertullian* was published in 1833.

and Cyprian,[157] and Augustine,[158] and Luther, and Calvin,[159] and Melancthon,[160] and Cranmer,[161] and Latimer,[162] and Ridley,[163] and Hooper."[164] Even so considerable a man as Bishop Hobart, in language, true indeed in the letter, but very paralogistic[165] in the sense, speaks of "our Zion," to use the Americanism, "as adorned with the intellect and erudition of Chillingworth,[166] Hooker, and Horsley,[167] by the eloquence of Barrow,[168] Tillotson,[169] and Porteus,[170] and the piety of Andrews,[171] Taylor,[172] and Horne.[173]"[174] But the most remarkable instance of this figure of speech is afforded us by that powerful writer, Dr. Chapman,[175] who, speaking of our Church's champions, enumerates among the archbishops and bishops, "the weight of whose learning and piety no pen can adequately tell, no wealth of words exaggerate," Cranmer, Leighton,[176] Tillotson, Wake,[177] Andrews,

---

[156] *Chrysostom*: See above note on p.[298].

[157] *Cyprian*: See above note on p.[199].

[158] *Augustine*: See above note on p.[200].

[159] *Calvin*: See above note on p.[273].

[160] *Melancthon*: Philipp Melanchthon (1497–1560), German Protestant theologian and associate of Luther.

[161] *Cranmer*: Archbishop Thomas Cranmer (1489-1556), Archbishop of Canterbury who oversaw the English church's split from Rome under Henry VII, wrote the *Book of Common Prayer* and was burnt at the stake under Mary I.

[162] *Latimer*: Bishop Hugh Latimer (1487-1555); one of the leaders of the English Protestant reformation, burnt at the stake under Mary I.

[163] *Ridley*: Bishop Nicholas Ridley (1500-55), leading Protestant reformer of the Church of England, burnt at the stake under Mary I.

[164] *Hooper*: Bishop George Hooper (1640–1727), High Church Anglican divine and theologian.

[165] *paralogistic*: characterized by or involving false reasoning; fallacious. (*OED*)

[166] *Chillingworth*: See above note on p.[112].

[167] *Horsley*: See above note on p.[180].

[168] *Barrow*: See above note on p.[299].

[169] *Tillotson*: See above note on p.[111].

[170] *Porteus*: Bishop Beilby Porteus (1731–1809), Anglican divine, popular preacher and opponent of slavery.

[171] *Andrews*: Bishop Lancelot Andrewes (1555–1626), Anglican divine and apologist who oversaw the King James Authorised Version translation of the Bible.

[172] *Taylor*: See above note on p.[45.]

[173] *Horne*: Thomas Hartwell Horne (1780–1862) Low Church Anglican divine and apologist.

[174] P. 9. [N]

[175] *Dr. Chapman*: See above note on p.[329].

[176] *Leighton*: Bishop Robert Leighton (1611–84), Scottish Episcopalian divine who attempted reconciliation with Presbyterians.

[177] *Wake*: Archbishop William Wake (1657-1737), Anglican divine and apologist; see also above p.[206]n.

Atterbury,[178] Bull,[179] Burnet,[180] Butler,[181] Hall,[182] Hoadley,[183] Hopkins,[184] Horne,[185] Hurd,[186] Latimer, Louth,[187] Taylor,[188] Tomline,[189] Warburton,[190] and Watson.[191] And among "divines inferior to these in dignity alone,"[192] Balguy,[193] Barrow, Clarke,[194] Hales,[195] Hammond,[196] Hickes,[197] Jones,[198] Law,[199] Lightfoot,[200] Milner,[201] Paley,[202] Waterland,[203] and Whitby.[204]"[205] Let us not

---

[178] *Atterbury*: Bishop Francis Atterbury (1663–1732), High Church Anglican divine and controversialist.

[179] *Bull*: See above p.[75]n.

[180] *Burnet*: probably Bishop Gilbert Burnet (1643–1715), Anglican divine and historian, author of a three-volume *History of the Reformation*; or possibly Thomas Burnet (1635–1715), Anglican divine; his writings on the creation of the world, the Fall and the resurrection of the body were considered unorthodox.

[181] *Butler*: See above note on p.[51].

[182] *Hall*: Bishop Joseph Hall (1574–1656), Anglican divine, controversialist, satirist and devotional writer.

[183] *Hoadley*: See above note on p.[114].

[184] *Hopkins*: Bishop Ezekiel Hopkins (1634-90), Anglican divine and author of a number of theological and controversial works.

[185] *Horne*: Thomas Hartwell Horne (1780–1862), Anglican divine; his three-volume *Introduction to the Critical Study and Knowledge of the Holy Scriptures* was widely popular in America as well as in Britain.

[186] *Hurd*: Bishop Richard Hurd (1720–1808), Anglican divine; his works, both on literary and theological topics, fill eight volumes.

[187] *Louth*: Bishop Robert Lowth (1710–1787), Anglican divine and scripture scholar whose work on the structure of Hebrew poetry was influential.

[188] *Taylor*: See above p.[45]n.

[189] *Tomline*: See above p.[208]n.

[190] *Warburton*: Bishop William Warburton (1698–1779), Anglican divine, theological controversialist and literary critic.

[191] *Watson*: See above p.[94]n.

[192] *"divines inferior . . . :* Again, the point Neman is making by giving this list is that these divines have mutually contradictory theological standpoints, including some which are notably unorthodox, and not all of them were even Anglicans.

[193] *Balguy*: John Balguy (1686–1748), Anglican divine and moral philosopher; he wrote in support of Bishop Hoadley's views on the church (see above p.[114]n.).

[194] *Clarke*: See above p.[94]n.

[195] *Hales*: See above p.[111]n.

[196] *Hammond*: See above p.[208]n.

[197] *Hickes*: George Hickes (1642-1715), Anglican non-juring divine and scholar; his views were attacked by Bishop Hoadley.

[198] *Jones*: See above p.[231]n.

[199] *Law*: See above p.[94]n.

[200] *Lightfoot*: John Lightfoot (1602–1675), Anglican divine and influential biblical scholar.

[201] *Milner*: See above p.[298]n.

[202] *Paley*: See above p.[131]n.

[203] *Waterland*: See above p.[75]n.

[204] *Whitby*: Daniel Whitby (1638–1726), Low Church Anglican divine and theologian whose views were Arian.

seem to bear harshly upon our brethren. It is their kindness and affection towards us which makes them thus speak; they think nothing but good can come from the Church of their fathers; they love us and admire us; alas! That we deserved their [374] affection as fully as they give it to us; but we must not in love to them conceal from them what we really are, what our good, and what our evil, lest we be a stumbling-block in their way.

We know their brotherly feeling towards us, but we wish it shown in higher and nobler ways. Let the American Church take her place; she is freer than we are; she has but to will, and she can do. Let her, as Mr. Caswall in one place suggests, react upon us, according to the light and power given her. Let her not take our errors and increase them by copying, but let her be, as it were, our shadow before us,—the prophecy and omen, the mysterious token and the anticipated fulfilment of those Catholic principles which lie within us more or less latent, waiting for the destined hour of their development.

10.

There are other formulæ popular in the American Church, besides that on which we have been principally commenting, which symbolize the same defective apprehension of her true position, and grievously wound our ears. What, for instance, shall we say to the contrast so frequent between "Scripture" and "Liturgy," "Protestant" and "Episcopal"? Our brethren speak as if all Protestants were scriptural, but were wanting in the *corona* of a Liturgy; and as if all of themselves were Protestants, *but* of the Episcopal denomination. Thus Mr. Caswall speaks of a large and growing portion of the Church, as "rising up under the full influence of the Liturgy and Episcopacy" (p.333); and of "the *conservative* influence of the Episcopate and the Liturgy" (p. 335). But of all combinations, that of Protestant-Episcopal is the least pleasant; yet we are met with this compound everywhere. We hear of the Protestant-Episcopal [375] Church, Protestant-Episcopal creed, Protestant-Episcopal press, Protestant-Episcopal societies, Protestant-Episcopal unions, Protestant-Episcopal clergy, and Protestant-Episcopal bishops.

---

[205] P. 326. [N]

Above all, Mr. Caswall speaks, as a creature indeed of the imagination, but still as a thing *in posse*,[206] of a "Protestant-Episcopal Cathedral"! Well may he doubt whether a cathedral "would strictly comport with the American Episcopal system" (p. 288). Let him take our word for it, such a vision never can be realized. The eyes of men will never see it. Sooner shall we set eyes on a griffin, or a wivern,[207] than so gross a violation of all the laws of unity and entireness. No possible style of architecture could embrace the idea. Not that the American Church will never have cathedrals, but when she has, as we trust she will have them, it will be because she is a Church, not because she works with such modern spells and under such unpriestly titles.

It may seem harsh thus to speak of "Episcopacy" and "Episcopalian," yet we hope it will not shock any one if we say that we wish the words, as denoting an opinion and a profession, never had been invented. They have done great mischief to their own cause. We are "of the Church," not "of the Episcopal Church;" our bishops are not merely an order in her organization, but the principle of her continuance; and to call ourselves Episcopalians is to imply that we differ from the mass of dissenters mainly in Church government and form, in a matter of doctrine merely, not of fact, whereas the difference is that we are *here*, and they are *there*: we in the Church, and they out of it.

We are quite sure that all this is not a matter of words; nothing practically is so chill and unnatural, or gives us churchmen such an air of technicality, pedantry, and narrowness with the many, as this insisting so earnestly upon what we at the same time own to be a form or point of Order added to Evangelical Truth, a portion of extraneous and dead matter, which will not graft into Protestantism, but must irritate and inflame it while it remains, and in the event must be cast out. If indeed the Church is to remain a genteel and fashionable communion for the rich and happy, as indeed it has been in its measure in our own large towns for a long while, then it may

[376]

---

[206] in posse: potentially, but not yet actually

[207] *griffin or a wyvern*: fabulous beasts which combine elements of different animals; the former is part eagle and part lion, the latter part dragon and part reptile.

preserve any incongruity or monstrosity for any length of time; but if it is to be, what we trust it is both in America and among ourselves, *earnest*,—if it is to be real, and to encounter the realities of human life, need, sickness, pain, affliction, sin, doubt, despair,—if it is to match the giant evils which it was sent into the world to overcome,—it must take up a simple and consistent doctrine, and will either make Episcopacy more than a form or an opinion, or will give it up.

So much we are bound to say about Episcopacy; as to "the Liturgy," we have lately taken up one of Mr. Cooper's[208] novels, and we find so apposite an illustration of what we would say, that before concluding we are tempted to quote one or two passages from it. It shows the *impression* produced by the existing American Church system on a clever man who, whatever be his views on the whole, for we know absolutely nothing of them except from this one novel, evidently has a proper respect and love for the Church.

In a sketch then of a clergyman in a rising colony in the woods, among churchmen and sectarians, squatters and Indians, whom he is trying to "organize" into an Episcopal Protestant parish, we have the following touches. The clergyman says to a stranger:—

"'It is so unusual to find one of your age and appearance in these woods, at all acquainted with *our Holy Liturgy*, that it lessens at once the distance between us."—*Pioneers*, p. 125. [377]

"'You have then resided much in the cities, for no other part of this country is so fortunate as to possess the *constant enjoyment of our excellent Liturgy*.' The young hunter smiled as he listened to the divine, etc., but he made no answer. 'I am delighted to meet with you, my young friend, for I think an ingenuous mind, such as I doubt not yours must be, will exhibit all the advantages of a settled doctrine and *devout Liturgy*. . . . Tomorrow I purpose administering the Sacrament. Do you commune, my young friend?' 'I believe not, sir,' returned the youth. 'Each must judge for himself,' said Mr. Grant, 'though I should think that a youth who had never been blown about by the wind of

---

[208] *Mr. Cooper*: James Fenimore Cooper (1789–1851), American novelist. His *The Pioneeers: or The Sources of the Susquehanna* was published in 1823. He was a devout Episcopalian.

false doctrines, and who has *enjoyed the advantages of our Liturgy* for so many years in its purity, might safely come.'"—*Ibid.*, p. 129.

"He seated himself and hid his face between his hands, as they rested on his knees. 'It is the hereditary violence of a native's passion, my child,' said Mr. Grant in a low tone to his affrighted daughter, who was clinging to his arm. 'He is mixed with the blood of the Indians, you have heard: and neither the refinements of education, nor the *advantages of our excellent Liturgy*, have been able entirely to eradicate the evil."—*Ibid.*, p. 134.

Now Mr. Caswall carefully reminds us that "*excellent* as are its general *arrangements*, and *venerable* as are its services, the Prayer Book in America or in England constitutes no *essential* part of the ecclesiastical fabric. The Church of England, in the Preface to the Prayer Book, has laid down a rule that 'the particular *forms* of divine worship, and the *rites* and *ceremonies* appointed to be read therein, being things in their own nature *indifferent* and *alterable*, and so acknowledged, it is but reasonable, that upon weighty and important considerations, such changes should be made therein as seem either necessary or expedient."—P.234. Very well; but, if so, there is some deficiency somewhere, when what is but an accident of a

[378] system, though a necessary accident, and a most salutary provision, assumes in the eyes of the world the appearance of being its one essential characteristic. Every religious body must be known by some badges; but if we must be ridiculed, we had rather it should be for preaching the "Holy Catholic Church," than for preaching the "Liturgy." If indeed we maintain that the Liturgy *is* necessary and essential, and, on the whole, *not* an alterable form, *as we well may*, particularly and singularly as regards certain portions of our Communion Service, that is another thing; but the incongruity we are insisting on is the confessing that the Liturgy is not *divine* and *necessary*, and yet making it our special characteristic.

We should be able to illustrate more fully what we mean by the scene toward the end of the same novel of the death of an old Indian, at which Mr. Grant is present:[209] but we could not

---

[209] *the scene . . . is present*: In this scene, at the end of chapter 38, the Episcopalian priest, Mr. Grant, asks the dying Indian, Mohegan (also known as Chingachook, the last of the Mohicans), 'do you wish the prayers appointed by the church at this trying

do justice either to the subject, or to our meaning, without using more words than we can afford here.

In taking leave of our American brethren, we congratulate both them and our own countrymen on the increased interest which is felt in both countries in the early Fathers of the Church. Two bishops, as far as our knowledge of America extends, have especially exerted themselves in encouraging this most promising symptom of advancement in Christian truth. Dr. Doane,[210] Bishop of New Jersey, has, among other excellent works, published editions of the Apostolical Fathers, Clement, Ignatius, and Polycarp; and Bishop Hopkins,[211] of Vermont, is the able author of several works, more or less controversial, one of which has lately been re-published in England.

We ought not to be sanguine about anything; the right rule [379] is to hope nothing, to fear nothing, to expect nothing, to be prepared for everything. The course of Religion is guided through the world far otherwise than human conjecture determines. Yet looking at the sincerity, zeal, and activity of the Anglo-Catholic clergy, both here and in America, the pleasing thought will suggest itself to us, that, since to him that hath more is given,[212] they are about to receive a reward for the good thing in them, however poor and worthless it be, by some greater good to come. A fuller gift of Apostolical light may be destined for them in the councils of divine mercy; they shrink from it at present and close their eyes, for it dazzles them. Still in time they may be enabled to bear it: and then it will be seen that in the ranks of popular Protestantism, nay, and of

---

moment?' But Mohegan ignores him and speaks of his imminent death in traditional Indian terms: 'my fathers call me to the happy hunting grounds.'

[210] *Dr. Doane*: Bishop George Washington Doane (1799–1859), High Church episcopalian divine; his *The Apostolical Fathers, Clement of Rome, Polycarp, and Ignatius* had been published in 1837 and is one of the books listed at the head of Newman's article (see the Textual Appendix).

[211] *Bishop Hopkins*: John Henry Hopkins (1792–1868), first Episcopalian bishop of Vermont and eighth Presiding Bishop of the American episcopal church. His *The Church of Rome in her Primitive Purity compared with the Church of Rome at the Present Day* which had been published in the U.S.A. in 1833 and been reprinted in London in 1839 is one of the books listed at the head of Newman's article (see the Textual Appendix).

[212] *to him that hath more is given*: cf. Mark 4:24; Matthew 13:12.

Dissent, there have been many Crypto-Catholics unknown to themselves,—many who, by patient continuance in well doing, are earning for themselves, against their will, to be—what they as yet in ignorance condemn, under the names of Popish, or even Pagan—Catholic believers in the Catholic Church of Christ.

October, 1839.

NOTE ON ESSAY VIII.[213]

THERE is an argument, in the foregoing pages, in behalf of the Anglican Church, which perhaps calls for remark from a Catholic. It is this:—that the Anglican Church is able to propagate its kind, and that fecundity is a sign of life, and life a sign of a divine origin, according to the words, "If this counsel or this work be of men, it will come to nought."[214]

And in the Essay which is soon to follow upon "the Catholicity of the Anglican Church,"[215] it is said "Life is a Note of the Church; she alone revives, even if she declines; heretical and schismatical bodies cannot keep life;"[216] and I go on to insist on this proposition at great length. And it certainly expresses an important truth, when it is carried out in fulness in the instance of a particular principle or institution. For example, the idea of a Supreme Being may truly be said to be real, because of its obstinate vitality; but before the argument can be applied to in favour of the Anglican Church, the conditions under which it is valid must be investigated, and various emergent difficulties disposed of, which interfere with its availableness.

It must be recollected that in this very Essay, in which the vitality of Anglicanism is dwelt upon, it is conceded, that there are different kinds of life, and not all of them good kinds. Evil itself has a sort of life: and still more in cases in which good and evil are mixed together, in these good lives in spite of the [381] evil, and evil seems to live because of the good which interpenetrates it, and is its life. Accordingly I expressly say,

---

[213] Added in the 1871 edition.
[214] *"If this counsel . . . to nought."*: Acts 5:38.
[215] *the Essay which is soon to follow* . . . : in Volume II of *Essays Critical and Historical*.
[216] *"Life is a Note* . . . : p.[54].

"Each creature has its own life, and life is a principle of good or of evil according as it is in this creature or in that. And so with moral life; fanaticism implies life, so does bigotry, so does superstition; but none of them is true religion."—*Supr.*, p. 364.

It does not then at once follow that, if a religion has life of any kind, therefore it is true; and I have carried out this admission to the disadvantage of Anglicanism, in a later publication, thus: "Life?—is it the religious 'life' of England, or of Prussia, or is it Catholic life, that is, the life which belongs to Catholic principles, [which is found in Anglicanism]? Else, we shall be arguing in a circle, if Protestants are to prove that they have that life, which manifests [supernatural grace], because they have, as they are sure to have, a life congenial and in conformity with Protestant principles. If then 'life' means strength, activity, energy, and well-being of any kind whatever, in that case doubtless the National Religion is alive. It is a great power in the midst of us; it wields an enormous influence; it represses a hundred foes; it conducts a hundred undertakings; it attracts men to its service, uses them, rewards them; it has thousands of beautiful homes up and down the country, where quiet men do its work, and benefit its people; it collects vast sums in the shape of voluntary offerings, and with them it builds churches, prints and distributes innumerable Bibles, books, and tracts, and sustains missionaries in all parts of the earth. In all parts of the earth it opposes the Catholic Church, denounces her as anti-Christian, bribes the world against her, obstructs her influence, apes her authority, and confuses her evidence. In all
[382] parts it is the religion of gentlemen, of scholars, of men of substance, and of men of no personal faith at all. If this be life,—if it be life to impart a tone to the Court and the Houses of Parliament, to ministers of state, to law and literature, to universities and schools, and to society,—if it be life to be a principle of order in the population, and an organ of benevolence and almsgiving towards the poor,—if it be life to make men decent, respectable, and sensible, to embellish and refine the family circle, to deprive vice of its grossness, and to spread a gloss over avarice and ambition,—if indeed it is the life of religion to be the first jewel in the Queen's crown, and the highest step of her throne, then doubtless the National

Church is replete, it overflows with life; but the question has still to be answered, Life of what kind? Heresy has its life, worldliness has its life; is the Establishment's life merely national life, or is it something more? is it Catholic life as well? is it supernatural life?"—*Anglican Difficulties*, Lect. ii.[217]

The passage does not proceed to answer the last question; but it may be freely conceded by all Catholics, as it is conceded in other passages of the Lecture, from which the above is taken, that the Anglican body both has, and does apply to the benefit of the souls of its members, various divine doctrines and ordinances, which it carried with it, when it left its true home in the one only Church of God. As to that special Note of life, however, which the foregoing Essay insists on, growth and fecundity, this is in a certain sense possessed by heresies, as weeds thrive and spread more luxuriantly than wholesome and pleasant plants. One heresy too gives birth to a dozen. Then, as to success in various countries, which, when attaching to an idea or undertaking, is under conditions a genuine evidence of truth, it must be recollected that, if Anglicanism has spread [383] among its kindred population in the United States, there have been, I think, Wesleyans in Sweden, and Friends[218] in the Low Countries, places strange to England in climate, language, and mental habits. Nestorianism, a Greek heresy, lasted for many centuries, and extended from China to Jerusalem. It had twenty-five archbishops, and its numbers, with the Monophysites, surpassed those of the Greeks and Latins together. It would be a better sign of life for Anglicans, if they succeeded in their present efforts with the Italians, who seem just now in want of a religion, or with the Spaniards or French,[219] who also at this time offer something of a field for their exertions. That is real fecundity in an idea, which is capable of reproduction in many separate minds, strange or hostile to each other, in rival classes of society, and in various political

---

[217] p.[47].

[218] *Friends*: the Religious Society of Friends, known as Quakers, founded by George Fox (1624-91).

[219] *the Italians . . . the Spaniards or French*: The new Italian state had enacted many anti-church laws since unification in 1870, and there were strong anti-clerical movements in both France and Spain.

constitutions and successive centuries. I have drawn out this argument elsewhere, and will here extract portions of it:—

"Catholics act according to their name; Catholics are at home in every time and place, in every state of society, in every class of the community, in every stage of cultivation. No state of things comes amiss to a Catholic priest; he has always a work to do, and a harvest to reap.

"Were it otherwise, had he not confidence in the darkest day, and the most hostile district, he would be relinquishing a principal Note, as it is called, of the Church. She is Catholic, because she brings a universal remedy for a universal disease. The disease is sin; all men have sinned; all men need a recovery in Christ; to all must that recovery be preached and dispensed. If then there be a preacher and dispenser of recovery, sent from [384] God, that messenger must speak, not to one, but to all, he must be suited to all, he must have a mission to the whole race of Adam, and be cognizable by every individual of it. I do not mean that he must persuade all, and prevail with all—for that depends upon the will of each; but he must show his capabilities for converting all by actually converting some of every time, and every place, and every rank, and every age of life, and every character of mind. If sin is a partial evil, let its remedy be partial; but if it be not local, not occasional, but universal, such must be the remedy. A local religion is not from God . . . Judaism then was local because it was an inchoate[220] religion; when it reached perfection within, it became universal without, and took the name of Catholic.

"Look around, my brethren, at the forms of religion now in the world, and you will find that one, and one only, has this Note of a divine origin. The Catholic Church has accompanied human society through the revolution of its great year; and is now beginning it again. She has passed through the full cycle of changes, in order to show us that she is independent of them all. She has had trial of East and West, of monarchy and democracy, of peace and war, of imperial and of feudal tyranny, of times of darkness and times of philosophy, of barbarousness

---

[220] *inchoate*: just begun and so not fully formed or developed; rudimentary (*OED*).

and luxury, of slaves and freemen, of cities and nations, of marts of commerce and seats of manufacture, of old countries and young, of metropolis and colonies . . .

"How different, again I say, how different are all religions that ever were, from this lofty and unchangeable Catholic Church! They depend on time and place for their existence, they live in periods or in regions. They are children of the soil, indigenous plants, which readily flourish under a certain temperature, in a certain aspect, in moist or in dry, and die if they are transplanted. Their habitat is one article of their [385] scientific description. Thus the Greek schism, Nestorianism, the heresy of Calvin, and Methodism, each has its geographical limits. Protestantism has gained nothing in Europe since its first outbreak . . .

"There is but one form of Christianity, my brethren, possessed of that real internal unity which is the primary condition of independence. Whether you look to Russia, England, or Germany, this Note of divinity is wanting. In this country, especially, there is nothing broader than class religions; the established form itself is but the religion of a class. There is one persuasion for the rich, and another for the poor; men are born in this or that sect; the enthusiastic go here, and the sober-minded and rational go there. They make money, and rise in the world, and then they profess to belong to the Establishment. This body lives in the world's smile, that in its frown; the one would perish of cold in the world's winter, and the other would melt away in the summer. Not one of them undertakes human nature: none compasses the whole man; none places all men on a level; none addresses the intellect and the heart, fear and love, the active and the contemplative. It is considered, and justly, as an evidence for Christianity, that the ablest men have been Christians; not that all sagacious or profound minds have taken up its profession, but that it has gained victories among them, such and so many, as to show that it is not the mere fact of ability or learning which is the reason why all are not converted. Such too is the characteristic of Catholicity; not the highest in rank, not the meanest, not the most refined, not the rudest, is beyond the influence of the Church; she includes specimens of every class among her

[386]   children. She is the solace of the forlorn, the chastener of the prosperous, and the guide of the wayward. She keeps a mother's eye for the innocent, bears with a heavy hand upon the wanton, and has a voice of majesty for the proud. She opens the mind of the ignorant, and she prostrates the intellect of the most gifted. These are not words; she has done it, she does it still, she undertakes to do it. All she asks is an open field, and freedom to act. She asks no patronage from the civil power: in former times and places she has asked it; and, as Protestantism also, has availed herself of the civil sword. . . . But her history shows that she needed it not, for she has extended and flourished without it. She is ready for any service which occurs; she will take the world as it comes; nothing but force can repress her. See, my brethren, what she is doing in this country now; for three centuries the civil power has trodden down the goodly plant of grace, and kept its foot upon it; at length circumstances have removed that tyranny, and lo! the fair form of the Ancient Church rises up at once, as fresh and as vigorous as if she had never intermitted her growth. She is the same as she was three centuries ago, ere the present religions of the country existed; you know her to be the same; it is the charge brought against her that she does not change; time and place affect her not, because she has her source where there is neither time nor place, because she comes from the throne of the Illimitable, Eternal God."—*Discourses to Mixed Congregations*.[221]

---

[221] *Discourses to Mixed Congregations*: 'Prospects of the Catholic Missioner', pp.246-8, 249, 252-4.

IX.

SELINA, COUNTESS OF HUNTINGDON.

LITTLE as we can be supposed to agree with the theological views of Selina, Countess of Huntingdon,[1] the well-known friend and patroness of Whitfield,[2] we have risen from the perusal of her life, as lately published,[3] with feelings of interest,—kind, though sad,—or rather the more sad because of the kindness which we feel towards so many of the persons and things recorded in it. We proposed no more on taking it up, nor do we propose more now, than to select some passages from it illustrative of the religious transactions with which Lady Huntingdon was connected; but a number of musings have arisen in us, while engaged on it, which it is difficult wholly to suppress, yet impossible duly to draw out. The history of Methodism is, we do not scruple to say, the history of a heresy; but never surely was a heresy so mixed up with what was good and true, with high feeling and honest exertion,—never a heresy which admitted of more specious colouring or more plausible excuse,—never a heresy in which partizan must be more carefully discriminated from partizan, persons from their tenets, their intentions from their conduct, their words from their meaning, what they held of truth from what they held of error,

---

[1] *Selina, Countess of Huntingdon*: For details of her life, see the Editor's Introduction, p.liv.

[2] *Whitfield*: George Whitefield (both spellings were used) (1714–70), Anglican divine and revivalist preacher of Calvinist views who became a key figure in the Methodist movement. A member of the 'Holy Club' at Oxford with John and Charles Wesley, he preached extensively to huge crowds in America as well as in England. He became chaplain to Lady Huntingdon, to whom he bequeathed his slaves on his American plantation after his death.

[3] *her life, as lately published*: *The Life and Times of Selina, Countess of Huntingdon.* Vols. I & II, London: Simpkin, Marshall & Co. 1839.

[388] their beginnings from their endings. Being nothing short of a formal heresy, ultimately good could not come of it, nor will good come of it. We have not yet seen its termination, and therefore as yet can but partially argue *ab eventu*,[4] which in theological matters is an evidence so solemn, so conclusive. "Ye shall know them by their fruits,"[5] is our Lord's canon concerning all schemes of doctrine, however attractive or fair of promise, which come not of the Catholic Church. Already has one of the two branches of Methodism, and that the principal one,[6] borne, in the person of its most learned divine, the bitter fruit of error in the most sacred doctrine of theology. We hope nothing, then, we fear everything, from a religious movement, which nevertheless in its rise excites our sympathy, and of which we do not deny, as of any event in the world, the incidental benefits. Yet interest, pity and admiration we do feel for many of the principal agents in it; and if the choice lay between them and the reformers of the sixteenth century (as we thankfully acknowledge it does not,) a serious inquirer would have greater reason for saying, "Sit anima mea cum Westleio,[7]" than "cum Luthero," or "cum Calvino," and "cum multis aliis," as the grammar has it, "quos nunc perscribere longum est."[8]

What pleases us in the Volume before us is the sight of a person simply and unconditionally giving up this world for the next. This must be right, whoever does it, and whatever else is right or wrong. So far Lady Huntingdon gained a point, and sets Christians of all times an example. She devoted herself, her name, her means, her time, her thoughts, to the cause of Christ.

---

[4] *ab eventu*: from experience

[5] *"Ye shall know them by their fruits,"*: Matthew 7:16.

[6] *one of the two branches of Methodism, and that the principal one*: Methodism split into those who followed Calvin's doctrine of the predestination of the elect, taught by Whitefield, and those who followed the Arminian doctrine about grace for all, taught by Wesley.

[7] *Westleio*: John Wesley (1703-91), Anglican divine and founder of Methodism. He had a conversion experience and later followed Whitefield in preaching outdoors. He established Methodist meeting houses throughout England; although he insisted that he remained a member of the Church of England, he ordained ministers himself.

[8] *"Sit anima . . . longum est."*: "May my soul be with Wesley" than "with Luther," or "with Calvin" and "with many others . . . whom it would now take too long to write out.'" George Whitefield wrote in a letter (24th June 1749) 'Sit anima mea cum Methodistis.' The phrase originates in the philosopher Averroes (1126-98) who wrote 'Sit anima mea cum philosophis'.

She did not spend her money on herself; she did not allow the homage paid to her rank to remain with herself: she passed these on, and offered them up to Him from whom her gifts came. She [389] acted as one ought to act who considered this life a pilgrimage, not a home,—like some holy nun, or professed ascetic, who had neither hopes nor fears of anything but what was divine and unseen. And such she was in an age which particularly required a witness that such things could be, or that it was possible to love anything better than the goods of life,—an age of which Hoadly[9] was the bishop and Walpole[10] the minister, and Pope[11] the poet, and Chesterfield[12] the wit, and Tillotson[13] the ruling doctor. She was the representative, in an evil day, of what was, then as now, lost to the Church,—of the rich becoming poor for Christ, of delicate women putting off their soft attire and wrapping themselves in sack-cloth for the kingdom of heaven's sake. And moreover, though she was a partizan, and party feeling has at first sight nothing attractive, at least in the eyes of this generation, yet after all,—whatever be its evils, whatever its inherent faults, whatever unintentional but real opposition in a given case to the will of God,—there is something very stirring and touching in the sight of a number of persons loving each other disinterestedly, and co-operating one with another, whoever they are; and that for no object of earth, but with a view of advancing His cause whose servants they profess to be.[14] How far this high and pure motive existed among Lady Huntingdon's friends, we do not here decide; but as far as it was there, it arrests and subdues our feelings, though existing in the

---

[9] *Hoadly*: See above note on p.[114].

[10] *Walpole*: Sir Robert Walpole (1676–1745), Whig politician who was Prime Minister (though the title did not formally exist at the time) from 1721 to 1742. He strongly supported the Hanoverian Protestant establishment against the Jacobite rebellions.

[11] *Pope*: See above note on p.[12]. Despite being a Catholic, Pope expressed a humanist philosophy in his *Essay on Man*.

[12] *Chesterfield:* Philip Dormer Stanhope, 4th Earl of Chesterfield (1694–1773), statesman and man of letters. His famous *Letters to his Son on the Art of Becoming a Man of the World and a Gentleman* encourage a worldly outlook; Dr Johnson said that they 'inculcated the morals of a Strumpet and the manners of a Dancing-master'.

[13] *Tillotson*: See above note on p.[111]. He was Latitudinarian in theology and a staunch Protestant apologist, writing polemically against Catholicism.

[14] *a number of persons . . . :* Newman surely has in mind here his own experience of working with his colleagues in the Oxford Movement.

midst of what is in itself base and contemptible. When faith and love, or even their types and semblances, are in any measure met with in the history of religious error, they outweigh much of extravagance, much of absurdity, nay, of buffoonery, and [390] even of unreality, which somewhere or other will be sure to make its appearance in those who figure in it. However, we must pass on to the business which lies before us, and in doing so, we fear we must be laying aside in no small degree the amiable feelings in which we have been indulging. There is nothing in the Volume itself which has given rise to them to call for much of such sympathy; and though it is not worth while to make much of its faults, yet we must not seem to extend to it an expression of kindness which is due only to its subject.

1.

Selina, Countess of Huntingdon, being the second daughter of Washington, Earl Ferrers, was noble both by birth and marriage; and it will not be the fault of her biographers, if posterity is not fully aware of this fact. Before opening the volume, we encounter her arms, with coronet, supporters, and motto, in gilt, upon the side of it. We open it, and are met with her portrait, with the coronet above it, and her arms below, not however as before, but according to a second device. Then comes the title-page, and here a third representation of her arms presents itself, and according to a third device; and we are informed, in addition, that the memoir which is to follow is the work of "a *member* of the noble houses of Huntingdon and Ferrers." This is but a specimen of the whole book. In the Preface, which succeeds, we are told, that in deference to Lady Huntingdon's wish, "all attempts at the publication of her correspondence hitherto have been resisted by her noble relatives," till the present compilation of documents and papers in their possession, which has been made by a "*cadet of her illustrious family.*"[15] An Introduction follows, which tells us that [391] "she had magnanimity enough to break the ranks of her *order*;"

---

[15] *a "cadet of her illustrious family.":* He was Aaron Crossley Hobart Seymour (1789–1870), the son of a Church of Ireland minister who had married into the Shirley family; he joined the Countess of Huntingdon's Connexion and later became a popular hymn-writer.

and then comes the "Life and Times," which, not content with
giving a minute account of the ancestral peculiarities of the
house of Shirley, of which the Countess was a member, as high
as "Edward the Confessor," and as wide as "the Roman
Empire," or rather as "Christendom," contains genealogical
notes appended to the names of noble persons mentioned in the
text, so copious that, put together, they would go far to make
up a Lodge or Debrett.[16]

This is instructive. The truth is, poor human nature cannot
support itself without objects of honour and deference. Man is
born to obey quite as much as to command. Remove the true
objects, and you do not get rid of a natural propensity: he will
make idols instead; remove heaven, and he will put up with
earth, rather than honour nothing at all. The principle of respect
is as much a part of us as the principle of religion. It is the boast
of the section of Christians to which belong the "cadet of an
illustrious family," and the "conductors," as they call
themselves, of the work, not to mention "the reverend author
of the Introduction,"[17] that it has discarded the authority of
bishops;[18] and therefore, as a natural consequence, it ever has
bowed down, and does, and ever will, bow down to mere flesh
and blood. Disbelieving the existence of a divine priesthood, it
will ever gaze with awe and reverence at the high station or
splendid connections or noble birth of the children of men. If
its view of religion be true, this misfortune cannot be helped;
but anyhow, that is a misfortune, and not a privilege, about
which it is so proud. The following almost grotesque instance
of this earthly view of things incidentally occurs in a later place
in the Volume, in a notice of Dr. Haweis,[19] of whom by-and-by   [392]

---

[16] *Lodge or Debrett*: Lodge's Peerage, the popular name for *The Annual Peerage and
Baronetage*, later *Peerage of the British Empire*, published under the name of Edmund
Lodge (1756-1839), Herald at Arms, though he did not in fact write any of it. *Debrett's
Peerage of the United Kingdom of Great Britain and Ireland*, first published by John
Debrett (1753-1822) in 1769 and republished in many editions in subsequent years.
[17] *"the reverend author of the Introduction,"*: Jacob Kirkman Foster (1786-1861),
President of Cheshunt College, founded by Lady Huntingdon at Trefaca in Wales to
train ministers for her Connexion.
[18] *discarded the authority of bishops*: Methodists in Britain do not have bishops (though
they do in the United States).
[19] *Dr. Haweis*: Thomas Haweis (1734-1820), Anglican divine who underwent an
Evangelical conversion experience and became Lady Huntingdon's chaplain. He

we shall have more to say. This gentleman, on being deprived of his curacy in Oxford by the bishop of the day, appealed, but fruitlessly, to Secker the primate.[20] On which our biographer, protesting against the "abused authority of the bishop," observes—"In this way was Mr. Haweis deprived of his curacy without redress; *yet* he had influence, *and was of a good family*, long resident in Cornwall, and well known as Haweis of St. Coose. His mother, Miss Bridgman Willyams, was the only daughter of, etc. Her mother was a sister of the last Baron Sandys of the Vines, etc. etc., whose eldest sister, Hester, was granddaughter and heiress of, etc. etc. etc.—P. 414. It is quite clear that this "member of the noble houses of Huntingdon and Ferrers" has been taught by his own people, that whatever excuse may be made for a bishop's acting vigourously towards snobs[21] or *parvenus*,[22] none at all of any sort or kind can be made for his curbing the zeal of well-connected ranters[23] or gentlemanlike heretics: the very idea of which argues a degree of presumption which need but be recorded to receive the deserved condemnation of an impartial posterity.

Mr. Whitfield was not exempt from the same weakness,—weakness, that is, in men who had so little pity for those who deferred to ecclesiastical authority. He speaks, to take one instance out of many, of Lady Huntingdon's "condescending[24] letter;" he is "ashamed to think she will admit him under her roof," and is "quite astonished at her ladyship's condescension."—P. 91. Now was this the language of Elisha towards the Shunammite,[24] who was "a great woman?" Did he talk of *her* condescension, or did she fall down and "catch him by the feet?" Yet what was Elisha's power of miracles to that

---

withdrew when her Connexion became a dissenting body, though he was later reconciled with her, and his second wife was one of her friends.

[20] *Secker the primate*: Thomas Secker (1693–1768), Archbishop of Canterbury 1758-68.

[21] *snobs*: In Newman's time, this word did not have its modern meaning of one who looks down on lower social classes; here it means someone from a lower social class who aspires to be taken for a higher class person.

[22] parvenus: people who have only recently joined a higher social class from a lower one.

[23] *ranters*: Originally the name of a radical sect in the time of the Commonwealth, the term was later applied to any preachers who adopted an extreme, highly-charged, style of delivery, associated with evangelicalism or non-conformism.

[24] *Elisha towards the Shunammite*: Cf. 2 Kings 4:8-37

which Whitfield claimed for himself as being a minister of "the everlasting gospel"[25]—the instrument, in the hands of its Author, [393] of miraculous conversion to the souls of thousands? There is something painfully extravagant in the cast of the sentence, in which the words last quoted occur: He is "quite astonished at her ladyship's condescension, *and* the unmerited superabounding grace and goodness of Him who has loved me," etc. We do not wish to bear hard upon the words of a simple-hearted and grateful person, occurring in a note not intended for preservation; but seeing as we do in his school of religion a certain general leaning towards sycophancy, we may fairly take this casual instance of it as the result of a principle, not the less real because spontaneous.

One great deficiency in the work before us lies in the dates, which occur so scantily and irregularly, that were we ever so desirous, we should not be able to contemplate the Countess in herself, or determine what she was, and how she became such. As far as we can discover, she did not know nor had heard Mr. Whitfield for some years after what is called her conversion, which was mainly owing to her sister-in-law, Lady Margaret Hastings.[26] She is described by her biographer, (whose account would have been more interesting had he given the authorities on which it is founded,) as possessing "a highly intelligent mind, an extraordinary quickness of apprehension, a brilliant fancy, a retentive memory, a strong clear understanding, and a sound judgment, much improved by reading, conversation, deep thought and observation. Her knowledge of mankind, even at an early age," he continues, "and her penetration into the character of those with whom she was acquainted, were admirable. Though not a regular beauty, she possessed a large portion of the charms of her sex; her person was noble, commanding respect—her countenance was the living picture of her mind, and united in it, in a happy combination, both the [394] great and the condescending."—Pp. 9, 10.

---

[25] *"the everlasting gospel"*: Revelation 14:6.

[26] *Lady Margaret Hastings*: (1700–68); sister of the Earl of Huntingdon (1696-1746); she had married Benjamin Ingham, an independent dissenting preacher, whose preaching had converted her.

She had religious impressions from a very early age, and when she grew up she made it her prayer "that she might marry into a serious family. None," continues the Memoir, "kept up more of the ancient dignity and propriety than the House of Huntingdon; the family possessed a sort of decorum which she perhaps mistook for religion." Here then she found the solution of her pious anxiety, and was married, or, in our author's language, "united in love's inviolable bonds," in 1728, when she was of the age of 21, to Theophilus, ninth Earl of Huntingdon;—who, he accordingly tells us, "was descended in a direct line from Francis, etc. etc.,[27] who married Catherine,[28] eldest daughter and coheiress to Henry Cole, Lord Montacute,[29] son and heir to Sir Richard Cole,[30] Knight of the Garter, and Margaret, Countess of Salisbury,[31] daughter to George Plantagenet, Duke of Clarence,[32] etc. etc. etc."—P. 8. Our biographer then proceeds in the following strain:—

"At a very early period of life, Lady Huntingdon discovered an elevated turn of mind: she was impressed with a deep sense of divine things, a feeling which had a wonderful influence on her conduct, in leading her to read the Word of God with great diligence. She manifested an extraordinary turn for religious meditation; and repeatedly felt the most awful convictions of the certainty and eternal duration of a future state.

"Her conversation was modest, and her whole conduct marked with a degree of rectitude, not usually to be found in early life. After her marriage, she manifested a particularly serious deportment; and

---

[27] *Francis, etc. etc.*: Francis Hastings, 2nd Earl of Huntingdon, (1514–61), whose mother, Ann Stafford, had been the mistress of Henry VIII who created her husband George Hastings the first Earl of Huntingdon. It is thus possible that Francis was Henry's illegitimate son, thus making Lady Huntingdon of royal descent, though she was also of Plantagenet royal blood through Francis's wife, Catherine (see below).

[28] *Catherine*: Catherine Hastings, *née* Pole (1511-76).

[29] *Henry Cole, Lord Montacute*: a mistake for Henry Pole (1492–1539), 1st Baron Montacute (also spelt Montagu or Montague).

[30] *Sir Richard Cole*: a mistake for Richard Pole (1462-1505), a supporter and relative of Henry VII.

[31] *Margaret, Countess of Salisbury*: Blessed Margaret Pole (1473-1541), a peeress of royal blood, executed by Henry VIII, beatified as a martyr by Pope Leo XIII in 1886.

[32] *George Plantagenet, Duke of Clarence*: (1449-78), brother of Edward IV and Richard III, executed by Edward, allegedly by being drowned in a butt of malmsey wine.

though sometimes at Court, yet, in visiting the higher circles, she took no pleasure in the fashionable follies of the great.

"At Donnington Park,[33] she was the Lady Bountiful[34] among her neighbours and dependants, though, as she herself afterwards felt and declared, going about to establish her own righteousness, she endeavoured, by prayer and fasting and alms-deeds, to commend [395] herself to the favour of the Most High. For, notwithstanding the early appearance of piety in Lady Huntingdon, it is evident she continued for many years a perfect stranger to the true nature of that Gospel which is the power of God to every one that believes. She aspired after rectitude, and was anxious to possess every moral perfection—she counted much upon *the dignity of human nature*, and was ambitious to act in a manner becoming her exalted ideas of that dignity. And here her ladyship outstripped the multitude in an uncommon degree: she was rigidly just in her dealings, and inflexibly true to her word; she was a strict observer of her several duties in life; her sentiments were liberal, and her charity profuse; she was prudent in her conduct, and courteous in her deportment; she was a diligent inquirer after truth, and a strenuous advocate for virtue; she was frequent in her sacred meditations, and was a regular attendant at public worship. Possessed of so many moral accomplishments, while she was admired by the world, it is no wonder that she should cast a *look of self-complacency* upon her character, and consider herself, with respect to her attainments in virtue, abundantly superior to the common herd of mankind. But while the Countess was taken up in congratulating herself upon her own fancied eminence in piety, she was an absolute stranger to that inward and universal change of heart, wrought by the gracious operations of the Spirit of God, by which new principles are established in the mind, new inclinations are imparted, and new objects pursued."—Pp. 10, 11.

Now here we must stop and comment. It would be a great satisfaction to have been told the authority on which this rounded and effective description is given. Is it doctrinal or is it historical? is it founded on antecedent grounds or on evidence? is it what the biographer thinks must in its degree take place in *every* one, under Lady Huntingdon's

---

[33] *Donnington Park*: mistake for Donington Park, Leicestershire, bought by the 1st Earl of Huntingdon in 1595 who replaced the castle there with Donington Hall; the present Hall was built after Lady Huntingdon's time.

[34] *Lady Bountiful*: i.e. generously charitable, especially to the poor.

[396] circumstances, before conversion, and *therefore* did necessarily take place in her instance inclusively; or is it a statement of a plain matter of fact in the particular case, delivered to him on testimony, as it stands in his pages? If it is the latter, we have nothing to remark upon it, of course, except that we are very sorry that it should be so. We are truly sorry and shocked to be told that a young person, such as Lady Huntingdon, engaged in a course of such excellent deeds, should have been imbued with what is neither more nor less than the Pelagian[35] heresy. Far from doubting the possibility of such a state of mind, on the hypothesis of trustworthy testimony, and far from extenuating its guilt, we denounce it, we anathematize it. She was in that case, as we fully admit, a precocious young heretic, and was formally excluded from all Christian hope, while she so remained, except on the ground of invincible ignorance. However, what seems to us more probable is, that her biographer takes for granted the fact of her being what he describes her, on the ground, which he also takes for granted, and most unwarrantably, that *all* men will *confess* such to be in matter of fact the state of the soul of man before what he would denominate its conversion, however they may differ from each other, whether it is a praiseworthy state or not. We believe that he considers that theologians, for instance, who agree with ourselves, hold in express words just that doctrine, about their natural, moral integrity, which he attributes to Lady Huntingdon, only, of course, not allowing that it is unscriptural or Pelagian. We should say that he supposed us to hold, not only that it is right "to aspire after rectitude," and to be "anxious to possess every moral perfection,"—an opinion, to which we most humbly plead guilty,—but, that it is also right, as he proceeds, to "*count much* upon the *dignity of human nature,*" and to be "ambitious to act in a manner becoming that dignity," a tenet which, understood, as it must be, of the mere nature in which we are born, is, as we have just said, sheer Pelagianism.

---

[35] *Pelagian*: Pelagius (c.390-418), a British priest, denied the doctrine of Original Sin and taught that human beings could attain salvation through their own efforts rather than by grace.

However, all this is the mere illusion of persons who will [397] not inquire into facts. We do not believe that many persons, so exact as the Countess is described in the above passage, do habitually look with "self-complacency on their character, and congratulate themselves on their superiority to the common herd of mankind." We have never met with such, or heard of such on good evidence. In the first place, to go no further, it is not an everyday matter to find persons "modest in conversation,"— of "serious deportment,"—"Ladies Bountiful among their dependants,"—used to "prayer, fasting, and alms-deeds,"— "rigidly just,"—"inflexibly true,"—"strict observers of relative duties,"—"liberal in sentiment,"—"courteous in deportment,"— "diligent inquirers after truth,"—and "strenuous advocates for virtue." We should be curious to ascertain how many such persons our noble cadet himself has fallen in with; and next whether they were all, as he describes Lady Huntingdon, Pelagians; and further, whether they are sufficient to make so certain an induction of a general rule, that it is safe to pronounce, without special testimony to the point, which he will find difficult to give, that such Pelagianism deformed Lady Huntingdon. When persons who so speak are pressed on the subject, they sometimes proceed to tell us, that *they themselves*, before their conversion, are instances in point, having been at once thus endowed and thus inflated, and thus they reduce modest people to silence. Now, that they were at such a time of their life, as they say they were, self-conceited, arrogant, opinionative, and well satisfied with their religious prospects, we admit is very possible;—perhaps they are more or less so still. This is not our difficulty; but whether they were so wonderfully good, so angelically perfect, as they describe. We think the probability is, that they might be amiable, correct, benevolent, just, praiseworthy in their social relations, diligent [398] in their calling, observant of the forms of religion, in a certain way, but that they had a low standard of moral excellence, that they had no lively sense of the necessity of being reconciled to God, that they thought little about the next world, and had inadequate ideas of the corruption of their nature, that they were content to live as they were, and let religious matters take their chance.

This is very different from that perfection of virtue, on the one hand, and that extravagance of pride on the other, of which the writer before us conceives,—as if the better we were really, the better we always thought ourselves; and something like this probably, though on a higher scale of excellence, might be the Countess's state of mind in her first years. Probably she was, as afterwards, full of benevolent plans, and bent upon doing her duty, but with insufficient ideas of the nature and difficulty of Christian perfection, of her natural weakness, of the necessity of divine grace, of the imperfection and guilt adhering to her daily life, and of the great miracle of Divine Mercy in which the Gospel centres. She was shallow in her religion, as young people ever are and must be. She was neither so perfect nor so self-righteous as perhaps she afterwards painted herself in memory; exemplary indeed in conduct, yet ignorant of the depths of Christian truth and her own heart. However, we repeat, if her biographer's painting be correct, we say not a word in her defence. Were her excellence like an Archangel's, pride would utterly spoil it, or rather would prove that it was but hollow and counterfeit; we do not argue against doctrines or facts, when really such, we only are jealous of theories.

[399]

2.

Lady Huntingdon was far from being the only person of her own rank on whom, in that languid and dreary time, the freshness and earnestness of the Methodist movement exerted an influence. Many were permanently impressed by it, and more were affected; and she did her utmost to increase the number of its converts. She tried to persuade the celebrated Sarah, Duchess of Marlborough,[36] to go with her to hear Whitfield; but the Duchess had a "severe cold," which stood in the way. However, she observes to Lady Huntingdon, "God knows, we all need mending, and none more than myself. I have lived to

---

[36] *Sarah, Duchess of Marlborough*: Sarah Churchill (1660–1744), wife of John Churchill, 1st Duke of Marlborough, and confidante of Queen Anne; she wielded considerable political power.

see great changes in the world,—have acted a conspicuous part myself,—and now hope, in my old days, to obtain mercy from God, as I never expect any at the hands of my fellow-creatures. The Duchess of Ancaster,[37] Lady Townshend,[38] and Lady Cobham,[39] were exceedingly pleased with many observations in Mr. Whitfield's sermon at St. Sepulchre's church,[40] which has made me lament ever since that I did not hear it, as it might have been the means of doing me some good—for good, alas, I do want: but where, among the corrupt sons and daughters of Adam, am I to find it? Your ladyship must direct me. You are all goodness and kindness, and I often wish I had a portion of it."

The Duchess of Buckingham,[41] who was said to be a daughter of James the Second, complied with a like invitation from the Countess, and took the Duchess of Queensberry[42] with her; however, she candidly avows her unfavourable opinion of "the Methodist preachers. Their doctrines are most repulsive, and strongly tinctured with impertinence and disrespect towards their superiors, in perpetually endeavouring to level all ranks, and do away with all distinctions. It is monstrous to be told that [400] you have a heart as sinful as the common wretches that crawl on the earth. This is highly offensive and insulting; and I cannot

[37] *Duchess of Ancaster*: Mary Anne Bertie, *née* Layard (1733–1804), second wife of Brownlow Bertie, 5th Duke of Ancaster and Kesteven.

[38] *Lady Townshend*: Audrey Townshend, Harrison (d.1788), wife of Charles Townshend, 3rd Viscount Townshend. The author describes her as 'that would be wit and affected woman' who 'changed about from one opinion to another with singular velocity' (pp.104-5).

[39] *Lady Cobham*: Hester Temple, 1st Countess Temple, 2nd Viscountess Cobham (c. 1690 – 1752); the wife of Sir Richard Granville, after his death she inherited the Cobham title through her brother, Richard Temple, 1st Viscount Cobham.

[40] *St. Sepulchre's church*: St Sepulchre-without-Newgate in London. The vicar, Dr. White, was sympathetic to the Methodists.

[41] *Duchess of Buckingham*: Catherine Sheffield, *née* Darnley (c.1641-1743). After an unhappy first marriage which was dissolved, she became the third wife of John Sheffield, 1st Duke of Buckingham and Normanby. The author describes her as 'perfectly mad with pride' (p.26) about her claimed illegitimate royal descent and records that during her last illness Lady Huntingdon tried to visit her, but Lady Buckingham replied in a note that she was 'extremely obliged by her kind efforts and attention, but regrets exceedingly her entire inability to undergo the fatigue of conversion' (p.27).

[42] *Duchess of Queensberry*: Catherine Douglas, *née* Hyde (1701-1777), famous beauty, wit and patroness of writers; wife of Charles Douglas, 3rd Duke of Queensberry.

but wonder that your ladyship should relish any sentiment so much at variance with high rank and good breeding."

At a time when the Church showed her tokens so faintly, the bold and energetic preaching of such men as Wesley and Whitfield, expending itself moreover on the inculcation of one or two neglected truths, spoke to the consciences of rich as well as poor, whether they were dissatisfied or sated with the carnal state in which their lives were passing away. They were preachers of repentance to those who needed repentance; when they failed to persuade the will, still they convinced the reason, and were admired and revered, even if not followed. Frederic, Prince of Wales,[43] was among those of whom the Methodistic party had hopes. Various of his words and deeds, such as are commonly caught at and made much of in the case of princes, were adduced to prove that he favoured or even shared in the movement. When his difference with his father led him to keep his own Court, Lady Huntingdon attended it: her husband,[44] Lord Ferrers,[45] and other of her friends being the Prince's political supporters. One day the Prince inquired of Lady Charlotte Edwin,[46] "where my Lady Huntingdon was, that she so seldom visited the circle?" On Lady Charlotte replying that probably she was "praying with the beggars;" the Prince, turning to her, said, "Lady Charlotte, when I am dying, I think I shall be happy to *seize the skirt* of Lady Huntingdon's mantle, *to lift me up* with her to Heaven."—P. 175. Such a speech in a royal mouth surely gives a favourable impression of the speaker; such is *our* judgment of it; but we marvel that the Calvinistic biographer of Lady Huntingdon allows it to pass without a protest. Surely he must feel in his heart, that, under the language of Scripture, it savours of what he considers the leaven of Popery, that it interferes with the doctrine of justification by faith only, ascribes to Lady Huntingdon works of

[401]

---

[43] *Frederic, Prince of Wales*: Frederick Louis (1707–1751), eldest son of George II; he died before he could succeed his father as king.

[44] *her husband*: Theophilus Hastings (1696–1746), 9th Earl of Huntingdon.

[45] *Lord Ferrers*: Henry Shirley (1691-1745), 3rd Earl Ferrers; he suffered from recurrent bouts of insanity.

[46] *Lady Charlotte Edwin*: (d. 1774), a supporter of the early Methodists and friend of Lady Huntingdon; she was daughter of the 4th duke of Hamilton and husband of Charles Edwin, Esq., M. P. and was a Lady of the Bedchamber of Augusta, Princess of Wales.

supererogation, tends to saint-worship, and encourages the notion that the intervention of one man can be of service to the soul of another.[47] What indeed is the Prince's mode of speech but the "gathering us together under the feet of Thine elect,"[48] of the semi-popish Andrewes,[49] or "his soul is with the saints, I trust," of an earlier period?[50] We do not think it would have been passed without remark, had it been found in certain publications of this day which could be named.[51]

Upon the Prince's death the Countess wrote to Mr. Lyttelton,[52] who had been his principal secretary, to ascertain his feelings and sentiments at the close of life. Little could be ascertained about them, yet that little she considered satisfactory. "It is certain," she says, "that he was in the habit of reading Dr. Doddridge's[53] works, which had been presented to the Princess, and has been heard to express his approbation of them in the highest terms. He had frequent arguments with my Lord Bolingbroke,[54] who thought his Royal Highness fast

---

[47] *it savours of what he must consider the leaven of popery . . .* : Newman is of course writing ironically here; see Editor's Introduction p.lvi.

[48] *"gathering us together under the feet of Thine elect,"*: from Newman's own translation, published in *Tract 88 – The Greek Devotions of Bishop Andrews Translated and Arranged*, p.54, of one of the *Preces* of Bishop Lancelot Andrewes.

[49] *the semi-popish Andrewes*: Newman of course in reality greatly admired Andrewes (1555-1626) as one of the great High Church scholars whose teaching the Oxford Movement was trying to revive; but Methodists indeed regarded such earlier Anglican divines as too Catholic in their beliefs.

[50] *"his soul is with the saints . . .*: from Samuel Taylor Coleridge's 'The Knight's Tomb', l.11: 'The Knight's bones are dust, / And his good sword rust; / His soul is with the saints, I trust.' But many years before this poem was published by Coleridge in 1834, he had recited it to a friend who later repeated it to Walter Scott. Scott adapted the final three lines (*'The knights are dust,/ And their good swords are rust, / Their souls are with the saints, we trust.')* and used them, with acknowledgment to 'a contemporary poet, who has written but too little' in *Ivanhoe*, published in 1819, where Newman may first have read it. It is therefore not really 'of an earlier period' except insofar as it refers to mediaeval times.

[51] *certain publications of this day which could be named*: e.g. the *Tracts for the Times* or any other publications of the Oxford Movement.

[52] *Mr. Lyttelton*: George Lyttelton, 1st Baron Lyttelton (1709–1773); he was the Prince of Wales' Secretary from 1737 until the Prince's death. While trying to disprove the truth of Christianity he became converted to it. He later had a distinguished political career, becoming Lord Chancellor.

[53] *Dr. Doddridge*: Philip Doddridge (1702-1751), non-conformist minister; among his many works, *The Rise and Progress of Religion in the Soul* (1745) was very influential, and he was the author of over 400 hymns.

[54] *Lord Bolingbroke*: Henry St John, 1st Viscount Bolingbroke (1678–1751), English

verging towards Methodism, the doctrine of which he was very curious to ascertain."—P. 175. Lord Bolingbroke told her that he went more than once privately to hear Mr. Whitfield, with whom he said he was much pleased.

Lord Bolingbroke himself was practised upon by the zealous Countess, and happy would it have been for such as him, if the hopes she cherished of him had been fulfilled. She says of him and his wife, the Marchioness of Viletta,[55]—"Of Lord Bolingbroke and the Marchioness I sometimes have a hope; they attend with such regularity, and hear with such apparent attention." Whatever might be Lord Bolingbroke's opinion of the Countess's intellectual depth, which was perhaps not more respectful than her biographer's opinion of Lord Bolingbroke's, to judge by his mode of speaking of him,[56] Bolingbroke doubtless was struck by what was better than all philosophy, her singleness of purpose in subjecting all matters of this world to the interests of the world unseen. Unbelievers and sceptics, living apart from the action, as it may be called, of the religious world, are so far in a condition to judge impartially of the conduct and principles of those who are in it, and consistency is just the very quality to which they give that praise, which really belongs, and which they cannot give, to truth. Hence they will often admire and defend extreme thinkers of whatever cast of opinion, while they despise those who move forward, or rather sideways or crossways, on two or three principles at once. This seems to be the secret of Lord Bolingbroke's respect for Lady Huntingdon, Mr. Whitfield, and others of their party, and, as the following story shows, for Calvin.

"The Rev. Martin Madan,[57] in his Comments on the Thirty-nine Articles, relates the following curious anecdote of Lord Bolingbroke

[402]

---

statesman and political philosopher; he was a Deist and very hostile to Christianity.

[55] *the Marchioness of Viletta*: Marie Claire *née* des Champs (1675–1749), second wife of Lord Bolingbroke after previously being married to the Marquis de Villette. She was a close friend of Lady Frances Shirley, Selina's aunt, and became a strong supporter of Lady Huntingdon's Connexion.

[56] *his mode of speaking of him*: The author describes Bolingbroke's volumes of philosophy as 'wild and pernicious ravings' (p.181).

[57] *Rev. Martin Madan*: (1726–1790), former barrister who became a minister in Lady Huntingdon's Connexion.

and Dr. Church, on the authority of Lady Huntingdon, to whom it was communicated by his lordship himself. Lord Bolingbroke was one day sitting in his house at Battersea, reading Calvin's Institutes, when he received a morning visit from Dr. Church.[58] After the usual salutations, he asked the Doctor if he could guess what the book was, which then lay before him; 'and which,' says Lord Bolingbroke, 'I have been studying?' 'No, really, my lord, I cannot,' quoth the Doctor. 'It is Calvin's Institutes,'[59] said Lord Bolingbroke; 'What do you think of these matters, Doctor?' 'Oh, my lord, we don't think about such antiquated stuff; we teach the plain doctrines of virtue and morality, and have long laid aside those abstruse points about grace.' 'Look you, Doctor,' said Lord Bolingbroke, 'you know I don't believe the [403] Bible to be a divine revelation; but they who do, can never defend it on any principles but the doctrine of grace. To say truth, I have at times been almost persuaded to believe it upon this view of things; and there is one argument which has gone very far with me in behalf of its authenticity, which is, that the belief in it exists upon earth, even when committed to the care of such as you, who pretend to believe it, and yet deny the principles on which it is defensible.'"—P. 179.

And he speaks thus of Mr. Whitfield, in a letter to Lady Huntingdon: "He is the most extraordinary man of our times. He has the most commanding eloquence I ever heard in any person—his abilities are very considerable—his zeal unquenchable, and his piety and excellence genuine, unquestionable. The bishops and inferior orders of the clergy are very angry with him, and endeavour to represent him as a hypocrite, an enthusiast; but this is not astonishing, there is so little real good or honesty among them. Your ladyship will be somewhat amused at hearing that the King[60] has recommended to his Grace of Canterbury[61] that Mr. Whitfield should be advanced to the bench, as the only means of putting an end to his preaching."—Pp. 179, 180.

---

[58] *Dr. Church*: Thomas Church (c.1710-1756), Vicar of Battersea and Prebendary of St. Paul's; opponent of the Methodists against whom he published two works, and anonymous author of *An Analysis of the Philosophical Works of the Late Lord Bolingbroke* (1756).
[59] *Calvin's Institutes*: Institutes of the Christian Religion (1536), a seminal work of Protestant theology.
[60] *the King*: George II (1683-1760)
[61] *his Grace of Canterbury*: Archbishop Thomas Herring (1693–1757), appointed 1747.

3.

It is no proof that the bishops or clergy of Whitfield's day were in an inactive state because a king like George II. or a peer like Bolingbroke chose to be witty upon them; but we fear there is abundant evidence, without going for it to the work before us, of the incapable, or (if we may use a strong word) the imbecile policy of the Establishment of the day, in dealing with this living and vigorous offspring, of which to its horror and perplexity it had been delivered. The Catholic Church,[62]

[404] unfettered by time or place, and embracing by her very profession all nations, all classes, all professions, and all modes of thought and feeling, ought never to be at a loss how to treat any possible occurrence, which meets her in her onward course. Her territory is the world physical and moral: and to profess or show ignorance would be to abdicate the throne. Hers is the universal science which assigns to each fact or doctrine its true position, and the universal rule which places each individual mind at its proper post. She offers to engage all comers, whether they come as knights of chivalry, or with the weapons of the schools. But at the period in question she was under eclipse, or at least behind a thick fog, in these our northern parts.[63] She indeed herself was ever what she has been, for she is one; but the English Establishment, which is the aspect in which she looks and has looked upon us from her native heavens, sent out at that time a wan and feeble ray, and exerted a languid influence, and was as little able to warn and guide her children, as the moon is to cheer the shivering wayfarer, and to light him amid the perils of wilderness or morass. Wesley and Whitfield doubtless had their places in her economy, as truly as St. Francis,[64] or St. Philip Neri,[65] had there been minds able and free to solve the problem. Repentance and conversion have their

---

[62] *The Catholic Church*: Newman of course includes the Church of England in this, at the time of writing.

[63] *under eclipse . . . behind a thick fog . . .* : These metaphors are tellingly vague, showing Newman's struggle to express his belief that the Church of England really was Catholic, despite being under the control of the dominant Protestantism of the time.

[64] *St. Francis*: of Assisi (1181/2-1226).

[65] *St. Philip Neri*: (1515–95), founder of the Congregation of the Oratory which Newman was to join and bring to England in 1848. This reference is significant, showing Newman's interest in St Philip even at this stage in his Anglican life.

place in the gospel and the Church; field preaching has its place; the poor have their place; and, if that place cannot be found in an existing system, which claims to be the Church, that system is, so far, but the figure of the narrow Jewish polity, not of that which overshadows the whole earth and penetrates into the recesses of the heart.

But such seems to have been, more or less, the English Church at that day. It saw that there was excellence in the Methodistic system, it saw there was evil;—it saw there was [405] strength, it saw there was weakness;—it praised the good, it censured the faulty;—it feared its strength, it ridiculed its weakness: and that was all. It had no one clear consistent *view* of Methodism as a phenomenon: it did not take it as a whole—it did not meet it,—it gave out no authoritative judgment on it—it formed no definition of it—it had no line of policy towards it—it could but speak of it negatively, as going *too far*, or vaguely, as wanting in *discretion* and *temper*; whereas it on the contrary, defective as it was, was a living, acting thing, which spoke and did, and made progress, amid the scattered, unconnected, and inconsistent notions of religion which feebly resisted it. The Volume under review affords us a number of instances of this want of precision and consistency in the conduct of the authorities of the Established Church, some of which shall be given in illustration of what has been said.

The amiable Bishop Benson[66] of Gloucester had been Lady Huntingdon's tutor. On the Countess's adopting the sentiments of the two Reformers, her husband, says the author, (whose account, however, must of course be taken with allowance as that of an opponent,) "recommended her to converse" with the bishop, "and with this request she readily complied. The bishop was accordingly *sent for*," (we suppose as the Shunammite sent for Elisha,)[67] "and he attempted to convince her ladyship of the unnecessary strictness of her sentiments and conduct. But she," continues the narrator, "pressed him so hard with Scripture, brought so many arguments from the Articles and Homilies, and so plainly and faithfully urged upon him the awful

---

[66] *Bishop Benson*: Martin Benson (1689–1752), appointed Bishop of Gloucester 1735.
[67] *as the Shunammite sent for Elisha*: cf. 2 Kings 4.

responsibility of his station, under the Great Head of the Church, that his temper was ruffled, and he rose up in haste to depart, bitterly lamenting that he had ever laid his hands upon George [406] Whitfield, to whom he attributed the change wrought in her ladyship. 'My Lord,' said the Countess, 'mark my words: when you are on your dying bed, that will be one of the few ordinations you will reflect upon with complacence.'"—P. 18. He goes on to say that the bishop's conduct at that solemn season verified her prediction; for when near his death, he sent ten guineas to Mr. Whitfield as a token of his regard and veneration, and begged to be remembered by him in his prayers.

Bishop Lavington[68] of Exeter got into a difficulty which obliged him to send to Lady Huntingdon an apology, which was forthwith inserted in the papers, "for the harsh and unjust censures which he was led to pass on Messrs. Whitfield and Wesley from the supposition that they were in some measure concerned in, or had countenanced" an imposition, by which the Bishop had been made to seem favourable to their opinions; and he requested them to "accept his unfeigned regret at having unjustly wounded their feelings, and exposed them to the odium of the world."—P. 96. At another time, when Whitfield was preaching at Exeter, "the bishop and several of his clergy *stood near him*, and *saw* ten thousand people awe-struck by his appeals,"—p. 127: a type of the conduct of the Established Church during the whole movement.

On the other hand, no one can complain of Bishop Hurd,[69] in the following anecdote, on the score of his not enunciating a broad principle, but how it consists with that other principle upon which he was Bishop of Worcester, does not appear.

"The Venerable Dr. Hurd, Bishop of Worcester, being in the habit of preaching frequently, had observed a poor man remarkably attentive, and made him some little presents. After a while he missed [407] his humble auditor, and meeting him, said, 'John, how is it I do not see you in the aisle as usual?' John, with some hesitation, replied, 'My lord, I hope you will not be offended, and I will tell you the truth,—I

---

[68] *Bishop Lavington*: George Lavington (1684–1762), appointed Bishop of Exeter 1746.
[69] *Bishop Hurd*: Richard Hurd (1720–1808), appointed Bishop of Worcester 1781.

went the other day to hear the Methodists, and I understood their plain words so much better, that I have attended them ever since.' The Bishop put his hand into his pocket, and gave him a guinea, with words to this effect,—'God bless you, *and go where you can receive the greatest profit to your soul*."—Pp. 18, 19.

"An instance of episcopal candour," truly adds our biographer, "well worth recording."

On the other hand, the Bishop of Oxford[70] withdraws Mr. Haweis's license, the Bishop of Rochester[71] refuses to license him in Westminster, of which he also held the deanery; the Bishop of London[72] silences Mr. Romaine[73] in London, and refuses Mr. Fletcher[74] leave to preach to the French prisoners at Tunbridge.

But again, the Bishop of Derry[75] attends "the ministry of Mr. Whitfield, Mr. Romaine, and Mr. Fletcher," at Lady Huntingdon's chapel at Bath, and, on receiving Mr. Maxfield[76] at Mr. Wesley's particular recommendation, says, "Sir, I ordain you to assist that good man, that he may not work himself to death."—P. 33.

Contrariwise, Dr. Drummond,[77] Archbishop of York, says to Mr. Conyers[78] on his visitation sermon, "Well, Conyers, you have given us a fine sermon." "I am glad," replies the doctor,

---

[70] *the Bishop of Oxford*: John Hume (1703–1777), appointed 1756.

[71] *the Bishop of Rochester*: Zachary Pearce (1690–1774), appointed 1756.

[72] *Bishop of London*: Newman seems unaware that two bishops of London are involved here. The one who silenced William Romaine in 1763 was Bishop Richard Osbaldeston (1691–1764, appointed 1762). The one who refused John Fletcher permission to preach to French prisoners at Tunbridge in 1758 was Bishop Thomas Sherlock (1678-1761, appointed 1748).

[73] *Mr. Romaine*: William Romaine (1714–1795), evangelical Anglican divine and author, chaplain to Lady Huntingdon; his best known work was his *Treatises Upon the Life, Walk and Triumph of Faith*.

[74] *Mr. Fletcher*: John William Fletcher (1729-1785), Swiss-born evangelical Anglican divine, author of a number of theological works in controversy with Calvinists, such as his *Five Checks to Antinomianism*.

[75] *the Bishop of Derry*: William Barnard (1697–1768, appointed 1747).

[76] *Mr. Maxfield*: Thomas Maxfield (d.1784), the first Methodist lay preacher, later ordained; he subsequently split from the Methodists and became hostile to Wesley.

[77] *Dr. Drummond, Archbishop of York*: Robert Hay-Drummond (1711-1776), appointed 1761.

[78] *Mr. Conyers*: Richard Conyers (1725-1786), Anglican divine, vicar of Helmsley, in Yorkshire, where he underwent an evangelical conversion; he later became vicar of Deptford, in London.

"it meets the approbation of your grace." "Approbation! Approbation!" replied the archbishop, "if you go on preaching such stuff you will drive all your parish mad. Were you to inculcate the morality of Socrates, it would do more good than canting about the new birth."[79]—P. 280.

Again: the churchwardens of St. George's, Hanover Square, not being able to deprive Mr. Romaine of the lectureship, refuse to light the Church, or to suffer it to be lighted; while the Bishop of Peterborough[80] exerts his influence in the diocese of London to put an end to this vexatious opposition.—P. 361.

[408]

Mr. Berridge's[81] interview with the Bishop of Lincoln[82] shall be given in his own words:—

"'Soon after I began to preach the Gospel at Everton,' says Mr. Berridge, 'the churches in the neighbourhood were deserted, and mine so over-crowded, that the squire, who did not like strangers, he said, and hated to be incommoded, joined with the offended parsons, and soon after, a complaint having been made against me, I was summoned before the bishop. 'Well, Berridge,' said his lordship, 'did I institute you at Eaton or Potten? Why did you go preaching out of your own parish?' 'My lord,' said I, 'I make no claims to the livings of those parishes; 'tis true, I was once at Eaton, and finding a few people assembled, I admonished them to repent of their sins, and to believe on the Lord Jesus Christ for the salvation of their souls. At that very moment, my lord, there were five or six clergymen out of their own parishes, and enjoying themselves on the Eaton bowling-green.' 'I tell you,' retorted his lordship, 'that if you continue preaching where you have no right, you will very likely be sent to Huntingdon gaol.' 'I have no more regard, my lord, for gaol than other folks,' rejoined I, 'but I had rather go there with a good conscience, than be at liberty without one.' His lordship looked very hard at me, 'Poor fellow!' said he, 'you

[79] *the new birth*: the psychological experience of repentance, conversion and assurance of salvation which Evangelicals underwent, assuming that this was the meaning of John 3:3ff. Cf. John Wesley, Sermon 18, 'The Marks of the New Birth', *Sermons of John Wesley*.

[80] *the Bishop of Peterborough*: Richard Terrick (1710–1777, appointed 1757). He became Bishop of London in 1764 shortly after the incident mentioned here which perhaps explains his influence in London at this time.

[81] *Mr. Berridge*: John Berridge (1716–1793), evangelical Anglican divine, Vicar of Everton, author of numerous hymns.

[82] *the Bishop of Lincoln*: John Green (1706–1779), appointed 1761, author of the anti-Methodist pamphlet, *The Principles and Practices of Methodists Considered*.

are beside yourself, in a few months you will either be better or worse.' 'Then my lord,' said I, 'you may make yourself quite happy in this business; for if I should be better, you suppose I shall desist of my own accord; if worse, you need not send me to Huntingdon gaol, for I shall be better accommodated in Bedlam."[83]—P. 369.

Again: the excellent Archbishop Potter[84] in his last moments sends an affectionate and touching note to Lady Huntingdon, who, nevertheless, should surely in the eyes of a bishop, and must surely in the eyes of a theologian, have been none other than a heretic and schismatic, whatever private feelings he might have entertained towards her. When Bishop of Oxford, he had an opportunity of witnessing the rise of Methodism in the [409] University; and afterwards ordained the Messrs. Wesley, Ingham,[85] Hervey,[86] Broughton,[87] Clayton,[88] Kinchin,[89] etc., the first members of that Society. On one occasion he treated Mr. Charles Wesley[90] with great severity; but towards the close of his life his sentiments respecting the Methodist preachers seem to have undergone a favourable change. After writing the letter to Lady Huntingdon above referred to, he was walking with it to his scrutoire,[91] when (as his son Mr. Potter acquainted her)

---

[83] *Bedlam*: The Bethlehem Hospital for the insane in London.

[84] *Archbishop Potter*: John Potter (c.1674–1747), appointed Archbishop of Canterbury 1737; High Church theologian, known for his *Discourse on Church Government* and his controversy with Bishop Hoadly (see above note on p.[114]).

[85] *Ingham*: Benjamin Ingham (1712-1772), see above note on p.[393]; initially a Moravian, then a Methodist and latterly sympathetic to Sandemanianism.

[86] *Hervey*: James Hervey (1714–1758), Anglican divine and author; he was a member of Wesley's 'Holy Club' at Oxford but adopted strong Calvinist views with which Wesley disagreed.

[87] *Broughton*: Thomas Broughton (1712-1777), Anglican divine; initially one of Wesley's circle at Oxford, he distanced himself from the Methodists, finding Wesley too Moravian.

[88] *Clayton*: John Clayton (1709–1773), Anglican High Church divine; one of Wesley's Oxford circle, he was sympathetic to the Methodists but remained a Church of England clergyman. He held Jacobite views for which he risked prosecution after the 1745 rebellion.

[89] *Kinchin*: Charles Kinchin (1711-1742), evangelical Anglican divine, leader of the 'Holy Club' after Wesley; George Whitefield was one of his curates. He later espoused Moravianism.

[90] *Charles Wesley*: (1707-1788), Anglican divine; brother of John Wesley and one of the founders of Methodism, though he disagreed with John about its separation from the Church of England. He wrote over 6,000 hymns.

[91] *scrutoire*: writing desk

he was "seized with a sudden syncope,[92] dropped upon the floor, and expired with the letter in his hand."—Pp. 446, 447.

Once more, we are told that

"The bigoted and intolerant Warburton[93] took every occasion to rally her ladyship on her newly-adopted sentiments, and, with his characteristic rudeness, pronounced her an incurable enthusiast; for with him all personal experience of a divine witness by the Spirit of God in the heart was rank enthusiasm:[94] and this Lady Huntingdon maintained as the essence of truth and Christianity. She pleaded for the application and enjoyment of divine truth in the conscience; Warburton for bishops, priests, and deacons, and the two sacraments of sacerdotal administration, as essential to the being of a Christian. Through life this singular man was strongly prejudiced against, and warmly opposed and censured, both the principles and people that Lady Huntingdon honoured and respected: and on numberless occasions manifested an undeviating opposition, contempt of, and endeavour to suppress, what he was pleased to style Methodism, but which her ladyship loved and vindicated."—Pp. 444, 445.

4.

Now under such a variety of judgments from the Episcopal Bench, when York, London, Exeter, Gloucester, Oxford, Lincoln, and Rochester, stood in opposition to Worcester, [410] Derry, and Peterborough,—and Canterbury and an earlier Gloucester,[95] beginning with a censure, softened towards the Methodists, as they grew towards schism,—what was the necessary consequence to the new Reformers themselves, as regards their work whether of proselytism or protest? This great advantage attached to them over their antagonists: they had a message to deliver, a position to defend, and that one and the same to all: the latter had none. Their opponents did not maintain any definite, or aggressive, or opposite doctrine, such as the sacramental power of the Church, or the catholic character of their own creed; they did not even agree together in opinion practically. Now the natural effect of this must ever be to create

---

[92] *syncope*: loss of consciousness
[93] *Warburton*: See above note on p.[373].
[94] *enthusiasm*: pejorative term for over-emotional religious behaviour
[95] *an earlier Gloucester*: Bishop Elias Sydall (1672–1733, appointed 1731).

in the mind of assailants a great notion of their own superiority. They will consider their own view to be true because it is a view, and they will regard the opinions opposed to it, not as constituting one whole, but as random ideas, which mean nothing in themselves, and whose real place is only assignable according to their approximation to, or divergence from, their own. This is what we see before our eyes, or did till lately. Persons of what have been called evangelical sentiments have not deigned to contemplate or investigate the opinions of sounder Churchmen, except in relation to what they held themselves. They have condescended to applaud when others approached them in this or that point, and have called them "promising," or "interesting;" but they have not dwelt upon, so as to understand, or perhaps in charity they have dismissed from their minds, whatever was contrary to their own opinions. They have not thought it worth while to inquire whether such approach to themselves might not legitimately consist with an opposition to them in certain other points; they have not tried to enter into the system or frame of mind of a High-Church [411] opponent, but have thought that where he agreed with them in opinion, this was *pro tanto*[96] a move towards themselves. In the same way Milner[97] treats the early Fathers; a reader of his history would never dream that the said Fathers had aught of oneness and system in their teaching; he would think that they held a mass of disconnected notions, some good, some bad, as it might be; some Lutheran, others superstitious, some pagan, some Jewish, some philosophic; nothing of an integral creed which had to be mastered, nothing which could serve to set them on a level with himself, or impair his persuasion of his own right of criticising, selecting, and taking the lead.

Here, if we mistake not, we see the meaning of the style of certain publications,[98] to which the last seven years have given birth, and which have been accused, though more so at first than now, of intemperance and harshness, of repelling people, instead of attracting them. We suspect their writers thought[99] that the

---

[96] pro tanto: to that extent

[97] *Milner*: See above note on p.[298].

[98] *certain publications*: the Tracts for the Times; see Editor's Introduction, pp.lvii-lviii.

[99] *We suspect . . .* : Newman knows perfectly well what the writers thought, being one

very first point to be secured in the controversy, was the inflicting upon all readers that theirs was a whole positive consistent objective system, which had to be mastered, not one which men already partly held and partly not, and from which they might pick and choose as they pleased, but one which they had to approach, study, enter upon, and receive or reject, according to their best judgment. They wished it to be recognized as a creed, and to gain from others the attention due to one. This they desired in the case of all hearers, whether they were what has been called evangelical, or of the school of Bishop Marsh[100] and Bishop Tomlin.[101] They perhaps wished to inform the public, as a first piece of information, that the said public had something to learn. They knew that comprehension [412] or compromise was simply beside the mark. They felt that it was no gain, if they so explained away their own words, that the parties addressed could consider that after all they meant by them no more than those parties meant already. They knew that there was a difference between the one side and the other, and that the other must come over to the one, not to set asleep upon the notion that the one *is* the other. We have made this allusion, in illustration of what we would convey concerning the history of Methodism. Had it been met with a definite theology, with an analysis of its errors, and a precise discrimination of what was true in it from what was false, its supporters would have felt that the Church had a meaning in its words, and they would have been necessarily thrown on the defensive; but the vague, unsystematic mode in which they were encountered did but create in their minds an impression of their own superiority, as if their own view must unavoidably be taken by all who would be religious, for none other could be found.

---

of them himself. His pose here of the detached observer is thus ironic.

[100] *Bishop Marsh*: Herbert Marsh (1757–1839), appointed Bishop of Llanduff 1816 and the Bishop of Peterborough 1819; a High Churchman, he was a scripture scholar of the new school of Higher Criticism and was hostile to evangelicals, especially Calvinists.

[101] *Bishop Tomlin*: Sir George Pretyman Tomline 1750–1827), another High Churchman; friend of William Pitt the Younger, appointed Bishop of Lincoln in 1787 and Bishop of Winchester in 1820. His *Elements of Christian Theology* (1799) was a standard textbook for ordinands, and he also wrote against Calvinism.

The other more obvious evil resulting from the then condition of the Church in relation to Methodism, was her abandonment of authority in her dealings with them. As we have already said, man craves for an object of veneration: and if not supplied with those which God has appointed, he will take what offers. The office of ecclesiastical authorities is to lead and guide to their rightful issues the great movements of the human mind, which are ever characterized by passion and error, but ever based on some portion of truth. If these guides will not act, others will act for them. So it was in the case before us: the rulers of the Church did not understand her mission, and Lady Huntingdon became acting bishop instead of them. This unconscious assumption on her ladyship's part of an hierarchical position is confessed by Whitfield in so many words. "Good Lady Huntingdon," he says in a letter to the [413] Countess Delitz,[102] "goes on acting the part of a mother in Israel more and more. For a day or two she has had five clergymen under her roof, which makes her ladyship look *like a good archbishop, with his chaplains around him.* Her house is a Bethel:[103] to us in the ministry it looks like a college. We have the sacrament every morning, heavenly conversation all day, and preach at night. This is to live at court indeed!"—P. 163.

The following passage is to the same purpose, showing that what the Church will not do well, others will do ill instead:

"When the great leaders had once admitted the assistance of lay-preachers, volunteers in abundance offered their zealous services. If they had been disposed to be nice in their selection, it was not in their power. They had called up a spirit which they could not lay; but they were still able to control and direct it. They had taken no step in their whole progress so reluctantly as this. The measure was forced upon them by circumstances, and *by the strong remonstrances of Lady*

---

[102] *Countess Delitz*: Anna Louise née von der Schulenburg (1692-1773) was the illegitimate daughter of George I and Melusine von der Schulenburg, Duchess of Kendal and Duchess of Munster, his long-term mistress. She married Ernest August Philipp von dem Bussche zu Ippenburg and was the sister-in-law of Lord Chesterfield. She experienced a conversion under the influence of George Whitefield and became his patroness.

[103] *Bethel*: the place where Jacob had a dream of a ladder stretching up to heaven and which he named Bethel because it was 'the house of God', cf. Genesis 28: 11-22.

Huntingdon, whose penetrating mind perceived that, if these men were not permitted to preach with the sanction of Mr. Whitfield and Mr. Wesley, they would not be withheld from exercising the power which they felt in themselves. *Her ladyship had coolly and impartially considered the difficulties of the case*; and upon the calmest view of it, notwithstanding her educational prejudices in favour of the Established Church, and her repugnance to the irregularity which was sanctioned by this step, she *still thought that those who were called only of God, and not of man, had more right to preach.*"—Pp. 60, 61.

Another decision, *conceptis verbis*,[104] is addressed to a clergyman of well-known and respected name, whose preaching did not quite please her. Thus she speaks *ex cathedrâ*,[105]—Selina Episcopa, dilecto filio Henrico Venn: [106]

[414] "Oh, my friend, we can make no atonement to a violated law—we have no inward holiness of our own. Cling not to such beggarly elements—such filthy rags—mere cobwebs of Pharisaical pride, but look to Him who hath wrought out a perfect righteousness for His people ... My dear friend, *no longer let false doctrines disgrace your pulpit*. Preach Christ crucified as the only foundation of the sinner's hope. Preach Him as the author and finisher, as well as the sole object, of faith ... May His gracious benediction rest upon your labours! and may you be blessed to the conversion of very many, who shall be your joy and crown of rejoicing in the great day, when the Lord, the righteous Judge, shall appear."—Pp. 225, 226.

In like manner she says of Cheltenham:[107]

"I sincerely hope that *I may be enabled to pay much attention* to this interesting field of labour. There is certainly an incorrigible apathy prevalent among the gay who frequent this place ... Nevertheless, not a few have given manifest proofs of the reality of their conversion ... Over such *we* do and will rejoice as the *fruit of our humble efforts*."—P. 434.

---

[104] *conceptis verbis*: in precise words, in terms

[105] *ex cathedrâ*: literally, 'from the chair', i.e. from the authority of a bishop or pope.

[106] *Selina Episcopa, dilecto filio*: 'from Bishop Selina, to her beloved son Henry Venn'. Henry Venn (1725-97), Anglican divine; originally High Church, he became Evangelical in his views and was later well known as the author of *The Compleat Duty of Man* (1763).

[107] *Cheltenham*: a spa town and, like Bath, a fashionable venue for the idle wealthy.

Again, about her students in the same place.—

"I wrote to (Shenstone)[108] *to order him* to France, as having a more able one *to employ* while the company was there. But he sent him back, and said he would not go. I then repeated *my orders* to both to change ... The wicked and most shameful confusion they have made in Wales must be no longer continued ... *My own* ministers must *have the lead* through all the work. Such reproach makes my heart ache, and often makes me, like him under the juniper tree, say, 'It is better for me to die,' but strength comes for the next day of trial."—P. 435.

Might not this be a translation from St. Basil,[109] bating[110] the proper names, or the allocution of some Pope, whose legates had been insulted?

5.   [415]

She, as other persons, had many cares of office, from the misconduct or waywardness of those over whom she presided. One awkward matter concerned Dr. Haweis,[111] though we are not sure that we rightly apprehend her biographer's account of it. "In the number of those," he says, "who stood forth in the midst of abounding reproach and hostility, and bore a fearless and faithful testimony to the grace and atonement of the Redeemer, was the late venerable Dr. Haweis, who had entered the University as a gentleman-commoner of Christ Church, but afterwards removed to Magdalen Hall. Early in life he was awakened under the powerful ministry of that good man, Mr. Walter,[112] of Truro."—P. 226. Eventually he had the living of Aldwinckle, in Northamptonshire, and Mr. Newton[113] said that

---

[108] *Shenstone*: This could be the poet William Shenstone (1714-63), since there are other references to him in *The Life and Times of Selina Countess of Huntingdon*, though he does not appear to have ever been a church student.

[109] *St. Basil*: See above note on p.[372].

[110] *bating*: with the exception of.

[111] *Dr. Haweis*: See above p.[393].

[112] *Mr. Walter*: Samuel Walker (1713-1761), Anglican divine, who underwent an Evangelical conversion and was sympathetic towards the Methodists, while remaining firmly in the Church of England; despite being the curate rather than the vicar of Truro, he had immense religious influence over the town's inhabitants.

[113] *Mr. Newton*: John Henry Newton (1725-1807), evangelical Anglican divine and abolitionist. He had been a captain of slave ships before undergoing the first of two conversion experiences which led to his eventually entering the Anglican ministry. He

his preaching there "sounded like the report of a cannon through the country" (p. 420), and in consequence he attracted vast congregations to his church. One instance of its success is recorded by our biographer. There was an old innkeeper, who, having entered the church for the singing, closed his ears with his hands when the sermon was to begin: when, a fly stinging his nose, he suddenly removed them just in time to hear the text given out "in a voice that sounded like thunder." The words were, "He that hath ears," etc.; he listened, and he was converted in consequence. Such was the incumbent of Aldwinckle's powers. And now let us review the circumstances under which he found himself in this influential position.

The former incumbent, a Mr. Kimpton,[114] had fallen into difficulties, and, becoming a prisoner in the King's Bench,[115] proposed to sell the advowson,[116] which it appears was his, in order, by the price it might fetch, to release himself from his painful situation. As he could not be dispensed from residence, he had no option but to sell the living at once; and, as delay occurred in finding a purchaser, he put in Dr. Haweis, at Mr. Madan's suggestion, to keep it meanwhile, lest the presentation

[416] should lapse to the Bishop of the diocese. The circumstance of immediate possession increased of course its money value, and before many months had elapsed it was sold for a thousand guineas. The bargain, however, could not take effect without Dr. Haweis; and he, on being informed of it, refused to resign, and denied he had made any promise to do so. On this, he was asked at least to make some compensation to Mr. Kimpton, for the loss he would sustain, but he answered, rightly enough, that he could not be party to any such simoniacal[117] proceeding; moreover, he had already laid out £300[118] on the parsonage. Then

---

became an outspoken opponent of slavery and influenced Wilberforce; he is the author of the hymn 'Amazing Grace'.

[114] *Mr. Kimpton*: John Kimpton, the family of whose wife Elizabeth, *née* Fleetwood, had owned the right of appointment to this benefice (church living) for several generations. When her brother died without heir, she obtained her sister's shares, and under the law of the time the benefice thus became the property of her husband.

[115] *the King's Bench*: a debtors' prison in London.

[116] *advowson*: the right to appoint someone to a benefice, subject only to confirmation by the diocesan bishop. After the Reformation many of these rights were held by lay people, typically the local lord of the manor.

[117] *simoniacal*: The sin of simony is the buying or selling of church appointments.

Mr. Kimpton turned to Mr. Madan, insisting that on the face of the matter he never could have intended to give so valuable a property out and out to Dr. Haweis, a stranger to him, and a young man, to the depreciation of its market value, which of course he needed to raise to the utmost; but Mr. Madan took a contrary view, and as there had been no third party in the transaction, who might have been a witness in the matter, Mr. Kimpton gained nothing by his appeal. Then Dr. Hawies gave him his *coup de grace*[119] by laying the case before the Lord Chancellor,[120] to whom Mr. Madan was chaplain, and who decided that Mr. Kimpton had no remedy in law. Indeed, no other decision was possible; and the poor man remained a prisoner in the King's Bench, with a son driven out of his mind, and his family nearly starving.

All this shocked Lady Huntingdon; and, as it was a money matter, she had both a plea and a meaning when she interfered. She purchased of Mr. Kimpton for £1000[121] what she could not take away from Dr. Haweis; and thus gained a claim for exercising her ecclesiastical functions, and giving both him and his friend, her views of the transaction. She addressed herself to Mr. Madan, "On having your representation read over," she [417] says in it, "my sentiment on that point I most freely gave, and thought, as the matter stood, I could not see how Mr. Haweis, as an honest man, could continue to hold that living." Then, after relating how she had herself purchased the advowson, and released Mr. Kimpton from confinement, she continues, "It remains now only for me to pray God to enable both you and Mr. Haweis to make every proper and public concession to the world for any conscious infirmity, weakness, temptation, or mistaken step, through this transaction. May you stand by the cross of Christ in this humbling and trying instance," etc.—P. 418. Mr. Madan, however, was equal to the occasion. He wrote back, "As to the concessions your ladyship is pleased to mention, as we do not conceive we have any to make so we may assure you that none can ever be made."

---

[118] *£300*: equivalent to over £50,000 in today's money
[119] *coup de grace*: finishing blow
[120] *the Lord Chancellor*: at this time Henry Bathurst, 2nd Earl Bathurst (1714–94).
[121] *£1000*: equivalent to £167,000 in today's money.

Such was the issue of an affair, in which, whatever we think of Mr. Madan, Dr. Haweis does not particularly shine; but, if faith, such as he was considered to have, blots out all, even the most enormous sins, it is not wonderful if Lady Huntingdon and her friends considered it a sovereign prophylactic against any prospective mischief happening to his soul from mere peccadillos against the law whether of charity, generosity, equity, or honour. Accordingly our biographer gently observes,—supposing Dr. Haweis "to have erred in this, let the mistakes of such men be beacons for our admonition and warning, while their fidelity and devotedness inspire us with the zeal of imitation and arouse us to exertion."—P. 421. He tells us too that "Mr. Romaine, Mr. Venn, as well as Mr. Newton, visited him in his living; the friendship of such men is unequivocal testimony to the *piety* of Dr. Haweis." Nay, even as regards Lady Huntingdon herself, we are struck to find that "however severe might be her ladyship's opinion of this transaction at the moment, she had always entertained a high opinion of the *piety* and *moral worth* of Mr. Haweis; he became one of her preachers, then her chaplain, and he was appointed by her will one of the chief managers of her chapel."—P. 414.

[418]

A word must be added about Mr. Madan on his own score, who was Dr. Haweis's associate in the foregoing transaction. He was "a friend and intimate of Lady Huntingdon," who, as the noble cadet informs us, "had been well acquainted with his mother-in-law, Lady Hale,[122] relict of Sir Bernard Hale,[123] etc., the friend, etc., of her ladyship's grandfather, Sir Richard Levinge,[124] etc., and uncle to a lady who married Sir E. Dering, Bart.,[125] Lady Huntingdon's cousin, and grandson to Lady Anne Shirley."[126] He was originally bred to the bar, but being sent by some gay companions to hear Wesley, by way of affording them

---

[122] *his mother-in-law, Lady Hale*: Anne *née* Thoresby; Martin Madan married her daughter Jane in 1751.
[123] *Sir Bernard Hale*: (1677-1729), one of the best paid barristers in England; he later became Lord Chancellor of Ireland.
[124] *Sir Richard Levinge*: 1st Baronet (1656–1724), Irish politician and judge.
[125] *Sir E. Dering, Bart*: Sir Edward Dering, 7th Baronet (1757–1811). He was Selina's first cousin once removed.
[126] *Lady Anne Shirley*: Anne Furnese, *née* Shirley (d. 1779), wife of Sir Robert Furnese, Selina's aunt (her father's half-sister).

amusement, he was converted on the spot by that wonderful preacher, and when his friends asked him, on his return, whether "he had taken off the old Methodist," he answered, "No, gentlemen, but he has taken me off." Mr. Madan was the founder and first chaplain of the Lock Hospital.[127] Our author's eloquence rises almost to the sublime in his description of this well-connected divine:

"The lawyer turning divine was novel—curiosity prevailed among the million of the metropolis. The manly eloquence of the preacher drew general attention and excited applause. The poor heard the Gospel with gladness, and the rich were not sent empty away. Many were filled with wonder. The croaking cry of prejudice was silenced— her raven voice sunk amidst the loud acclaims of the friends of religion, who heard the doctrines of the Reformation nobly defended by an able advocate, whose knowledge was equal to his zeal. Like Boanerges,[128] a son of thunder, he proclaimed the law from the flaming mountain;[129] and from the summit of Zion's hill, he appeared a [419] Barnabas, a son of consolation.[130] Mr. Madan was rather tall in stature, and of a robust constitution; his countenance was majestic, open, and engaging, and his looks commanding veneration; his delivery is said to have been peculiarly graceful. He preached without notes; his voice was musical, well-modulated, full, and powerful; his language plain, nervous, pleasing, and memorable; and his arguments strong, bold, rational, and conclusive; his doctrines were drawn from the sacred fountain; he was mighty in the Scriptures—a workman that needed not to be ashamed of his labours, rightly dividing the word of truth."—Pp. 166, 167.

After a time he itinerated in Wiltshire, Gloucestershire, Oxfordshire, Warwickshire, and Nottinghamshire, and he and another are spoken of by Mr. Ryland[131] as being "like men

---

[127] *the Lock Hospital*: Founded jointly with the surgeon William Bromfield in 1747 as the first hospital to treat sexually transmitted diseases. The name comes from the rags or 'locks' originally placed on leprosy sores, since Lock Hospitals were originally for the treatment of lepers.

[128] *Boanerges, a son of thunder*: the name given by Jesus to James and John the sons of Zebedee, cf. Mark 3:17.

[129] *the flaming mountain*: where Moses delivered the Ten Commandments to the people of Israel, cf. Deuteronomy 5:22.

[130] *a Barnabas, a son of consolation*: Cf. Acts 4:36.

[131] *Mr. Ryland*: John Ryland (d.1822), Anglican divine.

baptized with the Holy Ghost and with fire, fervent in spirit, and setting their faces as a flint."—P.431. An account of a sermon is also given us, in which "he showed what regeneration was not, but more especially what it *was*," with great power.—P. 432. And he himself speaks, in a letter to Wesley, of Lord and Lady Darmouth,[132] as "*breathing after inward holiness*, as the hart panteth after the waterbrooks."[133]—P. 433. At a later date, this gentleman, thus paralleled to St. John and St. Barnabas, baptized with fire and enlightened in the nature of regeneration, actually wrote a book, called "Thelyphthora, or a Treatise on Female Ruin," in which he advocates polygamy, as an expedient for setting things straight.[134]

If Luther found his representative in Mr. Madan as regards a point of Christian morality,[135] he had a disciple as regards a far more conspicuous peculiarity of his mind in a better man, Mr. Berridge, of Everton.[136] This gentleman, of whom an anecdote has already been told, amid many good points of character, was totally destitute of reverence, and can hardly [420] rebut the severe censure of Mr. Southey, that he was "buffoon as well as fanatic."[137] The author of the work before us maintains that he was neither, on the following grounds, first, because "Lady Huntingdon invited him repeatedly to meet at her house the eloquent and the courtly;" secondly, because "Mr. Whitfield called him an Angel of the Church, and employed him as his substitute at Tottenham Court Chapel,[138] and the Tabernacle;" thirdly, because Mr. Simeon "preached his funeral sermon;"

---

[132] *Lord and Lady Darmouth*: [sic] William Legge, 2nd Earl of Dartmouth (1731–1801), statesman, friend of Thomas Haweis; he married Frances *née* Nicoll (1733–1805).

[133] *as the hart panteth after the waterbrooks*: Cf. Psalm 42:1.

[134] *Thelyphthora . . . things straight*: Madan thought that a married man who had an adulterous relationship with another woman and made her pregnant should take her as an additional wife in order to accept financial responsibility for her. Published in 1780, unsurprisingly this book caused considerable controversy, eliciting nineteen published replies.

[135] *Luther found his representative . . .* : Luther advocated polygamy in cases where the first wife was ill and thus unable to have sexual relations with her husband; he approved the bigamous marriage of Philip of Hesse.

[136] *Mr. Berridge of Everton*: See above p.[408].

[137] *Mr. Southey that he was "buffoon as well as fanatic."*: see *The Life of Wesley; and the Rise of Progress of Methodism* (1820), Vol. II, p.274.

[138] *Tottenham Court Chapel*: Whitefield's Tabernacle, Tottenham Court Road, London, built in 1756.

fourthly, because Clare Hall[139] "presented him to the vicarage of Everton;" and fifthly, because he served the "office of moderator."—P. 367. However, he allows that Mr. Berridge "often *caused* a smile that he might *create* a tear;" we do not fully enter into the antithesis; "a hazardous," he continues, "if not an unwarrantable experiment in the pulpit;" but he excuses it on the ground that "his *perfect scholarship* as a classic enabled him to give point to piquant thoughts," and that "there will be some buffoonery *wherever* Aristophanic Greek[140] is understood;" that is, we suppose, among all distinguished scholars in both Universities. We are told that he was inferior in learning to very few of the most celebrated men of literature and science in the University, and "that from his entrance to Clare Hall to his being vicar of Everton, he regularly studied fifteen hours a day."

"His stature was tall, but not awkward—his make was lusty, but not corpulent; his voice deep, but not hoarse,—strong, but not noisy; his pronunciation was distinct, but not broad. In his countenance there was gravity without grimace. His address was solemn, but not sour—easy, but not careless—deliberate, but not drawling—pointed, but not personal—affectionate, but not fawning. He would often weep, but never whine. His sentences were short, but not ambiguous; his ideas were collected, but not crowded. Upon the whole, his manner and person were agreeable and majestic.

"For twenty-four years he continued to ride nearly one hundred miles [421] and to preach some ten or twelve sermons every week. At home, for his hearers who came from a distance, his table was served, and his stables open for their horses; and abroad, houses and barns were rented, lay preachers supplied, and his own expenses paid out of his own pocket. His ear was ever attentive to the tale of woe; his eye was keen to observe the miseries of the poor; the law of kindness was written upon his heart, and his hand was always ready to administer relief. The gains of his vicarage, of his fellowship, and of his patrimonial income (for his father died very rich), and even his family

---

[139] *Clare Hall*: the older name for Clare College, Cambridge. Oxford and Cambridge colleges still own the rights to some Church of England livings and can appoint their own candidates to them.

[140] *Aristophanic Greek*: Aristophanes (c. 446 B.C.–c. 386 B.C.), author of comedies such as *The Frogs*. His comedy includes indecency, so Newman is highlighting the incongruity of this praise of a clergyman.

plate, were appropriated to support his liberality. He was also a favourite with Lady Huntingdon. To her he was indebted for much spiritual light, and her liberality in other matters was felt and acknowledged by him."—Pp. 368, 369.

There is much in this account which raises respect for the subject of it: but to have a full view of his character, we should read the following strange letter to Lady Huntingdon, which seems to be a fair specimen of the author's style:

"My Lady,—Your letter just suited my case: it was a bleeding plaister for a bleeding heart. These many months I have done little else but mourn for myself and others, to see how we lie among the tombs,[141] contented with a decent suit of grave-clothes. At times my heart has been refreshed with these words, 'On the land of my people is come up briars and thorns, until the Spirit be poured out upon them from on high;'[142] but the comfort soon vanisheth, like gleams of a winter sun. I cannot wish for transports such as we once had, and which almost turned our heads; but I do long to see a spirit poured of triumphant faith, heavenly love, and steadfast cleaving to the Lord.

"Before I parted with honest Glasscott,[143] I cautioned him much against petticoat snares. He has burnt his wings already. Sure he will not imitate a foolish gnat, and hover again about the candle? If he should fall into a sleeping-nap, he will soon need a flannel night-cap, and a rusty chain to fix him down, like a church Bible to the reading-desk. No trap so mischievous to the field preacher as wedlock, and it is laid for him at every hedge corner. Matrimony has quite maimed poor Charles [Wesley], and might have spoiled John [Wesley] and George [Whitfield], if a wise Master had not graciously sent them a pair of ferrets.[144] Dear George has now got his liberty again, and he will 'scape well if he is not caught by another tenter-hook.

"Eight or nine years ago, having been grievously tormented with housekeepers, I truly had thoughts about looking out for a Jezebel myself. But it seemed highly needful to ask advice of the Lord. So falling down on my knees before a table, with a Bible between my

[422]

---

[141] *among the tombs*: Cf. Mark 5:3

[142] '*On the land . . . from on high;* ': Isaiah 32:13

[143] *Glasscott*: Cradock Glasscott (1743-1831), Evangelical Anglican divine of strongly Calvinist views who became a minister in Lady Huntingdon's Connexion; he later broke with her and returned to the Anglican ministry, becoming Vicar of Hatherleigh, Devon. He ignored Berridge's warning against matrimony, marrying Mary *née* Edmonds in 1784.

[144] a *pair of ferrets*: Both Wesley and Whitfield made unhappy marriages.

hands, I besought the Lord to give me a direction. Then letting the Bible fall open of itself, I fixed my eyes immediately on these words, 'When my son was entered into his wedding chamber, he fell down and died.'—2 Esdras x. 1. This frightened me heartily, you may easily think; but Satan, who stood peeping at my elbow, not liking the heavenly caution, presently suggested a scruple that the book was apocryphal, and the words not to be heeded. Well, after a short pause, I fell on my knees again, and prayed the Lord not to be angry with me, whilst, like Gideon, I requested a second sign,[145] and from the canonical scripture.[146] Then letting my Bible fall open as before, I fixed my eyes directly on this passage, 'Thou shalt not take thee a wife, neither shalt thou have sons or daughters in this place.'—Jer. xvi. 2. I was now completely satisfied; and being thus made acquainted with my Lord's mind, I make it one part of my prayers. And I can look on these words not only as a rule of direction, but as a promise of security: 'Thou shalt not take a wife;' that is, 'I will keep thee from taking one.'

"This method of procuring divine intelligence is much flouted by flimsy professors who walk at large, and desire not that sweet and secret access to the mercy-seat which babes of the kingdom do find. During the last twelve years I have had occasion to consult the oracle three or four times on matters that seemed important and dubious, and have received answers full and plain."—Pp. 388, 389.

What Lady Huntingdon thought of this singular style does not appear; but we have to thank her biographer for a very striking and friendly remonstrance, addressed to the same person by Mr. Thornton;[147] which, though too long to quote, shows us that not all, who agreed in religious sentiments with Mr. Berridge, agreed with him in his peculiar mode of enforcing them

5.   [423]

It is sometimes urged that our Church is much indebted to Whitfield and Wesley; and that if we will not praise them, we must either be ungrateful to good men, or paradoxically deny

---

[145] *Gideon . . . a second sign*: Cf. Judges 6:36-40.

[146] *from the canonical scripture*: 2 Esdras is one of the apocryphal books and therefore not part of the biblical canon.

[147] *Mr. Thornton*: John Thornton (1720–1790), businessman and philanthropist of evangelical views; he was a financial supporter of Lady Huntingdon's Connexion. Glasscott had written to Thornton in a humorous style asking for a loan of £10 to pay for a visit to the dentist. His humour was reproved by Thornton in a letter which *The Life and Times of Selina, Countess of Huntingdon* quotes in full, pp.371-3.

their instrumentality in bringing about the present seriousness and activity which exists within its pale. Now we fully grant that they have been instruments in the hands of Providence of raising the standard and extending the influence of religion in the land, and yet we do not see that the Church should be called their debtor at all. In the view indeed of their followers, the Church is indebted to them of course; for what is the Church, as they would say, but an earthly and voluntary society, and what were they but immediately commissioned ministers of grace acting upon it? But though their conclusion is clear enough upon their principles, it does not follow that it is clear upon ours; on the contrary, that it is plainly illogical and unsound a very little consideration will show. For churchmen would maintain, as a first principle in the question, that whatever spiritual gift Whitfield and Wesley possessed, it came, as from the Most High, so through His Church. By the Church they were baptized, by the Church they were ordained; from the Church they received the creed, whatever portion of it they preserved inviolate: they have nothing to boast of, nothing which they did not receive through her, who was providentially made their greatest of earthly benefactors. As well may a son have a claim on a parent, or a servant attempt works of supererogation[148] towards his master, as ministers of the Church become her patrons. What Scripture says of meritorious works of a servant

[424] towards his master, applies to the relation of these great preachers towards her whose Sons and ministers they were. "Doth he thank that servant because he did the things that were commanded him? I trow not."[149] She gave them the grace of baptism, *in order* that they might show forth their light, or rather her light in them; she ordained them, *in order* that they might preach repentance and gather souls into her bosom. As far as they did this, they only did what they had vowed to do; as far as they did something else, they did not benefit her, but were unnatural children and false priests. They had devoted themselves to her service for God's sake: whatever natural gifts

---

[148] *works of supererogation:* good deeds which go beyond what is required by law or moral duty
[149] *"Doth he thank . . . I trow not."*: Luke 17:9

they might possess were made over to her, who had made these gifts (what by nature they were not) gracious.

All this of course will not be granted for an instant by those who do not allow that the Church can forgive sins or convey grace; but, because they refuse to accept our doctrinal principles, it is very hard that they should think it incumbent upon us to acquiesce in theirs. Now we are persuaded that the Church is a living body; it will ever have life unto the end; any branch of it that does not show life is no real part of it. The English Church *could not but* have had a revival, if it be a branch of the true Church; that Wesley and Whitfield were the instruments of that revival (as far as they were such), was what may be called an accident of Providence, but that the Church should revive is an inspired promise from the beginning. The Church Established, if so be, may not be a true branch; the English people, if so be, may have forfeited the gift; and surely we are all most unworthy of it, and have abundant cause for thankfulness, so far as we have reason to suppose that we still have it. But, taking for granted, what we all maintain, that she is a true branch, then it [425] is no strange accident, no unusual Providence, no deed of Wesley's or Whitfield's that has roused her from her lethargy, but a consequence of the great, ordinary, and universal law of the Gospel, that "all her children shall be taught of the Lord,"[150] and that "their ears shall hear a word behind them, saying, This is the way, walk ye in it,"[151] and that "His words in her mouth shall not depart out of her mouth for ever."[152]

In a word, these men either spoke truth or falsehood; if and as far as they spoke falsehood, they have nothing to boast of; if and as far as they spoke truth, they did but receive from the Church a gift, and they did but fulfil for the Church a prophecy. What they did ill was their own, what they did well was hers. They were honoured, not she benefited. With this suggestion to those whom it may concern, we lay down this copious and not uninteresting, but ill-digested and ill-arranged Volume.

October, 1840.

---

[150] *"all her children . . . of the Lord,"*: Isaiah 54:13

[151] *"their ears shall . . . walk ye in it,"*: Isaiah 30:21

[152] *"His words in . . . mouth for ever."*: Isaiah 59:21

Note on Essay IX[153]

The "France" mentioned in p. 414 *supr.* seems to have denoted the Independent Meeting in the late Mr. Thomas Keble's[154] Parish in Gloucestershire near Chalford, which, he once wrote to tell me, "was certainly built about Lady Huntingdon's time, and was always in his time called by the people 'France.'"[155]

---

[153] Newman added this Note in the Sixth Edition of this volume (1885).

[154] *Mr. Thomas Keble*: (1793–1875), Vicar of Bisley, Gloucestershire, 1827-73, younger brother of Newman's close friend, John Keble (see above note on p.[12]).

[155] *he once wrote to tell me* . . . : Such a letter is not found in the *Letters and Diaries*.

TEXTUAL APPENDIX

The following list contains variants in the 1885 sixth edition (except for the Notes added by Newman at the end of each essay) from the original articles published 1829-1839. Where words in the '1885 text' column have nothing equivalent in the '1829-1839 texts' column, they are additions to the earlier text; and where words in the '1829-1839 texts' column have nothing equivalent in the '1885 text' column, they were omitted from the later text. Trivial variations in capitalising, punctuation and spelling have been ignored, as have insignificant verbal variations which do not affect Newman's meaning. The page numbers are as in the 1885 text which are in square brackets in the margins in this edition.

Page	1885 text	1829-1839 texts
1	POETRY, WITH REFERENCE TO ARISTOTLE'S POETICS	ART. VII.-*The theatre of the Greeks; or the History, Literature, and Criticism of the Grecian Drama. With an Original Treatise on the Principal Tragic and Comic Metres.* Second Edition. Cambridge. 1827.
	WE propose to offer some speculations of our own on Greek Tragedy, and on Poetry in general, as suggested by the doctrine of Aristotle on the subject.	
	1.	
	Aristotle considers the	THIS work is well adapted for the purpose it has in view – the illustration of the Greek Drama. It has been usual for the young student to engage in a perusal of this difficult branch of classical literature, with none of that previous preparation or collateral assistance which it pre-eminently requires. Not to mention his ordinary want of information as regards the history of the drama, which, though necessary to the full understanding the nature of that kind of poetry, may still seem too remotely connected with the existing Greek plays to be an actual deficiency; nor, again, his ignorance of the dramatic dialect and metres, which, without external helps, may possibly be overcome by minds of superior talent while engaged upon them; at least without some clear ideas of the usages of the ancient stage, the Greek dramas are but partially intelligible. The circumstances under which the representation was conducted, the form and general arrangements of

the theatre; the respective offices and disposition of the actors, the nature and duties of the chorus, the proprieties of the scene itself, are essential subjects of information, yet they are generally neglected. The publication before us is a compilation of the most useful works or parts of works on the criticism, history, and antiquities of the drama; among which will be found extracts from Bentley's Dissertation on the Epistles of Phalaris and from Schlegel's work on Dramatic Literature; the more important parts of Twining's Translation of Aristotle's Poetics, and critical remarks, by Dawes, Porson, Elmsley, Tate, and writers in the Museum Criticum.

If we were disposed to find fault with a useful work, we should describe it as over-liberal of condensed critical information. Such ample assistance is given to the student, that little is left to exercise his own personal thought and judgment. This is a fault of not a few publications of the present day, written for our universities. From a false estimate of the advantages of accurate scholarship, the reader is provided with a multitude of minute facts, which are useful to his mind, not when barely remembered, but chiefly when he has acquired them for himself. It is of comparatively trifling importance, whether the scholar knows the force of οὐ μὴ or ἀλλὰ γάρ; but it may considerably improve his acumen or taste, to have gone through a process of observation, comparison, and induction, more or less original and independent of grammarians and critics. It is an officious aid which renders the acquisition of a language mechanical. Commentators are of service to stimulate the mind, and suggest thought; and though, when we view the wide field of criticism, it is impossible they should do more, yet, when that field is narrowed to the limit of academical success, there is a danger of their indulging indolence, or confirming the contracted views of dullness. These remarks are not so much directed against a valuable work like the present, the very perusal of which may be made an exercise for the mind, as against an especial fault of the age. The uses of knowledge in forming the intellectual and moral character, are too commonly overlooked; and the possession itself being viewed as a peculiar good, short ways are on all subjects excogitated for avoiding the labour of learning; whereas the very length and process of the journey is in many the chief, in all an important advantage.

But, dismissing a train of thought which would soon lead us very far from the range of subjects which the theatre of the Greeks introduces to our notice, we propose to offer some speculations of our own on Greek tragedy and poetry in general, founded on the doctrine of Aristotle as contained in the publication before us. A compilation of standard works, (and such in its general character is the Greek Theatre,) scarcely affords the occasion of lengthened criticism on itself; whereas it may be of use to the classical student to add some further illustrations of the subject which is the common basis of the works compiled.

Aristotle considers the

1	settlement	arrangement
2	are found	is placed
3	Then again,	
3	of Clytemnestra in the Electra	the Clytemnestra of the Electra

427

4	transcendent	Divine
4	fable	Plot
5	as to which	Where
6	the mad fire	the mad and merry fire

7 | A Bull, thou seem'st to lead us; on thy head
Horns have grown forth: wast heretofore a beast?
For such thy semblance now. | καὶ ταῦρος ἡμῖν πρόσθεν ἡγεῖσθαι δοκεῖς
καὶ σῷ κέρατι προσπεφυκέναι
ἀλλ᾽ ἦ ποτ᾽ ἦσθα θήρ; τεταύρωσαι γαρ οὖν

	absolute decisions which came of his vigorous talent for thinking through large subjects	large and connected views which his vigorous talent for thinking through subjects supplied

	for it. The sudden inspiration, surely, of the blind Œdipus, in the second play bearing his name, by which he is enabled, "without a guide," to lead the way to his place of death, in our judgment, produces more poetical effect than all the skilful intricacy of the plot of the Tyrannus. The latter excites an interest which scarcely lasts beyond the first reading—the former "decies repetita placebit."	for it.* * The sudden inspiration, e.g. of the blind Œdipus, in the second play bearing his name, by which he is enabled, ἄθικτος ἡγητῆρος, to lead the way to his place of death, in our judgment, produces more poetical effect than all the skilful intricacy of the plot of the Tyrannus. The latter excites an interest which scarcely lasts beyond the first reading—the former *decies repetita placebit.*

9	"The spectators are led to recognize and to syllogize what each thing is."	συμζαίνει θεωρούννας μανθάνειν καὶ συλλογίζεσθαι, τί ἕκαστον.
10	formulæ of physics, before they are	formula of physics, before it is
10	atmosphere	gravity
11	disparage	condemn
11	gift	talent
11	the Choephorœ, are in themselves	the Choephorœ, or perhaps of the grave-diggers in Hamlet, are in themselves
12	pensive imagination. It is the charm of the descriptive poetry of a	pensive mind.* *It is the charm of the descriptive

religious mind, that nature is viewed in a moral connexion. Ordinary writers, for instance, compare aged men to trees in autumn—a gifted poet will in the fading trees discern the fading men.*
* Thus:—
"How quiet shows the woodland scene!
 Each flower and tree, its duty done,
 Reposing in decay serene,
 Like weary men when age is won,"
etc.

poetry of a religious mind, that nature is viewed in a moral connexion. Ordinary writers (e.g.) compare aged men to trees in autumn—a gifted poet will reverse the metaphor. Thus:—
'How quiet shows the woodland scene!
 Each flower and tree, its duty done,
 Reposing in decay serene,
 Like weary men when age is won,' etc.

14 Miss Edgeworth's

Miss E.'s

15 of fiction.

of fiction.*
*See this point more fully explained p. 26 of the present Number.

15 in some characters

of character

17 Byron's Childe Harold.

Byron's Childe Harold.*
*We would here mention Rogers's *Italy*, if such a cursory notice could convey our high opinion of its merit.

17 verses

sentences

18 Such is the character of Campbell's Pleasures of Hope; it is in his minor poems

In the Pleasures of Hope we find this done with exquisite taste; but it is in his minor poems

18 sermon

oration

18 for poetry.

for poetry.*
*The difference between oratory and poetry is well illustrated by a passage in a recent tragedy.
  Col. Joined! By what tie?
  Rien. By hatred –
  By danger – the two hands that tightest grasp
  Each other – the two cords that soonest knit
  A fast and stubborn tie; your true love knot
  Is nothing to it. Faugh! the supple

touch
Of pliant interest, or the dust of time,
Or the pin-point of temper, loose or rot
Or snap love's silken band. Fear and old hate
They are sure weavers – they work for the storm,
The whirlwind, and the rocking surge; their knot
Endures till death.
The idea is good, and if expressed in a line or two, might have been poetry – spread out into nine or ten lines, it yields but a languid and ostentatious declamation.

21	good feeling	feeling
21	some explanation.	some explanation.*

*A living prelate, in his Academical Prelections, even suggests the converse of our position – '*neque enim facile crediderim de eo qui semel hac imbutus fuerit disciplinâ, qui in id totâ mentis acie assuefactus fuerit incumbere, ut quid sit in rebus decens, quid pulchrum, quid congruum, penitus intueretur, quin idem harum rerum perpetuum amorem foveat, et cum ab his studiis discesserit, etiam ad reliqua vitæ official earum imaginem quasi animo infixam transferat.*'

21	depraved	bad
22	this is instanced	it is exhibited
22	only poetry	only such
22	the characteristics	the $\tilde{\eta}\theta o\varepsilon$, the physiognomy
22	conscience	the heart
22	refined	delicate
22	delicate	refined

22	drama	fable
23	Rousseau, it may be supposed, is an exception to our doctrine.	Rousseau is not an exception to our doctrine, for his heart was naturally religious.
23	great poetical genius	much poetical talent
24	However	
24	is manifestly	is however manifestly
24	may, in some poetical minds, be very feeble	is in some poetical minds entirely wanting
26	a similar gift	a similar internal gift
26	affected	affects
31	THE RATIONALISTIC AND THE CATHOLIC TEMPERS CONTRASTED	*The Rationalistic and the Catholic Spirit compared together*

31   RATIONALISM is a certain abuse of Reason; that is, a use of it for purposes for which it never was intended, and is unfitted. To rationalize in matters of Revelation is to make our reason the standard and measure of the doctrines revealed; to stipulate that those doctrines should be such as to carry with them their own justification; to reject them, if they come in collision with our existing opinions or habits of thought, or are with difficulty harmonized with our existing stock of knowledge. And thus a rationalistic spirit is the antagonist of Faith; for Faith is, in its very nature, the acceptance of what our reason cannot reach, simply and absolutely upon testimony.

There is, of course, a multitude of cases in which we allowably and rightly accept statements as true, partly on reason, and partly on testimony. We supplement the information of others by our own

To rationalize is to ask for *reasons* out of place; to ask improperly how we are to *account* for certain things, to be unwilling to believe them unless they can be accounted for, i.e. referred to something else as a cause, to some existing system as harmonizing with them or taking them up into itself. Again, since whatever is assigned as the reason for the original fact canvassed, admits in turn of a like question being raised about itself, unless it be ascertainable by the senses, and be the subject of personal experience, Rationalism is bound properly to pursue onward its course of investigation on this principle, and not to stop till it can directly or ultimately refer to self as a witness, whatever is offered to its acceptance. Thus it is characterized by two peculiarities; its loves of systematizing, and its basing its system upon personal experience,

knowledge, by our own judgment of probabilities; and, if it be very strange or extravagant, we suspend our assent. This is undeniable; still, after all, there are truths which are incapable of reaching us except on testimony, and there is testimony, which by and in itself, has an imperative claim on our acceptance.

As regards Revealed Truth, it is not Rationalism to set about to ascertain, by the exercise of reason, what things are attainable by reason, and what are not; nor, in the absence of an express Revelation, to inquire into the truths of Religion, as they come to us by nature; nor to determine what proofs are necessary for the acceptance of a Revelation, if it be given; nor to reject a Revelation on the plea of insufficient proof; nor, after recognizing it as divine, to investigate the meaning of its declarations, and to interpret its language; nor to use its doctrines, as far as they can be fairly used, in inquiring into its divinity; nor to compare and connect them with our previous knowledge, with a view of making them parts of a whole; nor to bring them into dependence on each other, to trace their mutual relations, and to pursue them to their legitimate issues. This is not Rationalism; but it is Rationalism to accept the Revelation, and then to explain it away; to speak of it as the Word of God, and to treat it as the word of man; to refuse to let it speak for itself; to claim to be told the *why* and the *how* of God's dealings with us, as therein described, and to assign to Him a motive and a scope of our own; to stumble at the partial knowledge which He may give us of them; to put aside what is obscure, as if it had not been said at all; to accept one half of what has been told us, and not the other half; to assume that the contents of Revelation are also its proof; to frame some gratuitous hypothesis

on the evidence of sense. In both respects it stands opposed to what is commonly understood by the word Faith, or belief in Testimony; for which it deliberately substitutes System (or what is popularly called Reason) and Sight.

I have said that to act the Rationalist is to be unduly set upon *accounting* for what is offered for our acceptance; *unduly*, for to seek reasons for what is told us, is natural and innocent in itself. When we are informed that this or that event has happened, we are not satisfied to take it as an isolated fact; we are inquisitive about it; we are prompted to refer it, if possible, to something we already know, to incorporate it into the connected family of truths or facts which we have already received. We like to ascertain its position relatively to other things, to view it in connection with them, to reduce it to a place in the series of what is called cause and effect. There is no harm in all this, until we insist upon receiving this *satisfaction* as a necessary condition of believing what is presented for our acceptance, until we set up our existing system of knowledge as a legitimate test of the credibility of testimony, until we claim to be told the mode of reconciling alleged truths to other truths already known, the *how* they are, and *why* they are; and then we Rationalize.

about them, and then to garble, gloss, and colour them, to trim, clip, pare away, and twist them, in order to bring them into conformity with the idea to which we have subjected them.

37   testimony   witness

37   Prophetic Records. How nobly

Prophetic records. It has pleased the 'Lord and Governor' of the world, in his inscrutable wisdom, to baffle our enquiries into the nature and proximate cause of that wonderful faculty of intellect, - that image of his own essence which he has conferred upon us; - nay, the springs and wheelwork of animal and vegetable vitality are concealed from our view by an impenetrable veil, and the pride of philosophy is humbled by the spectacle of the physiologist bending in fruitless ardour over the dissection of the human brain, and peering in equally unproductive enquiry over the gambols of an animalcule. But how nobly

37-   The writer of these sentences cannot
39   be said exactly to rationalize, because he neither professes belief in Revelation, nor dresses up any portion of its contents into a scientific, intelligible shape. But he lays down the principle on which rationalists proceed, and shows how superior, that principle being assumed, astronomy is to the Gospel. He tells us that knowledge, or what he calls truth, elicits "the best and highest feelings of the soul;" that the "love" and "craving" for such knowledge is the most noble of "passions," and a "glorious instinct;" that the attainments of such knowledge, say for instance, about the Milky Way or the Lost Pleïad (supposing it were possible), is emphatically "Revelation," not a mere inkling, conveyed in figures and parables like "other"

Here desire after Truth is considered as irreconcilable with acquiescence in doubt. Now if we do not believe in a First Cause, then indeed we know nothing except so far as we know it clearly, consistency and harmony being the necessary evidence of reality; and so we may reasonably regard doubt as an obstacle in the pursuit of Truth. But, on the other hand, if we *assume the existence of* an unseen Object of Faith, then we already possess the main truth, and may well be content even with half views as to His operations, for whatever we have is so much gain, and what we do not know does not in that case tend at all to invalidate what we do know.

A few words may be necessary to bring together what has been said. Rationalism then, viewed in its

Revelations, but "soothing, and yet how elevating!" opening upon the scientific "excursionist" the most splendid "scenery," a "compensation" for "metaphysical darkness;"—moreover, that the "physical universe" "eminently" gifts the astronomer with "the privilege of foreknowledge," and is converted for his use into a "prophetic record." No partial knowledge, he implies, can be so transporting as this unclouded light,—the subject-matter of our contemplations, of course, never having any bearing at all upon the transport which the contemplations create. To know the God of nature in part is a poor thing in comparison of knowing the laws of nature in full. To meditate on His power or skill, on His illimitable being and existence, on His unity in immensity, is a mere nothing compared with the ecstasy which follows on the infallible certitude of the physical philosopher, that particles of matter are attracted towards each other by a force varying inversely as the square of their distance. I do not say that the writer in question would thus express himself, when brought to book; but it is the legitimate sense of his words, and the secret thought of his heart, unless he has but enunciated a succession of magniloquent periods.

I have said he is not a rationalist; I do not call him so, because he does not own to a belief in Revealed Religion, or tamper with its contents. Rather he tends, how little soever he may realize it, to discard even Theism itself from his list of *credenda*. The only truth which he seems to think it worth while pursuing, is the knowledge of the universe; for a system can be more easily and thoroughly mastered than an Infinite Mind. Laws are stable; but persons are strange, uncertain, inexplicable. "Ex pede Herculem;"

essential character, is a refusal to take for granted the existence of a First Cause, in religious inquiries, which it prosecutes as if commencing in utter ignorance of the subject. Hence it receives only so much as may be strictly drawn out to the satisfaction of the reason, advancing onwards in belief according to the range of the proof; it limits Truth to our comprehension of it, or *subjects* it to the mind, and admits it only so far as it is subjected. Hence again it considers faith to have reference to a *thing* or *system*, far more than to an *agent*, for an agent may be supposed as acting in unknown ways, whereas a system cannot be supposed to have existence beyond what is ascertained of it. Hence moreover it makes the credibility of any alleged truth to lie solely in its capability of coalescing and combining with what is already known.

Mr. Hume, as has been observed, avowed the principle of Rationalism in its extent of Atheism. The writers, I shall have to notice, have religious sensibilities, and are far less clear-sighted. Yet even Mr. Erskine maintains or assumes that the main *object* of Christian faith is, not Almighty God, but a certain work or course of things which He has accomplished; as will be manifest to any reader either of His *Essay on Internal Evidence*, or *on Faith*. He says, for instance, in the latter of these works, if I know one fact about the physica*l* world, I know a million others; but one divine act and no more carries me but a little way in my knowledge of "Summum illud et æternum, neque mutabile, neque interiturum." There is some chance of our analyzing nature, none of our comprehending God.

Such is the philosophy of the writer whom I have quoted; and such is Rationalism in its action upon Scripture and the Creed. It considers faith to consist rather in the knowledge of a system or scheme, than of an agent; it is concerned, not so much with the Divine Being, as with His work. Mr. Erskine is one of the writers who are presently to engage my attention; here I will anticipate my mention of him by citing a passage from his Essay on Faith, in illustration of the parallelism, as I read him, between him and the Reviewer. He assumes the very principle of the latter, viz., that clear knowledge is the one thing needful for the human mind, and by consequence that Christian faith does not really consist in the direct contemplation of the Supreme Being, in a submission to His authority, and a resignation to such disclosures about Himself and His will, be they many or few, distinct or obscure, as it is His pleasure to make to us, but in a luminous, well-adjusted view of the scheme of salvation, of the economy of grace, of the carrying out of the Divine Attributes into a series of providential and remedial appointments. He writes as follows:—

40 That is, I cannot believe anything which I do not understand; therefore, true Christianity consists, not in "submitting in all things to God's authority," His written Word, whether it be obscure or not, but in understanding His acts. I must

Every word of this extract tells in illustration of what has been drawn out above. And it is cited here merely in illustration; what judgment is to be formed of it shall be determined in its place. To resume the thread of our discussion.

understand a scheme, if the Gospel is to do me any good; and such a scheme is the scheme of salvation. Such is the object of faith, the history of a series of divine actions, and nothing more; nothing more, for everything else is obscure; but this is clear, simple, compact. To preach this, is to preach the Gospel; not to apprehend it, is to be destitute of living faith.

Of course I do not deny that Revelation contains a history of God's mercy to us; who can doubt it? I only say, that while it is this, it is something more also. Again, if by speaking of the Gospel as clear and intelligible, a man means to imply that this is the whole of it, then I answer, No; for it is also deep, and therefore necessarily mysterious. This is too often forgotten. Let me refer to

40   a doctrine *lying hid* in language, to be received in that

We shall now perhaps be prepared to understand

49   MR. ERSKINE'S "INTERNAL EVIDENCE."

Remarks on Mr. Erskine's "Internal Evidence."

49   After speaking

We have an intuitive perception, that the appearances of nature are connected by the relation of cause and effect; and we have also an instinctive desire to classify and arrange the seemingly confused mass of facts with which we are surrounded, according to this distinguishing relationship." pp. 1,2.

He then speaks

50   "If the actions attributed to GOD, by any system of religion, be really such objects as, when present to the mind, do not stir the affections at all, that religion cannot influence the character and is therefore utterly useless." – P. 23

51   the end of ends

τελος τελειοτατου

53- 54	Again: he says that "the reasonableness of a religion seems to him to consist in there being a *direct and natural* connexion between a believing the doctrines which it inculcates, and a being formed by these to the character which it recommends." But surely it is conceivable that reasons may exist in the vast scheme of the Dispensation (of the bearings of which we know nothing perfectly), for doctrines being revealed, which do not directly and naturally tend to influence the formation of our characters, or at least which we cannot see to do so. Here again we have the authority of Bishop Butler to support us, in considering that, "we are *wholly ignorant what degree of new knowledge* it were to be expected God would give mankind by Revelation, upon supposition of His affording one; or how far, or in what way, He would interpose miraculously, to qualify them to whom He should originally make the Revelation, *for communicating the knowledge given by it*; and to secure their doing it to the age in which they should live, and to secure its being transmitted to posterity."
54	What was the burning bush to Moses? The Almighty indeed so displayed Himself with a view to the deliverance of His people from Egypt; but Moses did not know that, when he went to see it; that was not his motive for going.

54	The author says: "These terms	The author says :- "The *reasonableness* of a religion seems to me to consist in there being a direct and natural connexion between a believing [its] doctrines, and being formed by the character which it recommends." "These terms

55   expresses himself? The immediate

expresses himself? Further, does he not also tell us the "reasonableness" of a religion seems to consist in there being a *direct and natural* connexion between a believing the doctrines which it inculcates, and a being formed by these to the character which it recommends? We need not dwell on the assumption hazarded in this passage; for surely it is conceivable that reasons may exist in the vast scheme of the Dispensation, (of the bearings of which we know nothing perfectly,) for doctrines being revealed which do not directly and naturally tend to influence the formation of our characters, or at least which we cannot see to do so. We have at least the authority of Bishop Butler to support us in considering that "we are *wholly ignorant what degree of new knowledge* it were to be expected GOD would give mankind by Revelation, upon supposition of His affording one; or how far, or in what way, he would interpose miraculously to qualify them to whom He should originally make the Revelation, for *communicating the knowledge given to it*; and to secure their doing it to the age in which they should live, and to secure its being transmitted to posterity."

But even though Butler, and other deep thinkers, had not said a word on the subject, the immediate

61   of Christianity." It is not

of Christianity. Any person who draws his knowledge of the Christian doctrines, exclusively or principally from such sources, must run considerable risk of losing the benefit of them, by overlooking their moral object; and, in so doing, he may be tempted to reject them altogether, because he will be blind to their *strongest evidence, which consists in their perfect adaptation to these objects.* The bible is the only perfectly pure source of Divine knowledge, and the man who is unacquainted with it, is, in fact, ignorant of the doctrines of Christianity, however well read he may be in the schemes, and systems, and controversies, which have been written on the subject.... The habit of viewing the Christian doctrine and the Christian character as two separate things has a most pernicious tendency. A man who in his scheme of Christianity, says, 'here are so many things to be believed, and here are so many things to be done,' has already made a fundamental mistake. The doctrines are the principles which must excite and animate the performance &c."

It is not

64   the character of Man? .... There is something

the character of Man? ...The first of these questions leads us to consider the Atonement as an act necessarily resulting from , and simply developing principles in the Divine mind, altogether independent of its effects on the hearts of those who are interested in it. The second leads us to consider the adaptation of the history of the Atonement, when believed, to the moral wants and capacities of the human mind...There is something

64   lucky coincidence," etc. – P.97. These last

lucky coincidence, not an adjustment contrived by the precarious and temporizing wisdom of this world, but that it is stamped with the uncounterfeited seal of the universal Ruler, and carries on it the traces of that same mighty will, which has connected the sun with his planetary train, and fixed the great relations in nature, appointing to each atom its bound that it cannot pass." pp. 97-100.

These last

65-   of danger," etc. – P.74.
66   The view

of danger, &c. " p. 74.
Again :

"The design of the Atonement was *to make mercy towards this offcast race consistent with the honour and the holiness of the Divine Government.* To accomplish this gracious purpose, the Eternal Word, who was God, took on himself the nature of man, and as the elder brother and representative and champion of the guilty family, he solemnly acknowledged the justice of the sentence pronounced against sin, and submitted Himself to its full weight of woe, in the stead of His adopted kindred. *God's justice found rest here;* His law was magnified and made honourable, &c." pp 102.103.

The view

66f
n

This passage has been misunderstood from the word *manifestation* not being taken in the sense intended by the writer. The word may either mean the making a *fact evident,* or making the *reason* of it *intelligible*; it is used above in the latter sense. Christ's atoning death does indeed proclaim the fact that God's justice *is* satisfied, but it does not contain in it an explanation *how* it came to be a satisfaction. In the former sense then it may properly be called a manifestation of God's justice; not in the latter, though it is often said to be so. The Atonement is a satisfaction to God's justice, in that His just anger was in matter of fact averted thereby from us sinners; but we do not know in what way it satisfied His justice to afflict Christ instead of us. This is a mystery, though many persons speak as if they *saw* the fitness of it. It *manifests* to our *comprehension* the love and holiness of God; it is a *proof* of love towards man, and of hatred of sin; it is not a *proof* to us that He is just; but must be taken *on faith* as a *result* of His being so. (Ed. 1838.) [On this point vide the Author's Discourse to Mixed

440

Congregations, No. 15, *init.*, p. 306, etc., ed. 4.]

67   the Divine character from nature and Scripture – a result which

the character, - which the Catholic Church has ever considered, but which

67   professed Revelation.

    Mr. Erskine attempts to explain away this remaining Mystery of the Dispensation, as others have done before him: they have suggested that the vicarious satisfaction of Christ acts as a salutary lesson, how severe God might be to those who sin, did they receive their deserts, a lesson to all races of intellectual beings, present and to come, in order to the stability of His moral government:

    "The design of the Atonement was to make mercy towards this offcast race *consistent with the honour and the holiness of the Divine Government.* To accomplish this gracious purpose, the Eternal Word, who was God, took on Himself the nature of man, and as the elder brother and representative and champion of the guilty family, He solemnly acknowledged the justice of the sentence pronounced against sin, and submitted Himself to its full weight of woe, in the stead of His adopted kindred. *God's justice found rest here*; His law was magnified and made honourable," etc.—Pp. 102, 103.

    Thus justice comes to be almost a modification of benevolence, or of sanctity, or the carrying out of a transcendent expediency. To such conjectures it is sufficient, as against Mr. Erskine, to answer, that a human hypothesis is not a divine manifestation.

    An illustration, somewhat to the same effect, is used in the Essays of Mr. Scott, of Aston Sandford.

    "The story

professed revelation.

    An additional remark is in place.* The difficulty here pointed out has been felt by writers who agree with Mr. Erskine, and they have contrived to get rid of the remaining Mystery of the Dispensation, resulting from the question of justice, as follows. They refer GOD's justice to the well-being of His creation, as a *final end,* as if it might in fact be considered a modification of benevolence. Accordingly, they say GOD's justice was satisfied by the Atonement, inasmuch as He could them pardon man consistently with the good of His creation; consistently with the due order of His government. This should be carefully noted, as showing us the tendency of the Rationalistic principle under review towards Utilitarianism. The following passage is given in illustration, from the Essays of Mr. Scott of Aston Sandford.

    "The story

68   The mystery remains, that the Innocent satisfied for the guilty.

71   real meaning; I do not see what else they can mean; however, let it be observed, that the principles which have been laid down in this discussion are not at all affected by any failing, if there be failing, in the illustration of them which I have been drawing by contrast, on this or any other point, from the work of Mr. Erskine.

real meaning; in the meanwhile, let it be observed that nothing which has been said in the former portions of this discussion is at all affected by any failing, if so, in having fully elicited it.

72   MR. ABBOTT'S "CORNER STONE."

Remarks on Mr. Abbot's "Corner Stone."

74   a recent Unitarian author

a Socinian writer

76   City after city, etc ... Our globe itself

City after city, &c. As the last breath of its atmosphere draws off from us, it leaves us in the midst of universal night, with a sky extending without interruption all around us, and bringing out to our view, in every possible direction, innumerable and interminable vistas of stars... Our globe itself

77   described them. .... God is

described them...The conception of childhood, and it one which clings to us in maturer years, that above the blue sky there is a *heaven* concealed, where the Deity sits enthroned, is a delusive one. God is

77   *all controlled?*"—Pp. 6-14.

This is eloquent writing; but this is not the place for dwelling on this quality of it; as to its doctrine, to speak plainly, it savours unpleasantly of pantheism. It treats the Almighty, not as the great God, but as some vast physical and psychological phenomenon. However, we are immediately concerned with the author's views, not on Natural, but on Revealed Religion. He continues thus:
"He is

all controlled ? pp.6-14.

It is impossible to do justice to one's feelings of distress and dismay on studying this passage, - to explain what one thinks of it, and why, - to convince a careless reader that one's language about it is not extravagant. Nor is it necessary perhaps, as it does not directly bear upon the subject before us,- to which I will hasten on. I interrupt the course of this exposition merely to put in a protest against the doctrine of it, which, to speak shortly and plainly, is pantheistic, and against the spirit of it, which breathes an irreverence approaching

on blasphemy. Should the reader think the tone of this paragraph is out of keeping with the remarks as yet made, he will see in a little time that Mr. Abbott does not allow one to preserve that didactic or critical air, which is commonly appropriate to a discussion such as the present. To proceed, however, with our immediate subject, the author's views, not of natural, but revealed religion :-
"He is

80   the *origin* of sin, the state of   as the origin of sin."
Does this mean original sin ?
  "the state of

80   of infants, the *precise*   of infants."
Is it possible he should thus talk ?
  "The *precise*

80   Is Almighty God Himself then, in Mr.Abbott's view, *physical*?

84   doing evil;" –
  (God punishes

doing evil;"
How unspeakably bold; when God says He does punish

84   a mere hypothesis   an altogether gratuitous statement

86   crucified Him." – Pp. 50, 51.

crucified Him." – Pp. 50, 51.
I put aside the utter unreasonableness of this last remark.

86   low   grovelling

87   we have utterly no warrant to speak

87   Mr.Abbott's way.

Mr.Abbott's way. In saying this, I am quite aware that the sensitiveness of a Christian mind will at once, without argument, shrink from a passage such as that commented on, but I say it by way of accounting for its aversion, which, perhaps, it may not be able to justify to others.

89	*hegemonic*	Ἡγεμονίκον

90 Surely such passages as these are simply inconsistent with faith in the Son of God.

Surely such passages as these are direct evidence of Socinianism.

95 especially opposed.

especially opposed.

OXFORD,
The Feast of the Purification.

N.B. For reasons, not necessary here to explain, it may be proper to observe, that this Tract was written before the commencement of 1836.

98 "Of his view of the Trinity, we may at least say that *it is intelligible*. But who will venture to say, that any of the definitions heretofore given of personality in the Godhead in itself considered, I mean such definitions as have their basis in the Nicene or Athanasian Creeds, are *intelligible and satisfactory* to the mind?" – P. 277.

99 *February 2,* 1836.

102 APOSTOLICAL TRADITION

ART. VIII. – *The Brothers' Controversy, being a genuine Correspondence between a Clergyman of the Church of England and a Layman of Unitarian Opinions.* London. 1835.

102 -4 A SMALL volume has just now made its appearance which well deserves notice, as being the record of what the title-page styles a "Brothers' Controversy"—that is, an interchange of letters between a clergyman and his Unitarian brother-in-law on the subject of the cardinal doctrine which separates them in religion.

The disputants are men of education and ability: the clergyman orthodox, serious, amiable; his opponent a man of candour and good sense; and "the whole"

This small volume consists, in accordance with its title, of a series of letters between a Clergyman and his brother-in-law upon the Trinitarian question, or rather upon those previous questions which the controversy involves, such as the mode of seeking the truth, the use of reason, and the like. It is certainly interesting, but painfully, so; and that because it presents the picture of two well-meaning men disputing about sacred subjects on insufficient or mistaken grounds, and so leaving off as they began. In

correspondence professes to be sent to the press "faithfully, without comment, without altering a word or syllable" on one side or on the other.

If men are to argue with each other, they must, of course, find some common ground to argue upon. What gives this controversy to us a painful interest is that this common ground, accepted on either side in this case, is nothing short of a common error, so that in the event the combatants leave off pretty much where they were when they began. It is better, certainly, to hold the truth on wrong grounds than not to hold it at all; but it is better still to hold it on grounds which, not being erroneous, cannot be made a starting-point for distinct religious error in the long run. If the principles on which a controversy is conducted are false or uncertain, it is likely to be little more than a trial of strength between the parties engaged in it, and is doomed to failure from the first.

Such is the judgment that we are obliged to pass on the assumptions on which these friends are content to place their issue. They take it for granted, as beyond all question, that, if we would ascertain the truths which Revelation has brought us, we have nothing else to do but to consult Scripture on the point, with the aid of our own private judgment, and that no doctrine is of importance which the Christian cannot find for himself in large letters there. Not, of course, that, in calling this a mere assumption and a mistake, we would for an instant deny that Scripture has one, and but one, teaching, one direct and definite sense, on the sacred matters of which it treats, and that it is the test of revealed truth; but, as Anglicans, we maintain that it is not its own interpreter, and that, as an historical fact, it has ever been furnished for individuals with an interpreter which is external to its readers and infallible, that is, with

thus speaking we should be grieved indeed to seem to imply that their respective opinions are, in any point of view, to be put on a level, the one not higher or better than the other. Socinianism is a deadly heresy, full of everlasting evil to its wilful professors, and influential moreover on their moral character; still there is a way of opposing it, which does but seem to justify, and does but conform them in it. And such in the main is that which is now exhibited in the work before us.

Both the disputants are men of some education and ability. The Clergyman is an orthodox, serious, and amiable man; and there is much of candour and good sense in his Unitarian adversary. The Editor professes to send their correspondence to the press, "giving the whole faithfully without comment, without altering a word or syllable;" and it is but fair to add that "the internal evidence," as he anticipates, is a voucher for the correctness of his representation.

Both parties acquiesce in the fundamental position, that truth of doctrine is to be gained from Scripture by each person for himself; and here lies the $\pi\rho\tilde{\omega}\tau o\nu$ $\psi\epsilon\tilde{\upsilon}\delta o\varsigma$ of the controversy, which in consequence becomes a trial of *strength* between the two individuals. The (so-called) Unitarian claims the right of assuming that -

an ecclesiastical Tradition, derived in the first instance from the Apostles—a Tradition illuminating Scripture and protecting it; moreover, that this Tradition, and not Scripture itself, is our immediate and practical authority for such high doctrines as these friends discuss. To attempt to prove against adversaries our Lord's Divinity and Incarnation by Scripture without Tradition, seems to us a mistake as great as that of attempting to speak a living language by studying its classics, or to ascertain physical facts by pure mathematics without experiment or observation.

We have said that the common ground, on which these disputants erect their arguments, admits of being used in behalf of error; but we must go further. Their first principle really is inconsistent with there being any certainties in Revelation whatever; for, if nothing is to be held as revealed but what every one perceives to be in Scripture, there is nothing that can be so held, considering that in matter of fact there is no universal agreement as to what Scripture teaches and what it does not teach: and why are one man's opinions to be ruled by the readings of another? The right which each man has of judging for himself *ipso facto* deprives him of the right of judging for other inquirers. He is bound to tolerate all other creeds by virtue of the very principle on which he claims to choose his own. Thus ultra-Protestantism infallibly leads to Latitudinarianism.

However, our proper business here is not to prove what is so very much of a truism, but to fulfil an intention which we expressed some time since, of attempting an exposition and an explanation of the Anglican doctrine on the subject. First, however, by way of introduction, we mean to devote a few pages to the volume which has given us the opportunity of redeeming our pledge.

The Unitarian, then, as we have said, claims the right of private judgment, and the clergyman grants it to him. Says the former, -

104   Says the clergyman in response, -

The Clergyman responds as follows: -

105 -6

Manifestos such as these profess to enunciate some large principle, maxim, or law, of axiomatic or enthymematic force, carrying its proof in its very wording; yet how evident an assumption is involved both in the former of these two statements and in the latter! If by "the Gospel" the Unitarian means the written document of Matthew or of Mark, of Luke or of John, then he has to prove, what he takes for granted, that that document is addressed to every individual inquirer of all times and places as a summary of the Christian religion; but, if he uses the word in its primary sense of "good tidings," then his "understanding," whether "powerful" or not, need in no sense be taxed by what is in its very idea nothing else than an oral message of peace, requiring on his part no sagacity, labour of thought, perseverance, or learning,—in short, no intellectual effort at all beyond that of faith. And in like manner, the clergyman must be asked on his part why it is that he advocates "the duty of free inquiry," and yet withdraws the "authority of Scripture" from its action? If inquiry is a healthy exercise as regards the creed, why not as regards the canon? but if we may not "tamper with" the authority of "Scripture," why with the authority of Tradition?

Of course both disputants will maintain that in fact no authoritative Tradition now exists, so as to admit of any such appeal to it as we have supposed; but they ought to bear in

Now these statements are true in one sense, false in another, and in this consists the fallacy of the reasoning. If by "the Gospel" the (so-called) Unitarian means the text of Scripture without note or comment, it is not true that this is "addressed to every individual;" but, unless he assumes this, it does not at all follow that "he, who does not use his most serious and powerful understanding in endeavouring to comprehend it, hides his best talent." Surely "the Gospel" which is "addressed to every individual" is the Gospel as dispensed by primitive teaching, as we shall show in the sequel, and this does not require "the powerful understanding" of any one. The true sense of Scripture, as regards all high theological points, has been determined by an unerring authority from the beginning. Again, it is a mistake in our clerical controversialist, to "advocate the duty of free inquiry." Those, of course, who are competent to the task may fairly inquire whether the teaching received in the Church from the first is, in matter of fact, Apostolic, as they may inquire whether the New Testament be the writing of Apostles and Evangelists; but unless they have first examined and disproved its claim to be so considered, they have so far no duty of free inquiry upon the text of Scripture. It will be observed that, in so saying, we are advancing no pretensions in behalf of the Clergy, as such, to the power

447

mind that others believe in its existence, if they do not, whereas the layman is so supremely unsuspicious that Anglicans hold it, as to bring it against us, as *a reductio ad absurdum*, that we grant St. Paul never to have taught the orthodox creed in his catechizings and preachings, but solely in certain *obiter dicta* of his extant Epistles. He asks with reference to the Book of Acts,—

of interpreting Scripture more than in behalf of the laity; we subject them both to an existing Apostolical teaching, explanatory of Scripture.

But the "Layman" goes further. Not only does he consider that we have no existing records of Apostolic teaching but those preserved in the Canon, but he seems most preposterously to think that St. Paul never taught his converts orally, that he instructed them only through his extant epistles. He takes this strange position for granted, and founds upon it an argument against the doctrine of our Lord's divinity. He asks—

106 Strange that a grave controversialist should impute to a school so sober as the Anglican so unnatural and poor a view of the process by which the Catholic truths were first presented to the world! Yet he reiterates,—

Strange, indeed, that any religionists should be able to satisfy themselves with so unnatural and meagre a view of the actual propagation of the Gospel! Yet it is parallel to an observation of Mr.Abbot, the American, that our Saviour was under the "disadvantage" of having "no press," whereby to act upon "the different portions of the community." Again -

106 An additional remark is in place here. Our disputant in this passage insists on the *silence* of the Apostles, year after year, on the subject of our Lord's Divinity, while protesting nevertheless that they had "taught *all* the gospel." Let it be observed, then, that in that very address delivered at Miletus, to which the Unitarian specially refers, as being that in which St. Paul declares that he has preached "the whole counsel of God," far from being silent as to our Lord's Divine nature, he even declares it with startling explicitness. He exhorts the elders whom he had called around him to "feed the flock of God, whom He hath purchased with His

It is inconceivable, doubtless, and incredible that he should have brought out a new and stupendous truth for the first time "in so cursory and elliptical a manner;" but then there *is* an explanation which the "Layman" overlooks. Perhaps it was *not* for the first time; this is surely *as* probable as that "God over all" in Rom. ix. 5, does not apply to Christ. Perhaps whoever converted the Romans had *taught* them this doctrine by word of mouth, as human beings might do now-a-days, and perhaps St.Paul knew it. Surely oral instruction is not one of modern" advantages," as Mr.Abbot would term them, as well as "the press."

448

own blood."

109	Elsewhere he enlarges on this view in a genuine Protestant tone: -	What follows, however, shows he *has* another reason for quoting the Fathers; viz. to make it clear *they cannot be used against him*. Dr.Priestly had pretended to assign the *date* of the first corruption of the Church's doctrine. "Justin Martyr is the first writer who mentions the miraculous conception." – (*Hist. Early Op.* vol. iv. P.107.) Our controversialist meets this assertion; and is employed accordingly, not in showing that the tradition of the Trinity is apostolic, but that it is *not* Justin Martyr's. His inadequate notion of the primitive creed has already been shown. But one or two extracts in addition will be in point: -
109	All this is true, but not the whole truth.	All this is most true, but not the whole truth. It is most true that Scripture is the sole verification of the creeds, as of all professed Apostolical traditions whatever; but it is as true that the creeds are the legitimate exposition of Scripture doctrine. Revealed truth is guaranteed by the union of the two, the creeds at once appealing to Scripture, and developing it. To take Scripture as the guide in matters of doctrine is as much a mistake as to take the Apostolical Tradition as the rule. What is written is a safeguard to what is unwritten; what is unwritten is a varied comment on a (necessarily) limited text.
110	After all, he takes the desperate step of referring the personal reception of the orthodox truth to a supernatural influence—a resolution of his difficulty which of course dispenses with the necessity of arguing altogether. At length his unlucky first principle is after all too strong for	After all, he refers the reception of the orthodox doctrine to the influence of the Holy Ghost, vouchsafed to the individual student of Scripture; a position which, of course, dispenses with the necessity of any formal proof of the doctrine at all. At the same time, consistently or inconsistently with

him; and, in spite of his appeal to Heaven and its inscrutable grace, overcome by the logic of his adversary, he allows himself to accept, however hesitatingly, those latitudinarian views which are the legitimate issue of the ultra-Protestantism with which he started. He condemns

this last belief, but in truth betraying a conviction of the insufficiency of his own arguments for the conversion of another, he condemns

112-3 Leaving, then, this halfway house to latitudinarianism, which this anxious clergyman has in all good faith done his best, on a Protestant basis, to put into habitable condition, let us go on to our proper subject—that is, to try whether, as regards such sacred dogmas as relate to our Lord's Person, a better stand against the liberalism of the day cannot be made by the Anglican theology. This theology teaches the existence, the uninterrupted continuance from the time of the Apostles, of a tradition of our Lord's Divinity—a tradition interpretative of what is also said of Him in Scripture, and dispensing, as far as its subject-matter extends, with the need of private judgment on the sacred text, as being the voice of Christendom in every time and place. This is the hypothesis which, *apropos* of Mr. Blanco White's recent work, we pledged ourselves some months back to consider; and, though our most careful treatment of it must be worse than imperfect, yet we shall gain as much as we aim at, if we succeed in any measure in directing the attention of our readers to an important subject, especially important in this day.

Much as we differ from Mr. White in the main conclusions to which he has come, he fully bears out what we have been saying above; he denies an Apostolical tradition of doctrine, and therefore he is consistently a Unitarian. He thinks that Scripture has no authorized interpreter, and that dogmatic

And here we take leave of a work which cannot but give pain to all who sympathise in our own views, the pain of seeing one who sincerely holds the truth of the Gospel, so little conscious of the grounds on which he holds it as to be unable to instruct a brother in error.

The argument for the existence of a known Apostolical Tradition on the subject of the Trinity, and therefore an unerring interpreter of Scripture so far, which has been taken for granted in the above remarks, was briefly stated in our January number in a review of Mr. Blanco White's late work. We then expressed an intention of treating the subject more fully than our limits admitted at the time, and we have now a fit opportunity of redeeming our pledge. That writer, it may be recollected, entirely dismissed the notion of any existing Apostolical interpretation of the sacred text, and maintained, on the contrary, that Scripture has no authorized interpreter of any kind, and that dogmatic statements are not part of the revelation. This is the ground long ago taken by Chillingworth and Locke; nor would Mr. Blanco White think we paid a bad compliment to himself to remark it. He would, of course, maintain that all clear-headed reasoners on the popular Protestant basis must necessarily proceed onwards to his own latitudinarian conclusions, if they are but fair to their own minds, and free from the

statements are no part of Revelation. Chillingworth and Locke thus spoke before him, nor would he consider that we paid him a bad compliment in saying so. Every clear-headed thinker, he would say, must so determine. Bible religion, so called, and a creed with anathemas never can stand together, except at the bidding of the law of the land, or under the prejudices of education, or with the inducements of self-interest. Men in general, it is true, are ruled by habit, by authority, by prejudice, by associations, and against these ordinary motives of action philosophers indeed may strive in vain; but still there is no doubt what will ever be the result, when an age or a people begins to think.

prejudices of education, and the inducements of interest. He would maintain that what is called "Bible religion" and the imposition of dogmatic confessions were irreconcilable with each other, except in a system, (if it deserved the name,) which was imposed by the law and intimately bound up with the security and well-being of the community. And thus he would account both for the acquiescence of the majority in what is in itself absurd, and the recurrence of the same objections and arguments, from time to time, on the part of men of more independent and enlarged minds. In consequence, he would rather exult than otherwise in finding the following passages in Chillingworth and others, anticipating his recent publication.

114   the semi-Arian,

114   And lastly, Dr. Hampden, to whose lot it has fallen to state objections to Catholic Truth in a more distinct shape than they have been found in the works of Churchmen for some time. He says:—

The argument contained in these extracts stands thus: "Scripture is the sole informant of religious truth; there is no infallible interpreter of Scripture, therefore every man has a right to interpret it for himself, and no one may impose his own interpretation on another." If it be objected that learning, scholarship, judgment, and the like, conduce to the understanding of this as of any other ancient book, it is replied, that true as this may be, these qualifications are on all sides of the doctrinal controversy, there being no opinion entertained by any party which has not been advocated at one time or another by confessedly learned, scholarlike, judicious, and able men. This being the case, no one has a right to say that his own opinion is important to anyone besides himself, but is bound to tolerate all other creeds by virtue of the very principle on which he has leave to form his own. The imposition, therefore, of dogmatic confessions on others by any set of religionists, is inferred to be an encroachment upon the Christian liberty of their brethren, who have in turn a right to their own private judgment upon the meaning of the Scripture text. Such is the latitudinarian argument.

Now we might put it to the common sense and manly understanding of any number of men taken at random, whether this, at first sight, is not a very strange representation, and such as they would never use in any ordinary matter of importance, any business they took an interest in or were earnest about. Surely no one in a confidential situation, on receiving instructions from his principal, which he could not altogether understand, would think himself at liberty to put any sense he pleased on them, without the risk of being called to account for doing so. He would take it for granted, that whether the instructions given were obscure or not, yet that they were intended to have a meaning, that they had one and one only meaning; and in proportion as he considered he had mastered it, he could not but also consider fellow-agents wrong who took a different view of it; and in proportion as he considered the instruction important, would he be distressed and alarmed at witnessing their neglect of his own interpretation. He might, indeed, if it so happened, doubt about the correctness of his own opinion, but he never would think it a matter of indifference whether he was right or wrong, he would never think that two persons could go on contentedly and comfortably together who took opposite views of their employer's wishes. Now all this fairly applies to the Scripture disclosures concerning matters of faith. First, it is plain, that faith is therein insisted on as an important condition of salvation; next, it is faith in certain heavenly and unseen truths; and this faith is expressly said to be "one," and is guarded by an anathema upon those who reject it. Now let us asks the disciples of Latitudinarianism *how* do they understand, in what assignable manner do they fulfil, the passages in which all this is conveyed? *What* is the doctrine therein spoken of, and belief in which is pronounced to be necessary for divine favour? Does it not consist of certain mysterious truths, and these undeniably propounded in the form of dogmas, (as in the beginning of St.John's Gospel,) so as to utterly preclude the notion of faith being but an acceptable temper of mind or character? And if so, is it not perfectly wild to imagine that knowledge of these doctrines is altogether unattainable? Can we conceive the allwise Governor of man to have made a solemn declaration of a doctrine which, after all, is so obscurely expressed, that one sense of it is not more obvious and correct than another? These strong arguments in favour of the determinateness and oneness of the doctrinal revelation contained in Scripture, can only be met by appealing to the fact that men do take different views of it; but this surely proves nothing; no more than the vicious or secular lives of the majority of men are a proof that one line of conduct is as pleasing to the Creator as another. No one denies that the revealed doctrines *may* be understood variously; but whether this possibility arises from God's indifference to such variety, or answers the purposes of a moral probation (which is the Catholic mode of accounting for it), is not at all decided by the mere fact of its existing.

But here Mr. Blanco White meets us with an objection which strikes at the root of our entire system. He is not content with denying the existence of an unerring guide for determining the theology of Scripture; he boldly advances a step, and maintains that no form of human language can possibly reveal in one certain sense those doctrines which we commonly suppose revealed; that words are necessarily the representatives of things experienced, and are simply words, and nothing but words, and not the symbols of definite and appropriate ideas, when used of things belonging to the next world. Now let it be observed clearly that this objection brings us upon quite a new ground; here it is that this ingenious writer seems to add something to the arguments of his predecessors in the same philosophy. Hitherto the position maintained by latitudinarians has chiefly been, not that Scripture may not possibly reveal to us heavenly truths in any measure, but that we cannot be sure that we individually have correctly ascertained them. The existence of an authorized interpreter, not the possibility of the revelation itself, has been questioned. But Mr. Blanco White denies of unseen truths, as well that they *can* be, as that they *have* been revealed to us under any one determinate view. Under these circumstances we shall claim of the reader the liberty of some little discursiveness, not so much, however, with the view of refuting an evident paradox, as of illustrating the subject itself. We call it a paradox, for if anything is plain, it is that Scripture does from time to time speak dogmatically on heavenly subjects. The writer in question, tells us that nothing respecting these subjects can be conveyed in language so definitely, as not to admit of the maintenance of the most contradictory theories respecting its meaning. With what *purpose,* then, does St. John, for instance, propose for our belief, "The Word was with God and was God," if nothing definite is gained by saying it, if the matter is left as vague as if he had not said? He cannot but have meant to convey something such, that it could not be anything else; and it is surely a paradox, to use a mild word, to maintain that Scripture attempts that which it cannot possibly accomplish.

It is a paradox for another reason. Would Mr. Blanco White deny that Christians of the English Church at this day, or again, that the Catholics of the fourth and fifth centuries, had embraced one certain view of the doctrine of the Trinity, and not another ? We do not say how far definite, complete, consistent; but still, so far forth as they had any view, a view of a certain kind, ascertainable, communicable, capable of being recorded? It seems hard to deny it, yet deny it he must, or else it will follow that human language *is* able to convey, circulate and transmit one certain sense of a mystery—a position which he denies in the abstract.

But this is not all. Human language, he says, cannot stand for *ideas* concerning the Divine Nature, i. e. for definite conceptions such as may be imparted to *us.* Let us, for argument's sake, grant it. Yet even then, at least it may stand for the real objects themselves. Nothing is more common in the usage of the world than what logicians call *words of second intention,* which mean nothing at all to those who are not conversant with the sciences which employ them for their own purposes. Almighty God might surely put His own meaning on human words, if it may be reverently said, and might honour them by making them speak mysteries, though not conveying thereby any notion at all to us. Here then at once we are admitted to the privilege of a dogmatic creed, in spite of Mr. Blanco White. Granting we do not *at all* understand our own words; nor did the Apostles when they were told their Lord should "rise from the dead:" they questioned *what it meant*. Still it is something after all to be intrusted with words which have a precious meaning, which we shall one day know, though we know it not now. Is it nothing to have a pledge of the next world? to have that given us which involves the intention of future revelations on God's part, unless His work is to be left unfinished? We will be bold to say that this is no slight point gained, if nothing else follows; a principle of mysteriousness, a feeling of deep reverence, of solemn expectation and waiting, is at once introduced into our religion. Allow, for argument's sake, that we have no data for disputing about the interpretation of the Scripture enunciations; well, then, we have an obligation for that very reason to preserve them jealously, to regard them awfully. Is it nothing that human words have been taken into the dialect of angels, and stand for objects above human thought? Is it nothing that when thus consecrated for a supernatural purpose, they have been given back to us to know and gaze upon, even though the outward form of them be the same as before? Let all "denominations of Christians" unite as far as this, to set apart and honour the very formulae contained in Scripture, keeping silence and forbidding all comment upon them, and they will have gone a considerable way towards the adoption of the Catholic *spirit* respecting them.

But again. We are told that human words *cannot* convey to us any idea, one and the same, of heavenly objects. Supposing it; but what then are we to say about the doctrines of natural religion? Has all the world gone wrong for ages in supposing it had a meaning in saying that God is *infinite* and *eternal?* Yet what known objects do these words stand for? It will be answered that they stand only for negative ideas; that we know what is finite, and we say that the Almighty is *not* finite either in His attributes, His essence, or His existence. Truly said; but may not we gain just this from the doctrinal formulae of the Gospel, whatever else we gain beside, viz. the *exclusion* of certain notions from our idea of the Son and Spirit? Thus when Christ is said to be the *Son* of God, we conclude thence that He is *not* a creature, *not* of a created essence, *dissimilar* from all created natures. Whether this be the right interpretation of the word *Son,* a fair inference from it, is another question; the instance is adduced here only with a view of exemplifying what is at least the negative force of the Scripture figures concerning divine objects. So again, the words "in the bosom of the Father," surely may suffice to exclude from our theology the notion of the Son being distinct in substance and existence from the Almighty Father. We assert it is possible that human language, as used in Scripture, should do as much as this,—it may make the truth of doctrine lie in one direction, not in another, whether there be an unerring arbiter of controversies or not,—it may have a *legitimate* meaning, so as to involve readers in guilt if they reject it, and make them amenable hereafter for not having had an unerring and sufficient judge of the Scripture text in their own breasts. And let it be observed that one great portion of the Catholic symbols and expositions actually is engaged in this department of limitation and admonition. Thus, in the creed of the Nicene Council, the anathema was attached to those who rejected these negative attributes of our Lord, viz. His having *no* beginning, being *not* of a created essence, and being unchangeable. Again; the following remarks of a recent writer on the conduct of the Fathers in the controversy are altogether in point, the more so as being incidentally introduced into his work. "They did not use these [figures] for more than shadows of sacred truth, symbols *witnessing against* the speculations into which the unbridled intellect fell. Accordingly, they were for a time inconsistent with each other in the minor particulars of their doctrinal statements, *being far more bent on opposing error than forming a theology.*" To the same purpose are the remarks of Gibbon, who thought he was exposing the Catholic creed, when he was really illustrating the foundation of all our doctrine concerning the Divine Nature, whether in natural or revealed religion. "In every step of the inquiry, we are compelled to feel and acknowledge the immeasurable disproportion between the size of the object and the capacity of the human mind. We strive to abstract the notions of time, of space, and of matter, which so closely adhere to all the preceptions of our experimental knowledge. But as soon as we presume to reason of infinite substance, of spiritual generation, *as often as we deduce any positive conclusions from a negative idea,* we are involved in darkness, perplexity, and inevitable contradiction."—*Gibbon,* ch. xxi. Yet, strange to say, this very author, who so unhesitatingly blames positive statements concerning the mysterious essence of God, shortly after indirectly assails the Catholics at Nicaea for being more eager to denounce the Arians than to explain the formula of the Homousion, and for allowing the Sabellians to shelter themselves under it, so that they would help them in subduing those who denied it. We do not by any means allow the correctness of this charge, but at least it represents the Catholics as doing the very thing which he had shortly before by implication recommended, confining their symbol to the expression of "a negative idea," and excluding from it "any positive conclusions." Gibbon probably was not aware (unless he was too much prejudiced to admit) that the doctrine he puts forward in the above extract with so much pomp and authoritativeness, was a principle taken for granted by the Catholic Fathers, and acted upon in their discussions. St. John Damascene, (e. g.) after speaking of Almighty God as immaterial and spiritual, proceeds, "But even this attribute gives us no conception of His *substance,* (ὐσία) any more than His eternity, unchangeableness, and the rest; for these declare not what He is, but what He is not; whereas, when we speak of the substance of any being, we have to say what it is, not what it is not. However, as relates to God, *it is impossible to say what He is as to His substance;* and it is rather more to the purpose to contrast Him with all beings (ὄντων) when we speak of Him The Divine Nature, then, is infinite and incomprehensible; all we can know about it is, that it is not to be known; and *whatever positive statements we make concerning God, relate not to His nature,* but to the accompaniments of His nature. For instance, where one calls Him good, just, wise, and so on, one does not speak of His nature, but of what belongs to it."* *[Footnote:* *

De Fid. Orthod. i. 4. n 2*]* It is clear, then, that in all their discussions concerning the *ὐσία, ὁμούσιον*, and the other subjects of the Trinitarian controversy, the Fathers started with the admission that they were arriving after all at no positive conclusions on the subject, only guarding against the introduction of error.

These observations seem to have carried us as far as this; first, that whereas the New Testament contains dogmatic statements concerning the Divine Nature, proposes them for our acceptance, and guards them with anathemas, it is clearly our duty to put them forth formally, whether we be able in our present state to attach a distinct meaning to them or not, just as the Blessed Virgin pondered our Lord's words, or the Apostles His prophecy of His resurrection, or the Prophets what "the Spirit of Christ signified," without understanding what they received. Next it would appear that these statements, however inadequate to express the divine realities, yet may convey to us at least some negative information about them, whatever else they convey,—in fact, may reveal to us the mysteries of the Trinity and the Incarnation in the same sense in which natural religion teaches us the truths connected with the being and attributes of God; so that we are under no necessity of giving up our interpretations of the Scripture statements, unless we are bound to go further, unless we are to be forced from our notions of religion altogether—forced into Pantheism, or some more avowed form of atheistical speculation.

But we do not mean to stop here, we mean to prove the existence of an authorized interpreter of Scripture, as well as the intrinsic definiteness of its text. The obvious remark on what has hitherto been said, would be, that it justified the use, not the imposition, of extra-scriptural statements; whereas some of the articles of the creed are not simply deduced from Scripture, but are made the terms of Communion, invested with the terrors of the invisible world, and so raised from human comments into the rank of inspired truth. Let us hear Dr.Hampden* *[Footnote: *This article was written before Dr.Hampden's appointment to the Divinity Professorship at Oxford, and has been in type since March last.]* on this subject, a writer who is introduced, not from any wish to come into collision with him, but because it has fallen to him.

115
-
122

We agree then with these writers in their strong protests against the assumption that private judgment is compatible with dogmatic certainty; but a man need not be a liberal because he is not a Protestant. Granting that Scripture does not force on us its full dogmatic meaning, that cannot hinder us looking for that meaning elsewhere. Perhaps Tradition is able to supply both interpretation and dogma. For that there should really be no definite, no dogmatic meaning at all in Scripture in its sacred revelations, is, to say the least, a very paradoxical position.

This is what these authors forget when they write so magisterially and fluently. They agree in ignoring the existence, in fact—nay, the probability, or the very possibility—of an Apostolical Tradition, supplementary to and interpretative of Scripture. The idea of such an aid to Christian teaching does not seem even to enter into their comprehension. They take for granted that the accumulated knowledge about our Lord and His religion which must have flowed from the lips of the Apostles upon

Now we quote this passage for the sake of meeting it; it contains a fair argument, which ought to be met. If a Christian is pained at it, as he may well be, it is not on account of the argument itself, or the putting it forward, or the necessity of encountering it, but to see an author so confident of its correctness as to allow himself in consequence to speak evil of that which others consider as the very word of God. Those who consider that the Creeds are the word of God, as truly, though not in the same sense, as the Scripture, and derived in the same way from transmission from the Apostles, of course will be shocked at finding their expressions treated as a "dogmatical and sententious wisdom." It is surely not modest or becoming in any one, so to connect his own opinions with the truth itself, as to assume that what *he* does not consider as the true view of the case, may be at once treated with contumely; it is, in fact, but a specimen in Dr. H. of the very error which he conceives he has detected in the Church Catholic itself. We suppose he would object to a controversialist who, in arguing

461

their converts, in their familiar conversations, catechizings, preachings, ecclesiastical determinations, prayers, was clean swept away and perished with the closing of the canon and the death of St. John. All the information of the great forty days came to nought, except so far as it accidentally strayed into one or other passage of the Apostolic Epistles. No one had ever any curiosity to ask the Apostles, during the remnant of their lives, any point of faith; no one had felt interest enough to ascertain from them who their Master was, why He died, and with what results. No one retained any memory of their teaching concerning God, or the human soul, or the unseen state, or the world of saints and angels, or the Church on earth; no one had sought for explanation of any verse in St. Matthew or St. Luke, of the doctrine contained in the first or in the sixth chapters of St. John, or of the symbol of "the Lamb," or of the nature of "the Spirit"; or, anyhow, nothing had been asked, nothing answered, but what already was recorded by a singular chance in the books of the New Testament, or at least nothing that was of the slightest importance and worth preserving. The great Churches of the day, at Corinth, Rome, Antioch, and Ephesus, the learned school of Alexandria, knew in the year A.D. 100 and onwards as much of all these matters as we do now, and no more. Their interpretations of the sacred writings were just on a par with the private judgments of clever commentators, orthodox or heterodox, now—one as good as another, conjectural, personal, inferential, unauthoritative. "Pious opinions," as they have been called, "theories upon facts," "dogmatical and sententious wisdom," "hieroglyphics, casting shadows," "metaphors explanatory of metaphors," "vain conceits,"

against a Calvinist, maintained, that if his opponent's view was the true one, the course of Providence was unjust and tyrannical. He would protest against hazarding the mercy and equity of the Divine dealings on the accident of the correctness of any human reasonings. On somewhat a similar ground we are offended at the above passage; not for the argument itself, which he is at liberty to put forth if he will; but at the lightness (as we view it) of his expressions about what others consider sacred statements, expressions which are not excusable, except a line of argument be true which we think a fallacy. "Let not him that girdeth on his harness, boast himself as he that putteth it off;" and let not the writer now in question assume the very position in debate, lest haply he be found to be scoffing against that very wisdom, which, "dogmatical and sententious" or not, has come by direct transmission independent of Scripture, from the Apostles themselves. We say, from the Apostles; and thus we advance a claim, which if substantiated, overturns the argument of Mr. Blanco White, Dr. Hampden, Chillingworth, Hoadly, Locke, and the rest from its very foundation. The doctrinal statements of the creeds are not to be viewed as mere deductions from Scripture, any more than the historical statements of those creeds,—the article of the Homousion any more than that of the Resurrection; but as the appropriate expressions and embodying of apostolical teaching, known to be such, and handed down in the Church as such from age to age. If this be so, it is in vain to argue about "various interpretations of Scripture," "pious opinions" and "theories" upon "facts," and of "differences of fallible judgments;" it is equally vain to talk of "hieroglyphics

"presumptuous impositions,"—it seems nothing better than these remains to us, these are all the leavings, if we are to credit Chillingworth, Locke, Hoadley and the rest, of the contemporaries and the disciples of our Lord.

Dr. Hampden, however, is bolder still, and goes farther: in order to deprive us of the barest dream of enjoying an Apostolical voice in illustration and confirmation of an Apostolical writing, he assures us that the very idea of Tradition is a mistake, that there is no such thing as a succession of preaching and hearing, that what is called Tradition teaches us—nay, professes to teach us—nothing more than Scripture, nothing at all, true or false; that it has nothing to do with the transmission of knowledge, and for this plain reason—because it is but the judgment of ecclesiastics exercised on Scripture. He says, "Tradition is *nothing more* than expositions of Scripture, *reasoned out* by the Church, and embodied in a code of doctrine" (p. 4). It is but the gold and silver of inspired writers taken out in coppers.

This surely is a most startling and paradoxical statement. We had fancied that St. Paul "*delivered*" to his converts "that which he also *received*;" we had fancied that St. Irenæus enumerated the succession of Bishops, through whom the tradition of gospel doctrine had come down to his day, and that Tertullian testified to a like tradition, and that Vincent of Lérins had even gained a name in theological history by appealing to the testimony, not of Scripture, but of antiquity and catholicity, as the warrant for the creed of his day. But it seems, after all, that the celebrated "Quod semper, quod ubique, quod ab omnibus," means nothing more than "The Bible, and the Bible only, is the religion of Protestants." Nor shall we surely be singular in being

casting shadows" and "metaphors explanatory of metaphors," and so forth. These "interpretations" turn out to be authoritative and original statements ; these "opinions" are doctrines; these so-called secondary metaphors are primary symbols given by Apostles or expressive of their known teaching. Will it be here said that now in turn we are boasting before our proof? No: we are complaining, and on this score, that this view which we consider the true one, has not attracted the attention either of Mr. Blanco White or Dr. Hampden.

This is the more remarkable in the case of the latter of these two writers, for he approaches the view in question, but strangely enough in one who has a name for learning, he notices it only to misunderstand it. He speaks thus of the doctrine of the Church of Rome. "In the Roman Catholic Church .... the question" (whether conclusions from Scripture have in themselves the authoritative force of real divine truth) "is formally decided in the affirmative, by the authority assigned to tradition in conjunction with Scripture; for *tradition is nothing more* than expositions of the text of Scripture, *reasoned out by the Church* and embodied in a code of doctrine."—p. 4. This, we confess, is to us information ; as we suspect it would be to Bellarmine also or any other Roman controversialist. We suspect that they would altogether disavow all claim to impose mere deductions from Scripture, as divine truths, in spite of their assumed infallibility in matters of doctrine. Rather it is one of their charges against Protestant communions, that these do impose, as matters of faith, what after all they believe only on the assurance of private judgment. They profess that their traditions exist quite independently of Scripture; that had Scripture never

thus surprised at such an issue of this great controversy. It will sound strange, we think, to the hosts of Protestant controversialists, especially to Hales and to Chillingworth, to Tillotson and Newton, who have in good faith taunted the Pope and his Bishops for so long a time as determining their creed by traditions of men and lying legends. Nor will it be a less surprise to the theologians of Rome themselves, whose very profession and boast it is that their Church has ever preserved inviolate, and is ever transmitting to posterity, not merely by the canon of Scripture, but by a living observance, that very religion of which the Apostles commenced the delivery, and which, they would say, Protestant doctors have supplanted by that process of deduction which after all is, according to Dr. Hampden, simply identical with Tradition itself.

Had Scripture never been written, Tradition would have existed still; it has an intrinsic, substantive authority, and a use collateral to Scripture. This surely, and nothing else, is the doctrine of Bellarmine and his co-religionists. "Totalis regula fidei," he says (*De V. D. non Scr.* 12), "est Verbum Dei, sive Revelatio Dei ecclesiæ facta, quæ *dividitur* in duas regulas partiales, Scripturam et Traditionem." And he has a chapter on the tests by which we ascertain what traditions are Apostolical; and among the uses of Tradition he places that of interpreting Scripture doctrine. He says, "It happens very often that Scripture is ambiguous and perplexed, so that, unless there be an interpreter who cannot err, it cannot be understood. Examples abound: the equality of the Divine Persons, the Procession of the Holy Ghost, etc. ... and many similar points admit, indeed, of being *deduced* from the sacred writings; but with such difficulty that, if Scripture

been written, they would have existed still, and that they form a collateral not a subordinate source of information to the Church. We must repeat our utter surprise at such a statement as the above, from such a quarter, when even the popular work of Bishop Jebb would have warned Dr. Hampden of its incorrectness. "The Church of Rome maintains," he says in his Essay on the Peculiar Character of the English Church, "not only that there are two rules of belief, but these two rules are *co-ordinate;* that there is an *unwritten,* no less than a written *word of God;* and that the authority of the former is *alike definitive with the authority of the latter.*" Reluctant as we may be to set before our readers a truth as plain as the fact of the existence of the Roman Church itself,—its maintenance of the *intrinsic* and *independent* authority of the unwritten Word,—yet we must insist upon it when writers indulge themselves in so extravagant a liberty of speculation. Let us turn to the words of Bellarmine. "Totalis regula fidei," he says, (De Verb. Dei non Script. 12), est Verbum Dei, sive *revelatio* Dei Ecclesiaa facta, quas dividitur in duas regulas partiales, Scripturam et *traditionem.*" And he has a chapter on the tests by which we ascertain what traditions *are* apostolical. Again, among the uses of tradition he places that of *interpreting* Scripture doctrine. "Saepissime Scriptura ambigua et perplexa est, ut nisi ab aliquo, qui errare non possit, explicetur, non possit intelligi; igitur sola non sufficit. Exempla sunt plurima: nam aequalitas divinarum personarum, processio Spiritus Sancti à Patre et Filio, ut ab uno principio, peccatum originis, descensus Christi ad inferos, et multa similia *deducuntur quidem ex sacris litteris, sed non adeofacile,* ut si *solis* pugnandum

testimonies were the sole weapon, the controversy with heady men would never come to an end." And Bossuet in like manner (*Expos.*, ch. xvii., xviii.): "Jesus Christ, having laid the foundation of the Church by preaching, the unwritten word was consequently the first rule of Christianity; and, when the writings of the New Testament were added to it, its *authority was not forfeited on that account*; which makes us receive with *equal veneration* all that has been taught by the Apostles, whether in writing or by word of mouth." Yet Dr. Hampden rules it absolutely in half a sentence, that "Tradition is *nothing more* than expositions of Scripture *reasoned out* by the Church."

Nor will Anglican writers be less surprised at a statement which, if it can be maintained, is fatal to the authority of Vincent of Lérins, and to the corner-stone of our theology. Certainly, if Tradition is but a subtle mode of arguing and deducing from the Bible, the interference of critics of our theological school in "the Brothers'" controversy is a simple blunder, as we shall have no case as against the combatants and the first principle which they hold in common. But what would Bishop Jebb say to the doctrine that Tradition was nothing else than Scripture inference? Jebb considers that the Church of Rome has erred, not certainly in fancying Tradition to be all one with Scripture, but in considering the former as so separate from the latter, and so independent of it, that it may be true and authoritative, though it says what Scripture is silent upon. "The Church of Rome," he says, "maintains, not only that there are two rules of belief, but that these two rules are co-ordinate; that there is an unwritten, no less than a written Word of God, and that the authority of the former is alike definitive with the authority of the

sit Scripturae testimoniis, *nunquam lites cum protervis finiri possint.* Notandum est enim, duo esse in Scripturâ, voces scriptas, et sensum in eis inclusum Ex his duobus primum habetur ab omnibus; quicunque enim novit litteras, potest legere Scripturas: at secundum non habent omnes, nee possumus in plurimis locis certi esse de secundo, *nisi accedat traditio.*—Ibid. 4. In like manner Bossuet, (Exposition, ch. 17, 18,) "Jesus Christ having laid the foundation of his Church by preaching, *the unwritten word was consequently the first rule* of Christianity; and, when the writings of the New Testament were added to it, its *authority was not forfeited on that account;* which makes us receive with *equal veneration all that hath been taught by the Apostles,* whether in writing or by word of mouth .... And a most certain mark that a doctrine *comes from the Apostles,* is, when all Christian Churches embrace it, without its being in the power of any one to show when it had a beginning .... Bound inseparably, as we are, to the authority of the Church, by the Scriptures which we receive from her hand, we learn tradition also from her; and by means of tradition the true sense of the Scriptures. For which reason *the Church openly professes, that she says nothing from herself; that she invents no new doctrine;* she only *declares* the Divine Revelation, by the interior direction of the Holy Ghost, who is given to her as her teacher." Here mention of the third person of the Blessed Trinity is introduced, not as aiding the Church to interpret Scripture, but as guiding her into a right discrimination and application of apostolical tradition. The reader probably is by this time tired of authorities, or we might refer to the words of the Tridentine Decree,

latter." What, again, must the present Bishop of Lincoln think of this same doctrine, who is still more explicit than Jebb in enunciating Jebb's principle, and whose language is so strong and so apposite to the course of thought which we are pursuing, that we cannot refrain from setting it before the reader?

"If we mistake not the signs of the times," says Dr. Kaye, in his work upon Tertullian, "the period is not far distant when the whole controversy between the English and Romish Churches will be revived, and all the points in dispute again brought under review. Of those none is more important than the question respecting Tradition; and it is therefore most essential that they who would stand forth as the defenders of the Church of England should take a *correct and rational view* of the subject—the view, in short, *which was taken by our divines at the Reformation. Nothing was more remote from their intention than indiscriminately* to condemn all Tradition ... What our Reformers opposed was the notion that men must, upon the mere authority of Tradition, receive as necessary to salvation doctrines not contained in Scripture ... In this, as in other instances, they wisely adopted a middle course: they neither bowed submissively to the authority of Tradition, nor yet rejected it altogether."—P. 297, ed. 1826.

In another place he speaks still more distinctly. "Tertullian," he says, "appeals to Apostolical Tradition, to a rule of faith, not *originally* deduced from Scripture, but delivered by the Apostles orally to the Churches which they founded, and regularly transmitted from them to his own time. How, I would ask, is this appeal inconsistent with the principles of the Church of England, which declares *only* that Holy

upon which the foregoing passages are the comment.* *[Footnote:* * Sacro-sancta .... Tridentiiia Synodus . . . omnes libros tam veteris quàm novi Testaraenti .... necnon *traditiones* ipsas, turn ad fidem turn ad mores pertinentes, tanquam *vel ore terms à Christo* vel *à Spiritu Sancto dictatas,* et *continuâ successione in Ecclesiá Catholicá conservatas,* pari pietatis affectu ac reverentiâ suscipit et veneratur.- *Sess. quart.]* And this matter is perfectly understood by clear-headed men, as Hales and Chillingworth, who, though they deny the fact, yet understand the Roman Church's assumption, that its tradition comes directly from the Apostles, independently of Scripture; whereas Dr. Hampden has ruled it in half a sentence that "tradition is *nothing more* than expositions of the text of Scripture, *reasoned out by the Church,* and embodied in a code of doctrine;" stating what is neither agreeable to the fact nor to the Roman view of it; for no one will say, for instance, that the doctrine of indulgences either is and is professed by the Romanists to be primarily reasoned out from Scripture. Nay the decree of the Council of Trent expressly says "Cum potestas conferendi indulgentias *à Christo Ecclesiæ concessa sit,* atque hujusmodi potestate, divinitus sibi traditâ, *antiquissimis temporibus ilia usa fuerit,*" &c, not a word being said of any Scripture sanction for the use of them. Indeed this is the very point of difference between the Romanists and ourselves. The English Church no where denies the existence of apostolical traditions, and their authority in the interpretation of Scripture; so far we do *not* dissent from the Romanists. But what we do deny is the independent and substantive power of tradition in matters of faith, where Scripture is silent,—the

Scripture *contains* all things necessary to salvation? Respecting the *source* from which the rule of faith was *originally* deduced, our Church is silent."—P. 587.

This is the doctrine of genuine Anglicanism; and surely it embodies a principle as consonant to the considerateness of Revealed Mercy, as it is welcome to those who would profit by that Revelation to the full. Certainly there are strong reasons, prior to evidence for weak human nature to desire, nay, almost to expect such an informant as we are supposing, to help them in determining the meaning of Scripture where the clearness of its teaching is not on a level with its importance. Such a guide is not a superfluity. Scripture is not written in a dogmatic form, though there are dogmatic passages in it; it contains portions and tokens, nay, the promise, of a boon, which nature so intimately desiderates that it betakes itself to false teachings if it cannot get true. To the millions for whom Redemption has been wrought, creeds and catechisms, liturgies and a theological system, the multitudinous ever-sounding voice, the categorical, peremptory incisiveness, the (so to say) full chime, of ecclesiastical authority, is a first necessity, if they are to realize the world unseen. Yet, strange to say, this need is denied by writers, because they cannot have it supplied just in the way they wish. Dr. Hampden here again distinguishes himself by paradox. He "asks," in his *Bampton Lectures* with the Unitarian above quoted, "whether it is *likely* that an Apostle would have adopted the form of an epistolary communication for imparting *mysterious propositions* to disciples with whom he enjoyed the opportunity of personal intercourse, and to whom he had already 'declared the whole counsel of God'" (p. 375). This argument, let it

right of the Church to impose doctrines on the *mere* authority of tradition, which the Council of Trent has done, for instance, in the above cited decree on indulgences. So that it would seem that Dr. Hampden has not only passed over the question of the apostolicity of the creeds, in which we conceive lies the refutation of his peculiar theory; but he has actually missed that very point in the Roman Church's doctrine, in which she differs from our own.

Here we take leave of Dr. H. for the present, and should feel pleasure if we could be saved the necessity of recurring to him. Other objections will be made to the notion of the authority of the creeds, as a contemporaneous comment upon Scripture, which we must try to clear off as expeditiously as we can. When an educated man of the present day first hears it said that the creeds are the expressions of apostolical traditions, he is at once annoyed, and listens with suspicion. Now why is this? First it is because he has never heard the view stated before, and he feels that doubt which spontaneously rises when the mind is put out of its usual way of thinking. He does not know what the principle may lead to; he does not see how far it may carry him towards popery; he does not see its bearings, its limitations, or its grounds. This is all very natural; yet on second thoughts perhaps he will take heart and be more rational. We say "more rational," for there are certainly fair grounds of reason, prior to evidence, to desire, nay almost to expect, such an informant as we are offering to him about the meaning of Scripture. Such a guide is surely very much wanted. Scripture is not written in a dogmatic form, though there are dogmatic passages in it; it contains the portions and tokens of a

be observed, is intended to prove that Christianity is not dogmatic, because Scripture is not dogmatic in its form or its profession. Let us suppose that there was not one dogmatic sentence in the New Testament—let the argument be, Christianity is not dogmatic, because its Scriptures are not dogmatic,—is it not far more reasonable to argue that, considering the need, if Christianity is not dogmatic in its books, we must look for its dogmas elsewhere?

We shall think it safe to assume the latter proposition as a sound one, and under its controversial force and the countenance of the learned Prelate whose words are given above, we now proceed to apply the doctrine of Apostolical Tradition to the purposes of that controversy which "the Brothers" attempted to settle on the ground of private judgment.

theological system, without itself being such. It promises dogmatic statements without fully supplying them. What then is so natural as to suppose that Divine Mercy has somewhere or other supplied this desideratum? and what antecedent improbability is there in the creeds containing the heads and subjects of the teaching required? It is worth remarking, however, that this very character of Scripture, which seems by its form and matter to point at the creeds and the traditionary teaching connected with them as its due complement, has been paradoxically brought as an argument for dispensing with them. *Assuming* that in Scripture we have the model and type of all Christian teaching, it has been decided, that since the creeds, as being dogmatic, are unlike Scripture, that therefore they are no part of Christianity, which is about as rational as to conclude (according to St. Paul's illustration) that because the eye is not the hand, therefore it is not of the body; or because England has a king, therefore its constitution is a development of the monarchical principle; or that because it has popular institutions, therefore it has no king. We must surely take things as we find them in matter of fact, we must deny ourselves in theories, (latitudinarian as well as what Dr. Hampden calls "scholastic,") and use *a priori* reasonings not to prove but to recommend our conclusions. Moreover, in the present instance, it is humbly conceived that antecedent probability, as far as it goes, is for, not against, the apostolical authority of the creeds. Dr. Hampden came into our minds in this last sentence, because here too he has indulged in a seeming paradox as on other points. Speaking in depreciation of dogmatic statements, he uses an argument which tells so fatally against himself, that readers must look over it twice to be sure that they have not mistaken his meaning. "I ask," he says in his Bampton Lectures, in a passage which has been much quoted of late, "whether it *is likely* that an Apostle would have adopted the form of an epistolary communication for imparting mysterious propositions to disciples with whom he enjoyed the opportunity of personal intercourse, and to whom he had already 'declared the whole counsel of God?'" —p. 374. This argument, let it be observed, is to go to prove that Christianity is not dogmatic, because Scripture is not; and we do not know which most to admire— the boldness of the main position, or the felicity of a mode of handling it, which oversets the reasoning on which it is founded. It presents a curious contrast to the reasoning of the present Archbishop of Dublin in his Essay on Creeds; who advocates the same theory on the ground that there *is* no Apostolical teaching now extant, thus failing characteristically, not in the reasoning, which is most intelligible, but in the matter of fact.

It will serve at once to explain and to defend the position we have taken up against Dr. Hampden, to express ourselves in the language of the learned and soberminded prelate, who is at present in the possession of the see of Lincoln. "If we mistake not the signs of the times," he observes in his work upon Tertullian, "the period is not far distant when the whole controversy between the English and Romish Churches will be revived, and all the points in dispute again brought under review. Of those none is more important than the question respecting tradition; and it is therefore most essential that they who stand forth as the defenders of the Church of England should take a correct and rational view of the subject, the view in short which was taken by our divines at the Reformation. *Nothing was more remote from their intention than indiscriminately to condemn all tradition. . . .* What our reformers opposed was the notion that men must, upon the *mere* authority of tradition, receive, *as necessary to salvation,* doctrines *not contained in Scripture* .... With respect to the particular doctrines, in defence of which the Roman Catholics appeal to tradition, our reformers contended that some were directly at variance with Scripture ; and that others, far from being supported by an unbroken chain of tradition from the apostolic age, were of very recent origin, and utterly unknown to the early Fathers ... In this, as in other instances, they wisely adopted a middle course; they neither bowed submissively to the authority of tradition, nor yet rejected it altogether. We at the present day must tread in their footsteps and imitate their moderation, if we intend to combat our Roman Catholic adversaries with success."—p. 297, ed. 1826. In another place he speaks still more explicitly. "Tertullian," he says, as if citing the statement of a writer he was animadverting on, "appeals to apostolical tradition, to a rule of faith, not *originally* deduced from Scripture, but delivered by the Apostles orally to the Churches which they founded, and regularly transmitted from them to his own time. How, I would ask, is this appeal inconsistent with the principles of the Church of England, which declares *only* that Holy Scripture *contains* all things necessary to salvation? Respecting the source, from which the rule of faith was *originally* deduced, our Church is silent."—p. 587.

Granting, however, there was such an apostolical tradition (e. *g.*

concerning the doctrine of the Trinity) it may be a question with many persons whether we at this day know for certain what it was. The Creed indeed bids fairest for being reputed such ; but though definite in its articles and of primitive antiquity, a question might arise as to its strict apostolicity. On the other hand it might be plausibly asked, if even the Creed be not for certain of apostolic origin, what doctrinal statements can safely be considered as such. It may be right therefore in this place to offer some brief remarks on the *relation* existing between the Creed and apostolical tradition; and here again we encounter at once an observation of Dr. Hampden's. He observes that "it will be said by some advocates of our Church that .... the doctrines expressed in its formularies .... are derived from the confessors and doctors of the primitive ages of the Church—they have descended to us in pure stream from the fountains of orthodoxy, &c." To this he replies; "Is this correct in matter of fact? Are the doctrines *as expressed in our formularies,* (for this is the point at issue, and not whether the divine truths which they are intended to guard, are the same or not,) precisely those which the primitive Church declared ? If we look to the course of controversy we must see, I think, that the dogmas have taken their mould and complexion from the discussions of subsequent periods, until they reached a speculative accuracy of expression to which subsequent discussions could not add."—*Obs.* pp. 23, 24.

Not for the sake of interfering with Dr. Hampden, but for the sake of an important question, we will here say a few words in explanation of this subject; are the dogmatic statements of the Creeds, or are they not, of Apostolic origin? the case seems to be as follows:—

It is quite certain from the writings of Irenaeus, Tertullian, and Vincent, not to mention other authorities, that from the times of the Apostles, there was a certain body of doctrine in the Church Catholic called the dogma fidei or depositum transmitted from bishop to bishop, and taught to every member of it. It was too vast, too minute, too complicated to be put into writing, at least in times of persecution and proselytism; it was for the most part conveyed orally, and the safeguard against its corruption was, first, the unanimity of the various branches of the Church in declaring it; next the canon of Scripture which acted as a touchstone, not indeed measuring it and limiting it, but coinciding with it in all its greater points and verifying both its outlines and occasionally its details also. As regards its outlines this dogma, or regula fidei, as it was called, was from the first fixed in a set form of words called the Creed, the articles of which were heads and memoranda of the Church's teaching, and as such were rehearsed and accepted by every candidate for baptism by way of avowing his adherence to that entire doctrine which the Church was appointed to dispense. These articles varied somewhat in the different branches of the Church; but, inasmuch as they were but heads and tokens of the Catholic doctrine, and when developed and commented on implied each other, this argued no difference in the tradition of which they were the formal record. This account of the matter, if correct, shows us the mistake of considering, as some have done, that the fact of the Creed being the initiatory confession of the Church, involved a latitudinarian principle in primitive times. This is maintained by

Episcopius, who argues as if because the words "Son of God" stood nakedly in some of the early creeds, therefore they might allowably be taken in any sense which the humour of individuals imagined, as well as in that one Catholic interpretation in which the Nicene fathers afterwards developed it.* *[Footnote:* * "Symbola certe Ecclcsiæ ex ipso Ecclesiæ sensu, non ex hæreticorum cerebello exponenda sunt. Svmbola Ecclesiæ non tenet, qui aliter quam Ecclesia intelligit."— Bull. Judicium Eccl.Cath. c. 5, § 10.*] Bishop Bull shows this was not true as regards that high article of doctrine, and the same might be showed of all the rest; so that if one wished a clear and available definition of heresy, perhaps one could not find a better than this, that it is a wilful rejection of any article of the Creed in that sense in which the early Church understood and taught it. And here, by the bye, we have light cast at once on a question which may, for what we know, perplex us in this day before many years are over. It is notorious there are persons in the Church who wish its recognition of baptismal regeneration to be removed. Now inasmuch as one of the articles of the Nicene Creed witnesses to the "one baptism for the remission of sins," and since any how the doctors of the early Church would so explain the less complete form of words which occurs in the Apostles' Creed, "the forgiveness of sins," it follows, if the above view is correct, that to deny baptismal regeneration is *heresy,* and that a Church which indulged its members in such denial would have forfeited its trust and have done much to deprive it of any claim upon our allegiance. But to return to the subject immediately before us:—it would seem from what has been said that the very articles of the Creed are not Apostolic in such a sense that we can pronounce them to be literally spoken by the Apostles; but they are some among a great multitude of statements of a similar kind, none of which indeed can be identified as literally Apostolic, but which altogether go to convey that view which is Apostolic, and might be ascertained to be Apostolic in the same way in which we become acquainted with each others' views in any matter, not relying on this or that expression, but mastering it from the general bearing and scope of each others' conversation; and this is the view to be taken of certain words, as *ὁμούσιος*, *θεοτόχος* and the like, which at different times were assumed as the criterion of certain doctrines which required the seal of public authority. They are representations, more or less arbitrary, as the case might be, of the Apostolical tradition on the subject of them. They were assumed after a careful consideration and ascertaining of the doctrine which they symbolized. Received opinions were compared together, between the Churches, as they might now-a-days. Bishop compared notes with bishop, and brought out his meaning in the clearest and fullest form. This implied time and accurate thought, freedom of discussion, questioning, reviewing, and all not for the sake of forming a new doctrine, but in order to ascertain the old. The next question was how this one and the same sense in which all parts of the Church were found to agree could be best expressed and perpetuated; and the word or phrase selected for the purpose, and generally from the diction of antiquity, became the expression and representative of the Apostolical tradition, without having any special claim above others to be considered of

Apostolical origin itself.*
[Footnote: * Vide Vincent. Lerin. Comm. 32 fin.*]*

It has taken a long time indeed to clear our ground; but now at length we hope to proceed without impediment to the *proof* of the doctrine which we have been hitherto explaining. After all, it will be asked, *it* there any ascertainable Apostolical Tradition ? Let us see.

122
-5

First, then, every one knows that a definite doctrine concerning our Lord's origin and nature is taught at this day all over the Church, and that this doctrine, in matter of fact, was, strictly speaking, *taught* to the present generation—not learned by it so much as taught it—*taught* it by the generation immediately before it, not gathered in the first instance by its own inferences from Scripture. This was the fact; and there is as little doubt that that previous generation of men was in like manner taught in the same matters by their own predecessors; and further, that this process of transmission and acceptance—that is, of tradition—has gone on for many centuries: nay, we might say, up to the very first or Apostolic century; but (not arbitrarily to place it so high), at least to the fourth century of our era—that is, up to little more than 200 years from the death of St. John. We will stop, then, at the year 325, being sure that no one will deny that our Lord's Divinity has ever since the fourth century been an article of the Christian creed, and has ever since been acknowledged through the whole extent of Christendom as a fundamental, or rather as the cardinal, doctrine of revealed religion. The question is, whether the events of A.D. 325 and the following years do not bear conclusive testimony to the fact that this great {123} article of faith, then

First, every one knows that a certain doctrine concerning our Lord's nature is taught at present all over the Church, and that this, in matter of fact, was not gained from Scripture in the first instance by the existing generation (though it is fully attested and verified by Scripture), but from the teaching of the generation immediately preceding. This process of transmission and reception has gone on, at least for many centuries; nor is there anything antecedently absurd in the notion, nay it is agreeable to what meets us at first sight, that the process should have been so conducted, independently of Scripture, from the first. Of course, when we come to examine into the course of the history, decisive objections to this supposition may, for what we know, present themselves; but there is nothing in the actual face of things to throw discredit upon it. On the contrary, there is this strong probability against the doctrine ever having been strictly deduced from Scripture, that it is not sufficiently on the surface of the sacred text to force itself as Scriptural upon the observation of men at large. At first sight it is not likely, to say the least, we think no candid man will say it is likely, that the Catholic doctrine, systematized as it is, should be in matter of fact a mere deduction from Scripture, even though it be (as it most surely is) quite

publicly acknowledged, was also taught 200 or 250 years before by St. John and St. Paul—whether the year 325 does not transmit to 1800 what it had received from A.D. 60 or 90. We answer this question in the affirmative, and our reasons are as follows:—

In the second decade of the fourth century a controversy arose in Alexandria about our Lord's proper Divinity. It was brought before the Bishop, and, when his authority was unequal to the settlement of it, it led to the summoning of the first Ecumenical Council at Nicæa, in A.D. 325, which was attended by 318 bishops from all parts of the world, as representatives of the whole Church Catholic. Out of this number so collected more than 300 at once pronounced that that doctrine concerning our Lord, such as we hold it now—viz., that He was "God of God"—was the doctrine taught by the Apostles in the beginning. This was their concurrent and energetic testimony, as history records it; and now, was or was not that testimony practically decisive on the question what it was that after our Lord's departure the Apostles had taught about our Lord in Jerusalem, Antioch, Ephesus, Alexandria, and Rome?

Here, then, first let it be observed that no external authority interfered to incline them to the doctrine to which they subscribed. Constantine had originally considered the dispute which led to their meeting as little better than a question of words, and had written to Alexandria to order both parties engaged in it to tolerate each other and keep quiet. On finding, however, both before and at the Council, the general opinion to be against Arius, the originator of the disturbance, he changed his course in favour of orthodoxy, at the cost of abandoning thereby his personal friends, and zealously defended the side

consistent with it. To use a familiar illustration, it is like a key to a lock, of independent workmanship, but subordinate use. We do not say that no acute and subtle mind, no as individual, might not draw it forth and develope it from Scripture as we find it in the Church, nay, add other and more complicated distinctions to it; it is its general adoption from so early an age which proves incontrovertibly, that, whether it be by revelation or not, whether it be (as we believe) from the Apostles, or (as others have said) from the Platonists, or Paganism, or in whatever way, it is from sources historically distinct from the written word which is the verification of it. The instances which happen daily of the differences of view which take place as to the doctrine, when men, however learned and clearheaded, do attempt to deduct from Scripture their "pious opinions," as Dr. Hampden terms them, prove that the knowledge of it which we enjoy does not come from the mere study of Scripture. Let us now approach nearer to this phenomenon and view it at that date, when even heretics will allow it did exist, whatever questions they raise about the earlier centuries, we mean in the fourth century. Assuming that the Church's belief now is the same as its belief then, let us observe what took place in the year 325. At that date, in consequence of a controversy which occurred on the subject of our Lord's Divinity between the bishop of Alexandria and one of his clergy, a council was held of 318 bishops collected from all parts of Christendom. No such general meeting had ever before taken place; no opportunity had before occurred for adjusting their notions one with another. Yet out of this number so collected above 300 agreed in the maintenance of that doctrine which is now known by

professed by the majority. After a few years he changed back again, and exposed the Bishops and populations of the Church to the revenge of an exasperated faction. Constantius, who succeeded him, also sided with the heretics, and far more decidedly. He fiercely persecuted the orthodox, assembled Council after Council to destroy the authority of the Nicene, and at the end of his reign dragooned 400 bishops in the West and 150 in the East into giving an indirect denial to the doctrine witnessed to and solemnly professed in 325. Thus political influences told strongly against, not for, the triumph throughout Christendom of the tradition of orthodoxy. The creed of Nicæa was not the imposition of secular power.

Nor did it proceed from a powerful coalition of mutually sympathizing and allied hierarchies. On the contrary, there were long-existing rivalries between those several Churches which took part in the Council. There had been at an earlier date serious disputes between Rome and Ephesus, Rome and Carthage, Rome and Antioch, Rome and Alexandria; and, if it be said that the Bishop of Rome himself was not at Nicæa—only delegates from him—in the same degree as his influence would not be felt there, is it remarkable that he should have so zealously co-operated in the West in carrying out the determinations of the East. Moreover, whatever local influence there was of a theological character at Nicæa was in favour of the heresy, for a member of the original Arian party, and a friend of Arius, was in possession of its see. Further, there was an old jealousy between Alexandria and Antioch, which, as far as it was allowed to act, would tell powerfully in the direction of blunting or thwarting any such keen assertion of the orthodox doctrine as the Council

the title of Orthodox. This is the phenomenon, and on it we make the following remarks.

First, then, let it be observed that no external authority interfered to incline them to the doctrine to which they subscribed. Constantine had originally considered the dispute which led to their meeting as little better than a question of words, and had written to Alexandria to order both parties engaged in it to tolerate each other and keep quiet. On finding however the general opinion before and at the council in favour of orthodoxy, he changed his course, though he abandoned thereby his personal friends, and zealously defended the side professed by the majority. After a few years he gradually changed back again, and exposed the cause of orthodoxy to the revenge of a disappointed faction, Constantius, who succeeded him, took a still more decided part against it. Thus no political influences can be assigned as the cause of the general agreement, such as for instance may be objected to the unanimity at Trent.* [*Or again, as at Ariminum, where (A. D. 359) four hundred bishops *under compulsion from Constantius*, signed a formulary short of the Nicene.] On the other hand there were known and long existing rivalries between the separate Churches which took part in the council. Before this era there had been serious disputes between Rome and Ephesus, Rome and Carthage, Rome and Antioch; and if it be said that the bishop of Rome himself was not at the council, only delegates from him, in the same proportion as his influence did not act there, is it remark able that he should have so cordially and zealously co-operated in the West in carrying its decrees into effect? Further, there was an old jealousy between Alexandria and Antioch.

carried out. Moreover, there was at that time a schismatical communion called the Novatian, of about seventy years' standing, spreading through Asia Minor and Africa as well as Italy, bitterly opposed to the Catholics and the see of Rome, and representing at the Council the theology of A.D. 250. This communion is known to have held the dogmatic symbol adopted at the Council as zealously as its Fathers, and afterwards suffered persecution from the Arians.

Moreover, there was at that time a schismatical communion, called the Novatian, of about 70 years standing, spreading through Asia Minor and Africa, as well as Italy; and represented at the council, at Constantine's instance, by one of their bishops. This communion is known to have held the Homousion as zealously as the Church Catholic, and to have afterwards suffered persecution on that account from the Arians.

125
-8

Again, it must be borne in mind that the great Council at Nicæa was summoned, not to decide for the first time what was to be held concerning our Lord's nature, but, as far as inquiry came into its work, to determine the fact whether Arius did or did not contradict the Church's teaching, and, if he did, by what sufficient *tesserae* he and his party could be excluded from the communion of the faithful. That authoritative and formal interpretation of the written word, which we have above treated as a probability, is in truth a matter of history in the early Church. The fact of a tradition of revealed truth was an elementary principle of Christianity. A body of doctrine had been delivered by the Apostles to their first successors, and by them in turn to the next generation, and then to the next, as we have said above. "The things that thou hast heard from me through many witnesses," says St. Paul to Timothy, "the same commit thou to faithful men, who shall be able to teach others also." This body of truth was in consequence called the "depositum," as being a substantive teaching, not a mere accidental deduction from Scripture. Thus St. Paul says to his disciple and successor Timothy, "Keep the deposit," "hold fast the form of sound words," "guard the noble deposit." This important principle is forcibly insisted on by Irenæus and Tertullian before the Nicene era, and by Vincent after it. "'O Timothy,'" says Vincent, "'guard the *depositum*, avoiding profane novelties of words.' Who is Timothy today? Who but the universal Church, or, in particular, the whole body of prelates, whose duty it is both themselves to have the full knowledge of religion, and to instruct others in it? What means 'guard'? Guard the deposit because of enemies, lest, while men sleep, they sow tares upon the good seed, which the Son of Man has sowed in His field. What is 'the deposit'? That which hath been intrusted to you, not that which thou hast discovered; what thou hast received, not what thou hast thought out; a matter, not of cleverness, but of teaching, not of private handling, but of public tradition."

This doctrine of a deposit leads to another remark. It involves in its idea a teaching which had no natural limit or circuit. Such teaching, carried on as it might be in the lifelong contact of master and scholar, was too vast, too minute, too complicated, too implicit, too fertile, to be put into writing, at least in times of persecution; it was for the most part conveyed orally, and the safeguard against its corruption was the number and the unanimity of its witnesses. The canon of Scripture was an additional safeguard—not, however, as limiting it, but as verifying it. Also it was kept in position, and from drifting, by the Creed: that is, by a fixed form of words, the articles of which were the heads and main points, and memoranda for the catechist and preacher, and which were rehearsed and accepted by every candidate for baptism, by way of avowing his adherence to that entire doctrine which the Church was appointed to dispense. The Divinity, then, of our Lord could not have been asserted and recorded at Nicæa, unless the separate Churches there represented had severally found it in their *depositum fidei*.

A further remark is in point. It followed from the very Catholicity of the Church that its tradition, as now described, while one and the same in its matter everywhere, or at least in its substance, was manifold, various and independent in its local manifestation. Each Branch of the extended body had its own distinct line of traditional teaching from the Apostles; and each branch was loyally, nay, obstinately, attached to its own traditions, whatever their peculiarities might be, and reluctant, on grounds of conscience, to yield any portion of them in favour of the traditions of other churches, even when they related to what was indifferent or of minor moment, or at least only of expedience. Thus the dispute between Ephesus and Rome related to the time of keeping Easter. Thus there was a question of the authority of the Apocalypse and other books of Scripture, and a more serious question relative to the baptism of heretics. In such controversies the one party religiously refused to yield to the other. The unanimity at Nicæa, then, was not a mutual sacrifice of views between separate churches for the sake of peace; not merely the decision of a majority; but simply and plainly the joint testimony of many local bodies, as independent witnesses to the separate existence in each of them, from time immemorial, of that great dogma in which they found each other to agree. Indeed, it is hard to suppose that they could be found to disagree in what was obviously so primary and elementary a question in the revealed system.

130
-1

If, then, our Lord after all was by the Apostles accounted and preached as a mere man, are we to believe in the phenomenon of this one and the same substitution everywhere of a new doctrine about Him, in the course of 220 years (nay, perhaps of only 70), in times of persecution, among peoples of different languages, characters, attachments, and religious attainments, and in spite of the safeguard of episcopal transmission? All this, moreover, without record of the change, or assignable reason why it should be made anywhere, or what brought it about:—lastly, with the unaccountable belief on the part of the Fathers in the Council that the view which they enforced was that which the Apostles had bequeathed them.

We have been viewing the argument on its hierarchical side; the witness of the Christian people for the orthodox truth is not less striking—nay, more so—than that of the Bishops. One or two of the great cities were corrupted as time went on, but the mass of the laity was decided and fervent in its maintenance of the sacred truth that was in jeopardy. The population of Alexandria, Antioch, Edessa, Cæsarea, Rome, and Milan, were even patterns in their profession of the dogma to the distressed, menaced, and hardly-used ecclesiastics.

So much, then, on the argument in behalf of our Lord's Divinity from Apostolical Tradition; and perhaps the reader may consider that enough has now been said upon the subject: but, before dismissing it, he must be prevailed upon to attend to one or two collateral illustrations of it, by way of showing, in corroboration of what was observed above, how natural and reasonable this argument

We are not at this moment determining *which* side in the dispute was taken by the apostles and their immediate disciples,—we only say that the after questions *were* questions then; so that the Catholic doctrine, if not apostolic, is not a mere *addition* to apostolic statements, but a plain going counter to them, in one way or another,—whether, that is, the Apostles be supposed to have shut up these questions in the words of the creed, or to have explained them differently. Thus, on this supposition, we have to account for the phenomenon of this one and the same substitution every where of a new doctrine, in the course of 220 years, in times of persecution, in times of doctrinal controversies, among people of different languages, attachments, and religious attainments, and in spite of the safeguard of episcopal transmission; all this, moreover, altogether silently, without record of the change, or assignable reason why it should be made any where, on tenable reference to any external school or doctrine; lastly, with the unaccountable belief on the part of the fathers in the council, that their own view was that which the apostles had bequeathed them. Still further, it must be recollected, that they had in their different Churches the writings of Christian teachers during the intermediate time, much of which is lost now, but which made them judges, virtually infallible, of the doctrine of the Church from the first. Hence too an additional argument results even at this day; for what remains of these writings serves the purpose of verifying the correctness of the tradition attested at Nicaea, just as we might inspect a money account, and, to satisfy ourselves, here and there cast up a sum, or make a calculation, in a balance sheet, which checks itself without such

from Tradition must be considered.

experiments. Alexandria, Carthage, Syria, Gaul, and Rome, thus bear independent witness, during the interval of 200 years, to the unanimous testimony extant at the end of it. And what adds incalculably to this testimony of the Ante-Nicene writers, is their stating the Catholic doctrine, not on the sole authority of their own respective Churches, though that were sufficient, but as the one doctrine even then preached and confessed all over Christendom.

This, then, is what is meant by Catholic tradition, and thus it attests the proper divinity of Christ, and anathematizes Socinianism and all other heresy on the subject; not by arguing and deducing from Scripture, as Dr. Hampden would say, but as being a separate apostolic information, parallel with Scripture, verified by, but not subsisting in it. We know from Scripture that there was a certain doctrine called "the doctrine of Christ," which was enforced by an anathema; we find it contemporaneously described in the primitive creed by the words the "Son of God;"—we find it tried, discussed, and sifted by the Gnostics, who arose even in apostolic times;—we find it committed to the keeping of the bishops of the Church as a perpetual legacy, and all along in connexion with the creed; at the end of 200 years after the last apostle's death, we find it publicly declared, .still with reference to the creed, and attested by 300 bishops from various parts of the world, as that which had ever been preached and taught among them; lastly, we hear of no other doctrine on the subject, even professing to come from the apostles. Can we for an instance doubt, what shadow of pretence have we for doubting, that the doctrine so declared was that very truth which the apostles consigned to the Churches as saving? What cause of alarm have we, though it be proved by Chillingworth, or Mr. Blanco White, ever so convincingly, that Protestant communities, as such, have no right to impose articles of faith, or that uninspired men have no power to add to the metaphorical expressions found in Scripture? By this review of the case, we are as certain that the apostles had that definite view which we call orthodoxy, as we are that we ourselves have it; as certain that Arians or Socinians do not agree with the apostles, as that they do not agree with us; as much bound to apply to them the apostolic anathema, as we are sure that there were speculators to whom the apostles applied it.

And here it occurs to us to notice the obvious mistake of many writers who argue against *Catholic* tradition from the errors of the fathers, whatever they are, in recording, as *individuals,* matters of fact. Thus the notion entertained by Irenaeus that our Saviour lived to be near fifty years old, Clement's assertion that St. Paul was married and the like, are urged as if a valid argument against doctrines built, not upon reports or rumours, but on the *agreement* of Christians in all times and places. Even Beausobre is not free from this mistake.

Perhaps the reader may consider enough has been said on this subject; yet, before dismissing it, he must be prevailed on to attend to one or two illustrations of it, which may press on him the *naturalness* of the argument.

133   "If the catholicity of the fourth century is not in substance the catholicity of the first, can we feel sure that our present MSS. of the New Testament in substance agree with the MSS. of St. Jerome?"
Further,—

135   the Apostles' death or not, etc." It seems, then, that those who deny the force of the argument from Catholic Tradition discard the true and sufficient interpreter of Scripture, not only according to the Roman Bellarmine, but according to the Anglican Wall.

the Apostles' death or not, because the fathers of some of them, and grandfathers of most of them, were born before that time, and were themselves infants in the Apostles' days, and so were baptized then in their infancy, if that were then the order, or their baptism deferred to adult age, if that were the use then," etc. Thus it is plain that those who deny the force of the argument from Catholic tradition in the case of the great gospel doctrines, go far to deprive us of the privilege of administering baptism to our children.

137   to heresies? ....

to heresies? Influenced by the very fact, that he sees you have hitherto gained no ground, and stand even with your adversary in denying this point and defending that, he will undoubtedly leave this level contest in still greater uncertainty, not knowing which side he is to judge to be heresy. For surely nothing can hinder them retorting upon us, if they are minded, the charges we bring against them. Nay, they must, in self-defence, maintain that we rather introduce corruptions of Scripture and false expositions, in order to support their own pretences to the truth.

138   FALL OF DE LA MENNAIS

ART. I. – *Affaires de Rome*. Par M. F. de la Mennais. Bruxelles. 1836.

138   M. F. DE LA MENNAIS has given us an account of what passed between him and the Papal See in 1831-1832, in a small volume entitled "Affaires de Rome." It is a curious

THIS is a very curious

140   of no particular religion

an infidel by profession

147   the temporal establishment of religion

the temporal establishment of the Papacy

147	Catholics are one	the Church is one
148	maturing	Realizing
148	for God: the king protects him	for God's cause, the king protects it
148	their Church	Romanism
149	the communion of Rome	Romanism
152	broiling	Burning
152	and long precedent	
153	imperial	
153	in order to establish image-worship	for a most unjustifiable object, and in, apparently, a most unjustifiable way. They became rebels to establish image-worship. However, even in this transaction, we trace the original principle of Church power, though miserably defaced and perverted, whose form – "Had yet not lost All her original brightness, nor appeared Less than Archangel ruined, and the excess Of glory obscured."
154	that the power consisted in	it was in
154	mooted	agitated
154	are agitating	kindle
154	concerning their duties, nay, concerning your own rights	their duties, nay, your rights
154	sentence	decision
154	shackle, nay break	shackle and break
155	relative	
155	carried away	drawn

155	an energy all heavenly	a heavenly energy
155	Have we here	Is this
155	knows no bounds	has no limits
155	they have reduced you	you have been reduced
155	can she have	can it have
155	she will be persecuted, she will be kept down	it will be persecuted, it will be oppressed
155	has she not	has it not
155	she made her greatest and most rapid advance	it made its first greatest and swiftest advance
155	Has she not	Has it not
156	proper	
157	out of place; and nothing	out of place. "Tempus abire tibi est" and nothing
159	the teaching of his own Church	the doctrine of his Church
159	a standing organ of revelation	a standing revelation
159	scarcely apparent yet	scarcely apparent
159	Go back	Retreat
159	getting quit of	leaving
160	utilitarianism to be the true philosophy of political action	expedience as the great rule of politics
161	the Roman population	they
162	the idea of happiness entertained by men	the happiness of men
162	has a universal influence in the shape of unworthy private interest	everywhere keeps it under by unworthy private interest
162	the Roman church	Romanism

163	from which we have been making extracts	which is the subject of this article
163	as to be worth dwelling on for its own sake	that we must not leave our readers altogether in ignorance of it
163	the dependence of the Church on the State	its dependence on the state
164	as de la Mennais says	
166	to Rome	to him
165 -6	the conductors of *L'Avenir*	they
166	in their journal	in L'Avenir
167	according to M. de la Mennais	
168	prudence tolerates error as the less evil	prudence requires it as the less evil
168	as good or desirable in themselves	as a good or a thing desirable
169	his journal	the L'Avenir
170	never should have I have admitted it	never had I admitted it
170	by Rome	from Rome
171	Now is it not really to annul a judgment, to assume the right, in any degree whatever, of forming a judgment on it?	Now does not in truth the subject matter of our reasonings, *ipso facto*, cease to have existence, directly we claim in whatever degree the right of reasoning about it? Lamennais wrote: 'Or n'est-ce pas là juger réellement ce qui n'existe plus, dès qu'on s'attribue, à un degré quelconque, le droit d'en être le juge?'
179	PALMER ON FAITH AND UNITY	ART. IV. – *A Treatise on the church of Christ, designed chiefly for the use of Students in Theology.* By the Rev. W. Palmer, M.A. of Worcester College, Oxford. 2 vols.

Rivingtons.

183
-4

These thoughts are suggested to us by a recent "Treatise on the Church of Christ, designed chiefly for the use of students of theology," by Mr. Palmer, of Worcester College, a work which, not only from the name of its author, but in connexion with the line of thought which we have been pursuing, deserves the attentive consideration of all who have at heart our Church's well-being. It does, in fact, as far as it goes, profess to provide a remedy for the fortuitous origin and personal characteristics of our classical works on theology, being a careful

The treatise before us is the work of a man who is evidently alive to this inconvenience, which attaches to our Church's present position; accordingly, it is a careful

191

Thence he goes on to assume as an axiom that there can be no real difficulty in finding the true Church.

192

He says:
"The Churches

He says, in defence of the English Church, -

"It is true that several of our doctrines are carped at by various communities around us. The Romanists accuse us of heresy on several points. We deny the charge most absolutely and peremptorily. *Is it necessary to go into an examination* of all these points on which the Church is assailed by her adversaries before we join her communion? *Were this the case, few men would ever be enabled to unite themselves to her,* even though she be the Church of God, in which salvation is offered; because their lives would be spent in investigating critically all these controversies of faith. It cannot be needful, for example, to enter into the controversies concerning the Trinity, incarnation, original sin, predestination, the sacraments, the power of the Roman pontiff, the forms of Church government, &c. &c., and to master them all before we unite ourselves to the Church.

This would impose an impenetrable bar in the way of those who are called by God to unite themselves without delay to the Christian and Catholic Church, and to receive from her, as "the pillar and ground of truth," that instruction and guidance which she is authorized by God and aided by his Holy Spirit to bestow."—vol. i. p. 244.

In the following passages, however, the same principle is merely assumed, viz., that no difficulty can exist really in finding the Church:—

The Churches

192	That is, Consistency in doctrine is not a Note of the Church: therefore the less the inquirer thinks about her changes, the better.	
192 -3	That is, It ought to be enough for the inquirer to know that we are *prepared* to prove our point, and have a case; for how can he be supposed able actually to *enter into* the proof? And again; "The English	And again: - "The mere fact of differences in religion, proves nothing as to the heresy of either party; and the English,
194	darkest	longest
194	political and civil watchwords	"National" or "by law established"
195	not Apostolic but "by law established"	
195	Unity and Sanctity	Catholic and Holy
195	"the Episcopal Church"	"the National Church"
195	Protestants of course will say that there are no Notes at all, for the Church is invisible; and, even if we suppose that Notes exist at this day, sufficient to determine for us the particular communion which is the very Church set up by the Apostles in the beginning, still what is the sense of ascertaining it, considering that our object in ascertaining is to	It may, at first sight, be thought almost a truism, that the Church, in any sense in which a Protestant can accept it, has no Notes at all in this day, or in other words has ceased to exist; or, if we suppose that Notes can be found, and the ancient divinely framed Church ascertained, still that inasmuch as it cannot be shown to teach one and

learn thereby the one true teaching, and she, the one true teacher, teaches one thing in this place, and another thing in that?

the same doctrine every where, whereas to learn the true faith was the very object of seeking for the Church, we are not at all better off after finding the Church than before.

196   dependent on time and place

197   "the Roman Obedience" as Mr.Palmer calls it

the Roman Body

197   theory

decision

197   one and the same body

the One Church

198   which does not exist

204   the discordant teaching of antagonist Christian bodies

the witness of the existing Catholic body

204   This is the theory of the *Via Media*. However, Mr.Palmer does not adopt it.

204   since Fundamentals do not exist thus absolutely true and universally received

since he does not admit the existence of any Fundamentals to which these properties can be confined

204   in Rome, London, Constantinople and St.Petersburg

205   ages; but, as no article

ages; but, it has been already observed, that the existence of some faults and imperfections by no means annuls the character of a Church; and, as in the present case, it arose from want of information and discussion, and besides, no article

208   superlative sanctity..... The Lutherans

superlative sanctity. It may be objected that this affords an inadequate view of the important changes made by the Reformation, and that if the difference between the faith of the Church of England before and after it, was not

490

profound and total, it could never have been worth while to suffer martyrdom for the truths of the Reformation, or to separate from the existing Church. But I reply that this proceeds on a totally erroneous view of facts. Those who suffered under Queen Mary suffered because they would not profess their belief in certain mistaken opinions, which their opponents erroneously asserted to be matters of faith; and therefore the fact of their suffering does not prove that there was in reality a total contradiction in matters of faith between them and their persecutors. The Lutherans

214   on the Church.....
       "That the whole Western Church

on the Church; but there are very reasonable grounds for doubting that the synod had such an intention. The Roman doctrine of Transubstantiation supposes the *whole substance* (in the Aristotelic sense, as distinguished from the *accidents)* of bread and wine to cease, by conversion into a different substance; so that the eucharist cannot be called bread after consecration, except in some figurative or tropical sense Though the term 'Transubstantiation,' as Bossuet observes, naturally implies 'a *change of substance*' this by no means settles the question; for it does not determine whether 'substance' is used in the Aristotelic or the popular sense; whether the change is physical, and in itself corresponding to other changes whether natural or miraculous, or entirely sacramental, spiritual, and ineffable; in fine, whether it be partial or total. Hence those who employed the *term* Transubstantiation with reference to the mystical change, might quite consistently hold that the substance of bread was not physically changed, or that it did not cease to exist, or that it was changed by union with the substance of Christ's body, or with His soul, or with the divine nature. All these opinions are consistent with the use of the term Transubstantiation, and all are contradictory to the common Roman doctrine on the subject.

In fact Pope Innocentius himself, in one of his books, having asserted that 'the matter of bread and wine .... is *transubstantiated* into Christ's body,' continues thus: 'but whether *parts* change into *parts,* or the *whole* into the *whole,* or the *entire* into the *entire,* He alone knows who effects it. As for me, I commit to the fire what remains; for we are commanded to believe; forbidden to discuss.' Thus Innocentius declares that the total change of the substance is not a matter of faith; and he mentions, *without any condemnation,* the opinion of some who held that the bread and wine remain after consecration together with the body and blood. He reserves the charge of heresy for those who held the bread to be only a figure of Christ's body. This renders it very probable, that Innocentius in the synod of Lateran did not intend to establish any thing except the doctrine of the real presence. In fact the question was not then with those who denied the modern doctrine of Transubstantiation: it was with the Manicbaeans, who denied the real presence of Christ's body in the eucharist. Nor was the term Transubstantiation introduced specially into the decree to meet any particular heresy, as the term 'consubstantial' had been introduced into the creed at the synod of Nice expressly to exclude the heresy of Arius. No one objected to this *term* at the Council of Lateran: no one had objected to it before; nor does it appear that it was disapproved of by any one till centuries afterwards, when it had been abused by some persons. Hence I conclude that the term was employed, not with any intention of establishing a specific view of the real presence; but simply as equivalent to 'conversion,' 'transformation,' 'change,' &c. which had been employed before, and continued to be employed afterwards to express the same thing.

"That this was so, and that the whole Western Church

214   The first is, etc .... Thus we see

The first is, that the *substance of bread is Christ's body;* the second, that the substance does not remain, but is reduced into matter existing by itself or receiving another form, &c.; the third, that the substance of bread remains; the fourth, and more common, that the substance does not remain, but simply ceases to exist. Thus we see

222   THE THEOLOGY OF ST. IGNATIUS

ART. II. - *S. Clementis Romani, S. Ignatii, S.Polycarpi, Patrum Apostolicorum, quæ supersunt. Accedunt S. Ignatii et S. Polycarpi Martyria. Ad fidem codicum recensuit, Adnotationibus variorum et suis illustravit, Indicibus instruxit,* Gul. Jacobson, A.M. Tom. 1, 2. Oxon. 1838.

222   The undertaking which

So small is the bulk, so few the extant manuscripts, and so careful the former editions, of the three Apostolical Fathers presented to the reader in these volumes, that at first opening them, he may be tempted to question whether he is to look for anything more than the superior convenience for mastering their contents which the octavo possesses over the folio form. But Mr. Jacobson has shown that no book can have been so well edited as not to admit of improvement in competent hands. The recommendations of his edition are mainly enumerated in the title page, consisting first in a recollation of the original MSS., next in a most elaborate Index, which is almost a reprint of the text under an alphabetical arrangement, and lastly in a selection of notes, partly from fresh sources, partly arranged anew, and partly the editor's own. Besides other valuable introductory matter, a careful account is given of preceding editions of the Three Fathers, in the original, Latin, English, German, French, Italian, and Dutch; and fac-similes of the MSS., to which we owe the preservation of these precious remains of antiquity. In procuring these the editor has visited the libraries of Paris, Florence, Rome, and Vienna. The last-mentioned of these has supplied him with a new and valuable MS. of the martyrdom of Polycarp.

Dissatisfaction has been expressed in some quarters that the University edition of the Apostolical Fathers should include the writings of only three of those who are commonly so considered, as if thereby tacitly deciding that the works attributed to St. Barnabas and St. Hermas were not genuine. But the University Press does not seem to us to be open to this charge; Mr. Jacobson at least is in no way concerned in it, for he has but undertaken a task put into his hands. As to the press, its directors only profess, as the title-page of the volumes expresses it, to publish "S.Clementis, S.Ignatii, S.Polycarpi, Patrum Apostolicorum, quæ supersunt;" that they are Apostolical Fathers, all persons must agree; and, in saying that they are, it is not said that others are not. It is open to the University to bring out, as its next publication, the works "S. Barnabæ, S. Hermæ, Patrum Apostolicorum," and to label the volumes "Patres Apostolici," as well as the present. We have been anxious to set this in what we consider to be its true light, lest a venerable body should seem to have yielded in this matter to the spirit of the age; which, in deciding upon what is truth, commonly dispenses with inquiry, and thinks that incredulity is the safer side in doubtful questions. The divines of Oxford have quite a right to think St. Barnabus not the author of the Epistle which goes by his name, but they have no warrant in philosophy, and no permission in piety, silently to reject what has been so widely received. To leave seeking is not the way to find; and to determine without reasons assigned, that Fathers and Doctors have been mistaken, argues little modesty or much weakness.

We do wish, however, that our editor was as entirely clear of all disrespect towards those ancient documents which he does edit as he is quit of it towards those which he does not. There are, it is obvious, cases in which those Fathers are happier whom an editor neglects, than whom he handles. This is far indeed from being true in the present instance; the very labour which Mr. Jacobson has spent upon the writings he has undertaken, being a sort of homage to them of a very marked kind. Yet it would have been well if this due act of reverence had been left unimpaired. It is hard to please all parties, as Mr. Jacobson must know full well; and therefore he will not be surprised to find that those who, like ourselves, profess to be more zealous in the cause of the fathers, whether apostolical or of a later age, than the world around us, should not have that satisfaction in some passages of the notes which they will afford to the many. There seems in them at times a want of realizing who the persons were and are, whose epistles, through divine condescension, are reserved for modern criticism.

With these remarks we shall close our notice of this very serviceable

		publication, which we feel sure will abundantly repay in the profit thence accruing to the Church, the anxious care of which it bears the marks. And now let us use it for one of the purposes to which it is calculated so well to minister. The undertaking which
222	in making some suggestions for its satisfactory accomplishment, which others may pursue for themselves, we shall deem it worth while to have attempted it.	in throwing out hints which others may pursue for themselves, it will have been worth while attempting it. We shall attempt then to show the mode in which the text of the Apostolical Fathers subserves the proof of the Catholic system of doctrine.
222	certain additions	certain additions really distinct from it
222 -3	The point debated between them has reference to the origin of this system,—when it began, and who began it. Those who maintain its Apostolic origin, are obliged to grant that it is not directly and explicitly inculcated in the Apostolic writings themselves. When they turn for aid to the generation next to the Apostles, they find but few Christian writers at all, and the information to be derived from them to be partial and meagre. This is their difficulty, and the difficulty which we purpose here to meet, by considering how the text of those writers who have come down to us—the Apostolic Fathers as they are called—is legitimately to be treated, and what light, thus treated, it throws upon the question which is in dispute between Catholics and their opponents.	The point debated between them is, whether or not the Apostolical Fathers sanction or confirm this system; the difficulty in determining it arises from their remains being scanty and their statements concise; and the question here to be considered is, *how, under* this difficulty, they may best be used, in what way put forth and treated, in confirmation of it.
224	proposition	proposition or measure
225	for him	
229	must be	considered *to be*

230	Certainly, this is a general truth, but what is that to the purpose in a particular case?	And so it may; but what then in a particular case?
230	a critic	Persons
230	in theology	
232	his own	
232	admit of question	are not conclusive
234	We feel, indeed, a difficulty in entering upon the subject, both from the impossibility of doing justice to it in a few words, and on account of the especially sacred character of the doctrines which it will introduce. On both accounts it is unsuitable to a Review; nevertheless we trust	We feel, indeed, a difficulty in entering upon the subject, both from the impossibility of doing justice to it in the pages of a review, and also from the sacredness of the topics into which we shall be led; but we trust
235	interpretation	comment on
235	proprius	propius
235	born and unborn	with beginning and without beginning
238	"the Mother of God."	"the Mother of God"* * When persons object to this translation of the word θεοτόκος, they are bound, if they would not open the door to Nestorianism, to say how else it can be translated.
242	and a gratuitous gloss upon his meaning	
243	but the great work of Irenæus *contra Hæreses* is also evidence to the same effect, not to speak of the various passages to be found in Origen, and the fragments of Hippolytus. However, perhaps the general tone of the Epistles themselves will be considered a most satisfactory proof, if we believe that in any sense they are his, that Ignatius had an eye to	who applies even the word "persona" to Christ, a word which, as far as we happen to know, is not found in its Greek equivalent with the same sense in any undisputed work till the later years of Athanasius. However, perhaps the following passages of St. Ignatius himself will be considered a most satisfactory proof of his having had an eye to heretics in his Epistles,

heretics in what he wrote, and of his judgment upon them.

and of his judgment upon them.

243
-4
*[St.Ignatius speaks of those who had known the truth and left it (as St. Peter, about the immoral sects, in the terrible words, "It had been better for them not to have known," etc.), not of those who are born and educated in error, and never had reason to doubt about what they had received.]

244	is heresy	are sectaries
244	unsuitable language	irreverence
245	or, as sometimes, a corrupt reading	
246	unkind	overkind
246	his words	ourselves
247	the disciples and friends of the sacred writers	
248	the risen Lord	Christ
248	"rekindling in the blood of God"	"ἀναζωπυρήσαντες ἐν αἵματι Θεοῦ"
248	the *body* and *blood*	the σὰρξ and αἷμα
248	"union with the flesh and spirit of Jesus Christ"	"ἕνωσις σαρχος και πνεύματος Ι. Χ."
248	an *Indivisible Spirit*	the Spirit, ἀδιάκριτον πνεῦμα
248	*flesh*, which is *spirit*	σὰρξ which is πνεῦμα
248	which is flesh of Jesus Christ	ὅς ἐστι σὰρξ Ι. Χ.
248	His blood	τὸ αἷμα αὐτοῦ'
248	symbol	Type
249	a literal interpretation of the phrases in question	taking the phrases in question literally
249	includes	*leads* to

250	union	Oneness
256	"Maintain the honour of thy post,	"Do honour to thy see," he says to Polycarp, "ἐκδίκει σου τὸν τόπον,
256	foreign	another man's
257	of united prayer. – Trall. § 12.	of united prayer: "Continue in your unanimity, and your mutual prayer." – Trall. § 12.
257	unnecessary and headstrong	Blind
260	on the hypothesis of these objectors	
260	been corrupted	been incidentally corrupted
261	And thus we take our leave of St. Ignatius.	But to enlarge on this subject more, would be entering upon a separate disquisition.

263 PROSPECTS OF THE ANGLICAN CHURCH

ART.V. - I. *Revival of Popery; a Sermon preached before the University of Oxford, at St. Mary's, on Sunday, May* 20, 1838. By Godfrey Faussett, D.D., the Lady Margaret's Professor of Divinity. Parker, Oxford.

2. *Letter to the Rev. G. Faussett, D.D., on certain Points of Faith and Practice.* By J. H. Newman, B.D., Fellow of Oriel College. Parker, Oxford.

3. *Strictures on some Parts of the Oxford Tracts ; a Charge delivered to the Clergy of the Archdeaconry of Ely.* By Rev. J. H. Brown, M.A., Archdeacon. Hatchard, London.

4. *A Charge delivered to the Clergy of the Peculiar of Allerton and Allertonshire.* By G. Townsend, M.A., Vicar of Northallerton.

5. *The Present State of the Controversy between the Protestant and Roman Catholic Churches.* By Hunter Gordon, of Lincoln's Inn, Esq. Whittaker, Loudon.

6. *A Call to Union on the Principles of the English Reformation; a*

Sermon preached at the Primary Visitation of Charles Thomas, Lord Bishop of Ripon. By W. F. Hook, D.D. Rivingtons, London.

7. *Dr. Hook's Call to Union, answered.* Fraser, London.

8. *Essays on the Church; with some Observations on Existing Circumstances and Dangers.* By a Layman. New Edition. Seeley, London.

9. *Travels in Town.* By the Author of Random Recollections of the Lords and Commons. 2 vols. Saunders & Otley, London. 1838.

10. *Plain Sermons.* By Contributors to the Tracts for the Times. Rivingtons, London. 1839.

11. *Letters on the Writings of the Fathers of the Two First Centuries, with Reflexions on the Oxford Tracts.* By Misopapisticus. Seeley, London.

12. *Episcopacy, Tradition, and the Sacraments considered, in reference to the Oxford Tracts.* By Rev. W. Fitzgerald, B.A.

13. *The Oxford Tract System considered, with reference to the Principle of Reserve in Preaching.* By Rev. C. S. Bird, M.A., late Fellow of Trinity College, Cambridge. Hatchards. 1S38.

14. *Letter to the Bishop of Oxford on the Tendency to Romanism imputed to Doctrines held of old as now in the English Church.* By E. P. Pusey, D.D. Parker, Oxford. 1839

263	at the present moment, when a controversy is in progress, which has so powerfully arrested the attention, and excited the feelings, of its members.	in the present state of the controversy to which the publications which we have just been enumerating belong.
265	the amusing writer	the silly gossiping writer
266	mere churches	mere (!) churches
266	*even*	*even* (!)

266	long	
266	how gradually and certainly they	the gradual and certain progress which
267	survey that state of religion	examine those opinions
267	forfeited	Disabled
268	what they ought not	what not
269	were once seen	did appear
271	the work of furthering	the advancement
272	really	
274	forcibly	
275	easily resist	can pass by
275	satisfy them	repose on
275	divine love	divinely planted love
275	the disposition to confide which they involve	the character of reliance which they manifest
275	in a given case	
276	we have no intention of disputing	it must of course be confessed
276	phantasiæ	φαντασίαι
276	the shape in which it addresses them	only for the sake of its vehicle'
277	close	seek it
277	ordinary development	regular developing
279	the writer to whom we have above referred	Mr. Townsend
279	says	reads a charge to the clergy of the peculiar of Allerton and

Allertonshire, that is, to one or two of his curates, one or two very respectable, but perhaps not university men, certain churchwardens and a clerk; and it is published at their "request". The following is a specimen of it: -

279 fn	. . . .	when the doctrine of toleration might have been supposed to have become an axiom with governments and individuals, that this learned and laborious member of the University of Oxford,
279 fn	castigation	overthrow
280 fn	in argument. As a person	in argument. However he proceeds – *"Could the Church of Rome require any other defence of its persecutions?* Who would believe that in the very same page in which *this atrocious sentence* is uttered we should read this passage also? "The heresiarch should meet with no mercy. He assumes the office of the tempter, and so far as his error goes must be dealt with by the competent authority as if he were embodied evil. To spare him is a false and dangerous pity. It is to endanger the souls of thousands, and it is uncharitable to himself.' *Could the spirit of St, Dominic animate the inquisition with more intolerable language?* Is it to be endured in the present day among a people who rightly and justly seek for liberty as well as truth.... that the Episcopal Church should be rendered odious by such language?" As a person
281	the truth of their doctrine	their doctrine
281	by no means clear of moral extravagance in the case of individuals	not unmixed with what

281	which the movement presents	
283	quality in Catholicism	principle
285	when they hear it recommended	which they hear recommended
285	severely animadverted	reflected
286	be idiosyncratic	differ from one another
286 fn	Dr. Kaye	
286	of the truth	
286	The Fathers	They
286	Moderns	We
287	such servility is	it would seem
287	otherwise do. Even the Fathers	otherwise do. However the contingency here is not one we need be very solicitous about. The danger unfortunately lies the other way; in the way, that is, of superficial and disrespectful criticism on the Fathers. The truth is, we are sadly in want, after all our boasting, of that real liberality of mind which can acknowledge and admire the excellent wherever found, even though it may sometimes be of a kind which we do not sympathize with ourselves or feel called on to imitate. Granted that there are points in the divinity of the Fathers which were not designed to be followed up in the present age, why should men disdain the Fathers in consequence? Are we to admire nothing but what we are ourselves? Is our own age, its character, tastes, opinions, habits, to be the only admissible or tolerated standard of what is good? None but ignorant vulgar people laugh at every thing that is foreign. There is a rule of modesty, we rather think, which would take us

quite the other way. A practical age should admire a contemplative one, even more than it would one of its own character; on the principle on which, in actual life, persons are often found to admire and attach themselves to those who are most different from themselves.

"alterius

Altera poscit opem res, et

conjurat amicè."

For our own part we cannot but think that different schools of theology were meant to rise up from time to time in the Christian world according as change was wanted, nay in order to bring out, and give fulness and expression to the truth itself; the inward basis and substance of truth in doctrine and discipline of course continuing the same all along. Even the Fathers

287   the Schoolmen. And there have been other great changes

the Schoolmen. And in the same way what is there to prevent the growth amongst us, at the present day, of a school of Church divinity to follow in the train of its predecessors of old time, but not to be bound in the letter to any one of them? or to be an harmony of them all? or again a development? or a particular aspect? Much has taken place in our Church, since the days of the schoolmen, to give reason for such a modification of ecclesiastical doctrine, and more since the days of the Fathers. There have been the middle ages, then the Reformation, then Puritanism, then Dissent in the multitudinous and overwhelming form in which it has manifested itself in recent times. All these have been great changes

288   [Of course it is true that the past
fn   never returns, and that reactions are always in one sense innovations. But what is said above goes further than this, further than I habitually went myself as an Anglican, and in my deliberate judgment. The

hypothesis about the *depositum fidei* in which I gradually acquiesced was that of doctrinal development, or the evolution of doctrines out of certain original and fixed *dogmatic truths*, which were held inviolate from first to last, and the more firmly established and illustrated by the very process of enlargement; whereas here I have given utterance to a theory, not mine, of a certain *metamorphosis* and recasting of doctrines into new shapes,—"in nova mutatas corpora formas,"— those old and new shapes being foreign to each other, and connected only as symbolizing or realizing certain immutable but nebulous principles.]

288   that we are born in the nineteenth century, not in the fourth not in the fourth. We are tempted

that we have not the power. And that all this is understood by the writers who are at present attracting attention, is plain from the following explicit avowal of one of them, which, whatever may be worth of the views it puts forward, is far indeed from implying any blind antiquarian adherence to early times. "Primitive doctrine," says Mr. Newman, speaking of the labours of *English* divines, "has been explored for us in every direction, and the original principles of the Gospel and the Church patiently and successfully brought to light. But one thing is wanting We have a vast inheritance, but no inventory of our treasures. All is given us in profusion; it remains for us to catalogue, sort, distribute, select, harmonize, and complete.... What we need at present for our Church's well-being is not invention, nor originality, nor sagacity, nor even learning in our divines, at least in the first place,— though all these gifts of God are in a measure needed, and never can be unreasonable when used religiously,— but we need peculiarly a sound judgment, patient thought, discrimination, a comprehensive mind, an abstinence from all private fancies and caprices and personal tastes,—in a word, divine wisdom."— *Romanism,* p. 30, ed. 2.'

We are tempted

288	reduction of	throwing
288 -9	the tastes, opinions, passions, and aims of a particular audience	another man's tastes, opinions and affections
290	If another illustration of these economies (as they may be called) is wanted	If, in addition to this illustration, which has been extended somewhat beyond its due limits, another is wanted
290	Such in its origin and nature, though not such in its magnitude	Not so much, of course, as the difference which these instances imply, but such in its origin and nature'
290	teaching	truth
290	our common nature	human nature, which is always the same
291	the public	persons
291	times were modern. Identity of appearance	times were modern. We should be as unwilling to anticipate that any one age of the world was meant to be exactly like any other, as to set about proving that every flower of the earth was like every other. Identity of appearance
292	spasms	convulsions
292	It is wrong, indeed, to have longings or schemes for being let off easily; and doubtless there are those with whom all duty is up-hill work	and those who do indulge them, may be assured that they do *not*. To such persons all is uphill work
293	not infected	uninfested
294 fn	[It must be confessed, however, these formularies have not excluded	

it from the Anglican Church; still it has no stay in Anglicanism, or in any other religious communion, for it is a transition state, and is running its sure course, and in a great number of minds has already resolved itself into that avowed scepticism or infidelity which is its issue.]

294	creed	system
294	"Papists"	"Popery"
295	mutual trust and intimate fellowship	all trust
296	on this side or that	
300	less Protestant	un-Protestant
301	insane	utter
303	Rationalism	Liberalism
303	Erskinism	Jacob-Abbotism
307	the best of a bad matter, or not the worst, if not the best	and to use them as pilots to guide you through it κατὰ τὸν δεὐτερον πλᾶν, in not the worst way'.
307	cut your coat according to your cloth	to make your shoe out of the leather provided for you
307	Do they not thus recognize in us their real and most formidable opponents?	We had intended, after these high discussions, to furnish the reader, by way of conclusion, with some light matter which may be considered as a sort of desert after dinner. In plain English, he was to be regaled with some interesting specimens from certain of the works which we have prefixed to this article, but our necessary limits have frustrated our intentions towards him.
309	THE ANGLO-AMERICAN CHURCH	1. *America and the American Church*. By the Rev. Henry

Caswall, M. A., Rector of Christ Church, Madison, Indiana. London: Rivingtons.1839.

2. *Memoirs of the Protestant Episcopal Church in the United States of America.* By William White, D. D.. Bishop of Pensylvania. Second Edition. New York. 1836.

3. *Journal of the Proceedings of the Bishops, Clergy, and Laity of the Protestant Episcopal Church in the United States of America, in General Convocation held in the City of Philadelphia from Sept. 5th to Sept. 17th, inclusive,* A. D. 1838. New York. 1838.

4. *Sermons to Presbyterians of all Sects.* By G. T. Chapman, D.D. Hartford. 1836.

5. *The Church of Rome in her Primitive Purity compared with the Church of Rome at the Present Day.* By John Henry Hopkins, D.D., Bishop of Vermont. Burlington. 1837. [Reprinted, London. 1839.]

6. *The Primitive Church compared with the Protestant Episcopal Church of the Present Day.* By John Henry Hopkins, D.D., Bishop of Vermont. Burlington. 1836.

7. *The Apostolical Fathers, Clement of Rome, Polycarp, and Ignatius.* Burlington. New Jersey. 1837.

309	United States, fortunes which have a still greater promise in the future, than a present accomplishment.	United States of America, and still more, as appears probable, hereafter on retrospect, even than now.
312	shedding	Uttering
313	would not cease to be, though she were protected by the State no longer	too could bear to be deserted by it
314	To Mr. Caswall, an Englishman by birth, an American by his Orders,	And now leaving these reflections, let us to the publications which

we are indebted for the most graphic and circumstantial, as well as the latest account which has been published of the present state of the American Church. This gentleman is in all respects a man of note. He has the energy of a missionary, the curiosity of a traveller, and the sobriety of a man of letters.

have given rise to them. The first, and that on which we shall mainly dwell, is a graphic and circumstantial account of the present state of the American church, by Mr.Caswall, an Englishman by birth, but a presbyter in the American Church.

315 Elsewhere he tells us, that this young Church "is increasing

The following remarks too are *apropos* of what was said above:- "The American church is probably destined to become one of the most important and serviceable churches in Christendom. While it is unquestionably growing in piety, in resources, and in unity of action, so also it is increasing

315 of the States."

of the States." That it possesses the proper elements for a healthy increase is proved by the fact, that among the clergy and laity there exists a growing disposition to return as closely as possible to the primitive model, in doctrine, in discipline, and in worship. From the surrounding sects it has nothing to fear, but everything to hope. The more severely it is scrutinised, the brighter it will shine; and the more clearly its principles are developed, the more powerfully it will commend itself to public estimation." – *Caswall*, p. 356, 357.

315 We shall not understand the full force of these statements, until we look back at the condition in which Episcopacy found itself at the end of the revolutionary war.

Now compare this with her state at the close of the revolutionary war, which he elsewhere thus describes:-

315 and a half. The Propagation

and had not Omnipotence interposed, the ruin would have been complete. The fostering hand to which the American Church owed a long continuance of care and protection, was withdrawn; and the Propagation

315	'on the ground of their ecclesiastical connexion with the liturgy of the Church of England.'	on the ground of their ecclesiastical connexion with the liturgy of the Church of England.
315	unconstitutional sentence, ultimately despoiled the clergy of Virginia of their glebes and churches; while, in addition to all these calamities, Episcopalians in general became subject to unmerited political prejudices. Most of their churches were emptied; there was no centre of unity, no ecclesiastical government.	unconstitutional sentence, obtained through the efforts of sectarians and infidels, ultimately despoiled the Church of Virginia of its glebes and houses of prayer. Most of their churches were destitute of worshippers; their clergy had departed, or were deprived of maintenance; no centre of unity remained, and no ecclesiastical government existed.
316	this summary: "Few colleges	this summary: "Hitherto all persons desirous of preparing for the ministry of the church had laboured under great disadvantages. Few colleges
317	fifty and sixty." In Kentucky	fifty and sixty. Kenyon College has lately received from England, through Bishop McIlvaine, further donations amounting to about 12,000 dollars, besides many valuable books. In Kentucky
317	a bishop was consecrated	the Rev. Mr. Smith of Lexington was consecrated bishop
318	and to receive a bishop	and, accordingly, in the same year the Rev. Dr. Hopkins was elected and consecrated its bishop
318	highly probable, that before	highly probable, as I have mentioned in a former chapter, that before
318	enumerated	Specified
318	became £12,431. From these	became £12,431. "This increase is to be ascribed in a great measure to the growing prevalence of systematic contributions, in the form of weekly or monthly offerings. To Bishop Doane of New Jersey belongs the credit of having brought the latter

subject fairly into notice. It had become sufficiently obvious that with all the complicated machinery of agencies, charity sermons, newspaper appeals, and other expedients, the amount contributed to missionary purposes was exceedingly small, compared with the actual capabilities of the Church. It was plain also that the benevolent public was not so much indisposed so give, as under the influence of bad habits in giving. Excitement was a grand resource, and when this failed, the task of arousing to liberal action was difficult. Under these circumstances Bishop Doane and other influential clergymen conceived the plan of establishing a more ample, permanent, and effective supply. The idea was derived from the system recommended to the Corinthian Christians by St. Paul, when pleading in behalf of the impoverished churches of Judea; "Now, concerning the collection for the saints, as I have given orders to the Churches of Galatia, even so do ye. Upon the first day of the week, let every one of you lay by him in store as God has prospered him, that there be no gatherings when I come." It was justly concluded, that if but a comparatively small portion of the members of the Church could be induced to adopt this primitive practice, the funds thus raised would be sufficient to sustain on a liberal scale the missionary operations of the General Convention. Accordingly in 1833 Bishop Doane introduced the system into the diocese of New Jersey, and it was soon afterwards recommended and partially introduced in other dioceses."—pp. 2G2, 263.

From these

319   of the Church, at New York especially. If there is

of the Church. Mr. Caswall says-"The New York Episcopalians are pre-eminently distinguished for their disposition to assist all the institutions of the Church. If there is

319   says Mr. Caswall

320   trifling decorations. —P. 145. Elsewhere he tells us that in one of the eastern cities,

trifling decorations. In one of the windows is a striking painting of the Ascension, executed, as I was informed, in Italy." – pp. 145, 145. Mr. Caswall gives the following account of a church in one of the eastern cities, he does not say which: -

320   138 feet high. The pulpit

138 feet high, supported by angular buttresses of four stages, and finished at the top with eight pinnacles, each 30 feet high, crocketed and crowned with finials. Buttresses are also attached to the walls of the main building, the ends and sides of which and of the top of the tower, are crowned with embattled parapets. The roof is covered with metal; on each side of the tower is an open screen of rich tracery-work 30 feet high, supported by octagon towers, surmounted by pinnacles, and crowned by finials. There are five pointed windows on each side, and a large oriel window in the south end; the large window in front of the tower is 24 feet high and 12 feet wide. The galleries in the church are supported by clustered columns and Tudor arches, trimmed with projecting pendentives, filled between with rich traceiy and ornamental carving. The ceiling is composed of double-groined arches, springing from massive pendants. The pulpit

320   of design. The ground

of design. On each side of the pulpit, in the end wall, is a handsome niche, the design of which was taken from Henry the Seventh's Chapel at Westminster.

The ground

| 320 | depth 13 feet. The number | depth 13 feet. The case is a very rich specimen of the Gothic, and is furnished with three sets of keys (compass from GG to F alto), and pedals from GGG to an octave below the manuals to D, making the compass of the pedals one octave and a fifth. The number |

| 320 | draw-stops is 34. The cost of this organ was 5,000 dollars (£1,125)." – P. 283.

At Rochester | draw-stops is 34, distributed as follows. In the great organ, 12 stops, namely, large open diapason, second open diapason, stopped diapason, clarabella, night horn, principal, twelfth, fifteenth, sesquialtra of three ranks, cornet of four ranks, trumpet, and clarion. In the choir organ, 7 stops, namely, open diapason, viol, de gamba, stopped diapason, flute, principal, and cremona. In the swell, 9 stops, namely, open diapason, stopped diapason, dulciana, flute, principal, fifteenth, cornet of three ranks, trumpet, and hautboy. In the pedals, 3 stops, namely, double open diapason, open diapason, and principal; making in all 31 stops of pipes. The remaining three are coupling stops, one of which unites the great and choir organs; another, the choir organ and swell; and the third, the pedals, with the bass of the choir organ. The largest pedal pipes are 21 by 24 inches inside, and 22 feet long; the largest metal pipe is 10 inches in diameter, and about 12 feet long. The cost of the organ was 5000 dollars (1125*l.*)" – pp. 283, 284.

At Rochester |

| 322 | interesting description of a Sunday expedition in its vast and wild territory:

"We rise early, | interesting description of the literally pastoral, or, what may be called, the *nomadic* habits of the clergy in its vast and wild territory. "It may be interesting to you," he writes to a friend, "to hear a little more on this subject: I will, therefore, give you an account of |

my regular Sunday expedition, in which I am accompanied by a worthy collegian, my intimate friend. You must suppose the season to be summer, when the country appears to advantage, and the days are long. We rise early

323   of a family. Upon the abundant

of a family. Around the cabin are several acres upon which gigantic trees are yet standing; but perfectly deadened by the operation of girdling. Their bark has chiefly fallen off, and the gaunt white limbs appear dreary though majestic in their decay. Upon the abundant

323   gently undulating. After an hour

gently undulating. Our pathway is plain, and conversation enlivens our walk. Occasionally we pass a log hut surrounded by a small clearing; and after an hour

324   deepest attention. We then instruct

deepest attention. This, although not strictly regular, is permitted by the bishop to candidates for orders, on account of the exigency of the case. We then instruct

324   to stop. He wishes

to stop. He tells us that he has felt deeply interested in the services, that he desires more information, and that he wishes

324   to new efforts."-Pp. 35-39 (abridged). It is encouraging

to new efforts. I have mentioned that a number of the young men are engaged in a similar manner; and you will at once perceive that on account of the distance of their schools, they can but rarely be present at the regular morning and evening service at the college. The great majority of the students are, however, punctual attendants at Divine worship, and the bishop and profesors are faithful in their sermons and exhortations." – p.35-39.

Selection is difficult in a book so full of information as Mr.

Caswall's; in conjunction with the last extract the following will be read with interest. It relates to the individual to whom, under providence, the existence of the Church at Portsmouth in Ohio is owing.

"Samuel Gunn was born at Waterbury, in Connecticut, in the year 1763, and baptized by a clergyman sustained by the 'Society for Propagating the Gospel in Foreign Parts.' The war of the American Revolution commenced while he was a child, and consequently, he took no part in that fearful struggle. But the Church suffered severely during the momentous period in question, and became, in many places, but a name; a name, too, of obloquy and reproach. Yet Samuel Gunn continued faithful to his spiritual mother. He loved the vine which he believed the Son of God and his Apostles had planted; and though now broken and spoiled, he hoped to see the time when it would cover the land with its spreading branches, and when its leaves would be for the healing of the nations. The war having at length terminated, the clergymen in Connecticut rallied their remaining forces, and elected a bishop, who was consecrated in 1784 by the Scottish prelates. Bishop Seabury was soon actively engaged in the great work of reviving the enfeebled parishes committed to his charge. He ordained pastors, and was the first who performed the solemn ordinance of Confirmation in the United States. Among the numbers who hastened to receive this holy rite was the subject of our memoir, who had now attained the age of manhood, and had given unquestionable signs of a Christian character.

"The parish of Waterbury was, at that time, without a clergyman, and Mr. Gunn, being a man of unimpeachable morals, was appointed a lay-reader. During the week he was engaged on his farm, but on Sunday be occupied the desk, and conducted the devotions of a few zealous Christians according to the venerable forms of the Liturgy. Sometimes a clergyman visited the little flock; but such opportunities were not frequent, and for ten or twelve years Mr. Gunn continued his useful labours without fee or reward. But his family was now increasing, and his circumstances were greatly straitened. At length he determined to seek a home in the western country, which already presented a wide field to enterprise and industry. He first removed, about the year 1793, to Windham, in the western part of the state of New York. Here he established a small shop, which yielded him a livelihood sufficient for his moderate wants. He soon found means to collect a few persons together, and to persuade them to unite with him in the performance of divine worship. He commenced, a second time, his vocation of lay-reader; and soon experienced the gratification of finding that his efforts were not in vain. The number of attendants gradually increased, until finally they organized a parish and obtained a clergyman. But Providence did not permit the subject of our memoir to enjoy the spiritual advantage of a pastor. He seemed destined to be a lay-reader; and by the silent influence of a blameless life, no less than by his direct exertions, he was to promote the truth among those who had few opportunities of hearing an official ambassador of God.

"His circumstances becoming again embarrassed, he decided on removing into the fertile, but at that time, almost uninhabited region, bordering on the Ohio.

Accordingly, having punctually paid his debts, he sallied forth with a light heart and a light purse, in quest of new toils and new means of usefulness.

"It was in the autumn of 1805, that Mr. Gunn, with a wife and five children, commenced his long and fatiguing journey. An occurrence of a most distressing character soon wrung the affectionate heart of our lay-reader, and tried his faith to the utmost. While passing through the deep forest, one of his children fell from the waggon, and in a moment was crushed to death beneath the wheels. With his own hands the afflicted father dug a grave by the road-side, and having read the solemn burial-service of the Church, committed the remains of his beloved offspring to their kindred dust. In the month of November be reached the banks of the Ohio, and embarked with his family and little property on the noble river which was to bear him to his destination.

"No steam-boat then ploughed the western waters; and it was only in long and narrow vessels, propelled by poles or dragged by ropes, that the hardy boatmen could ascend the current. The passengers and goods destined for places down the stream were conveyed in flat-boats of a temporary construction, which were broken up and sold when the voyage was completed. In a vessel of this latter kind, Mr. Gunn, with his little all, floated slowly to his future home.

"At length, his boat was made fast near the village of Portsmouth, a place containing at that time not more than n dozen dwellings. There was, however, a dock-yard in the vicinity where a large ship was afterwards built, which descended the river 1500 miles to the Gulf of Mexico, and was employed in the trade with Europe.

"In   so   enterprising   a

517

neighbourhood, Mr. Gunn was not idle. He purchased a small farm, and diligently employed himself in felling the trees, breaking up the rich soil, and sowing the seeds from which he hoped to provide his children's bread. And now the Liturgy was heard probably for the first time on the shores of the Ohio. Every Sunday, the lay-reader collected his family around him, and united with them in worship and praise. For many years, none but his domestic circle attended on these occasions; but a providential circumstance soon enlarged his congregation. He thought it expedient to sell his farm and remove into the village of Portsmouth, where he established himself as a cooper. He soon found that he was not the only churchman in the place; but that there were a few others who had been taught to believe in one Catholic and Apostolic Church. These gladly attended his reading, and assisted with their responses. About this time, namely, in the year 1819, he received the grateful intelligence that a diocese had been organized in Ohio, and a bishop elected and consecrated. To complete his gratification, he learned that the new prelate was no stranger to him. The Rev. Philander Chase, the same missionary who, on more than one occasion had slept under his roof, and dined at his table at Windham, in New York, was now his bishop in the Far West. Mr. Gunn immediately took his pen, and wrote to his chief shepherd. He stated the importance of directly commencing regular services in Portsmouth. He mentioned the comfort which the few members of the Church in that increasing village would derive from an episcopal visit; and he concluded with earnestly requesting the bishop either to come himself, or send some clergyman to visit them at an early season."—p. 92—97.

The bishop came, organized a parish, and, in the want of a clergyman, appointed Mr. Gunn lay-reader; the narrative proceeds—

"For the third time, our lay-reader occupied the desk; but the people were, to a great extent, destitute of prayer-books, and could not, of course, join in the responses. It was soon discovered that a printer in the village was in possession of a large number of these invaluable manuals of devotion, which he had long since laid away as unsaleable. They were immediately purchased, and some at high prices. Money was then scarce, and one person actually gave twenty bushels of corn for a single prayer-book. For three years Mr. Gunn regularly performed the services. During this period, the village was visited most severely by disease. Many who had taken a deep interest in the Church militant below were removed to the Church triumphant above; and after several unhealthy seasons, few of the little congregation remained. In the year 1823, a clergyman residing in Chillicothe, fifty miles distant, consented to officiate once a month in Portsmouth. This was a great benefit to the people, and a great relief to Mr. Gunn, who had now attained his sixtieth year. The latter, notwithstanding, conducted worship, and read a sermon on the intervening Sundays; and after two years, when Mr. Kellogg, the clergyman, left Ohio, he again took the entire labour upon himself. All this, it must be remembered, was entirely gratuitous, and the only recompense was that of a good conscience.

"The congregation, now exceedingly small, was often a subject of ridicule to the thoughtless and the prejudiced. The members of other denominations also frequently importuned the few Episcopalians to unite with them, on the assurance that a Church minister could never be obtained. But the little community, attached by conviction to the distinctive principles of Episcopacy, never ceased to persevere in what they believed to be the way of truth. In 1831, they obtained a convenient room for their worship. They fitted it up with commodious seats and a pulpit; and here, after his recovery from a severe illness, the aged lay-reader, with a trembling voice, continued to conduct their devotions. In the month of July, in the same year, he officiated for the last time.

"Having been just ordained a deacon, by Bishop Chase, I was sent by him to Portsmouth, where I received and accepted an invitation to take charge of the feeble congregation. My compensation was fixed at 200 dollars (45*l.*) a year, which, with an additional hundred from the Diocesan Missionary Society, was enough to support existence at the low prices which then prevailed. But scarcely had I officiated once in my new sphere of labour, when a frightful accident befell the good Mr. Gunn, which hastened his departure from the world. A fire-engine had recently been purchased by the inhabitants of Portsmouth, and the old man, with many others was observing its operations. The person who directed the jet unfortunately permitted the tube to fall, and in an instant the whole stream of water struck Mr. Gunn in the face, crushing his right eye, and completely destroying its power of vision. For some time his condition was extremely precarious; and it was feared that a total loss of sight would be the result. At length nature rallied, and he recovered strength to walk. One eye was spared to him, but his former health was never restored. Yet the hope of immortality brightened upon him, and his conversation became more and more solemn and edifying. The Church, too, was dearer to his heart than ever; and it was not long before he gave a proof of his sincerity, which was the last crowning act of a life devoted to the service of God.

"During the winter following the accident, he one day requested as many of the parishioners as could attend, to meet him on important business. A number of them accordingly assembled, and the old man, rising from his seat, represented to them in strong terms the importance of building a church. He showed them that no considerable accessions to their number could be expected until a distinct building, of sufficient capacity, and easily accessible to all, had been obtained. He concluded almost in the following words: 'You know, my friends, that I am not rich, and that twice I have lost my all. Yet Providence has given me enough, and my property is now a little more than two thousand dollars. Of this, I will give one-third towards the erection of the proposed edifice, on condition that you will contribute the remainder of the necessary amount.' This offer was accepted with admiration and gratitude, and a sufficient sum was promptly subscribed.

"But the lay-reader lived not to see the church erected, nor even its corner-stone laid. A few months after his generous gift, his form became emaciated, and he was soon confined entirely to his bed

"A clergyman, in priest's orders, visiting Portsmouth about this time, Mr. Gunn expressed his desire to partake of the holy communion. The sacred rite was accordingly administered to him, and he expressed the liveliest joy and consolation. Five days afterwards, he breathed his last in perfect peace, having almost completed his seventieth year. Many hundred persons accompanied his remains to the burial ground; for he had been a friend to all, and had been long regarded as an example of uprightness and integrity."—pp. 98—103.

It is encouraging

326   Mr. Caswall's words: "Their delusion

Mr. Caswall's words: "The Mormonites are the vicitims, and, to a certain extent, the actors, of one of the grossest impostures ever palmed on the credulity of man. Their delusion

327   of Mormon.' There are fifteen

of Mormon.' This is a singular tissue of absurdities, not wholly devoid of ingenuity. There are fifteen

327   New York. It is needless

New York. It is said to have been originally intended as a hoax, with the further object of deriving profit from the sale of the book. It is needless

327   tenets

doctrines

328   An examination

A candid examination

328   tremarkable change. Then in his nineteenth year he resolved to devote himself to the clerical office. Accordingly, after

remarkable change. Philander Chase, then in his nineteenth year, being seriously inclined, and viewing with sorrow the feeble state of the Church, resolved to devote himself to the clerical office. Accordingly, after

329   of that sect. At length

of that sect, and some time elapsed after his appointment as professor in the Lexington Medical School, before any further change was effected in his sentiments. At length

330   the early Church. He therefore connected

the early Church, and found it still existing in the Greek and Roman Churches, as well as in the

522

episcopal Churches of England and America. A Romanist he could not become, because ecclesiastical history had shown him the origin of Roman Catholic errors, and the superior purity of antiquity. He therefore connected

330   powerful advocates. We will quote a passage from one of his sermons, both for the view given in it of the religious state of the country, and for the force and liveliness with which it is given:

"On the supposition that the original Apostles were to re-appear for the purpose of converting the heathen to the knowledge of the true God and Jesus Christ whom He hath sent, what, I demand, would be the course adopted by them, the system they would deem it advisable to employ? If the Apostles

powerful advocates. We have put one of his works at the head of this article; and it will contribute to inform the reader of the present state of the American Church, (which is one chief reason for our selecting the subject,) if we here set before him some specimens of Dr. Chapman's writings. If we chose to be hypercritical, we should confess that we are not altogether pleased with the tone of all that occurs in the following quotations; but we make them to show the effective way in which American preachers urge the unity and stability of the Church against the discordance and variations of the sects around her.

Take, for instance, the following noble passage.

"I will even suppose that the Scriptures were silent upon the subject so as to leave it optionable with us to have the ministry we pleased, and only insisting upon uniformity, yet would there be insuperable difficulties attending a resort to that which is Presbyterian, owing to the immense number of rival claims, which would forthwith make their demands upon our choice. Decision must be had between two and three hundred sects, and as many creeds. Out of such a labyrinth of confused and devious paths, which is to be preferred? Ye cannot tell, for that would to agree, and to agree ye will not. Were the selection to be made by us, the clamour of the unselected would never be appeased, because the pretensions of many are about equal, and the residue are indisposed to abate a fraction of their crudest dogmas. But were the question first narrowed down to the ministry alone, and ye were to select the episcopal on the ground of its apostolic origin, there would not be two or three hundred, there would not be two churches to distract your attention. Our Church is one and indivisible. Had it as many creeds as your Presbyterianism admits of, it could not be the pillar and ground of the truth. A great many good things may be extracted from your several communions. But what of this? We want them all in one, and the Church is that one. Come then, beloved brethren, all ye who have hitherto wearied yourselves with endless divisions and heresies, come, renounce them all, and enter into the ark which God bath prepared for the salvation of his saints, when the deluge of wrath shall overwhelm the host of the ungodly. Never should ye suffer it to escape from your memory, that 'Christ also loved the Church, and gave himself for it, that be might sanctify and cleanse it with the washing of water by the word.' It may satisfactorily account to you for the zeal with which her cause is advocated, and the immensity of her blessings tendered to your acceptance. But whatever may be your thoughts, and whatever your decision, however ye may acknowledge or withstand the institutions of God, unite with or keep aloof from the Bride of his Anointed, the strength of my attachment will not be impaired, it can only increase with increasing years, only fail to glow within my heart, when that heart shall become cold and still for ever. 'For Zion's sake will I not hold my peace, and for Jerusalem's sake I will not rest, until the righteousness thereof go forth as brightness, and the salvation thereof as a lamp that burneth. Amen.'"—p. 374.

In another place he says,

"I believe it was the learned Dissenter, Selden, who said 'Scrutamini Scripturas' (Search the Scriptures), these two words have undone the world; because Christ spoke them to his disciples, therefore we must all, men, women and children, read and interpret the Scriptures.' He does not mean to cast reproach on their general perusal; or, if he does, God forbid! that any man should countenance the insanity of such a project. But the crude and fanciful interpretations of ignorance, these, certainly, should call out the marked disapprobation of every true friend of Jesus. They have brought into existence the many sects of Shakers, Ranters, Sandomanians, Dunkers, Southcotians, Mormonists, with a long, long list of equally blind fanatics. And when private individuals have followed up their miserable glosses upon the sacred text, by assuming the clerical office, or the more enlightened denominations have conferred it upon the merest drivellers in biblical knowledge, then, indeed, we may feel with Selden, that if the world be not undone, the Christian part of it is sadly annoyed and disfigured by all manner of strange conceits and superstitious practices. In these United States, there are hundreds of preachers who cannot even read the Bible they undertake to expound. The qualification of others is limited to vociferation and riot, excitement and passion, incredible tales and incoherent exclamations. Sermons have degenerated into a disconnected series of anecdote, and pastoral visits into convenient vehicles for the retail of gossip. For the form of sound words we have jargon. For the excellency of sound doctrine, multitudes are destined to listen to the vagaries and the cant of empiricism."—p. 349.

In another sermon, when engaged in answering the position which is the *reduction ad absurdum* of sectarianism, that the Church is the better for division, he thus speaks:

"Far the largest part of the world is still unenlightened by its only moral luminary. And on the supposition that the original Apostles were to re-appear for the purpose of converting the heathen to the knowledge of the true God and Jesus Christ whom he hath sent, what, I demand, would be the course adopted by them, the system they would deem it advisable to employ? Would they fashion themselves after their former conduct, or be induced to avail themselves of the experience ye have had, in new, and, to them, untried developments. Consider, then, that if the Apostles

331   preserved by them. [But] supposing them to be now

preserved by them, unless indeed the rebuke should be given, to which reference was made in my prior publication. 'Every one of you saith, I am of Calvin, and I, of Brown, and I, of Munzer, and I, of Wesley, is Christ divided?' He must have known the most eligible mode of propagating the religion he came to reveal, and they would not venture to claim the honour of discovering a more lively and experimental way. Great difficulties also, brethren, would necessarily attend the preference on their part of your ecclesiastical polity. Not more than twenty Apostles are mentioned in the Scriptures. Many of you insist that there were thirteen only who enjoyed this high dignity. And supposing these to be now

331   the Christian world. Not only must

the Christian world. In what strange inconsistency therefore would all this involve the chosen of Christ. It would not be enough for the Apostles to set up severally some one of the principal religious denominations, putting the whole college at irreconcileable variance with each other. Not only must

331 make you free.'"—Pp. 333, 334. And now, having said

make you free.'

"Where then is the sectarian so entirely void of reason, as to believe that were the Apostles now conversant with men, they would proceed to Christianize the heathen, on this antagonizing plan, rather than confide in the old paths, wherein they were once divinely trained to go forth conquering and to conquer? Placed in an attitude so glaringly absurd, it is scarcely possible to conceive of a fatuity of intellect, excessive and incurable as this. Madmen only could subscribe to such madness; knaves alone, to its coming within the bounds of credibility. It is one thing to eulogize disunion and contradiction, when, in the revolution of ages, they have been gradually introduced, and another to ascribe their origin to the instruction of holy men of God, who spake as they were moved by the Holy Ghost. Often does the natural world bring forth monsters, and in the nursery of schism their parturition is by no means rare. But inspiration is an infallible security against all error. Inspired men could not be left to fasten a medley of contradictions upon the Divine decree. The Church proclaimed by them, whether it were yesterday, to-day, or to-morrow, must of necessity be one, even as God himself is one."—pp. 333, 334.

And now, having said

332 as regards its consequences

as regards itself

332 is undeniable

every one will admit

335 its full proportions

totis numeris absoluta'

336 pile placed aside of pile

337 cotton-crops

337 a season

338 into consideration.
First let us have recourse to Dr.
Seabury of Connecticut, the first
who was consecrated diocesan
bishop. What makes his sermons
more interesting is that they seem

338 derived from him." – Vo. i. p.12.
He thus speaks

mass placed aside of mass

sugar-canes

a time

into consideration.
We shall refer to three bishops of
their Church; and first to the
sermons of Dr. Seabury, the first
consecrated diocesan bishop. What
makes them more interesting is that
they seem

derived from him. It would be
tedious to quote particular texts to
prove that the Apostles did exercise
this power in the church. The
whole tenour of the history of their
Acts and their Epistles clearly show
that they did institute a plan of
Church government, enact laws,
appoint governors and officers to
regulate the economy of the Church
as a society, as well as to preach the
doctrines of the Gospel. And from
ecclesiastical history, it appears that
the government and officers
instituted by them do continue in
their successors at this present time,
notwithstanding the utmost force of
persecution which the malice of
evil men and wicked spirits could
bring upon it. Though in some
places veiled in poverty and
obscurity; in others, encumbered
with worldly pomp and
ceremonious superstition, the
Church of Christ still continues in
the world preserved by His
Providence who promised that 'the
gates of hell shall not prevail
against it;' and we trust to rise
again with splendour, and to shine
forth, delivered from the shackles
of worldly power and systematic
superstition, in the full lustre of the
beauty of holiness, both in its
public offices, and in the faith and
piety of its members." – vol. i. p.
12. He thus speaks

339   evidently appears." – P. 156.

evidently appears. As a priest, Christ offered Himself a sacrifice to God, in the mystery of the Eucharist, that is, under the symbols of bread and wine, and He commanded His Apostles to do as He had done. If His offering were a sacrifice, theirs was also. His sacrifice was original, theirs commemorative. His was meritorious through His merit who offered it, theirs drew all its merit from the relation it had to His sacrifice and appointment. His, from the excellency of its own nature, was a true and sufficient propitiation for the sins of the whole world, theirs procures remission of sins only through the reference it has to His atonement. When Christ commanded His Apostles to celebrate the holy Eucharist in remembrance of Him, He with a command gave them power to do so, that is, He communicated His own priesthood to them, in such measure and degree as He saw necessary for His Church, to qualify them to be His representatives, to offer the Christian sacrifice of bread and wine as a memorial before God the Father of His offering Himself, once for all, of His passion and of His death, to render the Almighty propitious to us for His sake, and as a means of obtaining, through faith in Him, all the blessings and benefits of His redemption.

"The Eucharist is also called the communion of the body and blood of Christ, not only because by communing together we declare our mutual love and good will, and our unity in the Church and faith of Christ, but also, because in that holy ordinance we communicate with God through Christ, the Mediator, by first offering or giving to Him the sacred symbols of the body and blood of Christ, not only because by communing together we declare our mutual love and good will, and our unity in the Church and faith of Christ, but also, because in that holy ordinance we communicate with God through Christ, the Mediator, by first offering or giving to him the sacred symbols of His dear Son, and then receiving them again *Blessed and sanctified by His Holy Spirit*, to fest upon at His table, for the refreshment of our souls, for the increase of our faith and hope, for the pardon of our sins, for the renewing of our minds in holiness, by the operation of the Holy Ghost, and *for a principle of immortality to our bodies as well as to our souls.*" – p. 156.

339 learned foreigners."* He speaks of

learned foreigners."* Bishop Seabury's feelings on the subject may be learned from a circumstance which Bishop White has preserved to us. On the Sunday morning during the session of the Convention in the course of which the restoration was made, the latter wished Bishop Seabury to consecrate. He declined. On the offer being repeated just before the service, he again declined, and smiling, added, "To confess the truth, I hardly consider the form to be used as strictly amounting to a consecration." This of course was a strong saying; but no wonder it was the means of effecting the desirable change.

In another sermon he speaks thus of both sacraments: -

"We are by the grace of Holy Baptism taken out of the world and put into the church of Christ, the ante-type of the garden into which Adam was put when god took him from the world in which he had been created. The same Holy Spirit is given to us at our baptism, as the governing principle of life, which was given to Adam at his creation, as the principle of his life. The

530

Holy Eucharist, the sacrament of the body and blood of Christ, is appointed for us, as the tee of life was for Adam, to be to us the principle or means of immortality." – p. 220.

He speaks of

339   the final retribution. *On this ground*

the final retribution; that this was the belief of Jews and Christians, might be fully proved from Jewish authors, and from the old liturgies and writings of the Fathers, did the compass of this discourse permit it. *On this ground*

339   day of judgment." – P. 196.
-40   Next we will mention Bishop Hobart: he thus speaks of the Christian ministry in a ordination sermon:

day of judgment; and to give us grace to follow the example of their faith and patience, that with them we might be made partakers of his heavenly kingdom, through the merit of Jesus, the Saviour. This they supposed necessary on their part, to keep up the communion of saints or fellowship with the Church of Christ; which is still one and the same, whether suffering here on earth, or at rest in paradise, and waiting in hope for perfect consummation and bliss, both in body and soul, when the judgment of the last day shall give them their portion in that life eternal, which God hath promised to all who obey the Gospel of his Son.

"*Every one who will consider the subject without prejudice, must feel the force of such a principle* in promoting the faith and holiness, which the Gospel requires; and will lament that the Church of Rome, by grafting the absurd errors of purgatory and prayers to departed saints, instead of for them, on *this old pious, and Catholic, Christian doctrine*, hath almost banished it out of the minds of Protestant Christians." —p. 196.

It is scarcely necessary to add that he was not behind these truly apostolical sentiments in his views of Confirmation.

"In baptism, He (the Holy Ghost) is given for the purpose of regeneration—to effect that new birth, by which we are born into the Church of Christ, obtain remission of all past sins and a new nature; in Confirmation, He is given for the purpose of sanctification or renovation of the heart in holiness. In Baptism, we are created anew in Christ Jesus, by the operation of the Holy Ghost; in Confirmation, the new creation is animated and enabled to live according to its new nature, by the energy of the same most Holy Spirit. As in the original creation of man, God made the body first, and then breathed into it the breath of life, to animate the body which he had made, and enable it to answer the purposes for which he designed it; so in our new creation, being buried with Christ in Baptism, we die to the former life of the old man, and rise again to a new life; and, in Confirmation, the Holy Ghost, as the principle of that regenerated, new or spiritual life, is infused into us from above. In Baptism, we are made Christians; but yet the new baptized is but an infant in Christ; in Confirmation, he is advanced to the rank of adults and made a perfect man in Christ Jesus."—p. 135.

Now to turn to Bishop Dehon and Hobart; and, first, of the latter. He thus speaks of the Christian ministry in an ordination sermon.

340 in holy things." – P. 13. In one of his posthumous

in holy things." – p. 13.

Accordingly we find him in 1818 addressed by, and addressing, the chiefs of the Oneidas, thus:

"Right Reverend Father, - As head and father of the Holy and Apostolic Church in this state, we entreat you to take a special charge of us. We are ignorant, we are poor, and need your assistance. Come, Venerable Father, and visit your children, and warm their hearts by your presence in the things which belong to their everlasting peace. ... My children, - I beseech you to attend to the instructions of your faithful teacher and brother, Eleazar Williams; to unite with him in the holy prayers of our Apostolic Church, which he has translated into your own language; to listen with reverence to the Divine word which he reads to you; to receive, as through grace you may be qualified and may have an opportunity, the sacraments and ordinances of the Church; and at all times and in all places to lift up your hearts in supplication to the Father of your spirits, who always and everywhere hears and sees you, for pardon and grace, to comfort, to teach, and to sanctify you through your divine mediator, Jesus Christ." *Life*, p. 221-223.

In another of his posthumous

340   of His Body.' – P. 308. Thirdly, we will quote the glowing language of the eloquent Dehon:

"What tokens

of his Body.' The blessings which Christians derive from Christ, *by virtue of their union with the Church*, which is his Body, may be summed up in the following:—

"1. Pardon of sin, through the merits of his blood.

"2. Spiritual life, holiness and protection, through the power of his grace.

"3. A title to that inheritance of glory, to which the Church will finally be exalted.

"Behold then, brethren, what exalted blessings are conveyed and pledged to us, *through the Church*. The merits of the Redeemer's blood is applied to us, and thus we are assured of the forgiveness of our sins; the influences of his Holy Spirit are bestowed upon us, by which we are renewed to holiness, and strengthened to resist temptation and to overcome in our Christian warfare; and it is as faithful members of Christ's

Church militant on earth, that we become heirs of the glory and bliss of his Church triumphant in heaven.

"It would be great presumption indeed to confine salvation to the Christian Church. God is not 'a hard master, reaping where he has not sown, and gathering where he has not strawed;' and therefore, where the Gospel is not proclaimed, he will not exact, as the condition of salvation, communion with that Church, into which men have no opportunity of entering. The influences of that grace, which Christ hath purchased for all men, may extend where it is not made known, or conveyed by visible signs and pledges; and those who endeavour to act according to the dictates of reason and conscience, will finally be judged according to what they have, and not according to what they have not; *but the rewards conferred on them will not be as great* as those adjudged to those faithful members of Christ's mystical body, who, through their communion with the Church, enjoy the means and pledges of his grace and mercy. "Still, wherever the Gospel is proclaimed, *the Church is the appointed mode of salvation*, for it is that mystical body, of which Christ is the Head and Saviour, to which he applies the merits of his blood, which he sanctifies by his Spirit, and which he will exalt, with its faithful members, to immortal glory." – p. 308.

He carries out his idea of the Church spiritual into those local habitations in which she is allowed to manifest herself.

"Particularly does God manifest his presence in the sanctuary, by the ordinances which are there administered; these are the means and pledges of his mercy and grace. In the sanctuary, the subjects of sin, the children of wrath, the heirs of mortality, coming with true repentance and faith, are translated by the Sacrament of Baptism, into that fold of the Redeemer, his mystical Body, the Church, where his mercy encircles them, his grace guides and sanctifies them, and makes them heirs of glory. They are continued in their title to the celestial privileges, and advanced to still higher degrees of bliss in the laying on of hands, that ordinance of Confirmation, in which they personally seal their baptismal vows. In the sanctuary is spread that holy table, in which, under lively symbols, Christian believers commemorate the stupendous sacrifice of the cross, and spiritually participate of that lifegiving body and blood, which preserve their bodies and souls unto everlasting life."—p. 303.

No wonder that in an address to his Convention in 1817, he thus recommends to his brethren an observance, which he yet found it impracticable to introduce.

"Let the minister, as frequently as circumstances will admit, assemble his congregation for divine worship. . . . No opinion is more unfounded than that there is a deficiency as to the means of pious instruction and devotion in the forms of our Church. She has provided *daily morning and evening prayer*; and hence her ministers, when circumstances admit and require, can assemble their flocks for any purposes of Christian edification, not only daily, but twice in the day, and lead their devotions to heaven, &c."—Life, p. 201.

Let us now turn to the glowing language of the eloquent Dehon: - he is pleading the cause of a religious society in his diocese.

"What tokens

340   of our love? We must espouse

of our love? We cannot 'pour upon his head a box of the most precious ointment,' we can procure; nor 'wash his feet with our tears and wipe them with the hair of our heads;' we cannot watch with him while he sorrows or sleeps, nor say to him personally, 'Thou knowest that we love thee,' 'All that we have is thine.' How then shall we manifest palpably our affection towards him? We must espouse

341   any such thing.'" – P. 266. Again: "Says the holy Chrysostom

any such thing.' And if what is 'done to one of the least' of the members of this his Body, is considered 'as done unto him' with what gracious satisfaction will he behold your gratitude employed in increasing the general health and vigour of the Body; in 'lifting up its hands which hang down, and strengthen its feeble knees,' and adding, by your munificence, to its reputation and beauty. You see then, my hearers, that this institution presents itself before you as an infant friend of your Redeemer. It stretches out its hands to you for your smiles and your help. It says to you, I would be strong, that I might go forth and build up the waste places of the city of God, and bring much people to the enjoyment of his peace and salvation. The spirits of those worthy laymen, who anciently sought the prosperity of the Church in these parts, seem to me to look down upon it, from their places of rest, and say, Jehovah prosper you. The spirits of the mild and pious Johnson, of the sensible and dignified Garden, and of those patient and intrepid clergymen, who, in the difficult years of the settlement of these regions, laboured in the word and doctrine, seem to me to lean from their seats of bliss and behold with delight the appearance of an institution, which will take up the work, in which they expended their labours and their lives. The spirits of your fathers, who once worshipped in the temples, which are desolate, and whose ashes rest in their cemeteries, seem to me to call to you from the skies to patronize in their steads this infant advocate of the Church which they loved. Yea! The Spirit of Jesus seems to me to be here, saying to you from his throne, 'Take this child and nurse it for me, and I will give thee thy reward.' Daughters of Jerusalem! love ye your Lord; I know that you love him. When you have read of the faithful, the happy women, who embalmed his body, you have envied them their felicity. To share it with them is not in your power. But he hath a mystical Body, the Church. Upon that you may bestow the expressions of your regard for him. And how can you do it so effectually, as through the instrumentality of this institution, which, as Joseph cherished in his humiliation his earthly body, would cherish the mystical one, in which he delights to dwell. Sons of the Church! love ye your Lord; I trust that ye love him. When ye behold the wise men coming to-day to bring to him their 'gifts, gold, frankincense and myrrh,' ye are struck with the grandeur of the scene, and are ready to say to the Author of so much good to our race, would we could do likewise. To bring your gifts to his presence, who has died that your sins might be pardoned, and is gone into heaven to intercede for you there, is not in your power. But you may bestow your gold, your frankincense and your myrrh, upon the Church, which is his Body. And how can you do it so effectually, as through the instrumentality of this institution, which, as the angels ministered in the days of his humiliation to his earthly Body, would strengthen his mystical one, with all the services it can devise?"—pp. 266—371.

Again:

"It has already been observed to you, that wherever the Deity is particularly present, it is with the retinue of his angels. This was eminently the case in the Jewish temple. And the Gospel favours the opinion that it is so in the places of Christian worship, in which God receives the homage of his redeemed creatures. In the earliest ages of the Church, before man had exalted himself above all created intelligence, this sentiment was carefully cherished. 'Hear thou me,' says one of the most eloquent of the Fathers, 'hear thou me and know that angels are everywhere, and that chiefly in the house of God they attend upon their King.' 'Doubt not,' says another of these primitive disciples of our Lord, 'that an angel is preserved, when Christ is offered.' And again, says the holy Chrysostom

341   One other short passage may be allowed us from a writer who would be found to be most eloquent, if we had room to quote him at length. Speaking of

One more passage may be allowed us from so natural and warmhearted a preacher: speaking of

341   His visible Church. It is presumable

... his visible Church. 'Go,' said he, when about to leave our earth, to the Apostles, whom for this purpose he had chosen, 'go ye, therefore, and teach all nations, baptizing them in the name of the Father, and of the Son, and of the Holy Ghost, teaching them to observe all things whatsoever I have commanded you, and lo, I am with you alway, even unto the end of the world.' There arises, from the nature of the Christian ordinances, a peculiar necessity for an authorized ministry. The sacraments are of high and holy import, like the ark of the Covenant they are not to be carried by unhallowed hands. They are seals of an engagement between God and men. They are compacts between the Almighty Father and his repentant children, in which he pledges himself, upon condition of their faith and obedience, to give them the pardon of their sins, the blessing of his Spirit, and the enjoyment of eternal life. And who can sign the covenant of such mercies unto men, but they who act in God's behalf? And who can act in God's behalf, but they who act by God's authority? Not, oh not, that in those to whom this ministry is committed, there is any relation above the ordinary qualities of their fellow-beings. Every priest appointed to this service must be taken from among men, and, consequently, be subject to like passions with the rest of their race. It is, indeed, infinite condescension in the great God to employ, in the accomplishment of his mighty and gracious purposes, beings frail as we are; but perhaps, we may say, it is also wisdom. For hereby is secured to him, to whom alone it belongs, all the honour, all the praise, all the glory of the efficacy of the ministrations. 'We have this treasure in earthen vessels,' says St. Paul, speaking of the great Christian behest, entrusted to the ministry, 'we have this treasure in earthen vessels, that the excellency of the power may be of God and not of us.' It is presumable

341   coming again." –P. 48, etc.
      It is pleasant

coming again. Not that a mere outward and formal observance of the sacraments of Christianity will accomplish in us the purposes of the mission of the Son of God. But in the sacraments are deposited the mercy, the gifts, the refreshments, the renewals, the hopes, which we need, of all which they who resort to them with the requisite qualifications cannot fail to participate. On this account it was that attendance upon them constituted so large a part of the religious business of the primitive

Christians, and that they spake of them in such lofty terms as the *laver of regeneration*, the *seed of immortality*, the *earnest of a resurrection*. Far different was the estimate of these ordinances in their days, from that which seems to prevail in ours. They were then the Christian Bethesdas, by which the penitent and believing waited, that when the angel moved the waters, they might wash in them from sin and uncleanness, and be restored to hope and soundness and vigour. And should we go about to ascertain why the Gospel is not now productive, in so great degree, as in the apostolic times, of its proper peace, and joy, and holiness, we shall probably find among the chief causes the uninformed manner in which some go to its sacraments, and the entire disregard with which the many neglect them. For besides the general reasons to observe them, there are to every individual peculiar motives for this obedience. The sacraments of Christianity are ordained, not only to be of general use, but also for his individual benefit. He himself is washed in its baptism from the defilement of sin, and in its supper he himself is nourished with *the bread of immortality, which came down from heaven*. These ordinances are, to every man, the channel of divine mercy, the resort where the Church findeth her Lord. Here he leadeth her by the still waters. Here he causeth her to lie down in green pastures. Here he maketh his flock to rest at noon. Enjoined by Divine authority, we may not question their necessity; crowned with a Divine promise, we cannot doubt their efficacy; but we do owe it to ourselves, as well as to the Redeemer, who appointed them, and the Christian community to which we belong, to endeavour to walk after the footsteps of his ancient servants, 'in all his

		commandments and ordinances, blameless.'"—pp. 48—51. It is pleasant
348	self-importance	self-satisfaction
349	"idea"	'ἰδέα'
350	this view of things is	they are
352	"extraneous influences"	extraneous influences
352	whose history Mr. Caswall gives at great length	Whose history has been given above in Mr. Caswall's words
352	Mr. Caswall thus speaks	Mr. Caswall, as our readers will have observed, thus speaks
353	without having any right or wish to suppose it	which we have no right or wish to suppose
353	Again:	
353	Again, he says,	
353	great extent." – P. 337. "The practice	great extent; but some extenuation of this omission may be found in the circumstance that the custom is not enjoined by canon as it is in England." – p. 337. "The practice
354	All this suggest that	Here
354	what we have called	
354	Again:	
355	that it is so	about the fact
355	the one never-dying priest, without break	the one, ὁ ἀεὶ, the never-dying priest continual
355	strangers on a visit	visitors
356	viz.	

358	or unmixed. As to the third	or unmixed. He speaks as follows: - "The American people are accustomed to republican modes of procedure, and, accordingly it has been shown that the American Church is conducted almost entirely on the popular principle. But this is not all. While the benefits of a republican administration are secured to the Church, its evils are not wholly excluded. Hence the conventions, both diocesan and general, have occasionally been the scenes of intrigue, while in the election of a bishop there is sometimes an exhibition of the same party spirit which always accompanies the election of a governor or a president. I am far from asserting that these evils prevail equally in the church as in the state. On the contrary, Christian courtesy, gentlemanly feeling, and the absence of many conflicting interests, tend greatly to restrain the spirit of faction; I only state the fact, that such an influence is exerted, felt, and acknowledged." – p. 329. As to the third
358	with himself	with him
359	the "Memoirs"	the pamphlet
361	seldom takes place	is seldom exercised
361	so constituted, are the conditions	so constituted, are the mode of trying clergy accused of heresy, the conditions
361	theological education, and the mode of trying clergy accused of heresy. The Standing	theological education. The Standing
361	can give ordination except to such	can ordain except such
362	has the oversight of	oversees
364	the morrow!	the morrow!

At the General

"He was raised up," says Mr. Caswall, "by Providence at a crisis when a person of his description was pre-eminently necessary. Steady and sober from his youth, he was prepared to advise in time of peril and excitement. Conciliatory in his measures, he was a man perfectly adapted to the promotion of harmony, at a time when diversity of opinions, and high claims respecting the independence of dioceses, threatened to rend the Church in pieces. Under the influence of his blended meekness and wisdom, objections to the Liturgy and Articles melted away; and many a root of bitterness was plucked up and allowed to die. The General Convention is the offspring of his prudence and brotherly love; from its first organization till the last meeting before his death, he was always at hand with his pacific counsels, superior to paltry manœuvre and selfish policy. His humility and piety were evinced more by actions than by words; and he always acted on the maxim, that for any man to assume dictatorial airs, on the ground of ecclesiastical distinction, is in America most unwise, and in every country most unbecoming. Hence while he lived, he was venerated as a patriarch and loved as a man, and when he died, the event was regarded by the Church as an irreparable loss, and by the nation as a public calamity."
– pp. 193, 194.
At the General

364   and spiritual,"

and spiritual."*
fn * P. 86.

364   his communion.
     One other illustration

his communion. Bishop Meade, too, in his sermon at the opening of the convention, speaks of

"The venerable patriarch of our Zion who lived and died in this city of brotherly love (Philadelphia) to whose peace he so greatly contributed, by whose citizens he was so highly honoured, so sincerely beloved, - whose death created a general pause along all its streets, and whose funeral procession was one long unbroken line from the door of his house to the mouth of his sepulchre – May he worth," he continues, "descend not on one of us but on all. Imbibing his truly catholic spirit, adhering to his judicious, moderate, and true interpretation of our standards, avoiding all metaphysical discussions and doubtful disputations, we shall agree on all subjects where agreement is necessary, and readily consent to differ where difference is unimportant."†

fn † Vide also the Missionary for August 19, and November 11, 1837, for some interesting accounts of Bishop white.

One other illustration

364	"development"	development
365	and only trained	but trained
365	is found to exist in	is found in
365	a principle of good or of evil	a blessing or a curse
365	creature or in that; no one accounts highly the life of a tiger or a toad. And so with	creature or that. And so with
366	"Evangelical Truth;" or like the "politeness, " the charge for which in some dames' schools used to be an extra two pence. Sectarians of	"Evangelical Truth." Sectarians of
366	*completion*	ἐπιτελείωσις
366	nor the Apostolic without the Evangelical	and *vice versâ*
366	"in sincerity", to use St. Paul's words	uncorruptly

366	except for	all but for
367	orthodox who denies the truth of the Incarnation, though he professed to believe the Atonement, as one who preaches divine grace, yet denies the gifts and powers of the Church	an orthodox believer who denies the truth of the incarnation as one who denies the divine appointment of the Church
367	"I believe in the Catholic Church"	the latter article
367	does not really hold Evangelical Truth	does not really hold apostolical truth
368	we view indeed under two aspects	we view separately
368	as excellent men speak	as Mr. Caswall would speak
369	to man." – P. 326. Hence, again, it is a favourite	to man." – p. 326. And still more so when he observes that "Party spirit is by no means so strong as it has been; the high Church generally admitting that the low Church are growing more consistent, and the latter conceding that the former are becoming more 'evangelical.' Both classes have done much in the great work of extending religion; the former by learned and dispassionate arguments for Apostolic truth and order; and the latter by zealous personal efforts, united with direct and faithful addresses to the conscience. The former labour with energy in the promotion of missions within their own country; and the latter with equal energy in the propagation of the Gospel abroad." – pp. 340, 341. Again it seems a favourite
369	the American Revolution	the Revolution
369	Perhaps this language is defensible	This is defensible
370	a certain *form* of government	a *form*
370	Our author	Mr. Caswall

370	who profess them	under them
371	cannot be looked for	will not be
371	the clothes indeed	clothes
371	(whom, we repeat, we do not make personally responsible for every word he uses,)	
371	boon	benefit
372	strictest	exactest
372	be allowed to	
372	temper	tone
376	at the same time	
376	affliction, sin, doubt despair	doubt, despair, affliction
377	carefully	
378	re-published	published
379	to expect nothing	to expect anything
387	SELINA, COUNTESS OF HUNTINGDON.	ART. I. – *The Life and Times of Selina, Countess of Huntingdon.* Vol. 1. London: Simpkin, Marshall & Co. 1839.
387	LITTLE as we can be supposed to agree with the theological views of Selina, Countess of Huntingdon,	LITTLE as we agree with the theological views either of the subject herself, or of the editors of this volume,
387	her life	it
387	so many	the many
387	partizan	agent
388	ultimately	

388	yet can but	yet but
388	as we	which we
388	passed these	passed them
389	faults	imperfections
389	in a given case	
389	unreality	dishonesty
390	Volume	Work
390	much of such	any such
390	Earl Ferrers	Earl of Ferrers
391	Shirley	Shirly
391	propensity	tendency
391	mere	
391	that	it
393	me	
393	a principle	it
393	is founded,) as possessing "a highly	is founded. "Lady Huntingon was unquestionably formed for eminence. Her tender age exhibited a fine dawn of her mature excellence, and she gave early presages of proving highly useful and ornamental to society, if permitted to arrive at those years necessary for maturing the powers of the human mind. She possessed a highly
393	age," he continues, "and	age, and
393	were admirable. Though not	were admirable. Though she was obliged , from her situation in life, to mix with others in fashionable

547

		amusements, an attachment to them, or to the ornaments of dress, was not the foible of her discerning and contemplative mind. Though not
394	condescending."—Pp. 9, 10. She had	condescending. This engaging exterior was animated by a soul, lively and ardent in its pursuits, and enriched with those qualities which the world highly esteems and pronounces very good."—Pp. 9, 10. She had
395	in life;	in every relation of life;
396	Far from doubting the possibility of such a state of mind, on the hypothesis of trustworthy testimony, and far from extenuating its guilt, we denounce it, we anathematize it.	Far from denying the possibility, as we are, on the supposition of alleged testimony, admitting the fact; and far from extenuating its guilt, we denounce it..
396	a precocious	an absolute
396	biographer takes for granted the fact	her biographer takes the fact for granted
396	*all* men	*all* parties in the Church
396	the soul of man before what he would denominate its conversion	persons before what he would denominate conversion
396	theologians	persons
396	hold in express words just that doctrine, about their natural, moral integrity, which he attributes to Lady Huntingdon, only	hold such doctrine as he attributes to Lady Huntingdon, in express words, only
396	mere	
397	the point, which he will find difficult to give, that such Pelagianism deformed Lady Huntingdon	the point, that such was the case with Lady Huntingdon.
397	life, as they say they were, self-conceited	life very self-conceited

548

398 praiseworthy   exemplary

398 in a certain way

398 conceives,—as if the better we were   conceives; and something
    really, the better we always thought
    ourselves; and something

398 She was shallow in her religion, as   She was neither so perfect nor so
    young people ever are and must be.   self-righteous as perhaps she
    She was neither so perfect nor so   afterwards painted herself in
    self-righteous as perhaps she   memory; exemplary indeed in
    afterwards painted herself in   conduct, yet partially ignorant, as
    memory; exemplary indeed in   all young people must be, of
    conduct, yet ignorant of the depths   Christian truth and her own heart.
    of Christian truth and her own heart.

398 excellence   holiness

398 when really such

398 of theories.   of theories.
-9   Lady Huntingdon was far   We suppose the following
                                                narrative belongs to what the author
                                                would call her time of darkness, but
                                                it is not easy to determine the point.
                                                It is curious, if it does not.
                                                   "At one period of her life, Lady
                                                Huntingdon appears to have been
                                                much occupied with political
                                                questions. Her sentiments were
                                                conformable with those of sir
                                                Robert Walpole and his
                                                administration; and she was much
                                                connected with the courtiers of that
                                                day. A little incident which
                                                occurred at this period will serve to
                                                mark the natural ardour of her
                                                character. There were some stormy
                                                debates in the House of Lords in
                                                May, 1738, on the depredations of
                                                the Spanish, in which Lord
                                                Huntingdon, and others of his
                                                intimate friends took a leading part.
                                                Her ladyship expressed her
                                                intention of being present, though
                                                ladies were excluded. 'At the last
                                                warm debate in the House of
                                                Lords,' says Lady Mary Wortley
                                                Montague, 'it was unanimously
                                                resolved that there should be no

unnecessary auditors; consequently the fair sex were excluded, and the gallery destined to the sole use of the House of Commons. Notwithstanding which determination, a tribe of dames resolved to show, on this occasion, that neither men nor laws could resist them. These heroines were, *Lady Huntingdon*, the Duchess of Queensberry, the Duchess of Ancaster, Lady Westmoreland, Lady Cobham, Lady Charlotte Edwin, Lady Archibald Hamilton and her daughter Mrs. Scott, Mrs. Pendarves, and Lady Frances Saunderson. I am thus particular in their names, since I looked upon them to be the boldest assertors and most resigned sufferers for liberty I ever read of. They presented themselves at the door at nine o'clock in the morning, when Sir William Saunderson respectfully informed them that the Chancellor had made an order against their admittance. The Duchess of Queensberry, as head of the squadron, 'pished' at the ill-breeding of a mere lawyer, and desired Sir William to let them up stairs privately. After some modest refusals. He swore he would not admit them. Her Grace, with a noble warmth, answered, they would come in, in spite of the Chancellor and the whole House. This being reported, the Peers resolved to starve them out; an order was made that the doors should not be opened till they had raised the siege. These Amazons now showed themselves qualified for the duty even of foot-soldiers; they stood there till five in the afternoon, without sustenance, every now and then plying vollies of thumps, kicks and raps, with so much violence against the door that the speakers of the House were scarce heard. When the Lords were not to be conquered by this, the two duchesses (very well apprized of the use of stratagems in war) commanded a silence of half an hour; and the Chancellor, who thought this a certain proof of their absence (the Commons also being very impatient to enter), gave orders for the opening of the door, upon which they all rushed in, pushed aside their competitors, and placed themselves in the front rows of the gallery. They stayed there till after eleven, when the house rose; and during that debate gave applause, and showed marks of dislike, not only by noisy laughs and apparent contempts, which is supposed the true reason why Lord Hervey spoke so miserably."" – pp. 23-4.

Lady Huntingdon was far

399 were affected; and she did her utmost to increase the number of its converts. She tried to persuade the celebrated Sarah, Duchess of Marlborough, to go with her to hear Whitfield; but the Duchess had a "severe cold," which stood in the way. However, she observes to Lady Huntingdon, "God knows,

were affected. We will extract two very different letters of noble ladies, neither of whom, however, were persuaded by the solicitations of the zealous person whom they address. The first is from the celebrated Duchess of Marlborough.

"My dear Lady Huntingdon is always so very good to me, and I really do feels very sensibly all your kindness and attention, that I must accept your very obliging invitation to accompany you to hear Mr. Whitfield, though I am still suffering from the effects of a severe cold. Your concern for my improvement in religious knowledge is very obliging, and I do hope I shall be the better for all your excellent advice. God knows

399 portion of it."

The Duchess of Buckingham, who was said to be a daughter of James the Second, complied with a like invitation from the Countess, and took the Duchess of Queensberry with her; however, she candidly avows her unfavourable opinion of

Portion of it. Women of wit, beauty, and quality, cannot bear too many humiliating truths – they shock our pride. But we must die – we must converse with earth and worms!

"Pray do me the favour to present my humble service to your excellent spouse. A more amiable

"the Methodist

man I do not know than Lord Huntingdon." – p. 25.

The second note is from the Duchess of Buckingham, who was said to be a daughter of James the Second.

"I thank your ladyship for the information concerning the Methodist

400 breeding."
At a time

breeding.

"Your ladyship does me infinite honour by your obliging enquiries after my health. I shall be most happy to accept your kind offer of accompanying me to hear your favourite preacher, and shall wait your arrival. The Duchess of Queensberry insists on my patronizing her on this occasion; consequently she will be an addition to our party." – p. 27.

At a time

400 they were dissatisfied

men were wearied

400 when they

while they

401 about them

402 apparent attention." Whatever might

apparent attention."

"He was seldom in her company," says our biographer, "without discussing some topic beneficial to his eternal interests, and he always paid the utmost respect and deference to her ladyship's opinion. One one occasion he said. 'How does your ladyship reconcile prayer to God for particular blessings with absolute resignation to the Divine will?' 'Very easily,' replied the Countess, 'just as if I was to offer a petition to a monarch of whose kindness and wisdom I have the highest opinion. In such a case my language would be, I wish you to bestow on me such a favour; but your majesty knows better than I how far it would be agreeable to you, or right in itself to grant my

		desire. I therefore content myself with humbly presenting my petition, and leave the event of it entirely to you.'" – p. 180.
		Whatever might
402	Lord Bolingbroke's	this unhappy man's
402	opinion of Lord Bolingbroke's	opinion of Lord Bolingbroke's* *He is said to have approved and advised the publication of a Treatise on the Inutility and Inefficacy of Prayer, written by Middleton.
402	speaking of him	relating the anecdote
402	that praise, which really belongs	the praise, which belongs
403	of Mr. Whitfield, in a letter to Lady Huntingdon	in a letter to Lady Huntingdon of Mr. Whitfield
403	his preaching."—Pp. 179, 180. It is no	his preaching. What a keen, what a biting remark! But how just and how well earned by those mitred lords."—Pp. 179, 180. It is no
404	narrow	
405	faulty	bad
405	defective	faulty
405	feebly resisted	were feebly opposed to
405	the authorities of	
406	with complacence.'"—P. 18. He goes on to say that the bishop's	with complacence.' The bishop's
406	a difficulty	circumstances in
406	the Bishop	he
406	that other	the
407	Again:	

408   in Bedlam."—P. 369.
       Again: the excellent

in Bedlam.' His Lordship then pathetically intreated me. As one who had been and wished to continue my friend, not to embitter the remaining portion of my days by any squabbles with my brother clergymen, but to go home to my parish, and so long as I kept within it, I should be at liberty to do what I liked there. 'As to your conscience,' said his lordship, 'you know that preaching out of your parish is contrary to the canons of the Church.' 'There is but one canon, my lord,' said I, 'which I dare not disobey, and that says, - Go preach the gospel to every creature.'

"The bishop was displeased, but Berridge gave himself little uneasiness on the subject; in the meanwhile an old friend, a fellow of Clare hall, who was very intimate with Pitt (afterwards Lord Chatham), stimulated him to exert his influence with a nobleman who had been the means of the bishop's promotion. This noble lord immediately applied to the bishop in behalf of Berridge, and, notwithstanding the efforts of his numerous enemies, the good man was suffered to occupy 'the lines which had fallen to him in pleasant places.' Although, however, Mr. Berridge attributes his triumph over the 'squire and his party to the influence of Mr. Pitt, we must not forget that Lord Chancellor Henley, who had promoted the bishop (Dr. John Green) to the see of Lincoln, was the friend of Lady Huntingdon, and that to her ladyship's application Mr. Berridge owed the interference with the bishop of his immediate patron, an influence not inferior to that of the renowned Earl of Chatham. To this Mr. Grimshaw alludes in a letter of this period, when he says, - 'May the Lord eternally bless that dear, good, honourable Lady Huntingdon, who would defend a persecuted minister of Christ to the last gown on her back, and the last shilling in her pocket.'" —pp. 369, 370.

Again: the excellent

408   towards her. When Bishop

towards her. The whole passage deserves to be quoted, as a specimen of the vacillations of the Church of the period, and of the conquest in a good man's mind of personal feeling over principle. Had the Church's principles, which she was transgressing, ever been set before her conscience by any one, at least in the commencement of her career, with that force with which such men as the editor of Clement could have inculcated them?

"In 1747 Lady Huntingdon again visited Bath for the benefit of her health. Previous to her ladyship's leaving London she called on Dr. Potter, Archbishop of Canterbury; and as he was then in his 75th year, and in a declining state, her ladyship, with the utmost tenderness and fidelity, spoke of the near approach of that last solemn event which would terminate all earthly friendships. He appeared sensibly affected, and at parting took her ladyship's hand, and said with great earnestness, 'May the Lord God of Abraham, of Isaac, and of Jacob, bless thee.' For many years she enjoyed the friendship of this learned divine, who succeeded Dr. Wake in the see of Canterbury, which high and important office he supported with much dignity for a period of ten years. When Bishop

409   Methodist preachers

Methodists

409   favourable change. After writing the letter to Lady Huntingdon above referred to, he was walking

favourable change. His long intimacy with Lady Huntingdon may have contributed to this end.

"On the death of Lord Huntingdon he visited her frequently, and always treated her with parental tenderness. Not long after her ladyship left London for Bath, his grace was seized with an alarming illness, from which he never entirely recovered. The last act of his life was writing the following note to her ladyship, on the 10th of October, 1747: -

"'Dear Madam, - I have been very ill since I last saw you. I hope soon to hear from you that your health is better for your being at Bath. Continue to pray for me until we meet in that place where our joy shall be complete. I am, as ever, your affectionate friend, 'JOHN CANT.'"

"After his grace had written the above, he was walking

409	acquainted her) he was	acquainted Lady Huntingdon), being
410	towards schism	worse
410	new	
410	proselytism or protest	persuasion or attack
410	a High-Church opponent	their opponents
410	he	the latter
411	an integral	a
411	persuasion	sense
411	readers	people
411	objective	external
411	they had to approach, study, enter upon, and receive or reject	must be approached, studied, entered upon, and received or rejected
411	gain from others	have
411	Bishop Marsh and Bishop Tomlin. They	Bishops Marsh and Tomlin. These writers

411 | They knew that comprehension or compromise was simply beside the mark. |

412 | they meant by them no more than those parties meant | they meant no more than they themselves meant

412 | side | religionist

412 | the history of |

412 | in its words | in it

412 | unavoidably be taken by all who would be religious, for | be taken in religion, or

412 | these guides | they

412 | of an hierarchical position |

413 | clergyman of well-known and respected name | well-known and respected clergyman

413 | our own. Cling not | our own – the Lord Jesus Christ is the Lord our Righteousness. Cling not

414 | His people ... My dear | his people. You find it a hard task to come naked and miserable to Christ – to come divested of every recommendation but that of abject wretchedness and misery, and receive from the outstretched hand of our divine Immanuel the riches, the superabundant riches of redeeming grace. But if you come at all, you must come thus, and like the dying thief, the cry of your heart must be, 'Lord, remember me.' There must be no conditions; Christ, and Christ alone, must be the only mediator between God and sinful men. No miserable performances can be placed between the sinner and the Saviour. Let the eye of faith be ever directed to the Lord Jesus Christ; and I beseech him to bring every thought of your heart into captivity to the

414	of faith ... May His	obedience of our great High Priest. "And now, my dear
		of faith, that faith which is the gift of God. Exhort Christless impenitent sinners to fly to this city of refuge – to look to him who is exlated as a Prince and Saviour, to give repentance and the remission of sins. Go on thus, and may your bow abide in strength. Be bold, be firm, be decisive. Let Christ be the alpha and omega of all you advance in your addresses to your fellow-men. Leave the consequences with your Divine Master. He will be with his faithful ministers to the end of time. May his
414	to change ... The wicked	to change, and the France [?] student went to Cheltenham..... The wicked
414	or waywardness	
414 -5	One awkward matter concerned Dr. Haweis, though we are not sure that we rightly apprehend her biographer's account of it. "In the number of those," he says,	One very serious case, which attracts attention, from the names of the persons implicated in it, shall be set before the reader. "Among the number of those," says the author,
415	abounding reproach and hostility	reproach and hostility to
415	a gentleman-commoner	a student [?] and gentleman-commoner
415	Eventually he had	He had afterwards
415	biographer. There	biographer in one of his lighter moods, to judge by the language he employs. There
415	ears," etc.; he listened, and he was	ears," &c and he was
415	Aldwinckle's powers	Aldwinckle
415	incumbent, a Mr. Kimpton, had	incumbent had

415   order, by the price it might fetch, to   order to

415   As he could not be dispensed from
-7   residence, he had no option but to
sell the living at once; and, as delay
occurred in finding a purchaser, he
put in Dr. Haweis, at Mr. Madan's
suggestion, to keep it meanwhile,
lest the presentation should lapse to
the Bishop of the diocese. The
circumstance   of   immediate
possession increased of course its
money value, and before many
months had elapsed it was sold for a
thousand guineas. The bargain,
however, could not take effect
without Dr. Haweis; and he, on
being informed of it, refused to
resign, and denied he had made any
promise to do so. On this, he was
asked at least to make some
compensation to Mr. Kimpton, for
the loss he would sustain, but he
answered, rightly enough, that he
could not be party to any such
simoniacal proceeding; moreover,
he had already laid out £300 on the
parsonage. Then Mr. Kimpton
turned to Mr. Madan, insisting that
on the face of the matter he never
could have intended to give so
valuable a property out and out to
Dr. Haweis, a stranger to him, and a
young man, to the depreciation of its
market value, which of course he
needed to raise to the utmost; but
Mr. Madan took a contrary view,
and as there had been no third party
in the transaction, who might have
been a witness in the matter, Mr.
Kimpton gained nothing by his
appeal. Then Dr. Hawies gave him
his *coup de grace* by laying the case
before the Lord Chancellor, to
whom Mr. Madan was chaplain, and
who decided that Mr. Kimpton had
no remedy in law. Indeed, no other
decision was possible; and the poor
man remained a prisoner in the
King's Bench, with a son driven out
of his mind, and his family nearly
starving.

As the relation, however, has some
obscurities in it, we will continue it
in the author's words.

"A long absence from his parish
could not be dispensed with by his
superior, and as he was unable to
return to Aldwinckle, the living was
in danger of lapsing to the bishop of
the diocese. It therefore became
necessary for Mr. Kimpton either to
sell the advowson, or to obtain the
bishop's leave for some clergyman
to hold it for a limited time. Dr.
Haweis not having any preferment
from the time he had been driven
from his cure at Oxford, was
recommended to Mr. Kimpton by
Mr. Madan, who had been
introduced to him by the Rev.
Samuel Brewer; and as the bishop's
leave could not be obtained for any
person to hold the living for a
limited time, he presented it to Dr.
Haweis. The whole transaction was
concluded with Mr. Madan and Dr.
Haweis by Mr. Kimpton, when no
other person was present. Mr.
Madan and Dr. Haweis, no doubt,
acted in this business as upright and
conscientious men, but in the eyes
of those equally excellent, Lady
Huntingdon, Mr. Whitfield, and Mr.
Thornton, their conduct appeared
less pure.

"Some months after Mr. Kimpton
had signed the presentation, a
gentleman made him an offer of
one thousand guineas for the
advowson, whereupon he
immediately applied to Dr. Haweis,
intimating his hopes of a
resignation, or of having a
compensation in money. As no
promises, or even so much as a hint
of a consideration, were made when
Dr. Haweis was presented to the
living, he and Mr. Madan
peremptorily refused a resignation
or compensation. The distress
which this refusal brought upon Mr.

All this shocked Lady Huntingdon; and, as it was a money matter, she had both a plea and a meaning when she interfered. She purchased of Mr. Kimpton for £1000 what she could not take away from Dr. Haweis; and thus gained a claim for exercising her ecclesiastical functions, and giving both him and his friend, her views of the transaction. She addressed herself to Mr. Madan, "On having your representation read over," she says in it, "my sentiment on that point I most freely gave, and thought, as the matter stood, I could not see how Mr. Haweis, as an honest man, could continue to hold that living." Then, after relating how she had herself purchased the advowson, and released Mr. Kimpton from confinement, she continues, "It remains Kimpton was almost without parallel: Mr. Kimpton himself being still a prisoner in the King's Bench, his son driven out of his mind, and the rest of his family nearly starving.

This affair soon became very public, and the foulest aspersions were thrown on the characters of Mr. Madan and Dr. Haweis by Mr. Kimpton and his friends. On the part of Dr. Haweis, it was contended that Mr. Kimpton presented him to the living without any pecuniary consideration whatever, either at the time of his acceptance of it, or the least promise or engagement for any future recompense. Mr. Kimpton and his friends did not deny this; but said it must be presumed that when the patron first waited upon Mr. Madan for his advice in the unfortunate situation he was in, that he told him his case, and that Mr. Madan must have known what he wanted; and though no promises, or even so much as a hint of a consideration, were made at the time the presentation was signed, yet Dr. Haweis must have known that Mr. Kimpton wholly relied on his honour, and could not think he would be willing to give his living away absolutely to a man he never saw before, and to one who was likely to enjoy it a great many years, when he might have found a person of more than twice the age of Dr. Haweis to have given it to.

Mr. Madan sought the advice of the first legal authorities, and having himself been an able practitioner at the bar, felt confident that he had acted in the most conscientious and honourable manner by Mr. Kimpton. Lord Apsley, afterwards Lord Bathurst, then Lord High Chancellor of England, to whom Mr. Madan was chaplain, decided in his favour, as did also several persons conversant with ecclesiastical law." – p. 414,

415.

Matters were in this state when Lady Huntingdon came to London; and she considered that the best mode of ending so scandalous an affair was for herself to purchase the advowson, and thereby both to release the suffering party out of prison, and set her reverend friends straight with the public. This she did for the sum of 1000*l.*; and then addressed a letter to Mr. Madan, which, together with his reply, shall be set before the reader.

"London, March 1st, 1768

"Rev. Sir, - some time in last April was a year, in my lodgings at Chelsea, you were so good as to inform me of this unhappy affair of Aldwinckle. On having your representation read over, my sentiments on that point I most freely gave, and thought, as the matter stood, I could not see how Mr. Haweis, as an honest man, could continue to keep that living. The objection then made against giving it up was the charge of simony, which might in that case be brought. To avoid even the suspicion of this, it instantly occurred to my mind that you and Mr. Haweis immediately taking Mr. Kimpton to the bishop, and proving yourselves free from the charge that was or might be brought against you, necessarily obliged him (the bishop) either to allow the resignation of the living in testimony of your innocence, or acquit your characters in keeping it, if he refused to accept it. From the inferior objection of the 300*l.* laid out on the house by Mr. Haweis (and which was afterwards offered to be paid by a friend on a resignation of the living), it did not then seem expedient too you that the living should be given up. I then had no more to say, and became satisfied to share in the certain shame and reproach so many of Go's people have had on this

561

occasion; but from the conviction of my mind, I could take up no weapons of defence on this subject. It remained from your own testimony to me, just the same under every various and future appearance to the world. Since I last came to town I have found a severe scourge indeed upon the Church of God, and which by going on must end in every evil word and work. To deliver, therefore, a miserable family, and to stop all further grief to God's people, who are alike in all parts affected by this blow, I had but one thing that suggested itself to me to its relief, and whereby these best motives might be explained. In order to do this the most effectually in my power, I have commissioned Mr. Thornton, Mr. Whitfield, Mr. West, and Mr. Brewer, (by this day giving them a note for 1000*l*.), to purchase the advowson of Aldwinckle, and they are now gone to see Mr. Kimpton released from prison, restored to his family, and the debts relative to the advowson, and all his other debts, punctually discharged. Thus far I have gone, but alas! I can go no farther. It remains

417   trying instance," etc.—P. 418. Mr. Madan, however, was equal to the occasion. He wrote back, "As to the concessions your ladyship is pleased to mention, as we do not conceive we have any to make so we may assure you that none can ever be made."

Such was the issue of an affair, in which, whatever we think of Mr. Madan, Dr. Haweis does not particularly shine; but, if faith, such as he was considered to have, blots out all, even the most enormous sins, it is not wonderful if Lady Huntingdon and her friends considered it a sovereign prophylactic against any prospective mischief happening to his soul from

trying instance. It will be sufficient to support and carry you victoriously through all, and bring back the love, the just love and honour due to you from the Church of God, and in the end can alone preserve that character, whose defence from man has wanted that success which God only can give. Should I ever live to see this happy day of peace proclaimed, you will then find me that faithful and affectionate friend I desire to be found by you both. Till then, I can only say, I remain, &c."—p. 418, 419.

To this excellent letter the person addressed returned the following answer:

mere peccadillos against the law whether of charity, generosity, equity, or honour. Accordingly our biographer gently observes

"Madam,—When I had the honour of your ladyship's letter I was confined to my bed, and therefore could not answer it by your servant. I am at present very unfit for writing or business of any sort; but lest any longer silence should be misconstrued into disrespect, I trouble your ladyship with the following answer.

Your ladyship acquaints me that you have sent a thousand pounds for the purchase of the advowson of Aldwinckle. This step your ladyship may have taken with the best intentions; but, under all the cicumstances of the case, it is very evident to me that the necessary consequence of it will be an increase of reproach and injury to my friend Mr. haweis's character and my own; and therefore I hope your ladyship will do us the justice upon all occasions to declare that this step has been taken without or knowledge, privity, consent , or approbation.

"As to the part which Mr. Haweis and I have taken, it has been, all things considered, a very disagreeable one for us; and nothing could have supported us under the oppression and persecution we have met with, but a consciousness of our having acted uprightly and sincerely. This has enabled us to stem the torrent of abuse which hath been poured on us from all quarters, and I trust will enable us to assert our integrity as long as we live.

"As to the concessions your ladyship is pleased to mention, as we do not conceive we have any to make, so we must assure you that none can ever be made, - by us I mean, for I by no means despair that some may appear on the other side of the question, when conscience shall do its office with respect to the wrongs we have sustained, and our just dealing shall be as the noonday sun.

"When evil is spoken of us falsely we are commanded to rejoice; when any can be said truly, I shall hope that you will find none more ready to acknowledge and lament it than dear Mr. Haweis, and, madam, your ladyship's humble servant, &c." – p. 420.

It would be little charitable to draw attention to the faults of those who have long since passed into another state, were it not for the moral they convey to us. Such a transaction as the above seems at first sight incredible to us in the case of persons of such high religious professions as the principals in it, and is the less to be forgotten at this time, because a volume of Dr. Haweis's sermons has lately been honoured with a new edition, and his preparation for Holy Communion is, if we mistake not, in popular use. We do not think it harsh or unfair in such a case to make use of our Saviour's maxim, already quoted, about knowing a tree by its fruit, as a reason for keeping clear of such an author. Yet the writer before us, candid as he is in stating the facts above recorded, does not, after all, venture "to offer any opinion on the affair of Aldwinckle," and gently observes

417 to exertion."—P. 421. He tells

to exertion."—P. 421. We consider that no creed but that of Calvin would thus coolly dispose of what seems to us pretty nearly a case of fraud. He tells

417 of Dr. Haweis." Nay, even as

of Dr. Haweis," yes, such piety can exist unruffled, unsoiled, full of heaven, full of spirituality, full of assurance, in the midst of what the catechism calls "lying" and "stealing." Nay, even as

418 on his own score

also

418 associate in the foregoing

companion in usefulness as well as

transaction	in moral perceptions
418	Our author's eloquence rises almost to the sublime in his description of this well-connected divine: "The lawyer	Our author rises almost into the sublime in his description of this well-connected divine. "Possessing a thorough knowledge of the Scriptures in the original languages, and having embraced those evangelical views of Gospel truth, of which he was afterwards so zealous a defender, Mr. Madan was desirous of diffusing amongst his fellow-men the savour of that name which he loved. Master of an independent fortune, he entered the ministry without any mercenary views; and though his brother, Dr. Spencer Madan, was successively Bishop of Bristol and Peterborough, he never accepted any benefice or emolument in the Church. In consequence of his religious sentiments, and the open avowal he made of the faith once delivered to the saints, he experienced some difficulty obtaining orders; but through the perseverance and interest of lady Huntingdon and some others, he was at length successful." Soon after his ordination, Mr. Madan was called to preach his first sermon in the church of All-hallows, Lombard Street. The lawyer
419	the waterbrooks."—P. 433. At a later	the waterbrooks." p. 433. Now one specimen of his own nice feeling in a moral matter has been given above; but it will scarcely be believed by those who have neither been in the way of hearing of this preachers from their contemporaries, nor have gone out of their way to master the literature of that day, that at a later
419	advocates polygamy, as an expedient for setting things straight. If Luther	advocates polygamy, thus renewing in the history of Methodism the same grave phenomenon which occurs in the instance of Milton and

of Luther.
If Luther

419   rebut   escape

420   was neither, on the following grounds, first, because "Lady Huntingdon   was neither, on the ground, first, that "Lady Huntingdon

420   fully

420   a day."
       "His stature

a day."
     "The mode of his public ministrations was emphatically original. He evidently observed method in all his sermons; but it was unhackneyed. It was not his custom to arrange his subjects under general heads of discourse; but when he made the attempt, his divisions would be particularly natural, and rigidly adhered to. As he rarely allegorized or accommodated the Scriptures, he was less liable to mistake their meaning: he seldom referred to their original text, but when he did, his remarks were pertinent. In his discussions of general topics, his figures were new, his illustrations apposite, and his arguments conclusive. Though he obtained the just reputation of being a learned man, and was conversant with all the beauties of language, so ardent was his desire of doing good to his most illiterate hearers, that he laid aside an affected style of elegance, and from principle cultivated an easy and familiar diction.
     "His stature

420   Lady Huntingdon. To her   Lady Huntingdon. Her conversation and correspondence with him were greatly blessed to his profit and advantage, and instrumental, under the divine blessing, in leading him to clearer and more consistent views of the plan of salvation, and of preaching the whole counsel of God with greater boldness and

clearness. To her

421   subject of it: but to have a full view
of his character, we should read the

subject of it: yet to see how sadly
the good in Methodism was alloyed
with evil, it is only necessary to
read the

421   style:
"My Lady,

style:
          "Everton, March 23, 1770.
"My Lady,

422   singular

strange

422   Mr. Thornton; which, though too
-3   long to quote, shows us that not all,
who agreed in religious sentiments
with Mr. Berridge, agreed with him
in his peculiar mode of enforcing
them.
             5.
  It is sometimes

Mr. Thornton; with which we shall
bring our extracts to an end. Mr.
Thornton writes as follows:-
   "In some discussions we have had
as to 'the Christian World
Unmasked,' I could not help
laughing with you, though at the
same time I felt a check within:
your reasons silenced, but did not
satisfy me. Your view of humour
and mine seem much alike. If there
is any difference between us, it lies
here; I would strive against mine,
while you seem to indulge yours. I
fight against mine, because I find
that the ludicrous spirit is just as
dangerous as the sullen one; and it
is much the same to our great
adversary whether he falls in with a
capricious or facetious turn of
mind. I could not forbear smiling at
your humourous allegory about the
tooth, and was pleased at trhe good
sense displayed in it; yet something
came across my mind – Is this
method agreeable to the idea we
ought to entertain of a father in
Israel? It would pass mighty well in
a newspaper, or in any thing
calculated for public entertainment;
but it certainly wanted that solidity
or seriousness that a Christian
minister should write with. What
the Apostle said, in another sense,
will apply here; 'When I was a
child, I spoke as a child,' &c. An
expression of yours in your prayer
before sermon, when at Tottenham

Court, struck me,— 'that God would give us new bread, not stale, but what was baked in the oven that day.' Whether it is that I am too little or you too much used to such expressions, I won't pretend to determine; but I could not help thinking it savoured of attention to men more than to God. I know the apology frequently made for such language is, that the common people require it; it fixes their attention, and affords matter for conversation afterwards, for a sentence out of the common road is more remembered than all the rest. This may be true; but the effect it has is only a loud laugh among their acquaintances; not one person is edified, and many are offended by such like expressions. Some ministers I have known run into the other extreme, and think something grand must be uttered to strike the audience; but it seems to me as unnecessary as the other, and both have a twang of self-conceit and seem like leaning to carnal wisdom. Truth, simple truth, requires no embellishments, nor should it be degraded; we are not to add to or take from it, but to remember the power is of God wholly. My reverend friend, as an old man, might be indulged in his favourite peculiarities, if they would stop with him; but others catch the infection, and we find young ministers and common people indulging themselves in the same way: they think they are authorized so to do by such an example. Wit in any person is dangerous, and often mischievous, when used improperly, and especially on religious subjects; for as the professing part of an audience will much longer retain a witty or a low expression than one more serious, so will the wicked part of it too, and turn it to the disadvantage of religion. I recollect but one humourous passage in all the Bible, which is that of Elijah with the Baalites; and when the time, place and circumstances are properly considered, nothing could be more seasonable, nothing so effectually expose the impotency of their false god, and the absurdity of their vain worship. The prophets often speak ironically, sometimes satirically, but I do not remember of their ever speaking ludicrously. Our Lord and his apostles never have recourse to any such methods. The short abstracts we have of their sermons and conversations are all in serious strain, and ministers cannot copy after better examples. I dare not say that giving liberty to a man's natural turn, or an endeavour to put and keep the people in good humour, is sinful; but this I may assert, such a method is universally followed on the stage, and in all places of public entertainment; and therefore it seems to me to savour much more of the old man than of the new.

"I remember you once jocularly informed me, you was born with a fool's cap on: pray, my dear sir, is it not high time it was pulled off? Such an accoutrement may suit a natural birth, and be of service, but surely it has nothing to do with a spiritual one, nor ever can be made ornamental to a serious man, much less to a Christian minister. I waive mentioning Scripture injunctions, such as 'Let your speech be with grace,' &c. as you know these better than I do. Surely they should have some weight, for idle and unprofitable words stand forbidden. If it should please God to give you to see things as I do, you will think it necessary to be more guarded; but should you think me mistaken, I trust it will make no interruption in our friendship that I am thus free with you, and it proceeds from a sincere love and regard. The Tabernacle people in general are wild and enthusiastic, and delight in anything out of the common; which is a temper of mind, though in some respects necessary, yet should never be encouraged. If you and some few others, who have the greatest influence over them, would use the curb instead of the spur, I am persuaded the effect would be very blessed. Wild fire is better than no fire, but there is a divine warmth between these two extremes, which the real Christian catches, and which, when obtained, is evidenced by a cool head and a warm heart, and makes him a glorious shining example to all around him. I desire to be earnest in prayer that we may be more and more partakers of this heavenly wisdom, and ascribe all might, majesty and dominion to the Lord alone."—pp. 371—373.

It is sometimes

| 425 | that has roused | that she has roused |
| 425 | from the Church a gift, and they did but fulfil for the Church a prophecy | from her a gift, and they did but fulfil for her a prophecy |